Lecture Notes in Computer Science 14024

The series Lecture Notes in Computer Science (LNCS), including its subseries Lecture Notes in Artificial Intelligence (LNAI) and Lecture Notes in Bioinformatics (LNBI), has established itself as a medium for the publication of new developments in computer science and information technology research, teaching, and education.

LNCS enjoys close cooperation with the computer science R & D community, the series counts many renowned academics among its volume editors and paper authors, and collaborates with prestigious societies. Its mission is to serve this international community by providing an invaluable service, mainly focused on the publication of conference and workshop proceedings and postproceedings. LNCS commenced publication in 1973.

Pei-Luen Patrick Rau

Editor

Cross-Cultural Design

15th International Conference, CCD 2023
Held as Part of the 25th International Conference, HCII 2023
Copenhagen, Denmark, July 23–28, 2023
Proceedings, Part III

Editor
Pei-Luen Patrick Rau
Department of Industrial Engineering
Tsinghua University
Beijing, China

ISSN 0302-9743   ISSN 1611-3349 (electronic)
Lecture Notes in Computer Science
ISBN 978-3-031-35945-3   ISBN 978-3-031-35946-0 (eBook)
https://doi.org/10.1007/978-3-031-35946-0

This Springer imprint is published by the registered company Springer Nature Switzerland AG
The registered company address is: Gewerbestrasse 11, 6330 Cham, Switzerland

Foreword

Human-computer interaction (HCI) is acquiring an ever-increasing scientific and industrial importance, as well as having more impact on people's everyday lives, as an ever-growing number of human activities are progressively moving from the physical to the digital world. This process, which has been ongoing for some time now, was further accelerated during the acute period of the COVID-19 pandemic. The HCI International (HCII) conference series, held annually, aims to respond to the compelling need to advance the exchange of knowledge and research and development efforts on the human aspects of design and use of computing systems.

The 25th International Conference on Human-Computer Interaction, HCI International 2023 (HCII 2023), was held in the emerging post-pandemic era as a 'hybrid' event at the AC Bella Sky Hotel and Bella Center, Copenhagen, Denmark, during July 23–28, 2023. It incorporated the 21 thematic areas and affiliated conferences listed below.

A total of 7472 individuals from academia, research institutes, industry, and government agencies from 85 countries submitted contributions, and 1578 papers and 396 posters were included in the volumes of the proceedings that were published just before the start of the conference, these are listed below. The contributions thoroughly cover the entire field of human-computer interaction, addressing major advances in knowledge and effective use of computers in a variety of application areas. These papers provide academics, researchers, engineers, scientists, practitioners and students with state-of-the-art information on the most recent advances in HCI.

The HCI International (HCII) conference also offers the option of presenting 'Late Breaking Work', and this applies both for papers and posters, with corresponding volumes of proceedings that will be published after the conference. Full papers will be included in the 'HCII 2023 - Late Breaking Work - Papers' volumes of the proceedings to be published in the Springer LNCS series, while 'Poster Extended Abstracts' will be included as short research papers in the 'HCII 2023 - Late Breaking Work - Posters' volumes to be published in the Springer CCIS series.

I would like to thank the Program Board Chairs and the members of the Program Boards of all thematic areas and affiliated conferences for their contribution towards the high scientific quality and overall success of the HCI International 2023 conference. Their manifold support in terms of paper reviewing (single-blind review process, with a minimum of two reviews per submission), session organization and their willingness to act as goodwill ambassadors for the conference is most highly appreciated.

This conference would not have been possible without the continuous and unwavering support and advice of Gavriel Salvendy, founder, General Chair Emeritus, and Scientific Advisor. For his outstanding efforts, I would like to express my sincere appreciation to Abbas Moallem, Communications Chair and Editor of HCI International News.

July 2023   Constantine Stephanidis

HCI International 2023 Thematic Areas and Affiliated Conferences

Thematic Areas

- HCI: Human-Computer Interaction
- HIMI: Human Interface and the Management of Information

Affiliated Conferences

- EPCE: 20th International Conference on Engineering Psychology and Cognitive Ergonomics
- AC: 17th International Conference on Augmented Cognition
- UAHCI: 17th International Conference on Universal Access in Human-Computer Interaction
- CCD: 15th International Conference on Cross-Cultural Design
- SCSM: 15th International Conference on Social Computing and Social Media
- VAMR: 15th International Conference on Virtual, Augmented and Mixed Reality
- DHM: 14th International Conference on Digital Human Modeling and Applications in Health, Safety, Ergonomics and Risk Management
- DUXU: 12th International Conference on Design, User Experience and Usability
- C&C: 11th International Conference on Culture and Computing
- DAPI: 11th International Conference on Distributed, Ambient and Pervasive Interactions
- HCIBGO: 10th International Conference on HCI in Business, Government and Organizations
- LCT: 10th International Conference on Learning and Collaboration Technologies
- ITAP: 9th International Conference on Human Aspects of IT for the Aged Population
- AIS: 5th International Conference on Adaptive Instructional Systems
- HCI-CPT: 5th International Conference on HCI for Cybersecurity, Privacy and Trust
- HCI-Games: 5th International Conference on HCI in Games
- MobiTAS: 5th International Conference on HCI in Mobility, Transport and Automotive Systems
- AI-HCI: 4th International Conference on Artificial Intelligence in HCI
- MOBILE: 4th International Conference on Design, Operation and Evaluation of Mobile Communications

List of Conference Proceedings Volumes Appearing Before the Conference

1. LNCS 14011, Human-Computer Interaction: Part I, edited by Masaaki Kurosu and Ayako Hashizume
2. LNCS 14012, Human-Computer Interaction: Part II, edited by Masaaki Kurosu and Ayako Hashizume
3. LNCS 14013, Human-Computer Interaction: Part III, edited by Masaaki Kurosu and Ayako Hashizume
4. LNCS 14014, Human-Computer Interaction: Part IV, edited by Masaaki Kurosu and Ayako Hashizume
5. LNCS 14015, Human Interface and the Management of Information: Part I, edited by Hirohiko Mori and Yumi Asahi
6. LNCS 14016, Human Interface and the Management of Information: Part II, edited by Hirohiko Mori and Yumi Asahi
7. LNAI 14017, Engineering Psychology and Cognitive Ergonomics: Part I, edited by Don Harris and Wen-Chin Li
8. LNAI 14018, Engineering Psychology and Cognitive Ergonomics: Part II, edited by Don Harris and Wen-Chin Li
9. LNAI 14019, Augmented Cognition, edited by Dylan D. Schmorrow and Cali M. Fidopiastis
10. LNCS 14020, Universal Access in Human-Computer Interaction: Part I, edited by Margherita Antona and Constantine Stephanidis
11. LNCS 14021, Universal Access in Human-Computer Interaction: Part II, edited by Margherita Antona and Constantine Stephanidis
12. LNCS 14022, Cross-Cultural Design: Part I, edited by Pei-Luen Patrick Rau
13. LNCS 14023, Cross-Cultural Design: Part II, edited by Pei-Luen Patrick Rau
14. LNCS 14024, Cross-Cultural Design: Part III, edited by Pei-Luen Patrick Rau
15. LNCS 14025, Social Computing and Social Media: Part I, edited by Adela Coman and Simona Vasilache
16. LNCS 14026, Social Computing and Social Media: Part II, edited by Adela Coman and Simona Vasilache
17. LNCS 14027, Virtual, Augmented and Mixed Reality, edited by Jessie Y. C. Chen and Gino Fragomeni
18. LNCS 14028, Digital Human Modeling and Applications in Health, Safety, Ergonomics and Risk Management: Part I, edited by Vincent G. Duffy
19. LNCS 14029, Digital Human Modeling and Applications in Health, Safety, Ergonomics and Risk Management: Part II, edited by Vincent G. Duffy
20. LNCS 14030, Design, User Experience, and Usability: Part I, edited by Aaron Marcus, Elizabeth Rosenzweig and Marcelo Soares
21. LNCS 14031, Design, User Experience, and Usability: Part II, edited by Aaron Marcus, Elizabeth Rosenzweig and Marcelo Soares

22. LNCS 14032, Design, User Experience, and Usability: Part III, edited by Aaron Marcus, Elizabeth Rosenzweig and Marcelo Soares
23. LNCS 14033, Design, User Experience, and Usability: Part IV, edited by Aaron Marcus, Elizabeth Rosenzweig and Marcelo Soares
24. LNCS 14034, Design, User Experience, and Usability: Part V, edited by Aaron Marcus, Elizabeth Rosenzweig and Marcelo Soares
25. LNCS 14035, Culture and Computing, edited by Matthias Rauterberg
26. LNCS 14036, Distributed, Ambient and Pervasive Interactions: Part I, edited by Norbert Streitz and Shin'ichi Konomi
27. LNCS 14037, Distributed, Ambient and Pervasive Interactions: Part II, edited by Norbert Streitz and Shin'ichi Konomi
28. LNCS 14038, HCI in Business, Government and Organizations: Part I, edited by Fiona Fui-Hoon Nah and Keng Siau
29. LNCS 14039, HCI in Business, Government and Organizations: Part II, edited by Fiona Fui-Hoon Nah and Keng Siau
30. LNCS 14040, Learning and Collaboration Technologies: Part I, edited by Panayiotis Zaphiris and Andri Ioannou
31. LNCS 14041, Learning and Collaboration Technologies: Part II, edited by Panayiotis Zaphiris and Andri Ioannou
32. LNCS 14042, Human Aspects of IT for the Aged Population: Part I, edited by Qin Gao and Jia Zhou
33. LNCS 14043, Human Aspects of IT for the Aged Population: Part II, edited by Qin Gao and Jia Zhou
34. LNCS 14044, Adaptive Instructional Systems, edited by Robert A. Sottilare and Jessica Schwarz
35. LNCS 14045, HCI for Cybersecurity, Privacy and Trust, edited by Abbas Moallem
36. LNCS 14046, HCI in Games: Part I, edited by Xiaowen Fang
37. LNCS 14047, HCI in Games: Part II, edited by Xiaowen Fang
38. LNCS 14048, HCI in Mobility, Transport and Automotive Systems: Part I, edited by Heidi Krömker
39. LNCS 14049, HCI in Mobility, Transport and Automotive Systems: Part II, edited by Heidi Krömker
40. LNAI 14050, Artificial Intelligence in HCI: Part I, edited by Helmut Degen and Stavroula Ntoa
41. LNAI 14051, Artificial Intelligence in HCI: Part II, edited by Helmut Degen and Stavroula Ntoa
42. LNCS 14052, Design, Operation and Evaluation of Mobile Communications, edited by Gavriel Salvendy and June Wei
43. CCIS 1832, HCI International 2023 Posters - Part I, edited by Constantine Stephanidis, Margherita Antona, Stavroula Ntoa and Gavriel Salvendy
44. CCIS 1833, HCI International 2023 Posters - Part II, edited by Constantine Stephanidis, Margherita Antona, Stavroula Ntoa and Gavriel Salvendy
45. CCIS 1834, HCI International 2023 Posters - Part III, edited by Constantine Stephanidis, Margherita Antona, Stavroula Ntoa and Gavriel Salvendy
46. CCIS 1835, HCI International 2023 Posters - Part IV, edited by Constantine Stephanidis, Margherita Antona, Stavroula Ntoa and Gavriel Salvendy

47. CCIS 1836, HCI International 2023 Posters - Part V, edited by Constantine Stephanidis, Margherita Antona, Stavroula Ntoa and Gavriel Salvendy

https://2023.hci.international/proceedings

Preface

The increasing internationalization and globalization of communication, business and industry is leading to a wide cultural diversification of individuals and groups of users who access information, services and products. If interactive systems are to be usable, useful and appealing to such a wide range of users, culture becomes an important HCI issue. Therefore, HCI practitioners and designers face the challenges of designing across different cultures, and need to elaborate and adopt design approaches which take into account cultural models, factors, expectations and preferences, and allow development of cross-cultural user experiences that accommodate global users.

The 15th Cross-Cultural Design (CCD) Conference, an affiliated conference of the HCI International Conference, encouraged the submission of papers from academics, researchers, industry and professionals, on a broad range of theoretical and applied issues related to Cross-Cultural Design and its applications.

A considerable number of papers were accepted to this year's CCD Conference addressing diverse topics, which spanned a wide variety of domains. A notable theme addressed by several contributions was that of service and product design for the promotion of cultural heritage and local culture. Furthermore, a considerable number of papers explore the differences in cultural perceptions of technology across various contexts. Design for social change and development constitutes one of the topics that emerged this year, examining the impact of technology on society, for vulnerable groups, for shaping values, and in promoting social movements and folk beliefs. Another growing topic is that of sustainable design, which delves into methodologies, cultural branding, and design for sustainability in various areas such as travel, transportation and mobility, climate change and urban public spaces. Emerging technologies, future-focused design and design of automated and intelligent systems are also prominent themes, exploring culturally informed innovative design methodologies, User Experience aspects and user acceptance angles, as well as evaluation studies and their findings. Furthermore, papers emphasized the design of technological innovations in domains of social impact such as arts and creative industries, cultural heritage, immersive and inclusive learning environments, and health and wellness.

Three volumes of the HCII 2023 proceedings are dedicated to this year's edition of the CCD Conference:

- Part I addresses topics related to service and product design for cultural innovation, design for social change and development, sustainable design methods and practices, and cross-cultural perspectives on design and consumer behavior.
- Part II addresses topics related to User Experience design in emerging technologies, future-focused design, and culturally informed design of automated and intelligent systems.
- Part III addresses topics related to cross-cultural design in arts and creative industries, in cultural heritage, and in immersive and inclusive learning environments, as well as cross-cultural health and wellness design.

Papers in these volumes were included for publication after a minimum of two single-blind reviews from the members of the CCD Program Board or, in some cases, from members of the Program Boards of other affiliated conferences. I would like to thank all of them for their invaluable contribution, support and efforts.

July 2023   Pei-Luen Patrick Rau

15th International Conference on Cross-Cultural Design (CCD 2023)

The full list with the Program Board Chairs and the members of the Program Boards of all thematic areas and affiliated conferences of HCII2023 is available online at:

http://www.hci.international/board-members-2023.php

HCI International 2024 Conference

The 26th International Conference on Human-Computer Interaction, HCI International 2024, will be held jointly with the affiliated conferences at the Washington Hilton Hotel, Washington, DC, USA, June 29 – July 4, 2024. It will cover a broad spectrum of themes related to Human-Computer Interaction, including theoretical issues, methods, tools, processes, and case studies in HCI design, as well as novel interaction techniques, interfaces, and applications. The proceedings will be published by Springer. More information will be made available on the conference website: http://2024.hci.international/.

General Chair
Prof. Constantine Stephanidis
University of Crete and ICS-FORTH
Heraklion, Crete, Greece
Email: general_chair@hcii2024.org

https://2024.hci.international/

Contents – Part III

Cross-Cultural Design in Immersive and Inclusive Learning Environments

Cross-Cultural Health and Wellness Design

Cross-Cultural Design in Arts and Creative Industries

A Study on the Emotional Awareness of Lacquer Art Dyeing Applied to Fan

LuoYu Chen[✉] and Jun Chen

Graduate School of Creative Industry Design, National Taiwan University of Arts,
New Taipei City 220307, Taiwan
ooorangelolo@gmail.com

Abstract. With the rapid development of modern society, traditional handicrafts are gradually replaced by new products of technology. With the rise of the national trend, it has become an important cultural proposition to recreate the culture of lacquer art through the art of momentum. The paper fan, which can be seen everywhere in life, is often used as one of the design vehicles for cultural and creative products, which can be both communicative and practical. As a new expression of the lacquer language, the lacquer bleaching technique integrates traditional lacquer techniques while retaining the creativity of modern lacquer art. This study uses literature analysis and questionnaire survey as the main research methods. First, we collate the development value of lacquer art through literature collection, and integrate the fan and lacquer art into a symbiosis. We hope that the development of cultural and creative industries will also allow traditional lacquer art to be passed on in a new way.

Keywords: Lacquer Art · Cultural and Creative Goods · Emotional Awareness

1 Introduction

1.1 Research Background

The history of lacquer art is a history of material-related development, while lacquer painting has developed alongside lacquer ware and has only recently become a new genre of painting in its own right. Traditional lacquer painting focuses more on the expression of craftsmanship, unlike modern lacquer painting, which focuses on conceptual expression [1]. Cross-border, diversified, fusion, symbolic, abstract, and composition are the trends in the development of lacquer art, and as a new expression of lacquer language, the technique of bleaching lacquer has integrated traditional lacquer techniques and provided new creative possibilities for the development of lacquer art. Traditional art needs to be preserved and developed in a creative way, and modern elements need to be added to attract the attention of the public. In many contemporary creative arts, artists often use the concept of conception to design the development of the birth of their works. In the creation of the traditional craft integration in the modern cultural and creative industry, not only can inject a rich cultural connotation into contemporary fashion, but also provide an important basis and momentum for the promotion of cultural and creative design industry.

P.-L. P. Rau (Ed.): HCII 2023, LNCS 14024, pp. 3–12, 2023.
https://doi.org/10.1007/978-3-031-35946-0_1

Therefore, through the application of lacquer art techniques in the fan culture and creative industry, this study aims to understand the color preferences of consumers, promote cultural diversity, draw out the essence, and integrate design innovation and cultural innovation, so that traditional lacquer art can be integrated into contemporary culture and creative design.

1.2   Motivation and Purpose of the Study

The study aims to collect and collate relevant literature on lacquer art, to understand the differences between traditional and contemporary lacquer art, and the cultural value of contemporary lacquer art, to apply the emotional design of the mother lacquer to the floating lacquer fan, to understand consumers' emotional perceptions when purchasing cultural and creative goods, and to promote the development of cultural and creative industries.

Through this study, we hope to integrate contemporary lacquer art into cultural and creative design, so that lacquer art can be better passed on and promoted in modern society.

2   Literature Review

2.1   Cultural Value of Lacquer Art

In the Neolithic era, our ancestors discovered a liquid that could secrete high viscosity and corrosion resistance. When people used lacquer, a natural liquid, to paint objects, they gradually discovered its decorative effect on objects, and through the pursuit of art, the accumulation of experience, the refinement of techniques, and the use of the characteristics of pigments such as bonding and painting, a special craft and technique called "lacquer art" was formed [2]. Lacquer art is the craft of lacquer. In a broad sense, when it comes to lacquer, it can be classified as lacquer art. The technique of lacquer bleaching began in the 1990s by Fuzhou lacquer artist Mr. Zhi-Qing, L., The drifting lacquer art skillfully blends its randomness with the technical skills of lacquer painting. Through different techniques, lacquer art reveals different painting languages and values, and at the same time, the form of lacquer painting's linguistic expression is constantly being innovated, and "floating lacquer" is a modern representation technique developed from traditional lacquer art techniques.

With the development of society, contemporary art interventions have expanded the circle of traditional lacquer art to include traditional lacquer ware, modern lacquer paintings, contemporary lacquer sculptures, and lacquer installations, among other arts associated with lacquer. Li (2021) argues that "we can distinguish the period of lacquer art works by their expression and characteristics because they were created in a time when the cultural context and techniques corresponded to them. Especially in the contemporary era, the application of decorative and rich expressions in lacquer art creations has nearly overturned people's perception of the traditional lacquer art textural expressions before them. Contemporary lacquer art has undergone radical changes from form to technique, from materials to tools, and from consciousness to form. Contemporary lacquer art is composed of three parts: lacquer ware, lacquer painting and lacquer sculpture, breaking the traditional concept of lacquer ware as a unified world. It straddles two fields: decorative art and pure art. Compared with metal, glass and ceramics, lacquer is a material given life by human beings, but lacquer itself is taken from natural tree lacquer and is alive. During the process of production, it shows different beauty depending on the environment, weather, temperature and technique, and it is a sustainable and eco-friendly material. Meng Wu. [3] believes that lacquer art is a treasure of Chinese culture, and its integration with modern diversified design can not only produce new design ideas, but also effectively convey the cultural connotation of lacquer art, which can satisfy people both materially and spiritually, thus enhancing people's sense of identity with lacquer art culture. The works of each era have traces of the corresponding era, and this is especially true for contemporary lacquer works, which, while pursuing aesthetic expression, show more of the creator's personality and characteristics, and the development of lacquer art has gradually transformed from the traditional figurative functionality to the decorative nature of contemporary aesthetics.

2.2 Emotional Awareness of Cultural and Creative Goods

In art theory, it is often said that "art comes from life and is higher than life". "Emotional cognition" is the essence and life of art, which requires the artist to have his own unique personality and aesthetic vision, and to consciously feel the beauty and emotion from life. Similarly, emotional cognition is also an essential intrinsic characteristic of artists in painting creation. If the object conveyed in lacquer art lacks the emotion of the creator, it will lack artistic infectiousness, and only works that move the heart can cause rational thinking of aesthetic beauty and promote the emotional value of consumers in purchasing cultural and creative goods [4]. The commonly recognized theory of product emotional design is Donald Arthur Norman's three-level theory of emotion (Fig. 1) [5], namely the instinctive layer, the behavioral layer, and the reflective layer. The instinctive layer is the brain's emotional response to the product, which is expressed as the influence of visual factors on people, specifically the shape, color, material and texture of the product. The behavior layer is mainly the feelings of people in the process of use, mainly expressed as the satisfaction and pleasant experience of product function, specifically the efficiency and pleasure of product use. The final product rises to the reflective layer, is the highest stage of emotional design, specific performance can be expected of the product with social attributes, cultural connotations, etc.. The realization of the emotional design of the product is a multi-layered and complex process of interaction between the various levels, not only with the physical level, but also the spiritual level of design. In the contemporary lacquer fan applied to the emotional awareness of cultural and creative products, the first thing consumers will see is to see its shape, color, material and texture on the favorite visual experience, when consumers become interested in the product will consider the convenience of the use of lacquer fan and functional value of the behavioral layer, and finally from the lacquer fan to feel the temperature of the lacquer art craftsmanship of the inner spiritual level of reflection layer design.

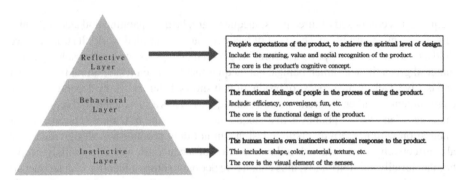

Fig. 1. Donald a. Norman emotional three-level theory

2.3   Emotional Design Factors in Cultural and Creative Goods

Commodity styling design includes three major elements: form, color, and texture, each of which is closely related to the emotion of the product [6]. When providing products to customers, we clearly understand that products need to have a perfect blend of practicality, ease of use, and aesthetics, and on top of that, more emotional elements are needed to stimulate customers' emotions [7]. The specific performance of emotional elements of cultural and creative goods can be divided into two major categories: external emotional elements and internal emotional elements [8]. The external emotional elements of products include semantic, color, and material elements to promote communication with consumers (Fig. 2). Attractive color can strengthen the product to promote consumption; the material of the product can enrich the texture of the product itself to promote the aesthetic economy, thus achieving the effect of gilding the lily. The appearance of the commodity is the skeleton of the product modeling design, then the brand culture of the product, social culture, etc. This is the soul of the product modeling design [9]. The appearance of the product shape is the skeleton of the product, brand culture and social culture is the inner emotional soul. Designers convey culture to consumers through goods, and promote the value of cultural and creative industries while purchasing. The sense of belonging to the product better reflects a sense of spiritual solace. Designers find elements in the corresponding design that match the consumer's sense of value. Among the people with purchasing power, they are free to choose products according to their own interests and personalities, and such may reflect the identity, taste, and pursuit of consumers. Such products are mostly characterized by simple and generous shapes, and at the same time, the brand culture can be found to fit in the shape. This study uses the shape and functionality of the doughnut fan to give the value of traditional lacquer art cultural connotation in the form to meet the function of the This study uses the shape and functionality of the doughnut fan to give the value of traditional lacquer art culture to the product, while satisfying the function of the form, and to compare and associate the form with the specific environment, so that we can understand the needs of consumers and promote communication.

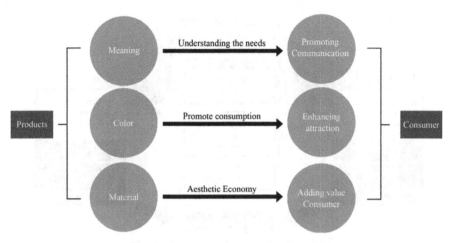

Fig. 2. Desmet product emotional model

3 Research Methods and Procedures

3.1 Research Methodology and Framework

This study uses literature analysis and questionnaire survey as the research method. Firstly, the literature on the historical origin of lacquer bleaching technique, cultural value and emotional cognition of cultural and creative commodities was sorted out, communication theory analysis was conducted by 10 samples of lacquer bleaching dough fans (Fig. 3), and cognitive model questionnaire was designed. In the process of quantitative research, a multi-dimensional questionnaire survey was conducted for different consumer groups on three levels: color modeling, perception cognition, and emotional feelings of lacquer fans, and the related results were analyzed to draw conclusions and recommendations.

In the product emotion model discussed by Dutch scholar Desmet, the process of product emotion generation is explained from a cognitive perspective. The model includes three levels of variables that influence emotion generation: product, product evaluation, and attention. The "product" is the external stimulus for emotion generation and is the emotional object of the product; the second level is the automatic subjective perceptual evaluation of whether the product is relevant to personal interests; and the third level is the reference hidden behind the product evaluation. In 2015, Lin, R. T. explored the reader's cognitive model in depth. Therefore, his cognitive model of "turning poetry into painting" is used as a model case reference in this study [10]. In many contemporary creative arts, artists often use the concept of "maternal fetus" to conceptualize and reflect on the development of the birth of their works. In this study, samples were selected under the theme of "mother fetus to lacquer art" to integrate emotions into the design of lacquer fans, hoping to pass on the traditional lacquer culture while injecting a new soul into cultural and creative design.

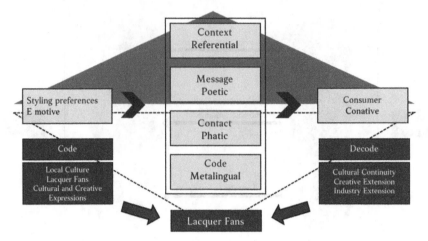

Fig. 3. Lacquered fan propagation cognitive model

3.2 Data Analysis Process

In many contemporary creative arts, artists often use the concept of "mother-born" to think about the birth and development of their works, and natural lacquer itself is a kind of life, and "detachment" is a form of lacquer art creation. In this study, the main viewpoint is applied from the attributes of cultural and creative transformation product design proposed by Xu and Lin [11], which is summarized and integrated in this study to form the framework of cultural and creative product design (Fig. 4), from the conception level of the mother fetus, the rhythm level and the connotation level to the color and shape, perception and cognition, and emotional feeling of the lacquer fan, and from the expression of creation, creative concept and creative result to the design of the fan. In addition, we decoded consumers' emotional awareness of purchasing from the perspectives of cultural creativity, joyful consumption, and how to drive the aesthetic economy in the creative expression, creation concept, and creation results. These nine key words were used as the key words for the subsequent questionnaire survey of consumers, in the hope of integrating emotions into the design of lacquer fans, so that the traditional lacquer art culture can be passed on and the cultural and creative design can be given a new soul.

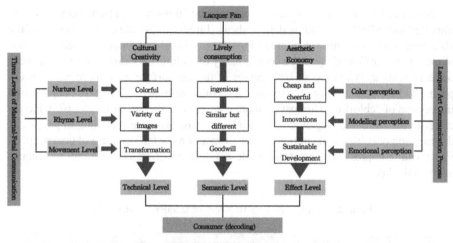

Fig. 4. Data analysis process of urban imagery poster sentiment study

4 Research Results and Analysis

In this study, 10 lacquer fans of five different shapes and colors were used as sample elements (Table 1). 9 questions were designed for each of the 10 lacquer fan sample elements based on: technical, semantic, and effect levels, and rated on a 5-point scale.

Table 1. 10 samples of lacquer fan

A total of 135 valid questionnaires were collected through social networks, and were imported into SPSS for multiple data analysis. Table 2 shows the average scores of the 10 lacquer fans in the nine attribute ratings. It was found that among the ten fans, four of them were "different", giving a commonality of feeling, each different from the other but each similar. When the abstract curves of the fan surface were more pronounced, people had a deeper feeling of "vibrancy" and more saturated colors gave people a first impression of "colorful". Compared to other adjectives, the fan surface of p7, which is closer to the fresh and elegant colors of ink and wash, is more appealing to people, as the collision of colors with appropriate white space on the fan surface will give people a transforming impression. The 10 works do not differ much in terms of craft techniques and practicality.

Table 2. Average score of 10 pieces of lacquer fan properties

	p1	p2	p3	p4	p5	p6	p7	p8	p9	p10
1 Colorful	3.74	4.22	3.99	3.90	4.30	4.04	4.18	3.79	4.10	3.49
2 Variety of images	3.80	4.03	3.95	3.86	3.93	4.12	4.03	3.99	4.13	3.99
3 Transformation	3.93	3.91	3.90	3.75	4.04	4.01	4.10	3.82	4.07	3.82
4 Ingenious	3.74	3.97	3.89	3.84	4.01	4.04	4.07	3.85	4.04	3.81
5 Similar but different	3.84	4.01	3.87	3.83	3.85	4.03	3.93	3.84	3.93	3.85
6 Goodwill	4.08	4.13	4.05	3.82	3.90	4.09	4.14	3.88	4.10	3.97
7 Cheap and cheerful	3.68	3.86	3.86	3.78	3.96	3.95	4.04	3.86	4.03	3.93
8 Innovations	3.98	4.07	4.00	3.84	3.81	4.13	4.05	3.87	4.00	3.88
9 Sustuinable development	3.89	4.01	3.91	3.78	3.92	4.01	4.00	3.89	4.07	3.93

After inputting the data in Table 2 into the MDS multivariate analysis, the multivariate structure of cognitive differences was presented, as shown in the Fig. 5 below, where P1–P10 are the 10, F1–F9 are the 9 attributes, and the 10 posters are divided into four vectors. From the figure, it can be seen that P5 has the best performance in colorful, P7 and P9 have better performance in artisanal, ingenious and pushing the boundaries, p6 has good performance in the remaining attributes, while P1, P4, P8 and P10, on average, do not have too significant differences in performance comparison.

Among the 10 samples of lacquer fans studied, P7 was the one with the best performance in terms of shape, color and cognitive feeling, and it also had the highest rating among the survey results. 78% of the consumers in the survey thought that seeing this lacquer fan would bring good feelings, 65% of them were attracted by it, and 67% of them would recommend it to their friends and relatives when they saw this cultural and creative product, and more than 72% of them More than 72% of consumers think that the cultural and creative goods that incorporate lacquer art into the fan are innovative

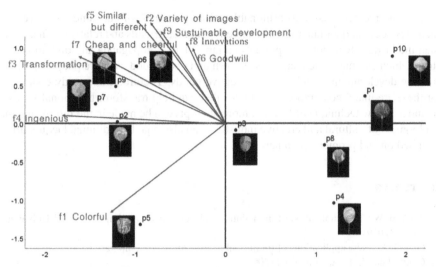

Fig. 5. MDS Analysis of Spatial Structure

and developable. After analyzing the data, we found that there was not much variation in the color and shape of the 10 samples, but more of a preference of people. It also provides new thoughts and references for future creative research.

5   Results and Discussion

This study, using literature analysis and questionnaire, is a cognitive study of the attributes of city posters based on cognitive models, through literature exploration and cognitive theory, we first conducted a case study on the design differences of city posters, constructed six attribute rating models, analyzed the variability of respondents' ratings after viewing these posters and the visual defects of the posters, and finally investigated through questionnaires which individual of these attributes can enhance the perception and identity of the city where they are located, and the following are the results of the study.

This study uses literature analysis and questionnaire survey as the main research method, based on the cognitive model to study the attribute cognition of lacquer art into the fan, firstly, through literature collection and expert scholars' cognitive theory as the basis, the development value of lacquer art is organized, and then through questionnaire to understand the emotional motivation of consumers to purchase this lacquer fan, from the perspective of three levels of lacquer fan's color shape, perceptual cognition and emotional feeling, and constructs A five-point scale rating model was constructed for nine attributes, and finally, a questionnaire survey was conducted to understand whether it is feasible to integrate lacquer art into the new vehicle of communication with fans that can be seen anywhere in life.

Based on the analysis of the literature and the questionnaire survey, it can be understood that the development of contemporary lacquer art has cultural value. Contemporary lacquer fans are generally considered as cultural and creative goods that can bring good feelings and are practical and fashionable. More than 68% of consumers believe that when they see a lacquer fan, they will share it with their friends and relatives. Therefore, when the lacquer technique is applied to a fan, it has a propaganda and dissemination effect, which can make the lacquer art known and understood by more people and promote the development of cultural and creative goods. Therefore, this study concludes that there are many contemporary vehicles that can help transform traditional lacquer art, and as a new technique of lacquer, more attempts can be made in the future, and the development of cultural and creative industries can also enable traditional lacquer art to be passed on and promoted in a new way.

References

1. ShuYan, W.: The implication of ink painting in lacquer painting. Fujian Normal University, Fujian (2019)
2. Qian, L.X.: New applications of traditional lacquer art in contemporary handi-crafts (2013)
3. Chong-hua, Z.: Lacquer and Art (2008)
4. Meng, W.: A Brief Introduction to the Application of Product Design Thinking in the Big Lacquer Craft (2020)
5. Donald, A.N.: Design Psychology. CITIC Press (2012)
6. Zhu, H.Z.: A Study of Female Perfume Bottle Design Based on Emotional Per-ception and Measurement (2018)
7. Chun, S.: Research on the use of emotional factors in product design (2016)
8. Cheng, Z.Z., Jin, Z.Y.: Research on emotional factors of product design (2009)
9. Xia, J.J.: Product Form Design-Design, Form, Psychology (2012)
10. Lin, R., Sandy, L.: Poetic and Pictorial Splendor. National Taiwan University of Arts, New Taipei (2015)
11. Hsu, C.H., Lin, R.: A study on cultural product design process. J. Des. **16**(4), 1–18 (2011)

Viewer's Perceptual Difference in NFT Aesthetics – A Case Study of Popular NFT Avatars (PFPs) at the Opensea

Bin Chen[✉]

Creative Industry Design, National Taiwan University of Arts, 59, Sec. 1, Daguan Rd., Banqiao, New Taipei 22058, Taiwan
yeshanhua825@gmail.com

Abstract. Although creating AI-generated art is still a process of trial and error, the future of AI painting is unstoppable. For exploring the differences in the aesthetic perceptions of the general audience towards the popular NFT avatars, this study investigated the popular avatars on the Opensea platform and collated the four major NFT avatars (PFPs) and their corresponding 12 aesthetic attributes through this study. The results show that although most of the audience are not familiar with NFT avatars, most of them agree with their expectations on the aesthetic attributes of NFT avatars, and that NFT avatars are only a change in form compared to traditional artworks, but the aesthetics of the art itself remains unchanged. The results of this study provide a new insight to the design of the visual style of the NFT avatars, or the aesthetic perceptions of the audience and the preference factors for their work.

Keywords: NFT Avatars · Aesthetic attributes · Perceptual difference

1 Introduction

In recent years, NFT (Non-Fungible Token) has grown stronger and stronger. The virtualization of art, or the combination of art and AI, is one of the future trends. Gareth Jenkinson [1] released a report on 14 July stating that the NFT market will reach US$231 billion by 2030, according to Verified Market Research (VMR), a global research and advisory firm. At the same time, A variety of famous fashion brands and celebrities have collaborated with the NFT artist team to produce co-branded products and enjoy the dividends of the times. Although creating AI-generated art is still a process of trial and error, the future of AI painting is unstoppable.

NFT avatars, or NFT profile pictures (PFPs), are usually images of a character, often above the chest, and are often used as digital profile pictures. The low barrier of access to the NFT trading platform has led to the growth of a large pool of creators, resulting in a rich diversity of styles and derivatives of NFT avatars. The low barrier of access to the NFT trading platform has led to the growth of a large pool of creators, resulting in a rich diversity of NFT avatar styles and derivative values. The NFT avatar is a high-tech product of the future metaverse and a major experiment in artificial intelligence

P.-L. P. Rau (Ed.): HCII 2023, LNCS 14024, pp. 13–24, 2023.
https://doi.org/10.1007/978-3-031-35946-0_2

technology. With the explosion of NFT art, it has also led to an in-depth discussion in the academic field. However, there is a lack of research on the visual aesthetics and cognitive differences of NFT avatars. Will the aesthetics of popular NFT avatars be recognized by the general audience? This is an issue worth discussing.

The results of the study provide an important reference for the design of the visual style of the NFT avatars, the viewer's aesthetic perception of their works and the preference factors. Two research questions raised in this study:

1. To study the cognitive process of the aesthetic experience of NFT avatars, which is the decoding process of the viewer's aesthetic experience.
2. To investigate the differences in the recognition of the aesthetic qualities of various NFT avatars and the aesthetic orientation of the general viewers on both sides of the Taiwan Strait.

2 Theoretical Background and Literature Review

2.1 Style Features of NFT Avatars (PFPs)

Artistic style is one of the most important indicators of cognitive differences in artworks. Stylistic perception is closely related to the aesthetic characteristics of a work of art. In a study by Lakoff and Johnson [2], it was argued that categorization in psychology is a way of identifying an object or trait by strengthening some traits, reducing others, and hiding more of them, so that style is more likely to be recognized if the artwork has more of them. Regardless of the changing times, the study of the stylistic characteristics of artworks requires an understanding of the expressive techniques and compositional elements of the works themselves, as well as familiarity with the types and characteristics of artistic styles. The study explores how "artistic creation" is perceived, involving theories related to semantic cognition, communication theory, and mental models; through the application of "cognitive engineering", the study explores how the art created by artificial intelligence allows the audience to enjoy the emotional experience of art in the field of sensual technology, appreciate the sensual creative content, and achieve the recognition of "artistic creation" by artificial intelligence [3].

In the visual arts, style is a distinctive manner that permits the grouping of works into related categories [4], and it refers to similar critical features for recognition, such as characteristic subject matter or materials, distinctive ways of drawing or applying paints, preferences for specific color combinations, brushstrokes, distortion, and exaggeration. The perception of visual art is a complex performed by the brain to perceive different elements' features in the painting [5, 6]. The various painting attributes, such as colors, shapes, and boundaries, are selectively redistributed to the brain for processing [7].

Free from meta-universe identities or technical aura, the aesthetics of NFT avatars are essentially based on the elements of artistic creation, namely color, shape, composition, and texture. There is no doubt that the style of NFT avatars is closely related to the current art market preferences and the technological influences of the times. Most of the NFT avatars currently exist as digital illustrations, either in the form of artificial intelligence (AI) paintings, digital screen paintings, or partially in the form of traditional paintings. The digitalization of illustration has brought a rich variety of artistic styles and visual expressions to the NFT world, but at the same time, the birth of digital AI platform painting has brought unprecedented market impact and pressure on traditional painting.

2.2   Aesthetic Experience of Artwork

The aesthetic design and experience behind a successful art product is essential to its success. According to Holbrook [8], aesthetic perception is initially a perceptual influence of the human brain on the design of a product. According to neurological research, this is because a key area of the brain, the ventral prefrontal cortex (the area that processes pleasure and reward), is enhanced by aesthetic messages, and visual stimuli with a high degree of aesthetics are rewarded at the brain level with higher associated values than ugly visual stimuli [9, 10].

The viewer enjoys aesthetic works because beauty itself provides an immediate experience of pleasure, a process that occurs naturally [11, 12]. In relation to aesthetic judgements of works of art, Immanuel Kant (1724–1804) refers to the analysis of aesthetic judgements in terms of quality, quantity, relationship, and manner in the 'Analysis of Beauty' chapter of the Critique of Judgement. In the plastic arts, texture generally refers to the artist's perception of different objects using different techniques. Scholars Fang [13] have reorganized and redefined the sense of beauty, dividing it into three aspects: beauty of image, beauty of imagery and beauty of intention.

The aesthetic experience of the NFT avatars is a fusion of the aesthetics of the times and the beauty of the blockchain technology, as well as the aesthetic embodiment of the artist and the appreciator. In addition, from a communication point of view, the aesthetic experience of the NFT avatars is inseparable from the communication, which needs to satisfy three aspects: the technical, the semantic and the effect level. The difference in the aesthetic perception of the NFT avatars comes from the viewer's aesthetic experience of it. The NFT artist transforms the creative concept and stylistic approach to form an aesthetic imagery to express the artwork, and the viewers will have an emotional exchange through the aesthetic experience of the NFT avatars. The audience decodes the aesthetic experience, and as followers of the artist's thoughts, how can they truly understand the artist's original intention of creation, through the connection of experience and the touch of the beauty of image, imagery and idea on emotion, the process of their perception is precisely the process of decoding, and the aesthetic feeling is born in response to the desire of art [13]. The audience's perception of the popular NFT avatars is essentially an aesthetic experience of the artwork, and the resulting difference in perception depends on whether the aesthetic expression and stylistic characteristics of the artwork are preferred by the audience.

2.3   Viewer's Cognitive Process of the Artwork

With the rapid development of technology in recent years, cognitive-related issues are becoming a very important research topic in the field of human factors engineering [14]. Cognitive engineering is closely aligned with the future development of artificial intelligence. At the same time, the style of an artwork is recognized by the general audience and is dependent on the cognitive process of the viewer. Baumberger [15] points out that artworks have a cognitive function and that their cognitive function partly determines their aesthetic value. Norman's conceptual model, including the design model, the user model, and the systemic impression, represents the artist model, the listener model, and the artwork, respectively, and provides insight into the cognitive model of the viewer, i.e., the process of perceiving the external aesthetic and emotional meaning of the artwork, helping the artist to use the familiar symbols of the listener to create artworks with a common experiential mental model for evaluating artworks [16].

In terms of the programmatic school of communication theory [17], there are three levels of communication that must be met for a successful 'artistic creation' to be communicated from the artist (the sender) creating the artwork (the message) to the audience (the recipient): the first is the technical level, where the recipient can see, hear, touch, and even feel the message. The first is the technical level, where the message is seen, heard, felt, and even sensed by the recipient. The second is the semantic level, which is how to make sure that the recipient understands the meaning of the message without misinterpretation, misunderstanding or even ignorance, that is, how to make sure that the reader understands the original meaning of the message. The third is the effect level, how to get the receiver to take the right action according to the message's original meaning, that is, how to effectively influence the intended behavior [18]. Visualizing and mental imagery are pictorial identifications of cognitive states, reflecting different states of aesthetic activity of the listener [19]. For the listener, there are three key steps to understanding the meaning of a work of art: recognition (attracting attention), awareness (understanding and perception) and reflection (deep emotion). On the one hand, the viewer's aesthetic experience of art is a dynamic process, in which the 'inner feeling' is stimulated by the 'perception of form' of the aesthetic object, resulting in a holistic experience [20]. On the other hand, artistic creation is an expression of the artist's pursuit of beauty, which has the characteristics of experiencing 'form' with 'content' and enriching 'form' with 'content', complementing each other. Therefore, exploring the perception of 'artistic creation' from the perspective of the reader's 'decoding' can help to understand the mental journey of the artist's creation [21].

Understanding the stylistic and cognitive process of NFT's avatar works will not only help to realize the decoding process between NFT artists' artistic creation and the audience, but also provide a cognitive research context for the development of AI painting and a solid theoretical basis for subsequent experimental creation.

3 Materials and Methods

To investigate the difference in the general audience's perception of the aesthetics of NFT avatars, this study investigated the popular avatars on the Opensea platform.

3.1 Case Introduction

The case studies were sourced from the Opensea platform (the world's largest NFT trading platform) and were prepared for the expert review and questionnaire by surveying the top 30 popular NFT avatar artworks on Opensea. The following is an overview of the Opensea platform, the source for NFT cases. Opensea is currently the world's largest NFT trading platform, bringing together mainstream NFT players and is also the comprehensive and open trading platform of choice for beginners to get started. It has a low threshold, good user experience, strong inclusiveness, and complete control of the

Table 1. This study cases' Introduction and Aesthetics attributes

Characteristics	Aesthetics attributes	NFT Avatar (PFP)	Team Introduction
Pixelated	Composition	CrytoPunks #9998	CrytoPunks, one of the world's first NFTs, was released in June 2017 as a first-generation application on Ether and is widely regarded as the starting point of the modern 'crypto art' movement.
	Fantasy	Moobirds#2080	Moonbirds is a set of 10,000 pixelated owl NFT items to be released on 16 April 2022, Moonbirds will act as an avatar for the PROOF community, driving brand communication and attracting more mid-level players.
	Fun	CrypToadz by Gremplin#6704	CrypToadz by Gremlin is an avatar NFT (PFP) project consisting of 6969 small pixelated frogs, conceived and created by the famous anonymous artist Evil King Gremlin at the saturation of the PFP and Punk derivative projects.
Three-dimensional	Space	Meebits#17522	Meebits are 3D characters rendered in voxels, upgraded from large stickers to dynamic voxel figures, consisting of a variety of different elements commonly used in NFT collectibles. The project is due for release in May 2021.
	Fashion	HapePrime #3980	HapePrime launches in January 2022, these 8192 HAPE NFTs are unique NFTs made by Digi mental Studios using 3D modelling techniques, and these 3D ape NFTs are cleverly designed to incorporate many common street elements.
	Science fiction	Clone X#4583	Clone X is a collection of 20,000 algorithmically generated 3D characters designed for metaverse interaction launched on the Ethereum blockchain. The project is due for release in November 2021.

(*continued*)

Table 1. (*continued*)

Comic	Comics	Bored Ape Yacht Clubs#5602	The Bored Ape Club, a 10K project launched in April 2021, has become the most expensive and influential series of NFT collectibles.
	Japanese manga	Azuki#1468	Azuki, a 10k project launched in January 2022, has become one of the most successful projects in NFT thanks to its innovative Japanese manga style.
	Weird	Goblintown.wtf #5948	A collection of 10,000 NFTs released in May 2022, depicting the various unpleasant animals one might encounter in Goblin Town. An ironic description and sigh of relief, the 'ugly' and 'grotesque' allude to the current cold market conditions.
Simple	Childish	Cool Cat#3995	Cool Cat is a 10k project launching in July 2021 and the creative team has created a utopian world with cool cats as the main characters in a lively and bright cartoon style.
	Minimalist	Doodles#813	Doodles NFT is a 10k project launching in October 2021, based primarily on the work of Burnt Toast, and Doodles intends to create a collaborative ecosystem that spreads happiness and creativity.
	Casual	Mfers#6704	Mfers is a well-known NFT project in Web3, with a total of 10,021 projects. It was the first project to voluntarily relinquish its intellectual property rights, respecting a bottom-up philosophy and growing wildly without any project owners.

platform. The choice of Opensea for this study ensures the authenticity, accuracy, and longevity of the study.

This study categorized the top 20 most popular NFT avatars on the Opensea platform and selected the most popular or the highest priced one from these works. The samples were then screened for four broad categories of character, and within each of these four categories, the aesthetic attributes of the work were identified in three directions, resulting in a total of 12 aesthetic attributes. 4 main characteristics of the NFT avatars at the Opensea are Pixelated, Three-dimensional, Comic and Simple. The 12 aesthetic attributes are Composition, Fantasy, Fun, Space, Fashion, Science fiction, Comics, Japanese manga, Weird, Childish, Minimalist and Casual (see Table 1). The questionnaire was finally revised through expert evaluation to complete the sample selection.

3.2 NFT Avatars (PFPs) Cognitive Model

Based on the solid foundation of literature and theory, as well as the content of this study, a preliminary cognitive model of NFT avatar works was constructed for this study (see Fig. 1). The aesthetic experience of the NFT portraits combines the viewer's intuitive perception of the images and their judgement of their specific style and aesthetic features. The whole process is a sublimation from perception to cognition, a cognitive process from the most basic stylistic impression to its fundamental semantic impression. It's also a process of perceiving the aesthetic experience of a work of art from the beauty of the image to the beauty of the imagery and then to the beauty of the ideas generated.

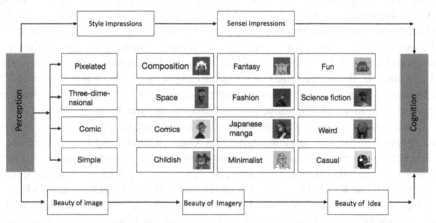

Fig. 1. NFT Avatars(PFPs) Cognitive Model

3.3 Questionnaire Design

To examine the accuracy of the audience's perception of the attributes and the differences in perceptions of the samples, the strength of the selected works was questioned in terms of their aesthetic attributes. In the questionnaire, the questions were set up in the form of a matrix, and the target audience was the general audience on both sides of the Taiwan Strait. By asking them to make intuitive judgments on the 12 aesthetic attributes of each of the 12 works, it was possible to quickly see the general audience's identification with these aesthetic attributes and the communicative effect of the NFT avatars.

For the fairness of the questionnaire, the subjects were informed of the purpose of the experiment. They are then asked to assess the sample artwork for this study based on the questions by intuition. In this study, their assessment of the suitability of each piece of artwork consisted of 2 questions. Question 1 explored viewers' identification with the aesthetic attributes selected for this study, using a 5-point Likert scale with scores ranging from 1 ('strongly disagree') to 5 ('strongly agree'), while question 2 explored viewers' preference for the style of their work or the images themselves, ranging from 0 to 100%, with higher scores associated with higher identification.

In this study, 130 questionnaires were collected, and 127 valid questionnaires were sent to the public in Taiwan and Mainland China. A total of 46 questionnaires were collected from people living in Taiwan, while 81 questionnaires were collected from people living in Mainland China. The gender breakdown was 48 for males and 79 for females; the age breakdown was 15 for those aged under 18, 57 for those aged 18–25, 25 for those aged 26–35, 16 for those aged 36–45, 7 for those aged 46–55, 3 for those aged 56–60 and 4 for those aged over 60.

4 Results and Discussion

Based on the analysis of the above research results, the findings reflect that the cognitive model and evaluation matrix of the aesthetic experience of the NFT avatars is reasonable, and the findings reflect the process of the general audience's aesthetic experience of the NFT avatars, which provides a theoretical basis for the aesthetic judgement of the NFT avatars and allows for an intuitive attribute analysis of the aesthetic evaluation of the NFT avatars. In the future, this study will investigate the relationship between NFT avatar preference and viewers' aesthetic experience, as well as the relationship between subjects' background and cognitive factors, based on the questionnaire data.

Consequently, A spatial analysis of the audience's aesthetic cognition was conducted, on a sample of 12 NFT avatars embodying 12 aesthetic attributes and 4 stylistic features, and a confusion matrix of the aesthetic cognition of the NFT avatars (see Table 2). From the results of the MDS statistical analysis, the stress index and the absolute coefficient were found to be Kruskal's Stress = 0.16911 and RSQ = 0.89674, which indicates that the two vectors are suitable for describing the spatial relationship between the 12 aesthetic attributes, the 4 stylistic characteristics, and the multi-vectors in this study. This shows that the two vectors are appropriate for describing the spatial relationship between the 12 aesthetic attributes, the 4 stylistic characteristics and the 12 NFT avatars and the multi-vectors in this study.

The following conclusions are drawn from the confusing matrix of this study:

(1) p2, p5, p6, p8, p9, p10 and p11 performed in line with the strength of the aesthetic attributes as expected.
(2) p1 was expected to have the strongest sense of composition, but the result was not high, instead it scored highest in the sense of randomness, while p12 was expected to have the strongest sense of randomness, but in the end, there was a difference of 0.08 with p1, indicating that the sense of randomness of p12 was very strong and did not exceed the strength of p1.

Table 2. NFT avatars and the confusing matrix of aesthetic properties

	p1	p2	p3	p4	p5	p6	p7	p8	p9	p10	p11	p12
f1 Composition	2.97	3.01	2.94	3.35	3.41	3.04	2.94	3.32	2.50	2.63	3.21	2.28
f2 Fantasy	2.09	3.54	2.25	2.20	2.61	2.39	2.20	3.24	1.97	2.18	3.38	1.85
f3 Fun	2.92	3.15	3.33	2.98	3.35	2.43	3.17	2.74	2.43	3.01	3.30	2.93
4 Space	2.24	2.48	2.39	3.41	3.58	3.02	2.43	2.76	2.03	2.11	2.49	2.04
5 Fashion	2.65	2.72	2.62	2.69	3.76	2.95	2.74	3.50	1.96	2.41	3.09	2.33
f6 Science fiction	2.54	3.12	2.47	2.46	2.95	3.17	2.22	2.76	2.15	2.02	2.68	1.96
f7 Comics	2.61	2.58	2.81	2.57	3.46	2.85	3.42	2.79	2.49	2.25	2.94	2.57
f8 Japanese manga	2.06	2.21	2.11	1.91	2.07	2.53	2.09	3.43	2.04	2.49	2.28	1.90
9 Weird	3.15	2.92	3.51	3.21	3.30	3.36	3.30	2.34	3.79	2.51	2.80	2.93
f10 Childish	2.68	3.07	3.04	2.41	2.35	2.14	2.59	2.31	2.05	3.39	3.38	2.74
f11 Minimalist	3.16	2.68	2.46	2.24	2.24	1.91	2.30	2.49	1.96	3.02	3.32	2.57
f12 Casual	3.28	2.93	2.65	2.50	2.54	2.22	2.51	2.72	2.72	2.84	3.02	3.20

(3) p5 had the highest selection rate among all the works, and scored highest in f1 sense of composition, f3 sense of fun, f4 sense of space, f5 sense of fashion, f6 the highest scores were achieved in f1 composition, f3 interest, f4 space, f5 fashion and f6 aesthetics.

Based on the results of the confusion matrix (see Fig. 2), a cognitive-spatial analysis of the 12 aesthetic attributes of the viewers in the 12 works was conducted, and the angle between each aesthetic attribute and the three-way axial diagram of the avatars was analyzed in terms of multiple vectors. This is the conclusion drawn from the multi-directional analysis diagram:

(1) The study shows that p11 and p2, p4 and p6, p3 and p7 are more closely related as one group, while p10 and p1 are more closely related as one group.
(2) f2 Dreaminess, f8 Japanese Manga and f3 Fun are interrelated, with p2 and p11 having higher strengths in Dreaminess and Fun; f1 Simplicity, f10 Childishness and f12 Casualness are interrelated, with p1, p10 and p12 having higher strengths in Casualness, Simplicity and Childishness; f4 Spatiality and f7 Manga are interrelated, with p5, p6 and p4 having higher strengths in Spatiality and Manga.

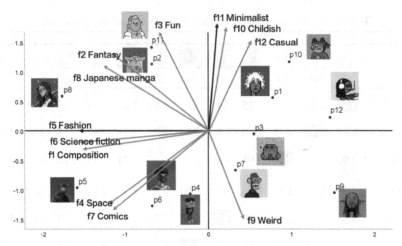

Fig. 2. Multi-dimensional cognitive analysis of NFT avatars

(3) p9, p12 and p3 are weaker in all aesthetic attributes, and the angle between p9 and each aesthetic attribute is too large, indicating that the audience's recognition of their aesthetics is low.

5 Conclusion

The development of the metaverse in the field of art, the explosion of NFT avatars is only the beginning of AI painting, and the rapid development of AI painting in the future is an inevitable trend, but in the life of the public, NFT art has not yet reached popularity, and most of the audience are quite unaware of NFT avatars, or even unheard of. Even so, the viewer's aesthetic experience of the NFT avatars is the same as that of other works of art, so AI painting and traditional painting are both variations of form, the aesthetics of the art itself remains the same. Therefore, although there are some discrepancies in the results of this study, the overall finding is that most of the audience's perception of the aesthetic properties of the NFT avatars is consistent with expectations. The audience's choice reflects whether the effect level of the artwork is well expressed in relation to the semantic and technical levels. The effect layer of an artist's work affects the audience's intuitive experience and choice to a certain extent. It embodies the artist's own aesthetic feelings and stylistic characteristics, awakening the audience's experience of beauty. Also, the definition of aesthetic attributes also affects the semantic perception of the different stylistic features of the NFT avatars. There is a correlation between the aesthetic attributes of different NFT avatars and the style of their images, and the audience's assessment of different works also reflects their specific aesthetic recognition.

Based on the analysis of the above research results, the findings reflect that the cognitive model and evaluation matrix of the aesthetic experience of the NFT avatars is reasonable, and the findings reflect the process of the general audience's aesthetic experience of the NFT avatars, which provides a theoretical basis for the aesthetic judgement of the NFT avatars and allows for an intuitive attribute analysis of the aesthetic evaluation of the NFT avatars.

As a fresh product of this era, the popularity of NFT avatars is inevitably due to the perceptual design and aesthetic experience of the images behind them, and Chen [22] also points out that NFT viewers' purchases can reflect their own aesthetic qualities and aesthetic experiences to influence their attitudes and tastes. The essence of beauty is expressed through objects (artworks), as well as viewers achieve aesthetic, meaningful and emotional experiences through the process of viewing artworks. This will help to explore the audience's mental models in appreciating NFT avatars and provide a basis for artists to create artworks that convey emotional elements and inner meanings through artworks. This study is one of the few research projects on the aesthetic awareness of NFT avatars. The core argument of this study is that the central thesis of this study is the difference in the recognition of the aesthetic qualities of various NFT avatars and the aesthetic orientation of the general audience on both sides of the Taiwan Strait. The results of this study provide a new insight to the design of the visual style of the NFT avatars, or the aesthetic perceptions of the audience and the preference factors for their work.

References

1. Gareth Jenkinson. https://cointelegraph.com/news/nft-market-worth-231b-by-2030-report-projects-big-growth-for-sector. Accessed 30 Dec 2022
2. Lakoff, G., Johnson, M.: The metaphorical structure of the human conceptual system. Cogn. Sci. **4**(2), 195–208 (1980)
3. Gao, Y., Jiede, Wu., Lee, S., Lin, R.: Communication between artist and audience: a case study of creation journey. In: Rau, P.-L. (ed.) Cross-Cultural Design. Culture and Society: 11th International Conference, CCD 2019, Held as Part of the 21st HCI International Conference, HCII 2019, Orlando, FL, USA, July 26–31, 2019, Proceedings, Part II, pp. 33–44. Springer International Publishing, Cham (2019). https://doi.org/10.1007/978-3-030-22580-3_3
4. Fernie, E.: Art History and its Methods: A Critical Anthology, pp. 27–28. Phaidon, London (1995)
5. Solso, R.L.: Cognition and the Visual Arts, pp. 34–36. MIT Press, Cambridge (1996)
6. Shamir, L., Macura, T., Orlov, N., Eckley, D.M., Goldberg, I.G.: Impressionism, expressionism, surrealism: automated recognition of painters and schools of art. ACM Trans. Appl. Percept. **7**, 1–17 (2010)
7. Steenberg, E.: Visual Aesthetic Experience. J. Aesthet. Educ. **41**, 89–94 (2007)
8. Holbrook, M.B., William, B.M.: Feature interactions in consumer judgments of verbal versus pictorial presentation. J. Consumer Res. **8**(2), 103–113 (1981)
9. Reimann, M., Zaichkowsky, J., Neuhaus, C., Bender, T., Weber, B.: Aesthetic package design: a behavioral, neural, and psychological investigation. J. Consumer Psychol. **20**(4), 431–441 (2010). https://doi.org/10.1016/j.jcps.2010.06.009
10. Nadal, M., Munar, E., Capo, M.A., Rossello, J., Cela-Conde, C.J.: Towards a framework for the study of the neural correlates of aesthetic preference. Spat. Vis. **21**(3–5), 379–396 (2008)
11. Dutton, D.: The Art Instinct: Beauty, Pleasure, & Human Evolution. Oxford University Press, New York (2009)
12. Reber, R., Schwarz, N., Winkielman, P.: Processing fluency and aesthetic pleasure: is beauty in the perceiver's processing experience. Pers. Soc. Psychol. Rev. **8**, 364–382 (2004)

13. Fang, W.T., Gao, Y.J., Zeng, Z.X., Lin, P.H.: A study of general audience's perception of aesthetic experience of dance art. J. Des. **23**(3), 23–46 (2018)
14. Wang, M.Y., Yeh, Y., Huang, R.C.: The application of cognitive psychology in Taiwan: from cognitive research to humanistic design in the context of technology. Chin. J. Psychol. **55**(3), 381–404 (2013)
15. Baumberger, C.: Art and understanding: In defense of aesthetic cognitivism. PhilPapers (2013)
16. Norman, D.: The design of everyday things: Revised and expanded edition. Basic Books, New York (2013)
17. Fiske, J.: Introduction to Communication Studies, pp. 5–6. Routledge, London (2010)
18. Lin, R.: An application of the semantic differential to icon design. In: Proceedings of the Human Factors Society Annual Meeting, pp. 336–340, Los Angeles, CA: SAGE. (1992).
19. Zeimbekis, J., Raftopoulos, A.: The Cognitive Penetrability of Perception: New Philosophical Perspectives. Oxford University Press (2015).
20. Beardsley, M.C.: Aesthetics, Problems in the Philosophy of Criticism. Hackett, Indianapolis (1981)
21. Lin, R.T., Lee, X.M.: Poetry, and Painting-The Beauty of the Immortal Cloud Project. National Taiwan University of Arts, New Taipei (2015)
22. Chen, Y.Y.: A study of brand value, aesthetic quality, and empowerment in influencing users' purchase of non-homogenized tokens (NFT). Master's thesis, National Taiwan University of Arts, Department of Graphic Communication Arts (2022)

Preferences for Chinese TV Dramas and Purchase Intentions of Southeast Asian Audiences

Ping-Hua Lee, Pin-Hsuan Chen, Dian Yu, and Pei-Luen Patrick Rau(✉)

Department of Industrial Engineering, Tsinghua University, Beijing 100084, China
rpl@mail.tsinghua.edu.cn

Abstract. TV dramas are an important medium for Southeast Asians to understand Chinese culture. Fashion dramas, however, are less innovative and competitive than costume dramas in terms of theme innovation. In order to grasp the audience's perceived preference and consumption willingness for Chinese TV dramas, this study conducted empirical research by recruiting 60 subjects from Thailand and Malaysia. The research is divided into two parts. Firstly, the perceptual preference design related to the plot (preference, viewing intention) and non-plot (dialogue speed, total duration of the drama) is learnt through the audiences' country, the plot era background and the content level of Chinese cultural elements. Next, the purchase intention of Chinese products (consumption, finance, science and technology) under different stimulus conditions is sorted out by the audiences' country, video viewing order, and video viewing quantity. The research results will put forward specific TV series design suggestions based on the background of the plot era, the content level of Chinese cultural elements, the order of video viewing (costume before fashion/fashion before costume), the number of video views (8/16 films) and the audiences' country, so as to enhance the cultural soft power and international influence of cross-cultural communication of TV dramas.

Keywords: Chinese TV dramas · Southeast Asian audiences · perceived preferences · purchase intentions

1 Introduction

Chinese TV dramas have been playing an essential role in promoting the country's culture and values to the global audience, particularly in many developing countries where Chinese TV dramas are becoming increasingly popular. However, despite their growing popularity, most of China's costume dramas generally lack Chinese features from character attire and makeup to plot themes. This is partly due to the low cultural confidence and consciousness and the insufficient exploration of core cultural competitiveness in China's media and film industry [3].

In contrast, Korean dramas have already established a stable base in Southeast Asia slightly a few years back [1]. With their unique storylines, stylish fashion, and captivating music, Korean dramas became the most popular TV programs in the region,

P.-L. P. Rau (Ed.): HCII 2023, LNCS 14024, pp. 25–37, 2023.
https://doi.org/10.1007/978-3-031-35946-0_3

challenging the hegemony of Hollywood and other western media. As a result, many Korean dramas have been successfully exported to Southeast Asia, boosting the Korean Wave or "Hallyu" in the region [8].

The growing popularity of Korean dramas in Southeast Asia raised important questions about the preferences and consumption patterns of Southeast Asian audiences [18]. Against this backdrop, the purpose of this study is to understand Southeast Asian audiences' perceived preferences of Chinese TV dramas, as well as their purchase intentions on Chinese products, and propose an audience-centered TV drama design that will meet their leisure and entertainment needs, enhance the viewing experience, and promote domestic and international economic development. The study will focus on the audience preferences and purchase intentions of Chinese TV dramas in two Southeast Asian countries, Thailand and Malaysia. Through this research, we hope to fill in the gap of designing Chinese TV dramas that can better satisfy the needs of overseas audiences.

2   Literature Review

2.1   Preference Design of Chinese TV Dramas

In the export markets of Chinese TV dramas, the era context and the integration of Chinese elements in the drama subjectively influence one's visual impression, while the dialogue speed and total duration of the show objectively affect the viewing experience of the audience.

Costume dramas typically feature characters whose clothing styles date back to before 1911 AD, while modern dramas are based on contemporary China, using realistic content and dialogue to uncover the mysterious veil of the country's rapid development. Costume dramas tend to pique the curiosity of overseas audiences who are unfamiliar with Chinese culture and lack personal experience. Modern dramas with less obscure language made it attractive to Southeast Asian audiences, due to their curiosity about the Chinese language [23]. African audiences, despite having significant cultural differences with China, also showed interest in understanding modern China's high-speed development through modern dramas [7].

Incorporating Chinese cultural elements into TV dramas can highlight the rich cultural heritage, foster cultural confidence and competitiveness, and ultimately realize cultural value. The "China National Image Global Survey Report 2016–2017" also mentioned that Chinese cuisine (52%), traditional Chinese medicine (47%), and martial arts (44%) were the most interested cultural aspects of the country. The demand for actual depiction and ecological information of China were met by integrating traditional features in TV dramas [6, 20].

In addition, linguists believed that Mandarin has a slower speech rate compared to Spanish. The rate of speech for syllables and consonant clusters were 34% and 49% slower respectively, while the amount of information covered was only 4% less. Therefore, Mandarin easily pulled off as a loose and imprecise impression to people [16]. Southeast Asian audiences may have a negative viewing experience and lower acceptance for TV dramas with slower dialogue speed, as their culture emphasizes fast and efficient working styles.

The total duration of TV dramas may also affect the perception of Southeast Asian audiences. The total duration of Chinese TV dramas had significantly increased in the recent years, from an average of 34 episodes in 2010 to an average of 43 episodes in 2017, while Southeast Asian TV dramas usually have around 20 episodes. This phenomenon highlighted the potential issues of excessive plot narration and slow pacing in Chinese TV dramas, which invisibly increase the amount of time engaged, eventually lead to a higher likelihood of viewers abandoning the drama. According to a big data report from iQiyi, the dropout rate for TV dramas with more than 45 episodes has been increasing year by year, reaching 56% in 2018 [17]. Therefore, regardless of the plot quality, the viewing willingness is closely related to the total duration of the drama.

2.2 Influence on Chinese Product Purchase Intentions

Television dramas serve as a medium for shaping the image of their place of origin, which can influence audiences and enhance their willingness to pay a premium for local products [10]. The images of the place of origin presented in costume dramas and fashion dramas differ to a large extent. There is a need to further analyze whether the "product placement" trend formed by TV dramas based on different time periods can enhance the willingness to purchase other products. A study conducted by Murphy et al. [15] divided consumer products into convenience product, preference product, shopping product, and specialty product, among which consumers would invest more to consume shopping and specialty products. Recognition of a product's value increases as consumers invested more money, time, and energy in it. Therefore, this study also explored the audiences' perception preferences for TV dramas and the motivation behind their willingness to purchase related products.

3   Research Framework and Questions

Plot era background (costume or modern drama) and content level of Chinese cultural elements (high or low) were selected as the two most interesting factors of Chinese TV dramas to be further analyzed, of their influence on preference and viewing willingness of Southeast Asian audiences. The next step was to evaluate how preference and viewing willingness affect the purchase intentions of consumers on different categories of Chinese products. At the same time, the direct influence of the two factors chosen at the start was also discussed on how they stimulate purchase intentions on Chinese products. Lastly, plot era background and content level of Chinese cultural elements were analyzed with dialogue speed and total drama duration.

Many studies and reports on Chinese TV dramas have pointed out that historical dramas and martial arts dramas are the most popular genres among overseas audiences, and costume dramas have become the best category for export [21, 22]. However, there is currently no research that empirically examines the reasons behind this. Therefore, this study starts from the perspective of Southeast Asian audiences to examine whether they really prefer Chinese costume dramas and the reasons behind their preferences. Under the strong influence of Western culture, Chinese film productions were seen to incorporate elements of Western culture, but Chinese cultural elements were still relatively rare. In the eyes of overseas audiences, China is still a mysterious and unfamiliar country, with more people hoping to obtain more information related to China. Therefore, Chinese film industry should reconsider whether to incorporate more elements with Chinese characteristics in film and television works, in order to enhance audience preferences and viewing willingness.

- RQ1. How do "plot era background" and "content level of Chinese cultural elements" in Chinese TV dramas affect Southeast Asian audiences' perceived preference and viewing willingness on these TV dramas?

Many studies have shown that a film or television work can convey plenty of information about a region. After audiences are exposed to a film or television work, they will perceive it and this will affect their perception or attitude towards a region [9, 19]. This part aims to observe if the perception one has will directly affect their purchase intentions.

- RQ2. How do the perceived preference and viewing willingness of Southeast Asian audiences on Chinese TV dramas influence their purchase intention of Chinese products?

In the study by Koschate-Fischer, Diamantopoulos and Oldenkotte [10], the researchers pointed out the with the influence of country of origin, a positive image can enhance consumption behaviors and increase the willingness to pay. There are currently no findings on the effect of driving sales between costume dramas and modern dramas.

- RQ3. After viewing Chinese TV dramas of different plot era backgrounds, how will this affect the purchase intention of Chinese products of Southeast Asian audiences?

With the difference in habit and preference of dialogue speed by Southeast Asian audiences, costume dramas may not be favorable to them as the difference in languages and culture could bring about discomfort when they listen to Chinese TV dramas. According to Hofstede sixth cultural dimension, ASEAN6 have higher indulgence score and tend towards short-term orientation as compared to China [5]. It is more likely for them to prefer fast-tempo and plot-intensive TV dramas, with higher preference on shorter total drama duration.

- RQ4. In the design of Chinese TV dramas, how do plot era background and content level of Chinese cultural elements influence Southeast Asian audiences' preference on dialogue speed and total drama duration?

4 Methodology

4.1 Participants

The study was conducted with a total of 60 participants from Thailand (30) and Malaysia (30), of which 80% were female, and the average age was 24.5 years (SD = 4.1). 44 participants (74%) had a bachelor's degree or above. As the population composition and culture differ to some extent between the two countries (percentage of ethnic Chinese in the local population: 14% in Thailand and 23.4% in Malaysia; uncertainty avoidance: 64 in Thailand and 36 in Malaysia; long-term/short-term orientation: 32 in Thailand and 41 in Malaysia), the study believed that the differences may cover more preferences of Southeast Asian audiences, which may facilitate the promotion to other countries with similar backgrounds.

4.2 Experiment Design

The experiment focused on the perceived preferences and viewing intentions of Southeast Asian audiences towards TV dramas at both the narrative-related and non-narrative-related levels. Narrative-related designs include the historical background of the plot and the inclusion of Chinese cultural elements, while non-narrative-related designs cover dialogue speed and total length of the drama. The influence on Chinese product purchase intentions is measured three times before, during, and after the experiment, focusing on three product types: consumer goods, finance, and technology [12, 14].

The experiment consisted of two 2 * 2 * 2 independent mixed designs: one focused on the perceived preferences of TV dramas, and the other discussed the purchase intentions Chinese product. The independent and dependent variables of the experiment are shown in Table 1.

Table 1. Experimental Variables

		Perceived Preference	Purchase Intention
Independent	Between-subjects	Target country (Thailand/Malaysia)	Video viewing order (costume then modern/modern then costume) Target country (Thailand/Malaysia)
	Within-subject	Plot era background (costume drama/modern drama) Content level of Chinese cultural elements (high/low)	Number of videos watched (8/16)
Dependent		Preference level [15] Viewing willingness [13] Dialogue speed [4] Total duration of drama [4]	Consumption willingness

4.3 Materials

According to Douban's rating list (as of 15 February 2020), the top four most viewed dramas under each category (costume and modern) were used as the experimental video in this study. Two one-minute clips were selected from each drama and labeled with high or low levels of Chinese cultural elements. At least one of the same lead actors was present in both clips. Based on the "China National Image Global Survey Report 2016–2017", Chinese cultural elements include, but not limited to, Chinese cuisine, traditional Chinese medicine, martial arts, traditional Chinese calendar, natural scenery of China, Confucianism, calligraphy and painting, products, architecture, cultural classics, clothing, and technological inventions. To ensure that the video clips sufficiently highlighted Chinese cultural elements, experts were recruited to validify prior to the experiment.

4.4 Procedure

The participants were evenly divided by country and assigned to two groups: one group watched 8 video clips from costume drama followed by 8 video clips from modern drama, while the other group watched 8 video clips from modern drama followed by 8 video clips from costume drama. The video order was determined using a Latin square design to avoid order effects. Each experiment consisted of 16 tasks, with each task containing a one-minute video clip and a survey on factors such as preference and viewing willingness. Participants will be informed of the total number of episodes and the length of each episode for the drama they have just watched, in order to measure their preference for total drama duration. Chinese product purchase intention was also measured using surveys before, during (after completion of 8 tasks), and after the experiment (after completion of 16 tasks). To ensure the experiment quality, a simple content test was conducted after each video. The complete experiment process is shown in Fig. 1.

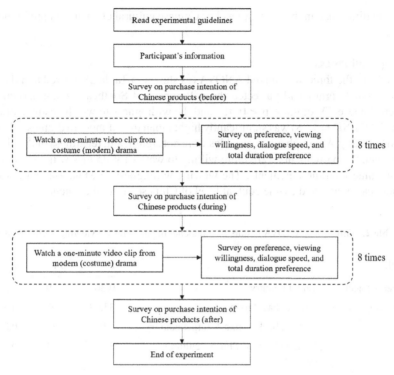

Fig. 1. Experiment Procedure

5 Results

5.1 Perceived Preferences of Chinese TV Dramas

The audience's perceived preference for TV dramas will be measured by indicators such as preference, viewing willingness, dialogue speed preference, and total drama duration preference based on factors such as the target country, plot era background, and content level of Chinese cultural elements. Among them, preference and viewing willingness are related to the plot, while dialogue speed and total duration of the drama are related to non-plot. According to the normality test, the degree of preference and the preference on dialogue speed will be tested by non-parametric tests, while the viewing willingness and the preference on the total duration of the drama will be tested by parametric tests.

Preference

The Kolmogorov-Smirnov Z test showed no significant difference in preference between the audience countries (p = 0.39). According to the results of Wilcoxon's test, the background of the plot era significantly affected viewers' preference (p < 0.01), and the participants' preference for costume dramas (Med = 4.69, IQR = 1.07) was significantly higher than that of modern dramas (Med = 4.03, IQR = 0.97). However, there was no significant difference in the content level of Chinese cultural elements on preference (p = 0.72).

Viewing Willingness
The results of the three-way mixed ANOVA (as shown in Table 2) showed that the plot era background significantly affected the willingness of Southeast Asian participants to watch Chinese TV dramas (p < 0.01), and the willingness to watch costume dramas (Mean = 3.82, SD = 1.38) was significantly higher than that of modern dramas (Mean = 3.13, SD = 1.28). Although other variables were not significant, regardless of the plot era background, the participants were more willing to watch TV dramas with high content level of Chinese cultural elements. The viewing willingness of Malaysian participants was more easily affected by the content level of Chinese cultural elements.

Table 2. Three-way ANOVA results of independent variables on viewing willingness

Variables		F	p	η_p^2
Between-subjects	Target country	0.30	0.59	0.01
Within-subjects	Plot era background	33.43	0.00*	0.37
	Plot era background * Target country	0.96	0.33	0.02
	Content level of Chinese cultural elements	2.38	0.13	0.04
	Content level of Chinese cultural elements * Target country	0.31	0.58	0.01
	Plot era background * Content level of Chinese cultural elements	0.02	0.89	0.00

Dialogue Speed Preference
The results of the Kolmogorov-Smirnov Z test showed that there was a significant difference in the preference on dialogue speed in the target countries (p < 0.01). Compared with Thailand (Med = 3.92, IQR = 0.72), Malaysian subjects (Med = 4.52, IQR = 0.93) significantly preferred faster dialogue speed. According to the Wilcoxon test results, there was no significant difference between the plot era background (p = 0.91) and the content level of Chinese cultural elements (p = 0.75) on the dialogue speed preference of the two groups of participants.

Total Drama Duration Preference
Based on the three-way mixed ANOVA, there is no significant impact of the three independent variables on total drama duration preference.

5.2 Purchase Intentions of Chinese Products

Consumer Products

Results of a three-way mixed ANOVA are presented in Table 3, showing that the order of video viewing significantly influenced participants' willingness to purchase Chinese consumer products (p = 0.03). Regardless of the number of videos viewed, the stimulus condition of first modern and then costume dramas (8 videos: Mean = 4.66, SD = 0.81; 16 videos: Mean = 4.72, SD = 0.95) led to significantly higher purchase intentions than the stimulus condition of first costume and then fashion dramas (8 videos: Mean = 4.13, SD = 0.91; 16 videos: Mean = 4.22, SD = 0.98). Furthermore, an interaction effect was found between the order of video viewing and the audiences' country. Thai participants who were exposed to modern dramas first (Mean = 4.87, SD = 1.02) showed a greater willingness to purchase consumer products compared to those who were exposed to costume dramas first (Mean = 3.89, SD = 0.86).

Table 3. Three-way ANOVA results of purchase intention for consumer products

Variables		F	p	η_p^2
Between-subjects	Video viewing order	5.13	0.03*	0.08
	Target country	0.23	0.63	0.00
	Video viewing order * Target country	4.14	0.05*	0.07
Within-subjects	Video viewing quantity	2.15	0.15	0.04
	Video viewing quantity * Target country	0.18	0.68	0.00
	Video viewing quantity * Video viewing order	0.11	0.74	0.00

Financial and Technological Products

The results of the Kolmogorov-Smirnov Z test indicate that the video viewing order, viewing quantity, and target country had no significant impact on the purchase intention of Chinese financial and technology products.

6 Discussion

6.1 Perceived Preferences of Chinese TV Dramas

Plot era background: Southeast Asian audiences showed significantly higher preference and willingness to watch costume dramas than modern dramas. This phenomenon could be attributed to the fact that costume dramas can fulfill entertainment desires like aesthetics and curiosity, which are closely linked to the local culture of short-term orientation and high indulgence. Costume dramas create a unique visual experience through scenes, attire, and landscapes, which stimulates the process of promoting rapid perception of freshness, unfamiliarity, arousing curiosity and aesthetic experience. From the perspective of the Uses and Gratifications Theory, costume dramas are more likely to satisfy prying and curiosity psychological needs. Compared to modern dramas, costume dramas presented Chinese architecture, vessels, artworks, and other contents which differed from the daily experience of overseas audiences, resulting in higher preference and willingness to watch costume dramas among audiences.

Content level of Chinese cultural elements: The amount of Chinese cultural elements did not affect participants' preference for TV dramas. Although there was no statistically significant difference in their viewing willingness, the experimental results showed that Southeast Asian audiences were more willing to watch TV dramas with high content level of Chinese cultural elements. Just like the Korean drama "My Love from the Star" in 2013 that sparked a Korean-style fried chicken and beer trend, exposure to positive information with local cultural characteristics can establish a rich and profound cultural impression, stimulate a sense of closeness and curiosity, and help drive cross-cultural communication cycles through TV dramas [11].

Target countries: The viewing willingness of Malaysian participants was more sensitive to the amount of Chinese cultural elements than Thai participants, although it did not reach statistical significance, it is still worth noting. In addition, people often react to unfamiliar languages with a fast pace that they cannot keep up with. The proportion of Chinese Malaysians is 1.7 times higher than that of Thailand, and their familiarity with Chinese may be higher as well. Therefore, this study speculated that the reason why Thai participants preferred slower dialogue speed than Malaysian participants may be related to the proportion of Chinese population within the country. Coupe et al. [2] also pointed out that the Thai language is slower in terms of the number of syllables per unit time compared to Mandarin, which may also affect the preference of Thai participants for dialogue speed.

Total duration of drama: According to the results of the perception preference for Chinese TV dramas, there is no significant difference in the preference for the total drama duration, which may be related to the dragging of the plot in recent years, and it is generally present in both costume dramas and modern dramas.

6.2 Purchase Intentions of Chinese Products

Based on the experimental results, the video viewing order led to different purchasing intentions among participants for different types of Chinese products, with significant differences in purchasing intentions for consumer products. Participants were more willing to buy consumer products after being stimulated by the modern dramas. In contrast, the effect of the costume dramas on increasing purchasing intentions for consumer products was limited, even when followed by the stimulation of modern dramas. This result suggested that modern dramas are helpful in establishing the audience's perception of the origin of consumer products, as they have the characteristic of directly conveying information about modern Chinese goods. This perception forms a first impression that expands from a specific to a comprehensive influence, which reflects the psychological halo effect. However, ancient objects in ancient dramas are difficult to promote or map onto modern consumer cognition, which not only made it difficult to resonate with the audience but also lowered their purchasing intentions. Moreover, Thailand's uncertainty avoidance is much higher than that of Malaysia, which may make it more challenging for Thai participants who first received stimulation from costume dramas to extend their impression of costume dramas to modern Chinese consumer products, resulting in lower purchasing intentions.

The experiment also explored the impact of Chinese TV dramas on the willingness to purchase financial and technology products. Even though the results did not reach statistical significance, it was found that participants were more inclined to purchase technology products. The research results showed that Chinese TV dramas had a positive impact on the willingness to purchase Chinese consumer products, which may be related to technology products gradually iterating as rapidly as consumer products, coupled with the influence of Chinese technology brands in the Southeast Asian market, making TV drama-driven Chinese technology products more popular than financial products.

7 Conclusion

This study explored the perceptual preferences of Southeast Asian audiences for Chinese TV dramas and the influence of Chinese TV dramas on the purchase intention of Chinese products through experiments conducted on Thai and Malaysian participants. The study was conducted from two aspects: plot-related and non-plot-related perceived preferences, and analyzed purchase intentions for three types of products: consumer, financial, and technological. Based on the results, the study summarized five key takeaways on perceived preferences and purchase intentions of Southeast Asian audiences for Chinese TV dramas.

Southeast Asian audiences had a significantly higher preference and viewing willingness for costume dramas than modern dramas. As Southeast Asian culture values quick results and short-term entertainment, the themes of costume dramas brought freshness and unfamiliarity to Southeast Asian audiences, and the audiovisual enjoyment was different from their daily experiences. Korean dramas were a benchmark for the development and overseas marketing of television dramas, and they remained a valuable reference for China's costume dramas. In recent years, Korean dramas such as "Itaewon Class" and "Hotel Del Luna" have adopted different themes and constantly created innovative visual experiences, quickly aroused the audience's curiosity. This study believed that even though costume dramas have their inherent attractiveness, modern dramas can still break through existing frameworks and tap into the potential of the Southeast Asian market through innovative themes and the inclusion of unique elements. At the same time, costume dramas should also strive for innovation to avoid audience aesthetic fatigue. In addition, the study also found that the content level of Chinese cultural elements had a positive impact on the level of preference and viewing willingness, even if the results were not statistically significant, it is still worth considering in practical applications.

The dialogue speed of Chinese TV dramas preferred by Malaysian audiences was faster than that of Thai audiences. The influence of audience's native language and country's population composition could result in significant differences in dialogue speed preferences. Therefore, knowing the local language and identify the difference in speed between the local language and Mandarin, can help the post-production team in adjusting the speed to fit the audience's habits. This can enhance the viewing experience and improve the communication effectiveness of non-plot related elements in the dramas.

Southeast Asian audiences preferred shorter TV dramas in total duration (total number of episodes). Chinese TV dramas exported to Southeast Asian market should adopt user-centered design, shorten the total drama duration to achieve the effect of fast-tempo, plot-intensive, and effective progress of the plot. The increase in usage and purchase of Chinese film productions can only be reached if we can cater to the viewing habits of both domestic and foreign audiences while retaining the high-quality features of television dramas.

China's modern dramas effectively promoted the purchase of consumer products and technology products by Southeast Asian audiences. According to the psychology of the halo effect, modern dramas are more effective in building an impression of Chinese consumer products and increasing the willingness to purchase them than costume dramas, especially for high-value Chinese specialty products (such as antiques and paintings) and shopping products (such as clothing). Although the purchase intention of technology products did not reach statistical significance, their mean value was higher than that of consumer and financial products, which may be related to the increased visibility of Chinese technology brands through the placement of advertisements and sponsorships in TV dramas. The study further speculated that high-value, high-investment products such as specialty and shopping products, and technology products can significantly enhance purchasing intention. In addition, designs such as co-branded products and IP marketing, which give products higher value, may also create higher sales and overseas market share.

For audiences in countries with high uncertainty and avoidance (Thailand), costume dramas did not easily promote the willingness to purchase consumer goods in China. Countries with a high uncertainty avoidance index tend to avoid unclear and unknown consumer behavior, especially when the audience cannot visually display information such as product quality and appearance design. Therefore, clearly displaying the image and portraying information of Chinese products in costume dramas will help to reduce the purchasing risk concerns of such audiences, essentially promote TV drama-driven consumer behavior, and purchasing intentions.

References

1. Ariffin, J.T., Bakar, H.A., Yusof, N.H.: Culture in Korean drama towards influencing Malaysian audiences. Int. J. Innov. Res. Eng. Manag. **5**(1), 10–14 (2018)
2. Coupé, C., Oh, Y.M., Dediu, D., Pellegrino, F.: Different languages, similar encoding efficiency: comparable information rates across the human communicative niche. Sci. Adv. **5**(9), eaaw2594 (2019)
3. Guan, W.: 国产电视剧海外传播建构中国国家形象的维度与偏差 [The dimensions and biases of constructing China's national image by overseas communication of domestic TV dramas]. J. Lover **7**, 37–39 (2017)
4. Hall, J.L., Flanagan, J.L.: Intelligibility and listener preference of telephone speech in the presence of babble noise. J. Acoust. Soc. Am. **127**(1), 280–285 (2010)
5. Hofstede, G., Hofstede, G.J., Minkov, M.: Cultures and Organizations: Software of the Mind: Intercultural Cooperation and its Importance for Survival, 3rd edn. McGraw-Hill (2010)

6. Hu, Z., Liu, J.: Nongovernmental identity, communication appeal, multimedia channels, multi-type programs: on the four dimensions of enhancing the international communication force of Chinese media. J. Commun. **4**, 5–24 (2013)
7. Jiang, D.: 中国当代题材电视剧对外传播的跨文化传播解读—以《媳妇的美好时代》在非洲传播为例. [Intercultural communication interpretation of the external communication of Chinese contemporary TV dramas - taking the communication of "a beautiful daughter-in-law era" in Africa as an Example]. Mod. Audio-Video Arts **02**, 9–11 (2014)
8. Kim, E.M., Ryoo, J.: South Korean culture goes global: k-pop and the Korean wave. Korean Soc. Sci. J. **34**(1), 117–152 (2007)
9. Kim, S., Kim, M.J.: Effect of Hallyu cultural products in Thai society on enhancement of Korean national image and intention to visit. Korean J. Tour. Res. **23**(4), 101–125 (2009)
10. Koschate-Fischer, N., Diamantopoulos, A., Oldenkotte, K.: Are consumers really willing to pay more for a favorable country image? A study of country-of-origin effects on willingness to pay. J. Int. Mark. **20**(1), 19–41 (2012)
11. Lee, S.T.: Film as cultural diplomacy: South Korea's nation branding through Parasite (2019). Place Brand. Public Dipl. **18**, 93–104 (2021)
12. Lee, S., Ha, S., Widdows, R.: Consumer responses to high-technology products: product attributes, cognition, and emotions. J. Bus. Res. **64**(11), 1195–1200 (2011)
13. Lee, J., Lee, M.: Factors influencing the intention to watch online video advertising. Cyberpsychol. Behav. Soc. Netw. **14**(10), 619–624 (2011)
14. Murphy, P.E., Enis, B.M.: Classifying products strategically. J. Mark. **50**(3), 24–42 (1986)
15. Murry, J.P., Lastovicka, J.L., Singh, S.N.: Feeling and liking responses to television programs: an examination of two explanations for media-context effects. J. Consum. Res. **18**(4), 441–451 (1992)
16. Pellegrino, F., Coupé, C., Marsico, E.: A cross-language perspective on speech information rate. Language 539–558 (2011)
17. Qiu, W.: 数据揭秘剧集长度与观众弃剧率关系, 短剧才是王道?. [Unveiling the Relationship Between TV Series Length and Audience Dropout Rate: Is Shorter Better?]. https://www.sohu.com/a/233746124_603727. Accessed 8 Apr 2020
18. Shim, D.: Hybridity and the rise of Korean popular culture in Asia. Media Cult. Soc. **28**(1), 25–44 (2006)
19. Su, H.J., Huang, Y.-A., Brodowsky, G., Kim, H.J.: The impact of product placement on TV-induced tourism: Korean TV dramas and Taiwanese viewers. Tour. Manag. **32**(4), 805–814 (2011)
20. Wang, B.: 走向世界的可能性与现实性—关于中国现实题材电视剧的出口问题. [The possibility and reality of going to the world—on the export of Chinese TV dramas with realistic themes]. China Telev. **3**, 59-65 (2004)
21. Zhang, S.: Exploring how Chinese TV dramas reach global audiences via Viki in the transnational flow of TV content. J. Transcult. Commun. **2**(1), 69–89 (2022)
22. Zhou, Q.: Review of China's film and TV drama export in recent years. In: Yue, F. (ed.) Translation Studies on Chinese Films and TV Shows, pp. 1–20. Springer, Singapore (2022). https://doi.org/10.1007/978-981-19-6000-0_1
23. Zong, Q.: The communication of China Mainland's TV dramas in Southeast Asia – based on the audience perspective. (Master's thesis). Zhejiang University, China (2014)

Analysis of Perceived Preferences and National Images for Chinese TV Dramas in Southeast Asia

Ping-Hua Lee, Pin-Hsuan Chen, Dian Yu, and Pei-Luen Patrick Rau[✉]

Department of Industrial Engineering, Tsinghua University, Beijing 100084, China
`rpl@mail.tsinghua.edu.cn`

Abstract. Southeast Asia accounts for more than half of China's total TV drama exports, but in recent years, with fierce market competition, the advantages of China's TV drama production have been challenged to some extent. Due to its delayed start in TV drama development, China's film and TV production is not as advanced as that of other countries. In order to improve the foresight and initiative of Chinese TV and film foreign communication, quantitative research on the viewing needs of overseas audiences can provide foreign marketing strategies centered on audience needs and preferences, ensure competitiveness and shape the national image through TV and film titles that best fit local market expectations. The questionnaire of this study investigated 151 Southeast Asian audiences' preferences for Chinese TV dramas and perceived national image to provide a quantitative basis for China's subsequent overseas marketing of TV dramas. Based on the results, this study summarized suggestions for audience-centered cross-cultural design of TV dramas to enhance the competitiveness of China's film and TV exports.

Keywords: Chinese TV dramas · Southeast Asia · perceived preferences · national image

1 Introduction

With the flourishing development of global trade and communication, the external projection of culture and image has become an important issue for countries. Compared to movies, TV dramas have a greater continuous and periodic implication on the audience. In addition, the cultural customs, social environment conditions, and values conveyed through TV dramas can contribute to cultural understanding between nations, which helps to improve impressions and reduce cultural differences [7, 14, 16]. Since 2001, China has proposed the "Going Global Project" of the cultural industry, and in 2007, it once again emphasized cultural soft power to encourage Chinese film and television to go overseas [11]. According to statistics from the State Administration of Radio, Film and Television of China in 2017, the national export of film and television products and services reached US$400 million, and TV dramas accounted for 70% of the export value of film and television works [32]. Exports were mainly directed to Southeast Asia and countries that are geographically close and culturally homogeneous with China, such as

P.-L. P. Rau (Ed.): HCII 2023, LNCS 14024, pp. 38–49, 2023.
https://doi.org/10.1007/978-3-031-35946-0_4

Japan and Korea, because the proximity of life and social culture easily resonates with audiences [29, 33]. However, compared with other relatively mature film and television works (American, Japanese and Korean dramas, etc.), the competitiveness of Chinese film and television industry is still lacking in terms of production level, plot novelty, core values, and cultural self-awareness [21]. It is not easy to have breakthrough growth in the highly competitive market of Southeast Asian film and television.

The purpose of this study was to explore the preferences and perceived national image of Southeast Asian audiences towards Chinese TV dramas. Past studies lacked quantitative measurement methods and data support, and did not systematically understand the impact of drama series structure on audience perceptions and attitudes. This study developed a questionnaire based on the structure of TV dramas to measure audiences' perceived preferences and national image, so as to effectively measure Southeast Asian audiences' perceptions of Chinese TV dramas and understand the strengths and weaknesses of the current development of Chinese TV dramas.

2 Literature Review

2.1 Country Image

Country image is a belief and impression of a region and can be considered as a strategic asset for brand marketing and needs to be managed in a focused manner [18]. Kim and Richardson [12] showed that the high-frequency and multi-directional exposure of films and TV shows can provide a multidimensional and intuitive perception of a region's culture, economy, technology, and politics. In addition, audiences' preferences for films and TV shows are likely to project their perceptions and attitudes toward a region [13, 14, 27]. When television has become an actively utilized medium of mass communication in countries, the dramas, shows, movies, etc. that it broadcasts will dominate social interactions and their audiences' perceptions of the country's image, status, and influence [9].

Beerli et al., [2] suggested that film and television productions can generate subjective impressions and emotional connections to a region. When audiences perceive the actors in a drama as a meaningful reference group, they not only represent a preference and affinity for the actors, but also a more positive attitude toward the cultural and regional context of the story in the drama [27]. In addition, liking is the most intuitive emotional response to a film or television production, focusing on the positive experience of the audience [23]. Japanese films and television productions sparked a trend of Japanese pop culture in the 1990s, making Japanese products, language, and lifestyle a part of everyday life [10, 20]. In addition, the spread of Japanese animations, such as "Case Closed" and "Dragon Ball Z", has positively influenced the feeling of closeness, favorability, liking, and perception of the national image of Japan, which in turn has led to the development of the tourism industry [15]. Many popular Korean films and TV shows in recent years have similar phenomena, and Lee et al. [19] used the Parasocial Interaction Theory proposed by Donald Horton and Richard Wohl to explain the influence of Korean dramas on the national image of Korea. The results of the study indicated that although Korean dramas only convey information to overseas audiences in a one-way manner, they invariably established an emotional connection between the audience and the characters of the drama, creating trust and dependence, which in turn promoted the national image of Korea.

In recent years, there were few successful cases of China's film and television works expanding overseas markets, and nearly half of them are historical dramas, and although this developed a positive impact on Chinese national image to a certain extent, the negative perceptions implied by them are also worth reflecting on. The historic traditional clothing, landscape, architecture, lifestyle, speech and behavior of historical dramas differ greatly from the modern society today [3, 30]. They satisfied audiences' curiosity about Chinese history and shape the image of China's cultural profundity, but the dramatic exaggerated rendering (harem scandals, etc.) and fictional plots (fatalism, ghosts, gods and demons, etc.) have also created biases and limitations on the moral or cultural connotations [25].

2.2 Characteristics of Southeast Asians

To capture the characteristics of Southeast Asian audiences, this study focused on the six Southeast Asian economies ASEAN6 (Thailand, Indonesia, Singapore, Vietnam, Philippines, and Malaysia) as defined by Oktaviani et al. [24].

Based on the six dimensions (power distance, individual/collectivism, masculinity/femininity, uncertainty avoidance, long-term/short-term orientation, and indulgence/constraint) sorted out by Hofstede's cultural dimension theory, it can be found that the two most significantly different dimensions of the six countries have from China are: long-term/short-term orientation and indulgence/constraint. In terms of long-term/short-term orientation, the six countries mentioned above are less motivated to plan for the future compared to China, they value quick results, and prefer fast-paced, plot-intensive, and information-rich dramas [25]. In terms of indulgence/constraint, it can be found that the six countries mentioned above seek simple pleasure and freedom, enjoyment of life, and focus on entertainment more than China. Studies on Southeast Asian audiences pointed out that leisure and entertainment are the most important motives for watching TV dramas in China [25].

It can be seen that the cultural differences between Southeast Asia and China are likely to affect the perceived preference for Chinese TV dramas and the national image of the country. Blindly promoting the development of film and television based on China's subjective perception of film and television works will cause difficulties for future film and television output.

3   Research Framework and Hypotheses

Numerous research studies have demonstrated that a film or television production has the ability to communicate information about a particular area. Once viewers have been exposed to such productions, they will develop perceptions which can impact their attitudes towards that region [13, 20]. According to Aristotle's six elements theory, preference has been further dissected into plot, fable, dialogue, actors, music and landscape [4, 8]. The national image has also been divided into eight dimensions, namely culture, people, product, technology, economy, diplomacy, policy, and military. This research explored the relationship between the drama elements, perceived preferences, and national image of China as a result of exposure to Chinese TV dramas by the Southeast Asian audiences. As such, three research questions were proposed to identify the link between the variables.

- RQ1. How do the six elements of Chinese TV dramas affect the perceived preferences of Southeast Asian audiences?
- RQ2. How does the perceived preferences of Southeast Asian audiences on Chinese TV dramas influence the national image of China?
- RQ3. After viewing Chinese TV dramas of different plot era backgrounds, how will this affect the national image of China?

4 Methodology

This study focused on audience perceived preferences for Chinese TV dramas and the national image in order to quantify the overall picture of audience perceptions of television dramas and the country in the context of drama. There are two basic reasons behind this: 1) perceived liking is used as a measure in many studies to understand the comprehensiveness of audience perceptions; 2) Drama has a significant influence on shaping the nation's image, assessing the audience's perceived national image will aid in understanding the impact of TV dramas on the national image.

For this study, a questionnaire was created with 65 questions based on the literature and the six dramatic elements outlined in Sect. 6 of Poetics by Aristotle, which are plot, fable, dialogue, actors, music, and landscape. Demographic variables and the participants' experience of watching Chinese TV dramas were also included in the questionnaire, as well as the overall perceived preference for each of the six elements, and the perceived national image for each element. The national image component of the questionnaire was developed based on eight dimensions identified from CIPG and related research, which are people, culture, science and technology, product, economic, diplomatic, political, and military [5, 22].

The measurement of perceived preference was designed based on the scales for TV program preferences developed by Barwise et al. [1], Murry et al. [23], and Lee et al. [19], along with the questionnaire items designed for drama structure. A 7-point Likert scale was used to collect the responses of the subjects (1: strongly disagree, 7: strongly agree). In terms of national image measurement, the item directly asked about the national image of China perceived by the participants. Participants answered based on a 7-level Likert scale (1: decrease greatly, 4: stay the same, 7: increase greatly), so as to reasonably quantify the impact of TV dramas on the country's image.

The questionnaire was written in English, and three Thai and Malaysian students from Tsinghua University were invited to pilot-test and optimize the items to ensure that they could understand the questions correctly and ensured the quality of the questionnaire.

The questionnaires were distributed on social media (WeChat, Facebook, Instagram) with active audiences in six countries in Southeast Asia (ASEAN6). All participants have watched more than two Chinese TV dramas. A total of 191 online questionnaires were collected, and out of which,151 were valid. Of these, 119 (79%) were women. In terms of target countries, 26 people from Thailand (17%), 27 people from Indonesia (18%),

23 people from Singapore (15%), 23 people from Vietnam (15%), 21 people from the Philippines (14%), 31 people from Malaysia (21%). The age distribution was mainly between 20–29 years old (120 people, 79%). In terms of education level, 105 people (70%) hold a bachelor degree or above. In terms of Chinese experience, 109 respondents (72%) have lived in China for more than one month.

According to the experience and statistics of watching Chinese TV dramas, most of them watched through online platforms (82%), and each participant watched an average of 3.6 (SD = 1.7) dramas, of which 1.9 are costume dramas (SD = 1.6) and 1.7 are modern dramas (SD = 1.4). Majority of the themes centered around love (86%), followed by the palace (55%), with history (52%) coming in close behind.

In order to judge the appropriate statistical method for the questionnaire data, this study used the K-S normality test to test the data normality. According to the results, all the variables in the questionnaire did not meet the normality assumption, therefore, the analysis of this study adopted non-parametric test (Spearman correlation analysis).

5 Results

In terms of measuring preference, this study referred to previously validated scales with good reliability, including those used in Murry et al. [23] with a Cronbach alpha of 0.89, Lee et al. [19] with a Cronbach alpha of 0.91, and Cowley et al. [6] with a Cronbach alpha of 0.87. Adjectives such as good, interesting, attractive, and well-designed were extracted to measure preference, ensuring the reliability of the questionnaire.

The questionnaire items were developed based on literature review, expert evaluation, and pre-testing to ensure the relevance between the items and the behavioral constructs to be measured, ensuring the internal validity of the questionnaire. As the sample group had sufficient experience with Chinese TV dramas and came from regions with relatively high economic development in Southeast Asia, the data obtained in the study is representative and helps to generalize the results to other audiences with Southeast Asian cultural backgrounds, ensuring the external validity of the questionnaire.

5.1 Analysis of Perceived Preference

The measurement of perceived preference was firstly done through the expression of participant's subjective perceptual liking on the six structural elements of drama, and then evaluated the overall perceived preference based on their responses.

Descriptive statistics revealed (as indicated in Table 1) that participants had the highest perceived preference for musical elements and relatively low reported preferences for fable. Overall, the participants had a positive evaluation of the general perceived preference for Chinese TV dramas. Moreover, Southeast Asian audiences preferred the sensory and aesthetic drama viewing experience to the TV series' fundamental design.

According to the results of Spearman correlation analysis (as shown in Table 2), the participants' overall perceived preference was moderately positively correlated with six structural elements, among which the actor had the highest correlation to overall perceived preference ($\rho = 0.74$). In terms of the correlation of the structural elements of Chinese TV dramas, fable was moderately positively correlated with the plot ($\rho = 0.74$)

and the same for fable and dialogue ($\rho = 0.61$). Plot and landscape ($\rho = 0.42$), as well as plot and music ($\rho = 0.42$) were positively correlated with low degree.

Combined with Table 1, the perceived likability of plot, fable, and dialogue were closely interdependent, representing that the core meaning conveyed by the drama affected the development of the plot and the design of dialogue. However, the low perceived likability of core meaning by the audience suggested a possible gap between the current arrangement of meaning in Chinese TV dramas and the expectations of Southeast Asian audiences, which may also affect dialogue and plot.

Table 1. Descriptive statistics of perceived preference

	Mean	S.D.
Plot	5.1	1.2
Fable	5.0	1.2
Dialogue	5.2	1.2
Actors	5.3	1.3
Music	5.4	1.3
Landscape	5.3	1.2
Overall	5.3	1.2

Table 2. Spearman correlation analysis based on the six elements of TV drama

	Plot	Fable	Dialogue	Actors	Music	Landscape	Overall
Plot	1	–	–	–	–	–	–
Fable	0.64	1	–	–	–	–	–
Dialogue	0.48	0.61	1	–	–	–	–
Actors	0.51	0.59	0.56	1	–	–	–
Music	0.42	0.51	0.45	0.55	1	–	–
Landscape	0.42	0.54	0.59	0.57	0.46	1	–
Overall	0.54	0.68	0.61	0.74	0.55	0.58	1

5.2 Perceived National Image

The influence of Chinese TV dramas on the perceived national image was measured through the use of six structural elements of TV dramas and eight dimensions of national image. The objective of this study was to gain an understanding of whether Chinese TV dramas positively or negatively impacted the perceived national image, specifically in terms of whether it has an elevating effect (scoring above 4 points) or a diminishing effect (scoring below 4 points) on perception.

Based on the descriptive statistical results, as shown in Table 3, there was a positive correlation between the enhancement of cultural image and the elements of plot, fable, music, and landscape. Additionally, the improvement of national image was positively correlated with the elements of dialogue and actors. On the other hand, dialogue, actors, music, and landscape had the least impact on improving the military image, whereas the elements of plot, fable, actors, and music had the least impact on improving the political image.

Table 4 showed the results of Spearman's correlation analysis, which indicated that the elements of fable, dialogue, actors, and landscape in TV dramas had a moderate positive correlation with China's national image, while music had a moderate positive correlation with China's cultural image. The element of plot, however, falls between a low positive correlation and no correlation with the eight dimensions of national image.

When combining the results from Table 3 and Table 4, it is evident that the elements of fable, dialogue, actors, and landscape can contribute to enhancing China's culture or national image, as the moderately positive correlation results suggest. This means that Chinese TV dramas with good meaning conveyed, clear dialogue design, distinctive actor arrangement, and exquisite landscape scenes can have a positive impact on China's culture or national image. Additionally, the music arrangement in TV dramas is an element that directly reflects the cultural image and plays a significant role in enhancing it. Music design is not only an element that can improve China's cultural image, but it is also a crucial carrier for TV dramas to showcase China's image.

Table 3. Descriptive statistics of six drama elements on national images

	Culture	Technology	Economic	Product	People	Diplomatic	Military	Political	Average
Plot	**5.5** (**1.2**)	5.3 (1.2)	5.1 (1.0)	5.1 (1.1)	5.1 (1.1)	4.8 (1.1)	4.7 (1.2)	**4.6** (**1.0**)	5.0
Fable	**5.3** (**1.1**)	5.1 (1.1)	4.9 (1.1)	5.2 (1.1)	4.9 (1.0)	4.7 (1.0)	4.5 (1.1)	**4.5** (**1.0**)	4.9
Dialogue	5.2 (1.2)	4.7 (1.0)	4.7 (1.1)	4.9 (1.0)	**5.2** (**1.1**)	4.6 (1.0)	**4.4** (**0.9**)	4.5 (1.0)	4.8
Actors	5.3 (1.2)	5.0 (1.2)	5.0 (1.1)	5.2 (1.1)	**5.4** (**1.2**)	4.8 (1.1)	**4.5** (**1.0**)	**4.5** (**1.0**)	5.0
Music	**5.4** (**1.1**)	4.8 (1.1)	4.6 (1.0)	5.0 (1.1)	5.2 (1.2)	4.5 (1.0)	**4.4** (**1.0**)	**4.4** (**1.0**)	4.8
Landscape	**5.4** (**1.1**)	5.2 (1.1)	5.1 (1.1)	5.2 (1.1)	5.1 (1.0)	4.8 (0.9)	**4.5** (**1.0**)	4.6 (0.9)	5.0

Despite the fact that the plot has had a more significant impact on improving China's cultural image among Southeast Asian audiences, the low positive correlation between cultural image and plot suggested that the plot itself did not significantly affect China's cultural image. Rather, the plot is a vehicle for conveying cultural features that are rooted in China's long and profound cultural heritage. These cultural features are potential dramatic elements that shape cultural images, but their effectiveness may be ambiguous due to variations in the audience's recognition of the plot and their perception of its moral aspects. Similar results were also found in the elements of fable and landscape.

Table 4. Spearman correlation analysis on perceived national image based on drama elements

	Culture	Technology	Economic	Product	People	Diplomatic	Military	Political
Plot	0.29	0.12	0.26	0.08	**0.32**	0.27	0.24	0.35
Fable	0.44	0.35	0.43	0.30	**0.63**	0.46	0.34	0.43
Dialogue	0.59	0.37	0.42	0.52	**0.61**	0.40	0.29	0.43
Actors	0.46	0.38	0.38	0.43	**0.63**	0.40	0.35	0.33
Music	**0.64**	0.40	0.43	0.47	0.59	0.41	0.26	0.40
Landscape	0.46	0.31	0.32	0.35	**0.53**	0.30	0.19	0.24

The audience's perception of these three elements was influenced by their individual perception of China, which may be affected by factors such as the length of their stay in China.

The findings suggested that the Southeast Asian audience has a positive attitude towards the depth and richness of Chinese culture. However, due to their limited awareness of China, they tend to project their affirmation of the cultural image onto the people image that is closer to them. In other words, their positive perception of Chinese culture is expressed through their perception of China's national image, rather than through a direct recognition and appreciation of the cultural elements within the Chinese TV dramas. This implied that efforts to promote China's cultural image among Southeast Asian audiences may benefit from a more targeted approach that emphasizes the cultural features that are most likely to resonate with the audiences.

6 Discussion

6.1 Perceived Preference

The current trend in the Chinese film and television industry is to invest most of its resources in hyped celebrities, fancy props, and special effects, while neglecting the importance of plot, dialogue, and fable design. This has led to problems such as protracted plots, illogical dialogue, and shallow meanings, which are not conducive to the long-term development of the industry. However, the moderately positive correlation between the overall perception preference of actors and the preferences of Southeast Asian audiences suggested that the current trend in the Chinese film and television industry, which focuses on promoting hyped celebrities, may be related to the preferences of this audience. In the future, it is important to focus on developing TV dramas that take into account the perceived preferences of Southeast Asian audiences while ensuring the depth of core elements, such as meaning. The Chinese film and television industry should pay more attention to this direction in the future.

6.2 Perceived National Image

Costume and modern dramas are two major genres in domestic TV productions in China. Costume dramas typically depict Chinese historical culture and court intrigues, with different themes giving audiences different impressions. However, themes that focused on the dark side of human nature, such as struggle and the underworld, may have a negative impact on the country image. Additionally, the palace buildings in these dramas, such as the Forbidden City, implied a closed-off and class-based society, which can negatively impact the image of China's economy and diplomacy.

In contrast to costume dramas, most modern dramas focused on the present China, incorporating elements of technology and the economy to portray a prosperous nation. By featuring high-tech products and fluent use of foreign languages, modern dramas like "Mr. Right" and "Women in Shanghai" have significantly improved their diplomatic image compared to costume dramas.

Regarding the impact of audience awareness on cross-cultural communication, the study found that "cultural freshness" had a more significant influence on the national image of Chinese TV dramas than "cultural proximity or familiarity". For example, audiences who have not been exposed to as much Chinese culture may find the landscapes and music with Chinese characteristics more beautiful and interesting due to their novelty, resulting in greater tolerance and interest. This, in turn, can lead to positive changes in the diplomatic and cultural images of China.

7 Conclusion

This study is based on a questionnaire of the perceived preferences and national image of different structural elements of Chinese TV dramas in Southeast Asia. According to the analysis results, the following five cross-cultural design suggestions for Chinese TV dramas to expand into the Southeast Asian market can be summarized.

Southeast Asian audiences tend to prefer the sensory elements of TV dramas such as music, landscape, and actors, rather than the core elements such as plot, fable, and dialogue. This is likely due to their different cultural background from that of China, so the TV drama arrangements that easily resonated with Chinese audiences may not necessarily be understood by Southeast Asian audiences. In the future, when marketing and selecting TV dramas for Southeast Asian audiences, it is important to consider the design of the plot and its implications, so as to arouse resonance and reflection among Southeast Asian audiences in terms of concepts and values.

Southeast Asian audiences tend to have a higher preference for actors compared to other aspects of Chinese TV dramas, with plot and preference have the lowest correlation. This suggested that the casting and portrayal of actors may have a significant impact on the attitudes of Southeast Asian audiences towards TV dramas. Therefore, when producing TV dramas for the Southeast Asian market, it is important to consider the design and selection of actors, as this can directly influence the success of the show in this region.

On top of the plot, the fable, dialogue, actors, music, and landscape preferences had a significant positive impact on the overall national image. When arranging the plot for Chinese TV dramas, it is important to consider the information it conveys rather than simply focusing on creating thrilling plots that could negatively impact the audience's perception. The plot arrangement of TV dramas should aim to objectively convey more positive plot information that encourages reflection and resonance, while drawing on China's rich cultural heritage.

While fable may have a lower perceived preference compared to other structural elements of TV dramas, it has been found to have a greater impact on enhancing the Chinese national image than dialogue and music. Morality, which is often the essence of a TV drama, is frequently overlooked. Therefore, incorporating meaningful and impactful allegory in the production process of Chinese TV dramas can greatly increase their core value and competitiveness, as well as leave a lasting impression on the audience. By focusing on the moral implications of the story, TV dramas can deliver deeper messages that resonate with the audience and ultimately contribute to a more positive national image.

Southeast Asian audiences tend to have a more positive perception of China's economic, technological, product, and diplomatic image when they watch more modern dramas. Despite that, costume dramas are still the most popular type of Chinese TV dramas in Southeast Asia. Nonetheless, the somber and isolated atmosphere often depicted in costume dramas can give viewers an outdated impression of China. Integrating ancient Chinese technology, economy, and international achievements into costume dramas will help improve the image of China portrayed in such dramas, especially in terms of economy, technology, products, and diplomacy. In recent years, costume dramas have incorporated various elements to achieve this goal. For instance, "Story of Yanxi Palace" featured the plot of Chinese medicine diagnosis, and cultural and technical exchanges between the imperial court and foreign visitors. The strict business logic and the interpretation of Chinese way of business in the dramas "To The Generation Meng Luochuan" and "The Merchants of Qing Dynasty" were all manifestations of China's national image in ancient scenes.

References

1. Barwise, T.P., Ehrenberg, A.S.: The liking and viewing of regular TV series. J. Consum. Res. **14**(1), 63–70 (1987)
2. Beerli, A., Martín, J.D.: Tourists' characteristics and the perceived image of tourist destinations: a quantitative analysis—a case study of Lanzarote, Spain. Tour. Manag. **25**(5), 623–636 (2004)
3. Cai, Q., Wen, Q.: 论古装剧的题材、叙事与意识形态 [Discussing the themes, narratives, and ideology of costume dramas]. Chin. Telev. **11**, 11–15 (2018)
4. Carlson, M.A.: Theories of the Theatre: A Historical and Critical Survey from the Greeks to the Present. Cornell University Press, Ithaca (2018)
5. China Foreign Languages Publishing Administration Research Center for International Communication. 中国国家形象全球调查报告2014 [2014 Global Survey Report on China's National Image] (2015)
6. Cowley, E., Barron, C.: When product placement goes wrong: the effects of program liking and placement prominence. J. Advert. **37**(1), 89–98 (2008)
7. Han, H.J., Lee, J.S.: A study on the KBS TV drama Winter Sonata and its impact on Korea's Hallyu tourism development. J. Travel Tour. Mark. **24**(2–3), 115–126 (2008)
8. Hatcher, J.: The Art and Craft of Playwriting. Penguin, London (2000)
9. Hou, M.: Television Program Brand Building Research–Based on the Example of Reality Show <Dad, Where Are We Going>. Master's thesis. Sichuan Normal University, China (2015)

10. Huang, S.: Nation-branding and transnational consumption: Japan-mania and the Korean wave in Taiwan. Media Cult. Soc. **33**(1), 3–18 (2011)
11. Jiang, Y.: 题材拓展, 抱团发力, 中国影视"出海"能量可期 [Expanding themes, working together, China's film and television industry has the potential for success in overseas markets]. Radio & TV Today, **2**(24) (2018)
12. Kim, H., Richardson, S.L.: Motion picture impacts on destination images. Ann. Tour. Res. **30**(1), 216–237 (2003)
13. Kim, H.J., Chen, M.H., Su, H.J.: Research note: the impact of Korean TV dramas on Taiwanese tourism demand for Korea. Tour. Econ. **15**(4), 867–873 (2009)
14. Kim, S.: Extraordinary experience: re-enacting and photographing at screen tourism location. Tour. Hosp. Plann. Dev. **7**(1), 59–75 (2010)
15. Kim, S., Kim, M., Agrusa, J., Lee, A.: Does a food-themed TV drama affect perceptions of national image and intention to visit a country? An empirical study of Korea TV drama. J. Travel Tour. Mark. **29**(4), 313–326 (2012)
16. Kim, S.S., Agrusa, J., Lee, H., Chon, K.: Effects of Korean television dramas on the flow of Japanese tourists. Tour. Manage. **28**(5), 1340–1353 (2007)
17. Kim, S.S., Kim, M.J.: Effect of Hallyu cultural products in Thai society on enhancement of Korean national image and intention to visit. Korean J. Tour. Res. **23**(4), 101–125 (2009)
18. Kotler, P., Gertner, D.: Country as brand, product, and beyond: a place marketing and brand management perspective. J. Brand Manag. **9**(4), 249–261 (2002)
19. Lee, B., Ham, S., Kim, D.: The effects of likability of Korean celebrities, dramas, and music on preferences for Korean restaurants: a mediating effect of a country image of Korea. Int. J. Hosp. Manag. **46**, 200–212 (2015)
20. Liou, D.Y.: Beyond Tokyo rainbow bridge: destination images portrayed in Japanese drama affect Taiwanese tourists' perception. J. Vacat. Mark. **16**(1), 5–15 (2010)
21. Liu, J.: 电影电视剧的对外传播对中国国家形象的影响分析 [Analysis of the impact of foreign transmission of Chinese films and TV dramas on China's national image]. TV Guide Chin. **10**, 36–38 (2017)
22. Meng, X., Guo, Z.: 新形势下国家形象塑造及对外传播策略研究—基于2012-2014年《中国国家形象调查报告》的分析 [Research on the shaping and foreign communication strategy of China's national image under new situations-based on the analysis of the "China National Image Survey Report" from 2012-2014]. Jiang-huai Tribune, (006), 99-104 (2016)
23. Murry, J.P., Lastovicka, J.L., Singh, S.N.: Feeling and liking responses to television programs: an examination of two explanations for media-context effects. J. Consum. Res. **18**(4), 441–451 (1992)
24. Oktaviani, R., Puspitawati Haryadi, E.: Impacts of ASEAN trade liberalization on ASEAN-6 economies and income distribution in Indonesia (No. 51). ARTNeT Working Paper Series (2008)
25. Qin, J.: 从观众心理看我国现实题材电视剧如何走向港台和东南亚 [How Chinese TV dramas with realistic themes can enter Hong Kong, Taiwan, and Southeast Asia: a perspective from audience psychology]. Chin. Telev. **1** (2004)
26. Ren, J.: Typification of palace fighting drama and its cultural identities on the improvement of its cultural taste. J. Chongqing Jiaotong Univ. (Soc. Sci. Ed.) **17**(3), 23–27 (2017)
27. Russell, C.A., Stern, B.B., Stern, B.B.: Consumers, characters, and products: a balance model of sitcom product placement effects. J. Advert. **35**(1), 7–21 (2006)
28. Su, H.J., Huang, Y.-A., Brodowsky, G., Kim, H.J.: The impact of product placement on TV-induced tourism: Korean TV dramas and Taiwanese viewers. Tour. Manage. **32**(4), 805–814 (2011)
29. Xu, M., Liao, X.: 中国电视剧的海外市场与对外传播策略研究 [Research on the overseas market and foreign communication strategy of Chinese TV dramas]. Int. Commun. **02**, 46–48 (2015)

30. Zhang, Z.: 论古装剧的主要特征 [Discussing the main features of costume dramas]. Chin. Telev. **07**, 26–30 (2008)

31. Zhu, C.: 我国电视剧"走出去"的历史、问题与策略 [The history, issues, and strategies of Chinese TV dramas' "going global"]. Youth Journalist **000**(021), 64–65 (2018)

32. Zhu, X.: 国产电视剧走出去: 正成为产业高质量发展的新动能 [Chinese TV dramas going global: becoming a new driving force for the high-quality development of the industry]. https://baijiahao.baidu.com/s?id=1651941490986844579&wfr=spider&for=pc. Accessed 8 Apr 2020

The Application of Cross-Cultural Context Fusion Virtual Reality Technology in the Course of Film Art Creation

Weilong Wu[1]([⊠]), YuLin Chen[1], and Xia Du[2]

[1] School of Film Television and Communication, Xiamen University of Technology, Xiamen,
China
wu_academic@163.com

[2] School of Computer and Information Engineering, Xiamen University of Technology,
Xiamen, China

Abstract. Objectives: Since the 21st century, with the rapid development of
science and technology, China's education level and educational technology have
been continuously improved, and the classroom model has been developed and
upgraded in innovation, but in the case that digital technology has not been fully
covered and China's educational resources are relatively scarce, there are still
many practical courses that cannot be taught in the traditional classroom to obtain
good educational effects.

The development of cinematography knows no borders, but the education of
cinematography is limited by the different educational environments of different
countries. As an international art, the education of cinematography can achieve
better quality development through cross-cultural communication. The use of virtual reality technology in the art of filmmaking can break the time and space limitations between countries and enhance the degree of integration and innovation
in education in a cross-cultural context. The study of film and television creation
often requires students to have a lot of practical experience, but the equipment and
venue funds required for its practical courses are more expensive and cannot meet
the needs of most schools to create specialized teaching equipment and venues.
The teaching equipment of film creation plus the course venue are two aspects that
require later management and maintenance expenses, therefore, most of the film
creation courses in domestic universities are still stuck in the traditional teaching
mode.

In addition, the continuous updating of film creation technology makes teaching resources, teaching materials and teacher training lag behind, which affects
teaching quality. The special nature of the film creation course makes it difficult
to effectively restore the filming process by traditional graphic, visual and audio
transmission methods, and the out-of-home practice is limited in terms of coordination, time and space. In the global epidemic environment, online learning is
gaining more and more attention, but the film and television industry is in a "winter", which makes most film and television students lack of practice places where
they can establish cooperation. Virtual reality technology in the film creation program for the restoration of the film set, that is, to build a virtual practice scene, is
a way to break the limits of time and space to provide students with experience.

W. Wu and Y. L. Chen—Authors contributed equally to this study.

P.-L. P. Rau (Ed.): HCII 2023, LNCS 14024, pp. 50–60, 2023.
https://doi.org/10.1007/978-3-031-35946-0_5

Virtual reality technology, as a more important technology in various industries in recent years, is widely used in many fields, such as medical, construction, fashion, military, etc. At present, the teaching advantages of virtual reality technology have gradually come into playing in the field of education. Using virtual reality technology to build experimental apparatus, scenarios and equipment, students are less constrained by equipment as well as scenarios, more able to stimulate interest in the midst of an immersive classroom, enhance practical perceptions through virtual reality technology instead of hardware facilities, immersive learning, and enhanced learning efficiency.

On the other hand, it will also reduce the pressure of teachers in teaching, and can view student dynamics through virtual experiments, timely adjustment of teaching programs. The virtual scene practice is complemented by the teacher's classroom lecture, combining practice and theory, transforming the teacher-led classroom into students' spontaneous experiential learning, showing the abstract concepts through virtual reality, restoring the real scene of the film set placed in the plane in front of their eyes, allowing students' audio-visual senses to have a more realistic experience, crossing time and space in the virtual reality situation, kinetic interaction, allowing the theoretical learning in the construction of The "imaginary film set" built in the theoretical learning can be immediately shown in front of the eyes.

Methods: A sample of 32 students from a film creation course in a Chinese university was selected and divided into two groups: the experimental group and the control group, with 16 students in each group (8 male and 8 female students in each group), to confirm their knowledge of virtual reality technology and familiarity with its operation before the experiment. The 16 students in the control group will be taught in a traditional film creation course, mainly by a multimedia teacher who will show the process of film creation in graphic form; the 16 students in the experimental group will be led by the teacher and will be taught in the first half of the course, while in the second half they will enter an immersive virtual reality scenario using VR technology to experience the process of filming on a real film set and become familiar with the operation of each position. A questionnaire will be used at the end of the experiment to investigate students' engagement, interest, initiative, classroom satisfaction and learning outcomes.

Results: Through the experiments of both groups, it was found that students in the experimental group would be more engaged and interested in the course, have a higher understanding of the structure and operation of the set than students in the control group, and have significantly better satisfaction and knowledge absorption in the course than students in the control group. More than half of the students in the control group were inattentive and uninterested in the course content, and the data on the learning effect in the post-test were also poor.

Conclusions: It is clear from this study that virtual reality technology can provide a greater degree of convenience to the teaching of film creation practice by restoring the actual scenes on the film set, and that the traditional teaching mode may make the teaching effect "superficial" and prevent students from understanding and experiencing the real scene. The integration of virtual reality technology and traditional teaching methods produces a $1 + 1 > 2$ effect, stimulating students' interest in learning, improving their learning efficiency, reducing lab construction costs, deepening students' understanding of realistic scenarios, and cultivating their innovative thinking and abilities.

Using the advantages of virtual reality technology to reform the classroom of film art creation in colleges and universities can improve students' intercultural communication skills while effectively supplementing the teaching content of international film creation, which helps promote the cultivation of intercultural excellent film talents. However, virtual reality technology can only be an "affordable substitute" for film creation practice courses. The unexpected events and responses that may occur in actual scenes cannot be restored yet, and students cannot learn to react and respond to unpredictable events in film creation in virtual reality scenes, so it should be combined with reality to make up for its shortcomings.

Keywords: AR technology · VR technology · Film art creation · Cross-cultural training · Teaching mode

1 Introduction

In the current teaching system of many universities, the teaching of film creation is a very important practical teaching course. For university majors related to film art, offering a course on film creation can not only further the image creation ability of film major university student groups and adapt to the current trend of image development, but also help to improve the quality ability of university students. However, the current situation of the film art creation course in universities shows that many students have deficiencies in their professional background, technical foundation and creative thinking, resulting in a great difference in the teaching effect of the film art creation course in universities among the student population. In particular, the high demand for equipment in film art has led to differences in the quality of education between universities of different economic strength, which requires universities to constantly explore new teaching methods in the process of teaching reform and research to address the problems in teaching film creation. The integration of virtual reality technology into the creative film arts curriculum is an emerging and effective way of reforming the creative film arts curriculum.

The film art creation course in higher education requires students to progress together in a number of areas including aesthetic expression, sound, editing, cinematography and scriptwriting, as well as to use a comprehensive range of skills in the process of film art creation practice. In a course like Film Art Creation Course, which is more practical than theoretical, it is difficult to achieve quality teaching in the traditional mode of teaching by practising and reproducing the process of filming on set. In traditional film art teaching, teachers usually guide students to work in teams to experience the whole process of film art from conception to text design to final formation. However, the constant development of the Internet and film-related technology in the new era has begun to make this traditional mode of teaching inefficient and time-consuming, and it is difficult for university students to obtain precise knowledge of film creation from the teacher's screen presentation or oral narration in a short period of time, so the teaching of film art creation has also taken on a higher level of demand. This means that the educators involved have to constantly update their teaching methods and course content systems in line with the developing market needs and industry standards, in order to prepare for a better adaptation to the social environment.

The practice of virtual reality technology in innovative classroom reform is the embodiment of new contextualized teaching and learning. Compared to traditional contextualized teaching, virtual reality technology-based teaching is more conducive to allowing students to have the ability to make up for the difference in subjective imagery in a contextualized setting, to gain a more intuitive visual memory in a virtual classroom, to retain more of the emotions brought about by visual images, and to be able to retrieve them in memory at any time, making the teacher's words and graphics in a traditional classroom figurative, allowing students to experience a real film set or film creation process from their visual senses, free of temporal and economic limitations. The emotions generated in the process and the exploration of the details of the learning content will be more beneficial. This study will analyse the feasibility of virtual reality technology in the future of film creation education through an experiment on the change of lectures involving virtual reality technology in a film art creation course. In a cross-cultural context, the application of virtual reality technology in film art education reform can also provide feasible solutions for film art education in different countries and regions, and provide theoretical support for the introduction of virtual reality technology in film art creation majors in different universities in different countries and regions.

2   Literature Review

2.1   Virtual Reality Technology

Virtual reality technology originated in the United States and has a wide range of applications in the field of education, providing educators with a new approach to teaching, deconstructing the traditional teaching model and offering unlimited possibilities for the development of people's educational technology. It expands the development of teaching methods and provides a new platform for pedagogical innovation [1]. Virtual reality (VR) technology and the interaction of 3D geometric models can put an end to the passive learning followed in traditional educational methods. They also facilitate useful exchanges between the different participants in the educational process [2]. The use of virtual reality in teaching is evident in medicine, the military, fashion, architecture and many more. A study by M Samadbeik, D Yaaghobi et al. exemplifies the feasibility of virtual reality in teaching clinical medicine, using virtual education technology for laparoscopic surgery training [3]. In addition to this, practical nursing training simulation software programs have been introduced in the USA where students can access electronic cases, make virtual appointments and can assess and then interact with patients in a virtual ward created by the program, as well as follow up on patient interventions, understand changes in the patient's condition in real time and be able to assess the patient and implement a care plan [4]. The practice of virtual reality technology in university physical education courses is also gaining good ground, as Yildirim, Gürkan's team combined VR technology with history education courses and found that interactive environments under VR virtual environments were found to be more effective in history courses and especially in presenting important events in history (e.g. wars, treaties, negotiations, discussions, etc.) compared to traditional teaching environments [5]. This visualization of non-concrete historical scenes also demonstrates the ability of virtual reality technology to reproduce what already exists in reality, but also to visualise what is imagined, providing a technological channel for the teaching of different subjects. Liu Guiwen's team used 3D modelling techniques, stereo sound synthesis and other technologies to slimly explain the specific operations of building a physical education model as well as special treatments, which is an important breakthrough in the combination of virtual reality technology and university classroom reform [6]. Jin Yadi uses the Internet+VR courseware to apply VR technology to the teaching of the guzheng. The key is the design, production and application of VR teaching courseware. She believes that VR technology is essentially a tool used to create virtual information environments. This approach is inexpensive and can avoid the need for specialist VR terminals (e.g. VR helmets, VR simulation pods, gesture sensors, VR projectors, etc.) and instead uses desktop VR functions in the courseware to produce an economical virtual realm using personal computer terminals and their conventional external devices, forming a non-contact VR remote teaching and learning environment based on the Internet [7]. Weilong Wu, Hsu Y, Yang Q F et al. developed a landscape architecture SV-IVR learning system using virtual reality technology as a tool to effectively improve students' academic performance, learning attitudes and self-regulation without negatively affecting them [8]. Virtual reality technology has now been gradually tried and practiced in multiple areas of university education and is an important tool for future educational reform. This study focuses on analysing the interest of university students majoring in the art of film creation in virtual reality immersive classes and their learning outcomes, to analyse the feasibility of using virtual reality technology in the art of film creation course.

2.2 Curriculum and Teaching of Film Art Creation

The Film Art Creation course was created to train excellent film practitioners and talents in all sectors of the film creation process, and is a highly practical and professional course, As a highly practical discipline, researchers are committed to reforming education in ways that enhance the effectiveness of practical learning in the area of innovation in teaching methods. Sasha A. Barab and Thomas M. Duffy of Indiana University explain the concept of "field of practice" from the perspective of educational psychology, which is a place of learning based on a campus or classroom environment, where functional learning situations or environments are set up and created to achieve certain learning objectives by setting up and creating functional learning situations or environments [9], From the point of view of the "field of practice", practical courses need to be developed in a functional and practical context, creating a professional learning context that can improve the inertia of knowledge caused by the traditional teaching model. The art of film creation, as an art of film and television, is itself a multimodal and comprehensive art, a discipline in which sound, image, animation, color and text are synergistically applied, especially in the current context of new media and media convergence, where new technologies and new ideas have become obsolete. The traditional teaching system of theoretical courses plus observation courses cannot meet the contemporary trends in film and television art education [10]. Therefore, the integration of virtual reality technology and film creation art courses can break the bottleneck of traditional teaching on top of practical classes and promote the reform of practical education with a hybrid teaching mode. Schuenemann's team has demonstrated in a study of the teaching methods in the subject of audiovisual language that students develop short films using a digital platform and then use the virtual platform again for post-production work after shooting, an innovative and effective practical teaching of audiovisual language that makes the film-making process more flexible in terms of workplace and time, optimising media production. In addition, the use of digital communications in the development and completion of a film is closer to professional filmmaking standards than putting audiovisual content on a classroom screen [11]. To sum up, as a practical course, what is needed is an innovation of the teaching method and a comprehensive training programme for talents, and a reform of the education method following the progress of film technology.

3 Experiment Design

3.1 Participant

In this study, 16 students (8 male and 8 female) were randomly selected from a school in China as the control group and 16 students (8 male and 8 female) as the experimental group. There were no major differences in the basic information of the two groups, and all of them had taken a preliminary course on film art creation and had a preliminary knowledge of film creation. The control group used the traditional teaching mode, with the teacher teaching knowledge and operating demonstrations, while the experimental group used virtual reality technology for teaching, with the teacher using virtual reality for classroom teaching and the students using VR for learning. All the teaching activities of this experiment were conducted by a professor with a high level of knowledge and experience in teaching film creation for many years, and it was ensured that there were no major differences in the prior knowledge of the two groups before the teaching activities began.

3.2 Measuring Tools

The research instrument for this study was a questionnaire measuring two aspects of students' interest in learning and their confidence in learning. The questionnaires were divided into two different questionnaires for the experimental and control groups, each containing eight questions on a scale of 1–5.

3.3 Experimental Process

The experimental process is shown in Fig. 1. Before the experiment began, the professor introduced the film art creation course and gave a preliminary explanation of the relevant knowledge. After the initial presentation, the students in the experimental group were taught using virtual reality technology, while the students in the control group were taught in the traditional way.

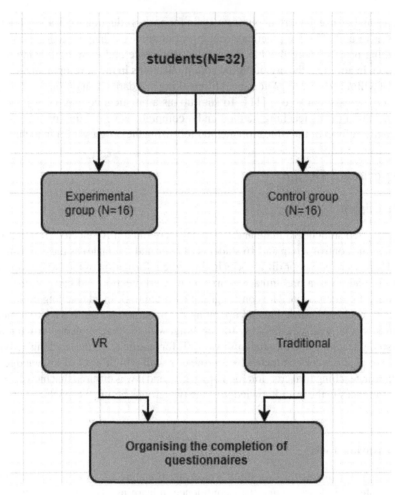

Fig. 1. The experimental process

4 Experimental Results

4.1 Analysis of Interest in Learning

The independent sample t-test was used to analyse the differences between the experimental and control groups in terms of both confidence in learning and interest in learning in the process of participation in the film art creation course. The analysis of interest in learning, using the independent sample t-test method to analyse the experimental and control groups' knowledge of the film creation process, as shown in the Table 1 of differences between the experimental and control groups, showed that the familiarity with the content of the film art creation course: showed a 0.01 level of significance ($t = -3.696$, $p = 0.001$), as well as specific comparative differences can be seen, the experimental group's mean (2.25), which was significantly lower than the mean of the control group (3.19). The level of interest in the film art and creative writing course was significant at the 0.01 level (t = −3.360, p = 0.002), and the difference in specific comparisons showed that the mean of the experimental group (2.13) was significantly lower than the mean of the control group (3.06). Satisfaction with the mode of delivery of the film art creation course: showing a 0.05 level of significance (t = −2.259, p = 0.031), as well as specific comparative differences, the mean of the experimental group (2.31) was significantly lower than the mean of the control group (2.94). Initiative in the film art creation course: showed a 0.01 level of significance (t = 2.936, p = 0.006), as well as a specific comparison difference which shows that the mean of the experimental group (2.31), was significantly higher than the mean of the control group (1.69). The total score showed a 0.05 level of significance (t = −2.654, p = 0.013), as well as a specific comparison difference that shows that the mean of the total score of interest in learning in the experimental group (9.00) is significantly lower than the mean of the control group (10.88). In conclusion, it can be seen that the experimental and control groups showed significant differences in the effects of their participation in the film art creation course in terms of interest in learning. Students who underwent immersive film art creation classes with virtual reality participation were generally somewhat more engaged, satisfied, interactive and knowledgeable than those who received traditional lectures. Students in the control group reported that the class was not very interesting, that it was difficult to be enthusiastic, and that they did not gain much knowledge of the basic content of the course, making them fewer effective learners. Students in the experimental group generally reported that they were more engaged in classroom inter-actions, gained more knowledge in the same amount of time, and were more satisfied and focused on the class than the control group.

Table 1. Research findings on learning interest

Learning interest	group	N	average	SD	t	p
Familiarity with the content of the film art creation course	Traditional	16	2.25	0.683	−3.696	0.001**
	VR	16	3.19	0.705		
Satisfaction with the mode of delivery of the film art creation course	Traditional	16	2.31	0.704	−2.259	0.031*
	VR	16	2.94	0.854		
Level of interest in the film art creation course	Traditional	16	2.13	0.806	−3.360	0.002**
	VR	16	3.06	0.772		
Initiative in the film art creation course	Traditional	16	2.31	0.602	2.936	0.006**
	VR	16	1.69	0.602		
Total	Traditional	16	9.00	2.066	−2.654	0.013*
	VR	16	10.88	1.928		

*$p < .05$** $p < .01$

4.2 Analysis of Confidence in Learning

The independent samples t-test was used to analyse the learning confidence of the experimental and control groups on the process of film creation, as shown in Table 2. The
results of the study showed that the knowledge of the process of film art creation: showed
a 0.01 level of significance (t = −3.220, p = 0.003), as well as specific comparative
differences can be seen that the mean of the experimental group (1.56), would be significantly lower than that of the control group mean (2.25). The level of difficulty of
the film art creation course was found to be significant at the 0.01 level (t = 2.825, p =
0.008), and the difference between the experimental group's mean (2.63) and the control
group's mean (2.00) was found to be significantly higher. Familiarity with the practical
venue of the film art creation course: a 0.01 level of significance (t = −5.222, p =
0.000), as well as a specific difference in comparison, shows that the mean of the experimental group (1.50) is significantly lower than the mean of the control group (2.56).
The total score showed a 0.051 level of significance (t = −2.693, p = 0.011), as well
as a specific difference in comparison, which shows that the mean of the total learning
confidence score for the experimental group (5.69) is significantly lower than the mean
of the control group (6.81). In conclusion, it can be seen that the experimental group
and the control group showed significant differences in their effectiveness in terms of
learning confidence after participating in the film art creation course. When comparing
the students in the experimental group with those in the control group, the students in the
experimental group generally outperformed the students in the control group in terms
of their knowledge of the film art creation process, their familiarity with film sets and
their perceived difficulty level of the film art creation course. The students in the control group, who were still receiving traditional lectures, had difficulty in understanding
specifically the knowledge of the film shooting process through written and oral accounts
of its It was also difficult for the control students to understand the professional filming
environment in their subjective imagination, and the course was more difficult for the
control students because most of the time the process was relayed by the teacher through
text and images, unlike the immersive participation of the experimental students. This

Table 2. Research findings on learning confidence

Learning confidence	group	N	average	SD	t	p
Level of knowledge of the process of creating film art	Traditional	16	1.56	0.629	−3.220	0.003**
	VR	16	2.25	0.577		
Perceived level of difficulty of the film art creation course	Traditional	16	2.63	0.619	2.825	0.008**
	VR	16	2.00	0.632		
Familiarity with the practical venue of the film art creation course	Traditional	16	1.50	0.632	−5.222	0.000**
	VR	16	2.56	0.512		
Total	Traditional	16	5.69	1.448	−2.693	0.011**
	VR	16	6.81	0.834		

$^*p < .05$ ** $p < .01$

shows that virtual reality technology can be very helpful in the delivery mode of practical classes, reducing the sense of tedium and boredom brought about by traditional classes, increasing students' interest, accessing information through more senses, improving the efficiency of learning and reducing the difficulty of learning.

5   Discussion and Conclusions

It is evident from this experimental study that, firstly, students who participated in the film art creation course with the integration of virtual reality technology were more interested and confident in learning compared to those who participated in the traditional classroom learning. Secondly, students who participated in a film art creation course with the integration of virtual reality technology were more proactive in interacting with the teacher and more satisfied with the way the class was taught with VR technology. Thirdly, students who participate in a film art creation course with virtual reality integration are able to acquire knowledge more efficiently and are more familiar with the practical environment than students in a traditional classroom. For practical courses such as film artistry, the traditional educational model, which relies on teacher-student interaction, is relatively boring and hardly satisfies the sense of vitality and engagement that practical courses should maintain. In teaching practice, film art creation often involves knowledge from many different majors and fields, so the requirements for students' practical ability and operational skills are relatively high. This requires university teachers to constantly change their teaching ideas, follow the current market development rules, and link the teaching method of combining virtual reality technology and traditional classrooms with film art creation courses, in order to cope with the film market's requirements for talents' abilities and meet the increasingly developing film creation technology. The integration of virtual reality technology into the university classroom not only enhances students' interest and confidence in learning, but also to a certain extent reduces human and financial resources for universities to carry out teaching activities, improves the quality of teaching in practical courses and cultivates higher quality and more technically proficient talents in the film industry. From a cross-cultural perspective, the current boom of the Internet, the innovative reform of virtual reality technology in film creation education also provides ideas and possibilities for teaching reforms in universities in different countries and regions around the world, and further promotes the advancement of professional education in film art creation worldwide. With the help of virtual reality technology, the reduction of geographical differences in education on the creative art of film can add to the further development of film education in the world in the future and can also contribute to the common development of global cinema.

Based on the results of this study, it is possible to offer some suggestions and perspectives for future research on VR practices in film art creation: the first point is that the use of virtual reality technology in practical classes should be adapted to different practical classes through different technical means, and that a single experiment still has limitations that are not interoperable. Secondly, too small a sample size can also lead to less precise experiments and should be more diverse, taking into account the different circumstances and roles of different samples to further enhance the professionalism of the experiment. Finally, the various technical problems that will arise in practice with virtual reality are still unpredictable and will need to be upgraded in the course of continuous pedagogical reform, and these are directions that can be studied and focused on later.

Funding. This work was supported by Social Science Foundation of Fujian Province, China (Funding Number: FJ2022C071).

And supported by Xiamen Education Scientific Planning Project: Application of VR in art design courses in the post-epidemic era Innovative Teaching Reform Study (Funding Number:22002).

And supported by High-level Talent Research Project of Xiamen University of Technology (Funding Number: YSK22018R).

References

1. Jiang, J., Zhi, L., Xiong, Z.: Application of virtual reality technology in education and teaching. In: 2018 International Joint Conference on Information, Media and Engineering (ICIME), pp. 300–302. IEEE (2018)
2. Sampaio, A.Z., Ferreira, M.M., Rosário, D.P., et al.: 3D and VR models in civil engineering education: construction, rehabilitation and maintenance. Autom. Constr. **19**(7), 819–828 (2010)
3. Samadbeik, M., Yaaghobi, D., Bastani, P., et al.: The applications of virtual reality technology in medical groups teaching. J. Adv. Med. Educ. Prof. **6**(3), 123 (2018)
4. Hester, R.L., Pruett, W., Clemmer, J., et al.: Simulation of integrative physiology for medical education. Morphologie **103**(343), 187–193 (2019)
5. Yildirim, G., Elban, M., Yildirim, S.: Analysis of use of virtual reality technologies in history education: a case study. Asian J. Educ. Train. **4**(2), 62–69 (2018)
6. Liu, G.: Research on physical education teaching model based on virtual reality technology. Electron. Test **0**(18), 63–65 (2014). https://doi.org/10.3969/j.issn.1000-8519.2014.18.026
7. Jin, Y.: The application of virtual reality technology in the teaching of Guzheng performance art. Art Eval. null(9), 108–110 (2022). https://doi.org/10.3969/j.issn.1008-3359.2022.9.yysk202209033
8. Wu, W.L., Hsu, Y., Yang, Q.F., et al.: A spherical video-based immersive virtual reality learning system to support landscape architecture students' learning performance during the COVID-19 Era. Land **10**(6), 561 (2021)
9. Barab, S.A., Hay, K.E., Duffy, T.M.: Grounded constructions and how technology can help. Tech Trends WASHINGTON DC **43**, 15–23 (1998)
10. Dai, N.: Innovation research on film and television art education reform based on multimodal environment. In: 7th International Conference on Arts, Design and Contemporary Education (ICADCE 2021) , pp. 681–686. Atlantis Press (2021)
11. Schuenemann, I., Kirch, J., Siehl, S.: How a new learning module supports a comprehensive learning with respect to film production and competencies of the future. In: EDULEARN20 Proceedings. IATED, pp. 4906–4912 (2020)

An Innovative Study on the Integration of Cross-Cultural Virtual Reality Technology in Art Practice Courses

Weilong Wu[(⊠)], Jiaqing Lin, and Zhiling Jiazeng

School of Film Television and Communication, Xiamen University of Technology, Xiamen, China
wu_acedemic@163.com

Abstract. Objectives: With the development of the times, the group of students who love art and participate in art practice activities is getting bigger and bigger, and the related courses in colleges and universities are getting more attention and financial investment. The traditional teaching of practical art courses requires students to have a certain knowledge base of the course, and then to operate it through practical tools to a venue with relevant conditions. Based on this, the art practice course need to take more manpower, material and time. In addition, considering the different cultural backgrounds of students, coupled with uncontrollable factors such as weather conditions, venue arrangements, and virus transmission, this also has a worse impact on the actual teaching. This study applies virtual reality technology to the art practice course, carries out virtual simulation experimental teaching, crosses the limitation of time and space, creates realistic learning situations for students, and achieves a high degree of integration of "virtual environment+real operation", so as to improve the teaching effect of the art practice course.

The development of art practice courses is an important process of combining theory and practice, but in the traditional teaching process there is a problem of "emphasizing theory but not understanding". The teachers' teaching method is single and ignores the importance of comprehension learning. In addition, the arrangement of the course takes a lot of teachers' efforts and the executability of the teaching is greatly reduced. Besides, in the context of globalization, intercultural design practice courses have come into the public eye, but the actual teaching effect is not good due to the problems of cultural span and the difference of understanding. How teachers can create the right context to make the transmission of intercultural design knowledge more profound and the teaching process more interesting and intuitive is an urgent problem to be solved.

The virtual reality technology with three characteristics of immersion, interaction and imagination has basically solved the existing problems of teaching art practice courses. It uses 3D graphics generation technology and multi-sensing interaction technology to generate 3D realistic virtual environments. Students enter the simulated virtual environment through the unique interactive equipment, and can feel the real teaching situation as well as the artistic atmosphere. In this way,

---

W. Wu and J. Lin—Authors contributed equally to this study.

P.-L. P. Rau (Ed.): HCII 2023, LNCS 14024, pp. 61–72, 2023.
https://doi.org/10.1007/978-3-031-35946-0_6

not only does it improve the feasibility of teaching and the cultural inclusiveness of the course, but it also improves the fun and interactive nature of the course.

Methods: The subjects of this study were selected from two classes of second-year art departments of a Chinese university, from which 30 students were randomly selected each, one group as the control group (15 male and 15 female students) and the other group as the experimental group (15 male and 15 female students). The students in both groups had the same curriculum-related education content, the same level, and had a preliminary understanding of the art practice curriculum. For the students in the control group, the traditional teaching method is adopted. The teacher teaches the knowledge in the classroom, and then goes to the designated place for practical operation; for the students in the experimental group, the teaching method of combining virtual reality technology with the curriculum is adopted, and the teacher completes the construction of the virtual practice scene through VR technology, and teaches the art practice in the virtual environment while explaining the knowledge. Before teaching, pre-test questionnaires of students' knowledge will be conducted to ensure that there are no major differences in the prior knowledge of the experimental subjects; after the teaching, relevant questionnaires will be conducted according to the students' learning situation and classroom effect. Finally, the questionnaire data were analyzed and the experimental results were recorded.

Results: The comparison of the experimental results shows that: in terms of questionnaire score, the average performance of the experimental group is significantly higher than that of the control group; in terms of teaching effect and feedback, students in the experimental group are significantly more interested and enthusiastic in learning, more satisfied, and hold more positive evaluation of the teaching method; In terms of cultural differences, students in the experimental group had a good acceptance and enjoyment of the course. In contrast, students in the control group all clearly indicated that the course content was boring and less attractive.

Conclusions: This study found that the introduction of virtual reality technology into art practice courses can improve students' motivation and largely solve the problem of traditional teaching methods being boring. The use of "virtual technology+reality teaching" can allow more students from different cultural backgrounds to enjoy the convenience of teaching and truly participate in the virtual environment, reducing the inevitable alienation problem of cross-cultural design teaching and enabling students to have a deeper and more comprehensive absorption and mastery of art practice knowledge.

In addition, because virtual reality technology has not yet reached the level of popular application, its technology is still being updated and iterated, and it is still to be examined in terms of stability and operability. Therefore, the actual teaching application needs to be more rigorous and serious dialectical treatment.

Keywords: VR technology · Art Practice Course · Intercultural Course Design

1 Introduction

The content of art practice courses covers a wide range of subjects, including music, exhibition, painting, sculpture, etc. It has good effect in cultivating the comprehensive quality, aesthetic ability and creative ability of contemporary students. This has also contributed to a certain extent to the rapid development of art practice courses in various universities in different cultural contexts [1]. However, the course requires not only the teacher to teach and explain the knowledge, but also the students to have real hands-on practice. The traditional art practice courses require offline venue arrangement, tool preparation, testing and other tedious aspects, which require greater effort in terms of manpower, material and time. In addition, the global spread of Covid-19 epidemic has reinforced the uncertainty of teaching and learning arrangements [2]. Despite the addition of online education, students are still unable to truly acquire knowledge of art practice in terms of practice acquisition [3]. Through the use of virtual reality technology, the required practical teaching environment can be provided to students. In addition to having the effect of immersion and strong realism, it brings a great improvement to the teaching feasibility and effectiveness. The purpose of this study is to explore the problems associated with traditional teaching by creating a three-dimensional, virtual practice environment to achieve a high degree of integration of "virtual environment+real operation". This study uses virtual reality technology to explore its impact on students' learning interests and learning outcomes in the application of cross-cultural art practice courses.

Art practice courses are an important part of developing students' artistic thinking as well as their artistic practice skills, which play an important role in their academic life [4]. However, in the traditional teaching mode, teaching is usually mainly lecture-based and practice is supplementary. The practical part of the course also has all kinds of problems, making students unable to really feel the charm of art practice. Eventually, students lose their enthusiasm and interest in the course, which reduces the teaching effect. At the same time, it is difficult to meet the learning needs of students with different cultural backgrounds and barriers by following a rigid teaching model. And with the development of globalization, the importance of intercultural teaching is also increasing [5]. How can we eliminate cultural differences to the greatest extent possible, so that the knowledge of art practice courses can reach people's hearts and minds is an imminent problem to be solved.

The introduction of virtual reality technology into teaching can create interactive three-dimensional dynamic visions and promote the integration of practice space and cyberspace [6]. It can more easily bring students into practice sites with an artistic atmosphere and lift the limitations of art practice courses in terms of space, time, weather, and other condition factors. Through the application of virtual reality technology, it is possible to break the inherent mode of traditional teaching and reproduce realistic, diverse and low-cost practice environments of all kinds. This allows students to create a variety of artworks through practical operations in a real-world environment with an artistic atmosphere, allowing them to feel the real sense of perceiving, understanding and creating beauty. This stimulates greater anticipation and enthusiasm for the class, and also enhances the learning experience and the learning effect.

2 Literature Review

2.1 Art Practice Courses and Teaching

The art practice curriculum is a new type of curriculum born in the experiment of basic education reform. It advocates that teaching and learning should have a hands-on, participatory component along with the transmission of knowledge. It is in the process of carrying out practical work in art courses that students can really put into practice the theories they have learned in textbooks through practical activities. Students learn from this experience, optimize their knowledge structure and achieve a learning outcome that unifies theory and practice [7]. In recent years, colleges and universities have been paying more and more attention to art education. In addition to the study of professional knowledge, students have to devote themselves to diverse art practice courses and participate extensively in art practice learning. As a result, it is possible to improve the practical and creative abilities of students in all aspects. This promotes the development of aesthetic education while bringing art back to life and giving it a new lease of life. In the midst of an epidemic around the world, universities and colleges around the world have launched an online education model of "classes suspended but learning continues" [8]. In Sehran Dilmac's study, it can be learned that students taking art classes through distance education have less problems with technology, especially some of those who need to be in art classes. Students believe that many educational frameworks and elements of art courses are already available online: for example, applied works performed during the course can be organized in virtual exhibitions, different drawing applications ("Autodesk SketchBook") can be used on their cell phones; virtual trips to museums and historical works can be guided by lecturers and students can conduct amateur research [9].

The art practice curriculum plays a very important role in the training of educational personnel. It develops students' ability to translate what they learn in the classroom into practical application skills [10]. From the actual teaching needs as well as teaching trends, the proportion of practical sessions has been greatly increased in the design of various art courses. The traditional art practice teaching is based on offline teaching mode, point to point, face to face with students. Various factors, such as the preparation of the venue, time schedule, weather and students' cultural background, can affect the course. In the learning process, the weight of theory and practice is not equally distributed. The practical part is often not as effective as it could be due to the limitations of the conditions, resulting in students not being able to access the appropriate practical environment at anytime and anywhere. The creation of art often requires the creation of an atmosphere and environment. In reality, it is difficult to achieve the ideal artistic environment with low cost and low investment. Most of the hands-on courses are briefly introduced through pictures, text and videos, without giving students the actual sensory experience to learn, experience and summarize. It is clear from numerous studies and surveys that the importance of teaching art courses cannot be underestimated. Many college courses and even art courses have introduced virtual teaching methods for teaching assistance, including online platform interaction, personal homework upload and correction, virtual exhibitions, virtual artworks, etc., to help teachers' teaching go more smoothly and students' knowledge absorption go deeper. However, innovation in the teaching mode of relevant practice courses has yet to be explored, and there is even less in art practice. This has resulted in students not being able to engage in the freedom of artistic practice in a good environment. Therefore, further exploration and innovation are still needed regarding the upgrade and change of teaching methods for art practice courses. In addition, the arrival of the Covid-19 epidemic also makes the development of offline practice much more difficult. Teaching arrangements have also had to shift from face-to-face lectures to an online virtual teaching model [11]. How to break through the traditional teaching mode and achieve the ideal teaching effect in the development of online education has become a problem that needs to be explored and solved.

2.2 Virtual Reality Technology

Virtual reality is a new practical technology developed in the 20th century. As the name implies, it combines virtual and reality with each other and generates a pre-defined simulation environment through high-speed computer computing, where users can immerse themselves in the simulation environment and experience the most realistic feelings [12]. And it combines with school informatization with unique charm, highlighting its unique advantages in educational applications. Due to the characteristics of virtual reality technology such as immersion, simulation, interaction, and conception [13], combined with the actual operation, it can create a learning environment of intelligent education in the educational process. It allows for more diverse teaching designs and higher feasibility of teaching environment creation. This is used to develop students' innovation and practical skills in the long term and to form different teaching methods and educational wisdom. In addition, research shows that educators want to take advantage of the immersive qualities that today's technology can provide as a way to engage students in a wide range of learning activities. Students have the opportunity to use the simulated environment to explore the dimensions and pitfalls of the scenario. It is this type of stimulating iterative process, learning by doing, that attracts today's educators to use VR technology to teach their courses. The use of virtual reality technology in teaching and learning is gradually becoming more and more common. In medicine, for example, it is possible to perform rapid three-dimensional (3D) reconstructions in virtual reality (VR) conditions. The surgical simulation allows a more visual and detailed understanding of the anatomical relationships of the surgical area. Although this technology can be better used for teaching skull base tumor neurosurgery [14], it is not widely available due to technical as well as financial reasons. Furthermore, in Edoardo DegliInnocenti's research, the VR4EDU framework was proposed. It is a VR-based learning tool that uses spatial learning and immersive listening to support hands-on music lessons in elementary school. It is at an early stage, but has some practical results in application [15]. In a study by Wei-Long Wu's team, a more accessible, interactive spherical video-based immersive virtual reality (SV-IVR) approach was used in a teaching model for a landscape planning course. They developed a landscape architecture SV-IVR learning system that helped students to improve and enhance their academic performance and attitude [16]. It is obvious that the teaching application of virtual reality technology has penetrated all aspects of society, and its advantages are highlighted in online education. However, the application of this technology is still mostly at the primary and secondary education level, and it has not been developed in all aspects. In addition, studies have shown that virtual reality is still underused in the teaching and learning process of university courses. Among them, the use of the technology in the integration of the practical part of art courses is almost absent. The essence of the application of virtual reality technology in education is to give full play to the advantages and role of online teaching from the internal needs of students, so as to achieve the sharing and interoperability of high-quality courses. Therefore, accelerating the application of this technology in art practice courses in higher education is also urgent and requires more exploration and research. Under the impact of the Covid-19 epidemic, it has become a necessary trend of the times to put technology into use in education and the innovation and expansion of all types of curricula [17].

3 Experiment Design

In order to fully investigate the effectiveness of virtual reality technology in art practice courses and to achieve the effect of improving teaching effectiveness, this experiment combined virtual reality technology with a practice course in the art department of a Chinese university. Among them, the art practice course as a mandatory course for college art students, the course is divided into two parts: theoretical knowledge teaching session and practical operation session. This experiment was divided into two groups: the experimental group and the control group. The experimental group's course content is the introduction of virtual reality technology into the art practice teaching process, through which students can listen and learn at the same time during the teaching process. The course content of the control group is taught by the teacher in the classroom through traditional teaching methods to explain the content exhibition of the art practice course. In this process, students learn accordingly. The purpose of this study is to investigate: the impact of the integration of innovative virtual reality technologies on students' learning experience and related aspects of learning outcomes in a hands-on art course.

3.1 Participant

The experimental subjects selected for this study were from two classes in the second-year art department of a university in China. From them, 30 students (15 male and 15 female) were randomly selected as the experimental group; 30 students (15 male and 15 female) were selected as the control group. These two groups of students had basically the same grades and similar knowledge of the art practice curriculum, and they both had a preliminary understanding of relevant art knowledge. The experimental group used virtual reality technology and integrated it into the teaching of art practice courses, allowing students to listen and learn in a created virtual environment. The control group used the traditional teaching method. The teacher teaches relevant art knowledge followed by appropriate explanations and demonstrations. Both groups were taught for the same length of time, in the same classroom setting, and by the same teacher with many years of teaching experience. Before starting the experiment, the two groups of students were given a relevant pre-experimental questionnaire to ensure that their existing relevant knowledge did not differ significantly. After the experiment begins, a post-experiment test questionnaire will be administered to analyze and summarize the learning experience and effects.

3.2 Measuring Tools

The measurement tools for this study were: a questionnaire for pre-experimental testing and a questionnaire for post-experimental testing. The questionnaire consists of 10 questions and is divided into two parts: learning feelings and learning effects. There are six questions in the learning perception section with a score of 1–5, and four questions in the learning effect section with a score of 1–5.

3.3 Experimental Process

The experimental procedure is shown in Fig. 1. Before the start of the formal course, pre-experimental test questionnaires were administered separately to students in the experimental and control groups as a way to ensure that their basic knowledge and knowledge base of the course did not differ significantly, and classroom instruction followed. Students in the experimental group were taught using virtual technology integrated with innovative teaching methods; students in the control group were taught using traditional teaching methods. At the end of the course, a questionnaire of the same length will be filled out and distributed. This is to ensure that each student fills in the questionnaire to test their learning experience and effectiveness.

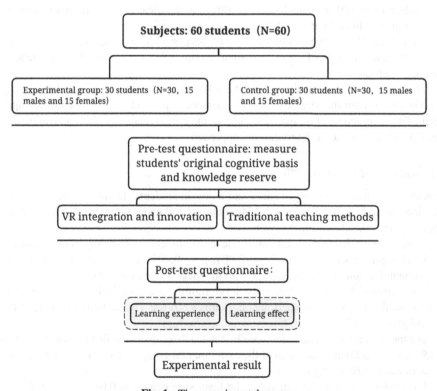

Fig. 1. The experimental process

4 Experimental Results

4.1 Analysis of Learning Experience

This experiment uses t-tests to analyze students' perceptions of learning in a hands-on art course using traditional teaching methods and using virtual reality technology integrated into the classroom.

From Table 1, for the overall classroom atmosphere: level significance of 0.01 ($t = -3.469, p = 0.001$), the mean of the experimental group (3.70) is greater than the mean of the control group (2.60).

For the effect of the introduction method of the new lesson: the level significance was 0.01 ($t = -4.172, p = 0.000$) and the mean of the experimental group (3.67) was greater than the mean of the control group (2.43).

For the degree of knowledge absorption: the level significance was 0.01 ($t = -4.137, p = 0.000$) and the mean of the experimental group (3.90) was greater than the mean of the control group (2.60).

For student participation in learning: level significance was 0.01 ($t = -2.939, p = 0.005$) and the mean of the experimental group (3.57) was greater than the mean of the control group (2.70).

For the idea that if the same type of class is taught next time, the students: the level of significance is 0.01 ($t = -3.572, p = 0.001$) and the mean of the experimental group (3.83) is greater than the mean of the control group (2.67).

for the overall effectiveness of the class: the level significance was 0.01 ($t = -4.083, p = 0.000$) and the mean of the experimental group (3.83) was greater than the mean of the control group (2.60).

The above combination shows that there is a significant difference in the learning experience between the virtual reality-in-classroom approach and the traditional approach. The mean scores of the questionnaire for the virtual reality-in-classroom approach were higher than those of the traditional approach.

4.2 Analysis of Learning Effect

This experiment used a t-test to study and analyze: students' learning effect in the art practice course using traditional teaching methods and using virtual reality technology integrated into the classroom, respectively.

From Table 2, it can be seen that the level of students' knowledge understanding: the level significance was 0.01 ($t = -2.901, p = 0.005$) and the mean value of the experimental group (3.57) was greater than the mean value of the control group (2.70).

For students' learning perceptions: level significance was 0.01 ($t = -4.139, p = 0.000$) and the mean of the experimental group (3.80) was greater than the mean of the control group (2.47).

For the learning assistance provided by the teacher: level significance was 0.01 ($t = -2.924, p = 0.005$) and the mean of the experimental group (3.53) was greater than the mean of the control group (2.63).

For students' learning enthusiasm: the level significance is 0.01 ($t = -2.967, p = 0.004$) and the mean of the experimental group (3.67) is greater than the mean of the control group (2.77).

Table1. Research findings on learning experience

Learning experience	group	N	average	SD	t	p
Overall classroom atmosphere	Traditional	30	2.60	1.28	−3.469	0.001**
	VR	30	3.70	1.18		
Effect of new lesson introduction method	Traditional	30	2.43	1.10	−4.172	0.000*
	VR	30	3.67	1.18		
Absorption of knowledge	Traditional	30	2.60	1.35	−4.137	0.000*
	VR	30	3.90	1.06		
Student participation in learning	Traditional	30	2.70	1.32	−2.939	0.005*
	VR	30	3.57	0.94		
The students' idea of taking the same class next time is	Traditional	30	2.67	1.42	−3.572	0.001**
	VR	30	3.83	1.09		
The overall effect of the classroom	Traditional	30	2.60	1.10	−4.083	0.000*
	VR	30	3.83	1.23		

$^{*}p < .05 ** p < .01$

The above synthesis shows that in terms of learning effectiveness, the teaching method using virtual reality technology integrated into the classroom shows significant differences from the traditional teaching method, and the mean of the questionnaires obtained using virtual reality technology integrated into the classroom is higher than that of the traditional teaching method.

Table 2. Research findings on learning effect

Learning effect	group	N	average	SD	t	p
Knowledge understanding	Traditional	30	2.70	1.32	−2.901	0.005**
	VR	30	3.57	0.97		
Learning Comprehension	Traditional	30	2.47	1.31	−4.139	0.000**
	VR	30	3.80	1.19		
Learning assistance provided by teacher	Traditional	30	2.63	1.33	−2.924	0.005**
	VR	30	3.53	1.04		
Learning enthusiasm	Traditional	30	2.77	1.19	−2.967	0.004**
	VR	30	3.67	1.15		

$^{*}p < .05 ** p < .01$

4.3 Result

The analysis of this experiment with the control group and the comparison of the experimental results shows that the mean values of the experimental group on the scores of each question in the questionnaire are greater than those of the control group. In terms of learning experience, for students using traditional teaching methods, the overall classroom atmosphere was relatively average, and the classroom was introduced in a way that lacked novelty. Students' absorption of knowledge is still shallow and their participation in classroom interaction is low. For students using virtual reality technology to integrate art practice, the introduction of the technology not only brings interest to the classroom and attracts students to listen carefully, but also allows them to feel the corresponding artistic atmosphere in an immersive way. The overall classroom atmosphere is good. In addition, the students showed that they have greater expectations for the upcoming classes. It is clear that students have a better feeling and are more enthusiastic about learning in a classroom where virtual reality technology is introduced. In terms of learning effect, students who use traditional teaching methods are more average in their perception of learning knowledge. They do not have a complete and full understanding of the knowledge, their overall motivation to learn is low, and they feel more boring about the teacher's teaching methods. For students who use virtual reality technology to integrate hands-on art learning, they feel that the knowledge is more accessible and have a deeper sense of learning. Most of the students were clearly interested in learning and thought that the teacher's teaching methods made the class fresher and more interesting. It is clear that students are more motivated, more focused, and therefore have better learning outcomes in a classroom with virtual reality technology. In summary, the introduction of VR technology helps students to have better learning performance in the classroom and make them feel better in learning. At the same time, the final learning effect achieved is also more considerable.

5 Discussion and Conclusions

From this study and the results of the study, we can learn that traditional teaching methods have gradually failed to meet the needs of students in the art practice course. In a traditional art classroom, the scheduling of a practical lesson involves more influencing factors: time, manpower, material resources and even weather conditions, which are more limited. In addition, the rapid development of the Internet has accelerated the self-evolution of education, making online education a hot commodity. This has added some difficulty to the development and popularity of offline courses. And because of the practical, hands-on nature of the art practice course, it makes the course much more difficult to teach. This study applies virtual reality technology to the art practice course and carries out virtual simulation experiment teaching, which breaks the limitation of traditional teaching methods and achieves a high degree of integration of "virtual environment+real operation". It helps students to immerse themselves in the corresponding environment, which makes students' learning interest and learning effect greatly improved. In addition, even when students from different cultural backgrounds are faced with the need to develop corresponding cross-cultural teaching, it becomes easier to achieve.

There is room for refinement in this study, and a larger and more diverse sample size would allow for a more comprehensive and in-depth study. In addition, virtual reality technology is not yet mature, and the application level is not yet popular. In the actual teaching application, this needs to be dialectically treated, and attention needs to be paid to teaching according to the material.

Funding. This research is supported by Xiamen Education Scientific Planning Project: Application of VR in art design courses in the post-epidemic era Innovative Teaching Reform Study (Funding Number: 22002).

References

1. Marshal, J., D'Adamo, K.: Art practice as research in the classroom: a new paradigm in art education. Art Educ. **64**(5), 12–18 (2011)
2. Hofer, S.I., Nistor, N., Scheibenzuber, C.: Online teaching and learning in higher education: lessons learned in crisis situations. Comput. Hum. Behav. **121**, 106789 (2021)
3. Peng, W., Li, X., Fan, L.: Research on information-based teaching and its influence on future education under the background of epidemic situation. In: 2020 IEEE 2nd International Conference on Computer Science and Educational Informatization (CSEI), pp. 340–343. IEEE (2020)
4. Heaton, R.: Cognition in art education. Br. Edu. Res. J. **47**(5), 1323–1339 (2021)
5. Sergeeva, M.G., et al.: Development of teachers' cross-cultural literacy in the system of further vocational education. Religación. Revista de Ciencias Sociales y Humanidades **4**(13), 249–254 (2019)
6. Jiang, J., Zhi, L., Xiong, Z.: Application of virtual reality technology in education and teaching. In: 2018 International Joint Conference on Information, Media and Engineering (ICIME), pp. 300–302. IEEE (2018)
7. Dolmans, D.H., De Grave, W., Wolfhagen, I.H., Van Der Vleuten, C.P.: Problem-based learning: future challenges for educational practice and research. Med. Educ. **39**(7), 732–741 (2005)
8. Nuere, S., de Miguel, L.: The digital/technological connection with COVID-19: an unprecedented challenge in university teaching. Technol. Knowl. Learn. **26**(4), 931–943 (2020). https://doi.org/10.1007/s10758-020-09454-6
9. Dilmaç, S.: Students' opinions about the distance education to art and design courses in the pandemic process. World J. Educ. **10**(3), 113–126 (2020)
10. Lampert, M.: Learning teaching in, from, and for practice: what do we mean? J. Teach. Educ. **61**(1–2), 21–34 (2010)
11. Martin, F., Budhrani, K., Kumar, S., Ritzhaupt, A.: Award-winning faculty online teaching practices: roles and competencies. Online Learn. **23**(1), 184–205 (2019)
12. Mihelj, M., Novak, D., Beguš, S.: Virtual reality technology and applications (2014)
13. Chavez, B., Bayona, S.: Virtual reality in the learning process. In: Rocha, Á., Adeli, H., Reis, L.P., Costanzo, S. (eds.) WorldCIST'18 2018. AISC, vol. 746, pp. 1345–1356. Springer, Cham (2018). https://doi.org/10.1007/978-3-319-77712-2_129
14. Hanson, K., Shelton, B.E.: Design and development of virtual reality: analysis of challenges faced by educators. J. Educ. Technol. Soc. **11**(1), 118–131 (2008)
15. Shao, X., et al.: Virtual reality technology for teaching neurosurgery of skull base tumor. BMC Med. Educ. **20**(1), 1–7 (2020)

16. Wu, W.L., Hsu, Y., Yang, Q.F., Chen, J.J.: A spherical video-based immersive virtual reality learning system to support landscape architecture students' learning performance during the COVID-19 Era. Land **10**(6), 561 (2021)
17. Martín-Gutiérrez, J., Mora, C.E., Añorbe-Díaz, B., González-Marrero, A.: Virtual technologies trends in education. Eurasia J. Math. Sci. Technol. Educ. **13**(2), 469–486 (2017)

A Study of Young Art Creators' Perceptions of Chinese Sex Symbolic Art

Xi Xu[✉] and Shuguang Xu

Faculty of Fine and Applied Arts, Khon Kaen University, Khon Kaen, Thailand
xuxiart@163.com

Abstract. Thousands of years of Chinese civilization have left a large number of written records and other works in the form of paintings and sculptures in the history of sexual culture. "Sexuality" is an expression of the primitive ancestors' pursuit of happiness and hope for a prosperous career. It is a praise and aspiration for the reproductive capacity of the biological world, a custom commonly prevalent in primitive societies, which is also the origin of sex symbol art. These sex-related works have been controversial in the development of society, so their historical and artistic characteristics have been marginalized and not well organized and protected, but it is undeniable that they are an integral part of the historical development. Therefore, this paper will analyze and discuss Chinese artworks related to sex symbols, and study the perceptions and opinions of young art creators about sex-related artworks, so as to understand whether such works have any influence on young art creators and their creative ideas. It can be concluded that most of the young art creators understand and know Chinese art works related to sex, and they are able to accept such works and are willing to experiment with sex-related symbols in their creations, and many young creators already have sex-related symbols in their works. They believe that art should not be influenced by the outside world and that art needs to be a true expression of their inner thoughts.

Keywords: Sexual art · Sexual symbols · Young art creators · Artworks · Symbolic perception

1 Introduction

The fact that eating and sex are basic human desires reflects the fact that ancient Chinese inhabitants placed sexual activities on the same footing as compared to daily eating activities [1]. Sexual artworks, such as literature, film and video, painting and other forms of expression, are a means of expressing human consciousness in extremes that do not exist in mainstream form [2]. In the process of changing national ideology, these works are also playing different functions and roles for social development, guiding people how to participate in social practices [3].

In sexual art works, we can often capture features such as buttocks, breasts, lips, thighs, etc. that can show the process of sex in progress, and these things not only represent their own properties, but also are given the meaning of "sex", thus constituting a sex symbol with cultural connotation. Every artistic image can be said to be a symbol or system of symbols with a specific meaning. In order to understand a work of art, the artistic image must be understood, and in order to understand the artistic image, the structure must be understood. As the denotative form of an object, the symbol has a unifying function that generates humanity and shapes human culture. Sexual symbolic art is created by the creator of art based on the analysis and interpretation of elements such as human feelings and sexual activity [4]. The purpose of sex symbol art is also to delight the viewer's eyes, tantalize the viewer's heart, and awaken the viewer's lust [5]. In the development of society, whether in the most popular or powerful sex symbol artworks, or in the sex symbol artworks in museums to the merchandise found everywhere in sex stores, all contain the function of arousing eroticism. Every social group has to be exposed to things related to sexual symbols [6]. In addition, sex symbolic art also reflects the social acceptance of sexual values and culture in the society [7].

Sexual symbolic art has many forms of expression. In the gears of history, the expressions of sex symbol art have continued to progress with social development, from intuitive figurative expressions to metaphorical abstract expressions [8], constantly enriching and reflecting people's daily lives, providing cultural and social values. This paper introduces and interprets the expression of artworks related to sex symbols, while conducting a social survey of young people such as scholars, students, and artists who create art in China based on the characteristics of sex symbol art, in order to gain a deeper understanding and explore the impact that sex symbol art brings to society and its future potential.

2 Peripheral Design in Chinese Symbolic Art

Art about sexual symbols is common in people's daily life, such as porcelain cups, snuff bottles, pillows, porcelain sculptures, Chun Gong Tu and other products [9]. These various forms of peripheral products, which appear in different forms of craft products, not only reflect the metal smelting technology and craft technology of the time, but also have great significance for further research on the historical development of Chinese sex symbol peripheral products. According to the different functions of these products, this paper divides them into three categories.

The first is the actual use of the function of sex tools. Such products are mainly direct imitation of the shape of the sexual organs, and have part of the sexual function of the product. The earliest of these was found in the tomb of King Jing of Zhongshan, known as the Bronze Ancestor, a sexual instrument. The shape of the bronze ancestor shows that it is mainly a symmetrical combination of the upper and lower male genitalia, and each group contains two cases of sexual organs. From the morphological point of view of the organ, its shape is mainly the simulation of the male genitalia of the penis, which has been able to reflect the basic morphological characteristics of the phallus more realistically. The inclusion of testicles makes the image of such sexual instruments more concrete, according to the shape of Han Dynasty sexual instruments from another period excavated. Based on the technical limitations of the Cold War era, the sexual instruments that emerged from the Han Dynasty were mostly represented by copper products, and occasionally other materials such as Chinese white jade, and in the Republican period, with the development of the industrial revolution in China, rubber products began to appear. In addition, the craftsmanship of the early sexual instruments was relatively low, only a rough imitation of the genitalia, but from the copper gilt sexual instruments and the rubber products of the Republican period presented below, the craftsmanship further increased and the aesthetic sense was no longer limited to figurative. Finally, given that most of these tools were produced during the feudal period, when patriarchal society was the system, most of the sexual tools are mainly based on the simulation of male genitalia (Fig. 1).

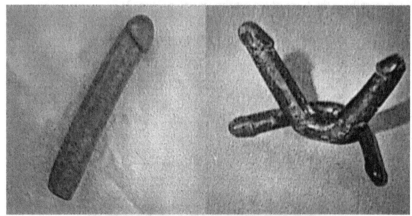

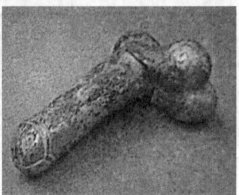

Fig. 1. Sexual instruments

The second is the imitation sexual instrument that symbolizes the sexual organ. These tools are actually imitations of a certain form of the sexual organ, which are less intuitive than the aforementioned sexual tools, and only invoke certain functions of the sexual organ or change the form of the sexual organ to emphasize its decorative role. As shown in the figure below, the porcelain cup on the left simulates the testicular form of the male genitalia, but its form is difficult to relate to the meaning of the sexual organ if not inferred from the decorative writing attached to its surface, while the second ceramic pot figure simulates the penis form of the male genitalia, whose body excludes the possibility of other representations of the sexual organ, retaining only the straight form and diminishing the utilitarian nature of the genitalia, and using sculptural techniques to achieve a decorative effect. Compared to the two drawings on the left, the two illustrations of Qing Dynasty products on the right show a more lifelike use of such imitation class tools. In the two boys form of the teapot, the top two-thirds of the pot is the upper body sculpture of two boys, but in the lower half of the pot extends out of the spout is located in a position that is generally the location of the male sex organs, which implies the morphological characteristics of the male genitalia, and the excretory function of the genitalia is linked to the pouring function of the teapot. In general, such tools are more lifelike, generally in the form of tea sets appear more (Fig. 2).

Fig. 2. Ceramic products

The third is the decorative tool that implies sexual culture. The distribution of such tools is more diverse, and because of the ease of manipulation of decorative elements, they appear in a larger range of products, generally appearing as ceramic vessels, sculptures, wood craft products, etc. According to the artistic shaping techniques of such tools, the article broadly classifies these products into two categories, one with pictorial-based products and the other with sculptural forms. In general, these products are mostly ceramic products, supplemented by simulated animal mating or male and female intercourse as decoration to show the form, its craft reached its peak in the Qing Dynasty. The two works of art shown below are Song dynasty clay pots, their surfaces engraved in relief with a scene of two fish mating, but in terms of form, the pots themselves are of a more rustic texture, and the coitus scene is depicted in a simpler manner (Fig. 3).

Fig. 3. Animal ceramic products

In addition, from the viewpoint of the excavated Qing dynasty products, the description of the sexual intercourse scene is not only more vivid and richer, but also more diverse in product form. In the porcelain product shown in the figure below, the painting form with the spring palace picture is used to describe the daily coitus scene of a man and a woman, with richer color expression and more erotic posture, while the subject matter is also decorated with decorative folding fans or daily objects next to the auxiliary decoration, showing a more decorative overall, showing a rich aesthetic sense of sexual intercourse. The porcelain pen container painted with sexual intercourse motifs on the right are integrated in a combined form, in which not only are there multiple groups of male and female intercourse scenes, but they are also decorated by the addition of rockery and bamboo, which appear more often in literati paintings. It is thus evident that these craft products of the Qing Dynasty, decorated with sexual culture, not only embody the basic art of sexual intercourse, but also reveal the unique scholarly sentiments of the Chinese literati (Fig. 4).

Fig. 4. Sex symbol painting daily necessities

3 Data Analysis

The survey for young art creators in this study was divided into two stages for data collection, in order to more accurately and scientifically understand the views and opinions of this group on artworks related to sex symbols. First, in the pre-survey stage, the main purpose was to test the applicability of the questionnaire, in order to make the content of the questionnaire clear to the public, without creating ambiguity, ambiguity and unintelligibility, in order to provide a reference basis for the subsequent revision and optimization of the questionnaire, and to lay the foundation for the development of a formal research program. Students and young art workers from several art colleges in China were used as the target population for this study. The pre-survey phase was conducted from December 23, 2021 to January 7, 2022, using offline questionnaire distribution to collect a random sample of students and young workers who had received art education. After conducting 20 surveys, this paper revised the questioning and presentation of some questions, which was able to make the presentation of the questionnaire easier to read for these groups. The official survey phase was conducted from April 5, 2022 to 2022, and 189 questionnaires were collected, of which 150 were valid and 39 were rejected. The 39 questionnaires included both homogeneous questionnaires with the same options and those in which the art students had not been exposed to sexual art education during their studies, so we excluded those who had not received such education in the questionnaire.

The following are the descriptive statistics of the sample for the general information collected from the study subjects. From these descriptions, we find that: among the group of respondents, there are 65 male groups, accounting for 43.3%, which is less in number than the female group, which accounts for 56.67%. In terms of age level, students aged 18–22 years old accounted for the largest number, 43.33%, while students aged 30 years old and above accounted for the smallest number, only 14.67%; in terms of education, the total number of young art creators with bachelor's degrees surveyed was 81, the In terms of education, the number of young art creators with a bachelor's degree was 81, accounting for 54% of the total, while the number of masters was 50, accounting for 33.33%, and the number of doctors was the lowest, at 19, accounting for 12.7%; when asked whether they had creative experience, only 57 art creators said they had such experience, while a total of 93 artists had no such experience. This indicates that the development of works related to sex symbolic art is still not in the mainstream in China, and although they have received education on sex art, they still lack relevant practices; when asked "do you actively pay attention to these works related to sex symbolic art", 103 art Finally, among the surveyed groups, we also categorized the professional fields of these young art creators, with painting accounting for the largest group, followed by design, and less by film and television.

The second part of the questionnaire, which is the focus of this paper, was divided into 10 questions. When asked if they had ever seen artworks related to sex symbols, 91 people said they had, while 59 people said they had never seen such artworks or art forms. When asked whether these works of art related to sex symbols could serve the purpose of sex education [10], 72 people thought that they could serve this function and could be used to teach adults or minors about sex, while 78 people thought that they would not use these works of art to teach themselves or their children about sex, but would use other methods When asked whether these works of art related to sexual symbols affect their perceptions of sexuality, 102 people thought that these works have made them think about sexuality, whether more openly or more conservatively. When asked whether these works of art related to sexual symbols are free to express themselves, 86 people thought that it is allowed, and that art related to sexual symbols can be expressed differently depending on individual differences, whether it is symbolic or not, while 64 people thought that its expression is bound by other factors, such as the shape of the male genitalia is fixed, and therefore its expression can only be limited by the shape of the male genitalia. And therefore its expression can only be expressed in the same or similar way as it, and if it is not, it cannot represent this symbol; when asked whether the symbols in these artworks related to sexual symbols are obvious, a total of 78 people think he can delicately capture the wonderful symbols, beautiful lines, usage of bold colors, etc. in these artworks, which together form a complete When asked whether these works of art related to sexual symbols could be appreciated by you, 112 people said they would be willing to buy them if they were accessible to them in their lives, while 38 people said that although these works were distinctive, they were not. When asked what kind of theme they could see in these artworks related to sex symbols, 15 people thought they were meant to be conservative and subtle, 24 people thought they were meant to be tense, and 68 people thought they were meant to be purely sexy. When asked what the main characteristics of these artworks related to sex symbols were, a total of 40 people thought that the form of creation was A total of 45 people thought it could convey a lot of content and let me learn more about it. 30 people thought these works had a strong traditional Chinese culture behind them, and were the product of a cultural society with depth and connotation. A total of 15 people chose this other option, and they thought the expression of these artworks should have more characteristics; when asked in what aspects these artworks related to sex symbols could do better, a total of 55 people hoped that the presentation of these artworks could be more diversified, and a total of 35 people hoped that the Chinese culture it represents could be better inherited and developed A total of 40 people hoped that the artworks would not show sexual desires too visually, but should be expressed in a more abstract way so that they would not be used in an awkward way, and 20 people hoped that the artworks would be presented in a more vivid way so that the public could easily understand their meaning and essence.

From the above results, we can learn that today's artworks related to sexual symbols have been carried out in the vision of many young art creators, who hope that sexual art with Chinese characteristics can be greatly developed, and they have also carried out many art creations related to sexual symbols and produced various art products. Among these groups, most of the young art creators understand and know Chinese sex-related art works, and are willing to accept such works and experiment with sex-related symbols in their creations, and many of them already have "sexuality"-related symbols in their works (Table 1).

Table 1. Sample description statistics

Category	Item	Quantity	Proportion
Gender	Male	65	43.3%
	Female	85	56.67%
Age	Age 18–22	65	43.33%
	Age 22–26	30	20.00%
	Age 26–29	33	22.00%
	Over 30 years old	22	14.67%
Qualifications	Undergraduates	81	54.00%
	Postgraduate	50	33.00%
	Doctor	19	12.70%
Experience in creating sexual artworks	Yes	57	38.00%
	No	93	62.00%

4   Conclusion

Sexuality, as one of the essential elements in people's daily lives, is an important topic explored by people all over the world, both in life practice and in academic research. Based on the understanding of Chinese sex symbolic art, this article describes the current peripheral products related to sex art that have social and cultural value, and introduces and interprets them in order to allow more people to gain insight into the unique Chinese sex and culture. In addition, the article initiates a social survey of young art workers through a structured questionnaire, leading to general conclusions. This group is the backbone of China's art discipline or art industry development and has an important role to play in the future development of Chinese sexual art, so it is feasible to select this group for the study. We found that young art creators believe that art in this area is valuable or has the potential to be valuable in the future, and that it can be used as an educational tool to transmit sexual knowledge and serve as an initiation tool. In addition, more young art creators believe that the expression of sexual art should be free and unrestricted, so that the essential characteristics of sexual art can be revealed as much as possible in the process of creation. Through these surveys, we can provide the general art workers and scholars with directions for creation and research, and make relevant suggestions based on them.

Chinese government departments, art associations, and higher education institutions should increase investment in sex-related art education and create a general education curriculum on sex art education for all students to guide them to a scientific understanding of sex. Sexual art education is still a weak link in school education, and there are many difficulties and problems. The situation of insufficient opening rate of art courses, small participation in related activities, and shortage of teachers has not been fundamentally improved, schools in remote areas lack basic art education, and the evaluation system of sexual art education has not been established, which restrict the full play of the nurturing function of sexual art education. In the face of the new situation and new requirements, schools must accelerate the development of sex art education from a new historical starting point. Secondly, we should screen the general vulgar pornographic works and noble sexual art works, to make students realize what the real sexual art is, so that students will not be confused in their youth, from the psychological real recognition of Chinese sexual symbolic art, generate a strong interest, and happy with to understand and research about sexual art topics or to create related art works out, only in this way, China Only in this way can Chinese sex art education flourish and gradually be recognized by the whole country or even the whole world.

References

1. Liu, D.L.: The History of Sexuality in the World. Zhengzhou University Press, Zhengzhou (2005)
2. Chen, X.M., Yang, L.: "Sex" and the preference of consumerism. Soc. Sci. Front **3**, 163–167 (2012)
3. Guo, F.M.: Research on sexuality theme painting. China Academy of Art (2009)
4. Chen, W.G.: Anti-theorist, "art pornography." J. Jianghan Univ. (Human. Edn.) **29**(2), 42–46 (2010)
5. Zheng, H.Y.: Analysis of the modernization and popularization trend of film and television art communication. Tomorrow's Style **19**, 62–65 (2022)
6. Lindberg, L.D., Kantor, L.M.: Adolescents' receipt of sex education in a nationally representative sample, 2011–2019. J. Adolesc. Health **70**(2), 290–297 (2022)
7. Rentschler, R., Fillis, I., Lee, B.: National identity and the future of branding the arts. Futures **145**(2–3), 1–45 (2023)
8. Peng, Y.X.: On Liu Haisu's practice on the road of "art for the people": The example of his art dissemination activities during the European tour. Chin. Art Res. **2**, 128–134 (2022)
9. Dai, Z., Bao, Y.H.: Sexual culture and sexual art: a study of Spring palace paintings. Chin. Sex Sci. **22**(8), 105–109 (2013)
10. Goldfarb, E.S., Lieberman, L.D.: Three decades of research: the case for comprehensive sex education. J. Adolesc. Health **68**(1), 13–27 (2021)

Cross-Cultural Design in Cultural Heritage

Creative Tourist Behaviors During the COVID-19 Pandemic

Shu-Hua Chang(✉) (iD)

Department of Arts and Creative Industries, National Dong Hwa University, Hualien, Taiwan
iamcsh0222@gms.ndhu.edu.tW

Abstract. In 2020, the world was affected by the COVID-19 pandemic. Because of the pandemic, consumers changed their lifestyles, becoming increasingly home-based and preferring consumption habits that facilitate a healthy life. Consequently, in numerous service industries that target on-site consumption, businesses were suspended, and because creative tourism emphasizes on-site tourism experiences, it was also substantially affected. Few studies have explored the consumer behaviors of creative tourists during the COVID-19 pandemic. Thus, this study aimed to characterize creative tourists and investigate their decisions and motivations to participate in creative tourism during the COVID-19 pandemic in Taiwan. Data were collected at six creative-tourism attractions, and convenience sampling was applied to perform a survey. The results revealed that women were predominant among creative tourists and that most tourists who traveled with their family members to creative tourism destinations were middle-aged, highly educated and middle-income or higher-income earners. Among the various characteristics of tourist behaviors, the three key factors that influenced decision-making were local characteristics, the atmosphere of a creative tourism destination, and personalized experiences pertaining to handmade products. By contrast, on-site COVID-19 prevention facilities were regarded as less important by tourists. These findings can facilitate the deployment of creative tourism management strategies in response to the COVID-19 pandemic.

Keywords: COVID-19 · Creative Tourism · Tourist Behavior · Consumer Behavior · Creative Life Industry

1 Introduction

1.1 Research Background

Creative tourism is regarded as a key strategy for promoting creative industries; examples of creative tourism include DIY Santa Fe in New Mexico, United States; the Nordic Model; the Maori workshops held in New Zealand; and the creative life industry in Taiwan [1, 2]. The Taiwanese government promoted Taiwan's creative life industry as a cultural and creative industry. A creative life industry is defined as an industry that uses creativity to integrate the core knowledge of the life industry and provide in-depth experiences and achieve high-quality aesthetics (e.g., food cultures, life aesthetics, natural ecologies, fashion, cultural heritage, and crafts) [3].

© The Author(s), under exclusive license to Springer Nature Switzerland AG 2023
P.-L. P. Rau (Ed.): HCII 2023, LNCS 14024, pp. 85–98, 2023.
https://doi.org/10.1007/978-3-031-35946-0_8

In 2020, the world, including Taiwan, was affected by the COVID-19 pandemic. Because of the pandemic, consumers changed their lifestyles, becoming increasingly home-based and preferring consumption habits that facilitate a healthy life [4]. Consequently, in numerous service industries that target on-site consumption, businesses were suspended, and because creative tourism emphasizes on-site tourism experiences, it was also substantially affected.

Studies have examined the overall effects of the COVID-19 pandemic on tourism, and they have explored areas such as tourism policies and tourist behaviors. Post-COVID-19 developments in the tourism industry, such as travel patterns that combine communities, ecology, and culture to improve quality of life, have been studied by researchers. For travel patterns, creative tourism is characterized by local in-depth experiences, which promote the continual development of local traditions and lifestyles [5]. Given the effects of the COVID-19 pandemic, a crucial aspect of contemporary tourism development is reconsidering the patterns of tourism and tourist behaviors, including the profiles and characteristics of tourist behaviors in the context of creative tourism. These topics can contribute to the formulation of recommendations for creative life industry policymakers and highlight the key role of creative tourism in Taiwan. Therefore, the profiles of creative-tourism tourists should be studied, and the factors that influenced their activity preferences and participation in creative-tourism activities should be identified.

1.2 Purpose

Few studies have explored the tourist behaviors in creative tourism following the COVID-19 pandemic. Therefore, the present study examined tourist behaviors in creative tourism from a demand-side perspective. The aim of the present study was to explore the consumer behaviors of creative-tourism tourists by determining the profile of tourists who visit creative-tourism sites and understanding the elements that influence the tourism-related decisions and motivations of tourists following the COVID-19 pandemic. In the present study, several creative tourism sites in Taiwan with distinctive characteristics were selected, and the tourists that visited them were surveyed to understand how their behaviors, motivations, preferences, and consumption tendencies were influenced by the COVID-19 pandemic.

The next subsection briefly reviews the theoretical literature on creative tourism and the effects of the COVID-19 pandemic on tourist behaviors. Thereafter, the research design of the present study is presented, followed by the results, discussion, and conclusions and suggestions.

2 Literature Review

2.1 Creative Tourism

The United Nations Educational, Scientific and Cultural Organization (i.e., UNESCO) defines creative tourism as "travel directed toward an engaged and authentic experience, with participative learning in the arts, heritage, or special character of a place, and it provides a connection with those who reside in this place and create this living culture"

[6]. Creative tourism involves creative activities such as those related to painting, crafts, pottery, cookery, winemaking, photography, dancing, and music. Smith [7] described the evolution of creative tourism as follows: (1) tourists develop their creative potential, interact with local people, and connect more strongly with the cultures of the countries that they visit; (2) tourists tend to explore and express their creative potential while they are on vacation, and they focus on activities and their relationships with themselves; (3) tourists enjoy attractions and activities that are more closely connected with creative industries. With the diversification of cultural tourism and the evolution of tourist motivations, the development of creative tourism has shifted from location-based creative activities to explorations and expressions of individual creative potential involving linkages with creative industries [7–11].

The evolution of creative tourism is linked to the creative industries, which provide novel ways for creative-tourism tourists to interact with their destinations, thereby increasing their engagement and generating new tourism demand [12]. Tourists engaging in creative tourism can participate in diverse forms of tourism, and how creative-tourism businesses determine the needs of tourists and develop creative-tourism models is a topic that warrants further exploration [13]. Galvagno and Giaccone [14] proposed a shift in research focus away from macro perspectives based on the creative economy and culture and toward the motivations, activities, and value creation pertaining to creative tourism (i.e., micro perspectives).

Wessels and Douglas [15] explored the potential of creative tourism as a medium for applying cultural and heritage resources in Kruger National Park (KNP) by determining the profile of tourists that visit KNP and assessing their needs in relation to their visit. They reported that tourists who traveled to KNP with their family were generally older, highly educated, and extremely loyal to the KNP brand. Cheng and Chen [16] conceptualized the construct of creative atmosphere in creative tourism and identified five types of creative atmospheres, namely novel, pleasurable, artistic, hedonic, and distinctive atmospheres. They expanded the concept of atmosphere from fixed interior spaces to open spaces and creative products, activities, and individuals in an environment with creative design characteristics. The literature on creative tourism indicates that a comprehensive understanding of tourism behaviors can contribute to our understanding of tourist needs in the context of creative tourism.

2.2 COVID-19 and Tourist Behaviors

Since 2020, tourism has been among the industries most severely affected by the COVID-19 pandemic. Scholars have investigated the effects of the COVID-19 pandemic on service industries, including the hospitality, retail, and leisure industries [17]. Studies have reported the effects of the COVID-19 pandemic on the tourism industries of various regions, such as Queensland, Australia [18]; Malaysia [19]; and Taiwan [20].

The COVID-19 pandemic changed the travel behaviors of tourists with respect to their habits and preferences; specifically, it motivated them to increase their engagement in outdoor activities [21], avoid overcrowded destinations, and go on local trips [22]. Assaf, Kock, and Tsionas [23] highlighted the necessity of understanding the psychology of tourists with respect to their tourist behaviors and changing tourism patterns (e.g., preference for rural destinations, online experiences, and virtual tourism).

Engel, Blackwell, and Miniard [24] defined consumer behaviors as the activities related to acquiring, consuming, and interacting with products or services and the decisions made before and after such activities. Schiffman and Wisenblit [25] proposed that studies on consumer behaviors should examine the products purchased by consumers, their reasons for purchasing such products, their means of purchase, their product usage frequency, their postpurchase product reviews, and their intention to continue purchasing such products. The values conveyed through consumer behaviors reflect the core meaning of marketing.

Remoaldo et al. [26] highlighted that research on the profile of cultural tourists is extensive, which contrasts with the limited literature on creative tourists. The profile and characteristics of creative tourists is a complex topic that involves efforts from various tourist groups (children, adults, and older adults) to seek authenticity, exclusivity, skill learning, and contact with local people.

Richards and van der Ark studied the dimensions of consumption among tourists [27]; they reported that women were more likely than men to exhibit a dynamic pattern of cultural consumption and that cultural tourists differed considerably in terms of their consumption of various types of cultural attractions. Huang, Chang, and Backman [28] administered 395 survey questionnaires to study three creative-tourism attractions in Taiwan; they discovered that individuals aged between 31 and 40 years accounted for the largest proportion of the surveyed tourists and that women were predominant in their sample (59.2%). Tan, Luh, and Kung [29] identified five types of creative tourists, namely novelty seekers, knowledge seekers, skill learners, relaxation-oriented tourists, and leisure-oriented tourists.

In 2020, Remoaldo et al. [26] conducted a study to investigate the motivations and profile of creative tourists. They identified three types of creative tourists in Portugal, namely novelty seekers, knowledge and skill learners, and leisure–creativity seekers. They reported that women (63.8%) and individuals aged between 36 and 53 years (37.6%) were predominant in their sample; they also discovered that most of their respondents had a higher education degree, had a monthly income of between €1,001 and €2,500 (43%), and traveled with other people (90%).

Overall, analyses of the profile of tourists with respect to their sociodemographic characteristics were based on in situ surveys of creative tourists. Because length of stay, creative tourism activities, spending, and the consumption preferences of tourists who could not visit tourist sites because of the COVID-19 pandemic were factors that appeared to have affected tourism patterns, they were examined in the present study.

3 Research Methods

The present study aimed to understand the profile of tourists who participated in creative-tourism activities and their motivations for doing so. A questionnaire was designed on the basis of a literature review of the research on creative tourism, tourist behaviors, and cultural tourist profiles. The questionnaire comprised 15 closed-ended questions that focused on clarifying the behaviors and profile of respondents (i.e., tourists).

Part 1 of the questionnaire focused on the demographic characteristics of the sampled respondents and included questions on a respondent's age, gender, occupation, level of education, income, place of residence, and the numbers of visits to a creative-tourism site. Part 2 of the questionnaire consisted of nine items that covered three basic dimensions, namely (1) the attitudes and motivations related to a visit to a creative-tourism site, (2) the spending behaviors of a tourist, and (3) the basic elements of a tour (e.g., presence or absence of travel companions). The questionnaire was refined through academic reviews and pretesting.

Data were collected from six creative life businesses in Taiwan, namely Jioufen Tea-house, the Taiwan Coal Mine Museum, Zhou Ye Cottage, The Cookies Expert in Taiwan, Minxiong Kumquat Factory, and Digangarden. Convenience sampling was performed, and both the paper-based and online versions of the questionnaire were administered to tourists. At each site, 150 self-administered tourist surveys were administered between August 11 and September 15, 2021. The surveys of tourists were conducted after they had completed their visit to a creative tourism site. In total, 775 valid questionnaires were collected and used in the data analysis of the present study. To analyze the collected data, frequency statistics was analyzed using SPSS Statistics 14.0.

4 Results and Discussion

4.1 Profile of Tourists

A total of 775 valid questionnaires were collected, and the profile of the questionnaire respondents is summarized in Table 1. Overall, 60.6% and 39.4% of the sample were women and men, respectively. Approximately 87.5% of the respondents were younger than 50 years, and only 12.5% were aged over 50 years. For age, the respondents aged between 30 and 39 years (30.5%) accounted for the largest proportion of the sample, followed by those aged between 40 and 49 years (29.0%), between 20 and 29 years (28.0%) and between 50 and 59 years (9.7%). For educational background, the respondents who held bachelor's degrees (65.2%) accounted for the largest proportion of the sample, followed by those who held master's or higher degrees (18.9%), those who received secondary school education (13.3%), and those who were not educated to the secondary school level (2.6%). Overall, 84.1% of the respondents received tertiary education, suggesting that creative tourists tend to be highly educated. The educational background and age of tourists can influence tourist behaviors in the context of creative tourism.

For monthly income, the respondents with a monthly income of NT$30,001–NT$45,000 (26.6%) accounted for the largest proportion of the sample, followed by those with a monthly income of NT$45,001–NT$60,000 (22.6%), NT$15,000–NT$30,000 (17.8%), <NT$15,000 (17.2%), and >NT$60,000 (15.9%). This finding suggests that the typical creative tourist is moderately wealthy. In total, 35% of the respondents had a monthly income of <NT$30,000, and 65% had a monthly income of >NT$30,000.

For place of residence, 53.5% of the respondents were from Northern Taiwan, 29.8% were from Central Taiwan, 13.4% were from Southern Taiwan, 3.0% were from Eastern Taiwan, and 0.2% were from the outlying islands of Taiwan. Most of the respondents were first-time visitors to the creative tourism destination where they were surveyed (71.2%), 16.8% were second-time visitors, 4.8% were third-time visitors, and 7.2% had visited the site where they were surveyed at least 4 times in 2 years.

The present study revealed that the tourists who visited creative tourism attractions were predominantly female (women vs. men, 60.6% vs. 39.4%). Most of the respondents were older adults, had a high level of education, and visited the creative tourism attractions with their families. These findings correspond to those reported by Huang et al. [28], Wessels and Douglas [15], and Remoaldo et al. [26]. In the present study, women were more interested than men in cultural consumption; this finding corresponds to the results reported by Richards and van der Ark [27].

Table 1. Demographic characteristics of respondents.

Variable	Category	Total	
		N	%
Gender	Female	470	60.6
	Male	305	39.4
Age	20–29 years	217	28.0
	30–39 years	236	30.5
	40–49 years	225	29.0
	50–59 years	75	9.7
	≥ 60 years	22	2.8
Educational level	Lower than secondary school education	20	2.6
	Secondary school education	103	13.3
	Bachelor's degree	505	65.2
	Master's or higher degree	145	18.9
Monthly income	≤ NT$15,000	133	17.2
	NT$15,001–NT$30,000	138	17.8
	NT$30,001–NT$45,000	206	26.6
	NT$45,001–NT$60,000	175	22.6
	> NT$60,000	123	15.9
Place of residence	Northern Taiwan	414	53.5
	Central Taiwan	230	29.8
	Southern Taiwan	105	13.4
	Eastern Taiwan	24	3.0
	Outlying islands of Taiwan	2	0.2
Numbers of visit	1	552	71.2
	2	130	16.8
	3	37	4.8
	≥4	56	7.2

4.2 Behavioral Characteristics of Tourists

Table 2 presents the respondents' attitudes and motivations with respect to their engagement in creative tourism. In terms of the creative activities of the respondents in the past 2 years, food-based experiential activities (e.g. tea tasting, do-it-yourself [DIY] pastry, and cooking; 35.9%) accounted for the largest proportion of such activities, followed by experiences pertaining to handmade botanical or aromatic products (e.g. perfume, horticulture, and floriculture; 18.6%), handicraft-related experiences (e.g. pottery, carpentry, dyeing, and weaving) (16.8%), fun activities (e.g., games for kids) (11.4%), visual creations (e.g., painting; 9.3%) and industrial culture experiences (8.0%).

The three key factors that influenced the respondents' decision to visit a creative-tourism destination were local characteristics (20.5%), the atmosphere of a creative-tourism destination (15.4%), and personalized experiences pertaining to handmade products (13.8%); the least crucial factor was the on-site COVID-19 prevention facilities of a destination (2.4%). These findings indicate that local cultural characteristics and the overall atmosphere of a destination site are key factors influencing the decision of tourists to visit a creative tourism destination.

For the respondents' motivations to visit a creative-tourism destination, 21.7% of them were motivated by the opportunities to relax while visiting these destinations, and 17.5% were interested in learning about different cultures; the other motivations were acquiring an enriching life experience (14.6%), relieving stress (12.2%), enjoying local landscapes (11.8%), increasing one's knowledge (10.8%), learning about local humanities and history (6.1%), and learning about local customs (5.3%).

For travel decisions, the present study revealed that the atmosphere of a creative-tourism destination was a key influencing factor; this finding is comparable to that of Cheng and Chen [16], who conceptualized the construct of creative atmosphere in creative tourism. The survey of the present study was conducted between August 11 and September 15, 2021. During this period, international travel was curtailed and no travel restrictions were imposed in Taiwan. The amount of on-site prevention facilities for COVID-19 at a creative tourism destination was the least crucial influencing factor. This result may be explained by the status of the creative tourism destinations (i.e., destinations selected for the survey), which are mainly located in unpopulated rural areas, as safe destinations for tourists. By contrast, on-site COVID-19 prevention facilities are a necessity for creative tourism attractions.

For the respondents' motivations to engage in creative tourism, the findings pertaining to relaxation and stress relief are similar to those identified by Remoaldo et al. [26] with respect to creative tourists who were leisure–creativity seekers. The findings of the present study with regard to increasing one's knowledge, learning about local culture and history, and learning about local customs correspond with those reported by Tan et al. [29] and Remoaldo et al. [26]. Tan et al. [29] asserted that tourists are motivated to visit a creative-tourism destination to gain knowledge. Remoaldo et al. [26] identified knowledge and skill learners as a type of creative-tourism tourist in Portugal.

The importance of interactions with local people and other visitors was emphasized in several studies, such as those conducted by Smith [7], Tan et al. [29], and Remoaldo et al. [26]. By contrast, the present study reported different results; specifically, it revealed that most respondents wanted to relax, learn about different cultures, and enrich their life experiences. Some tourists indicated that they were not highly motivated to learn more about the creative-tourism destinations that they visited. Thus, although tour operators should consider whether tourists are interested in learning more about creative tourism, they should be aware that some comprehensive tours can be exhausting for tourists.

With the imposition of COVID-19 travel restrictions, tourists tended to purchase experiential products or engage in home-based activities. Food-based experiential activities were most commonly cited by the respondents (e.g., tea tasting, DIY pastry, and cooking; 36.1%), followed by handicraft experiences (e.g., pottery, carpentry, dyeing, and weaving; 18.9%), experiences pertaining to handmade botanical or aromatic products (e.g., perfume, horticulture, and floriculture; 14.7%), visual creations (e.g., painting; 10.7%), fun activities (e.g., games for kids; 10.3%), and online guided tours (e.g., tours and exhibitions; 9.3%). The present study revealed that tourists were more likely to engage in life aesthetics-related experiences at home. Notably, online guided tours were the activity least cited by the respondents, suggesting that tourists still prefer physical guided tours.

A summary of tourist spending behavior is presented in Table 3. Approximately 29.1% of the respondents purchased products, followed by experiential activities (e.g., DIY; 23.7%), meals (22.0%), tickets (16.8%), accommodation (5.3%), and other products or services (3.0%). When creative tourism operators provide high-quality products and experiences, they are more likely to attract tourists to purchase their products or services. The accommodation provided by the creative-tourism sites examined in the present study were small and only accounted for a small proportion of tourism spending.

Among the respondents, 40.4% spent <NT$500, 34.5% spent NT$501–NT$1,000, 17.8% spent NT$1,001–NT$2,000, 4.3% spent NT$2,001–NT$3,000, and 3.1% spent ≥NT$3,001. The amount of money spent by the respondents was generally low. Notably, only a small proportion of the respondents spent a large amount of money on creative tourism (i.e., ≥NT$3,001).

For length of stay, most respondents (59%) stayed at the creative tourism sites that they visited for ≤2 h, and 31.5% stayed for 2–4 h. The present study revealed that the respondents were not highly interested in spending a considerable amount of time at a creative-tourism site. It also revealed that creative-tourism operators tended to provide short-term experiences.

Table 4 presents the basic elements of the tours conducted at the creative tourism destinations. For travel companions, most respondents (67.4%) traveled with their families, 11.9% traveled with their partners, 11.5% traveled with their friends, 7.0% traveled alone, and 1.0% traveled with their coworkers. Most respondents obtained information about the creative tourism sites that they visited through social networks (43.3%), family and friends (25.7%), other channels (12.7%), media (TV, radio, and online news; 12.6%), and print media (5.7%).

The present study revealed that 74.9% of the respondents spent <NT$1,000, 90% spent <4 h at creative-tourism destinations, and 59% spent <2 h at these destinations. With respect to traveling companions, the respondents who traveled with their families (including or excluding their children) accounted for the largest proportion of the sample (68.4%). These findings suggest that the products and services offered by creative tourism

Table 2. Dimensions of tourist attitudes and motivations.

Variable	Category	Total	
		N	%
Creative activities in the past 2 years (multiple-choice item)	Food-based experiential activities	449	35.9
	Handicraft experiences	210	16.8
	Visual creations	116	9.3
	Fun activities	143	11.4
	Experiences pertaining to handmade botanical or aromatic products	232	18.6
	Industrial culture experiences	100	8.0
Top three factors influencing decision to visit a destination (multiple-choice item)	Local characteristics	464	20.5
	Atmosphere of a creative-tourism site	348	15.4
	Featured goods	311	13.7
	Personalized experiences pertaining to handmade products	313	13.8
	Diverse experiential activities	204	9.0
	Brand reputation of a destination	142	6.3
	Characteristics of cultural history	185	8.2
	Accessibility of location	142	6.3
	Visit made as a side trip	103	4.5
	On-site COVID-19 prevention facilities	54	2.4
Motivation-related items (multiple-choice item)	Learning about different cultures	360	17.5
	Enriching one's life	300	14.6
	Increasing one's knowledge	221	10.8
	Seeking relaxation	446	21.7
	Relieving stress	251	12.2
	Enjoying local landscapes	243	11.8
	Experiencing local customs	108	5.3

(*continued*)

Table 2. (*continued*)

Variable	Category	Total	
		N	%
	Learning about local humanities and history	126	6.1
Purchases made at home during period in which travel restrictions were imposed	Food-based experiential activities	457	36.1
	Handicraft experiences	240	18.9
	Visual creations	135	10.7
	Fun activities	131	10.3
	Experiences pertaining to handmade botanical or aromatic products	186	14.7
	Online guided tours	118	9.3

Table 3. Dimensions of tourist spending behavior.

Variable	Category	Total	
		N	%
Purchases	Tickets	199	16.8
	Products	345	29.1
	Experiential activities	281	23.7
	Food	261	22.0
	Accommodation	63	5.3
	Others	36	3.0
Spending	<NT$500	313	40.4
	NT$501–NT$1,000	267	34.5
	NT$1,001–NT$2,000	138	17.8
	NT$2,001–NT$3,000	33	4.3
	≥NT$3,001	24	3.1
Length of stay	Under 2 h	457	59.0
	2–4 h	244	31.5
	4–8 h	35	4.5
	8 h to 1 day	26	3.4
	>1 day	13	1.7

may be more appealing to family travelers than to other types of travelers. To increase the contribution of tourists, the appeal of various items should be improved.

Table 4. Basic elements of tours.

Variable	Category	Total	
		N	%
Source of tourism information (multiple-choice item)	Media (TV, radio, and online news)	122	12.6
	Social networks	420	43.3
	Printed media	55	5.7
	Friends, relatives, and coworkers	249	25.7
	Others	123	12.7
Travel companion	Alone	54	7.0
	Family (excluding children)	163	21.0
	Family (including children)	367	47.4
	Partner	92	11.9
	Friends	89	11.5
	Coworkers	8	1.0
	Others	2	0.3

Word-of-mouth through social networks and family and friends was the main source of information for the respondents. Thus, assessing the satisfaction of tourists with their tourist experiences is a key task. Social networks are crucial, especially those formed through Facebook and Instagram. Media (television, radio, and online news) and print media were not regarded by the respondents as key sources or useful sources of information. Hence, strengthening the influences of social networks and tourist experiences can be effective marketing strategies for attracting tourists.

5   Conclusions and Suggestions

The objectives of the present study were to characterize the profile of creative-tourism tourists and their travel motivations and behaviors in Taiwan. The present study described the profiles and characteristics of the tourists who traveled during the COVID-19 pandemic, and it contributed to the limited research on Taiwan's creative tourism.

The results of the present study have several implications. With regard to the first objective of the present study, the tourists who traveled with their families to creative-tourism destinations were generally middle-aged and highly educated individuals who were middle-income or higher-income earners. In addition, given that almost a third of the respondents were <30 years old, they could represent a potential market for creative tourism in Taiwan. Among the respondents, most were from Northern Taiwan, and nearly a third of them visited a creative-tourism destination more than twice. Consequently, creative tourism operators should target tourists and focus on the key elements that can increase tourist loyalty.

For the second objective, which pertained to the behavioral characteristics of tourists, three key factors that influenced decision-making were identified, namely local characteristics, the atmosphere of a creative-tourism destination, and the personalized experiences pertaining to handmade products. Therefore, creative tourism operators should strengthen their local characteristics and creative atmosphere to address the concerns of tourists. In addition, on-site COVID-19 prevention facilities were regarded as a less important factor by the respondents. This result suggests that the respondents regarded these facilities as a necessity rather than a factor that could influence their decision and that the respondents preferred to visit creative-tourism attractions in rural areas. The present study also revealed that most tourists were motivated by opportunities to relax, learn about different cultures, and pursue enriching life experiences. Tourists have various concerns when they visit creative tourism attractions in Taiwan. To attract tourists, creative tourism operators should focus on their target tourists and the key motivators that influence these tourists' decision to visit a creative tourism destination.

The present study has several limitations. First, data were collected at six creative-tourism attractions, and convenience sampling was applied to perform a survey; thus, the results of the present study are not representative of the overall creative tourist populations in Taiwan. For the sample, various scales were applied across multiple Taiwanese regions, and the present study focused on specific rural areas and small- and medium-sized creative tourism attractions. In the future, studies should collect samples comprising various types of creative tourism attractions associated with various cultures to increase the generalizability of their results. Second, the tourist behavior variables examined in this study were established on the basis of the characteristics of creative life businesses in Taiwan; given the cultural differences, caution should be exercised when applying the results of the study to other countries. The present study used examined tourist behavior variables but did not involve a cross-analysis of variables. Thus, its findings can be extended by cross-analyzing visitor profiles and behavioral variables to better understand tourist behaviors in the context of creative tourism.

Acknowledgments. The survey conducted in this study was conducted as a part of the research project 2021 Creative Life Industry Development Plan – Industrial Development and Market Trend Analysis, which was funded by the Corporate Synergy Development Center and co-funded by the Industrial Development Bureau, Ministry of Economic Affairs, Taiwan, through the Creative Life Industry Development Program. The author would also like to thank everyone who has contributed to this research.

References

1. Richards, G., Raymond, C.: Creative tourism. ATLAS News. **23**, 16–20 (2000)
2. Tan, S.-K., Tan, S.-H., Luh, D.-B., Kung, S.-F.: Understanding tourist perspectives in creative tourism. Curr. Issue Tour. **19**(10), 981–987 (2016). https://doi.org/10.1080/13683500.2015.1008427
3. Chang, S.H.: A practical framework for designing creative tourism experiences. In: Agapito, D., Ribeiro, M., Woosnam, K. (eds.) Handbook on the Tourist Experience: Design, Marketing and Management, pp. 118–135. Edward Elgar, Cheltenham (2022)

4. Chang, S.H.: 2021 Creative Life Industry Plan - Industrial Development and Market Trend Analysis. Corporate Synergy Development Center, Taipei (2021)
5. Richards, G.: Creative tourism: opportunities for smaller places? Tour. Manage. Stud. **15**(SI), 7–10 (2019). https://doi.org/10.18089/tms.2019.15SI01
6. UNESCO: Towards sustainable strategies for creative tourism, http://unesdoc.unesco.org/images/0015/001598/159811E.pdf. Accessed 10 May 2019
7. Smith, M.K.: Issues in Cultural Tourism Studies, 2nd edn. Routledge, New York (2009)
8. DuBru, N.: A look at its origins, its definitions, and the creative tourism movement. In: Wurzburguer, R., Aageson, T., Pattakos, A., Pratt, S. (eds.) Creative Tourism: A Global Conversation: How to Provide Unique Creative Experiences for Travelers Worldwide, pp. 229–237. Sunstone Press, Santa Fe (2009)
9. Raymond, C.: Creative tourism New Zealand: the practical challenges of developing creative tourism. In: Richards, G., Wilson, J. (eds.) Tourism, Creativity and Development, pp. 145–157. Routledge, London (2007)
10. Richards, G.: The development of cultural tourism in Europe. In: Richards, G. (ed.) Cultural Attractions and European Tourism, pp. 3–29. CAB International, Wallingford (2001)
11. Richards, G.: Creativity and tourism: the state of the art. Ann. Tour. Res. **38**(4), 1225–1253 (2011). https://doi.org/10.1016/j.annals.2011.07.008
12. OECD: Tourism and the Creative Economy, OECD Studies on Tourism. OECD Paris (2014)
13. Tan, S.-K., Kung, S.-F., Luh, D.-B.: A model of "creative experience" in creative tourism. Ann. Tour. Res. **41**, 153–174 (2013). https://doi.org/10.1016/j.annals.2012.12.002
14. Galvagno, M., Giaccone, S.C.: Mapping creative tourism research: reviewing the field and outlining future directions. J. Hosp. Tour. Res. **43**(8), 1256–1280 (2019). https://doi.org/10.1177/1096348019862030
15. Wessels, J.-A., Douglas, A.: Exploring creative tourism potential in protected areas: The Kruger National Park case. J. Hosp. Tour. Res. **46**(8), 1482–1499 (2020). https://doi.org/10.1177/1096348020983532
16. Cheng, T.-M., Chen, M.-T.: Creative atmosphere in creative tourism destinations: conceptualizing and scale development. J. Hosp. Tour. Res. **June**, 1–26 (2021). https://doi.org/10.1177/10963480211012459
17. Williams, C.C., Kayaoglu, A.: COVID-19 and undeclared work: impacts and policy responses in Europe. Serv. Ind. J. **40**(13–14), 914–931 (2020)
18. Flew, T., Kirkwood, K.: The impact of COVID-19 on cultural tourism: art, culture and communication in four regional sites of Queensland Australia. Media Int. Australia **178**(1), 16–20 (2020). https://doi.org/10.1177/1329878X20952529
19. Foo, L.-P., Chin, M.-Y., Tan, K.-L., Phuah, K.-T.: The impact of COVID-19 on tourism industry in Malaysia. Curr. Issue Tour. **24**(19), 2735–2739 (2021). https://doi.org/10.1080/13683500.2020.1777951
20. Wu, L.-F., Achyldurdyyeva, J., Jou, W.-P., Foung, W.-T., Jaw, B.-S.: Relief, recovery, and revitalization measures for tourism and hospitality industry during Covid-19 pandemic: case study from Taiwan. SAGE Open **11**(3), 1–16 (2021). https://doi.org/10.1177/21582440211040805
21. Osti, L., Nava, C.R.: Loyal: To What Extent? A shift in destination preference due to the COVID-19 pandemic. Ann. Tour. Res. Empirical Insights **1**(1), 100004 (2020). https://doi.org/10.1016/j.annale.2020.100004
22. Zenker, S., Kock, F.: The coronavirus pandemic – a critical discussion of a tourism research agenda. Tour. Manage. **81**, 104164 (2020). https://doi.org/10.1016/j.tourman.2020.104164
23. Assaf, A.G., Kock, F., Tsionas, M.: Tourism during and after COVID-19: an expert-informed agenda for future research. J. Travel Res. 1–4 (2021). https://doi.org/10.1177/00472875211017237

24. Engel, J.F., Blackwell, R.D., Miniard, P.W.: Consumer Behavior, 6th edn. Dryden Press, Chicago (1995)
25. Schiffman, L.G., Wisenblit, J.: Consumer Behavior. 11th edn. Pearson, New York (2017)
26. Remoaldo, P., et al.: Profiling the participants in creative tourism activities: case studies from small and medium sized cities and rural areas from Continental Portugal. Tour. Manage. Perspect. **36**, 100746 (2020). https://doi.org/10.1016/j.tmp.2020.100746
27. Richards, G., van der Ark, L.A.: Dimensions of cultural consumption among tourists: multiple correspondence analysis. Tour. Manage. **37**, 71–76 (2013). https://doi.org/10.1016/j.tourman.2013.01.007
28. Huang, Y.-C., Chang, L.L., Backman, K.F.: Detecting common method bias in predicting creative tourists behavioural intention with an illustration of theory of planned behaviour. Curr. Issue Tour. **22**(3), 307–329 (2019). https://doi.org/10.1080/13683500.2018.1424809
29. Tan, S.-K., Luh, D.-B., Kung, S.-F.: A taxonomy of creative tourists in creative tourism. Tour. Manage. **42**, 248–259 (2014). https://doi.org/10.1016/j.tourman.2013.11.008

A Study on the Influence of Converting Cultural Elements into Pattern Design and Cultural Cognition

Jun Chen[✉] and Luoyu Chen

Graduate School of Creative Industry Design, National Taiwan University of Arts,
New Taipei City 220307, Taiwan
cheesejune@qq.com

Abstract. Local culture is equivalent to a kind of city colour, and the charm of a city is often reflected by the city image formed by the full expression and manifestation of its local cultural elements. For cultural and creative commodities, designers should focus on the "meaning" of commodities while focusing on the "form" of commodities, that is, "meaning" may make a commodity stand out. It is the most intuitive and vivid to convey the concept and behavior of the city to the public through cultural elements. At the same time, local cultural elements also enhance the people's sense of cognition and pride in the region, thus enhancing the cultural cohesion of the region. It is a new trend of consumption in modern society to draw consumers' attention and recognition to the commodities through unique cultural elements.

Therefore, this study will take the jasmine cultural elements of Fuzhou City, Fujian Province, China as the research object, and explore the application of local pattern design by extracting the local cultural elements. The study was conducted by literature analysis and questionnaire survey, and correlation analysis and multiple regression analysis were applied to analyze the questionnaire data. The results show that: 1. Pattern design has influence on consumers' purchase intention; 2. Pattern design has influence on consumers' cultural cognition; 3. Cultural cognition plays a part in mediating the effect between pattern design and purchase intention, which means that pattern design can influence consumers' purchase intention through cultural cognition; 4. Different styles of pattern design have different effects on cultural cognition.

Keywords: Cultural Element Conversion Design · Pattern Design · Cultural Cognition · Purchase Intention

1 Introduction

In the context of globalization of the economy, information technology provides us with rapid sharing of resources. People can quickly learn about the culture of a place through the Internet. The cultural and creative economic industry is also developing rapidly, and cultural symbols have become the most abstract and rich connotation bearer of culture, which is an important form of cultural connotation expression.

© The Author(s), under exclusive license to Springer Nature Switzerland AG 2023
P.-L. P. Rau (Ed.): HCII 2023, LNCS 14024, pp. 99–111, 2023.
https://doi.org/10.1007/978-3-031-35946-0_9

Culture is the calling card of a place, carrying irreplaceable humanistic values. Every brick and tile, every building and pavilion, every street and alley has a culture and a story. As Murphy Rhodes says, "the city is a container of great cultural significance" [1]. Culture is the most important intangible asset of a city, and it also influences the world's evaluation of the city. In today's society, the large amount of information makes it difficult for people to obtain useful information quickly, so the prominence of symbols is especially important. Symbols are found everywhere in people's daily lives, and each symbol has its own meaning. People use symbols to share and communicate with each other and to promote cultural development. Some of these symbols are historical marks, such as Chinese tea; some are forms of life, such as Chinese food and Chinese medicine; some are symbolic symbols, such as the dragon and the Great Wall; and some are communication tools, such as Chinese characters and names. The pattern design with cultural elements is also an extension of the local cultural connotation, constructing recognizable forms through cultural imagery, and systematizing, symbolizing and signifying the visual elements of the visible material entities and environment in the place [2].

With such a huge amount of information available, how do people receive cultural information from graphic design? With the above background and motivation, this study will serve as a pilot study to explore, from the perspective of cultural cognition, the combination of intangible cultural conversion pattern design and merchandise to improve the public's cultural cognition and enhance the popularity and fame of local characteristics, which is a very worthy topic in cultural communication.

2   Literature Review

2.1   Local Culture

Local culture is the culture associated with a specific region. Local culture reflects the economic, political, religious and other cultural forms of the society and people of the region, and contains the philosophy, art, religion, customs and the origin of the entire value system of the nation. The phrase "a place where water and soil nurture a people" describes the human characteristics of a region, reflecting the fact that each region of China has its own special history and characteristics. Local culture has an important and unique position as one of the traditional Chinese culture and folklore characteristics.

In China, different regions have their own cultural traditions, customs and habits. As people's awareness of local culture deepens, cultural and creative goods are gradually integrated with local culture. For example, the Palace Museum has incorporated the unique culture and characteristics of Beijing's Forbidden City into its cultural and creative products, making them popular. For example, lipstick from the Forbidden City, notebooks from the Forbidden City, keychains from the Forbidden City, and so on. The design of these cultural and creative goods is inspired by the human geography and natural landscape of Beijing and its surrounding areas. In recent years, many places not only attach importance to tangible culture, but also vigorously promote the development of intangible culture.

2.2 Cultural Elements Conversion Pattern Design

Patterns are essentially visual symbols, and their integration with the design of modern artworks means that traditional cultural elements and related content can be presented to audiences through an intuitive visual symbol. This intuitive visual experience can enhance the profundity and effectiveness of the audience's cognition of traditional culture, thus promoting traditional culture as a highlight and cultural promotion point in modern art design [3]. To apply shapes and patterns with regional characteristics to tourism products, the method of refining and transformation is often used. Based on the understanding of local cultural elements, designers extract shapes and patterns, extract recognizable and representative cultural symbols, retain their characteristics, and then form new shapes and patterns that meet modern aesthetics through simplification, transformation, abstraction, etc., so that consumers can understand the culture expressed by their elements based on the first impression [4].

When transforming cultural elements into pattern design, designers should focus on profound reflection on culture, so as to give the cultural and creative products a new connotation, improve the value and meaning of the products, and make the cultural elements fully present in the pattern content of the cultural and creative products. For example, words, symbols and other graphic shapes can be used as backgrounds or materials in the patterns of cultural and creative products; at the same time, words are integrated into the graphics for presentation; in addition, the artistic and decorative functions of graphic shapes should be given full play, and traditional patterns can be decorated and embellished with words, numbers and other shapes, so that the patterns of cultural and creative products have strong expressive and affinity power to attract more people to appreciate and buy. As scholars have suggested, how the correlation between "form" and "content" becomes a concept of creative development in painting. There seems to be a certain degree of correspondence between "form" and "content", that is to say, the threads of "content" can be found in "form" [5].

2.3 Cultural Cognition

Cultural cognition is the analysis of the process of receiving and processing cultural information with the help of cognitive science theories [6]. Cultural cognition is the acquisition, identification and application of external cultural information. Once the environmental information carries cultural symbols, then the process of identifying and processing information in the environment will acquire some kind of meaningfulness [7]. In their study, Wang Xinge et al. showed that tourists generally have a higher awareness of the cultural elements that are close to the real life of the residents and carry the collective memory of the local residents in the tourist destination [8]. With its special charm, tourism culture attracts people to explore and discover, and presents its own unique value and meaning in a unique way, thus attracting the audience groups to recognize, understand and resonate with the culture. To a certain extent, cultural cognition enables consumers to make value judgments about a particular destination, which in turn affects their attitudes toward that destination. Cultural cognition includes the recognition of history and the prediction of the future, and there are differences in people's understanding of the value of things in different times and regions. For example, historically, the urban environment has contained a large number of cultural symbols that are important sources of emotions, attitudinal judgments, and behavioral choices that residents make about social phenomena.

2.4 Purchase Intention

Purchase intention refers to the tendency of consumers before the consumer behavior takes place. According to Gilbert, tourists are influenced by motivation, personality, cognition, and learning to make purchase decisions [9]. According to Spears and Singh, purchase intention has three meanings: first, the consumer's willingness to consider the possibility of purchasing a good in the future; second, purchase intention represents what we want to buy in the future; and third, purchase intention is an assertion that links self and action [10]. Other scholars have also summarized the definition of purchase intention into three main points: first, it refers to the possibility, i.e., the possibility of consumers to purchase the goods; second, it refers to the evaluation or attitude, i.e., the evaluation or attitude of consumers towards the relevant goods, which can actively cooperate with external factors to stimulate the purchase decision; third, purchase intention can be regarded as an important indicator to predict the actual behavior of consumers [11]. The formation of purchase intention is a continuous process of change, and consumers tend to have different preferences and form purchase behavior at different stages.

3 Methodology

3.1 Research Hypothesis

From the semiotic point of view, "semiotics" itself is an open discipline that does not exclude the intervention of other disciplines. It is the versatility of symbols that also gives scholars from different disciplines the possibility of constant creativity in the study, discussion and development of this field. Therefore, the scope of this study was set by exploring the pattern design of different expression styles in visual symbols, conducting a preliminary study and analyzing its impact on consumers, and proposing a model of cultural visual integration based on the results.

The purpose of this study is to investigate the perception of culture and the perceptions and preferences of the consumer groups after the product has become a "cultural value-added" product by adding cultural elements. The research structure integrates the designer's visual processing process with the consumer's cultural cognition and consumption intention, and proposes a research structure diagram as shown in Fig. 1. This study uses questionnaire survey, data analysis, and inference of results as the basis for the study of "cultural value-added" goods. The study explores three parts: first, the feasibility of a scale to assess the design of cultural element conversion patterns; second, the relevance of the design of cultural element conversion patterns to consumers' cultural cognition; and third, the differences in the impact of different expressive styles of pattern design on cultural cognition. The following research hypotheses are proposed for the purpose of this study.

H1: There is an effect of design on consumers' purchase intention.

H2: Pattern design has an effect on the level of cultural cognition.

H3: Pattern design influences purchase intention by affecting cultural cognition.

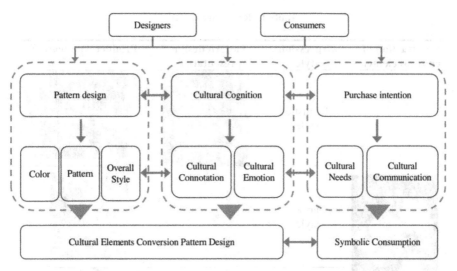

Fig. 1. Research architecture of cultural element conversion pattern design

3.2 Research Subject

This study is based on the jasmine culture in Fuzhou City, Fujian Province, China. In Fuzhou, there is a kind of city flower called jasmine, which has brought together the ingenuity of generations of Fuzhou people and precipitated the unique cultural meaning of Fuzhou. As early as 2000 years ago in the Western Han Dynasty, jasmine flowers came to Fuzhou from the distant ancient Rome via the Silk Road. Since the Ming Dynasty, Fuzhou people have been famous for their jasmine tea production, and it has become the birthplace of jasmine tea in the world. In the mid-1990s, jasmine tea in Fuzhou fell from its peak to an all-time low in just a decade, and most jasmine plantations have disappeared due to a number of factors, including urbanization, industrialization, and fierce competition from other regions [12]. Since 2007, Fuzhou has been working to revive the production of jasmine tea. In recent years, this effort has grown, with the official opening of Fuzhou Line 1 in January 2017, which became a sensation due to the special jasmine carriage with local cultural elements of Fuzhou, and the construction of the Fuzhou Strait Culture and Arts Center, a building themed on the local culture of jasmine.

How to bring back the glory of jasmine, which has a long history and cultural tradition in Fuzhou, is the original purpose of this research paper. Therefore, in this paper, we will discuss from the perspective of pattern design by collecting local products related to jasmine culture, analyzing the expression of design elements, and following the "visual expression of illustration design language" proposed by Gu and Liu [13]. The forms of expression are classified as realistic, abstract, cartoon, and decoration (See Table 1).

3.3 Experimental Design

In this study, the questionnaire design was conducted through literature research and data analysis of related studies, and the assessment items were developed based on the

Table 1. Research Subject

Extraction of cultural elements	Expression style	Pattern design presentation	Product Application
	Realistic style		
	Cartoon style		
	Abstract style		
	Decoration style		

research hypotheses, and the scale dimensions were used to develop assessment questions in three dimensions starting from their hypotheses, and the research surveys were conducted in different performance styles of pattern design respectively (See Table 2).

The scale of the assessment questions was a Liker-type 5-point scale, which consisted of "strongly disagree", "disagree", "average", "agree", and "strongly agree", and was given a score of 1, 2, 3, 4, and 5, respectively. A total of 12 questions were asked, and 180 valid questionnaires were returned, which is 15 times the number of questions in the questionnaire. Depending on the number of questionnaire questions, it is recommended that the sample size be 3 to 5 times or 5 to 10 times the number of questions [18, 19], in line with the needs of the sample size.

Table 2. Cultural element conversion pattern design scale structure and assessment questions

Dimension	Assessment Questions
A. Pattern Design	A1. This pattern design has a sense of beauty
	A2. This pattern design can convey the local culture
	A3. The color of this pattern design has a cultural connotation
	A4. This pattern design has a cultural connotation
B. Cultural Cognition	B1. This pattern design is unique to the local culture
	B2. This pattern design will cause me nostalgia or life memories
	B3. This pattern design will make me value the cultural connotation of the product
	B4. This pattern design will make me want to learn more about the culture and history of the place
C. Purchase Intention	C1. I will buy products with this pattern design
	C2. I will recommend products with this pattern design to my friends and relatives
	C3. I will buy products related to Fuzhou jasmine culture
	C4. I will recommend products with Fuzhou jasmine culture to friends and relatives

Reference source: [14–17].

4 Results and Discussion

4.1 Study Questionnaire Reliability and Validity Analysis

This study was mainly conducted by online questionnaire distribution, which took about 5–10 min to fill out and contained basic personal information, questions on each dimension of each pattern design, and personal preferences. The subjects were mainly local residents (with household registration and more than 10 years of residence) and foreign residents in Fuzhou. There were 180 people, including 84 males and 96 females; 68 local Fuzhou residents and 112 foreign residents, including local residents, for a total of 148 people who came to Fuzhou; their ages were mainly distributed between 18 and 35 years old.

The questionnaire in this study needs to be shown to be consistent and stable by using the results of reliability and validity analysis. In order to measure the adequacy of the questionnaire itself, SPSS 19.0 was used to test the reliability and validity of the questionnaire, and the Cronbach's alpha coefficient was used to check the constructs of the questionnaire. The results of the reliability and validity analysis are as follows: from the reliability of each dimension, the Cronbach's alpha coefficient is greater than 0.9 ($p < 0.001$), which indicates that this questionnaire has sufficient reliability; from the validity of each dimension, the factor loadings are between 0.8 and 0.9, which has good structural validity; and the explained variance of each dimension is between 81%

and 87%. Between 81% and 87%, and the overall results meet the criteria, showing the feasibility of this study instrument (See Table 3).

Table 3. Reliability and validity analysis of the questionnaire

Dimension	Title number	Cronbach's Alpha	Factor loadings	Explained variance
A. Pattern Design	A1	0.940	0.885	86.649%
	A2		0.938	
	A3		0.928	
	A4		0.929	
B. Cultural Cognition	B1	0.943	0.924	85.537%
	B2		0.908	
	B3		0.930	
	B4		0.937	
C. Purchase Intention	C1	0.925	0.900	81.694%
	C2		0.907	
	C3		0.897	
	C4		0.912	

4.2   Correlation Analysis of Cultural Elements Conversion Pattern Design

In order to find out whether there is a correlation between the cultural element conversion pattern design, cultural perception and purchase intention, this study used Pearson's correlation analysis to investigate, and the results showed that the facets were significantly correlated with each other (See Table 4).

Table 4. Correlation analysis

Dimension	Pattern Design	Cultural Cognition	Purchase Intention
Pattern Design	1	.919**	.829**
Cultural Cognition	.919**	1	.853**
Purchase Intention	.829**	.853**	1

**. Significantly correlated at the .01 level (two-sided)

4.3   Regression Analysis

In order to understand the influence relationship between cultural elements converted pattern design, and cultural perception, purchase intention, and predict the degree of cultural perception can play a mediating role. This study was explored by multiple regression analysis: the mediating role of cultural cognition (m) in the relationship between pattern design (x) and purchase intention (y) was examined. The specific methods are as follows: (1) Regression analysis was conducted to examine the predictive effect of pattern design on purchase intention with pattern design as the independent variable and purchase intention as the dependent variable. (2) Regression analysis was conducted with pattern design as the independent variable and cultural cognition as the dependent variable to examine the predictive effect of pattern design on cultural cognition. (3) Regression analysis was conducted with pattern design and cultural cognition as independent variables and purchase intention as dependent variables to examine the predictive effect of pattern design on purchase intention after adding cultural cognition variables (See Table 5).

Table 5. Regression analysis of the three dimensions of pattern design, cultural cognition and purchase intention

Steps	Standardized regression equation	Regression coefficient test	
Step 1	y = 0.829*x	SE = 0.021	t = 39.674**
Step 2	m = 0.919*x	SE = 0.016	t = 62.442**
Step 3	y = 0.290*x	SE = 0.048	t = 6.017**
	+ 0.557*m	SE = 0.046	t = 12.131**

Note: SE stands for standard error, t stands for t-test value; **. P < 0.01

The results of the regression analysis show that (1) the predictive effect of pattern design (X) on purchase intention (Y) is significant; (2) the predictive effect of pattern design (X) on the degree of cultural cognition (M) is significant; (3) the predictive effects of cultural cognition and pattern design on purchase intention are also significant when the degree of cultural cognition is included in the equation. Therefore, it can be concluded that cultural cognition plays a partial mediating effect between pattern design and purchase intention, which is a good verification of the hypothesis. And the proportion of the partial effect to the total effect is $0.919 \times 0.557 / 0.829 = 0.6175$, i.e. 61.75%.

4.4 Exploring the Influence of Different Expressions Styles of Pattern Design on Cultural Cognition

Four different expressive styles of pattern design were selected for this study to see if there are differences in the effects of different expressive styles of pattern design on the degree of cultural cognition. A regression analysis model was developed with pattern design as the independent variable and cultural cognition as the dependent variable (See Table 6).

Table 6. Analysis of the influence of different expressive styles of pattern design and cultural cognition

Pattern design style	Variable	Coefficient	T-statistic value	P-value	Goodness of fit	F-statistic
Realistic style	Constant	−0.066	−0.467	0.641	0.802	720.605(0.000)
	Cultural Cognition	0.993	26.844	0.000		
Cartoon style	Constant	0.103	1.102	0.272	0.883	1346.478(0.000)
	Cultural Cognition	0.942	36.694	0.000		
Abstract style	Constant	−0.052	−0.442	0.659	0.844	960.049(0.000)
	Cultural Cognition	0.988	30.985	0.000		
Decoration style	Constant	0.225	1.914	0.057	0.843	954.996(0.000)
	Cultural Cognition	0.946	30.903	0.000		

From the above results, the F-statistics of all four equations passed the significance test, the goodness-of-fit was greater than 0.8, and the regression coefficients of the independent variables passed the significance test, indicating that the equations were well constructed.

From the regression coefficients, it shows that the influence of different expressive styles of pattern design on cultural cognition is from high to low: realistic style, abstract style, decorative style, and cartoon style.

4.5 Summary

Based on previous studies, this paper synthesizes previous views and expands the research perspective on this basis to obtain the results of this paper through questionnaire survey and validation analysis. In addition to the reliability analysis of the scale structure, this paper will also investigate and analyze the dimensions to draw the final main conclusions as listed below.

1. The results of the analysis of reliability, validity and correlation met the requirements of the test and proved the reasonableness of the scale. Also, the scale can be used as a reference and application for the relevant design teaching and industry assessment.
2. From the results of the study, all three hypotheses proposed in this study are valid. It can prove that cultural and creative goods can enhance users' visual experience to improve the added value of products and increase cultural value, thus enhancing their purchase intention and cultural cognition. The cultural uniqueness of cultural and creative goods can make them more easily accepted by the public and create a sense of identity. This provides a good theoretical basis for subsequent research on cultural identity.

3. Regarding the influence of different expressive styles of pattern design on cultural cognition, the results of this study concluded that, in descending order, they are: realistic style, abstract style, decorative style, and cartoon style. A cross-tabulation analysis of consumers' preference for pattern design and purchase intentions revealed that consumers' preference and purchase intentions for pattern designs with different expression styles differ from those that enhance cultural cognition. Therefore, this study emphasizes the importance of communication between design and consumers. The process of transforming cultural elements into design requires designers to understand and grasp the cultural connotations, and should align design with consumer preferences and enhance the value and meaning of products.

5 Conclusion

The study is intended to serve as a pre-study to examine the impact of consumers' cultural identity, expecting that cultural and creative products can become an important tool for spreading culture, deepening consumers' cognitiveness and memorability of traditional culture, and stimulating the public's sense of cultural identity, and the audience's identification with culture further stimulates the consumption of cultural symbols.

The study extends the research structure and results by means of literature analysis, decomposes the process of designers' conversion of cultural elements into pattern design and consumers' cultural cognitive process, and divides it into three stages: sensory stimulation, visual processing and cultural match. Designers refine cultural elements, use color and pattern to stimulate consumer vision, so that consumers have an initial impression of the cultural elements; then use pattern design so that consumers through the processing of visual information, by different forms of expression and the formation of characteristics of the representation; pattern design with obvious cultural characteristics can trigger visual associations, so that consumers in memory, experience the cultural prototype to produce a fit and then emotional projection; finally, consumers because of cultural identity and the role of cognitive, emotional, aesthetic, social and other levels, and then promote consumer behavior. And referring to the value-added model of cultural creative commodity design proposed by Lin, the value-added of cultural creativity is divided into three stages [20], trying to propose the cultural vision integration model, as shown in Fig. 2. In order to integrate cultural elements with modern art design in the subsequent design of cultural and creative industries, the value and meaning of product patterns can be enhanced, and more cultural elements can be displayed in the pattern content of cultural and creative products in a visible and disposable form.

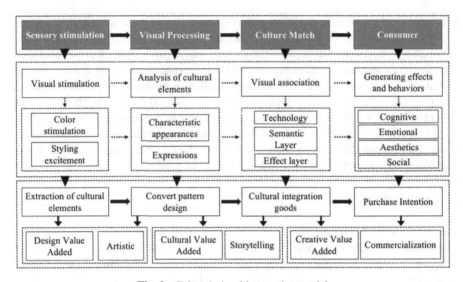

Fig. 2. Cultural visual integration model

References

1. Rhodes, M.: City as a Mirror of Society. In: Agnew, J.A., Mercer, J., Sophen, D.E. (eds.) The City in Cultural Context. Routledge, p. 189, New York (2007)
2. Wang, P.H., Hung, M.H.: Research of local visual iconography system and using the present situation-with Taiwan's southern areas as a case study. Kaohsiung Normal Univ. J. **24**, 105–137 (2008)
3. Gao, X.K.: Intangible heritage protection as a national development strategy: fractal heritage and public products. J. Jiangsu Admin. Inst. **1**, 25–32 (2020)
4. Chen, W.W.: Design strategy of integrating regional cultural elements into tourism products of Dujiangyan Dam. Pack. Eng. **43**(24), 269–276 (2022)
5. Lyu, Y., Lin, P., Lin, R.: A pilot study on audience's cognitive model of neural style transfer. J. Des. **26**(3), 61–84 (2021)
6. Xie, X., Xu, X.: Color design of subway station interior based on cultural cognition. Pack. Eng. **41**(8), 239–245 (2020)
7. Wang, Z., Li, D., Li, G.: Research on the renewal of public space in the life circle of old blocks with cultural cognition: take Laodao Nanjie District of Qinhuangdao as an Example. Urban Develop. Stud. **29**(4), 34–29 (2022)
8. Wang, X., Zhang, X., Chen, T.: Influencing factors of tourists' cognition of local nostalgic cultural elements: take Huizhou region as a case study. Geogr. Res. **39**(3), 682–695 (2020)
9. Gilbert, D.C.: An examination of the consumer decision process related to tourism. In: Cooper, C.P. (ed.). Progress in Tourism, Recreation and Hospitality Management, vol. 3, pp. 78–105. Belhaven Press, London (1991)
10. Spears, N., Singh, S.N.: Measuring attitude toward the brand and purchase intentions. J. Curr. Iss. Res. Advertising **26**(2), 53–66 (2004)
11. Chao, P., Chao, L.: The effects of cause-related marketing on brand image and purchase intention. J. Univ. Kang Ning **7**, 27–82 (2017)
12. Huang, Y., Weng, W.: Moli xuncheng- Fuzhou moli huacha zuowei wenhua chanpin de shijian ji tantao. Xueshu pinglun **1**, 116–120 (2017)

13. Gu, M., Liu, H.: Chahua sheji yuyan de shijue biaoxian. J. Chifeng Univ. **35**(11), 233–234 (2014)
14. Yen, H.Y.: Factors in transforming cultural elements into fashion design: a case study of the fashion exhibition china: through the looking glass at the metropolitan museum of art in New York. J. Des. **22**(2), 1–24 (2017)
15. Chen, X.: Wenhua rentong yu fuhao xiaofei: bowuguan wenchuang de fuhao jiangou yanjiu. Southeast Commun. **1**, 86–88 (2022)
16. Kuo, S., Lin, P.: The perceptive difference of color harmony: a case study on homage to the square by Josef Albers. Journal of Design **25**(2), 1–18 (2020)
17. Liau, S.: A preliminary study of consumption values and characteristics on Hakka Cultural Goods. J. Arch. Plann. **17**(1), 53–74 (2016)
18. Tinsley, H.E., Tinsley, D.J.: Uses of factor analysis in counseling psychology. J. Couns. Psychol. **34**, 414–424 (1987)
19. Comrey, A.L.: Factor analytic methods of scale development in personality and clinical psychology. J. Consult. Clin. Psychol. **56**, 754–761 (1988)
20. Lin, R.: Cultural creativity added design value. Art Appreciation **1**(7), 26–32 (2005)

Kansei Marketing Strategies for Cultural and Creative Products

Zhen-Yu Chen$^{(\boxtimes)}$ ⓘ and Yen Hsu ⓘ

The Graduate Institute of Design Science, Tatung University, New Taipei, Taiwan
d11117007@o365.ttu.edu.tw, yhsu@gm.ttu.edu.tw

Abstract. With the oversupply of goods, people began to pay attention to a higher level of emotional consumption. The pursuit of increasingly higher aesthetic quality has driven the popularity of the aesthetic economy and experience economy in recent years. The public has begun to pursue products with warm feelings and connotations. In particular, high-quality personalized handmade goods with sentimental value, warmth, and unique texture that are derived from regular handmade goods are popular in many countries and gradually become a trend. However, under the wave of globalization, high value-added products are produced through the trend of branding. Art and aesthetics are integrated into handmade goods to maximize their value, with the expectation of being stood out in such a competitive market. This study analyzed and summarized the current status of handicraft brands from the perspective of brand marketing and product design. It highlighted the handicraft characteristics by combing the brand power to achieve the effect of value-added goods to use it as a reference to strengthen the competitiveness of handicraft brands in the future.

Keywords: Cultural and Creative Goods · Handcrafted · Brand · Marketing Strategies · Design Strategies

1 Introduction

In a world that is becoming increasingly mechanized, increasingly homogenized, and almost completely exposed to the scrutiny of the Internet, it is logical to assume that the unique, the individual, and the culturally resonant will acquire ever more appeal and luster (Liebl & Roy, 2004). Lash, Urry, and Urry (1993) pointed out that there is a reciprocal relationship between culture and economy. Culture is presented in a commercialized way due to the economy. In the meantime, the economy makes products more beautiful and connotative through culture and improves the quality of life and cultural identity. Cultural features then are considered to be unique characteristics to embed into a product both for the enhancement of product identity in the global market and for the fulfillment of the individual consumer's experiences (Lin, 2005). Although it is difficult to produce handicrafts on a large scale due to long working hours and small output, new retail channels have been developed due to the emergence of online platforms and social media (Luckman, 2015). Market opportunities for craft industries are emerging based on this trend in consumption diversification and the traditional economic weaknesses of craft industries are becoming strengths (Campbell, 2005; Chartrand, 1989). In recent years, with the trend of an aesthetic economy as well as cultural and creative industries, handicrafts have become popular in various countries and a wave of handicrafts has sprung up, making the emotional endowments of products extremely significant. American design expert Norman (2004) stated that affective/emotional factors are the ultimate determiner of the success or failure of product design.

Emotion is the most significant factor that attracts consumers to pay for goods, while beauty is the most important inducement that can evoke pleasant memories as well as experiences and make people desire to own goods (PostrelVirginia, 2004). Kotler (2012) said "The art of marketing is largely the art of brand building. When something is not a brand, it will probably be viewed as a commodity." Great brands present emotional benefits, not just rational benefits (Kotler, 2003). Customization and uniqueness of handicrafts can strengthen consumers' desire to purchase them, thus creating their additional value, increasing the importance of beauty to products, and making products more competitive, which also bring consumers a pleasant mood and satisfy their potential needs (Veryzer Jr & Hutchinson, 1998). In the past, the research on handicrafts focused on their texture as well as the development of cultural and creative markets, rather than on brand marketing and design strategies. Therefore, the goal of this study was to help handicraft entrepreneurs create product diversity by understanding the current development situation of the existing handicraft brands, the problems they face, and their differences in the design of handicraft products. The aesthetic economy and brand marketing were taken as the added value of handicraft entrepreneurship with excellent marketing strategies for the promotion and inheritance of handicrafts to improve the competitiveness of handicraft brands.

With regard to cultural and creative products, this study explored perceptual marketing based on the characteristics of handicrafts and discussed the development of Taiwan's handmade brand companies. It attempted to understand the operation of handmade brands and the direction of brand marketing strategies through case interviews. It further analyzed as well as summarized the practices of product designs based on case products as a reference for future research on enhancing the competitiveness of handmade brands in cultural and creative products. According to the above statement, the main purposes of this study are as follows:

(1) To explore the development of Taiwan's handmade brand companies.
(2) To analyze the marketing strategies of handmade brand companies.
(3) To explore the practices of product design based on the cases of handmade brand companies.
(4) To summarize the relevance between the marketing strategies of the handcraft brands and the product designs.

2 Literature Review

2.1 Cultural Originality

Culture is viewed as men's way of maintaining life (Baldwin, Faulkner, Hecht, & Lindsley, 2006) In a world that is becoming increasingly mechanized, increasingly homogenized, and almost completely exposed to the scrutiny of the Internet, it is logical to assume that the unique, the individual, and the culturally resonant will acquire ever more appeal and luster (Liebl & Roy, 2004). Cultural features then are considered to be unique characteristics to embed into a product both for the enhancement of product identity in the global market and for the fulfillment of the individual consumer's experiences (Lin, 2005). Lash, Urry, and Urry (1993) pointed out that there is a reciprocal relationship between culture and economy. Culture is presented in a commercialized way due to the economy. In the meantime, the economy makes products more beautiful and connotative through culture and improves the quality of life and cultural identity. In the global market-local design era, connections between culture and design have become increasingly close. For design, cultural value-adding creates the core of product value. It is the same for culture; designs are the motivation for pushing cultural development forward (Ho, 1996).

2.2   Value of Handmade Goods

In the cultural and creative industries, handmade goods are considered as a unique existence. Although it is difficult to produce handicrafts on a large scale due to long working hours and small output, new retail channels have been developed due to the emergence of online platforms and social media (Luckman, 2015). According to the Crafts Council in the UK, since 1998 the crafts have been identified as an industrial sector with the highest growth potential (Schwarz & Yair, 2010). With the development of the global market, most companies gradually realize that the keys to product innovation are not only market and technology aspects but also emotional design (Hsu, Chang, & Lin, 2013). Market opportunities for craft industries are emerging based on this trend in consumption diversification and the traditional economic weaknesses of craft industries are becoming strengths (Campbell, 2005; Chartrand, 1989). When product safety and comfort have been satisfied, emphasis can shift toward the decorative, emotional, and symbolic attributes of design (Crilly, Moultrie, & Clarkson, 2004). Incorporating "feeling" into product design to present the emotional communication of user experiences has become a design trend of the twenty-first century (Hsu, Chang, & Lin, 2013). For consumers, understanding and knowing the whole production process of objects, as well as the time and labor spent by artisans in that process, indirectly endow commodities with deeper meaning (Frayling, 2012). Customization and uniqueness of handicrafts can strengthen consumers' desire to purchase them, thus creating their additional value, increasing the importance of beauty to products, and making products more competitive, which also bring consumers a pleasant mood and satisfy their potential needs (Veryzer Jr & Hutchinson, 1998). (Greenhalgh, 2003) indicates that crafts straddle between the art and design economies and often get the worst of both worlds. Handcrafts meet the deep desire of consumers, and scholars see the ultimate existence state of consumers' desire as "value" (Rokeach, 1973). Therefore, an optimal product is a craft that opens a discourse with people through its sensation-evoking image and inspires them (Hsu, Chang, & Lin, 2013). American design expert Norman (2004) stated that affective/emotional factors are the ultimate determiner of the success or failure of product design.

2.3 Marketing Strategies

Marketing is an organizational function and a set of processes for creating, communicating, and delivering value to customers and for managing customer relationships in ways that benefit the organization and its stakeholders (Rownd & Heath, 2008). Marketing management is the art and science of choosing target markets and getting, keeping, and growing customers through creating, communicating, and delivering superior customer value (Kotler, 2003). Marketing as culture is a basic set of values and beliefs about the central importance of the customer that guides the organization (Webster, 1992). Kotler (2012) said "The art of marketing is largely the art of brand building. When something is not a brand, it will probably be viewed as a commodity." Great brands present emotional benefits, not just rational benefits (Kotler, 2003). Wang, Chen, Hu, and Ye (2008) proposed that a brand is abstract and spiritual, and is the sum of all consumer feelings toward products, reflecting their mood, knowledge, attitudes, and behaviors. Branding means giving a distinct individuality to a product (Kotler et al., 2000). Therefore, emotional product design characteristics and brand emotion are crucial (Yen, Lin, & Lin, 2014). Emotion is the most significant factor that attracts consumers to pay for goods, while beauty is the most important inducement that can evoke pleasant memories as well as experiences and make people desire to own goods (PostrelVirginia, 2004).

3 Research Methods

3.1 Research Process

This study adopted a qualitative research method to divide the research process into three stages (see Fig. 1). In the first stage, after the purpose of this study was established, the theoretical framework was formed through literature discussion as the basis for the follow-up analysis of this study. In the second stage, the finalists of the Pop Up Asia Makers were seen as the research scope, the willingness of the interviewees was collected over the phone, and ten cases were further selected as the research subjects. Moreover, the relevant secondary data of the cases were collected, the first draft of the interview was prepared, the interview test was carried out, the relevant details of the interview were revised according to the expert advice, and the formal interview manuscript was formed. Semi-structured interviews were conducted for ten cases to obtain more complete data. After the formal interviews, the content of the case interviews was transcribed into a verbatim draft. In the third stage, the content analysis method was applied for organization and analyses, and the content was divided into two parts, companies and their products, for discussion. In terms of companies, the strategies of the cases in brand marketing and marketing combination were analyzed. The cases were grouped and the group names were given according to the analysis results. In terms of products, the practices of product designs based on the launch motivation, design appeal, development type, and design focus were analyzed. The research results and suggestions based on the above comprehensive analysis were put forward.

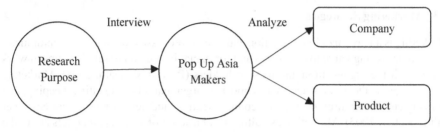

Fig. 1. Research process

3.2 Case Sample

The purpose of this study is to explore the marketing strategies and features of product designs used by handmade brand companies. Therefore, the Pop Up Asia Maker Award with the theme of handcraft entrepreneurship was taken as the research scope, and the brand companies under the same market economy background were selected as the research samples for convenience. Furthermore, the Taiwanese companies of the shortlisted brands from 2017 to 2020 were selected as the research scope and subjects by multiple case methods. The researcher contacted the cases in person to inquire about their intention of being interviewed and eventually selected ten cases willing to be interviewed.

Since 2017, the Pop Up Asia Maker Award has hoped that through entrepreneurship exhibitions and online communities, more people can see the business model of hand-craft entrepreneurship. Through the four thematic categories of manufacturing locally, handcrafted, personalized mass production, and customized service, it selects the greatest Asian handcraft entrepreneurship spirit and special representatives. It encourages those who have been working hard to share stories from creation to entrepreneurship and supports them through business exhibitions with the exchange of artisans as the core (Pop Up Asia Makers, 2020). The four major theme categories make the case samples possess diverse industrial patterns and business modes, so that the case study can explore the marketing strategies and product design features of Taiwan's handcraft brands more comprehensively.

3.3 Interviewees

According to the purpose of this study and the relevant theoretical framework collated in the literature review, this study drafted an interview manuscript and conducted an initial interview test. The subjects of this preliminary interview were the founders of the Taiwanese cultural and creative brands of handicrafts, who are also the operators. With more than ten years of relevant handcraft brand management experience, they are competent to serve as the expert consultation subjects of this study. The interview places are their workshops. After communication, the unclear part of the interview questions was found, and the manuscript was revised based on experts' advice and became a formal interview draft.

The interview cases in this study were listed in the case code (see Table 1) according to the interview sequence. The interviewee in each case is the founder of the cultural and creative brand of handicrafts or an internal senior executive, having a considerable understanding of the brand's business model.

Table 1. Brands interviewed

Case A takes the promotion of lacquer art as its core, returns to the original folk art tradition, abandons the gorgeous and complex decoration, and integrates the traditional craft culture into the modern life utensils, bringing more people to know and feel the inheritance of this in generations; Case B integrates the landscape design background with the design and production of cement products, changes the rough image of cement, and combines the aesthetic sense and function of space to express the delicate taste; Case C turns culture into totem and presents it in commodities, conveys the connotation and belief of culture through paper writing, and integrates it with the traditional cross-stitch technology of aborigines; Case D prefers wood, selects the most natural painting process, and attaches attention to the curve and overall proportion of each product, highlighting the nature of wood; Case E uses various kinds of claw beads and composite materials to display different festivals and seasonal themes, and can be applied to various soft fabrics to present interesting styles; Case F makes pocket items through soft clay and other materials, and also endows soft clay with practicality; Case G combines embroidery lace cloth with fashion and modern elements, and matches life accessories with soft colors; Case H takes the performance of log material as its core through the technology of local industry and fine manual grinding, and develops the exclusive patent combination technology to more complete the unique wooden wrist watches full of life; Case I combines carpentry and metalwork, creates more practicality and beauty by originality, has unique characteristics of handicrafts, and advocates handmade travels; Case J mixes the handmade yarn weaving and factory production, pays attention to practicality and durability, bright color matching geometric graphics, and warm and thick knitting materials utilized, highlighting the characteristics of Nordic style.

3.4 Content Analysis

This study mainly adopted a qualitative analysis method to analyze the content of the interview. Afterwards, it analyzed the use of case brands' marketing strategies and the design practices of their products, and compared the results by cross analysis to conclude the relevance of case marketing strategies and product designs.

The transcript of the interview was written into a verbatim version, then, the data were checked sentence by sentence, and open coding was conducted. Because the interview data were large and scattered, the data were read repeatedly, the content related to the research topic was extracted, and the paragraphs were marked as the basis for analysis. As for the coding principle in the interview content, the first letter is the code of the interview case, the second letter and number is the item of the questions answered by the interviewees, and the third number is the order of paragraphs marking in the answer items (see Table 2).

Table 2. Coding diagram

Code	Meaning
A-Q06–1	Symbolizing the first paragraph marked in interviewee A's answer to question 6
C-Q13–2	Symbolizing the second paragraph marked in interviewee C's answer to question 13

In addition to the in-depth case interviews, this study also took advantage of common data collection methods of case studies through those companies' official websites, past interview information, and exhibition data to obtain various data and improve the analysis of this study. Due to the different types and nature of interview cases, there are differences between cases, and they have different strategic plans for their development of brand management. Therefore, differentiation analysis can be carried out. Because the cases are all in the industries related to the handmade industry, which are faced with the same economic market, similar channels, as well as consumers, their common points could be analyzed. This study utilized the aspects extracted from theories as a reference and analyzed the similarities and differences of the ten cases, as well as the product analysis of the entity cases. This way, we could have a detailed understanding of the marketing strategies and product design practices of the rival brand companies, and make a further summary.

4 Analysis and Discussion

4.1 Summary and Naming of Brand Marketing Strategic Groups

Before marketing planning, the market environment and consumer behaviors should be understood first, and a remarkable job of target marketing should be finished to facilitate the formulation of the marketing mix so that marketing resources can be utilized most effectively. Therefore, according to the results of brand marketing and product mix analysis, the strategic groups of brand marketing could be divided into three groups, and then each group was given an appropriate name to facilitate the relevant comparison of subsequent analyses (see Table 3).

Table 3. Summary of brand marketing strategy groups

		Group 1			Group 2			Group 3			
		A	E	G	F	H	D	J	B	I	C
Background motivation	Industrial expansion	●	●	●							
	Self-actualization				●	●	●	●	●	●	●
Brand strategy	Multiple brands	●	●	●	●	●	●				
	Single brand							●	●	●	●
Market positioning	Life culture	●	●	●				●	●	●	●
	Special emotion				●	●	●				
Product strategy	Material	●	●	●	●						
	Finished product	●	●	●	●	●	●	●	●	●	●
	Experience	●	●		●	●			●	●	
Price strategy	Cost-oriented		●	●	●	●		●			
	Customer-oriented						●		●	●	
	Competition-oriented	●									●
Promotion strategy	Mainly offline						●				
	Mainly online	●	●	●		●		●	●		
	Half online and half offline				●					●	●
Channel strategy	Mainly real	●	●		●	●	●				
	Mainly virtual							●	●		
	Both virtual and real			●						●	●

"●" refers to "mainly used".

Companies in Group 1 were all transformation and inheritance of traditional industries. With the rise and fall of the times, having gone through several generations of inheritance and transformation, they enjoy a deep business foundation. Although the transformation from traditional industries to brand development is a new start, they have relatively rich experience in relevant resources, and also have developed multiple brands for different market segments. Their principle of market positioning is being close to life. Besides, Most of their products are practical. According to the above findings, the brand marketing of Group 1, focusing on the combination of products and people's lives, is characterized by industrial management background and rich technical resources. In this study, Group 1 was named the technique inheritance group.

The companies in Group 2 are relatively abundant in capital operation, with more than five human resources, assisted by a basic team. These companies combine interests with business and achieve good performance. With abundant enterprise resources, they develop different brands for various target markets and adopt their own marketing mix strategy. In terms of market positioning, they are also distinguished by their unique feature and emotional connotation. From the above, it was found that this group's brand marketing, focusing on the transmission of specific consumer groups and emotions, has a clear segment market positioning and development objectives. In this study, Group 2 was named the spontaneous originality group.

In Group 3, the companies' entrepreneurial motives are all oriented towards interest, but the difference is that their use of funds is relatively limited, their development scale is small, and most of them are organizations of one to three people. Because of the lack of experience, the process of developing interest into a business has no prior planning of brand positioning, target market, and operation strategy, but through repeated trading experience and customer feedback, they gradually find their own development basis. To shape personal brand positioning and style, through professional technology and innovation, they provide the most favorable service for the single market demand, to resist the resource-rich competitors, and also take daily life as an investigation factor in market positioning, with interest and preference as the development motivation, has specific development market and professional technical innovation. In this study, Group 3 was named the interest and preference group.

4.2 Case Product Analysis and Discussion

Based on the research results, ten case brand companies were classified into three groups according to the brand marketing strategy. This step is for the purpose of further analyzing the differences in the design practices used by each group in the implementation of product designs, and understanding their consideration on product designs when formulating marketing strategies. Among the ten case brands, three typical goods cases were listed for each case respondent, with a total of 30 products. The design practices of the case products were explored. The items for discussion included product introduction motivation, product development type, product design focus, and product design appeal (Table 4).

Table 4. Case product

4.3 Launch Motivation and Design Appeal of Case Product

After a discussion on the 30 products, according to the main introduction motivation, these products were divided into three types, namely, practical life, unique sentiment, and technical innovation. Based on the literature, the case products were divided into four design appeals of handcrafted products, namely, high quality, well-being, practicality, and uniqueness, which were further analyzed and summarized (see Table 5).

From Table 5, it could be found that among the 30 case products, high quality and well-being were the main product design appeals, accounting for nine products each, followed by uniqueness totaling eight products, and practicality was in last place, totaling four products. High quality means that the consumer's perception and feeling for a product was from the aesthetic appearance of the product. The essence of the material was manifested, and the details and quality were emphasized so that the product had an attractive and good image. Well-being means that the consumers felt the sentimental value, warmth feeling, hand-feel, and other elements extended by the product through sense experience. Meanwhile, it brought a pleasant mood, triggered interest and satisfaction, and satisfied their potential needs. Practicality refers to the design based on life observation and understanding. Practical and innovative ingenuity were combined to increase the substantive use value and stay close to the daily needs of consumers;

Table 5. Launch motivation and design appeal of product

	High quality	Well-being	Practicality	Uniqueness
Practical life				
Unique sentiment	None		None	
Technical innovation				
Total	9	9	4	8

while uniqueness was different from the simple reproducibility of products under mass production. Combined with high originality and aesthetic value, special production characteristics were used to highlight the uniqueness, individuality, and limited quantity of each work, thereby creating the added value of the product and bringing unique feelings to consumers.

4.4 Focuses of Development Type and Design of Case Products

According to the development type, the products were divided into four types. New creation refers to the first revolutionary new product in the world. Creative breakthrough refers to goods created by integrating existing products on the market but different from the ideas and technologies on the market. The same type of extension refers to the extension of a company's existing product types by different subjects. New application of the same technology refers to products whose old production techniques are applied to different dimensions. The design focus was divided into three types: material, color, and shape, which were analyzed and summarized in Table 6.

In the product development type, no case with the development type of new creation has been found, and thus, there were no products of this development type in the cases. In respect of the case products whose development type was a creative breakthrough, a total of four pieces emphasize that their design focus is mainly on shape; two pieces on

Table 6. Launch motivation and design appeal of product

	Material	Color	Shape
Creative breakthrough			
same type of extension			
New application of the same technology			
Total	11	4	15

material; and then one piece on color. As for the case products whose development type is the same type of extension, eight pieces emphasize that their design focus is mainly on shape; six pieces on material; and two pieces on color. With regard to the case products whose development type is a new application of the same technology, three pieces each emphasize that their design focus is mainly on material and shape, followed by color, accounting for one piece.

4.5 Relationship Between Brand Marketing Groups and Product Design Practices

After the making of Table 5 and Table 6, it was found that the strategic groups of brand marketing and product design practices in 30 product cases included four major items: product launch motivation, product design appeal, product development type, and product design focus.

The launch motivation of the products is mainly practical life (M1). The number of it is 17; the number of unique sentiment (M2) is eight; the number of technological innovation (M3) is five. The cases with technique inheritance as the strategy group mainly focus on practical life (M1), accounting for 77.8%; the cases with spontaneous originality as the strategy group unique sentiment (M2), accounting for 44.5%; the cases with interests and preference as the strategy group practical life (M1), accounting for 66.7% (see Fig. 2).

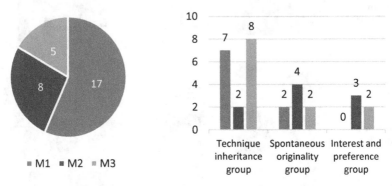

Fig. 2. Analysis of product launch motivation

In terms of product design appeals, well-being (S1) took up the major, accounting for ten products, followed by high quality (S2) and uniqueness (S3), respectively accounting for eight products, and practicality (S4), accounting for four products. The cases with technique inheritance as the strategy group mainly focused on well-being (S1), accounting for 44.5%; the cases with spontaneous originality as the strategy group focused on uniqueness (S3), accounting for 66.7%; the cases with interest and preference as the strategy group focused on high quality (S2), accounting for 41.7% (see Fig. 3).

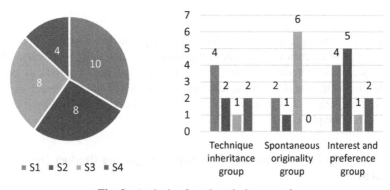

Fig. 3. Analysis of product design appeal

In terms of the product development type, the "same type of extension" (P3) is in the largest proportion, with a total of 16; next are "new application of the same technology" (P4) and "creative breakthrough" (P2), with 7 each; the number of "new creation" (P1) is zero. The cases with "technique inheritance" as the strategy group, mainly focus on "same type of extension" (P3), accounting for 66.7%; the cases with "spontaneous originality" as the strategy group "creative breakthrough" (P2) and "same type of extension" (P3), accounting for 44.5% respectively; the cases with "interest and preference" as the strategy group "same type of extension" (P3), accounting for 50% (see Fig. 4).

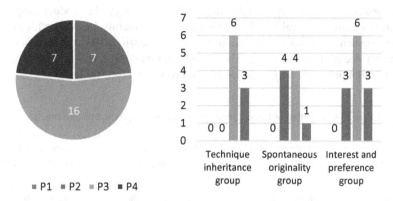

Fig. 4. Analysis of product development type

In terms of the product design, "shape" (K3) is in the largest proportion, with a total of 15; the second is "material" (K1), with a total of 11; the last is "color" (K2), with a total of 4. The cases with "technique inheritance" as the strategy group mainly focus on "shape" (K3, accounting for 55.6%; the cases with "spontaneous originality" as the strategy group "material" (K1) and "shape" (K3), accounting for 44.5% respectively; the cases with "interest and preference" as the strategy group "shape" (K3), accounting for 50% (see Fig. 5).

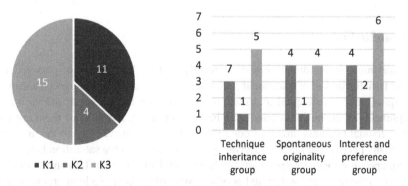

Fig. 5. Analysis of product design focus

Specifically, for companies classified as the technique inheritance group by the brand marketing strategy, the product introduction motivation was the practical life. The design appeal was mainly focused on the feeling of well-being. The development type was mostly the same type of extension. The product design focus was mainly focused on the shape. For companies classified as the spontaneous originality group by the brand marketing strategy, the product introduction motivation was the unique sentiment. The design appeal was mainly focused on the uniqueness. Equal attention was paid to the same type of extension and the creative breakthrough in terms of development type, and to the material and the shape in terms of product design focus. For companies classified as the interest and preference group by the brand marketing strategy, the product introduction motivation was the practical life. The design appeal was mainly focused on high quality. The development type was mostly the same type of extension. The product design focus was mainly focused on the shape. The three brand marketing groups with their main product design practices were summarized and compared (see Table 7).

Table 7. Comparison of brand marketing groups and product design practices

Brand Marketing Groups	Technique inheritance group	Spontaneous originality group	Interest and preference group
Product Introduction motivation	Practical life	Unique sentiment	Practical life
Product Design appeal	Well-being	Uniqueness	High quality
Product Development type	Same type of extension	Creative breakthrough Same type of extension	Same type of extension
Product design focus	Shape	Material Shape	Shape

5   Conclusion

The investment in handmade brands is mostly due to the practice of personal ideas and the transformation of traditional industries. Since handmade entrepreneurship does not require enormous capital and manpower. Based on the economic strength of the entrepreneurs, their business scales can be large or small, but most of them are based on the personal business model of one to three people. However, due to the investment of too many people, the market survival space is narrow and the saturation is high. As a consequence, homogeneous products fill the market. Consumers in Taiwan are not highly receptive to the price of handcrafted goods. In spite of the cost of a long production time for each piece of goods, consumers are not willing to pay for it, which is attributed to the weak perception of handmade goods and the lack of aesthetic cognition. Therefore, brand and marketing strategies play a critical role. In the era of the rising experience economy, handcraft companies are allowed to take advantage of the trend of branding to maximize the value of handmade goods.

Through the analysis of ten cases' interviews, it can be seen that brand marketing in Taiwan's handcraft market can be divided into three strategic groups, namely, the technique inheritance group, the spontaneous originality group, as well as the interest and preference group. This study divided product design practices into four major items,

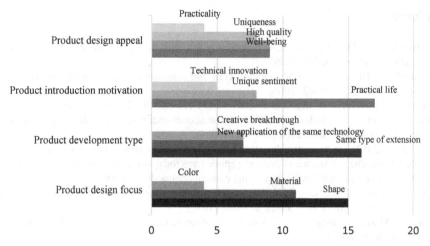

Fig. 6. Product design practices of handmade brand companies

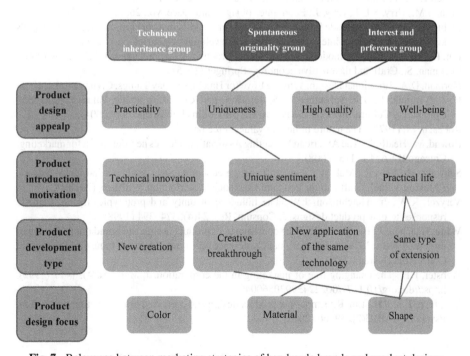

Fig. 7. Relevance between marketing strategies of handmade brands and product designs

including product launch motivation, product design appeal, product development type, and product design focus. The design practices of 30 products (see Fig. 6) were collated, and the relevance between the marketing strategies of the handmade brands and the product designs was also sorted out (see Fig. 7).

References

Baldwin, J.R., Faulkner, S.L., Hecht, M.L., Lindsley, S.L.: Redefining Culture: Perspectives Across the Disciplines. Routledge (2006)

Campbell, C.: The craft consumer: culture, craft and consumption in a postmodern society. J. Consum. Cult. 5(1), 23–42 (2005)

Chartrand, H.H.: The crafts in a post-modern market. J. Des. Hist. 2(2/3), 93–105 (1989)

Crilly, N., Moultrie, J., Clarkson, P.J.: Seeing things: consumer response to the visual domain in product design. Des. Stud. 25(6), 547–577 (2004)

Frayling, C. (2012). On craftsmanship: towards a new Bauhaus: Bloomsbury Publishing

Greenhalgh, P.: The persistence of craft: the applied arts today. Rutgers University Press (2003)

Ho, M.-C.: Some speculations on developing cultural commodities. J. Des. 1(1), 1–15 (1996)

Hsu, C.-H., Chang, S.-H., Lin, R.: A design strategy for turning local culture into global market products. Int. J. Affect. Eng. 12(2), 275–283 (2013)

Kotler, P.: Marketing insights from A to Z: 80 concepts every manager needs to know: John Wiley & Sons (2003)

Kotler, P.: Kotler on Marketing. Simon and Schuster (2012)

Kotler, P., et al.: Introducción al marketing: Pearson Prentice Hall (2000)

Lash, S.M., Urry, S.L.J., Urry, J.: Economies of signs and space, vol. 26. Sage (1993)

Liebl, M., Roy, T.: Handmade in India: Traditional craft skills in a changing world. Poor people's knowledge: Promoting intellectual property in developing countries, 53–74 (2004)

Lin, R.: Creative learning model for cross cultural product. Art Appreciation 1(12), 52–59 (2005)

Luckman, S.: Craft and the creative economy: Springer (2015)

Norman, D.A.. Emotional Design: Why we Love (or Hate) Everyday Things. Civitas Books (2004)

PostrelVirginia, I.: The Substance of Style: How the Rise of Aesthetic Value is Remaking Commerce, Culture, and Consciousness. Harper Collins Publishers, NY (2004)

Rokeach, M. (1973). The nature of human values: Free press

Rownd, M., Heath, C.: The American Marketing Association releases new definition for marketing. Chicago IL: AMA, 1–3 (2008)

Schwarz, M., Yair, K.: Making value: craft and the economic and social contribution of makers. •'Making Value', Craft and the economic and social contribution of makers (2010)

Veryzer, R.W., Jr., Hutchinson, J.W.: The influence of unity and prototypicality on aesthetic responses to new product designs. J. Consum. Res. 24(4), 374–394 (1998)

Wang, H., Chen, J., Hu, Y., Ye, M.: The consistency of product design and brand image. In: Paper presented at the 2008 9th International Conference on Computer-Aided Industrial Design and Conceptual Design (2008)

Webster, F.E.: The changing role of marketing in the corporation. J. Mark. 56(4), 1–17 (1992). https://doi.org/10.1177/002224299205600402

Yen, H.Y., Lin, P.H., Lin, R.: Emotional product design and perceived brand emotion. Int. J. Adv. Psychol. (IJAP) 3(2), 59–66 (2014)

A Study on the Model of Experience Activities in Wineries

Yifan Ding[✉] and Chi-long Lin

Graduate School of Creative Industry Design, National Taiwan University of Arts,
New Taipei City 220307, Taiwan
2929904428@qq.com, cl.lin@ntua.edu.tw

Abstract. The winery is a relatively new industry and has certain research value. We have used theories of experiential marketing and experiential value in past studies of the tourism industry. However, in the literature in the past, wineries characteristic integration, cultural communication, and ways to achieve economic benefits of experience activities have been less explored. This study examines the successful winery cases and summarizes the models behind those successful experience activities. This study used a case study approach to analyze the secondary data collected through wineries characteristics, experience activities, and visitor participation at four wineries: Changyu Winery, Samuel Adams Winery, Macallan Winery, and Miguel Winery to present relevant results. The results of the study show that the wineries usually use the production methods of wine, the use of historical buildings, and the scenery of the wineries as components in their experiential activities. The wineries also need to deploy the resources required according to their circumstances, and on this basis, the design, operation, and other marketing of winery events are achieved through event planners' planning, marketing, and promotion. Besides the regular wine-making activities, the winery offers entertainment and educational activities such as wine-tasting courses to meet the needs of visitors and make the winery experience model more effective in terms of entertainment and education, thus attracting more visitors to the wineries.

Keywords: Wineries Features · Experience Activities · Visitor Participation

1 Introduction

In recent years, there has been a growing interest in winery industry. Nowadays, economic development can be divided into the agricultural economy, industrial economy, service economy, and experience economy. When an industry develops into an experience economy, the companies concerned will create good experiences for their customers, bringing them unforgettable memories and making them loyal to the brand [1]. Experience design is the extend of product design and service design. Experience design focuses on the quality of the user experience and is applied to the design of products, services, processes, events, and environments to provide customers with an elaborate and complete experience [2]. By transforming the history and culture of wine into creativity and designing a good experience, we can provide a good opportunity for the development of wineries. Thus, incorporating the experience economy perspective into the planning and management of winery experiences is an important issue in the development of wineries.

Researchers have found that researchs on wineries exist around the world, but with different emphases. In the current academic research environment, there is a lot of literature on wine, wineries, and experiential marketing, but there is a lack of research on experiential design to drive winery visitor experience, participation, and experiential activity models. How can wineries spread from local markets to foreign markets through their unique cultural markets? Faced with this problem, the culture, customs, and business environment of different regions differ, so adjustments need to be made according to the actual situation, and a more effective way is to construct a reasonable experience model for wineries.

The objectives of this study are. (1) To examine the successful cases of wineries. (2) To summarize the successful models of wineries experience activities and provide theoretical and practical references for subsequent research and wineries management.

2   Literature Review

2.1   Wineries Features

In the past, studies on wineries have focused on the wine industry. Researchers have emphasized the importance of the physical environment of wineries [3]. Wine tourism involves many physical features of the wineries, and the physical atmosphere of the wineries, often constructed from vineyards, landscaping and architectural features, plays an important role in the satisfaction of visitors who come not only for the wine but also for leisure and relaxation [4, 5]. Wineries need to showcase their own identity, but they also need the support of visitors. Wine tourists can seek unique experiences when visiting wine-producing areas or wineries. Wine tourism is based on visits to vineyards, wineries, festivals and wine shows, where tasting, learning and experiencing the attributes of the wines produced are the main motivating and entertaining factors for tourists [6]. Therefore, the researcher believes that three conditions are required for the development of a winery. The first is to have an area suitable for growing or storing raw materials for wine making; the second is that the winemaking and bottling process must take place in the winery itself; and the third is to refine, transform, and develop its own characteristics into experiential elements.

2.2   Experiential Activities

The tourism field is now placing more and more emphasis on quality travel experiences, and therefore, more tourism-related research is being conducted in experience design. Related tourism companies have focused on visitor experience interaction and high-quality management strategies, so that we regard the tourism experience as the core of their products and services. However, the nature of tourism experience differs from the view of tourism service, such as the interaction of tourists with local landscape and local people can increase their experience of local exploration, which needs to be designed, so experience design is more applicable to tourism experience [7]. We can divide the elements of experience design into relational and physical contexts. Relational contexts emphasize the design of interactions between customers and service staff, and between customers and others, which helps to promote recognition between service providers and customers. Physical context is the tangible aspect of experience design, such as service facilities, convenience items, meals, sensory design, etc. Through the design or atmosphere of these tangible aspects, the information and theme of the service area can be conveyed [8].

We can realize the purpose of implementing the experiential design in the application of scenery. Good scenery can make a good experience for visitors, such as tourists who look for authentic experiences in wine tours because they want to see how wine is produced and how the vineyards are managed [9]. It has also been argued that this is a reproduction of an authentic experience, noting that visitors' authentic experience of a winery needs to take place in a satisfying and 'matched' service context to enhance positive emotions, satisfaction and behavioural intentions [10]. In terms of the composition of the winery experience, the main sources are traditional production activities and festivals, which still build on traditional production activities but are more attractive. Festival activities form the central focus of the festival and are what visitors do during the festival [11, 12]. A large festival event at the University of Iowa included educational presentations and entertainment, resulting in two constructs, an educational experience and an entertainment experience [13]. Alcohol is also an essential part of the festival, and its presence adds to the atmosphere of the event. An Australian cultural festival focuses on ethnic food and wine experiences, with event variables defined as food, wine, and entertainment [14]. Therefore, the wineries' experiences activities could be conducted in an appropriate service setting as much as possible, introducing an educational function alongside the entertainment experience, which would make the event impactful and meaningful.

2.3 Visitor Participation

The participation of tourists is the test of tourism results. Using experience design in the tourism experience is mainly reflected in the interactivity. Interactivity includes the interaction between tourists and objects (e.g., art scenes, heritage), between tourists and social elements of the destination (e.g., other tourists, locals, tourism provide staff, other relevant social networks), and between tourists and media (e.g., mass media, marketing media, etc.) [7]. Similarly, experience design elements for cultural venues can be explored at the level of touchpoints, customer journeys, social environments, and physical environments. It mainly focused these experience elements on the social and physical environment levels, with the social environment level emphasizing the interaction between customers and service staff and the design of interactions between customers; the physical environment refers to the design of the interior architecture and atmosphere [15]. Most of the good wineries have good architectural design and ambience, which helps to create the right conditions for their own experience, and also facilitates the participation of visitors.

Most of the research on winery visitor engagement is based on a wine-based, Western visitor perspective. In terms of wine tourism alone, the potential motivations for wine tourism are different between Chinese and Western tourists [16]. The wineries model has been a tradition in the West for many years and is a "traditional product" for Western consumers, but it is still a novelty for Chinese consumers. Even though many wineries exist in China, and China has a long history of wine production [17]. Major wineries in China, such as the Changyu Winery, are designed in an European style, as Chinese consumers have an image of European wineries associated with tradition and prestige [18]. In the past, they theorized that tourists' unforgettable memories of the experience would leave a good impression on the company providing the travel service. When tourists have a quality and memorable experience in a tourist venue, it will eventually help to form tourism brand loyalty [1, 7]. Therefore, it is important for tourism companies to design quality experiences and deliver values to visitors through tourism-related resources [19]. In the literature of past wineries, tourists can check the authenticity of the winery during the trip through specific elements related to its physical atmosphere, namely the wine production methods used, the use of historic buildings, and the winery landscape [20]. The architecture and landscape of a winery can significantly affect the enjoyment and arousal of winery visitors [5]. Therefore, the researcher believes that visiting wineries and wine production areas allows visitors to experience the authenticity of wine production through various activities offered by wineries, such as wineries and production tours and walks through the wineries. Therefore, the natural environment (e.g., gardens, raw material areas, or winery buildings) affects visitor satisfaction.

3 Methodology

3.1 Case Study

This study adopted the case study approach to investigate the experience design of wineries' experience activities in a focused manner. A multiple case study approach was adopted for the following reasons: First, this study was conducted on four cases, which quantitatively meets the requirements of a case-oriented comparative research approach. We focused on the relationship between experience activities and wineries, identified what strengths are needed in the experience activities, and examined the effects of experience activities on wineries. Case study method can help researchers investigate the theoretical logic in terms of the "how" and "why" behind the questions; thus, this method is helpful for exploring the potential patterns of the development of wineries. Second, in terms of testing the feasibility of the theories, this study focused on well-noted wineries. The multiple case studies method emphasizes the identification of key theoretical concepts from phenomena and empirical data, and can be phenomenon-or problem-driven. This is helpful for interpreting the process of the development of wineries, from pioneering to maturity, comprising such wineries' characteristics and experience activities [21].

3.2 Cases Selection

We selected four wineries as research objects: Changyu Winery, Samuel Adams Winery, Macallan Winery, and Miguel Winery. We focus on the leading wineries in wine, beer, whisky, and yellow wine to be more representative, as shown in Table 1. In addition, research shows that companies in the cultural and creative field of wineries are increasingly combining their business model of creativity to enrich their clients' travel experience.

Table 1. Study samples.

Case Subjects	Case Photos	Case Characteristics
Changyu Winery		Ltd. was established in 2001 as a joint venture between Yantai Changyu Winery Co., Ltd. and Castel Group, France. In North Yujia, Yantai Economic and Technological Development Zone, Changyu-Castel Winery is a modern winery integrating wine-making, tourism, leisure, and entertainment.
Samuel Adams Winery		Samuel Adams Brewery is the original American craft beer brewery, in Boston, U.S.A. Samuel Adams Brewery has been named "America's Best Beer" four times and is represented by Samuel Adams Boston Lager.
Macallan Winery		Macallan winery was formerly owned by Alexander Reid, who got one of the few winemaking licenses in Scotland at the time in 1824.
Miguel Winery		In 2016, Miguel Winery was established in Nantong. Miguel Winery is based on combining the strengths of internationally renowned areas such as beer, wine, and sake, and then refining them with the traditional Chinese yellow wine process, and then doing a boost to speed up this industry.

Source: [22–25]

3.3 Data Collection and Analysis

A set of relevant secondary data were collected from October 1, 2022 to January 22, 2023. The data sources included academic journals, official accounts, industry websites, public annual reports of listed companies, and interview videos of relevant wineries. Data from multiple sources achieve a level of objectivity, starting with the research question, guided by evidence-based sources for content interpretation and in-depth analysis, carefully seeking and building a chain of evidence to support the ideas presented here. This study ensured that the data complement and cross-validate each other by diversifying the data sources and triangulating the data using multiple sources, thereby improving the reliability and validity of the cases [21]. This study's analytical approach is based on the analytical viewpoints and explanations using the logical relationships generated by the multiple cases in order to achieve intrinsic validity. To establish an analytical general rule, this study observed and compared the creative and experience activities practices of the four cases in their operations, continuously analyzed the logical relationships between the concepts, and went through an iterative process of building explanations through continuous comparison. We thus identified the patterns and structures of the experience activities of the four cases.

4 Findings and Discussion

4.1 Winery Experience Activities

Changyu Winery is designed in a European style from the point of view of visitor experience. The square and interior decoration of the winery, as well as the professional tasting room, are the work of Marcel Mirande, a top French architect, who has expressed his strength through architecture [22, 26]. Amuel Adams Winery brings visitors to Boston through advertising and marketing, and they believe the best way to experience it is to be there in person [23]. Macallan Winery has transitioned the industry, distillation and brewing of the winery to the human, natural, and harmonious. They hope to create a post-modern humanism of industrial architecture with its unique design, advanced concept and strict construction [24, 27]. Miguel Winery has changed its traditional approach to yellow wine brewing and will focus on the transformation of the yellow wine process, so that the yellow wine, which is rich in Chinese culture, can reach the international market [25].

All four wineries have made experience their main strategy for development, which is consistent with Tussyadiah's [7] findings that visitors' interaction with the local landscape and local people can enhance their experience of local exploration. In the literature, Pullman & Gross [8] point out that they can design the experience design for interaction between customers and service staff or between customers and other people; They can also design it in terms of service facilities, convenience items, meals, and sensory design to create an atmosphere to convey information and themes related to the winery venue. This is the same as what they did at Changyu Winery, Samuel Adams Winery and Macallan Winery from the planning of the architectural space, through the planning of excellent designers, marketing and promotion to achieve the design, operation, and other marketing operations of winery activities.

Changyu Winery aims to establish the cultivation and brewing norms with Chinese origin standards, to build a modern large industrial winemaking demonstration area and a 5A-level scenic spot for Chinese wine industry tourism, with entertainment and educational functions [22, 26]. The Samuel Adams Winery will introduce its history and educate visitors about craft beer while they visit the brewery [23]. Macallan Winery has set up a related theme to design the experience with the spiritual home, small stills, fine cores, and quality European oak barrels as the attributes on which it relies [24, 27]. Miguel Winery through the use of a smart chemical plant, the winemaking process can be started at the touch of a button, and the winemaking process can be made smart, bringing stability to the quality of yellow wine production [25].

As discussed earlier in the literature, Roberts & Sparks [9] point out that in applying scenarios to find authentic experiences, tourists on winery tours want to see how wine is produced and how the vineyards are managed. In their study, Manthiou et al. [13] noted that festivals can include educational presentations and entertainment activities, making the festival an educational experience and an entertainment experience. Savinovic et al. [14] suggest that festivals can focus on ethnic food and wine experiences, and therefore, the event variables are defined as food, wine, and entertainment. It represented these two scenarios at Changyu Winery, Samuel Adams Winery, and Macallan Winery. Besides the regular experiences, the wineries offer entertainment and educational activities to meet the needs of visitors. All four wineries have transformed their wine production into a communication symbol with their own characteristics, further realizing the currency through the operation of the experience process and activities, thus integrating and optimizing the wine products and even the industry chain for their own better development.

4.2 Winery Visitor Participation

The underground cellars of the Changyu Winery are divided into three storage areas, which are carefully managed with state-of-the-art equipment to ensure the full brewing and slow maturation of the various wines stored, and are also available for visitors to inspect [22, 26]. Samuel Adams Winery offers a space for visitors to explore a variety of Belgian-style brews, providing an introduction to beer making [23]. Macallan Winery has created a new experience center inspired by the old Scottish round stone towers that blend in with the beautiful natural landscape around them. The exterior, functionality, and interior configuration are a far cry from the distillery of old [24, 27]. Miguel Winery has established a production line with separate winemaking, low temperature fermentation and precise temperature control through technology, and the production process can be visited by visitors [25].

According to Tussyadiah [7], he use of experience design in the tourism experience is noted to be interactive and consistent with the processes that the four wineries offer for visitor participation. In terms of visitor interaction with art scenes and artifacts, the idea of providing experiences for visitors through winery scene-making. The interaction of visitors with other visitors, locals, tourism provider staff, and other relevant social networks, through wine making and experience, provides relevant experiences. The interaction between visitors and the mass media and marketing media allows the wineries to promote the event and themselves through online publicity. The other four wineries were able to mobilize the resources they needed to operate smoothly in their own situations.

The development of Changyu Winery will help Changyu Industrial Park enhance its international competitiveness in terms of capacity scale, brewing equipment automation, grape growing technology, brewing technology, and brand promotion, adding a new urban highlight to Yantai Asia International Grape and Cine City [22, 26]. The innovative and experimental core fermentation cellar at Samuel Adams Winery is not open to the public. Inside the winery's Barrel Room, visitors can learn what made these and other unique beers possible, as well as learn expert high-end beer identification techniques and aging varieties [23]. Macallan Winery has guarded the Macallan winery as it has developed in its original environment and uses good brewing equipment to make the wine appear rich, full, and fruity [24, 27]. Miguel Winery brings some changes to the traditional yellow wine industry, using modern equipment and standardized processes to bring new life to the yellow wine industry [25].

Pine II & Gilmore [1] and Tussyadiah [7] have suggested that when visitors have a quality and memorable experience in a tourism venue, it ultimately contributes to the formation of tourism brand loyalty. This is in much the same way that the four wineries bring good experiences to visitors during their experiential activities hoping to establish their brands in the minds of consumers. However, this study argues that the four wineries are not small businesses and that capital and talent are prerequisites, so what the wineries need is the ability to plan strategically, and that the success of brand promotion through events will lead to better business development and operations. Beverland has also discussed earlier the section on wineries providing interactive resources for visitors [20]. He found visitors can examine the authenticity of a winery through special elements related to wine production methods, the use of historic buildings, and the physical atmosphere of the winery's landscape. Changyu winery has captured this by explaining wine production methods to visitors, redesigning and using the historic buildings, and expanding the winery, which ultimately makes up good conditions for forming experiential activities. The results are consistent with the insights presented by the three scholars mentioned above. All four wineries have followed the principle of creating a good experience for brand loyalty in their operational development, both in terms of experience process, event design, and promotional marketing, to be close to visitors' lives and to attract their goodwill.

4.3 Winery Visitor Participation

Their constituent elements and activity design support the formation of the wineries' experience activities. We showed the experiential activities of the four wineries in Table 2 below. As a whole, the winery culture has a deep foundation in the West, so Changyu Winery, Samuel Adams Winery, and Macallan Winery are more mature in their development, specifically because the process technology related to the three categories of wine, beer, and whiskey is already mature and can be mechanized to make wine products, making the wineries have a stable income. As a yellow wine category, Miguel Winery is still on the go to revamp the yellow wine process, looking forward to using modern technology to achieve international standards for their wine. Once the winery has many high-quality wines, it usually plans further experiences, such as opening experience spaces, visiting underground cellars, and offering wine-tasting courses.

Table 2. Essential elements of the Case Winery Experience campaign model

Case Subjects	Constituent Elements	Activity Design
Changyu Winery	The European-style manor house incorporates the best of Chinese and European architecture Enhancement of wine-making equipment to improve production techniques Creation of a wine landscape	Open the underground wine cellar for visitors Wine-tasting classes are available for visitors
Samuel Adams Winery	Shape the winery experience space	Promote the history of the brewery and knowledge of craft beer during visitors' tours Provide visitors with an experience space to make brewed beer Provide professional high-end beer-tasting courses for visitors
Macallan Winery	Create a new experience center Use of high-end wine-making equipment	Take visitors on a tour of the newest experience space Provide visitors with the opportunity to taste and enjoy
Miguel Winery	The focus will be on the transformation of the yellow wine process	Visitors can tour the latest yellow wine production line

Source: Compiled by this study

All four wineries differed in their experience models, and a reasonable winery experience model can be derived by bringing together the different points of difference. We show the structure of the wineries experience activities in Fig. 1. As mentioned above, the model takes the winery as the source and the visitor as the goal. We should equip the winery with experience activities that focus on the production methods of wine, the use of historical buildings, and the creation of wineries landscapes. In terms of activity design, we can divide it into four directions. The first is to design a reasonable wine-making process for visitors to practice and experience the charm of wine-making. The second is to take visitors to the newly built wineries experience center to understand the historical background and relevant features of the wineries. Third, we will hold courses on wine appreciation and tasting to make the experience educational and attract more visitors to the wineries besides wine lovers. The wineries can allow local people to take part in the activities to guide visitors to become familiar with the local culture and increase their interaction with the local landscape and local people. In the end, the wineries experience model will achieve the effect of entertainment and educational experience, thus attracting more visitors.

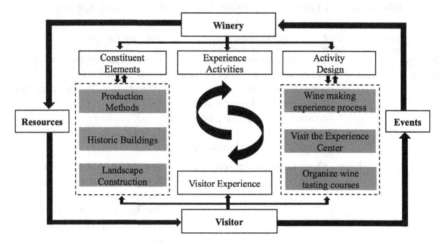

Fig. 1. Winery experience activity model.

In terms of the specific implementation, the wineries must first fully deploy the required resources according to their situation to make their operation smoother. On this basis, the design, operation, and marketing of the wineries' activities are carried out through the planning and marketing of the event planner. Besides the regular winemaking activities, the winery offers entertainment and educational activities, such as wine-tasting classes, to meet the needs of visitors. The wineries need to transform their wine production into a unique communication symbol that can be further monetized through the operation of the experience process and activities. Visitors gain experience through winemaking and experience. They can also interact with other tourists, local people, and tourism workers who are taking part in the experience and post the experience on social networks, which also promote the winery through the network.

5   Conclusion

We summarize the results of the above studies in this study, and we derive the framework of the wineries experience activity model. Theoretically, most studies related to wineries focused on business development strategies and industry chains of wineries. Few studies addressed the activities patterns of game wineries' operations. This study sought to address these research gaps. Thus, this study identified the experience activities of wineries, winery visitor participation, and experience activities model of wineries. These findings can provide a theoretical basis for future research that further distills the provide theoretical basis for future research on components of wineries experience design and how to construct the wineries experience activities model. Our work also has some managerial implications. The design of experience activities may differ between wineries and general companies. In terms of the design of the experience activities process, wineries place greater emphasis on the service attitudes and international visions of managers, and how they can properly use the resources and capabilities that the wineries possess. Regarding future research directions, researchers should adopt a combination of qualitative and quantitative approaches. The study can be conducted by adding wineries of the same wine category from different regions. The results of this study can also be verified with wineries in other regions to further improve the ideas presented in this study.

References

1. Pine, B.J., II., Gilmore, J.H.: The Experience Economy: Work Is Theatre and Every Business A Stage. Harvard Business School Press, Boston, MA (1999)
2. Shedroff, N.: Experience Design. New Riders, Indianapolis, IN (2001)
3. Quintal, V.A., Thomas, B., Phau, I.: Incorporating the winescape into the theory of planned behaviour: examining "new world" wineries. Tour. Manage. **46**, 596–609 (2015)
4. Byrd, E.T., Canziani, B., (Jerrie) Hsieh, Y.C., Debbage, K., Sonmez, S.: Wine tourism: motivating visitors through core and supplementary services. Tourism Manage. **52**, 19–29 (2016)
5. Bufquin, D., Back, R.M., Park, J.Y., Nutta, M.: The effects of architectural congruence perceptions on winery visitors' emotions and behavioral intentions: the case of Marqués de Riscal. J. Destin. Mark. Manag. **9**, 56–63 (2018)
6. Bruwer, J., Pratt, M.A., Saliba, A., Hirche, M.: Regional destination image perception of tourists within a winescape context. Curr. Issue Tour. **20**(2), 157–177 (2014)
7. Tussyadiah, I.P.: Toward a theoretical foundation for experience design in tourism. J. Travel Res. **53**(5), 543–564 (2014)
8. Pullman, M.E., Gross, M.A.: Ability of experience design elements to elicit emotions and loyalty behaviors. Decision Sci. **53**(5), 35(3), 551–578 (2004)
9. Roberts, L., Sparks, B.: Enhancing the wine tourism experience: the customers' viewpoint, CABI Books. CABI International, Wallingford UK, Cabi (2006)
10. Park, J.Y., Back, R.M., Bufquin, D., Shapoval, V.: Servicescape, positive affect, satisfaction and behavioral intentions: the moderating role of familiarity. Int. J. Hosp. Manag. **78**, 102–111 (2019)
11. Yoon, Y., Lee, J., Lee, C.: Measuring festival quality and value affecting visitors' satisfaction and loyalty using a structural approach. Int. J. Hospital. Manage. **29**(2), 335–342 (2010)
12. Lee, J., Lee, C., Choi, Y.: Examining the role of emotional and functional values in festival evaluation. J. Travel Res. **50**(6), 685–696 (2011)
13. Manthiou, A., Kang, J., Schrier, T.: A visitor-based brand equity perspective: the case of a public festival. Tourism Rev. **69**(4), 264–283 (2014)
14. Savinovic, A., Kim, S., Long, P.: Audience members' motivation, satisfaction, and intention to re-visit an ethnic minority cultural festival. J. Travel Tourism Market. **29**(7), 682–694 (2012)
15. Ponsignon, F., Durrieu, F., Bouzdine-Chameeva, T.: Customer experience design: a case study in the cultural sector: J. Service Manage. **28**(4), 763–787 (2017)
16. Lee, K., Madanoglu, M., Ko, J.Y.: Developing a competitive international service strategy: a case of international joint venture in the global service industry. J. Serv. Mark. **27**(3), 245–255 (2013)
17. Lee, K., Madanoglu, M., Ko, J.Y.: Exploring key service quality dimensions at a winery from an emerging market's perspective. British Food J.l **118**(12), 2981–2996 (2016)

18. Zhang Qiu, H., (Jessica) Yuan, J., Haobin Ye, B., Hung, K.: Wine tourism phenomena in China: an emerging market. Int. J. Contemp. Hospital. Manage. **25**(7), 1115–1134 (2013)
19. Diller, S., Shedroff, N., Rhea, D.: Making Meaning: How Successful Businesses Deliver Meaningful Customer Experiences. New Riders, Berkeley, CA (2008)
20. Beverland, M.: The "real thing": branding authenticity in the luxury wine trade. J. Bus. Res. **59**(2), 251–258 (2006)
21. Yin, R.K.: Case Study Research and Applications: Design and Methods. 6th edn. SAGE, Los Angeles (2018)
22. Changyu Homepage. http://changyu.com.cn/explore/city.html. Accessed 19 Jan 2023
23. Winery Design. https://cj.sina.com.cn/articles/view/5974261090/16417fd6200100a0nr. Accessed 19 Jan 2023
24. WeiCho. https://zhuanlan.zhihu.com/p/536757803. Accessed 20 Jan 2023
25. Good Wine Geography Bureau. https://baijiahao.baidu.com/s?id=1715461710234925467& wfr=spider&for=pc. Accessed 21 Jan 2023
26. Yantai City Culture and Tourism Bureau. https://m.thepaper.cn/baijiahao_12963210. Accessed 22 Jan 2023
27. Retourism. http://www.retourism-cn.com/newsinfo/43-46-633.html. Accessed 22 Jan 2023

A Study on the Differences of Consumers' Emotional Experience of Cultural Creative Products in the Palace Museum of Beijing

Lijuan Guo[1] ⓘ, Yingying Hang[1] ⓘ, and Jun Wu[2(✉)] ⓘ

[1] School of Art and Media, Taishan College of Science and Technology, Tai'an 271000, Shandong, China
[2] School of Fine Arts and Design, Division of Art, Shenzhen University, Shenzhen 518060, Guangdong, China
junwu2006@hotmail.com

Abstract. Under the development trend of globalization, the cultural creative industries in various countries began to develop towards localization, striving to present their local cultural characteristics to the world through various products and enhance their own cultural soft power. Against this background, museums around the world began to seek new ways of communication. The Palace Museum, which has more than 10 million followers in Sina Weibo, is relatively more influential among the top ten museums in China. Therefore, this study takes the 10 cultural creative products with the highest sales volume in the new categories of the official flagship store of the Palace Museum in China as the subjects, and explores the differences in the emotional experience of Chinese consumers on the cultural creative products of the Palace Museum. The study shows that (1) The emotional experience of consumers of different ages is similar, and the emotional identification of males is significantly higher than that of females; (2) The emotional experience of different age groups is similar; (3) The emotional experience of those with college degree is stronger; (4) Design-related majors have the lowest scores, while liberal arts majors have higher scores; (5) Low-income groups have more obvious emotional experience of cultural creative products.

Keywords: The Palace Museum · Cultural Creative Products · Cultural Codes · Purchase intention

1 Literature Review

1.1 Cultural Creative Products

In 2016, The cultural creative products of museums led by the cultural creative products of the Palace Museum bring opportunities to the whole cultural creative industry of museums. At present, thousands of museums, art galleries and memorial halls have developed cultural creative derivatives based on their collections. The market size of cultural creative industry has reached 41.35 billion yuan. In 2021, the market size of

Chinese cultural creative industry was 87.267 billion yuan, a year-on-year increase of 15.57% [1]. The production of cultural creative products involves transformation from local history and culture into cultural images, and creative design, so that they can become products boasting both culture and creativity. With the vigorous development of knowledge-based economy, consumers begins to pay more attention to the spiritual value attached to products instead of their functions alone. Their cognition and purchase intention of cultural creative products play a decisive role in the development of the cultural creative industry. "Culture" is a shape of life like thought, and "Industry" is a production and marketing mode [2]. Culture also generally refers to various forms of human activities and their symbolic structures [3]. Through cultural creative industries and the impact of Eastern and Western arts, countries around the world create a social atmosphere in pursuit of freedom, so that local arts can develop and culture can penetrate into people's daily life. Furthermore, cultural contents are also used as an investment tool to make profits, and the cultural creative industry has thus transformed into a new business form.

1.2 Emotional Experience of Cultural Creative Products

Products can be regarded as a medium to stimulate users' emotions. When products concern what users pay special attention to, they can stimulate their emotions, which also affects users' cognition of whether they have special views and preferences for the products [4]. Lynch and De Chernatony [5] believed that emotion can enhance the brand value and tap the potential of creativity, and it can create sustainable differential advantages, that is, when the product can meet the basic needs of consumers and provide a joyful process, then consumers can develop positive emotion for the brand through emotion for the product [6]. The research on emotions in art and design has attracted more and more attention. Don Norman [7] pointed out in the book *Emotional Design* that emotional design is divided into three levels, namely, visceral, behavioral and reflective. The visceral level focuses on user's visual, auditory and tactile experience; In the behavior level, users focus on the function, understandability, usability and physical feelings of products; The reflective level focuses on the information, culture and meaning in use brought by products to users. Therefore, under the guidance of Donald A. Norman's theory, this study takes the cultural creative products sold in the official flagship store of the Palace Museum in Taobao as the subjects, and studies consumers' emotional experience and purchase preference.

1.3 Purchase Intention of Cultural Creative Products

Reflective level. In addition to clearly positioning and segmenting the products, the way for enterprises to gain competitive advantage in the market is to appeal to customers' aesthetic feeling and emotional needs, so that products are no longer pure products, but can win consumers' hearts [8, 9]. The product that can be successfully sold is often determined by its beautiful appearance, the feelings of pleasure it produces and the sense of satisfaction it has brought to customers [10, 11]. Good product design can not only attract consumers' attention and promote communication with consumers, but also enable consumers to increase their purchase intention by their user experience [12]. Purchase intention means that consumers have preference for purchasing designated products or certain services and are willing to pay for such products or services. That is to say, consumers insist on purchasing the products after a series of evaluations, which means, they have purchase intention. Consumers' behavior tendency is closely related to their purchase intention and actual purchase behaviors, which can reflect every process of each consumer in obtaining products [13]. Engel, Blackwell and Miniard [14] believed that purchase behavior is a psychological decision-making process. Consumers would seek relevant information for their own needs. After further evaluation and comparison of information collected, they would make purchasing decisions, and use this experience as a reference for future purchasing decisions, that is, consumers' "purchasing decision-making process". Purchase intention is the possibility of consumers to buy a certain product or service, and the higher the purchase intention, the greater the probability of consumers to buy it [15].

This study selected the cultural creative products of the Palace Museum as the subjects. In Taobao's official flagship store for online sales, those with the highest sales volume in each product category were selected for case studies. For example, 10 cultural creative products were regarded as the research objects, such as twelve-flower-scented solid perfume in fragrance series, lucky rabbit red agate bracelet and necklace in jewelry series, the Imperial Palace snow relief lipstick in make-up series, Vast Land travel tea set in tea set series, palace cat notebook in stationery series. As shown in Table 1, the differences in purchase preferences of users from different backgrounds are explored through independent samples T-test and ANOVA analysis. The research purposes are briefly described as follows:

a. Differences in emotional experience of cultural creative products in the Palace Museum for consumers from different backgrounds;
b. Differences in emotional experience of cultural creative products in the Palace Museum for consumers with different incomes.

2 Research Methods

In this study, questionnaire surveys are adopted for statistics and analysis. The purpose of the questionnaire is to understand the consumer's value orientation of cultural creative goods in the Imperial Palace. The subjects are asked to fill in the structured questionnaire. A total of 135 valid questionnaires were collected in this study. There were 51 males and 84 females in terms of gender; There were 29 people aged 19 and below, 68 people aged

Table 1. Subjects of study.

Category	P1 Fragrance	P2 Jewelry	P3 Make-up	P4 Tea Set	P5 Stationery
Item Name	Twelve-Flower-Scented Solid Perfume	Lucky Rabbit Red Agate Bracelet and Necklace	Imperial Palace Snow Relief Lipstick	Vast Land Travel Tea Set	Palace Cat Notebook

Category	P6 Souvenir	P7 Household Products	P8 Mascot	P9 Fan	P10 Paintings and Calligraphy
Item Name	Rabbit children's portable lantern	The animal year red socks	Baby reunion doll ornaments	Mini moon-shaped fan	New year peace and safety hanging paintings

20–29, 19 people aged 30–39, 11 people aged 40–49, and 8 people aged 50 and above in terms of age; There were 30 people of design-related majors, 43 people of art-related majors, 11 people of liberal arts majors, 20 people of science and engineering majors, and 31 people of other majors in terms of majors; There were 5 doctors, 17 masters, 77 undergraduates, 12 junior college graduates, and 24 people with senior high school degree and below; in terms of educational background, There were 62 people with no income, 12 people with 2,000 yuan or less, 14 people with 2,000–3,000 yuan, 19 people with 3,001–5,000 yuan, 21 people with 5,000–10,000 yuan and 7 people with 10,000 yuan or more in terms of monthly income. The questionnaire consists of two parts. The first part is basic information, including gender, age, educational background, major, income and 4 question items, that is, general evaluation of the cultural creative products of the Palace Museum. The second part takes 10 representative cultural creative products in Table 1 as examples, and four questions: cultural connotation, creativity, recommendation willingness and your preference for the creative products as the general evaluation items, uses the 5-point Likert scale which gives 1 to 5 points to response options "strongly disagree", "disagree", "neither agree nor disagree", "agree" and "strongly agree", and puts relevant product information in the questionnaire, so that consumers are clear about the basic information of products when filling out the answers.

3 Research Results

3.1 Reliability and Validity Analysis

Statistical analysis found that the Cronbach's alpha was 0.971. Sapp pointed out that the Cronbach's alpha was acceptable when it was 0.8–0.9, and when it was above 0.9, it meant it had good reliability [16], which indicated that the questionnaire had good reliability. The total correlation for each dimension and item was from 0.576 to 0.765, and the "Cronbach's alpha after deletion" was 0.970 to 0.971, which can be seen that the internal consistency between the topics is relatively high and the topic selection is reasonable. Through the validity analysis, it can be seen that the KMO value was 0.905, which was of high value, the Sig value was 0.000, which was very significant, and the eigenvalue was 18.907.The factor loadings of each question were from 0.603–0.788, and the commonality was from 0.363–0.621. Sapp pointed out that it is good when the factor loading is above 0.5, it was ideal when it is above 0.7. It is good when the commonality is above 0.3, and it is ideal when it is above 0.5. The factor loading and commonality of each question are both higher than the ideal value, indicating good validity.

3.2 Analysis on the Differences in Variables Due to Different Genders

Taking the gender of the subjects as the independent variable and the four general evaluation questions as the dependent variables, this study adopted independent samples T-test to explore the differences in emotional experience of consumers of different genders for cultural creative products. The results are shown in Table 1. Consumers have cognitive differences in the creativity and cultural connotation of Twelve-Scented-Flower Solid Perfume, and the score of males is significantly higher than that of females. Twelve-Scented-Flower Solid Perfume takes the cloisonné enamel box collected in the Palace Museum as the shape of the perfume, and is decorated with flower goddess dress which goes with corresponding fragrance. Flower goddess dresses are costumes worn by ancient actresses when they play flower goddesses in each month. Each dress shows the seasonal characteristics of the current month and integrates the key elements of the season, such as the August laurel theme of Mid-Autumn Festival, in which the main patterns are white rabbits and sweet-scented osmanthus. This solid perfume is full of creativity in appearance design, and incorporates cultural connotation of Chinese traditional festivals. Its unique creative design is closely connected with people's lives. The features and design thinking of cultural creative products of the Imperial Palace are not only about creativity. What's more, along the 5,000-year history of the Imperial Palace, they have dug out the hidden elements of "Forbidden City Culture" as the carrier of communication and made continuous development. Thus, the consumers have obvious emotional experience. Compared with females, males are more rational in aesthetic psychology, so they pay more attention to creativity and cultural connotation in purchase behaviors, and female consumers pay more attention to the appeal of the appearance features of products when consuming cultural creative products. Therefore, males have greater emotional experience than females (Table 2).

Table 2. T test analysis of gender and characteristic differences.

Product	Variable	LEVEN Test for Equal Variance		Mean Versus T Test	
		F	Significance	T	Coefficient of Comparison
P1	creativity	3.784	0.054*	1.981	Man > women
	cultural connotation	0.016	0.898*	2.036	Man > women

*p < .05.**p < .01. ***p < .001

3.3 Analysis on the Differences in Variables Due to Different Ages

Variance differences test was respectively carried out on ages and four aspects of general evaluation. It turned out that consumers' scores on creativity, cultural connotation, willingness to recommend to relatives and friends and preferences of these 10 cultural creative products were relatively consistent. It can be seen that consumers of different ages have close scores in the above-mentioned four aspects, there is no significant difference in these scores, and they have gained relatively consistent emotional experience. In this study, the series of fragrance, jewelry, make-up, tea set, stationery, souvenir, household products, mascot, paintings and calligraphy, and fans of cultural creative products of the Imperial Palace are selected as the research objects. Compared with monotonous and simple products, cultural creative products basically contain cultural connotations, which are both practical and aesthetic. The cultural creative products of the Imperial Palace have realized creative entertainment, paid attention to reshaping the brand image of being fresh, young and down-to-earth, attracted consumers of all ages, catered to the entertainment needs of consumers, and enabled the public to obtain relatively consistent emotional experience after consumption experience.

3.4 Analysis on the Differences in Variables Due to Different Majors

Variance differences test was respectively carried out on majors and four aspects of general evaluation. It turned out that the consumers had cognitive differences on the creativity, cultural connotation, willingness to recommend to relatives and friends and preferences of 10 cultural creative products. The results are shown in Table 3. Consumers show differences in emotional experience regarding scores of P1, P4, P7, P9 and P10. For P1 Twelve-Scented-Flower Solid Perfume and P4 Vast Land travel tea set, regarding the scores of recommendation willingness and creativity, consumers of "other" majors have higher scores, while those of design majors have the lowest scores. The cultural creative products are all adapted from the buildings and collections of the Imperial Palace and the details of court culture, which are based on sufficient historical sources and full of creativity and bright ideas of the development team. Consumers of design majors have a higher pursuit of beauty, so in the consumption activities of cultural creative products, they can deeply understand and analyze the design of products, thus getting lower scores. For P7 the animal year red socks, regarding the creativity of design, those of science and engineering majors have the highest scores, and those of design related majors have the lowest scores, because consumers of design majors attach more importance to the application of creativity. For P9 mini moon-shaped fans and P10 new year peace and safety hanging paintings, those of liberal arts majors have the highest scores. The Palace Museum is at the forefront in creating cultural products, digging deep into the rich royal cultural elements of Ming and Qing Dynasties. By integrating the 5,000-year-old buildings of the Palace Museum, the cultural relics of the Palace Museum and the stories behind them, with fashion expression concept that modern people like, it has been turned into a museum with the cultural connotation of the Palace Museum and distinctive characteristics of the times, that caters to the actual needs of the republic. Compared with consumers of other majors, those of liberal arts related majors have much more knowledge of history and culture, so they can sense the cultural connotation and historical beauty in the process of purchasing and appreciating the cultural creative products of the Imperial Palace, thus enhancing the overall level of preference.

Table 3. ANOVA analysis of differences between specialty and characteristic evaluation.

Product	Variable	LEVEN Test for Equal variance		Mean Versus T Test	
		F	Mean	St	post hoc
P1	recommendation willingness	2.972*	3.86	0.874	
P4	creativity	2.469*	4.00	0.838	
P7	creativity	2.729*	3.76	1.002	
P9	cultural connotation	2.584*	4.10	0.866	
P10	preference	2.636*	4.12	0.873	

$*p < .05.**p < .01. ***p < .001$ (1= Design correlation , 2= Art correlation , 3= Liberal arts correlation , 4= Science and technology correlation , 5= Other major)

P1 recommendation willingness : 5(4.16)>4(4.15)>2(3.79)>3(3.64)>1(3.53)

P4 creativity : 5(4.29)>4(4.25)>3(4.00)>2(3.84)>1(3.77)

P7 creativity : 4(4.20)>5(4.03)>3(3.82)>2(3.53)>1(3.50)

P9 cultural connotation : 3(4.45)>4(4.35)>5(4.29)>1(4.03)>2(3.81)

P10 preference : 3(4.36)>5(4.39)>4(4.30)>2(4.02)>1(3.77)

3.5 Analysis on the Differences in Variables Due to Different Majors Analysis on the Differences in Variables Due to Different Educational Backgrounds

Variance differences test was respectively carried out on educational backgrounds and four aspects of general evaluation, and the results were shown in Table 4. Consumers show significant differences in emotional experience regarding scores of P1, P4, P6, P7, P8, P9 and P10. For P1 Twelve-Scented-Flower Solid Perfume and P4 Vast Land Travel Tea Set, there were significant differences in creativity and recommendation willingness of products, and those with high school degree and below had higher scores than consumers above bachelor's degree. For P6 Rabbit Children's Portable Lanterns, consumers with junior college degree had higher scores than undergraduates in terms of cultural connotation and consumption willingness of products. The consumers with junior college degree had the highest scores in creativity for P7 animal year red socks and in cultural connotation for P8 baby reunion doll ornaments. For P9 mini moon-shaped fan and P10 new year peace and safety hanging paintings, the junior college graduates had the highest scores and the doctors had the lowest scores in terms of preference and recommendation willingness.

Table 4. ANOVA analysis of differences between educational background and characteristic evaluation.

Product	Variable	LEVEN test for equal variance		Mean Versus T Test	
		F	Mean	St	Post Hoc
P1	creativity	2.446*	3.87	0.888	
	recommendation willingness	3.504**	3.86	0.874	5>3
P4	creativity	2.490*	4.00	0.838	
	recommendation willingness	2.465*	3.83	1.004	
	preference	5.289***	3.87	0.937	4>3,5>3
P6	cultural connotation	2.944*	4.16	0.771	4>2,4>3
	recommendation willingness	3.493*	4.33	0.816	4>3
P7	creativity	3.198*	3.76	1.002	
	cultural connotation	4.148**	3.86	0.948	
P8	cultural connotation	3.252*	4.04	0.818	
P9	cultural connotation	3.577**	4.13	0.845	4>2
	preference	2.961*	4.07	0.895	
P10	recommendation willingness	2.945*	4.01	0.926	
	preference	3.039*	4.12	0.873	

*p < .05.**p < .01. ***p < .001 (1= Doctor degree , 2= Master's degree , 3= Undergraduate , 4= Junior College , 5= Senior high school and below)

P1 creativity:1(4.25)>4(4.20)>5(4.17)>2(3.94)>3(3.68)

P4 creativity: 5(4.38)>1(4.20)>4(4.17)>2(4.12)>3(3.82)
recommendation willingness: 4(4.25)>5(4.21)>1(4.20)>2(3.82)>3(3.62)

P7 creativity : 4(4.33)>5(4.21)>3(3.61)>2(3.53)>1(3.40)

cultural connotation : 4(4.50)>5(4.29)>1(3.80)>3(3.71)>2(3.47)

P8 cultural connotation : 4(4.50)>5(4.25)>3(3.61)>1(3.60)>2(3.59)

P9 preference : 4(4.67)>5(4.29)>3(4.03)>2(3.71)>1(3.60)

P10 recommendation willingness : 4(4.67)>5(4.25)>2(4.06)>3(3.84)>1(3.60)

preference : 4(4.67)>5(4.46)>2(4.00)>3(3.97)>1(3.80)

3.6   Analysis on the Differences in Variables Due to Different Monthly Incomes

Variance differences test was respectively carried out on monthly income and four aspects of general evaluation. Consumers of different income groups had obvious differences in emotional experience regarding P6 rabbit children's portable lanterns, but there was no significant difference in emotional experience of other nine cultural creative products. The results were shown in Table 5. Lanterns, also known as festive lanterns or colored lanterns, are a symbol of good fortune and festivity. They are often used in the court to enhance the festive atmosphere. Designers inspired by the images of palace cats and moon rabbits made exquisite and interesting lanterns. 2023 is the Year of the Rabbit in Chinese New Year. Consumers have special emotional experience for cultural creative products containing rabbit elements, and are more willing to recommend relatives and friends to buy them. Consumers with monthly incomes of 2000–3000 had the highest scores of emotional experience, and those with monthly income of more than 10,000 yuan had the lowest scores. The official price of rabbit children's portable lantern is 29 yuan, which is within the range of consumption level of ordinary income groups, so that they are more willing to recommend it to relatives and friends after consumption experience. However, consumers with monthly income of more than 10,000 yuan have higher living standards, pay more attention to product quality during consumption and are more capable, so they are less willing to consume and recommend rabbit children's portable lanterns.

Table 5. ANOVA test analysis of differences between income and characteristic evaluation.

Product	Variable	LEVEN Test for Equal Variance		Mean Versus T Test	
		F	Mean	St	Post Hoc
P6	recommendation willingness	2.685*	4.03	0.889	

1= Temporary absence of income , 2=2000yuan and below , 3=2000-3000 yuan , 4=3001-5000yuan ,
5=5001-10000yuan , 6=More than 10,000 yuan.
P6 recommendation willingness:3(4.50)>5(4.33)>2(4.25)>4(4.11)>1(3.77)>6(3.86)

4 Conclusions and Suggestions

On the basis of aforesaid studies, it can be seen that consumers from different backgrounds have both the same and significantly different emotional experience of cultural creative products in the Imperial Palace. The conclusions of this study are as follows:

1. Consumers of different genders have cognitive differences in the creativity and cultural connotation of Twelve-Scented-Flower Solid Perfume, and the scores of males are significantly higher than those of females. Compared with female's delicate thinking and feelings, males pay more attention to the creativity and cultural connotation of products when buying cultural creative products due to their rational thinking.
2. Consumers of different ages have relatively consistent emotional experience of cultural creative products, with no significant difference. The consumer groups of cultural creative products in China are mainly young people, and young people play a key role in consumption of cultural creative products in the Palace Museum. The younger generation has unique consumption concepts and behaviors. The cultural creative products of the Palace Museum are of economic value, cultural value, technical value, artistic value and practical value. For different age groups, there should be reasonable differences in the perception of economy, culture, technology and artistic connotations. In the future, cultural creative products can be designed and developed for different age groups to better meet the consumption needs of different age groups for them.
3. There are significant differences in the emotional experience of cultural creative products for consumers with different educational backgrounds. From the results above, it can be seen that those with junior college diploma have the highest scores in most aspects, and there are also significant differences in scores of groups with other educational backgrounds. Consumers have different educational backgrounds, knowledge reserve and perception of things, so there are great differences in their scores.
4. Consumers with different professional backgrounds have significant differences in emotional experience of cultural creative products. According to the results of this study, the scores of consumers of design-related majors are relatively low, while

those of liberal arts majors are relatively high. Consumers of design-related majors tend to pay more attention to the creativity of products when buying cultural creative products, while those of liberal arts-related majors tend to capture the connotation of history and culture. In the later period, the production of cultural creative products can start from the professional characteristics of science and engineering related majors and art related majors, create more cultural creative products that meet consumers of other majors, and enrich the diversity of players in the consumer market.

5. Different income groups have some differences in emotional experience of cultural creative products. Consumers' consumption capacity is determined by their income level. Consumers with lower incomes have more factors to consider during consumption, and their consumption level is within a reasonable range. In the future, some cultural creative products will be designed for consumers whose monthly income is more than 10,000 yuan, so as to enhance their consumption willingness. The factors that affect the consumption willingness of high-income groups for cultural creative products still needs further study and discussion.

In the future, the Palace Museum can cooperate with more high-quality enterprises with the same cultural concepts, good social reputation and economic strength. Through the strategies of complementary advantages, they can jointly develop creative products with added value of high-level creativity and representing excellent Chinese traditional culture, so that consumers can directly touch the Imperial Palace through these products, feel the profoundness and aesthetic connotation of the Forbidden City culture, and realize the inheritance and promotion of Chinese traditional culture. Follow-up research may focus on in-depth and systematic studies on the cultural creative products of provincial museums, and explore other factors that affect the differences in consumers' emotional experience.

References

1. Forward Industry Research. https://www.fxbaogao.com/archives/organization/ForwardIndustryResearchInstitute?keyword=ForwardIndustryResearchInstitute&creative=61180634640. Accessed 1 Feb 2023
2. Z, Z. H, YH & X, A.: Cultural Marketing. National Air University, Taipei (1995)
3. Leong, D., Clark, H.: Cultural-based knowledge towards new design thinking and practice – a dialogue. Des. Issues 19(3), 48–58 (2003)
4. Desmet, P.M.A., Hekkert, P.: The basis of product emotions. In: Green, W.S., Jordan, P.W. (eds.) Pleasure with Products, Beyond Usability, pp. 60–68. Taylor & Francis, London, England (2002). (Object recognition: Evidence for a common attentional mechanism. Vision Research, 36(12), 1827–1837)
5. Lynch, J., De Chernatony, L.: The power of emotion: Brand communication in business-to-business markets. J. Brand Manage. 11(5), 403–419 (2004)
6. D'souza, M.E., Hancock, P.A., Hoonhout, H.C., Krout, K., Ohme, P.J., Walline, E.K.: Designing products to evoke and emotional connection in users. Hum. Factors Ergon. Soc. 54, 1747–1751 (2010)
7. Norman, D.A.: Emotional Design: Why We Love (or Hate) Everyday Things. Basic Books, New York (2004)
8. Pink, D.H.: A Whole New Mind Moving from the Information Age to the Conceptual Age. Riverhead Books, New York (2005)

9. L, SY. H , YT, T, ZW.: A Preliminary study on aesthetic elements of marketing management. Market. Rev. **6**(3), 391–422 (2009)
10. Spillers, F.: Emotion as a cognitive artifact and the design implications for products that are perceived as pleasurable. In: Proceedings of the 4th International Conference on Design and Emotion (2004). http://www.designandemotion.org/
11. Khalid, H.M., Helander, M.G.: Customer emotional needs in product design. Concurr. Eng. **14**(3), 197 (2006)
12. Z, SW. C, YX.: The effects of brand familiarity and commodity characteristics on purchase intention and loyalty of similar sports shoes: personal traits as the interfering variable. J. Sports Leisure Manage. **10**(1), 44–63 (2012)
13. Hoyer, W.D., MacInnis, D.J.: Consumer Behavior. George T. Hoffman, United States of America (2007)
14. Engel, J.F., Blackwell, R.D., Miniard, P.W.: Consumer Behavior. Dryden Press, New York (1984)
15. Schiffman, L.G., Kanuk, L.L.: Comsumer Behavior, 7 edn. Prentice-Hall (2000)
16. Sapp, M.: Psychological and Educational Test Scores: What are They? Charles C Thomas Publisher, USA (2002)

Immersive Museum: Design and Develop an Interactive Virtual Museum Experience

Jiayi Xu(✉), Lei Yang, Meng Guo, Fei Gao, and Yujian Yin

China Mobile Research Institute, Beijing, China
xujiayi@chinamobile.com

Abstract. Shifting from an informational to experiential age, Virtual Reality (VR) represents a new revolution of natural human-computer interaction. However, pricey VR devices and the complicated setup greatly discourage the diffusion of VR and isolate users from one another. This paper proposes an interactive art installation titled *"Immersive Museum"*, which provides a theatrical virtual museum experience that engages sight, sound, touch, and behaviors. The proposed system focuses on enhancing interaction and immersion in a Virtual Environment (VE) by allowing a user to interact with the virtual museum through head orientations, body movements, and facial expressions.

Keywords: Virtual Environment (VE) · Body Center Interaction (BCI) · Immersiveness

1 Introduction

A museum is a collection of art history and human civilization. It classifies cultural evidence and then presents it in the form of statues, textiles, paintings, drawings, etc. When walking in a museum, surrounded by great art, we immerse ourselves in human civilization. However, our interaction with artworks is limited and unnatural. We can be easily distracted from our beautiful imagination of the art world. As immersive Virtual Reality (VR) technology matures, a number of existing museums like the Palace Museum in Beijing, MOCA Los Angeles, and the British Museum have begun to use VR for developing virtual museums and sharing their collections worldwide [1–4]. VR can transcend a physical location of a built environment [5] and has a formidable ability to immerse people in artistic illusions [6], but like any new technology, it brings challenges as well. Currently, VR headsets can produce the effect of real vision but can also cause anxiety and motion sickness because there is a disconnect between a user's physical body and sensory experience [7]. Moreover, VR devices are expensive and difficult to

This work was supported by the National Natural Science Foundation of China (Grant No. U21B2004).

P.-L. P. Rau (Ed.): HCII 2023, LNCS 14024, pp. 152–161, 2023.
https://doi.org/10.1007/978-3-031-35946-0_13

maintain. The VR headsets make direct contact with the eyes and skin, and this can easily transmit infections. On the other hand, vision has been considered an important sense for developing human perceptions and experiencing space. Therefore, most VR projects focused on visual development and high-resolution display to immerse people. However, immersion is not just a visual sense. There are different aspects to it. Building a museum in a Virtual Environment (VE) means there would be no limits to space, financial resources, and interaction methods. A virtual museum should have the potential to host the history of humanity and provide an enjoyable, immersive user experience.

Therefore, instead of being obsessed with visual development only, the *Immersive Museum* system creates immersion in three distinct ways: maximizing body interactions, associating visual displays with a user's behaviors, and reducing the response time of the virtual space. In addition, to avoid motion sickness, the proposed system eliminated VR headsets and allowed the human body to become the interface. It used portable devices such as sensors and a face-tracking system for digitizing human behaviors and facial expressions.

2   Related Works

2.1   What Interactions Can Make People Feel "immersed" in a VE?

Movement-Produced Stimulation. According to the vision experiment performed by Held and Hein in 1963, self-produced movement with its concurrent visual feedback is necessary for developing normal visual perception [8]. In this experiment, a pair of kittens was harnessed to a carousel, one of them could move freely by itself while the other one was placed in a gondola. They received the same visual stimulation with the important difference that one kitten could move actively, while the other kitten moved passively. The experiment results showed that only the self-moving kitten developed a normal visual perception. The other one, which was deprived of self-actuated movement, behaved as if it was blind.

Body Center Interaction (BCI). Based on a previous study, the degree of immersion in a VE is increased by adding additional, and consistent modalities, a greater degree of body tracking, richer body representations and decreased lag between body movements and result changes [7]. It is also necessary for the actions that a person makes in a VE to be intuitively associated with the corresponding actions that they would need to take in everyday reality [7]. This conclusion is supported by Schuemie et al.'s research on presence in VR. There were 246 people participating in this survey after using different VR devices. The results showed that "Body Movement" (ranked 4th) and "Head Tracking" (ranked 5th) can make users feel more immersed in a VE than "Illusory Interaction" (ranked 7th) and "Social Cues" (ranked 8th) [9].

2.2 How to Digitize Human Behaviors in a Virtual Museum?

The natural and common behaviors people perform in a museum include:

1. Walking/Movements: including both head pose and body movement, which enable a user to change view and position.
2. Taking photos: a user can use external devices (such as a camera or mobile phone) to "save" artworks.
3. Moving eyes and mouth: facial expressions that indicate a viewer's emotion. For example, a slight pupil dilation indicates being attracted.

Head Pose Estimation. In the context of computer vision, head pose estimation is the ability to infer the orientation and position of a head relative to a global coordinate system [10,11]. A head pose is limited to three degrees of freedom (DoF), which can be characterized by pitch, roll, and yaw angles.

Eye Aspect Ratio (EAR)/Mouth Aspect Ratio (MAR). Previous studies have proposed a real-time algorithm to detect Eye/Mouth state using facial landmarks [12,13]. According to the study, the value of the EAR and MAR can be calculated by using the key 2D facial landmarks [12]. When the EAR is less than 0.20, it means that the eye of a user is closed; when the MAR is greater than 0.60, it means that the mouth of a user is opened [13].

3 System Overview

The *Immersive Museum* includes three components, a 3D virtual museum developed with Unity3D software, a face-tracking system for monitoring a user's real-time facial expressions, and a motion-tracking system for a user to change viewpoints and move freely in the virtual museum (see Fig. 1).

A user could interact with the proposed system as follows:

1. When the system was launched, the user saw the virtual scene and digital artworks projected on the screen.
2. The user changed viewpoints in the virtual museum by slightly rotating his head. This interaction allowed the user to enjoy the details of each artwork from all points of view.
3. The user moved freely in the virtual museum by stepping on different foot pads.
4. The user heard a story about each artwork by stepping closer to it. The sound system corresponded to the distance between the user and the display. The sound would be louder when the user got closer.
5. Eye blinking triggered the "Take Photos" command. The system automatically took a screenshot of the current scene when the user blinked his eyes.
6. Mouth opening triggered the color change of the 3D sculptures. Under the default condition, the 3D sculptures were gray. When the user opened his mouth, the 3D sculptures would display the preset colors.

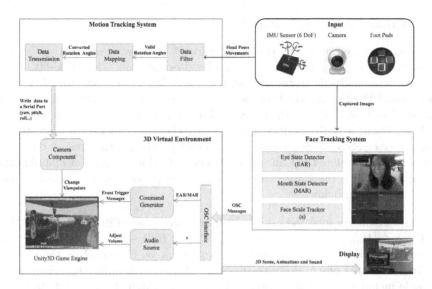

Fig. 1. System Construction: the proposed system includes a 3D virtual museum developed with Unity3D, a face-tracking system for monitoring a user's real-time facial expressions, and a motion-tracking system for tracking a user's head orientation and movements.

Fig. 2. Visual Elements: (a) 2D book illustrations (b) Interactive 3D sculptures.

3.1   The 3D Virtual Museum

The visual and audio elements in the virtual museum were developed with Unity3D software and contained:

1. Static images such as book illustrations created in the 18th century. (see Fig. 2(a))
2. Interactive 3D sculptures such as mythical beasts created by computer graphics. (see Fig. 2(b))
3. Audio sources [14] that were related to the art, history, and collections of the virtual museum.

3.2   Motion Tracking System

We first developed a motion tracking device (6 DoF) with an MPU-6050 sensor and Arduino for monitoring a user's head orientation. The MPU-6050 sensor combines a 3-axis gyroscope and a 3-axis accelerometer, together with an onboard Digital Motion Processor, which processes complex 6-axis Motion Fusion algorithms [15]. We then used Arduino for reading the sensory data such as Yaw, Pitch, and Roll values, and sending them to Unity3D via Bluetooth. Finally, we created a C# script in Unity3D for processing the sensory data and using it to manipulate the Camera component [16]. The process for mapping the sensory data with the Camera behavior (transform rotation and position) has been summarized below:

1. First, we determined the range of a user's head pose (Pitch, Yaw, Roll) [17], $Pitch \in [P_{min}, P_{max}]$, $Yaw \in [Y_{min}, Y_{max}]$, $Roll \in [R_{min}, R_{max}]$. The sensory data that was out of the range would not be processed by the system. According to a previous study, the range of head motion for an average adult male includes a sagittal flexion and extension (Pitch) from $-60.4°$ to $69.6°$, a frontal lateral bending (Roll) from $-40.9°$ to $36.3°$, and a horizontal axial rotation (Yaw) from $-79.8°$ to $75.3°$ [18].
2. Then, we used the map range formula to convert the incoming data into a rotation angle in the 3D virtual museum (nPitch, nYaw, nRoll). For example, if the sensory data $X \in [X_{min}, X_{max}]$ and the field of view in the 3D scene is [a, b], the formula for this transformation is:

$$X' = a + \frac{b - a}{X_{max} - X_{min}} * (X - X_{min}) \tag{1}$$

3. Finally, we created a local Quaternion variable in Unity3D and use it to manipulate the Camera rotation:

$$Q = Quaternion.Euler(-nPitch * RotationSpeed,$$
$$-nYaw * RotationSpeed, nRoll * RotationSpeed) \tag{2}$$

$$Camera.Transform.rotation = Q \tag{3}$$

This allowed a user to change viewpoints in the VE by slightly rotating the head. The real-time data transmission gave the user an accurate and immediate response.

There were four pads on the ground. A user could move forward, backward, left, and right in the virtual museum by stepping on different foot pedals.

3.3   Face Tracking System

The FaceOSC software [19] was selected to read facial data from a webcam and track an array of perceptual signals, including 68 facial landmark points (XY-pairs), face poses, and face gestures. The signals were in raw numerical form (e.g., raw/position 300.93, 168.44; pose/scale 0.23, 0.14, 0.10; eye/left 3.08) and forwarded to Unity3D over Open Sound Control (OSC, a communication protocol for sending information between computers, sensors, and multimedia devices) (see Fig. 3).

In Unity3D, we wrote a C# script to achieve the following goals:

1. It used key facial landmark points to calculate MAR and EAR:

$$MAR = \frac{\|P_{62} - P_{68}\| + \|P_{64} - P_{66}\|}{2 * \|P_{49} - P_{55}\|} \tag{4}$$

$$EAR(right) = \frac{\|P_{38} - P_{42}\| + \|P_{39} - P_{41}\|}{2 * \|P_{37} - P_{40}\|} \tag{5}$$

If the MAR value was greater than the threshold (set to 0.60), it means that the user opened his mouth and this would change the color of the 3D sculptures. If the EAR value was less than the threshold (set to 0.20), it means that the user blinked once and if the time between two blinks was less than 1 s, the system would take a screenshot of the current scene. (see Fig. 4)

2. It used the face scale ($0 < s < 1$) value to adjust the volume of the 3D sound system:

$$audioSource.volume = a_0 + s * a_0 \tag{6}$$

4 System Implementation

The setup of this system consists of a projector, a large screen, a webcam, a stereo system, a motion-tracking device, four foot pads, and a computer with an Intel Core i7 2.9 GHz processor, 16 GB of memory, and an Intel HD Graphics 630 graphics card (see Fig. 5). The participant put on the motion-tracking device and stood in front of the installation. The participant's facial data was captured by the webcam in real time.

5 Result and Discussion

The proposed system had been tested with people from different professional backgrounds. The representative quotes have been summarized below:

"I love that there are no VR goggles on my head. However, it would be better if I did not need to wear any sensor." (a graduate student in Digital Media Design)

"I need a cue that tells me what will happen next and what I should do...It would be great to have a storyline for this experience. The combination of technical capacity and emotional resonance can motivate people to dive deeper" (a professor of UX Design)

158   J. Xu et al.

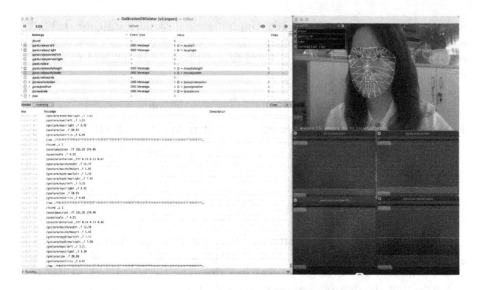

Fig. 3. FaceOSC software

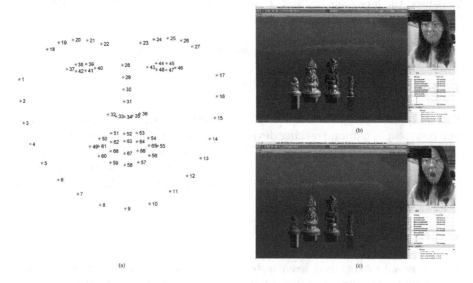

(a)   (b)

                                              (c)

Fig. 4. (a) 68 facial landmark points; (b) By Default, the 3D sculptures were gray; (c) Open mouth changed the colors of 3D sculptures.

"I didn't realize that I can take a photo by blinking my eyes. I need a response from the system to indicate this interaction." (a software developer)

"I felt awkward because I need to open my mouth to interact with the system. How can you immerse people by asking them to do this awkward behavior?" (a senior manager)

Fig. 5. Physical Setup

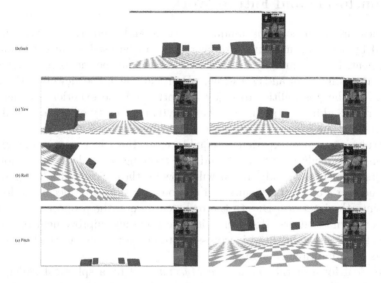

Fig. 6. A user's head orientation was tracked by a webcam and the real-time face tracking algorithm. A user changed viewpoints in the virtual museum by rotating her head. (a)Yaw: a head rotation to the left or to the right; (b)Roll: a downward or upward head rotation; (c)Pitch: a head tilt toward the shoulders.

Most participants loved the idea that there were no VR headsets but they also suggested reducing the size of the current motion-tracking device. Ideally, the tracking device should be light, wearable, and invisible. The size of the tracking device can be greatly reduced with a micro CPU and a tiny battery. In addition, we tried to remove all the sensors and measured a user's head orientation only by a webcam. We used the tracking data to change a user's viewpoints in the virtual museum (see Fig. 6). The system works well in most cases. However, the face tracker might lose track in complex background or poor light.

Some participants felt that "Moving" by both head orientation and foot movements broke the limitation of the space and made them feel immersed in the virtual museum. We also found that to avoid motion sickness, the amount of vertical head variation should be reduced and yaw behavior could be increased. These findings are consistent with Slater and Usoh's study [7].

"Changing the colors of virtual sculptures" by opening the mouth was effective for some participants. It made them feel that they were communicating with the virtual artworks. However, a few of the participants felt awkward about this interaction. The "eye blinking" interaction was not obvious and effective for most participants. It had been suggested to use a more accurate and smart sensory system and provide a response such as a flash or a sound to indicate this interaction. Finally, some participants suggested developing a storyline to make the experience more meaningful.

6   Conclusion and Future Work

A physical museum contains unique emotions and memories that cannot be replaced by a virtual museum. However, VR can be used as an extension and complement. People can stay in their own homes and see the exhibits remotely. This is more convenient and accessible. VR provides at-home viewers with perfect lighting, all the possibilities to enjoy artwork, and the experience of entering actual art. In addition, the interactive storytelling ability of VR can make the museum experience more appealing to the younger generation.

A truly immersive experience requires more than just convincing visuals. Replacing VR headsets with head and face tracking technologies, will not only free users from clunky headgear but will allow for the creation of VR experiences where the user's body movements and micro-expressions, can become fully integrated into the interface. Due to the technical limits, the proposed system still requires external sensors. However, with the accuracy improvement of the face and head tracking algorithms, it is possible to develop a human tracking system only based on multiple cameras.

The ideal form of the *Immersive Museum* will be a spherical gallery with a 360° video projection, a stereo system, and a multi-camera body tracking environment. Visitors can see the 3D replicas of the artworks all around them when they step inside. Under the default condition, the context of the video projection will evolve to show the chronological progression of artworks. The video projection can respond to the visitors' gestures, body movements, and subconscious facial reactions. For example, the visitor can choose, rotate and magnify an artwork by hand gestures. The visitor can hear a story about the artwork by stepping closer to it. Also, if the visitor becomes attracted by the current view (pupil dilations or a long-time staring), the system will automatically take a photo of what they are looking at.

References

1. Roussou, M.: High-end interactive media in the museum. In: ACM SIGGRAPH 99 Conference abstracts and applications (SIGGRAPH 1999), pp. 59–62. Association for Computing Machinery, New York (1999)

2. Lepouras, G., Katifori, A., Vassilakis, C., Charitos, D.: Real exhibitions in a virtual museum. J. Virtual Reality. **7**(2), 120–128 (2004)
3. Clini, P., Ruggeri, L., Angeloni, R., Sasso, M.: Interactive immersive virtual museum: Digital documentation for virtual interaction. Int. Arch. Photogrammetry Remote Sens. Spat. Inf. Sci. **XLII**(2), 251–257 (2018)
4. Huang, Y.-C., Han, S.R.: An immersive virtual reality museum via second life. In: Stephanidis, C. (ed.) HCI 2014. CCIS, vol. 434, pp. 579–584. Springer, Cham (2014). https://doi.org/10.1007/978-3-319-07857-1_102
5. Jung, T., tom Dieck, M.C., Lee, H., Chung, N.: Effects of virtual reality and augmented reality on visitor experiences in museum. In: Inversini, A., Schegg, R. (eds.) Information and Communication Technologies in Tourism 2016, pp. 621–635. Springer, Cham (2016). https://doi.org/10.1007/978-3-319-28231-2_45
6. Gulhan, D., Durant, S., Zanker, J.M.: Aesthetic judgments of 3D arts in virtual reality and online settings. J. Virtual Reality **27**, 573–589 (2022). https://doi.org/10.1007/s10055-022-00671-1. published online
7. Slater, M., Usoh, M.: Body centred interaction in immersive virtual environments. Artif. Life Virtual Reality **1**, 125–148 (1994)
8. Held, R.M., Hein, A.: Movement-produced stimulation in the development of visually guided behavior. J. Comp. Physiol. Psychol. **56**, 872–876 (1963)
9. Schuemie, M.J., Straaten, P.V., Krijn, M., Mast, C.V.: Research on presence in virtual reality: a survey. Cycberpsychol. Behav. **4**(2), 183–201 (2001)
10. Murphy-Chutorian, E., Trivedi, M.M.: Head pose estimation in computer vision: a survey. IEEE Trans. Pattern Anal. Mach. Intell. **31**(4), 607–626 (2009)
11. Neto, E.N.A., et al.: Real-time head pose estimation for mobile devices. In: Yin, H., Costa, J.A.F., Barreto, G. (eds.) IDEAL 2012. LNCS, vol. 7435, pp. 467–474. Springer, Heidelberg (2012). https://doi.org/10.1007/978-3-642-32639-4_57
12. Gavas, R.D., Karmakar, S., Chatterjee, D., Ramakrishnan, R.K., Pal, A.: Real-time eye blink detection using facial landmarks. In: 43rd Annual International Conference of the IEEE Engineering in Medicine and Biology Society (EMBC), pp. 4990–4993. Mexico (2021)
13. Zhu, T., et al.: Research on a real-time driver fatigue detection algorithm based on facial video sequences. Appl. Sci. **12**(4), 2224 (2022)
14. Unity Audio Source https://docs.unity3d.com/ScriptReference/AudioSource.html. Accessed 18 Jan 2023
15. MPU-6050. https://invensense.tdk.com/products/motion-tracking/6-axis/mpu-6050/. Accessed 18 Jan 2023
16. Unity Camera component. https://docs.unity3d.com/Manual/class-Camera.html. Accessed 18 Jan 2023
17. Selva, P., Morlier, J., Gourinat, Y.: Development of a dynamic virtual reality model of the inner ear sensory system as a learning and demonstrating tool. Model. Simul. Eng. **2009**(5), 1–10 (2009)
18. Ferrario, V.F., Sforza, C., Serrao, G., Grassi, G., Mossi, E.: Active range of motion of the head and cervical spine: a three-dimensional investigation in healthy young adults. J. Orthop. Res. **20**(1), 122–129 (2002)
19. FaceOSC Software. https://josephlyons.gitbook.io/face-control-digital-toolkit/tools/faceosc. Accessed 18 Jan 2023

A New Style of Meta-Cosmic Cultural Interaction: "Light Up" National Digital Museum

Jianing You[1](✉) and Gao Lin[2]

[1] College of Information and Electrical Engineering, China Agricultural University, Beijing,
China
yjn7777777@cau.edu.cn
[2] School of Public Administration, Guizhou University, Guiyang, China

Abstract. This paper analyzes the pain points faced by the museum industry today, interviews relevant museum exhibitors, and proposes the "Light Up"
national cloud museum app system, which is a practical tool for digital museum
construction that integrates the functions of theme creative design, collection collection and publicity, and space layout and exhibition, to create a thematic, diversified, and Thematic, diversified, flexible digital museum open platform. To build a
sustainable development system of digital museums with the important support of
cultural and museum experts, collection trading, museum community, etc. At the
same time, the study designs questionnaires based on usability testing, conducts
user research on the product, meanwhile, analyzes the operability, practicality,
and public acceptability of the product. The user usage of the APP is studied and
analyzed through questionnaires, user interviews, and user field tests to collect raw
data on user experience. It provides material support for the subsequent product
optimization and upgrading.

Keywords: Cloud museum · Human-computer interaction · Usability testing

1 Introduction

China has a long history with rich and profound traditional cultural resources. Since
the founding of the People's Republic of China, under the leadership of the Communist
Party of China, China has made remarkable achievements in economic social development and undergone profound changes [1–3]. In today's China, it is of great importance
and urgency to strengthen cultural construction, we also face a rare historical opportunity. Museums should play a greater role in preserving traditional values and inheriting
historical culture [4].

Since reform and opening up, the number of museums is increasing, the quality is
improving, and the functions of all aspects are constantly improving. It has played its
due role in cultural undertakings and social development. Museums are thriving and
prospering [5]. China has formed a museum system with national museums jointly built
by the central and local governments as the leading, national first, second and tertiary

P.-L. P. Rau (Ed.): HCII 2023, LNCS 14024, pp. 162–176, 2023.
https://doi.org/10.1007/978-3-031-35946-0_14

museums as the backbone, state-owned museums as the main body, and private museums as the supplement, to build a museum resource sharing platform that radiates to the whole country and faces the world [6]. Museums can be divided into comprehensive museums, archaeological museums, art museums, history museums, ethnic museums, etc. According to management classification, it can be divided into government museums, local museums, university museums, etc. [7]. At present, Chinese museums are mainly comprehensive museums and historical museums, accounting for 36.28% and 35.27% respectively. Details in Fig. 1.

Classification Method	Main Species
Classification by collection	Comprehensive Museum, Archaeological Museum, Art Museum, History Museum, Ethnographical Museum, Natural History Museum, Science Museum, Geological Museum, Industrial Museum, Military Museum, Museum of Intangible Heritage
Classification by management	Government Museum, Localized Museum, University Museum, Military Museum, Independent/ Charitable Foundation Museum, Enterprise Museum, Private Museum
By service area	National Museum, Regional Museum, Eco-Museum, City Museum, Localized Museum
Classification by audience	Comprehensive Museum, Educational Museum, Professional Museum
Classification by exhibition mode	Traditional Museum, Historic Structure Museum, Outdoor Museum, The Interactive Museum

Fig. 1. Museum Classification

At present, China has 767,000 immovable cultural relics [8], 56 World heritage sites, 5,058 key cultural relics under national protection [9], 36 national archaeological parks, and 137 national historical and cultural cities. The number of museums in our country is close to 5800. At the same time, there are more than 100 million pieces (sets) in the national collection of movable cultural relics. In 2019, museums nationwide held nearly 30,000 exhibitions and 335,000 educational events, receiving 1.227 billion visitors [10]. The "Internet Plus Chinese Civilization" action plan cultivates new business forms of cross-border financial platform, cloud exhibition, cloud education and cloud live broadcast continuously expand the radiation range of museum cultural services;From "National Treasures" [11] to "China Archaeology Conference" [12], from "I Built Cultural Relics in the Forbidden City" [13] to "If National Treasures Could Talk" [14], cultural relics are interacting with education, linking with science and technology, creativity and integrating, and constantly meeting the people's yearning for a better life.

In recent years, under the advocacy of the state, the society has gradually realized the importance of traditional culture, established intangible cultural heritage, and paid more and more attention to the protection and inheritance of traditional culture. As the form of traditional culture is relatively simple, and the current expression form of the network era is incompatible, the effect of traditional culture communication is not as expected. At the present stage, traditional culture mainly relies on physical objects and paper books, which requires the audience to enter a fixed cultural transmission place and a specific time to realize the cultural transmission function [15–17]. With the development of technology, people have higher requirements for information dissemination, and single media communication can no longer meet people's needs.

As early as 1998, the Palace Museum put forward the slogan of "Digital Palace Museum" and started the digital construction of the Palace Museum, which laid the foundation for the emergence and development of online exhibitions. In early 2020, the outbreak of the COVID-19 caused museums around the world to close. Since January 2020, the State Administration of Cultural Heritage has guided museums at all levels to actively expand online services for cultural relics. "Online exhibition" has become a landmark event for museums to creatively transform traditional exhibition methods in the era of "Internet +", and a new form of museum services in special times. Among them, 74.8 percent of museums have increased their digital content and online services. According to the official website of the State Administration of Cultural Heritage, more than 1,300 museums across China launched more than 2,000 online exhibitions during the Spring Festival in 2020, attracting more than 5 billion visitors. Since then, the online exhibition has officially entered the public's vision [18].

During the epidemic, online exhibitions, online classes, live interaction and other activities in museums around the country have appeared one after another [19]. In a way to break the isolation of the epidemic, the public's huge demand for "online services" in the culture and museum industry has been met, indicating the infinite possibilities of a new model of digital cultural services in the future. In this context, more and more museums are actively seeking new breakthroughs and improvements in value orientation. While providing high-quality cultural supplies, museums are opening their collection resources for the whole society to share, and innovative participatory and interactive learning experience projects are launched.

The museum in the future is not only the main space to display cultural relics, but also the cultural field to spread culture and improve the level of public culture and aesthetic education [20]. How to use digital technology to form a larger scope and more three-dimensional cultural promotion, tell good museum stories, attract more public attention to museum culture, maximize the social sharing of excellent cultural resources, will be the goal and vision of the future museum digital development.

In this context, based on the user-centered design, this project focuses on how to better develop the "online museum" and its supporting system, in order to supplement the lack of similar products in the market.

2 Methodology

This study follows the user-centered design steps to explore the possibility of developing an "online museum" and its supporting system. The specific steps of the research are shown in the Fig. 1: (1) Conduct interviews with museum enthusiasts to understand the public's attitude towards the digital transformation and upgrading of museums, put forward effective solutions and possible future development directions according to the answers of volunteers participating in the interviews. (2) Based on the interview results, we propose to build a multi-cultural gathering platform as wechat mini program, taking the step of all-round digital transformation and upgrading of museums in the digital era. (3) User tests are then conducted to investigate the feasibility of the information system.

3 Interview

This study mainly adopts a user-centered design and proposes a more effective system to solve the problems faced by the digital transformation and upgrading of China's offline museums to a certain extent. Through interviews with museum exhibition enthusiasts, the paper investigates the ways people acquire knowledge in daily life, the problems existing in offline museums, the necessity of online museums and the generally acceptable curatorial forms. The sample size of the interview is determined by the BJHP rule, which states that a sample of eight participants is suitable for exploratory research with a focus on identifying underlying ideas about the topic. In this study, eight exhibition enthusiasts participated in the interview.

The purpose of the interviews with the participants was to investigate the ways in which people acquire historical knowledge and the current situation of offline museums. In addition, the design of existing online museums, the influence of online museums on people's visits to offline museums, and the attitude towards further optimization of online museum system are also investigated. The interview questions were based on previous relevant research and reviewed by a panel of experts. Prior to conducting interviews, a preliminary study was conducted to refine the questions. This paper mainly examines the following research questions:

(1) What the concern and understanding of the existing digital museums?
(2) What do you think of the current status and deficiencies of offline museums?
(3) How about the influence of online digital museum on participation intention and behavior?

Interview questionnaires were posted on social media, and pedestrians interested in the topic could sign up for interviews.In total, eight volunteers participated in the interviews. Participants included students, office workers, parents, the elderly and children. All interviews were conducted in the Usability Lab and lasted approximately 1 h. Interviews with different participants were conducted separately.Participants came to the usability lab separately at the assigned times. Two staff members participated in the interviews: one conducted each interview and the other recorded it. Every interview was recorded and transcribed verbatim.

The volunteers' answers were divided into three parts: museum participation experience, the dissemination of Chinese cultural values and the necessity of multi-dimensional transformation in the digital age.

As for museum participation experience, every volunteer has visited offline museums (8/8), and some have visited online museums (3/8). They decide whether to visit an exhibition or not based on the number of visitors to the museum. Those who have no online exhibition experience will pay more attention to the exhibition form and scale of offline museums (2/8). In addition, except for one volunteer who was not yet an adult, all the other volunteers had the habit of using mobile phones in daily life (7/8). Although the current curatorial method of digital museum exhibition is not popular and needs to be developed, most people are still very interested in the concept of online museum. At the same time, most of the volunteers have the habit of watching pictures, texts and short videos on their mobile phones (6/8). Most of them think this is a way to relax and relax in daily life. Regarding the attitude towards visiting museums, all respondents (8/8) agree that visiting museums can enable people to have a deeper understanding of the displayed collections and the history related to the collections in a certain extent.However, most people think (5/8) after watching the offline pavilion due to lack of communication, the common interests of people get knowledge and can't absorb well.

As for the dissemination of Chinese cultural values, most of the volunteers believed that the current traditional offline museum form could not carry Chinese culture well. Some volunteers (2/8) thought that the organizational system of museums should strengthen the scientific interpretation and interpretation of the value of Chinese cultural relics, build a world window for the international expression of Chinese cultural relics. In addition, some people mentioned (4/8) that during the epidemic, online exhibitions, online classes, live interaction and other activities in museums around the country have appeared one after another. In a way to break the isolation of the epidemic, they have met the huge demand of the public for "online services" in the cultural industry, indicating the infinite possibilities of new models of digital cultural services in the future. In this context, more and more museums are actively seeking new breakthroughs and improvements in value orientation. While providing high-quality cultural supplies, museums are opening their collection resources for the whole society to share, and innovative participatory and interactive learning experience projects are launched.

As for the necessity of multi-dimensional transformation and upgrading of museums in the digital era, all volunteers (8/8) believed that transformation and upgrading of digital museums is the top priority of future museum reform. Some volunteers mentioned (5/8) that with the continuous progress of science and technology, the digital construction of museums faces huge public demand for "online services".

To sum up, the vast majority of volunteers believe that there are some problems in offline museums at present, and museum digitization is the trend of future development. Developing the cultural industry and enhancing the soft power of culture is an inevitable requirement for building a strong cultural country. It will also add strong impetus to economic development and open up broader space. In particular, museums can play an irreplaceable role in creating local cultural identifications, promoting the integrated development of culture and tourism, and promoting Chinese culture to go global. The digital transformation of museums is imminent.

4   Design of "Light Up" National Digital Museum

According to the interview results, it can be found that currently traditional museums are faced with a series of problems, such as single collection form, few contacts between exhibition participants, difficulties for individual collectors to build museums, and many collections with display value can only be stored in ashes. In the past few years, due to the impact of the epidemic, previous activities in the physical space of the museum were forced to stop, and the Internet has become an important link between the museum and the audience. During this period, many large museums have innovated cultural display methods, expanded communication channels through cooperation with new media platforms, aroused active participation of the public, and achieved good social response.

Unlike the existing online museums, our collections are not limited to physical objects, but can also be in the form of sound, video and pictures that can carry and express memories, so that people can display and share their collections, their common life memories, cultural resonance, and the same interests through thematic pavilions. The theme pavilion is a collection of people's collections, their common memories, their cultural feelings and interests. At the same time, according to the interview and practice results, the development plan of the small program form in the next ten years is speculated, as shown in Fig. 2.

Fig. 2. The Development Vision of the Program

"The project insists on the integration of "culture + technology" and independent innovation, system integration and application, relying on mobile Internet, Internet of things, big data, cloud computing, 5G, artificial intelligence, regional chain and other new generation Information technology, focus on individualized, small and medium-sized social museums and comprehensive museum exhibitions, in-depth research and development of the theme of creative design, collection collection publicity, space layout exhibition and other functions in one digital museum construction practical tools, to create thematic, diversified, flexible digital museum open platform, to build a digital museum expert library, collection trading, museum community as an important support. The "Light Up" program is a practical tool for digital museum construction. The main design functions of the "Light Up" program are shown below.

After users enter the system, the platform guides users through four entrances: "Building museums", "Visiting museums", "Cultural and museum expert pool" and

"Museum community". Users can access different functional areas according to their personal or corporate needs.

4.1 Building Museums

Individual or corporate users are required to register and submit information on the platform (individual users can authenticate by swiping their faces and scanning their ID cards, while corporations are required to submit copies of relevant business licenses for authentication), and accounts that have been approved by the backend can upload collections and create new museums. After the user uploads the collection successfully, the system will classify the collection and send it to the cultural and museum experts for review, and the final approved collection and museum will be displayed in the front-end. Through the "New Museum" portal, individual and corporate users can create personalized private museums and digitally share and exhibit their existing collections.

4.2 Visiting Museums

Users who choose this portal can browse the system has been shared collections and carry out cloud viewing exhibitions, browse through graphics, audio, video and VR panoramas and other browsing options classification, and have the right to comment, praise, report and other interactive rights. Realize the docking of collections and visiting users, benchmarking digital Forbidden City, digital cultural and creative products and blockchain technology, etc., for the dissemination of commercial value.

4.3 Cultural and Museum Expert Pool

Culture should dominate the integration of culture and technology. The library of cultural and museum experts is mainly through user applications and company hiring, inviting scholars in the society who have relevant research on planning and building museums to register as experts, and providing detailed introduction to the cultural and museum experts who are in the library. The members of the cultural and museum expert pool review the collections or new museums uploaded by users, propose modifications and rejections for collections and museums that do not pass, present the front-end for collections and pavilions that pass, and automatically generate thematic museums.

4.4 Museum Community

The museum community provides an interactive platform for users, with boards including Community Affairs, Blockchain Planet, BoG, Talking about the World, etc. The community is divided into visitor and user access, with both visitors and users browsing posts within it by selecting different boards. Users can accumulate points, activity and levels after logging in to gain more community power lines. As the user's reputation rises, he or she can apply to become an administrator. Users with administrator rights can manage posts, users and boards in the community, improve community services and optimize the user experience.

The initial version of the project demo is shown in the Fig. 3. The project has been implemented in the field of agricultural cultural heritage and red cultural heritage museums on a pilot basis, effectively verifying the practical functions and business operation mode of the "Light Up" digital museum software system for all people; on this basis, the next step will be to embed it into the public cultural service system of the cultural and museum industry in a high standing, deep and flexible manner, and promote its application in a wider scope and more industries to fulfill the vision and mission of our team based on the new era, helping to cultivate a new mode of digital cultural production and dissemination, empowering the public to have a new cultural life experience, telling the Chinese story vividly and enhancing the national cultural soft power.

Fig. 3. Program Interface

5 User Tests

5.1 Purpose of the Study

We invited 8 users to conduct usability research for the "Light Up" national digital museum App. We allowed the users to experience the product in real cell phone environment and conducting in-depth interviews after the usability test to obtain more detailed user experience and compile a product experience report to provide feasible solutions for subsequent prototype design and usability evaluation research [21].

5.2 Research Process

Study Subjects. Eight subjects were randomly selected for this study, and the specific information is shown in the Table 1 below.

Table 1. Subjects' basic information

NO.	Gender	Age	Education	Occupation
1	male	20	undergraduate	student
2	female	21	undergraduate	student
3	male	24	master	student
4	female	27	high school	employees of state-owned enterprises
5	male	45	junior high school	freelancer
6	female	43	high school	teacher
7	male	65	primary school	freelancer
8	female	35	primary school	civil service

Experimental Procedure. The usability test is divided into task tests and post-test interviews. The task test is divided into a total of 9 tasks to be completed, which are as follows:

(1) Download and register an account, change password, fill in personal information, etc.
(2) Browse each interface of the app, and use each function, view system messages, etc.
(3) Browse existing museums and visit collections.
(4) Create a new theme museum, upload materials (pictures) and improve information.
(5) Create a new gallery in the personal museum, upload materials (pictures) and improve information.

After the tasks are completed, the users' task performance is analyzed, and the degree of satisfaction with the completion of the tasks is scored from 1 to 5, indicating 1 - very dissatisfied, 2 - relatively dissatisfied, 3 - average, 4 - relatively satisfied, and 5 - very satisfied, respectively. The higher the average score of the subjects' completion of each task, the more the task can be completed successfully and the higher the satisfaction of the users.

After completing each task, subjects are interviewed about the "Light Up" national digital museum App.

The process tasks are as follows in Fig. 4:

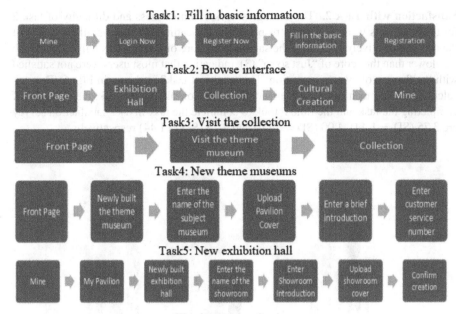

Fig. 4. Process of tasks

5.3 Research Results

Satisfaction with Task 1. The average satisfaction score of 8 subjects for the smoothness, difficulty and time spent on task 1 is above 4.5, which is higher than the score of "relatively satisfied" (4) and close to the score of "very satisfied" (5), indicating that the app is more perfect and the user satisfaction is higher. The results of task1 is shown in Fig. 5. Through calculation, the mean values of the smoothness of completing the task, the difficulty of completing the task and the time it took to complete the task in user satisfaction survey are 4.63 (SD = 0.23), 4.50 (SD = 1.00) and 4.50 (SD = 0.50) respectively.

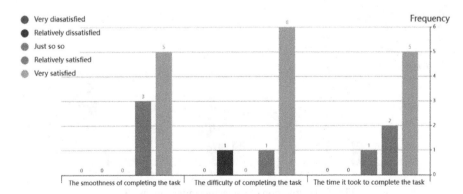

Fig. 5. Distribution of subjective ratings in task 1

Satisfaction with Task 2. The average scores of smoothness and difficulty of task 2 for the 8 subjects were 3.75 and 4 respectively, indicating that the overall page flow of the app was relatively good. But the satisfaction score of fluency was only 2.75, which was lower than the score of "Just so so" (3), indicating that most users were not satisfied with the fluency of system operation. The results of task2 is shown in Fig. 6. Through calculation, the mean values of the smoothness of completing the task, the difficulty of completing the task and the time it took to complete the task in user satisfaction survey are 3.75 (SD = 1.44), 4.00 (SD = 1.00) and 2.75 (SD = 1.44) respectively.

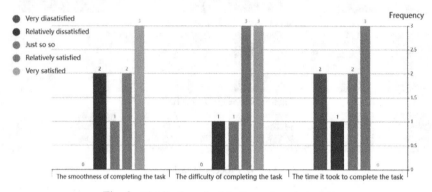

Fig. 6. Distribution of subjective ratings in task 2

Satisfaction with Task 3. The average satisfaction scores of 8 subjects for the smoothness, difficulty and time spent in completing task 3 were above 3.5, indicating that users had a high degree of completion of "visiting the collection" on the app. The results of task3 is shown in Fig. 7. Through calculation, the mean values of the smoothness of completing the task, the difficulty of completing the task and the time it took to complete the task in user satisfaction survey are 3.88 (SD = 0.61), 4.00 (SD = 1.00) and 4.25 (SD = 0.44) respectively.

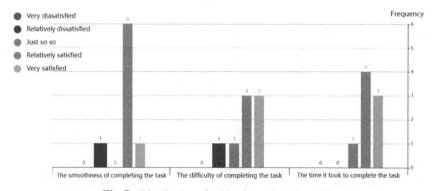

Fig. 7. Distribution of subjective ratings in task 3

Satisfaction with Task 4. The average satisfaction scores of the 8 subjects with the smoothness, difficulty, and time spent on Task 4 ranged from 3 to 3.5, i.e., which is between "Just so so" (3) and "quite satisfied" (4) and close to the average score of "Just so so" (3) indicates that users are not satisfied with the operation of "Create a new theme museum". The results of task4 is shown in Fig. 8. Through calculation, the mean values of the smoothness of completing the task, the difficulty of completing the task and the time it took to complete the task in user satisfaction survey are 3.25 (SD = 1.94), 3.38 (SD = 1.98) and 3.50 (SD = 1.75) respectively.

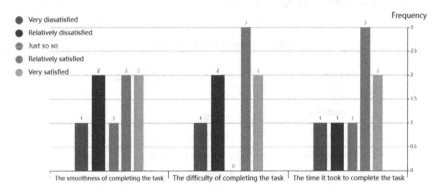

Fig. 8. Distribution of subjective ratings in task 4

Satisfaction with Task 5. The average satisfaction scores of 8 subjects for the smoothness, difficulty and time spent on task 5 ranged from 3 to 3.5, i.e. between "Just so so" (3) and "quite satisfied" (4), close to "The average satisfaction score for the smoothness of completing task 5 is only 3, which indicates that the operation of "New Showroom" is not smooth and the users are not very satisfied. The results of task5 is shown in Fig. 9. Through calculation, the mean values of the smoothness of completing the task, the difficulty of completing the task and the time it took to complete the task in user satisfaction survey are 3.00 (SD = 1.88), 3.25 (SD = 1.94) and 3.50 (SD = 2.25) respectively.

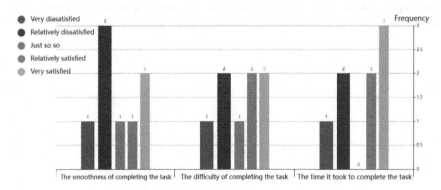

Fig. 9. Distribution of subjective ratings in task 5

5.4 In-Depth Interview Data

Overall Evaluation of the Product. In the in-depth interview, 5 out of 8 users indicated that the overall operation of the APP didn't run smoothly. For the overall page color, the majority of users said that the APP's page design was suitable for the style of the theme museum. While a few users said that the APP's page was monotonous and they hoped to customize the theme of the museum. For the practicality of the functions, 5 subjects thought that the functions were practical, while 3 subjects thought that the APP's functions were general and not innovative, and there were no novel functions to distinguish it from similar APPs (Table 2).

Table 2. Overall user evaluation

Question	Result	Frequency
overall smoothness of operation	satisfaction	1
	general	2
	dissatisfaction	5
page color design	satisfaction	6
	general	1
	monotony	1
functionality and usefulness	practicality	5
	general	3

Product Improvement Suggestions. From the interview results, it can be seen that although the majority of users are satisfied with the product, the APP still has problems such as the operating system is not smooth, the function keys are not properly positioned, and the functions are monotonous. The improvement suggestions made by users are as follows:

Improve page fluency, enrich page color, adjust function icon position, enrich theme museum type, enrich cultural and creative products, increase innovative functions, etc (Table 3).

Table 3. User Suggestion

Problems	Frequency
Improve page fluency	4
Adjust the position of function keys	2
Set showroom type	2
Enrich the color design of the page	3
Add different functions	1
Enrich cultural and creative products	3

6 Conclusion

Through interviews and questionnaires, we believe that the design of "Light Up" is practicable and actionable based on the following advantages.

Supported by Novel Architecture Design Concept. The vast majority of people believe that the current offline museums have certain problems, and the digitalization of museums is the trend of future development. The development of cultural industries and the improvement of cultural soft power are inevitable requirements for building a strong cultural country, and will also add a strong impetus to economic development and open up a wider space.

Powerful Series of Practical Functions Support. It's no longer a dream for everyone to have their own museum.

Human-Centered Human-Computer Interaction System. Our products are based on user interviews to design ideas and concepts, we further conduct a thorough product usability test to determine that the product can be put into practice.

References

1. Zhu, K.: Summary of symposium on Chinese excellent traditional culture and enhancing the party's "four self" ability. In: China Practical Studies Association Conference. China Practical Studies Society Conference Summary Compilation (2019)
2. Zhang, Y.: Research on the feelings of home and Country in Chinese excellent traditional culture. Jilin Agricultural University (2022)
3. Gao, D., Li, D.: Inheritance of excellent traditional culture and improvement of moral education effect – comments on Chinese traditional culture. Lang. Plann. **502**(22), 86–88 (2022)
4. Huang, Z.: On the role of museums in the protection of intangible cultural heritage – a case study of Qiandongnan ethnic museum. J. Kaili Univ. **30**(04), 182–184 (2013)
5. Chen, G.: Reflection on museum definition from the social function of museums in the 21st century. Museum **6**(06), 20–26 (2017)
6. Li, F., Gu, Z.: The industry characteristic and development trend of the new industry form of Chinese museum culture. J. Shandong Univ. (Philos. Soc. Sci.) **250**(01), 96–106(2022)

7. Gong, Y., Gao, H., Huang, Y., Pan, Y.: Discussion on the classification basis of museum types and the construction of classification standard system. Chin. Museum **149**(02), 36–42 (2022)

8. Shuren, H.: A study on the trends of conservation and management of museum relics. Inside Outside Lantai **371**(26), 61–63 (2022)

9. Zha, Y.: On the protection and management of immovable cultural relics. Daqing Soc. Sci. **233**(04), 61–63 (2022)

10. Wang, J.: The number of key cultural relics under protection increased by 115 percent over the past 10 years. In: People's Daily, no. 001 (2022)

11. Yin, X., Zhang, S.: The collision and fusion of excellent traditional culture and TV variety show – the innovation strategy of national treasure. Press **2022**(15), 106–107 (2022)

12. Pan, Y.: Visual construction and expression of cultural symbols in cultural and museological programs – a case study of Chinese archaeology conference. Chin. Radio TV Acad. J. **372**(03), 72–74 (2022)

13. Liu, B.: I repair cultural relics in the Forbidden City: a new form of documentary development in the context of internet. Chin. Radio TV Acad. J. **365**(08), 77–79 (2021)

14. Sun, Y.: Micro documentary communication of material cultural heritage in the new media environment – taking the first season of if national treasure could talk as an example. J. News Res. **10**(18), 9–10 (2019)

15. Ren, X.: On the significance and path of the protection of ancient architectural relics. Ident. Appreciation Cult. Relics **234**(15), 52–55 (2022)

16. Jinlin, F.: Thoughts on the protection of immovable cultural relics in Changting county museum. Ident. Appreciation Cult. Relics **240**(21), 47–50 (2022)

17. Liao, J.: Research on cultural relics protection under the background of rural revitalization – a case study of cultural relics in Gutian county. Ident. Appreciation Cult. Relics **225**(06), 150–152 (2022)

18. Yongzhe, Y.: Research on the development of Chinese digital Museum based on the perspective of globalization communication and cultural relic protection. Ident. Appreciation Cult. Relics **235**(16), 92–95 (2022)

19. Zeng, H.: Research on digital technology in Museum heritage protection. Cult. Ind. **243**(26), 112–114 (2022)

20. Zhiyong, W.: Looking into the future museum – thinking based on the operation practice of media museum. Media **377**(12), 19–21 (2022)

21. Tan, M.: Usability study of psychological service app. Zhejiang Sci-tech University (2021)

The Aesthetic Education of Traditional Chinese Mending Embroidery Technology in the Spread of Costume Culture

Hongwei Zhang[1,3](✉) and Jing Wang[1,2](✉)

[1] Beijing Technology Institute, Zhuhai, People's Republic of China
254783914@qq.com, 9155666@qq.com
[2] Studying School for Doctor's Degree, Bangkok Thonburi University, Bangkok, Thailand
[3] Institute of Innovation Design for Well-Being, Zhuhai City 519088,
People's Republic of China

Abstract. Because of the different geographical and cultural environment, the traditional Chinese mending embroidery craft is called silk embroidery, needle embroidery, silk embroidery, silk embroidery, cloth embroidery, etc. Modern commonly known as silk brocade. The palace repair embroidery is "based on mending and supplemented by embroidery". Throughout the history of human existence and development, various products and their functions are constantly changing due to the development of human physiological and psychological needs. Apparent embroidery was one of the traditional handicrafts that appeared in response to the needs of the imperial court and was handed down from generation to generation. To understand and master it, while inheriting and protecting it, we can introduce this materialized crystallization and humanistic idea into the aesthetic education of individual person, man and man, man and society, man and humanity under the modern thinking system, so as to understand ourselves and discover human's demand for truth. Goodness and beauty exist between good life and materialization, and the carrier is the internal force that promotes the orderly progress of society. As an intangible cultural heritage, its historical development is a continuation of China's 5,000 years of incense. Every stitch and thread can let the Chinese people feel the temperature of history, like a strong pulse of China's vitality. It is also an aesthetic education function of traditional skills in modern design and production life.

The writing of this paper is based on the comprehensive research method, through the essence of the traditional Chinese mending embroidery craft to reflect the correlation between various disciplines to state the development law and characteristics of things, mainly through works and literature, thinking and practice to raise questions, analysis and summary. It covers the research, investigation and visit of the regional, social production or research and development institutions involved in the traditional Chinese mending embroidery process in the early work, in order to obtain the relevant knowledge elements for paper writing and design creation, including the Beijing Institute of Yarn drawing and the Chaoshan region of China workshop. In addition, it also includes the collection, sorting and classification of materials related to the knowledge of Chinese traditional mending embroidery craft. Through systematic sorting, it is more intuitive to describe the influence of cultural origins and folk customs related to mending embroidery on

P.-L. P. Rau (Ed.): HCII 2023, LNCS 14024, pp. 177–185, 2023.
https://doi.org/10.1007/978-3-031-35946-0_15

people and things in the growth process. While sorting out and constructing the framework of this paper, it also considers whether the application of modern technology can be effectively grafted on the basis of the traditional aesthetic education creation of menshu embroidery, which may involve the traditional experimental methods of aesthetic education, such as material replacement, process promotion, style conversion and subject matter dabbling. In the conclusion part, it discusses the relationship between traditional Chinese mending embroidery and aesthetic education on the basis of theoretical maturity and social practice. At the level of creation, we need to pay attention to social hot topics and keep pace with The Times of modern creative thinking, to promote a value concept and survival criteria.

Keywords: Aesthetic Educatio · Chinese mending embroidery technology · spread of costume culture

1 Research Background of Mending Embroidery

1.1 Concept of Mending Embroidery

In the Southern and Northern Dynasties of ancient China more than a thousand years ago, the rudiments of mending embroidery, often called pick mending embroidery, developed in the Tang Dynasty and formed a unique handicraft called "pasting silk" and "making satin". Silk paste is a single layer of silk fabric cut into patterns flat paste, pile of silk or other silk fabric cut and stacked, to form a multi-level pattern. The poet Wen Tingyun of the late Tang Dynasty once described in his poems, "New embroidered Luo Ju, both golden partridges." He described putting on a popular silk short jacket and satin skirt jacket with a pair of golden partridges in a good pattern of gold thread, which was called "gilding." The most popular and mature period of this craft was the Qing Dynasty. To this day, robes, coats, chair cushions and purses made of this craft are still collected in the Imperial Palace. Broadly speaking, "mending embroidery" is an ancient Chinese embroidery technique. From a separate point of view, the technology of easy mending embroidery decorates the five-color thread and silk cloth piece on the bottom cloth (silk silk). Combined with the techniques of "making satin" and "pasting silk" in the Tang Dynasty, it developed into today's "court mending embroidery".

1.2 Sources and Causes

To study mending embroidery, we have to understand the splendid needlework culture of China. It is a great progress in human civilization that we have grown silkworms, grown cotton, spun yarn and woven cloth, and gone from threading a needle to sewing clothes. In the five thousand years of Chinese civilization, textile, clothing and needlework are closely related, difficult to separate. During the development of agricultural society in ancient China for more than three thousand years, women learned to draw flowers and embroider, spin yarn and weave cloth, cut clothes and sew at an early age, especially in the Jiangnan area. The "gong" among female workers is "female red", also known as the "gong of women". In the volume of the Book of Kao Gong, "the treatment of silk and hemp is called" Gong of women ", which refers to women's needlework and other work, which is regarded as the externalization of women's virtues, virtuous conduct and cultivation of knowledge. It is one of the four virtues of "appearance, speech, Gong and virtue" [1]. of ancient Chinese women. As one of the skills, mending embroidery also gradually matured and developed along with this flood. The traditional concepts of governance and development in ancient China created an environment that emphasized agriculture and oppressed commerce. As a scarce social resource, textile symbolized the attraction of social status and wealth level that was hard to resist at that time. In ancient China, the traditional women who were good at thrift would not waste the scraps of clothing. They were intelligent and could always find and create the beauty around them, clarify the practical functions of production and life, and make the best use of the household. Inadvertently, they in the cold lonely boudoir, with the visual aesthetic and functional aesthetic clothing gradually dissolve these production and life "fragments".

1.3   Aesthetic Education Status of Mending Embroidery

The application of raw materials in the creation of traditional Chinese mending embroidery is full of creativity and originality. Silk, satin, silk, tail yarn, cotton, etc. The final formation of the process is mainly due to the rich techniques. On the basis of the fabric, various techniques such as relief, weaving, embroidery, stitching, pile paste and drawing are combined. After years of research and practice, the development has broken the standard and limitation of traditional layering materials and techniques, and created a variety of new techniques such as painting. There are realistic patterns, deformation patterns, abstract patterns, freehand patterns and so on. In structure, it is mainly manifested as single pattern, corner pattern, suitable pattern, edge pattern, continuous pattern, etc. Its subject matter content is much more than the courage of the predecessors, such as plant pattern, animal pattern, figure pattern, landscape pattern, object pattern, text pattern, natural phenomenon pattern, geometric pattern and by a variety of themes combination or composite pattern. Among the themes and patterns it focuses on, the aesthetic education it involves involves the objective phenomenon and practical significance reflected by the ethics of Chinese traditional culture and the survival and development of society. Use a three-dimensional perspective to interpret the story and content behind a symbol. In a sense, it is part of the general linguistics, which will promote the study of the traditional embroidery more comprehensive, because the symbol itself has the function of language, which determines that the allegorical design of traditional Chinese patterns and patterns can not only speak, but also its words are worth thinking and self-examination.

2   The Content and Significance of Mending Embroidery in Modern Costume Aesthetic Education

The three-dimensional effect of traditional Chinese mending embroidery is very consistent with the relevant themes of contemporary fashion design, which is mainly reflected in the three-dimensional processing of vision and touch. Mending embroidery breaks through the limitation of two dimensions, and fabrics are not processed by any physical or chemical methods, making it possible to be three-dimensional. The popular 3D printing technology strengthens people's cognition of 3D products. Besides the avant-garde

3D effect, it will give people a brand new visual experience through the implantation of traditional elements and popular elements. Today's science and technology is enough to support the further improvement of the technological level, whether in the selection of materials or expression techniques, and the expression of style can also present diversified forms and contents. With the improvement of people's material level, the pursuit of beauty and the demand for taste are increasing day by day. From the perspective of technological inheritance and cultural edification, its educational significance involves the following aspects:

2.1 Entertainment Aspect of Life

In recent years, more and more folk custom Tours have been incorporated into the content of characteristic tourism, which first drives the recovery of regional folk culture. At the same time, exquisite and exotic folk culture has also sprung up like bamboo shoots in major cities in China, which is worthy of affirmation. Different cultures are rooted in the same region, which can well prove the third point below. Cultural diversity is quite necessary for the healthy demand and development of large cities. People from different regions, nationalities and beliefs under the same roof can greatly enrich their spare time life and form a good cultural atmosphere. The gradual and sound development after it takes root will also contribute to the mutual understanding and trust between people and between people and society, as well as greater tolerance and support. This will make the development planning of any country or city truly "tolerant and big".

2.2 It is Possible to Expand Employment

With regard to employment, we have to talk about the vanishing demographic dividend. A simple interpretation is that the income of working-age people is greater than the expenditure of retirees, and more and more young people are unemployed or idle, which is not conducive to social stability, unity, prosperity and stability. In the aging society is becoming more and more serious to form a problem, the rise of traditional handicraft such as mending embroidery is helpful to revitalize the development of traditional culture. Through this method of word and example, word of mouth can gradually expand the team of traditional craftsmen. Strictly speaking, it is not limited by age, but also need to be able to endure patience, calm down the heart of the "sunset red" to raise some young people, with the people who love it to carry the flag, this is one. Under the premise that the traditional craft such as mending embroidery can be integrated into people's social life and entertainment needs, it helps to the prosperity of regional handicraft industry. If a highly distinctive cultural and creative industry can be formed, it is not impossible to find new employment for those laid-off workers, retired people, unemployed people and unemployed people.

2.3 Reflect Cultural Diversity

People's education and rich social life have given rise to cultural diversity and changeability, and more choices means more space. The rapid development of communication and transportation has given people from different regions, countries and nationalities more time to communicate. P. Feyerabend, a famous contemporary American philosopher of science, explains the creation process of modern design in a way that can be understood in any way. Throughout the modern history of the world, the arrival of the industrial revolution has almost destroyed the living conditions of small commodity economy and traditional craftsmen. Industry represents machinery, law, uniformity and mass reproduction. While people enjoy the pleasure brought by cheap industrial products, more and more people are aware of the "ambiguity" of the loss of traditional culture. Literati try to transform the material culture needs into a "system" and "theory" that can be carried forward and developed to continue to guide the progress and survival of human society. In order to meet the growing material and cultural needs, people discuss new perspectives and concepts of artistic expression forms. And how the field of design can break through the traditional "box" and clarify what can and cannot be changed by liberating the creative process! The Peacock Revolution of the 1960s by fashion designer Hardy Ames about the diversity of men's wear also speaks to these issues. The development needs of the whole and the individual, the following and the individuality presented by the cultural diversity are unavoidable problems. Otherwise, with the rapid development of science and modern industrial technology, it is highly possible that humans will prove the existence of the uniform army of machines in Hollywood blockbusters such as Star Wars and I, Robot.

2.4 Education that Benefits People

The saying that diligence and frugality is the traditional virtue of the Chinese nation can be seen in most public Spaces of various cities in China. What kind of spirit and artistic conception is the complement character in the "complementing with complementing" feature mentioned in the article? It can turn waste into treasure, turn stone into gold, be pragmatic and honest, manage the family in a prudent way, be skilled in nature and make the icing on the cake. All these are the spirit passed down by our ancestors through materialization, which is also the educational significance for any nation or country to cherish the inheritance and development of traditional culture. Perhaps the skills may be lost. Even more precious is its language. A person's growth must have self-esteem, self-love, self-confidence, self-reliance, self-improvement these five characteristics, and the cultivation of culture and knowledge accumulation throughout. Without these, how can cohesion be achieved? How can you be patriotic? Where are feelings and thoughts? Therefore, the development of society and the progress of human civilization need not only strong people, but also "healthy" people.

3   Cases of Aesthetic Education

3.1   Significance of DIY Creative Study and Aesthetic Field

In recent years, more and more educational training institutions and cultural dissemination institutions have sprung up in cities and towns all over the world. Under the fast pace of modern people always take some time in their busy work to learn the traditional culture of various countries and feel the influence and perception of various cultural fields. DIY creative study is a very important part of it. Among many traditional Chinese embroidery crafts, methods, elements, styles and DIY creative study institutions can be found everywhere. For example, China Central Television, Chinese local satellite TV (documentary, archives, national treasure archives, Lecture room, etc.) treasure promotion, China's traditional embroidery study studio in Beijing Haidian District (Chinese Traditional embroidery Research Institute, Chinese Traditional embroidery skills training, Chinese traditional embroidery culture inheritors), a group of national arts and crafts masters in order to greatly promote traditional culture, We have successively held seminars on silk embroidery technology in Beijing University for the Aged, Beijing University for the Aged of Chinese Academy of Sciences, Beijing Railway University for the Aged, and General Logistics Department for the Aged, etc. The training course "High Finishing Hand Making and Flower Making" of Beijing Left Side Culture Communication Co., LTD. (Left Side Training Organization) will include the study and creation of traditional Chinese touch embroidery. Institutions such as Beijing Nanyi First-line Culture Communication Co., LTD., Beijing Wild Culture Communication Co., LTD., etc., also set up corresponding courses related to fabric transformation, study and creation, traditional embroidery craft and so on. In China's community life, such as universities for the elderly, community classes, community activities and other relevant city, district and county governments are also vigorously promoting traditional culture, actively carrying out offline classes and creative practices of traditional Chinese crafts, which not only greatly enrich people's material life, but also further enrich people's spiritual world. In addition to improving the quality of life and taste, in the process of continuous learning, communication and creation in this kind of institution based on community and small class, modern aesthetic education is constantly enriched at all levels from school-age education to social education, which is the cause of continuous inheritance and development of traditional culture. The more severe the regional restrictions of traditional culture on humanity, geography and environment are. The more it shows that traditional culture is one of the indispensable nutrients for modern aesthetic education.

3.2 The Significance of the Field of Professional Events

In the process of modern design education and aesthetic cognition, the field of aesthetic education has always been the top priority in the teaching practice of higher education departments all over the world. Learning to observe and understand life, and then obtaining better intuitive experience, at the same time by more appropriate perception, is one of the prerequisite elements of good design, but also a key link to carry out aesthetic education. In the field of design, there are a large number of professional-related competitions around the world every year, which provide a good platform for young designers to create and display. At the same time, it also continuously promotes young people from different regions, different age groups, different social roles, different cultural backgrounds and growing environments to learn from each other, communicate and compete. At the same time, The introduction of professional competitions is also a kind of examination and self-examination of the teaching achievements in the field of modern design education, so that more and more young people understand that the significance of aesthetic education is extensive and profound. Compared with modern aesthetic education, traditional craft itself is not a kind of vague and superficial, but has good content support, cultural continuation and formal expression. Life perception and other aspects, rather than a simple appearance design or a kind of inherited skills or methods to learn and digest, because it carries the experience and precious crystallization that human beings have accumulated and improved in the process of production and life for years and years, contains not only physical needs, but also spiritual sustains. It not only contains a certain way of life, but also represents a certain concept and thought of holding on to things.

3.3 Significance of Commercial Design and Application Field

The methods, elements, styles and ideas of traditional crafts are a very comprehensive and extensive existence in the modern market environment. The products of Chinese traditional repair embroidery process can also frequently appear in many product systems, mainly used in the garment industry and enterprises, clothing companies, home textile enterprises, transport vehicles (automobiles, ships, aircraft, trains, etc.) interior decoration manufacturers, clothing accessories (luggage, bags, shoes) enterprises and other fields. Some of its products in the process, elements, style, concept are involved in the repair embroidery technology related level, in the process of discussing the purpose and significance of this part, or to briefly elaborate on the designer's multi-angle thinking, about the traditional repair embroidery in the "repair" and "embroidery" the extended meaning of the two words. "Supplement" can be extended to be understood as a kind of supplement, filling, patchwork, supplement, repair, and supplement/subsidy of objects and objects. On the surface, it is a kind of connection (link) function. Its connotation is not only the increase of rich visual effects, the identification of different categories, the embodiment of enlargement and enhancement, but also a life use philosophy of making the best use of objects. "Embroidery" is a simple and clear technique. Through the basic carrier of textiles (or other materials), it uses different stitches and materials, and is supplemented by the aesthetic cognition of craftsmen (machines) under different regional cultures, customs and cultural backgrounds. A variety of products with different styles, tastes and sentiments have been formed (such as Li Ning brand in China, silk industry in Jiangsu and Zhejiang provinces), which makes clear the above contents. Then, looking back at textile products related to manufacturing industry in modern enterprises, it is clear that in the field of commercial design, from materialized products to the circulation of spirit and thought. It is a good confirmation of the eight-word motto of environment health, culture and people. Jonathan, Apple's chief designer, also said it's important to understand that our goal isn't just to highlight our products, but to create products that people will love in the future [14].

4 Conclusion

To sum up, as an important part of Chinese traditional needlework culture, the aesthetic educational significance of traditional mending embroidery is worth thinking about by every Chinese. It is inseparable from People's Daily life, closely connected with local national customs, in line with profound social culture, and a cultural crystallization integrating aesthetic appreciation value and practical education and use functions. Mr. Qian Mu, the master of Chinese studies, once said that the difference between civilization and culture is that civilization is outside, which belongs to the material aspect. Culture is part of the spiritual side [13]. Therefore, civilization can be spread and accepted, and culture must be produced by the accumulation of spirit within the group. The demands of modern society for products with functions such as fast, simple and comfortable make it gradually far away from the visual range of People's Daily life, which will inevitably result in the traditional mending embroidery process gradually losing its function and significance of aesthetic education, although in recent years, Some Chinese literati and educators who love collecting gradually brought the aesthetic education function of the traditional mending embroidery craft machine back to us through collection, cultural tourism, education and training and other fields. It aroused our memories of the past, our late appreciation, and our responsibility to preserve and care for it. On the basis of ensuring the virtuous cycle and development of traditional skills, technical innovation and breakthrough make it "live" in the present. Considering the respect and pursuit of traditional culture, the prospect of aesthetic education can be considered from the following levels for the features of theme, materials, techniques and techniques involved in menshu embroidery:

4.1 Cultural Diversity and Variation

"Zhouyi" said that when things have reached the extreme, they need to change. Only when changes occur, can the development of things not be blocked and things continue to develop. It shows that in the face of the situation that cannot develop, we must change the status quo and carry out reform and revolution. Different people's "taste" demands require creators to dare to integrate culture and tradition. The three elements of creation can be transformed to meet different needs.

4.2 Genes and Emotions

Under the traditional Chinese mode of thinking, the internal causes of the development of the forms of all things are objectively drawn to the logic of "poverty leads to change, change leads to prosperity, and general principles lead to attainment". This is also the significance of discussing the status quo of mending embroidery in the aesthetic education of clothing through its history. As Louise Wilson, the late Central Saint Martins professor, said in an interview: "A lot of people think you don't need to know history so you can create something new. I think we should understand history and destroy it." In a sense, innovation always has the suspicion of destruction, and of course, there is also the suspicion of fraud in the "constant response to change". In the collation and preservation of the source of cultural blood, we should dare to dig deep into the way of survival and the absorption and discarding of the internal causes of consumption. Everything can be transformed, but the spirit and style remain forever. It is engraved with the difference between you, me and "others". The real aesthetic education should be a hundred flowers blooming, not just one flower.

References

1. Jie, C.B.D.: 100 Years of Men's Wear in the World, p. 114. China Youth Press, Beijing (2011)
2. Schiller, F.C.S.: A Study of Humanism. Shanghai People's Publishing House, Shanghai (2010)
3. Ting, L.: The Way to Sustain: Design and Discussion of China's Sustainable Life Model, p. 11. Lingnan Fine Arts Press, Guangzhou (2006)
4. Zhidan, L., Qiumo, W.: Illustrated Silver Ornaments of the Qing Dynasty, p. 31. China Light Industry Press, Beijing (2007)
5. Jianhua, P.: The Art of Chinese Women's Boudoir, pp. 139–141. People's Fine Arts Publishing House, Beijing (2009)
6. Mu, Q.: Introduction to the History of Chinese Culture, p. 175. 1st edn. Kyushu Press, Fukuoka (2011)
7. Bre, R., Fangyi, L., Wei, L.: Critical Design, p. 19. China Renmin University Press, Beijing (2012)
8. Congwen, S.: Research on Ancient Chinese Clothing, pp. 127–134. Shanghai Bookstore Press, Shanghai (2011)
9. Gang, S.: A New History of Chinese Arts and Crafts, p. 54. Higher Education Press, Beijing (2007)
10. Kaiser, S.B., Hongwei, L.: Social Psychology of Clothing, p. 223. China Textile Press, Beijing (2000)
11. Papanaik, V.: Translated by Zhou Bo, Designing for the Real World, pp. 89–91. CITIC Press, Beijing (2013)
12. Yarong, W.: The Truth of Chapter Clothes. World Book Publishing House, Beijing (2013)
13. Li, W.: Common Sense of Ancient Chinese Culture (the fourth edition of the revised illustrations), p. 41. World Book Press, Beijing (2008)
14. Qiyue, W., Wenya, H.W.: Biography of Jonathan, p. 139. Citic Press, Beijing (2014)

Cross-Cultural Design in Immersive and Inclusive Learning Environments

Immersion and Intersectionality - Virtual Reality in Cross Cultural Art Exhibition Courses

Du Ao, Weilong Wu[(⊠)], and Xiaohua Guo

School of Film Television and Communication, Xiamen University of Technology, Xiamen, China
wu_academic@163.com

Abstract. With Virtual Reality (VR) and Augmented Reality (AR) technologies are becoming a trend in digital innovation in education due to their great strategic potential and are of great importance for many studies and programs. As a result, VR has become an indispensable tool in various fields such as science, geography, art and culture. VR creates a unique cross-cultural environment that enables deeper learning, stimulates interest and offers a very high educational potential. Today, new curatorial approaches are emerging alongside digitally activated modes of presentation and dissemination, characterized by permanent reproducibility and the sinking of physical space. Digitalization and global sharing of educational resources has been a hot topic of concern for arts management teaching. Cross-cultural courses on art exhibitions using virtual reality technology enable the integration of teaching resources from different cultural backgrounds and language environments.

Virtual simulation technology is truly applied to a wider range of exhibition planning and research, bringing more resources and practical opportunities for teaching and industry. Practical art curation training has limitations such as high teaching costs and high transportation risks. However, virtual art exhibition teaching can allow students from different cultural backgrounds and regions to break through the limitations of time and space and feel the context and cultural connotation of the exhibition more intuitively, which improves students' cross-cultural thinking and discernment awareness and cross-cultural communication ability.

In order to give students the opportunity to practice the tedious and highly specialized curatorial process visually. This study focuses on a virtual art exhibition experimental teaching system using VR as a carrier to provide students with opportunities to cognize theory and practice and to build a platform for effective practice. On the one hand, it improves students' exhibition planning ability. On the other hand, it gradually forms an integrated platform to promote the continuous updating of cross-cultural teaching of art exhibitions.

Through the system to accurately restore the exhibition space of domestic and foreign art institutions, a large number of artwork resources. It enables students to easily feel the exotic spaces and precious artworks that are out of their reach on a daily basis, which greatly increases the importance and interest of online learning during the epidemic. In the course of teaching virtual art exhibitions, students can further experience and understand spatial planning, artwork display,

---

D. Ao and W. Wu—These authors contributed equally to this study.

and other curatorial expertise while focusing on conceptual expression and spatial presentation.

Methods: This experiment adopts a quantitative research method, taking students of a school in China as the research object, randomly selecting 30 students (15 male and 15 female) as the control group and 30 students (15 male and 15 female) as the experimental group, the basic background of the two groups is similar, and all of them have initially studied the art exhibition course and have preliminary knowledge of the exhibition.

The control group adopts the traditional teaching mode, with the teacher teaching knowledge and operation demonstration, while the experimental group adopts virtual reality technology for teaching. A pre-test was given to the two groups of students before the teaching activity to ensure that there was no significant difference in the prior knowledge of the two groups. After the teaching, a post-test was conducted and a questionnaire survey on learning interest and learning confidence was organized.

By This study can be found by comparing the test scores, teaching questionnaire results and teaching satisfaction questionnaire between the control group and the experimental group. Students in the experimental group had higher average test scores than those in the control group, and students in the experimental group had higher classroom concentration, learning initiative, and satisfaction with classroom teaching than students in the control group.

Students in the control group indicated that the knowledge in the classroom was too boring and they did not pay attention in class, while students in the experimental group indicated that the classroom participation was high, the classroom was more interesting, and they hoped that more experimental courses could be taught in this way. Through the study, it was learned that virtual art exhibition teaching can enhance students' knowledge and classroom motivation about art exhibitions.

Conclusions: This study found that the traditional art curation teaching course is not able to fully meet the students' learning needs. Hands-on courses require more hands-on experience for students, and the use of virtual reality technology combined with traditional teaching can solve this problem well and improve students' learning efficiency. The application of virtual reality technology in art exhibition course teaching focuses on building real cross-cultural contexts for students and conducting comprehensive practical training, thus improving the interactivity and efficiency of experimental teaching in cross-cultural courses.

In addition, there are some noteworthy issues that need to be noted, whether the novelty of virtual reality technology will affect the actual operation and how to solve this problem remains to be examined.

Keywords: VR technology · Art exhibition · Cross-cultural training · Teaching model

1   Introduction

Virtual Reality (VR) and Augmented Reality (AR) are becoming increasingly popular in this digitally connected world due to their great strategic potential. Virtual reality technology is becoming a trend in digital innovation in education and is of great importance to many studies and programmers' creation of virtual art in a global virtual environment and the viewing and critiquing of virtual art in art exhibitions are huge advantages for conceptual learning and art education [1]. As a result, VR has become an indispensable tool in various fields such as science, geography, heritage, art and culture. VR creates a unique cross-cultural environment that enables deeper learning, stimulates interest and offers a very high educational potential. Today, the development of VR also offers new opportunities for art exhibitions [2]. Virtual simulation technology is truly applied to a wider range of exhibition planning and research, bringing more resources and practical opportunities for teaching and industry [3]. Immersion and integration have become the key words in the field of art exhibitions in recent years, and a single professional background and creation model can no longer meet the diversified development of today's art exhibitions. For art exhibition courses, exhibition is a comprehensive creative work, a creation of ideas and a production of knowledge. Compared to the traditional course model, the VR teaching model empowers the virtual scenario of the intercultural art exhibition course through the innovation and diversity of virtual reality technology, as well as building a platform for inter-temporal communication and discussion with experts and scholars from different fields. This research uses virtual simulation and digital interactive technology as a carrier to focus on a virtual art exhibition experimental teaching system, providing students with the opportunity to perceive artworks and exhibition theories perceptually and building a platform for effective training in the exhibition process. In order to give students a tangible understanding of abstract art exhibition theories and an opportunity to practice intuitively the tedious and highly specialized exhibition process, virtual art exhibition teaching provides teaching courses through virtual simulation technology and online teaching platforms to improve students' exhibition planning skills on the one hand; on the other hand, it gradually forms an integrated and linked platform to promote the continuous updating and progress of cross-cultural teaching of art exhibitions.

2 Literature Review

2.1 Virtual Reality Technology

The term "virtual reality" was coined by Jaron Lanier in the 1980s in the United States as "the immersion of humans in a synthetic world". Scavarelli, A argues that there is hope for more mainstream and diverse applications in the field of VR/AR, where we can push the limits of physical space and the physics of the known universe [4]. Alhalabi, W also recognised the increasingly important role that artificial intelligence, image processing techniques, simulation, and sensing virtual reality technologies are playing in people's work and learning [5]. Jerald proposed building an artificial environment through sensory stimuli (visual, auditory, sound) provided by computers, in which human behaviour partly determines what happens in the environment [6]. Technology plays an important role in the teaching and learning process, providing an interesting and engaging way of accessing information [7]. The integration of art exhibitions and education is therefore also a topic that has gained widespread attention. In the educational process, students face many problems with understanding the curriculum due to the complexity and necessity of abstract thinking and concepts. Based on research reports and literature, we found that virtual reality technology offers an immersive learning environment and experience in education unlike traditional 3D technology. Research by Elmqaddem, N. found that technological advances have made AR and VR more feasible and popular in many areas and that the nature of VR heralds new models of teaching and learning that can better meet the needs of 21st century learners [8]. Scavarelli, A argues that VR should also fulfil the task of imparting knowledge about cultural heritage at the intersection with art, and research points out that art exhibition venues as well as museums are now placing an unprecedented emphasis on education [4]. The Salvador Dali Museum's Dali's Dream uses VR/AR technology in its museum exhibitions to provide visitors and fellow teachers with an unprecedented virtual reality experience [9]. This research incorporates a variety of sensory experiences into our VR intercultural art exhibition course learning system, which will enhance the immersive experience for students. We will focus on the perceptual experience of the virtual reality system for students, with the aim of identifying important quality assessment factors for these applications from the perspective of the intercultural art exhibition curriculum, in an attempt to ensure the continued development and success of the augmented virtual reality SV-IVR system by attempting to give students a more innovative learning experience with a more comprehensive simulated sensory system. At the same time, many scholars have made equally relevant studies in the field of VR and art exhibitions, offering some very insightful ideas. Furthermore, immersion and presence have been described as "two extremely profound innovations of VR". The greater the number of technologies covering various sensory modalities, the more immersive it becomes [10]. A new exploration in the context of virtual museums and virtual spaces would be an innovative approach to teaching and learning [4]. Technological advances have created challenges for the online learning ecosystem in terms of applying immersive technologies to provide an educational and creative framework for students [11]. However, there is little insight into the potential of arts educators for system conceptualisation and classroom implementation [12]. Some research suggests that socially immersive media is very relevant to the context of VR in arts education [13]. Based on the literature and use cases that show that this technology is better accepted in many disciplines, we can learn that the application of VR technology in art courses is a promising area of research and that this study points to an unexplored area of VR intercultural art exhibition courses that can provide relevant and innovative perspectives for current research [14]. This study focuses on the impact that an intercultural art exhibition course featuring the use of immersive virtual reality can have on the perception levels of teachers and students. The use of immersive virtual reality systems can lead to more efficient learning and learning success than other learning methods, and teachers are able to summarise learning theories and student data more specifically and clearly in the course data [15]. The VR model of teaching and learning reduces unnecessary teaching costs in a more economically sustainable way, and increases the immersion and experience of the art exhibition course. At the same time, the VR course itself is a sustainable and valuable teaching resource as a knowledge carrier that can be reused for long-term learning [16]. Using technology to give students more imagination about space and construction in the teaching of art exhibitions can lead to better learning and understanding of the curriculum. Not only does it promote the development of art exhibition education, but it also spreads innovative technology to teachers and students, bringing a more scientific approach to teaching and learning skills. Overall, the results of this research will enable teachers to design classrooms that are better equipped to deal with many of the challenges that exist in the art exhibition curriculum, and to face the complexities of the post-epidemic educational environment with greater ease.

2.2 Intercultural Art Exhibition Course

Scholars such as Lily A. Arasaratnam-Smith have generally argued that intercultural competence has cognitive, affective and behavioural aspects. Due to the extensive interest in intercultural competence across multiple disciplines [17]. Holliday, A., in discussing intercultural education programmes, argues that the existing intercultural experiences that participants accumulate from an early age are an important resource. Interculturality is a reflective awareness of self and others when crossing boundaries, which echoes C. Wright Mill's 'sociological imagination' [18]. In an intercultural context, the art exhibition course, as a comprehensive discipline with an intercultural and interdisciplinary background, meets the need for the development of art talents and is one of the objectives of the construction of the art exhibition major. As a professional course that combines theory and practice, the course focuses on application and development, including design from two-dimensional to multi-dimensional, and the integration of figurative and logical thinking. Traditional teaching methods emphasise the "knowledge-based" approach, and the teaching mode of all majors in universities basically consists of teachers teaching theoretical knowledge in the classroom and then entering the practical stage. This mode of teaching tends to make students' lack of perceptual knowledge more difficult to understand and the learning process more prone to errors. In order to solve this problem, the application of 'technology-based' VR teaching methods has become an important issue in the teaching of art exhibition courses. Through innovative practice and analysis of VR art exhibition course teaching, this study explores the development direction and solutions of the course teaching reform. Combined with the practice and analysis of VR teaching models, the advantages of VR systems in cross-cultural art exhibition courses are exploited [19]. Britanny E. Reef-Stout's study argues that art exhibitions can embody various dimensions of art and sustainable fashion through the use of multimedia learning tools. This suggests that through experiential learning methods, students can learn as much, if not more, about art and sustainable fashion [20]. Since 2014, the School of Art Management and Education at the Central Academy of Fine Arts has been developing the Virtual Curatorial Lab for Art Museums, which also continues to promote the platform and teaching methods of virtual curation from a practical perspective. YohanHwang in South Korea linked education to the metaverse, and the analysis of the sentiments collected from students' showed that the composite results of their opinions, evaluations and attitudes towards the metaverse exhibition were generally positive [21]. Dilmaç Sehran scholars in Turkey studied the perceptions of 45 undergraduate students from different faculties of Izmir Katip Çelebi University regarding distance education in art courses. The results of the study showed that in some technologies that require art practice, the students believed that the use of software and systems in the course could enhance their interest in learning in the classroom [22]. The exhibition is the creation of a man-made environment, a subject with many strands of knowledge that are very cross-cutting in nature. However, under the current curriculum, it is difficult for teachers to balance theory and practice and to cater for the individual needs of students. This study uses a blended approach to cross-cultural art exhibitions, with the advantage of VR over traditional face-to-face or purely online learning, which allows students to master the basic content of the course in a variety of ways and through a variety of channels, without the constraints of objects, environments or equipment, and which better stimulates students' enthusiasm for learning and enhances their skills and creativity, while providing teachers with a better It also provides teachers with a better way of teaching and summarising after the lesson. On the one hand, the "Intercultural Art Exhibition Course" provides virtual exhibition experimental teaching courses through VR technology and online teaching platform to improve students' exhibition planning ability; on the other hand, it is based on the curriculum and is open to the world, and is dedicated to building a platform for teaching, communication and research of art exhibition cultural knowledge.

3 Experiment Design

The experiment used a quantitative research method with 30 students (15 male and 15 female) randomly selected as the control group and 30 students (15 male and 15 female) as the experimental group. Both groups had similar basic backgrounds and had all taken initial art exhibition courses and had a preliminary understanding of exhibition knowledge. The control group used the traditional teaching mode, with the teacher teaching knowledge and operating demonstrations, while the experimental group used virtual reality technology for teaching. The intercultural art exhibition course is a compulsory course for art exhibition majors, and it contains both theoretical and practical knowledge. In order to judge whether virtual reality technology can play an effective role in the intercultural art exhibition course, we combined virtual reality technology with the intercultural art exhibition course in a Chinese school. We arranged the experimental group's course to use virtual reality technology to learn the theoretical knowledge and practical operation of art exhibitions, and the control group's course to have the teacher talk about the theoretical knowledge, followed by a demonstration of the practical operation by the teacher. The aim of our study was to investigate the impact of virtual reality on learning attitudes and confidence in the intercultural art exhibition curriculum.

3.1 Participants in the Experiment

In this study, 30 students (15 males and 15 females) were randomly selected as the control group and 30 students (15 males and 15 females) as the experimental group. There were no major differences in the basic information of the two groups, and all of them had initially studied the art exhibition course and had preliminary knowledge of art exhibition. The control group used the traditional teaching mode, with the teacher teaching knowledge and operation demonstration. The experimental group used virtual reality technology for teaching, with the teacher using virtual reality for classroom teaching and the students using VR for learning. All teaching activities were carried out by the same professor with many years of experience in education and who had a strong theoretical knowledge of art exhibitions as well as a high level of practical art exhibition skills.

3.2 Measuring Tools

The research instrument for this study consisted of a questionnaire measuring students' attitudes towards learning and their confidence in learning. The questionnaire is divided into two sections, for learning interest and learning confidence, with the learning interest section containing five questions on a scale of 1–5 and the learning confidence section containing five questions on a scale of 1–5.

3.3 Experimental Procedure

The experimental process is shown in Fig. 1. Students in the experimental group were taught using virtual reality technology at the beginning of the course, while students in the control group received the traditional teaching model.

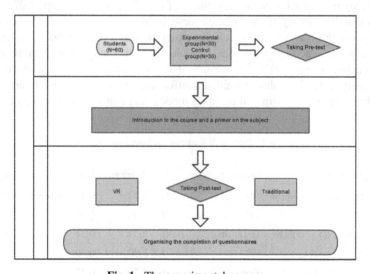

Fig. 1. The experimental process

4 Experimental Results

4.1 Analysis of Learning Interest

The independent sample t-test was used to analyse the students' interest in the inter-cultural art exhibition course under the traditional teaching mode and the virtual reality technology teaching mode, as shown in Table 1, the results of the study show that, as can be seen from the above table, using the t-test (fully known as the independent sample t-test) to study the specific analysis can be seen: for the level of interest in the course: showing a 0.01 level of significance ($t = -3.636$, the $p = 0.001$), as well as specific comparative differences can be seen that the mean of the traditional teaching group (3.57), would be significantly lower than the mean of the VR teaching group (4.03).For the degree of perceived innovation in this course: showing a 0.01 level of significance ($t = -3.101, p = 0.003$), as well as specific comparison differences it can be seen that the mean of the traditional teaching group (3.53), would be significantly lower than the mean of the VR teaching group (3.90). For the degree of integration of theory and practice in the course: it showed a 0.01 level of significance ($t = -2.875, p = 0.006$), as well as a specific comparison difference that shows that the mean of the traditional teaching group (3.70), would be significantly lower than the mean of the VR teaching group (4.13). For the level of difficulty of the course: it showed a 0.01 level of significance ($t = -3.743$, $p = 0.001$), as well as a specific comparison difference that the mean of the traditional teaching group (3.63), would be significantly lower than the mean of the VR teaching group (4.03). For the satisfaction of the subgroup of the course in which it was taught: it showed a 0.05 level of significance ($t = -2.038, p = 0.046$), as well as a specific comparison difference that shows that the mean of the traditional teaching group (3.70), would be significantly lower than the mean of the VR teaching group (4.07). For the evaluation of the learning method of the course: it shows a 0.01 level of significance ($t = -2.868, p = 0.006$), as well as a specific comparison difference that shows that the mean of the traditional teaching group (3.53), would be significantly lower than the mean of the VR teaching group (4.03). To conclude, it can be seen that students who learn using virtual reality technology show significant differences in their attitudes to learning from those who learn using traditional teaching modes, and that the mean value of learning

Table 1. Research findings on learning interest

Learning interest	Learning Styles	N	Average	SD	t	p
How interested are you in the course?	Traditional	30	3.57	0.50	−3.19	.009**
	VR	30	4.03	0.49		
How innovative do you think this course is?	Traditional	30	3.53	0.51	−3.101	0.003**
	VR	30	3.90	0.40		
How well do you think the course integrates theory and practice?	Traditional	30	3.70	0.47	−2.875	0.006**
	VR	30	4.13	0.68		
What is your satisfaction with the grouping of your course?	Traditional	30	3.70	0.70	−2.038	0.046*
	VR	30	4.07	0.69		
How would you rate the learning approach of the course?	Traditional	30	3.53	0.73	−2.868	0.006**
	VR	30	4.03	0.61		

$*p < .05 **p < .01$

using virtual reality technology is higher than that of students who learn using traditional teaching modes. All of them showed significant differences.

4.2 Analysis of Learning Confidence

The independent sample t-test was used to analyse the students' confidence in learning the art exhibition aerial survey course under the traditional teaching mode and the virtual reality technology teaching mode, as shown in Table 2. The results of the study show that for the classroom efficiency during the lessons: it showed a 0.01 level of significance ($t = -2.735$, $p = 0.009$), as well as the specific comparison difference can be seen that the mean of the traditional teaching group (3.67), would be significantly lower than the mean of the VR instruction group (4.03). For the level of learning initiative in the course: showing a 0.05 level of significance ($t = -2.470, p = 0.017$), as well as specific comparative differences it can be seen that the mean of the traditional teaching group (3.57), would be significantly lower than the mean of the VR teaching group (3.87). For the acceptance of the teacher's knowledge of the classroom: showing a 0.01 level of significance ($t = -2.977, p = 0.004$), as well as specific comparison differences it can be seen that the mean of the traditional teaching group (3.53), would be significantly lower than the mean of the VR teaching group (3.97). For the perceived level of teacher mobilisation of equipment and technology: showing a 0.05 level of significance ($t = -2.238, p = 0.029$), as well as specific comparison differences it can be seen that the mean of the traditional teaching group (3.53), would be significantly lower than the mean of the VR teaching group (3.83). For the perceived difficulty of the course: showing a 0.01 level of significance ($t = -3.743$, $p = 0.001$), as well as specific comparison differences it can be seen that the mean of the traditional teaching group (3.63), would be significantly lower than the mean of the VR teaching group (4.03). In conclusion, it can be seen that students learning with virtual reality technology showed significant differences in learning confidence from those learning with the traditional mode of instruction, with students learning with virtual reality technology perceiving the course to be less difficult than those learning with the traditional mode of instruction, and higher means in all other aspects of learning confidence than those learning with the traditional mode.

In In this study, by comparing the results of the teaching questionnaire between the control group and the experimental group, it can be found that the average classroom concentration, learning initiative and satisfaction with classroom teaching of the students in the experimental group were higher than those in the control group. Students in the control group indicated that the knowledge in the classroom was too boring and they did not concentrate in class, while students in the experimental group indicated that the classroom was highly participatory, the classroom was more interesting and the virtual reality technology effectively reduced the learning difficulty of the course. It is known from the study that teaching virtual art exhibitions can enhance students' knowledge and motivation in the classroom.

Table 2. Research findings on learning confidence

Learning confidence	Learning Styles	N	Average	SD	t	p
How effective are you in class?	Traditional	30	3.67	0.61	−2.735	0.009**
	VR	30	4.03	0.41		
What is your level of initiative in learning the course?	Traditional	30	3.57	0.50	−2.470	0.017*
	VR	30	3.87	0.43		
How receptive were you to the teacher's teaching of the class?	Traditional	30	3.53	0.63	−2.977	0.004**
	VR	30	3.97	0.49		
What do you think of the teacher's level of mobilization of equipment and technology?	Traditional	30	3.53	0.57	−2.238	0.029*
	VR	30	3.83	0.46		
What is your perceived level of difficulty of the course?	Traditional	30	3.63	0.56	−3.743	0.001**
	VR	30	4.03	0.18		

$*p < .05 **p < .01$

5 Discussion and Conclusions

This study found that the traditional intercultural art exhibition teaching curriculum does not fully meet the needs of students learning, students from different regions and cultural backgrounds cannot intuitively cognitive course knowledge, teaching the traditional teaching methods can only read history through paper and text, can only find fragments and information from the text and pictures, cannot be immersive to feel the impact of the art exhibition, and offline courses are more costly and more restricted in terms of space. Distance education in the context of the epidemic also still suffers from many problems, such as reduced student concentration, poor self-regulation, low initiative and marking difficulties [23]. And our proposed use of virtual reality technology combined with traditional teaching can be a good solution to this problem and further enhance the course content, learning efficiency and teaching methods. The application of VR art exhibition course teaching focuses on building realistic intercultural contexts for students and conducting comprehensive practical training, thus improving the interactivity and efficiency of experimental teaching in intercultural courses. In addition, there are a number of issues that need to be noted, and it remains to be seen whether and how this will be addressed due to the novelty of virtual reality technology and whether it will have an impact on practical operations. From this study we can find a few suggestions for future research based on the results of this study, the first being that the size of the research sample and the selection of the sample also needs to be more diverse and enriched. In addition, there are some issues that need to be noted, with the development of concepts such as virtual reality and metaverse in recent years, the relatively rapid iteration of technological development, as well as the novelty of virtual reality technology itself, whether it will have an impact on the actual operation and subsequent teaching methods. Teaching VR intercultural art exhibition courses still needs to be based on existing teaching ideas, continuous exploration in the professional space and continuous innovation.

Funding. This work was supported by Social Science Foundation of Fujian Province, China (Funding Number: FJ2022C071).

And supported by Xiamen Education Scientific Planning Project: Application of VR in art design courses in the post-epidemic era Innovative Teaching Reform Study (Funding Number: 22002).

And supported by High-level Talent Research Project of Xiamen University of Technology (Funding Number: YSK22018R).

References

1. Lu, L.: 3D virtual worlds as art media and exhibition arenas: students' responses and challenges in contemporary art education. Stud. Art Educ. **54**(3), 232–245 (2013)
2. Lin, C.L., Chen, S.J., Lin, R.: Efficacy of virtual reality in painting art exhibitions appreciation. Appl. Sci. **10**(9), 3012 (2020)
3. Kang, Y., Yang, K.C.: Employing digital reality technologies in art exhibitions and museums: a global survey of best practices and implications. In: Virtual and Augmented Reality in Education, Art, and Museums, pp. 139–161. IGI Global (2020)
4. Scavarelli, A., Arya, A., Teather, R.J.: Virtual reality and augmented reality in social learning spaces: a literature review. Virtual Reality **25**(1), 257–277 (2020). https://doi.org/10.1007/s10055-020-00444-8
5. Alhalabi, W.: Virtual reality systems enhance students' achievements in engineering education. Behav. Inf. Technol. **35**(11), 919–925 (2016)
6. Jerald, J.: The VR Book: Human-Centered Design for Virtual Reality. Morgan & Claypool Publishers and ACM Books, San Rafael (2015)
7. Kamińska, D., et al.: Virtual reality and its applications in education: survey. Information **10**(10), 318 (2019)
8. Elmqaddem, N.: Augmented reality and virtual reality in education. Myth or reality?. Int. J. Emerg. Technol. Learn. **14**(3) (2019)
9. Martinez-Conde, S., et al.: Marvels of illusion: illusion and perception in the art of Salvador Dali. Front. Hum. Neurosci. **9**, 496 (2015)
10. Bowman, D.A., McMahan, R.P.: Virtual reality: how much immersion is enough? Computer **40**(7), 36–43 (2007)
11. González-Zamar, M.D., Abad-Segura, E.: Implications of virtual reality in arts education: research analysis in the context of higher education. Educ. Sci. **10**(9), 225 (2020)
12. Bäck, R.M., Wenrich, R., Dorner, B.: Getting there? Together. Cultural framing of augmented and virtual reality for art education. In: 2021 7th International Conference of the Immersive Learning Research Network (iLRN), pp. 1–8. IEEE (2021)
13. Snibbe, S.S., Rafe, H.S.: Social immersive media—pursuing best practices for multi-user interactive camera/projector exhibits. In: Proceedings of the SIGCHI Conference on Human Factors in Computing Systems (2009)
14. Radianti, J., Majchrzak, T.A., Fromm, J., Wohlgenannt, I.: A systematic review of immersive virtual reality applications for higher education: design elements, lessons learned, and research agenda. Comput. Educ. **147**, 103778 (2020)

15. Concannon, B.J., Esmail, S., Roduta Roberts, M.: Head-mounted display virtual reality in post-secondary education and skill training. In: Frontiers in Education, vol. 4, p. 80. Frontiers Media SA (2019)
16. Wu, W., Zhao, Z., Du, A., Lin, J.: Effects of multisensory integration through spherical video-based immersive virtual reality on students' learning performances in a landscape architecture conservation course. Sustainability **14**(24), 16891 (2022)
17. Arasaratnam-Smith, L.A.: Intercultural competence: an overview. Intercultural Competence High. Educ. 7–18 (2017)
18. Holliday, A.: Designing a course in intercultural education. Intercultural Commun. Educ. **1**(1), 4–11 (2018)
19. Hodgson, P., et al.: Immersive virtual reality (IVR) in higher education: development and implementation. In: tom Dieck, M., Jung, T. (eds.) Augmented Reality and Virtual Reality. Progress in IS, pp. 161–173. Springer, Cham (2019). https://doi.org/10.1007/978-3-030-06246-0_12
20. Reef-Stout, B.E., Medvedev, K.: Multimedia exhibition teaches undergraduate students about sustainable fashion. In: Leal Filho, W., Brandli, L., Castro, P., Newman, J. (eds.) Handbook of Theory and Practice of Sustainable Development in Higher Education. WSS, pp. 83–101. Springer, Cham (2017). https://doi.org/10.1007/978-3-319-47868-5_6
21. Hwang, Y.: When makers meet the metaverse: effects of creating NFT metaverse exhibition in maker education. Comput. Educ. **194**, 104693 (2023)
22. Dilmaç, S.: Students' opinions about the distance education to art and design courses in the pandemic process. World J. Educ. **10**(3), 113–126 (2020)
23. Wu, W.L., Hsu, Y., Yang, Q.F., Chen, J.J.: A spherical video-based immersive virtual reality learning system to support landscape architecture students' learning performance during the COVID-19 era. Land **10**(6), 561 (2021)

Preliminary Research on the Design of the Evaluation Ruler for the Judge of the Higher Education CIE (Creativity, Innovation and Entrepreneurship) Competition

Chang-Wei Chang[✉]

Graduate School of Creative Industry Design of National Taiwan University of Arts, New Taipei City, Taiwan
ansondata@gmail.com

Abstract. Research background and purpose: Creativity, Innovation and Entrepreneurship (CIE) are important economic knowledge in recent years. The CIE competition is held in hope that students will demonstrate good competitiveness, and propose educational concepts and industry connections that achieves CIE thinking through practice. It remains to be discussed whether the evaluation criteria of existing CIE competitions in schools conform to the spirit of CIE. This study focuses on applying perception and science as evaluation rules to CIE competitions and proposing new evaluation standards based on the statistics of actual competitions. Method and tools: This study constructs an evaluation scale using communication theory, adopts the DIKW system theory as background, understands the process from theory to practice, and uses quantitative methods for verification. It is estimated that 100 cases will be accepted from participants in the fields of business management, research and development, design, and teaching and research. They will participate in the competition review through questionnaires, and compare the measurement results of the original review interactively. The study will count the state of perception and reception of the respondents through the three levels of appearance, meaning, and feeling, analyze the points of cognitive communication items in the presentation of works, and examine the process from learning to practice from various scores. Based on the statistical results, we will be able to obtain the new evaluation criteria in advance, which will be used as the scoring benchmark for CIE competitions in the future.

Keywords: Creativity · Innovation · Entrepreneurship · CIE · Review · Education

1 Introduction

In response to the purpose of CIE education, the Ministry of Education will organize the 2022 Higher Education Deep Cultivation CIE Competition. In view of the competition review, there is no effective scoring basis and structure to follow. In order to ensure the quality of education and the fairness and impartiality of grading, it is necessary to

P.-L. P. Rau (Ed.): HCII 2023, LNCS 14024, pp. 201–214, 2023.
https://doi.org/10.1007/978-3-031-35946-0_17

formulate an effective review mechanism. The term "CIE" emphasizes people as its core concept and is the three most important elements of competitiveness in the knowledge economy–creativity, innovation, and entrepreneurship (Chen Man Ling 2015). The connection between cultural perception and life skills is realized using creativity, innovation, and entrepreneurship through the process of exploration, interaction, sharing, learning, and creation in the competition. The essence of CIE is "cross-domain imagination", while its practice is "cross-domain implementation"–which also permeates the essence of CIE. Effective CIE competition evaluation methods not only make education fruitful, but also enable industries to enhance their competitiveness, and truly realize the value of CIE in cultural and economic strength.

In the book "Insight Out: Get Ideas Out of Your Head and Into the World" by Stanford University professor Tina Seelig, she proposed that the core concepts of "imagination", "creativity", "innovation", and "entrepreneurship" can effectively develop the processes of creativity, innovation and entrepreneurship in the "invention cycle" model (Tina Seelig/Lin Li Xue, translated 2016). The spirit of CIE is the use of imagination, the result of internal thinking and external skill performance. Imagination is the first step of creativity, which should be defined as encountering ideas that do not exist yet. Innovation is the use of imagination to solve events and problems. Entrepreneurship is dealing with human needs and can be continued as a method. Coincidentally, in the 25th year of Heisei, the Ministry of Education, Culture, Sports, Science and Technology of Japan put forward the key points of the current education revitalization plan in the second basic plan of education revitalization, expecting that every Japanese needs to actively invest in independence, cooperation, and creation to achieve Entrepreneurship-oriented learning activities (Ministry of Education, Culture, Sports, Science and Technology 2013). The development of CIE is also synchronized with the global thinking and learning mode.

Applied in the evaluation mechanism of the CIE competitions in higher education, the evaluation rule will shorten the distance between academia and industry and practice cross-domain business development, which is the goal that the evaluation rule expects to achieve in the process of review and learning. In this study, we will use the three essences of innovation: innovation, creativity, and entrepreneurship as the benchmark, and discuss the following topics:

1. Establish a fair, impartial and objective CIE review mechanism.
2. Effectively evaluate the learning process of higher education through the CIE review and scoring rule.

2   Literature Review

2.1   The Development and Purpose of CIE

Culture is the cornerstone of cross-domain thinking, and CIE are the practice of cross-domain design. From the perspective of perception, the development of culture to CIE is the embodiment of communication between CIE and the audience, and it is also the purpose of the development of cultural and creative industries. Students in the technical and vocational systems in Taiwanese society often lack self-confidence, and students feel frustrated and strenuous in their studies. In the workplace, employers report that technical and vocational students do not have the courage to accept challenges and dare not try new things (Chiou Huei Fang 2013). An effective evaluation mechanism is not only positive encouragement, but also a process of effective learning, and it is also the key to reestablishing the courage to try new things. Evaluation is a communication mode between education and learning. To jointly achieve the value expected by the society, the key lies in the degree of perception of two-way information. A good communication mode can effectively pass on the empathy information. The Ministry of Education of Taiwan has actively promoted related programs in recent years, hoping to allow innovation and entrepreneurship to take root on campus (Ministry of Education 2016). Encouraging the spirit of CIE is a trend vigorously promoted by advanced countries. Promoting a complete evaluation mechanism to establish a good communication model is a necessary condition for achieving the goals of education and knowledge building.

Starting from the construction point of creative education and knowledge presentation, we can understand the way of presentation through the DIKW system diagram (Data, Information, Knowledge, Wisdom), depending on the differences created by the materials and purposes of each level (Chen Jing Yi. 2022). CIE is like an information sharing system as information as a resource has the characteristics of being expandable, compressible, substitutable, transportable, diffusive, and shareable (Cleveland 1982).

The DIKW four-level system (data-information-knowledge-wisdom) proposed by Ackoff (1989) is applied in the field of knowledge management and educational development, and the cognitive process of cognitive behavior from ignorance to understanding (Zeleny 2005). In this study, on the basis of the DIKW framework model, the cognitive model of three-creation evaluation involved in "design creation" was developed, and integrated into a relationship map corresponding to the purpose of three-creation education (Fig. 1). From the perspective of research, theory and practice, we can find the corresponding class relationship, as well as the process of the application and development of knowledge and skills in the future.

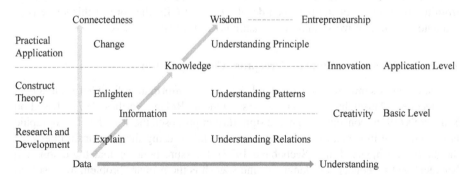

Fig. 1. The Performance Map of DIKW and the CIE Educational Purposes. Reference source: Lu Yan Ru, Lin Po Hsien, Lin Rong Tai (2021). Preliminary research on the general audience's cognitive model of "neural network-like" artistic style transfer. Journal of Design, 26(3), 61–84. 1.

As shown by the map hierarchy in Fig. 1, it shows the degree of knowledge application and the state of learning. Assessment is an area that can effectively understand the lack of knowledge absorption and learning, and it also systematically creates a fair and just competition stage to cultivate talents for CIE. An open and clear evaluation model can encourage the motivation of learning and strengthen the effectiveness, so that the CIE education can be implemented and rooted in schools (Huang Yi Liang, Wang Yi You 2019). The concept of CIE is to use new thinking, new technology and new communication, etc., to integrate with cross-field models, and then to upgrade the industry, to practice the value and spirit of CIE and to build a bridge for the future.

The three basic elements proposed in the book "Insight Out: Get Ideas Out of Your Head and Into the World", one of which is to have an "entrepreneurial mentality" and have the courage to challenge all established frameworks and assumptions. Furthermore, there must be a set of "clear methods" for solving problems and making good use of opportunities, using your internal and external environmental factors to open the way to create inventions. Third, a "clear roadmap" from inspiration to execution is required (Tina Seelig 2016). Implementation is the only way to achieve success; but effective evaluation is not only the correct way to learn, but also the best way to practice. Just like a book, "reading to know" and "reading to understand" are two different realms and meanings. The use of effective evaluation rules is an urgent and non-negligible link in education.

In the Journal of University Teaching Practice and Research, in the article "Discussion on the Teaching Process of Improving the Learning Effects of CIE General Education Courses - Taking "Life Creativity Ideas and Practices" as an example", it is proposed that "creativity is a kind of innovation in the existing field. Actions, ideas, product changes and updates" rather than just the self-feeling or personal evaluation of the instructor or leader. This has verified the theory (Amabile 1983) the emphasizing that "products or observable responses are the ultimate proof of creativity" in the evaluation of creativity (Huang Yi Liang Wang Yi You, 2019). Previous teaching research and seminars only focused on the creative teaching model, focusing on the process of promoting students' creativity (Dai Jian Yun, Chen Wan Fei, Yuan Yu Xi 2009). Starting from the perspective of the balanced development of CIE, the core of this study is to evaluate the value of works and the measurement of learning effects.

2.2 Semiotics and the State of Perceptual Communication

This study uses semiotics to understand the state of information flow between coders and decoders. Through symbol analysis, semiotician Roland Barthes (1977), based on Saussure's (1916) concept of sign and sign, further proposed the "two-level ideographic law" to deduce information and connotative meaning, using the relationship between the analyzed objects (Bally, Sechehaye 1977). Saussure believes that the distinction between the two concepts of language and speech is the primary problem to be solved in the study of linguistics in "General Linguistics Course". (Tsen Yun Chiang 2006). Saussure pointed out: "No matter which view we adopt, there are always two aspects of language phenomena, and these two aspects correspond to each other, and one of them needs the other to have its value. "In speech activities, language and speech correspond to each other (Shi Shu 2012). In the perception activities after symbols are converted into images, the corresponding communication behaviors are encoding and decoding.

This study confirms the effectiveness of learning through the evaluation of work competitions, and provides suggestions for the instructor's teaching direction. Taking audience perception as the evaluation, using the mode of semiotic message transmission and the process of expression as the basis of review to analyze the learning status. In semiotics, the perceptual performance of language activities can range from the external actual relationship of symbols, to feeling, emotional extension, etc., to express the strength of the message and the degree of message acceptance, which is an important process of empathy between the contestants' encoding and the judging's decoding. Integrating social and humanistic theoretical perspectives, at the same time collecting data on audiences and media content. It is emphasized that through the negotiation between the creator, the text of the work and the receiver (Hsu Jing Wun 2007), the individual consciousness actively constructed by the receiver has also become the main influence of criticism and review. However, the differences in geographical environment, knowledge experience and cognitive structure show different interpretation results. The thinking mode of judgment and approval is also a process of perceptual communication, and perception exists in the process of symbolic communication. The connotation of empathy is a part of society and culture, and it conveys a consensus cognitive message through narrative interpretation. From the perspective and process of the review, it is divided into the weighted comprehensive processing of cognitive and emotional changes of rational thinking to achieve the result of the review. There are many factors such as professional thinking, aesthetic experience, personal preference, emotional response and other psychological processes (Chen Xi Jing 2018), and then interpret the conclusion of the sum of the individual's perception and value. Like the problem of satisfying appearance perception, the semantic communication of meaning cognition and the effect level of inner feeling (Chen, Lin, & Lin, 2014, 2015; Lin, Chen, Chen, & Lin, 2015; Xu Qi Xian, Lin Rong Tai, 2011).

Between contestants and judges is a negotiation process of creators' encoding and judges' decoding. In Hall's view of text, the polysemy mentioned in the text is not completely pluralistic, and there are still specific restrictions on the interpretation of the audience. Hall adopts Parkin's "value meaning system" and proposes three reading positions for readers to read coded information. "Dominant-hegemonic Position": The listener fully accepts the connotation of the content of the message. "Negotiated Position": The correct combination of messages and specific or current situations under the hegemonic structure. "Oppositional Position": The listener has a good grasp of the connotation and meaning, but organizes or seeks a reference frame for another interpretation, resulting in opposite interpretations (Hall 1980). The semiotic concepts and perceptual communication modes are framed in the evaluation mechanism of "negotiation position", and the rulers based on this have clear goals and two-way empathy conditions. This can be used to establish the scope of review, reduce the uncertain factors in the evaluation of the heart syndrome, and achieve the effectiveness of the ruler. Combining the above theories, their relationships are integrated into a restricted cognitive model of "evaluation rules" (Fig. 2).

In this study, Lin Rong Tai (2017) puts forward six corresponding factors and functions of cultural and creative commodity communication, based on communication theory and perception model, as the design framework of the evaluation ruler. Divide the superficial factor into instinct, behavior and reflection, formulate the functional aspect below into three levels of information, contact, and code, and plan it in the review matrix

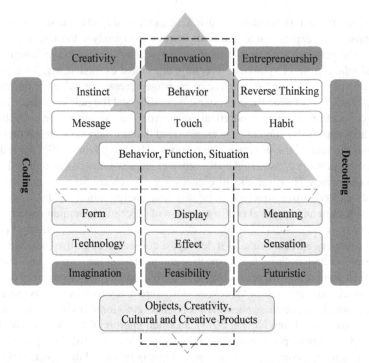

Fig. 2. Corresponding Factors and Functions of the Communication of the CIE Competition (drawn in this study).

structure, deconstructing the three-creation review rule The link that needs to be paid attention to (Fig. 3).

2.3   Evaluation Ruler Under the Framework of Social Equity Theory

The concept of judging role evaluation ruler design comes from the Social Comparison Theory proposed by Festinger (1954). The original intention is to believe that everyone has their own beliefs after observing the environment, and has the ability to evaluate their own abilities and social status, opinion needs (need), or driving force (drive) (Xiao Heng zhe 2012). Taylor and Lobel (1989) further identified broadly paying attention to other people's information and comparing specific behaviors with others as the category of social comparison theory, which measures not only the ontology but also external things. From the perspective of competition evaluation, it is the subjective consciousness generated through the ability and belief identified by the individual nature, which is used as the benchmark for evaluation. Social comparison theory is divided into upward, parallel, and self-comparison. By comparing with others, one can evaluate one's own ability and value (Seltzer 1980). Starting from the core of the essence of the CIE, and clearly summarizing the evaluation direction and value into the value of educational expectations, similar review conditions will be produced. Narrowing the scope of perception, excluding specific emotion, experience and other conditions of the social comparison

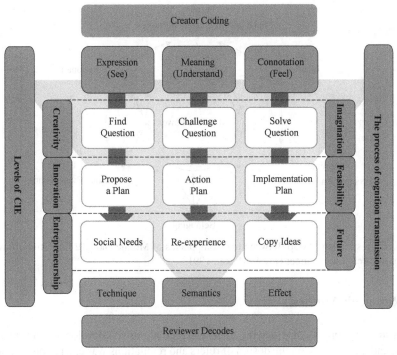

Fig. 3. Research Method and Process (drawn in this study) Review Role Assessment Ruler Design Perception Communication Matrix Structure Diagram.

theory model, setting the measured category as innovation, creativity and entrepreneurial awareness of sympathetic information, as the basis of social comparison, to reduce the generation of psychological evidence Biased.

Equity Theory belongs to the scope of social comparison theory. It was put forward by American psychologist Adams, J. S. in 1962 in the book "The Relationship of Worker Productivity to Cognitive Dissonance about Wage Inequities", focusing on Research the rationality and unfairness of wage distribution and its impact on employees' production enthusiasm. Among them, the factors for improving labor morale include three levels of identity, sense of belonging, and sense of rationality (Wu Zong Li 1997), which means the balance between goals, individuals, organizations, and expectations, and the same rationality also exists in the evaluation mechanism. In terms of sex and applicability, the following is an integrated map for the comparison of the elements of the fairness theory used in this study (Fig. 4).

Effective evaluation mechanism and rules, participation, learning, and education are interrelated. Educational goals increase the willingness to participate in behavior, improve the willingness to learn psychologically, and actually meet the expected educational outcomes of social expectations. The model of fairness theory can be effectively established in the CIE education, to achieve important teaching and progress between industry and academia, and to highlight the importance of product quality standards in education and social development.

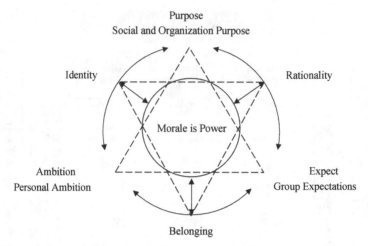

Fig. 4. Correspondence Map Between the Components of Morale and CIE Education (drawn in this study). Reference source: Hoy & Miskel, 1991.

3 Research Methods

In this study, the project of reviewing rulers and regulations was developed in a perceptual mode, and the research on the design of rulers and regulations was carried out in combination with questionnaire survey. In the process of encoding and decoding, explore the difference in the influence of rulers and gauges in the evaluation. The research process is shown below (Fig. 5). In the early stage of the research, the questionnaire survey method was used to deconstruct the reviewer's perception model of the CIE, and a communication matrix structure for the reviewer's role evaluation ruler design was constructed (Fig. 2). With educators and professionals in the fields of design, marketing, and advertising and with respect to the meaning, function, and development of the CIE; through eliminating subjectivity and preference, and thinking objectively and fairly, as a pilot questionnaire survey for perceptual deconstruction to confirm the perception of CIE, the validity of the perception and thinking of education and industry professionals on the recognition of the communication matrix structure, is used to construct the revision of the design model of the review ruler.

Subsequently, this study also divided the judging into two groups, namely the control group for competition judging and the experimental group for non-competitive judging. The original review is the control group, and the existing review method will be used, with the scoring methods of creativity (40%), fluency (30%), and completeness of conception (30%). In addition, the experimental group judged by the non-competition adopts the scoring method of the perceptual design model, and re-evaluates and records the competition works of this research with the method of questionnaire survey. Through this, we can understand the scoring status of the works, and analyze and discuss the similarities and differences between the original scoring mechanism and the review scale constructed by the CIE Perceptual Scoring Model.

3.1 Research Steps and Process

This study formulates a cognitive model as a design framework for the rubric. It creates a matrix structure evaluation rule for communication between creators and judges. A questionnaire is also designed to record points, so as to understand the gap between the rating status of the new reviewers and the original reviewers. Further confirmation and the effect in the learning process will become the basis for adjusting the direction in future teaching.

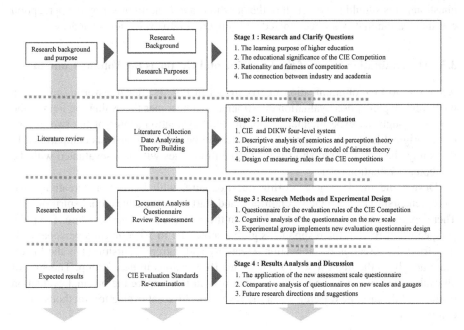

Fig. 5. Research Method and Process.

3.2 Contents of the Questionnaire on the Design of the CIE Assessment Perception Rulers and Gauges

The perception and identification of the score sheet is a layered deconstruction that needs to be obtained from the CIE education consensus in the previous research. Therefore, the content of the preliminary questionnaire is set to record three levels of innovation, creativity, and entrepreneurship, to confirm the linear recognition of the description and content of the CIE in the perception process, and the sense of identity with the proportion of CIE in one question, to ensure that the questionnaire is effectively filled out and interviewed. The differences in the common cognition of the participants are within the scope of control. Creativity, innovation, and entrepreneurship in CIE education are a cycle of thinking, practice, and continuation, so three-creation education should be a study that is equally important. While setting the questions, it also understands the cognition of the purpose of the CIE education.

Among the creativity-related question types, the identification and needs of discovery, challenge, and problem-solving are used as the starting point, and the purpose is to understand the source of creative thinking and the state of extensive learning and application in life. The innovation-related question type is to propose effective solutions and practice directions, understand the cognition of innovation in designers and reviewers, and in-depth learning experience of effective small problem solving. The spirit of entrepreneurship is also the focus of CIE, with the recognition of social needs, consumer experience and quantification, and the continuation of commercial thinking. The use of questionnaires should prove whether the questions and conditions set by the perception communication matrix are recognized and converted into evaluation standards.

3.3   The Evaluation Score of the Experimental Group as the Volume Content

According to the communication matrix model in Fig. 3, after transforming it into a mock review perception evaluation questionnaire, it becomes the evaluation item of the work. Through the experimental group, the total evaluation scores of the two groups of the original jury and the control group were obtained as an analysis comparison. In this study, the first to eight shortlisted competition cases will be re-evaluated with the perceptual evaluation ruler.

Design the mock review scoring questionnaire, with innovation, creativity and entrepreneurship as the review conditions, and start from the educational spirit of CIE. There are eight sets of one-minute videos in the review mock questionnaire. From the perspective of review, the respondents gave a score of 1 to 10 points and personal feelings from the direction of innovation, creativity and entrepreneurship (1 is the lowest score and 10 is the highest score). There are 10 questions in each group. The sum of all evaluation criteria is the ranking, which is used to compare the original evaluation results and discuss the differences in the results of different evaluation methods in the competition.

4   Results and Discussion

In the previous research, the perceptual model was used to formulate the content of the review rules, and the differences in cognition were understood by means of questionnaire survey. The number of returned questionnaires was 103. The obtained questionnaire responses are as follows.

77.1% of the surveyed data are related to the nature of the work and the development of CIE education. The study found that according to the questionnaire design of perceptual communication, there is a need for the overall educational goals of the CIE, and 69.9% of the respondents agree that from the perspective of education, the CIE must be balanced development. Based on this premise, the main content of the questionnaire is entered, and the three directions of creativity, innovation and creation are respectively carried out to reflect the thinking and identification questionnaires that the works need to present. The questionnaire is designed as a linear scale to understand the state of cognitive identification. In the creative survey questions, the linear scale diagram of the questionnaire responses is shown in Fig. 6 below.

Among the question items in Fig. 3 set by the conditions of the communication matrix structure diagram of the review role creator, as shown in Fig. 6, the linear scale percentage of the response to the perception questionnaire shows that the scale 1 to 3 is excluded. The average recognition rate of the creative perception evaluation items is as high as 71.3%. Responses to relevant questions agree with 75.1% of creative, 69.2% innovative, and 69.2% entrepreneurial. The research confirms that the project designed with the perception communication matrix not only agrees with the needs of CIE evaluation and learning, but also reaches a consensus on the needs of CIE by both creators and judges.

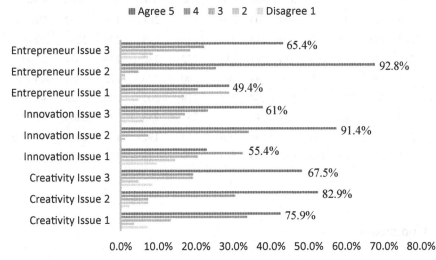

Fig. 6. Percentage Linear Scale of Responses to the CIE Perception Questionnaire (plotted in this study).

The review questionnaire is designed to be ranked in the order of 1st to 8th place in the original competition, and then the selection has a positive view on the learning balance of the CIE, and the non-original competition reviewers are 35 in the experimental group, and a new simulation review questionnaire is conducted. All the interviewees in the questionnaire summed up the individual questions in the individual works, and then re-ranked the accumulated total points to compare the statistics of the original competition review results, as shown in Table 1. In the data sheet, the work that ranked No. 1 in the original ranking will be reduced to No. 5, while the work that ranked No. 6 will be promoted to No. 1. The study found that there is a big difference between the rankings of the new judging rules formulated by the perceptual model and the original judging rules. The original number of reviewers was 5 people, and there were many testimonials and preference scores in the few and unclear project specifications. The clear perception project specification can effectively solve the biased criticism of the existing model. The large number of new test subjects also verifies the fairness of the new review rules formulated by the perception model.

In the creative test questions of items 1 to 3, it was also found that the original first place work and the first place after the new review results showed lower scores in the innovative projects. In the future teaching, it will help to analyze and strengthen the learning of lower scores, so as to present a more balanced reference direction for the development of CIE.

Table 1. Score Table of the CIE Film Competition Mock Review Project.

No.	Creativity			Innovation			Entrepreneurship					
	it.1	it.2	it.3	it.4	it.5	it.6	it.7	it.8	it.9	it.10	Score	Ranking
1	210	212	195	205	209	203	229	237	201	196	2097	5/1(old)
2	223	233	219	217	236	224	245	246	218	230	2291	3/2(old)
3	238	238	225	229	236	231	247	252	232	233	2361	2/3(old)
4	197	189	185	188	178	184	189	200	170	172	1852	8/4(old)
5	224	208	221	221	204	208	218	218	201	200	2123	4/5(old)
6	246	241	244	235	224	242	250	254	235	235	2406	1/6(old)
7	213	209	210	204	194	196	208	214	192	182	2022	6/7(old)
8	191	192	188	185	185	185	189	199	179	171	1873	7/8(old)

5 Conclusion

The purpose of this study is to establish a fair, impartial and objective review mechanism for the CIE, and to obtain recognition from the perception communication questionnaire. The goal of analyzing the teaching direction from the learning process is also achieved through the new review of the scoring rules.

After the grading rules for the CIE competitions are formulated, they can effectively produce a grading basis and structure that can be followed, and then modify the teaching direction, and improve the professional knowledge and thinking required by the industry. In addition to impartially reviewing the performance of works, the evaluation mechanism proposed in this study also understands the differences between the learning process and realistic goals, and then adjusts the teaching direction to realize the original intention of three-creation education. The design of the evaluation scale for the three innovation competitions in higher education only proposes a preliminary exploration of an effective evaluation model for educational development. The use of perception in the evaluation of three-creation education still needs to go through many trials and revisions before the effectiveness of perception evaluation can be verified. It is expected that CIE education will have more teaching development and thinking to improve learning effects, and discover models worth exploring and researching, so as to build the foundation for future international competitions.

References

Ackoff, R.L.: From data to wisdom. J. Appl. Syst. Anal. **16**(1), 3–9 (1989)

Amabile, T.M.: A consensual technique for creativity assessment. In: The Social Psychology of Creativity. SSSP, pp. 37–63. Springer, New York (1983). https://doi.org/10.1007/978-1-4612-5533-8_3

Amabile, T.M.: The social psychology of creativity: a componential conceptualization. J. Pers. Soc. Psychol. **45**(2), 357–376 (1983)

Adams, J.S.: Towards an understanding of inequity. Psychol. Sci. Public Interest **67**(5), 422–436 (1963)

Cleveland, H.: Information as resource. Futurist **16**(6), 34–39 (1982)

Hoy, W.K., Miskel, C.G.: Educational Administration, Theory, Research and Practice. McGraw-Hill, New York (1991)

Yi, C.J.: Visual Rhetoric, Aesthetics, and Narrative for Enhancing Reader Engagement in the Visualization of Interactive Information (unpublished doctoral dissertation). National Taipei University of Technology Design Doctoral Program, Taipei City (2022)

Ling, C.M.: Create a Year of Educational Innovation Action: Minister of Education Wu Sihua challenges Taiwan's education with "innovation". Educational Research Monthly, P5-P14 (2022)

Jing, C.X.:The Influence of Painting Display Media on Viewing Experience (unpublished doctoral dissertation). Institute of Creative Industry Design, National Taiwan University of Arts, New Taipei City (2018). https://hdl.handle.net/11296/pf6mec. Accessed 05 Oct 2022

Fang, C.H.: Research on Self-Concept, Learning Attitude and Employability of Students in Early Childhood Care Departments of Science and Technology Universities (unpublished doctoral dissertation), National Taipei University of Technology Technical and Vocational Education Research, Taipei City (2013)

Department of Higher Education, Ministry of Education of the Republic of China, Global Information Network of the Ministry of Education (2019)

Yun, D.J., Fei, C.W., Xi, Y.Y.: A case study of the influence of the inventor story teaching method on the integration of creativity into the teaching of professional subjects in electronics courses in higher vocational education. J. Tech. Vocat. Educ. **3**(2), 41–71 (2009). Department of Business Administration, National Taipei University, New Taipei City

Festinger, L.: A theory of social comparison processes. Hum. Relat. **7**, 117–140 (1954)

Wun, H.J.: Analysis of audience reception of music entertainment programs (unpublished master thesis). Institute of Communication, National Chiao Tung University, Hsinchu City (2007)

Hall, S., Xing, C.G.: Cultural Studies - Interview with Hall (Tang Weimin, translation). Yuan Zun Culture, Taipei (1998)

Liang, H.Y., You, W.Y.: The Second Basic Plan for Education Promotion (2013 Edition), **3**(1), 1–38 (2019)

Liang, H.S.: Probability Intensive Lecture Notes. New Taipei: Wensheng Bookstore (1995)

Yanru, L., Po, L., Tai, L.R.: Preliminary research on general audience's cognitive model of "neural network-like" artistic style transfer. J. Des. **26**(3), 61–84 (2021)

Sian, S.C., Tai., L.R.: Cultural product design program. J. Des.**16**(4), 1–18 (2011)

de Saussure, F.M.: Course in General Linguistics. In: Bally, C., Sechehaye, A., Harris, R. (eds.) Open Court, Chicago (1997). trans

Seltzer, V.C.: Social Comparison Behavior of Adolescents. In: Pepiton, E.A. (Ed.), Children in cooperation and competition. Lexington, Ma: Lexington Books (1980)

Shu, S.: Language and speech - rereading saussure's "course of general linguistics" and discussing the necessity of establishing linguistics. Russ. J. **19**, 1–15 (2012)

Taylor, S.E., Lobel, M.: Social comparison activity under threat: downward evaluation and upward contacts. Psychol. Rev. **96**, 569–575 (1989)

Seelig, T.: Insight Out: Get Ideas Out of Your Head and Into the World. (Lin Li Xue, translated). Taipei: Yuanliu (2016)

Chiang, T.Y.: Introduction to the Linguistics of Speech. Peking University Press, Beijing (2006)

The Second Basic Plan for Educational Promotion (2013 Edition) [The Second Basic Plan for Educational Promotion (Summary)]. Japan: Ministry of Education, Culture, Sports, Science and Technology of Japan. https://www.mext.go.jp/a_menu/keikaku/detail/1336379.htm, Accessed 10 Nov 2022

Li, W.Z.: School Administration Research, Kaohsiung Fuwen Books, Kaohsiung (1997)

Zhe, X.H.: A Social Comparison Theory of Tablet Adoption Intention - Moderated by Modes of Technology Acceptance (Unpublished Master's Thesis). Department of Business Administration, National Taipei University, New Taipei City (2012)

Zeleny, M.: Human Systems Management: Integrating Knowledge, Management and Systems. World Scientific, Singapore (2005)

Impact of Synchronous and Asynchronous Learning Approach: A Comparative Study of Graphic Design Students in a Developing Country (Botswana) Verses a Developed Country (UK)

Gerald Kennedy[✉]

University of Huddersfield, Queensgate, Huddersfield HD1 3DH, West Yorkshire, UK
geraldbkennedy@zohomail.eu

Abstract. The move to synchronous and asynchronous learning occurred during the extraordinary disruption of the Covid-19 pandemic. This case study, conducted by a self-completion questionnaire, aimed to provide a dual-perspective and comparative picture of the situation by investigating the impact of this new learning approach on graphic design students in a developing country (Botswana) verses a developed country (UK). This was done by comparing how teaching and learning were affected, how education stakeholders responded to the educational disruption, and how the students felt about it within the University of Botswana (Botswana) and the University of Huddersfield (UK).

Whilst research currently exists on teaching problems in developing and developed countries, they do not focus specifically on graphic design students in an internationally comparable way. A future benefit to this report, that would require further investigation and collaboration, is that academics who shift from one country to another could develop a framework to enable that shift to be seamless. This report presents data collected from two different universities in two different countries covering topics like previous experience with learning online, preferences with learning online, benefits, hindrances and how to address queries.

Whilst most of the students demonstrated a positive attitude towards online classes during the pandemic, with both country's liking the flexible and convenient way to study, only students from Botswana would be interested in staying online. This study further emphasizes that close monitoring and evaluation of the learning process is still required regardless of whether the programme has a synchronous and/or asynchronous learning approach.

Keywords: UK · Botswana · Graphic Design · Pedagogical knowledge · Technological literacy · Online tutoring systems · Online learning · Perception · Readiness · Preferences · Content analysis

P.-L. P. Rau (Ed.): HCII 2023, LNCS 14024, pp. 215–231, 2023.
https://doi.org/10.1007/978-3-031-35946-0_18

1 Introduction

At the peak of educational institutes closures, in early April 2020, 180 countries had implemented a nationwide closure of all educational institutes, affecting about 90% of the total enrolled learners (UNESCO, 2022). This was due to the Covid-19 virus spreading around the world. The virus was spread by being in close contact with an infected person, a scenario highly likely in an enclosed classroom. As it was impossible at the time to know how long these closures would be implemented both educational institutions, and students, were examining ways to complete their prescribed curriculums in line with the academic calendar. Globally, schools were fully closed for an average of 14 weeks, with Botswana (19.9 weeks) and the UK (25.9 weeks) exceeding that (UNESCO, 2021).

Whilst these measures caused an unprecedented crisis in education across the globe, they have also prompted new examples of educational innovation using digital interventions. This may be sanguine but considering the often reluctance within certain higher academic institutions for reforms, particularly in Botswana, it may well save them. Consider, for example, that for 500 years the book's historical role in learning has been based on the primacy of text over the visual.

Contemporary research shows that we learn faster through the use of visual media when utilized in learning (Parkinson, 2010). The Fourth Industrial Revolution (4IR) has arrived, bringing with it a dynamic, contextual, and linking environment. Pedagogy has become ever more reliant on technology and during the pandemic this transition was fast tracked, so teachers need to have a passion for and eagerness to experiment with these new modes of engagement and have thoughtful consideration of the tools that allow for this new deeper engagement. The impact of the Fourth Industrial Revolution (4IR) on design education and learning, and indeed teaching, has been profound. The majority of people are visual learners and retain far more when presented with an infographic than a paragraph (Parkinson, 2010). Graphic design students should not have to endure a body of content that must be learned off by heart but should appreciate a process of questioning and exploration. For contemporary educators the challenge between synchronous and asynchronous delivery becomes a significant one, as it calls for very different ways of student engagement. It can also offer more flexibility and opportunities to explore, discover, and find one's own way by self-guided instruction. This comes with even more class management challenges related to the calibre, and indeed technical ability, of the leaners.

As most countries are now open, reopening, or planning to reopen their education institutions, the priority is to ensure the return of all learners. However, experience from past crises and economic shocks suggest that not all students will be able to return. UNESCO projections, covering 180 countries and territories, estimate that Tertiary education will be affected the most, with an estimated 3.5% decline in enrolment, resulting in 7.9 million fewer students. The second largest share of learners (5.3 million) at risk of not returning are found in sub-Saharan Africa (Giannini, 2020).

Having lectured in the "University of Botswana" during the initial phases of the pandemic, and then the "University of Huddersfield" during its final phases, I have a unique insight into the challenges faced with synchronous and asynchronous learning approaches in a developing country and a developed country. This paper shares the results of a combination of a synchronous and asynchronous learning and teaching approach used for undergraduate graphic design students in a developing country and a developed country and compares them.

The study is important for two main reasons. Firstly, countries can learn from each other's approaches and mistakes. The curriculum of graphic design is such that practical aspects are a large and important part of the programme and adapting them to online platforms can be decidedly tricky. Secondly, educational intuitions can learn to adapt to students needs and preferences. At the end of the day, it is all about understanding how to best educate within a given socio-cultural context, and as this changes from place to place, our methods also need to change.

As there are now many ways to design and deliver asynchronous content, it is increasingly important to also take into consideration the preferences of the student to encourage, and indeed not hinder, participation. The Australian National Training Authority investigated the readiness of students for online learning mainly in terms of three aspects: (1) the online delivery preference of students; (2) the student's confidence in their technical ability; and (3) their capability to engage in autonomous learning (Warner et al. 1998). The student's perception is vital to accommodate any effort to improve the effectiveness of online learning. Whilst previous studies have identified basic frameworks and obstacles to asynchronous learning, not many have attempted to understand how the cultural and socio-economic situation might change a student's perception and preference in the context of a specific developed country comparatively to a specific developing country with primary research.

Furthermore, to the best of my knowledge, a study specifically in the field of graphic design education, with a very high share of practical learning in the curriculum, within the above context has not been attempted.

This paper is an attempt to try to fill this gap as well as used to further explore strategies that could be developed to create a more supportive learning environment. A case study approach recommended by Yin (2008) and Stake (1995) was employed because the phenomena being investigated had not been studied before within the context of the UK and Botswana. Baseline data was collected using a self-completion questionnaire. A questionnaire was chosen because the students represented a larger size of the sample. For purposes of gaining a holistic picture the research employed both quantitative and qualitative research instrumentation.

1.1 Methodology

Participants:

	University of Botswana (Botswana)	University of Huddersfield (UK)
Cohort	39	78
Responses	16 (41%)	29 (37%)

Graphic design students in their second-to-last year (in Botswana this would be 4th year students as the degree is five years, and in the UK, 2nd year students as the degree is three years) were chosen as the respondents for this study as they are in the semi-autonomous stage of their degree, not as inexperienced as 1st years, but not as confident as final years. Also, the subject is largely practical and requires students to use expensive studio equipment not always readily available at home, e.g., specialist printing (large format, 3D, silkscreen, RISO etc.), laser cutters, book binding machines etc.

117 students were eligible to participate (39 from Botswana and 78 from the UK) with 45 partaking (16 from Botswana and 29 from the UK). This represented 41% of all Batswana students and 37% of all UK students in their respective cohorts. 23 were Female, 21 were Male, and 1 identified as non-binary.

1.2 Procedure

A preliminary questionnaire was put together from discussions with students who were currently attending the online classes in Botswana. Pre-testing was done with a sample of four students (10% of the cohort) and their feedback were considered for the final questionnaire.

1.3 Domain of the Study

The online survey was built in Microsoft Forms and the link was sent to the UK students through Microsoft Teams (as I currently work here) and the link was sent to my former Batswana students through a WhatsApp group formed during the pandemic. I closed the form after 10 days of circulation.

1.4 Data Analysis

Data were collected on demographics, preferences, perceptions, advantages, disadvantages, and suggestions. To analyse and summarise the data frequency, percentages were calculated for most of the questions with statements being rated on a five-point continuum scale (five being most effective and one being the least effective).

2 Section 1: Demographic Details of the Students

This section was formed of sex, age, and place of residence. This question intended to see if the impact of synchronous and asynchronous learning affected the sexes differently, and/or, what sexes were more inclined to respond. The same logic applies to the age range and finally the place of residence sets the scene for the environment a student was in during the closures and how that may or may not affect them.

Botswana   UK

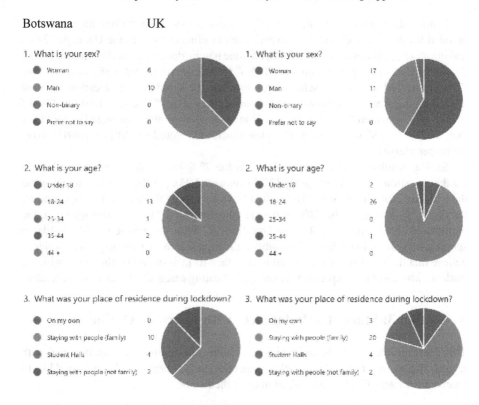

The majority of Batswana students who participated were Male (63%), aged between 18–24 (100%) and living at home with their family (70%).

The majority of UK students who participated were Female (59%), aged between 18–24 (88%) and living at home with their family (65%).

3 Section 2: Information Regarding Previous Experience with Learning Online

This question intended to see any if previous experience with online learning had an impact on a student's perception or ability to adapt to the new learning environment.

Botswana   UK

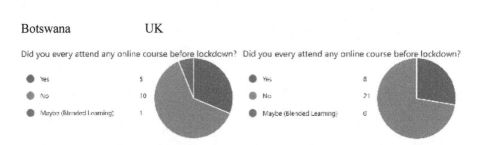

Among the respondents, only six (37%) from Botswana (with one having done a blended learning course) had prior experience of online classes. In the UK eight (28%) had prior experience of online classes (with none having done a blended learning course).

Of the 63% of people who answered "No" for this question (Botswana), the majority (70%) answered "As per the schedule to complete the syllabus" for Question 8, "How often did you expect the course tutor to conduct the classes?". However, of the 37% of people who answered "Yes" for this question, the majority (80%) answered either "Less than 2 h" or "2–4 h" for Question 10, "How much time would you like to spend in a day for online classes".

Similar results occurred in the UK with the 73% of people who answered "No" for this question (UK), the majority (72%) answered "As per the schedule to complete the syllabus" for Question 8, "How often did you expect the course tutor to conduct the classes?". However, the 28% of people who answered "Yes" for this question, the majority (63%) answered "2–4 h" for Question 10, "How much time would you like to spend in a day for online classes", possibly indicating that those with no prior experience believe that the duration of a class online and face-to-face should be the same, with the students who had prior experience of online indicating that a shorter class is preferable.

4 Section 3: Student's Preferences with Learning Online

This question intended to investigate what student's preferences, if any, they had with regards to how they connect to the class, what device they prefer, and how they'd like to receive the material and communication from their tutor.

Botswana   UK

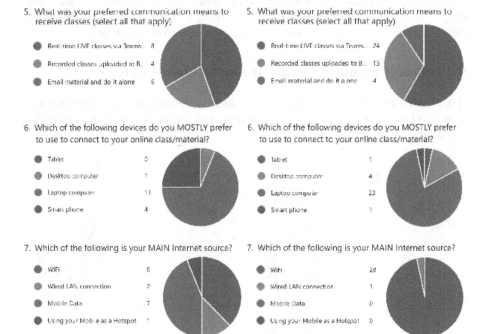

5. What was your preferred communication means to receive classes (select all that apply)

● Real-time LIVE classes via Teams   8

● Recorded classes uploaded to B..   4

● Email material and do it alone   6

5. What was your preferred communication means to receive classes (select all that apply)

● Real-time LIVE classes via Teams... 24

● Recorded classes uploaded to B..   13

● Email material and do it one   4

6. Which of the following devices do you MOSTLY prefer to use to connect to your online class/material?

● Tablet   0

● Desktop computer   1

● Laptop computer   11

● Smart phone   4

6. Which of the following devices do you MOSTLY prefer to use to connect to your online class/material?

● Tablet   1

● Desktop computer   4

● Laptop computer   23

● Smart phone   1

7. Which of the following is your MAIN Internet source?

● WiFi   6

● Wired LAN connection   2

● Mobile Data   7

● Using your Mobile as a Hotspot 1

7. Which of the following is your MAIN Internet source?

● WiFi   28

● Wired LAN connection   1

● Mobile Data   0

● Using your Mobile as a Hotspot 0

In Botswana 44% had a preference for "Real-time LIVE classes via Teams, Zoom etc. (synchronous)" with 87% accessing these classes via a "Laptop computer" using "Mobile Data" (43%).

Not too far behind, on 33%, was a preference for "Email material and do it alone" with 80% accessing these classes via a "Laptop computer" using "Wi-Fi" (60%).

The least preferred option, on 22%, was "Recorded classes uploaded to BrightSpace, BlackBoard, Moodle etc. (asynchronous)" with 66% accessing these classes via a "Smart phone" using "Mobile Data" (66%).

In the UK 58% had a preference for "Real-time LIVE classes via Teams, Zoom etc. (synchronous)" with 91% accessing these classes via a "Laptop computer" using "Wi-Fi" (100%).

The second most preferred option, on 31%, was a preference for "Recorded classes uploaded to BrightSpace, BlackBoard, Moodle etc. (asynchronous)" with 80% accessing these classes via a "Laptop computer" using "Wi-Fi" (80%).

The least preferred option, on 9%, was "Email material and do it alone" with 100% accessing these classes via a "Laptop computer" using "Wi-Fi" (100%).

Botswana had a much greater spread on how they wanted to engage with online learning with less than half of the students (44%) making up the majority of wanting "Real-time LIVE classes" and "Email material and do it alone" not too far behind (33%). This is in stark contrast to the UK where students overwhelmingly preferred (58%) "Real-time LIVE classes" and a very small minority (9%) "Email material and do it alone". The reasons for this would require further investigation but could have something to do with the majority of Batswana relying on using "Mobile Data" (50%) as opposed to 0% in the UK. Also, despite the majority of people in Botswana (68%) using a "Laptop computer" there was still 25% using a "Smart phone", suggesting that the chosen platform for delivery should be compatible with smart phones.

5   Section 4: Frequency and Duration of Online Classes

This question intended to investigate what student's preferences, if any, they had with regards to how often they were required to connect to the class, and for how long they would prefer to do so.

Botswana   UK

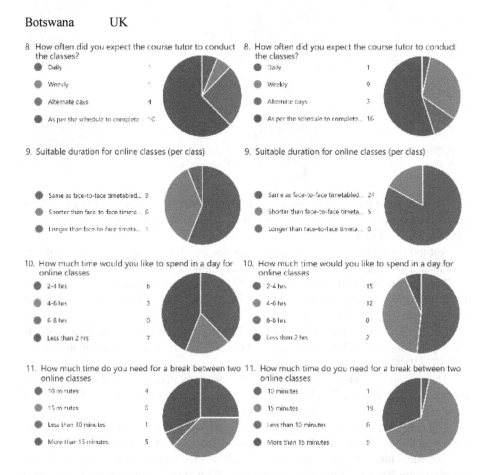

In Botswana 63% had a preference for "As per the schedule to complete the syllabus" in relation to the frequency of the classes, with 56% preferring the duration to be the "Same as face-to-face timetabled class" and 38% requiring a break of "15 min" between classes. The majority (44%) would like to spend "Less than 2 h" in a day for online classes. Classes tend to be timetabled all day in Botswana but 40% of the students who answered, "As per the schedule to complete the syllabus", also stated that they would like to spend "Less than 2 h" in a day for online classes, possibly indicating that they would like some autonomous time which is a large feature in a face-to-face graphic design course, especially as the programme of study progresses.

In the UK 55% had a preference for "As per the schedule to complete the syllabus" in relation to the frequency of the classes, with 83% preferring the duration to be the "Same as face-to-face timetabled class" and 66% requiring a break of "15 min" between classes. The majority (52%) would like to spend "2–4 h" in a day for online classes. Similarly, to Botswana, classes tend to be timetabled all day yet 68% of the students who answered, "As per the schedule to complete the syllabus", also stated that they would like to spend either "Less than 2 h" (6%) or "2–4 h" (62%) in a day for online classes.

6 Section 5: Addressing Queries

This question intended to investigate what student's preferences, if any, they had with regards to how to solve an issue they were having, and how long they expected to wait for clarity.

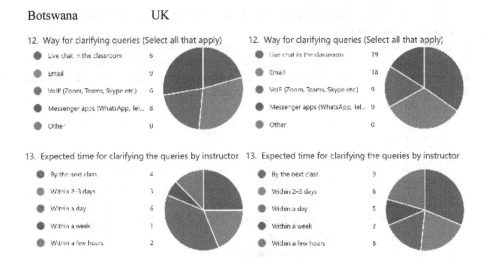

In Botswana the majority (31%) had a preference for "Email" in relation to ways for clarifying queries, closely followed by "Messenger apps (WhatsApp, Telegram, Messenger etc.)" at 28%. "Live chat in the classroom" and "VoIP (Zoom, Teams, Skype etc.)" came in the same at 21%.

The majority (38%) would like a response to their query "Within a day", however, 25% were happy to wait until the next class for clarity despite 50% of those students choosing "Email", "Messenger apps (WhatsApp, Telegram, Messenger etc.)" or "VoIP (Zoom, Teams, Skype etc.)" as their preferred way for clarifying queries. In other words, not "Live".

In the UK the majority (35%) had a preference for "Live chat in the classroom" in relation to ways for clarifying queries, closely followed by "Email" at 33%. "Messenger apps (WhatsApp, Telegram, Messenger etc.)" and "VoIP (Zoom, Teams, Skype etc.)" came in the same at 16%.

The majority (31%) would like a response to their query "By the next class" with 66% choosing "Live chat in the classroom" as their preferred way for clarifying queries indicating that they would like the response "Live".

7 Section 6: Student's Perception Towards Online Learning

This question intended to investigate what student's preferences, if any, they had with regards if they prefer face-to-face or online.

Seven statements were put to the students, and they were asked to rate them along a scale of a five-point continuum with 1 being "Strongly agree" all the way up to 5 being "Strongly disagree".

The seven statements are as follows:

1. I prefer my online courses as they are very structured with set due dates similar to face-to-face courses
2. Online classes help me to better comprehend the course materials compared to Classroom learning
3. Online environment makes it easier for me to communicate with my instructor than classroom environment
4. I am more comfortable responding to questions by email than orally
5. My technical skills (email/internet apps) have increased since attending online classes
6. I spend more time on my homework in comparison with regular classroom learning
7. My instructor understands the online environment and makes it easy to learn

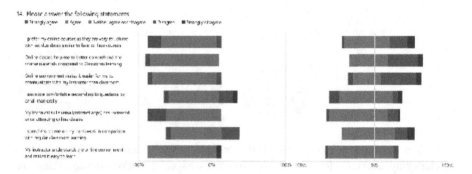

The results from Botswana would suggest a very strong preference for online learning across all seven statements with only two statements (4 and 7) getting a "Strongly Disagree" score, and even then, it was only 12% for both statements combined (6% each).

Botswana:
To statement (1) 81% of students chose either "Strongly agree" (19%) or "Agree" (62%), with only 6% choosing "Disagree", 12% being neutral and choosing "Neither agree nor disagree" and 0% choosing "Strongly Disagree".

To statement (2) 81% of students chose either "Strongly agree" (6%) or "Agree" (75%), with only 0% choosing "Disagree", 19% being neutral and choosing "Neither agree nor disagree" and 0% choosing "Strongly Disagree".

To statement (3) 81% of students chose either "Strongly agree" (6%) or "Agree" (75%), with only 6% choosing "Disagree", 13% being neutral and choosing "Neither agree nor disagree" and 0% choosing "Strongly Disagree".

To statement (4) 56% of students chose either "Strongly agree" (6%) or "Agree" (50%), with only 18% choosing "Disagree", 18% being neutral and choosing "Neither agree nor disagree" and 6% choosing "Strongly Disagree".

To statement (5) 75% of students chose either "Strongly agree" (25%) or "Agree" (50%), with only 0% choosing "Disagree", 25% being neutral and choosing "Neither agree nor disagree" and 0% choosing "Strongly Disagree".

To statement (6) 50% of students chose either "Strongly agree" (44%) or "Agree" (6%), with only 25% choosing "Disagree", 25% being neutral and choosing "Neither agree nor disagree" and 0% choosing "Strongly Disagree".

To statement (7) 81% of students chose "Agree", 0% selected "Strongly agree" or "Disagree", 13% were neutral and chose "Neither agree nor disagree" and 6% chose "Strongly Disagree".

UK:

The results from the UK were much more diverse compared to Botswana with 4/7 statements having preferences across all five options.

To statement (1) only 24% of students chose either "Strongly agree" (21%) or "Agree" (3%), with 25% choosing "Disagree", 41% being neutral and choosing "Neither agree nor disagree" and 10% choosing "Strongly Disagree".

To statement (2) only 17% of students chose "Agree" with 0% choosing "Strongly agree", 41% choosing "Disagree", 35% being neutral and choosing "Neither agree nor disagree" and 7% choosing "Strongly Disagree".

To statement (3) only 28% of students chose either "Strongly agree" (7%) or "Agree" (21%), with 48% choosing "Disagree", 17% being neutral and choosing "Neither agree nor disagree" and 7% choosing "Strongly Disagree".

To statement (4) only 38% of students chose either "Strongly agree" (14%) or "Agree" (24%), with only 7% choosing "Disagree", 48% being neutral and choosing "Neither agree nor disagree" and 7% choosing "Strongly Disagree".

To statement (5) 48% of students chose either "Strongly agree" (3%) or "Agree" (45%), with only 14% choosing "Disagree", 35% being neutral and choosing "Neither agree nor disagree" and 3% choosing "Strongly Disagree".

To statement (6) only 17% of students chose "Agree", 0% selected " Strongly agree", 17% choose "Disagree", 56% were neutral and chose "Neither agree nor disagree" and 10% chose "Strongly Disagree".

To statement (7) 41% of students chose either "Strongly agree" (3%) or "Agree" (38%), with only 7% choosing "Disagree", 52% being neutral and choosing "Neither agree nor disagree" and 0% choosing "Strongly Disagree".

I took all this information and put it into a table and highlighted in red any result which had a ≤5% difference. This happened on seven occasions highlighting the statements and feelings from each country were in synch with each other.

No.	Botswana / UK									
	Strongly agree		Agree		Neither agree nor disagree		Disagree		Strongly Disagree	
(1)	19%	21%	62%	3%	12%	41%	6%	25%	0%	10%
(2)	6%	0%	75%	17%	19%	35%	0%	41%	0%	7%
(3)	6%	7%	75%	21%	13%	17%	6%	48%	0%	7%
(4)	6%	14%	50%	24%	18%	48%	18%	7%	6%	7%
(5)	25%	3%	50%	45%	25%	35%	0%	14%	0%	3%
(6)	44%	0%	6%	17%	25%	56%	25%	17%	0%	10%
(7)	0%	3%	81%	38%	13%	52%	0%	7%	6%	0%

7.1 Similarities (≤5% Difference)

Statement (1) "I prefer my online courses as they are very structured with set due dates similar to face-to-face courses". Both countries had a similar percentage of students choose "Strongly agree".

Statement (3) "Online environment makes it easier for me to communicate with my instructor than classroom environment". Both countries had a similar percentage of students choose "Strongly agree" and "Neither agree nor disagree".

Statement (4) "I am more comfortable responding to questions by email than orally". Both countries had a similar percentage of students choose "Strongly disagree".

Statement (5) "My technical skills (email/internet apps) have increased since attending online classes". Both countries had a similar percentage of students choose "Agree" and "Strongly disagree".

Statement (7) "My instructor understands the online environment and makes it easy to learn". Both countries had a similar percentage of students choose "Strongly agree".

8 Section 7: Benefits of Online Learning

This question intended to investigate what students perceive as the benefits, if any, with online learning as opposed to face-to-face.

Botswana:

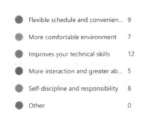

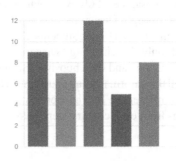

In Botswana "Improves your technical skills" was seen as the most beneficial aspect of online learning followed by "Flexible schedule and convenience". The results of the study would suggest that Batswana see asynchronous online learning as offering them the ability to study at their own pace and convenience, as well as improving their technical ability. "Self-discipline and responsibility", "More comfortable environment", and "More interaction and greater ability to concentrate" were ranked third, fourth and fifth respectively. No students selected "Other".

UK:

15. Benefits of online learning (Select all that apply)

More Details

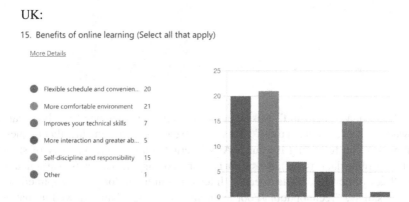

● Flexible schedule and convenien...	20
● More comfortable environment	21
● Improves your technical skills	7
● More interaction and greater ab...	5
● Self-discipline and responsibility	15
● Other	1

In the UK "More comfortable environment" was seen as the most beneficial aspect of online learning followed by "Flexible schedule and convenience". The results of the study would suggest that in the UK students see asynchronous online learning as offering them the ability to study in a more comfortable environment and at their own pace and convenience. "Self-discipline and responsibility", "Improves your technical skills" and "More interaction and greater ability to concentrate" were ranked third, fourth and fifth respectively". One student selected "Other" and stated, "I can't say there's any benefits in an online environment, I believe the best work is completed in a face-to-face environment/studio where I actually feel like I'm at work. It creates more structure, the process of getting up and going to the studio, treating it much like going to the office".

9   Section 8: Hindrances of Online Learning

This question intended to investigate what students perceive as the hindrances, if any, with online learning as opposed to face-to-face.

Botswana

16. Hindrance of online learning (Select all that apply)

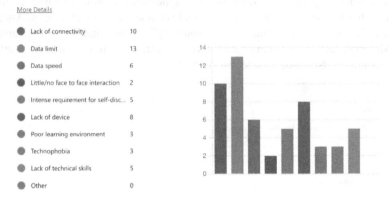

More Details

● Lack of connectivity	10
● Data limit	13
● Data speed	6
● Little/no face to face interaction	2
● Intense requirement for self-disc...	5
● Lack of device	8
● Poor learning environment	3
● Technophobia	3
● Lack of technical skills	5
● Other	0

In Botswana "Data limit" was seen as the biggest hinderance to online learning followed by "Lack of connectivity". This makes sense based off the fact that in question 7, "Which of the following is your MAIN Internet source?" the majority of students selected "Mobile data" (44%). Botswana is a rural country with many phone signal blind spots. "Lack of device", "Data Speed", "Intense requirement for self-discipline/Lack of technical skills", "Technophobia/Poor learning environment" all followed in that order with "Little/no face-to-face interaction" coming in last.

The study highlights that three out of the top four hinderances are limitations of the country's internet infrastructure, not helped by the country's landlocked status. The other member of the top four, "Lack of device" possibly highlighting Botswana's wealth divide and lack of equity in access to technology.

These gives an insight that if Botswana wants to move towards online education, and it's clear from this report that the students want to (81% of students indicated that they prefer online), then as a pre-requisite it should focus on its internet facilities and accessibility to technology, specifically "Laptops" as this is the device of choice for 69% of students as per question 6, "Which of the following devices do you MOSTLY prefer to use to connect to your online class/material?".

A lack of traditional face-to-face interactions in classrooms seems to be of little concern to the students. Further investigation is needed to establish why.

UK:

16. Hindrance of online learning (Select all that apply)

More Details

● Lack of connectivity	10
● Data limit	13
● Data speed	6
● Little/no face to face interaction	2
● Intense requirement for self-disc...	5
● Lack of device	8
● Poor learning environment	3
● Technophobia	3
● Lack of technical skills	5
● Other	0

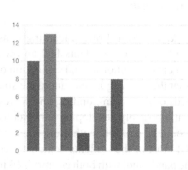

In the UK "Little/no face-to-face interaction" was seen as the biggest hinderance to online learning followed by "Lack of connectivity". This is somewhat surprising with 100% of the students in question 7, "Which of the following is your MAIN Internet source?" selecting either "Wi-Fi" (97%) or "Wired LAN connection" (3%), not to mention the UK having high speed fibre optic broadband readily available. I wonder if the students interpreted it as a physical lack of connection.

"Intense requirement for self-discipline", "Data Speed", "Poor learning environment", "Data limit", "Lack of device", "Other", and "Lack of technical skills" all followed in that order with "Technophobia" coming in last.

"Data Speed" showing up in fourth place is also surprising as question 6, "Which of the following devices do you MOSTLY prefer to use to connect to your online class/material?" showed only 3% connected with a "Smart phone".

Four students selected "Other" and stated:

1. "Feels less personal, asking questions to tutor is more difficult over online classes. Getting help isn't always instant, a second call may need to follow get help".
2. "I feel as if the more comfortable I am at home, the less likely I am to do any work, concentrate, listen and don't have the same feeling and connectivity with the tutors as I would if I was face to face".
3. "Email conversations become tiresome especially when it takes over a week to get a reply".
4. 'Cannot replicate the studio atmosphere needed for my course"

The study highlights that two of the top three hinderances in the UK are a lack of "Little/no face-to-face interaction" and an "Intense requirement for self-discipline", possibly indicating that the UK students are not yet comfortable working autonomously. The other member of the top three, "Lack of connectivity" is surprising for the above reasons and as previously stated, I wonder if the students interpreted it as a physical lack of connection. This requires further investigation but would be in keeping with the other top hinderances if true.

These gives an insight that if the UK wants to move towards online education, and it's not clear from this report that the students want to (only 24% of students indicated that they prefer online), then there will be issues around the lack of face-to-face interactions in classrooms. Working autonomously and self-discipline is also a major concern.

10 Conclusion

While the kind of self-directed learning in asynchronous approaches is supposed to be empowering, since the students feel an ownership over their learning, this study has shown that close monitoring and evaluation of the learning process is still required. This ensures that the learning is relevant to the students' world and to their interests, relevant to the needs of their communities, and solves problems that they need to solve. Further research into possibly developing a toolset for academics who shift from one country to another could be possible with more studies like this one.

Whilst most of the students demonstrated a positive attitude towards online classes during the pandemic, with both country's liking the flexible and convenient way to study, only students from Botswana would be interested in staying online.

Shifting to the online learning mode requires the interweaving of three knowledge bases, namely: subject matter knowledge, pedagogical knowledge, and technological literacy. Of the students, the UK most showed adaptation to the approach by submitting good quality outcomes on the set deadlines. A few had commitment issues with the asynchronous tasks and failed them. All students had a good grasp of the technology tools required for learning the course, with most of them using them effectively.

In contrast, the shift to online learning platforms was a relatively new phenomenon to both lecturers and students at the University of Botswana. Not all the lecturers were proficient in integrating technology into teaching and learning with many refusing to engage with the use of online learning platforms to deliver lessons. There are also challenges relating to broadband connectivity issues across the country which makes it a challenge for students to access the learning materials. This problem is further compounded by the fact that not all students or lecturers have their own computers or laptops at home and/or internet access.

Whilst digital content has undoubtedly explored new avenues for design and education by moving it well beyond the traditional chalk and talk classroom to create an interactive, engaged, and participatory classroom, it is clear that it is not panacea. This is especially true for graphic design students as they require workshop access and a large breadth of practical print processes that are unavailable to them online. In the non-virtual world people still must work together face-to-face, live together, and carry out projects. An acquisition of online knowledge, skills and even collaboration abilities have its place in this mix, but it is one part of a wide range of life skills needed to succeed and be happy in life.

Appendix

In total, 16 questions were asked to determine the impact of the synchronous and asynchronous learning approach adopted across the two countries.

Link to a summary of the Botswana Form results:

https://forms.office.com/Pages/AnalysisPage.aspx?AnalyzerToken=EfcufwNgV7MG
hjMvGkviQrk3e8VhLxId&id=2p8utZEGhUW9_FzK4c4YkFaJ03LGP6ZBrYNiW
0S9TlRUNjJHQVQ0WE5UUENNM0FPMTczTFNDRTg3Qi4u.

Link to a summary of the UK Form results:
https://forms.office.com/Pages/AnalysisPage.aspx?AnalyzerToken=6NR4dLdxkrtA
MF1xK3DrTS1RqmwELW7P&id=2p8utZEGhUW9_FzK4c4YkFaJ03LGP6ZBrY
NiW0S9TlRUNVBNV1AyR001V0NXU0YxWEE0WFBGOVBOMC4u.

References

Giannini, S.: UNESCO COVID-19 Education Response How many students are at risk of not returning to school? UNESCO Publishing (2020)
Parkinson, M.: Do-It-Yourself Billion Dollar Graphics. Pepperlip Pr. (2010)
Stake, R.E.: The Art of Case Study Research. Sage Publications (1995)
UNESCO: UNESCO figures show two thirds of an academic year lost on average worldwide due to Covid-19 school closures. UNESCO (2021). https://en.unesco.org/news/unesco-figures-show-two-thirds-academic-year-lost-average-worldwide-due-covid-19-school
UNESCO: The Impact of the COVID-19 Pandemic on Education. UNESCO Publishing (2022)
Warner, D., Christie, G., Choy, S.: Readiness of VET clients for flexible delivery including on-line learning. Australian National Training Authority (1998)
Yin, R.K.: Case Study Research: Design and Methods. Applied Social Research Methods, 4th edn. SAGE Publications (2008)

Design of an AR Application to Support Students with CVD in Learning Chemistry

Weijane Lin⬤, Pei-Luo Hung, and Hsiu-Ping Yueh(✉)⬤

National Taiwan University, No.1, Sec.4, Roosevelt Rd., Taipei 10617, Taiwan
{vjlin,r11126008,yueh}@ntu.edu.tw

Abstract. Color Vision Deficiency (CVD) is a common visual impairment. Research shows that CVD affects studying and life by facing difficulties in color distinction. However, it often relies on people having CVD to self-adjust or find alternative tools when resolving the problem or providing general color distinguishing support without considering the need for reading and learning in a specific subject. Therefore, this research dives into using augmented reality(AR), particularly its synchronous integration feature, to develop color vision support in science learning and design a system to support CVD students in high school chemistry reading. This research first reviewed existing technological approaches to support color vision, and the national curriculum of chemistry in secondary education. An exemplary lesson plan with the selected topic of the universal indicator was developed accordingly to test the AR color vision support with a texture-based approach. 8 high school students joined the user testing to assess the interface and flow of the prototype.

Keywords: Color Vision Deficiency · Augmented Reality · Texture Support · Chemistry Learning · Secondary Education

1 Introduction

Color is important for scientific practices and learning. Color Vision Deficiency (CVD), also known as color blindness or color weakness, is a common visual impairment that refers to a congenital or acquired deficiency in recognizing color. According to the local and global survey [1–3], although the degree and type vary, about 5%–8% of men and 0.8% of women around the world have color vision deficiency. However, their difficulty and inaccessibility were often overlooked because they looked the same as ordinary people and could often self-adjust, which may also be at the expense of their own needs, such as sacrificing their choices of colors in daily life or making decisions based on other cues instead of colors [4]. For example, they were unable to judge the ripeness of fruits, having difficulty in identifying skin rashes or reading map information due to similar colors. Some CVD patients were unable to drive due to the inability to tell traffic lights. In several critical learning or reading activities that required color recognition, CVD could significantly impact their learning competence and performance [5]. Students were unable to identify red characters written on the board, and it could even affect their mental health and career choices [6]. Furthermore, the flourishing online learning with screen technologies during the COVID-19 pandemic also posed significant challenges to reading and learning for students with CVD [7].

CVD has not been included in special education needs in most countries around the world, and a large body of previous research focused on instructional strategies such as teachers' awareness and instructional methods [6, 8, 9]. According to our survey of the related literature in Taiwan, there is a lack of local related studies, and there are even fewer educational studies investigating the learning of people with CVD. In the absence of a comprehensive picture of learners with CVD, the solutions proposed in previous studies were often scattered, such as studies focusing on classroom instruction that neglected students' self-learning after class. Despite the importance of the empirical evidence from other countries, due to different educational systems in terms of regulations, requirements, culture and norms, the applicability of foreign research findings to local settings requires further investigation. On the other hand, among the various subject area of learning, due to its subject attributes of conveying reality, science is one of the most challenging for learners with CVD. Kvitle [9] reviewed the learning issues of people with CVD to explore whether CVD should be considered as special education need; her review suggested that most mentioned learning difficulties were found in the subject area of art and science, especially when the colors of many natural materials cannot be changed or replaced. In learning Chemistry, which relies heavily on color information in determining and understanding the elements and reactions, it could be difficult to complement the difference of color vision anomalies with other perceptions. Therefore, auxiliary tools to assist people with CVD in recognizing and distinguishing colors would be required to reduce learning difficulty [10].

Previous studies in assistive technology have suggested different approaches of color aids, which could be categorized into three different types:

1. to remove specific color, related works such as Hasana and her colleagues [10] used color filters to filter out the easily confusing color. Their techniques have been adopted in a commercial product of EnChroma®.
2. to replace color, representative work like Tang et al. [11] developed augmented reality glasses that recolored pictures and images by converting the red, green, and blue into two-dimensional chromaticities.
3. use other visual cues instead of color, such as flashes [10] and textures [12], to help people with CVD discriminate colors.

The purpose of these approaches is twofold: one is to facilitate color recognition so that people with CVD can learn to distinguish color through comparison; the other is to develop color cognition that enables color vision abnormal people to have a correct interpretation of colors. However, the generalizability of these technologies and approaches in actual learning contexts and applications remained under-investigated. Taking chemistry experiments as an example, approaches of color removal and color replacement might create more difficulties and cognitive loads in these field-dependent tasks, which require further empirical investigations.

On the other hand, with the advancement of ubiquitous computing, it is now possible for computer interfaces to make possible casual use and provide information in small, easily understood portions without intervening users. Augmented reality (AR) interface technologies, in specific, are therefore gaining attention in its possibility to combine the aforementioned technologies to create direct, automatic, and actionable links between the physical world and virtual information. For AR provides a simple and immediate user interface to an electronically enhanced physical world, it may enable sensory access to the learning content by amplifying human perception and cognition through multiple and coordinated sensory channels [13]. Previous study [14] developed an AR application for chemistry education by using mobile AR to create metal structures and molecular models to visualize abstract concepts. Their findings suggested that the application was useful for students' acquisition of chemistry knowledge and skills. Tang et al. [11] designed a head-mounted AR device for CVD users to separate confusing colors by recoloring the viewed image in a timely manner. Rivera et al. [15] also adopted recoloring method with mobile AR technologies, while Ponce et al. [16] developed a texture module to add a layer of patterns to the viewed image in real-time.

However, while the empirical studies were still few, insufficient research attention has been paid to full examination of user experiences and interaction with the AR technologies in action in real settings. In educational contexts, how AR could be educationally assistive to improve instructional and learning experiences will be critical to be examined, especially when the advanced representations and expressions supported by currently available AR technologies could reasonably create cognitive load simultaneously. Accordingly, this study intends to adopt AR interface technology to assist the CVD learners' intellectual access to chemistry learning materials.

2   Research Design

This study aims to develop an assistive tool for chemistry learning adapted from the texture method with AR [16, 17], and conduct the empirical investigation with genuine learning materials. A within-subject design was adopted, the participants were assigned random tasks of color recognition with/without the AR tool. A usability test with secondary school students was conducted, and their interaction with the prototype, learning performance, and subjective perception of the system was recorded and analyzed. Considering the common CVD types in Taiwan, this study recruited only Type C (normal), Type P, and Type D participants. A total of 8 secondary school students, including 2 high school students and 6 junior high school students, joined the usability test. Two subjects with CVD, both of whom were mildly Type D. All participants were given a detailed description of the study, and their informed consent was obtained from the subjects before the test.

2.1   Experiment Materials

Learning Materials. In reviewing the current curriculum of chemistry in secondary education, it was found that the learning tasks of identifying natural colors were most often seen in hands-on chemistry experiments across different editions of textbooks in Taiwan [18]. According to the review, topics and lessons related to color recognition included acid-base reactions and oxidation-reduction reactions in basic chemistry, the relationship between gas volume and pressure in chemical equilibrium, and precipitation reactions. The experimental sections of these topics include the use of universal indicators to determine PH values, acid-base titration, oxidation-reduction titration, colorimetric determination of concentration, and the use of precipitates to determine unknown solutions. The experiment of using universal indicators to determine acid-base value was selected because it is common to all editions of textbooks as a fundamental and important skill. Universal indicators, on the other hand, contain a variety of hues and a rather wider color range, which could accommodate red (Type P) and green (Type D) colorblindness of different levels.

The instruction of the experiment was designed as a learning sheet and distributed to the participants. As shown in Fig. 1, the purpose, instruments, and steps of the experiment were illustrated, and a quiz with 2 questions was given at the end of the learning sheet. The three essential learning tasks in the experiment included a) preparation of reagents for different pH values, b) using the reagents to build a color chart of universal indicators, and c) determining the pH value of unknown solutions by referencing the color chart.

Fig. 1. The augmented feedback using the texture method adapted from ColorAdd [17]

Texture Coding System. This study is based on the ColorAdd texture method proposed by Neiva et al. [17] to provide natural color recognition aids. The approach of texture method is selected because the augmented texture information can be projected onto the real-time image without detracting from the original color characteristics. The coding rules are relatively simple and easy to understand to leverage learners' cognitive loads. However, we have adapted the original ColorAdd coding system to meet the needs of color recognition in this study. The original texture coding system could only classify colors into red, yellow, blue, orange, green, purple, and brown, in which brown was actually the mixed color of the above six colors. It would not be applicable when the colors of universal indicators are similar, such as colors between red and orange. In order to expand the capacity of color recognition, we extended the original ColorAdd texture codes to a composite pattern in groups of three, and the color gamut was subdivided into 18 divisions (see Fig. 2) based on the complexity of the texture and the ability to distinguish the color. On the other hand, while the original ColorAdd used triangles and diagonal lines to represent the RGB color model, in this study, the number and proportion of patterns are further used to define the color. For example, the color of orange on a yellow background is represented by a code of yellow wrapped around the code of orange to suggest the color leans toward yellow but with some orange and vice versa. In terms of the number of patterns, the difference between the color of orange and yellow could be found in the added small triangle in the middle representing the red color, which can be regarded as a yellow color with a trace of red.

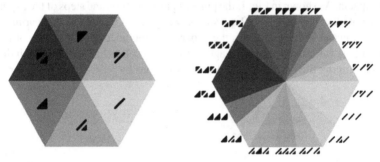

Fig. 2. Original ColorAdd coding system (left) and the adapted coding system of this study (right) (Color fgure online)

2.2 Experiment Apparatus and Procedures

A prototype of a smartphone app for Android OS is developed using Unity® with PhotoCapture API. As shown in Fig. 3, the users are able to operate the built-in camera of the smartphone to scan the universal indicators, and the system recognizes the color and augments the texture information to the image of universal indicators on the screen.

In order to confirm the type of CVD, all subjects underwent Ishihara Color Discrimination Test [19] in advance. The subjects were asked to read the introduction of the experiment, and the texture coding rules (see Fig. 3), after which the participants used the distributed cell phone and applications to interact with the prototype system. The whole process was recorded, and the participants were invited to think aloud and express their thoughts and opinions about the AR tool in each chemical experiment process. Lastly, in the quiz session, the participants were asked to compare the color chart with the color of the test indicators of the four unknown solutions to determine the PH value. Their accuracy and speed of making decisions were recorded for analysis.

The procedures and tasks are summarized as follows:

a) A real-time image of the reagent preparation is recorded as a tutorial video to introduce the idea of acid-base reaction, as shown in Fig. 4(a).
b) Participants use the built-in camera of the smartphone to capture the target image by placing it in the center of the camera field, as shown in Fig. 4(b).

Design of an AR Application to Support Students with CVD   237

Fig. 3. The augmented feedback using the texture method adapted from ColorAdd [17]

c) The application work to recognize the color (saturation and brightness) and overlay the virtual information of texture on the real-time image of universal indicator, as shown in Fig. 4(c).
d) The overlaid results would not disappear until the users clicked the X button to close it. So that the users were granted sufficient time to observe the indicator and the texture information, and also made judgments with reference to the learning sheet.

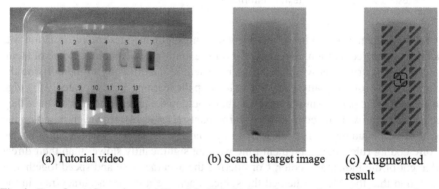

| (a) Tutorial video | (b) Scan the target image | (c) Augmented result |

Fig. 4. Experiment Procedure. (a) Tutorial video (b) Scan the target image (c) Augmented result

3 Preliminary Results and Discussion

The results of the usability test suggested that all subjects were able to complete the color recognition task smoothly with the aid of our system, confirming that the features and flows of our AR tool meet the users' expectations. As shown in Table 1, averagely all subjects had a high accuracy rate in color recognition for test indicators with pH values between 2 to 7 (testers A, B, C). The average accuracy rate was 75% without AR color aid, and increased to 83% with using AR color aid. For the test indicator with pH 10 (tester D), the accuracy rate dropped significantly with or without AR. It could be possibly affected by the capacity of universal indicators, the color change became small above pH 11 as shown in Fig. 4(a), so the participants had difficulty distinguishing the color by referring to the tutorial. Three subjects also emphasized in the interview that they had difficulty distinguishing the colors of testers with pH values of 10 and above. However, the average accuracy rate of the subjects with AR assistance (25%) was higher than those without AR tool (0%), suggesting the augmented texture information is still helpful in assisting learners in recognizing colors.

Table 1. Experiment Procedure. (a) Tutorial video (b) Scan the target image (c) Augmented result

Indicator	A	A*	B	B*	C	C*	D	D*
pH	4		7		2		10	
Color	Yellow-Orange		Green		Orange-Red		Blue	
Accuracy	75%	100%	50%	75%	75%	100%	0%	25%
Speed								
Max (sec)	7.53	10.59	9.78	8.82	14.07	11.57	12.4	10.78
Min (sec)	4.56	3.72	4.17	6.22	2.95	4.26	4.66	7.63
Average (sec)	5.975	6.28	7.0675	7.68	7.78	7.03	9.05	8.725

Note: * testers with augmented texture information

All participants agreed in the interview that the augmented texture information was useful for color recognition, especially for differentiating similar colors. Some of them, including one participant with CVD (J4), reflected on the difficulty of memorizing the textural coding rules initially. They had to look up the learning sheet repeatedly to judge the color. But the participants agreed that they could make judgments quicker once they became familiar with the coding rules (participants H1 and J4). However, based on the speed of color judgment, it is clear that even though the subjects had to look up the texture coding rules, their judgment time was not significantly slower than their direct judgment of the indicators' color. Considering the accuracy rate and speed together, it was found that the AR tool helped the subjects achieve a higher accuracy rate in the same color recognition task with a similar speed of judgment. The preliminary results confirmed that augmenting the texture information synchronously through AR enhanced students' effectiveness in color recognition in chemistry experiments.

Almost all the participants (87.5%) affirmed the designated AR tool of this study to provide color aids by mobile AR, as the natural colors of the images in the physical environment were preserved and presented simultaneously with the virtually added textural information. The proposed system satisfied the learners' needs in chemistry experiments and chemistry learning to emphasize natural colors and provided practical and effective aids in the interpretation of similar colors. A high school student (participant H2) mentioned that he missed the opportunity to win in the science fair because he could not judge the color of his homemade reagent. Participants H1, J4 and J6 shared that they had to ask their teachers or classmates repeatedly to solve the color recognition problems in their previous chemistry experiment classes. They all thought the AR tool developed by this study could be a promising solution to their learning problems.

4 Conclusion

This study reported our design and development of an AR tool to facilitate CVD learners' color recognition in chemistry learning by augmenting the textural information onto real-world objects synchronously and comprehensively. The approach of the texture method that does not disrupt original color information was adopted to develop the prototype system with reference to the ColorAdd texture system composed of simple geometric shapes to leverage users' cognitive loads. The prototype system was empirically tested in genuine chemistry experimental learning contexts with the current local secondary school curriculum. The results of this study support that the proposed AR tool is effective in helping the participants to achieve a higher accuracy rate of color recognition in a limited period of time, as well as in helping the subjects to recognize differences in similar colors while preserving the natural colors. Nevertheless, participants' perceived loads in understanding and memorizing the textural system are worthy of design attention, and memory aids on the screen might be considered in our future design. The implementation of the current study was affected by the COVID-19 pandemic, so the sample size was limited. User experiments on a larger scale with more CVD participants would be planned based on the preliminary findings in the future.

References

1. Wong, B.: Color blindness. Nat. Methods **8**, 441 (2011)
2. Birch, J.: Worldwide prevalence of red-green color deficiency. JOSA A **29**, 313–320 (2012)
3. Cheng, H.M., et al.: Characterising visual deficits in children of an urban elementary school in Taiwan. Clin. Exp. Optomet. **95**, 531–537 (2012)
4. Li, Y.-C., Tang, H.-H.: User experience design and research for the daily life of people with color vision deficiencies. In: The First International Symposium of Chinese CHI (Chinese CHI 2013), Paris, France (2013)
5. Espinda, S.D.: Color vision deficiency: a learning disability? J. Learn. Disabil. **6**, 163–166 (1973)
6. Chan, X.B.V., Goh, S.M.S., Tan, N.C.: Subjects with colour vision deficiency in the community: what do primary care physicians need to know? Asia Pac. Fam. Med. **13**, 1–10 (2014)
7. Kimble-Hill, A.C., et al.: Insights gained into marginalized students access challenges during the COVID-19 academic response. J. Chem. Educ. **97**, 3391–3395 (2020)
8. Albany-Ward, K.: Why colour really does matter. Prep School. Color Blind Awareness (2011)
9. Kvitle, A.K.: Should colour vision deficiency be a recognized special education need (SEN)? In: Transforming our World Through Design, Diversity and Education, pp. 832–838. IOS Press (2018)
10. Hasana, S., Fujimoto, Y., Plopski, A., Kanbara, M., Kato, H.: Improving color discrimination for color vision deficiency (CVD) with temporal-domain modulation. In: 2019 IEEE International Symposium on Mixed and Augmented Reality Adjunct (ISMAR-Adjunct), pp. 243–244. IEEE (2019)

11. Tang, Y., et al.: Arriving light control for color vision deficiency compensation using optical see-through head-mounted display. In: Proceedings of the 16th ACM SIGGRAPH International Conference on Virtual-Reality Continuum and its Applications in Industry, pp. 1–6 (2018)
12. Sajadi, B., Majumder, A., Oliveira, M.M., Schneider, R.G., Raskar, R.: Using patterns to encode color information for dichromats. IEEE Trans. Visual Comput. Graphics **19**, 118–129 (2012)
13. Azuma, R., Baillot, Y., Behringer, R., Feiner, S., Julier, S., MacIntyre, B.: Recent advances in augmented reality. IEEE Comput. Graphics Appl. **21**, 34–47 (2001)
14. Irwansyah, F.S., Nur Asyiah, E., Maylawati, D.S., Farida, I., Ramdhani, M.A.: The development of augmented reality applications for chemistry learning. In: Geroimenko, V. (ed.) Augmented Reality in Education. SSCC, pp. 159–183. Springer, Cham (2020). https://doi.org/10.1007/978-3-030-42156-4_9
15. Rivera, M.M., Padilla, A., Canul-Reich, J., Ponce, J., Ochoa-Zezzatti, A.: Realtime recoloring objects using artificial neural networks through a cellphone. Res. Comput. Sci. **148**, 229–238 (2019)
16. Ponce Gallegos, J.C., Montes Rivera, M., Ornelas Zapata, F.J., Padilla Díaz, A.: Augmented reality as a tool to support the inclusion of colorblind people. In: Stephanidis, C., Antona, M., Gao, Q., Zhou, J. (eds.) HCII 2020. LNCS, vol. 12426, pp. 306–317. Springer, Cham (2020). https://doi.org/10.1007/978-3-030-60149-2_24
17. Neiva, M.: ColorADD: color identification system for color-blind people. In: van Dijk, C.N., Neyret, P., Cohen, M., Della Villa, S., Pereira, H., Oliveira, J.M. (eds.) Injuries and health problems in football, pp. 303–314. Springer, Heidelberg (2017). https://doi.org/10.1007/978-3-662-53924-8_27
18. Ministry of Education: Curriculum Guidelines of 12-Year Basic Education for Elementary School, Junior High and General Senior High Schools: The Domain of Natural Science. Ministry of Education, Taipei, Taiwan (2018)
19. Ishihara, S.: Test for colour-blindness, 24 Plates Edition. Kanehara Tokyo, Tokyo, Japan (1987)

A Preliminary Study on Primary School Teachers' User Experiences in Distance Learning

Hsuan Lin[1]($\boxtimes$), Kuo-Liang Huang[2], and Wei Lin[3]

[1] Industrial Design, ChaoYang University of Technology, Taichung, Taiwan
t2020021@mail.cyut.edu.tw
[2] Department of Industrial Design, Sichuan Fine Arts Institute, Chongqing,
People's Republic of China
shashi@scfai.edu.cn
[3] School of Architecture, Feng Chia University, Taichung, Taiwan
wlin@fcu.edu.tw

Abstract. Affected by the coronavirus (COVID-19) pandemic, Taiwan has been at alert level 3. Schools at all levels and kindergartens have closed and switched to distance learning. While many kinds of free online video software are currently available, they are mostly designed for corporate meetings, with far less consideration given to learning environments and fields. Therefore, this study aims to design distance learning interfaces, regarding the task as the focus of online video software development. User experiences are examined to understand teacher-student interactions in the distance learning context. Furthermore, users' needs are suggested, with various distance learning activities provided and assisted. The research purposes include the following: 1) to explore the interface design elements of video software for primary school students involved in distance learning, 2) to grasp the interactions between primary school teachers and students employing video software for distance learning, 3) to propose the triggers of distance learning through user experiences, and 4) to put forward the environmental requirements of interfaces suitable for distance learning. The research methodology is divided into three stages. In the first stage, three sets of commonly-used free online video software are analyzed and compared to identify their functions and interfaces. In the second stage, participant observation is followed to recognize the interactions between primary school teachers and students engaged in distance learning, and triggers are proposed as interview topics in the next stage. In the third stage, through participatory interviews, primary school teachers are requested to describe the problems in class concerned with the triggers. The findings are as follows. 1) Students scramble to answer questions, which produces mutual interference and unclear hearing. 2) Changing the background and chat function of video software will distract students. 3) Increasing teacher-student interactions and reducing the distraction of students' attention can help to improve the quality of course-teaching. 4) Teachers and parents are worried that too much class time will worsen students' myopia. 5) The video software available now is more suitable for online meetings, with much less video software designed for distance learning. The findings can be provided as a reference for software interface design and development.

P.-L. P. Rau (Ed.): HCII 2023, LNCS 14024, pp. 241–254, 2023.
https://doi.org/10.1007/978-3-031-35946-0_20

Keywords: video software · interface design · user interface · digital learning · online learning

1 Introduction

1.1 Research Background

Impacted by the coronavirus (COVID-19) pandemic, many universities or colleges around the world were forced to close, with academic activities suspended or postponed. Teaching, research, examinations, international conferences, etc. were severely affected. Some students together with faculty members suffered from infection and even death in the worst case, which shows the plight of the global higher education system and the restricted flow in educational environments [1]. Taiwan was facing difficult challenges in the meantime, being at COVID-19 alert level 3. Schools at all levels and kindergartens closed and changed to distance learning. After-school care centers for children, cram schools, and other educational institutions also suspended classes simultaneously. All teachers and students had to adapt to this sudden wave of full-scale distance teaching. To reduce the risk of disease clusters, all schools and kindergartens on the island resorted to distance teaching. Thus, students could learn at home, and distance learning has been officially recognized as a mode of education [2].

1.2 Research Purposes

Plagued by this acute coronavirus pandemic, schools around the island have switched to distance teaching instead of physical teaching. Although there are many sorts of free online video software on the market, their main targets are corporate meetings, with learning environments and fields rarely taken into consideration. Therefore, improper operation of interfaces often affects the quality of course-teaching negatively. Despite many brands of online video software with different versions, no development and design of interfaces is directed at user experiences in online learning software. Surely, the poor usability of interfaces will slow down distance learning, waste teaching time, damage teaching quality, and reduce students' learning performance. In addition, people's learning methods have shifted because of the pandemic. Electronic or digital learning has changed from informal learning to a part of formal learning [3]. With the popularity of mobile devices as well as the continuous updating and development of mobile technology, mobile learning is gradually introduced as a form of education [4].

In the post-pandemic era, distance learning is sure to become one of the normal teaching modes. Consequently, this study takes the interface design of distance learning as the core of online video software development. Through user experiences, the author seeks to understand teacher-student interactions in distance learning environments, present the needs of users, and provide as well as assist various distance learning activities. It is the main focus of this study that students can improve their learning quality effectively by means of distance learning.

This study mainly analyses and discusses user experiences in video software applied to distance learning, with its purposes summarized as follows: 1) to explore the interface design elements of video software for primary school students in distance learning environments, 2) to understand how primary school teachers and students interact with one another while employing video software for distance learning, 3) to propose the triggers of distance learning based on user experiences, and 4) to put forward the environmental requirements of distance learning interfaces.

2 Literature Review

2.1 Distance Learning

With mobile devices affordable and the Internet increasingly popular, almost all college students in developed countries have a certain kind of mobile device [4]. Mobile devices include mobile phones, smartphones, tablet computers, wearable devices, etc. [5], and low-priced computers can be popularized in rural areas to improve local education [6]. As one of the learning modes at present, digital learning is divided into e-learning, web-based learning, online learning, mobile learning [7], and distance learning [8–10], with their own categories and definitions. In recent years, with the Internet developing rapidly, it has been gradually recognized to employ mobile devices as multi-functional tools both inside and outside the classroom [11]. Most schools adopt the learning mode mainly depending on classroom teaching, which is set according to the public's needs. Such a mode does not provide students with individualized learning plans or arrangements. Nevertheless, some scholars encourage students to try learning styles more diversified and personalized [7].

During the coronavirus pandemic, schools changed physical teaching to distance learning to combat the spread of the epidemic. Distance learning means that teachers and learners follow synchronous or asynchronous teaching methods to transmit educational courses to remote ends at the same time and different places or at different times and places. Online learning, video conferencing, online interaction, etc. are mainly used for that purpose [12, 13]. However, distance learning does not exclude the application of traditional classroom teaching. Actually, the definition of distance learning is broader than that of digital learning [14]. Being an emerging field, online learning is a growing trend from the perspective of distance learning. With the popularity of the Internet, online learning becomes more widespread [14, 15]. The most convenient way to learn online is to make use of apps on smartphones. Moreover, digital learning is not limited by time or space; as a result, it has become the best choice for most people eager for on-the-job training. Mobile equipment can be used for learning at any time and place [7].

For the higher education system, online teaching requires teachers to have innovative teaching modes and interests [12, 13]. The biggest difference between distance learning and other kinds of digital learning is that the latter lack purposeful teacher-student interactions. In recent years, many scholars have conducted research on distance learning. According to a survey of college students, the vast majority of them hold a positive attitude towards mobile learning, with 70% of them regarding mobile learning as highly convenient [7]. For students studying Italian in Australia, their teacher sends out the information they need to learn in the form of text messages. After receiving the text messages, they can learn independently in accordance with their personal preferences. Personalized learning enhances learners' interests and performances [16]. Students take much delight in exchanging and sharing real-time information through the popularity of the Internet and mobile devices. Mobile learning has brought great convenience, but there are some problems; namely, the abundance of information will divert learners' attention [7]. Additionally, it is difficult for students to maintain strong interests in learning without a teacher nearby [17]. According to Elaish et al., the problems associated with mobile English learning include poor motivation, learners' lack of concentration, absence of scientific theory in language apps, time needed to adapt to new learning styles, shortage of teacher-student interactions, and issues related to high costs [18].

2.2 Principles of User Interface Design

Users and computers or products need to maintain an interactive relationship satisfactory enough through interfaces. Poor interface design will not only increase users' mental load and operational pressure but also hinder the transmission of information, causing users' negative emotions in severe cases [19, 20]. Usability originated from human-computer interaction (HCI) [21]. Besides exploring the problems that users encounter while operating a device, usability experts focus on improving product design to meet users' actual needs. Being a design concept composed of multiple elements, usability serves as an indicator used to evaluate the effect of interaction between users and websites, interfaces, or apps. The usability of a system should include five indicators, i.e., learnability, efficiency, memorability, error, and satisfaction [22]. A design concept embracing usability makes the interface design more concise and definite, thereby elevating users' satisfaction levels. Thus, users are willing to spend more time on the interface [23]. In addition, when learners use smartphones to study, their attention will be distracted, with poor performance acquired [24]. In order to improve learners' performance and the efficiency of interaction between users and smartphones, it is necessary to follow the principles of user interface design [23]. Evaluating the interactions between humans and products through usability helps contribute to software development.

2.3 User Experience

User experience is one of the factors that determine whether digital technology can be popularized and applied, regardless of physical or virtual products; besides, its domain incorporates interactive devices, robots, social media, virtual reality (VR), augmented reality (AR), Internet of Things (IoT), etc. Technological development is inseparable from user experience (UX) [25]. User experience is a concept and method of product development that first appeared in the field of computer design, especially directed towards the relationship between functionality and usability [26]. In addition, user experience is the design concept extended from the user-centered idea, including such factors as product functions, usability, information content, and subjective satisfaction levels. These factors are interrelated to form user experience and affect how the user feels when operating a product [20]. There are many factors that affect user experience, including the user (his/her user experience, emotional response, ability, expected results, etc.), the product itself (its size, texture, appearance, etc.), usage context, culture and social factors [27–29].

A good design of a distance learning interface should not focus solely on the aesthetic or visual effect of the layout, nor should it center merely on the color, font, picture, or design of the layout. In this study, the evaluation of a distance learning interface is not exclusively based on its visual presentation, but the essence of its design must be explored to solve problems and achieve an interactive learning experience good enough. When distance learning is conducted, there are two users; namely, one is the teacher who teaches the learning content and the other is the student who is taught to learn. Furthermore, a good set of distance learning software is not only suitable for passive learning but also provides satisfactory interaction and experience. Completing a distance learning activity involves the usage procedures, so the design concept should be more complete to meet the needs of both teachers and students. However, in the current research on evaluating the usability of distance learning, most scholars mainly concentrate on learning performance without exploring the transmitted content or operation of the interface. Therefore, this study will probe the user experience in the distance learning software interface.

3   Methodology

To realize what happens in the process of distance learning, this study explores the operational relationship between the teaching and learning ends which use the video software interface. The research methodology is divided into three stages. In the first stage, the task is to provide an objective and comparative basis as well as theoretical framework founded on user experiences so that evaluating and analyzing the relevant literature can be carried out. Then, through the content analysis method, the operational functions and interfaces of the video software are investigated. After that, three commonly-used sets of free online video software are selected and operated, with their functions and interfaces analyzed and compared. In the second stage, based on usability theory and user experiences, participant observation is adopted to grasp the interactions between primary school teachers and students involved in distance learning. Meanwhile, the triggers are proposed as the interview topics in the next stage. In the third stage, through participatory interviews with primary school teachers, the actual happenings in class are identified, and the impact of distance learning on teaching is explored. The findings are organized, discussed, and presented as a reference for distance learning, learning interface environment, and software interface development.

3.1   Analyzing Operational Functions and Interfaces of Video Software

In this study, three sets of free online video software commonly used at present are sorted by English initials, i.e., Google Meet, Microsoft Teams, and Webex, with their operational functions and interfaces analyzed. The research steps are as follows: a) analyzing the functions of three sets of video software according to their operational sequence in distance learning, b) inviting three experts to classify the operational functions of video software through focus groups, c) finding the operational functions of the video software to be joining meeting, administration, discussion, information, and interaction, and d) creating a table showing the operational functions and interfaces of the video software, as shown in Table 1.

3.2 Observation of User Experience

Through participant observation, this study seeks to understand the actual situation and problems of teachers and students involved in distance learning. As participant observation is conducted in natural settings, researchers can collect rich and dynamic data [30]. Being an unstructured methodology, participant observation is a special form of fieldwork. The researcher participates in the events of the researched and becomes a participant [31]. In this qualitative observation methodology, the researcher, through field observation or direct observation, establishes and maintains a multifaceted and long-term relationship with the researched group in order to gain a scientific understanding of the group [32]. Therefore, before observing online courses in this study, the author explained the purposes and contents of the experiment to the participants, with the consent of teachers, parents and students obtained. After being connected to the teachers' classes, the author observed and videoed the actual happenings of teachers and students engaged in distance learning. The steps of observation are as follows: 1) to observe and video the happenings of distance learning as well as to compile and record the triggers of online teaching, 2) to convert triggers into problems and collect them, and 3) to use the observed results as the basis for interviewing the teachers about their experiences in the next stage.

Participants. The observed subjects engaged in distance learning are primary school teachers and students. In this study, three participants are primary school teachers, all of whom are female. Each teacher has more than fifteen years of experience in teaching. There are thirty-five fourth-grade students (seventeen boys and eighteen girls) participating in the experiment. The basic information of the participating teachers is shown in Table 2. In the next stage, three teachers will be interviewed further, with the students excluded.

Triggers. At this stage, three courses, i.e., Chinese, natural sciences, and English were taught online. What happened throughout the sessions was observed and videoed, and the triggers encountered by the three teachers during distance teaching were sorted out. Thereafter, the triggers were converted into eight problems, as shown in Table 3.

3.3 Participatory Interview

In the previous stage, the triggers gained through participant observation were converted into problems, which were used as the interview topics in the participatory interview subsequently. After the interviewee watched the video concerned with a trigger, she was asked to describe the situation of teaching at that time. The intensive interview in participant observation is a semi-structured method [30], by which the interviewer obtains analyzable materials from the rich data provided by the interviewee as well as understands the interviewee's thoughts or opinions on a trigger. Meanwhile, the interviewee's user experience in the form of feedback is respected [31]. Through the participatory interview, the participants' opinions on the research can be understood and collected more completely, becoming the basis for subsequent analysis and exploration.

Table 1. Operational functions and interfaces of video software

Function	Operational Step		Google Meet	Microsoft Teams	Webex
Joining meeting	Online software		●	●	●
	Moderator's account login		●	●	●
	Attendee's account login		●	●	●
	Ways of invitation to meeting	Internet connection	●	●	●
		Meeting code	●	–	●
		By email	●	●	●
		After creating a meeting, moderator can directly make targeted attendees join it	Together with Google Class	●	●
	Immediate meeting		●	●	●
	Scheduled meeting		●	●	●
	Supporting mobile device		●	●	●
Administration	Moderator's permission to join meeting		●	●	●
	Moderator's right to switch on/off microphone		●	●	●
	Meeting goes on after moderator is offline		●	●	●
	Videoing		Payable	●	●
Discussion	Sharing image		●	●	●
	Whiteboard		Jamboard to be installed	●	●
	Group discussion		Payable	Payable	●
	Remote control		–	●	●
	Emoji		–	●	●
	Hand-raising		●	●	●
	Instant subtitle		–	●	–
Information	Show/hide people		●	●	●
	Show/hide chat area		●	●	●

(*continued*)

Table 1. (*continued*)

Function	Operational Step	Google Meet	Microsoft Teams	Webex
	Attendee list	●	●	●
Interaction	Switch on/off webcam	●	●	●
	Switch on/off microphone	●	●	●
	Virtual background	●	●	●

Table 2. Interviewees' basic information

Teacher	Course	Years of service	Age	Gender
Teacher A	English	15	37	Female
Teacher B	Natural sciences	30	53	Female
Teacher C	Chinese	19	41	Female

The steps of the participatory interview are as follows. The interviewee was requested to think back after watching the video associated with the trigger, providing explanations about using video software for distance teaching. After the interview, its verbatim transcript was typed out, and its content was analyzed through inductive analysis to infer the functional requirements and reasons for the online learning software on the teaching and learning ends.

4 Results

After eight triggers were obtained through participant observation, the three teachers were asked to participate in the participatory interviews about the triggers they encountered. The interview results are set forth below:

Trigger 1: After the Fixed Course is Set for the First Session, the Teacher Need Not Reset It and Confirm the Students' Identities in Later Sessions. Through participant observation, it was found that Google Meet, Microsoft Teams, and Webex all offer three ways of invitation, i.e., Internet connection, meeting code, and email. As for meeting code, Microsoft Teams and Webex demand users to create a course or group first while Google Meet does not. In terms of joining meeting, Google Meet is comparatively unsuitable for course-teaching. The main reason is that the student group taking up a general course is composed of fixed members. As for Microsoft Teams and Webex, the teacher needs to create a course as well as name it in the first session and then to permit the students to log onto the course. Thereafter, the teacher need not manage or review the students' identities and qualifications in later sessions. To log onto a certain course, the teacher or student just needs to open the previously-set one. In other words, it is not necessary for the teacher to start the meeting first. Microsoft Teams and

Table 3. Summary of triggers

Teacher who encountered a trigger	Explanation of the trigger
Teacher A Teacher B Teacher C	After the fixed course is set for the first session, the teacher need not reset it and confirm the students' identities in later sessions
Teacher A Teacher B Teacher C	The teacher worries about network instability or delay, which will cause poor course-teaching quality
Teacher A Teacher B Teacher C	Just before a session, the teacher first confirms that the students have logged in. If a student is not online, the teacher needs to notify his/her parent through LINE communication apps
Teacher A Teacher C	The students scramble to answer a question. Speaking at the same time, they interfere with one another and can't hear clearly. It is impossible to know which of them is speaking. The teacher needs to stop all students from speaking before asking the question again
Teacher A Teacher B Teacher C	The student should avoid staring at the screen for too long
Teacher A	Some functions of the online software distract students. For instance, they change the dynamic background and type messages, so they cannot concentrate on the session
Teacher B	Distance learning makes a student who doesn't speak often keep silent online. If the teacher asks the student a question, he/she refuses to answer or goes offline directly
Teacher C	When a long-distance final exam is held, to prevent students from cheating is difficult

Webex are more suitable for fixed courses; by contrast, Google Meet is more suitable for temporary meetings, meetings with unfixed members, or discussions. To log onto a meeting on Google Meet, users only need to have the URL of the meeting. After the teacher confirms the students' identities, the students can join the meeting, but the URL of the meeting cannot be preserved. If students want a fixed course, the software needs to be set in conjunction with Google Class. Otherwise, every time students want to log onto a scheduled course, the teacher needs to open a meeting and to permit the students to do so.

Trigger 2: The Teacher Worries About Network Instability and Delay, Which Will Cause Poor Course-Teaching Quality. In the process of distance teaching, students' instant feedback is very important. If the teacher keeps teaching without interacting with students, he/she cannot immediately ascertain whether the network is unstable or delayed and whether the students grasp the taught content. As a result, the teaching quality is not satisfying, and students cannot understand the course content effectively. Therefore, the teacher should often ask questions about the course content to know whether students understand it. In this way, the teacher can ensure that the internet connection is normal and students are concentrating on the course.

Trigger 3: Just Before a Session, the Teacher First Confirms That the Students Have Logged In. If a Student is Not Online, the Teacher Needs to Notify His/Her Parent Through LINE Communication Apps. Through participant observation, it was found that when employing distance teaching, the teacher must first create a LINE group for students' parents. If there is an urgent message, the teacher can directly leave it along with its explanations by means of the group. Before starting online teaching, the teacher must first ensure that students can log in and use hardware smoothly. For example, does the computer work well or is the network speed stable? In the beginning, students may feel distance teaching to be different from physical teaching, but after a few classes, they will become adapted to the software interface. Whenever teaching a class, the teacher must confirm that all the students have logged in. If a student is not online, a message is sent to the student's parent through the LINE group. Thus, it is convenient to grasp the status of students. In addition, students who do not belong to the class occasionally log onto the course, and the teacher needs to deal with it immediately, restart the course, and send the new URL of the course through LINE.

Trigger 4: The Students Scramble to Answer a Question. Speaking at the Same Time, They Interfere with One Another and Can't Hear Clearly. It is Impossible to Judge Which of Them is Speaking. The Teacher Needs to Stop All Students From Speaking Before Asking the Question Again. In terms of online "classroom" order management, the most important thing is that the moderator should have the right to switch on/off a microphone. In the distance learning environment, students are often required to answer a question, and they frequently scramble to answer it. In such a case, the teacher can designate a particular student to answer. Alternatively, the teacher can ask the students to press the hand-raising button. There is a big difference between physical and online classes in terms of interaction. At first, not getting used to pressing the hand-raising button, students in the online class answer directly. As the students' microphones are constantly on and many students answer at the same time, the teacher cannot know which of them is speaking. With a number of voices resounding, the online class is plunged into chaos and does not go smoothly. At this point, the teacher can exercise the right to turn off the microphones of all students before restarting to teach. In addition, students in the online class often forget to turn off the microphone and need to be reminded of that. Likewise, the teacher often forgets turning off the microphones, and students have to remind the teacher that the microphones are off.

Trigger 5: The Student Should Avoid Staring At the Screen for Too Long. When the school implements distance teaching, it will notice that looking at the screen for long is not good for students' eyes or may lead to myopia, especially for developing children. This is also a matter of great concern for parents. Consequently, an online session lasts ten minutes less than the physical one and students take a break lasting ten minutes more. Namely, the distance learning session takes 30 min and the break takes 20 min so that students may not stare at the screen all the time. But the effect of this approach may not be very good. The main reason is that during the break, students ignore the teacher's advice and keep staying online until the next class if parents do not supervise nearby.

Trigger 6: Some Functions of the Online Software Distract Students. Students Change the Dynamic Background and Type Messages, so They Cannot Concentrate on the Session. In this study, the targets of distance teaching are primary school students. Whether students can concentrate on the session has always been a central part of the teacher's concern. In the distance learning environment, the teacher cannot know whether the participants are listening attentively. For instance, students open other web pages unrelated to the course at the same time or when the microphone and camera are turned off, students do something irrelevant to the course. In addition, the virtual background embedded in "interaction" of online software distracts both teachers and students. In the worst case, if a student changes to an exaggerated background, especially a dynamic background, the teacher and students unconsciously watch it and get distracted. Therefore, the teacher should demand the students not to change backgrounds.

Also, the chat area is prone to distract students. When the teacher is lecturing in class, some of the students send texts unrelated to the course concurrently. The other students find it very interesting to spot the texts or symbols in the chat area. Then, more and more students start to leave messages, which leads to distraction of attention during online teaching. Therefore, only with the teacher's permission can the students discuss the course content in the chat area. Generally, the teacher prohibits students from leaving messages in the chat area during class.

Trigger 7: Distance Learning Makes a Student Who Doesn't Speak Often Keep Silent Online. If the Teacher Asks the Student a Question, He/She Refuses to Answer or Goes Offline Directly. When the teacher asks his/her students to answer questions or wants to know whether the students have handed in their homework, those students who do not speak often refuse to answer. The teacher cannot instantly judge whether it is a network problem or a device problem. Because the class is not taught in a physical place, the teacher cannot understand the students' emotions. It is fairly difficult for the teacher to grasp the progress of the students' homework; besides, he/she cannot counsel or comfort the students. Therefore, in addition to reminding the students to hand in their homework, the teacher has to inform their parents through LINE of the students' missed homework. That will make it possible for the students to really grasp the homework status and avoid unfinished homework that will affect their grades.

Trigger 8: When a Long-Distance Final Exam is Held, to Prevent Students From Cheating is Difficult. Midterm exams and final exams are more troublesome. It is difficult for the current video software to solve this problem. Because the exams are held online, the teacher can only catch a partial picture through a small window on the screen, being unable to capture the actual situation of all the students answering the exam questions. Specifically, during the exam, the teacher has much difficulty preventing students from finding answers on the Internet, students flip through textbooks, and some other people tell answers to the students. Therefore, during the long-distance exam, the webcam and mac must be turned on and the examinees must not speak. As soon as the exam is completed, the student must notify the teacher. Then, the teacher should confirm that the student has finished answering the questions lest the latter go offline without uploading the answers and get no exam scores.

5 Discussion

Through participant observation and participatory interview, this study seeks to understand user experiences in distance teaching aided by video software. The triggers are obtained from the above observation, and the problems concerning user experiences are effectively clarified; in consequence, users can respond in a more focused manner.

The study finds that the biggest difference between distance teaching and physical teaching lies in the fact that the latter provides effective interactions. Enhancing the efficiency of interaction among users improves the learning performance of online learners [23]. The teacher can see the eyes and body movements of the students through physical teaching, which can enhance the interaction and atmosphere of the class effectively. Face-to-face communication makes it possible to understand the current speaker's emotions and ideas, to feel everyone's emotions, atmosphere and thoughts, and even to produce something amazing. In a physical class, the teacher can see the expressions and environments of students. In contrast, in a distance learning context, only the faces in front of the camera can be seen, the surrounding environment of students is invisible, and the teacher cannot judge the conditions of students. This study suggests that a twin-lens camera can be installed during distance teaching, with one lens showing the student's face and the other displaying the upper body and surrounding environment. If so, the teacher can observe the students' expressions and body movements more closely, which is beneficial to teacher-student interactions. Additionally, the teacher can obtain more information to realize whether students are really attentive.

According to Chen and Yan, when learners use smartphones for learning, their performance is not very satisfactory. The main reason is that attention will be distracted by the stimulation of multiple tasks. When receiving multiple pieces of information, the person will fall into a situation where attention does not pick up full information. Moreover, the individual only processes one information stimulus at a time, and some other information will be lost during the rapid information transmission [24]. This study finds that changing the dynamic background will distract users' attention and affect the course quality negatively. It is suggested that teachers should have the right to turn off the above-mentioned function. Also, it is suggested that an upload mode can be added to the chat room. Students can upload their answers after answering at home, and the pictures of all students answering the question will be displayed simultaneously. Such a measure facilitates it for teachers to know whether students clearly understand the course content, which is favorable to class interaction and teaching quality.

Getting used to distance learning is closely related to familiarity with the video software interface. Distance learning for primary school students is different from what college students need. At first, primary school students need to be accompanied by their parents to become familiar with the way to operate the video software. Besides, it is very important to make good use of communication software, which is beneficial to distance learning. In addition, most online students are used to talking without switching on the microphone, or some online students may stay in a noisy environment. Students are not conscious that their surrounding noise will be transmitted to the online course setting and interfere with other students' listening. Solving unwelcome noise effectively is an important issue in distance learning. Finally, when conducting distance teaching in primary schools, teachers as well as parents should care about the session time lest students should become short-sighted.

6 Conclusion

The challenge facing distance learning is not only the change of teaching modes but also the improvement of both software and hardware interfaces. This study focuses on distance learning employed by primary school teachers and students, seeks to understand their interactions, and explores the interface design as well as interface requirements. As shown in the findings, teachers attach great importance to the course-learning quality. Both increasing teacher-student interactions and reducing the distraction of students' attention help to improve the course quality. During distance teaching, it is very common for students to scramble to answer a question, which creates mutual interference and unclear hearing, damaging the quality of course-teaching. Changing the background and chat area on the video software distracts students' attention, thus affecting the course quality negatively. Teachers and parents worry that the long session in distance learning hurts students' eyesight. The current video software is more suitable for online meetings, with only a little video software designed for distance learning. The findings may serve as a reference for interface designers and software developers.

Acknowledgements. This study was subsidized and supervised by National Science and Technology Council, the Executive Yuan, with it coded MOST 111-2221-E-324-016. At the same time, the author hereby extends sincere gratitude to the reviewers who gave many valuable suggestions for revision of this paper.

References

1. Neuwirth, L.S., Jović, S., Mukherji, B.R.: Reimagining higher education during and post-COVID-19: challenges and opportunities. J. Adult Contin. Educ. **27**, 141–156 (2021)
2. Ministry of Education, R.o.C.T.: (2021/10/15)
3. Hao, Y., Lee, K.S., Chen, S.-T., Sim, S.C.: An evaluative study of a mobile application for middle school students struggling with English vocabulary learning. Comput. Hum. Behav. **95**, 208–216 (2019)
4. Klimova, B.: Impact of mobile learning on students' achievement results. Educ. Sci. **9**, 90 (2019)
5. Kukulska-Hulme, A.: Personalization of language learning through mobile technologies (2016)
6. Rosenzweig, E.: Successful User Experience: Strategies and Roadmaps. Morgan Kaufmann, Waltham (2015)
7. Zhang, Y., Zuo, L.: College English teaching status and individualized teaching design in the context of mobile learning. Int. J. Emerg. Technol. Learn. **14**(12), 85–96 (2019)
8. Anohina, A.: Analysis of the terminology used in the field of virtual learning. J. Educ. Technol. Soc. **8**, 91–102 (2005)

254   H. Lin et al.

9. Tsai, S., Machado, P.: E-learning, online learning, web-based learning, or distance learning: unveiling the ambiguity in current terminology. E-Learn Magazine (2002)
10. Stevanović, A., Božić, R., Radović, S.: Higher education students' experiences and opinion about distance learning during the Covid-19 pandemic. J. Comput. Assist. Learn. **37**, 1682–1693 (2021)
11. Lai, K.-W., Smith, L.A.: University educators' perceptions of informal learning and the ways in which they foster it. Innov. High. Educ. **43**, 369–380 (2018)
12. Elumalai, K.V., et al.: Factors affecting the quality of e-learning during the COVID-19 pandemic from the perspective of higher education students. COVID-19 Educ. Learn. Teach. Pandemic-Constrained Environ. **189**, 167–190 (2021)
13. McCormack, T.J., Lemoine, P.A., Waller, R.E., Richardson, M.D.: Global higher education: examining response to the COVID-19 pandemic using agility and adaptability. J. Educ. Dev. **5**, 10 (2021)
14. Zou, B., Li, J.: Exploring mobile apps for English language teaching and learning. Research-publishing.net (2015)
15. Chinnery, G.M.: Going to the MALL: mobile assisted language learning. Lang. Learn. Technol. **10**, 9–16 (2006)
16. Kennedy, C., Levy, M.: L'italiano al telefonino: using SMS to support beginners' language learning1. ReCALL **20**, 315–330 (2008)
17. Bhattacharya, S., Nath, S.: Intelligent e-learning systems: an educational paradigm shift (2016)
18. Elaish, M.M., Shuib, L., Ghani, N.A., Yadegaridehkordi, E., Alaa, M.: Mobile learning for English language acquisition: taxonomy, challenges, and recommendations. IEEE Access **5**, 19033–19047 (2017)
19. Wu, F.-G., Lin, H., You, M.: The enhanced navigator for the touch screen: a comparative study on navigational techniques of web maps. Displays **32**, 284–295 (2011)
20. Norman, D.: The Design of Everyday Things: Revised and Expanded Edition. Basic Books (2013)
21. Li, F., Li, Y.: Usability evaluation of e-commerce on B2C websites in China. Procedia Eng. **15**, 5299–5304 (2011)
22. Nielsen, J.: Usability Engineering. Morgan Kaufmann, San Francisco (1994)
23. Ishaq, K., Rosdi, F., Zin, N.A.M., Abid, A.: Usability and design issues of mobile assisted language learning application. Int. J. Adv. Comput. Sci. Appl. **11**(6), 86–94 (2020)
24. Chen, Q., Yan, Z.: Does multitasking with mobile phones affect learning? A review. Comput. Hum. Behav. **54**, 34–42 (2016)
25. Hsu, C.-C.: User experience research: an introduction. J. Inf. Soc. 27–38 (2019)
26. Edwards, E., Kasik, D.J.: User experience with the CYBER graphics terminal. In: Proceedings of VIM-21, pp. 284–286 (1974)
27. Knight, J., Jefsioutine, M.: Understanding the user: research methods to support the digital media designer. Res. Issues Art Des. Media (3) (2002)
28. Arhippainen, L., Tähti, M.: Empirical evaluation of user experience in two adaptive mobile application prototypes. In: Proceedings of the 2nd International Conference on Mobile and Ubiquitous Multimedia (MUM 2003), pp. 27–34. Linköping University Electronic Press (2003)
29. Kim, C., Self, J.A., Bae, J.: Exploring the first momentary unboxing experience with aesthetic interaction. Des. J. **21**, 417–438 (2018)
30. Wimmer, R.D., Dominick, J.R.: Mass Media Research. Cengage Learning, Boston (2013)
31. Babbie, E.R.: The Practice of Social Research. Cengage Learning, Boston (2020)
32. Lofland, J., Lofland, L.H.: Analyzing Social Settings–A Guide to Qualitative Observation and Analysis. Wadsworth, Belmont (1995)

How Scientific Illustration and Photography Aid Learners' Reading – Evidence from Eye Movements

Weijane Lin[1] , Koji Masumoto[2], Koh Kakusho[2(✉)], and Hsiu-Ping Yueh[1]

[1] National Taiwan University, No.1, Sec.4, Roosevelt Road, Taipei 10617, Taiwan
[2] Kwansei Gakuin University, 1 Gakuen Uegahara, Sanda 669-1330, Japan
kakusho@kwansei.ac.jp

Abstract. This study investigated how readers interacted with different visual elements of AR books and examined specifically the function of pictorial representations of scientific illustration and photography in scientific reading. Four visual elements, namely the original Latin texts, original botanical illustration, augmented Chinese translation, and augmented color photograph, were arranged in four different layouts. The valid eye movement data from 29 college students in reading botanical floras were analyzed. The participants were assigned into 4 groups to read the AR book with different layouts. Descriptive results of participants' reading behaviors regarding their gazes associated with the position and distance of the visual elements were reported and discussed. The preliminary findings of the study supported that color photography was a complementary aid to participants' reading of botanical illustrations.

Keywords: Scientific Illustration · Photography · Eye movement · Scientific Reading

1 Introduction

Pictorial representations such as diagrams, shapes, illustrations, and photographs are helpful in assisting reading by organizing readers' thinking while associating the words with the image [1]. Specifically, in scientific reading, visual inputs initiate the recognition and comprehension of domain-specific terminology and concepts [2–4], and pictorial representations with different graphic characteristics are proven to significantly affect readers' initiation and comprehension of scientific texts [5]. Taking the subject of botany as a typical example, botanical illustration and photography are viewed as essential references for systematic botany in terms of plant nomenclature and classification [6]. These visual representations have been carefully recorded as botanical illustration or photography in publication forms like monographs, revisions or floras [7, 8], serving as critical learning support in developing readers' conceptual knowledge. While previous studies have argued the roles of different types of botanical arts in systematics [9, 10], how photography and illustration actually work and function in scientific reading, however, requires further empirical investigation [3].

P.-L. P. Rau (Ed.): HCII 2023, LNCS 14024, pp. 255–264, 2023.
https://doi.org/10.1007/978-3-031-35946-0_21

On the other hand, a significant percentage of library collections have been digitalized with enhanced texts that enable readers of different levels or interests to interact extensively with the resources through critical reading behaviors of searching, annotating and cross-referencing [11]. To offer assistance to readers without sufficient prior knowledge, previous endeavors have been conducted to provide library users with content navigation aids [12], supplemental annotation and interpretation [13] using simulation technologies of virtual and augmented reality [14, 15]. Featuring 3D virtual objects and real-time interaction, AR technologies were adopted to visualize abstract concepts and invisible scientific phenomena by placing a virtual animation, image, text, and video on the real objects [16, 17]. In terms of the specific form of books, Grasset et al. [18] classified AR books into three types according to the layout of the content and the importance of original content in the book: Basic version using only AR markers to access virtual information, Multimedia side by side with virtual and real content display synchronously but spatially separated, and Multimedia-integrated that integrate multiple sources of information. The findings of their longitudinal studies [19] showed that readers who interacted with the multimedia-integrated layout performed significantly better than the other two types of layouts. But they have identified the research need to further investigate readers' detailed interaction with each visual element since the position and the distance between the elements could have a direct impact on the sense of integration [5, 19].

Motivated by the abovementioned issues and opportunities, the present study aims to investigate how readers interact with different visual elements of AR books in detail and to examine specifically the function of scientific illustration and photography in scientific reading by analyzing readers' eye movement with our previously developed machine learning techniques [20]. As a serial work in our long-term development of an adaptive reading system, the tracking results of readers' cognitive processing will contribute to the instructional design of guiding learners' attention and supporting learners with different levels of reading skills.

2 Research Design

2.1 Methodology

A between-group quasi-experiment design was adopted to investigate the causal relationship and interaction effect among different arrangements of visual elements. 35 undergraduate and graduate students volunteered to join the experiment by reading the designed AR book of medicinal herbs with their eye movements recorded by an unobtrusive eye-tracker. 6 of them were excluded owing to failed eye-tracking data, and the valid sample for analysis was 29 participants. The participants were randomly assigned into 4 groups to read the AR book with different layouts. The participants were tested individually in a single session lasting approximately 40 min. The participants were first administered the informed consent and an exemplary scientific passage for practice. After the practice session, they were allowed as much time as needed to read the texts. When the participants finished reading, they were asked to take the reading comprehension test.

2.2 Reading Materials

The reading materials were adapted from a rare book of the University Library's special collection entitled *De virtutibus herbarum* (The Nature of Herbs) [21], which is an incunabulum published in the 15th century. The book introduced more than 200 medicinal herbs in medieval Europe with illustrations and Latin text. Based on the accessibility of information and the level of difficulty, 7 herbs including daffodil, absinthe, acorus, alkekengi, bugloss, marrubium and verbascum were selected as the basis of reading materials for the experiment.

Two virtual pieces of information were augmented to the book: translated Chinese texts to the original Latin texts and the color photograph that illustrates the traits and habitats of the selected herb. Subject matter experts and linguistic professionals proofread the translated passages of each medicinal herb to ensure the accuracy of the content. And each translated passage was controlled to be in 100 Chinese characteristics to ensure the quantity and difficulty of reading content are equivalent across different herbs.

The 4 visual elements, namely the original Latin texts, original botanical illustration, augmented Chinese translation, and augmented color photograph, were then arranged in four different layouts. Sample pages describing absinthe with the four layouts are illustrated as Fig. 1.

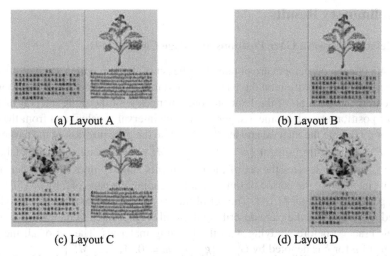

(a) Layout A   (b) Layout B

(c) Layout C   (d) Layout D

Fig. 1. Combinations of the components and their arrangement for different layouts of the page for absinthe as an example.

As shown in Table 1, to map the eye movement with the reading material, each page of the reading materials was firstly partitioned into four rectangular sections denoted by $S_{Ul}, S_{Ur}, S_{Ll}, S_{Lr}$, which occupied the upper-left, upper-right, lower-left, and lower-right quarters of the page, respectively. The set of these four sections is denoted by $S = \{S_{Ul}, S_{Ur}, S_{Ll}, S_{Lr}\}$. Each section was then assigned at most one of the four kinds of visual components, including the original text in Latin, its translated text in Chinese, the original illustration, and the color photograph.

The gaze positions of the participants on the pages of the learning materials were measured while the participants were reading through the learning materials by a commercial eye movement tracker Tobii EyeX [22]. Reading materials are displayed on a 22-inch LCD screen at a resolution of 1920 × 1080. To be less restrictive, the participants sit about 50–60 cm from the monitor in their preferred sitting postures, and no chin rest is used. The sampling rate of the Tobii EyeX is 50 Hz, which was sufficient for this study to collect the data samples of macro-saccadic eye movements per second.

Table 1. Layouts of the learning materials used for the experiment.

Layout	S_{Ul}	S_{Ur}	S_{Ll}	S_{Lr}
A	X	Illustration	Chinese text	Latin text
B	X	Illustration	X	Chinese text
C	Photograph	Illustration	Chinse text	Latin text
D	X	Photograph	X	Chinese text

3   Preliminary Results

3.1   Relation Between Gaze Positions and Page Components

Gaze data of each participant are obtained as the set of fixation points, each of which is described by its 2D position on the page and the duration of fixation at the position. To analyze how the position of the fixation point changes with the same interval of time, the gaze position at each moment separated by the interval is calculated from the gaze data. Let Δt denote the interval and let $g_h^p(m)$ denote the gaze position of the participant $p(p \in P)$ at the m-th moment $(m = 0, 1, \ldots, M_h^p)$ for reading the page of herb h $(h \in H)$, where P denotes the set of the participants and M_h^p does the number of the moments included in the period of time spent for reading the page of h by p. The length of this period is given by $M_h^p \Delta t$. The set of the six kinds of herbs without daffodils is denoted by H because the page describing daffodils is presented to the participant first for their practice before studying with the learning materials. The set of all the gaze positions of p for h is denoted by $G_h^p = \{g_h^p(m) \mid m = 0, 1, \ldots, M_h^p\}$.

Given the gaze data described above, it was first analyzed how the gaze positions taken by the participants at each moment for fixation and transition to reading through each page are related to its layout. Temporal change in the gaze position of participants p reading the page describing herb h during the period between m-th and $(m + 1)$-th moments are characterized by the pair of $g_h^p(m)$ and $g_h^p(m + 1)$, which are the initial and final gaze positions for the period. Thus, the four-dimensional vector, which is constituted by the components of $g_h^p(m)$ and $g_h^p(m + 1)$, is employed to represent the temporal change in the gaze position. This vector is named *gaze change vector* and is denoted by $\gamma_h^p(m)$. This vector represents fixation at $g_h^p(m)$ if $g_h^p(m) = g_h^p(m + 1)$, whereas it represents a transition from $g_h^p(m)$ to $g_h^p(m + 1)$ if $g_h^p(m) \neq g_h^p(m + 1)$.

Given the learning materials with the same layout, to obtain representative temporal changes in gaze position for reading each page by all participants, gaze change vectors of all participants reading each page with each layout are classified by clustering. Let P^L denote the set of participants given the learning materials with layout $L \in \{A, B, C, D\}$, and let Γ_h^L denote the set of the gaze positions of all the participants included in P^L for the page of herb $h(\in H)$ as follows:

$$\Gamma_h^L = \bigcup_{p \in P_L} G_h^p \tag{1}$$

The set of the gaze positions Γ_h^L of all participants reading the page describing one of the six kinds of herbs h with layout L were classified into some clusters including similar transition vectors by *K-means++* method [23], which is one of the most representative methods employed for clustering. From the result of this clustering, *representative gaze change vectors*, which represent the gaze change vectors included in the clusters, are obtained as their centroids. As shown in Fig. 2, examples of the representative gaze change vectors correspond to the centroids of the different clusters obtained for the pages of the six kinds of herbs in different layouts by the lines in different colors with the circles at the starting points of the representative gaze change vectors.

The positions of the visual components were found to affect participants' reading behaviors and integration. As shown in Fig. 2, the endpoints of the representative gaze change vectors are associated with the visual components of the page. Some representative gaze change vectors with their endpoints in the same component are arranged horizontally along with the rows of the texts as if reflecting reading behavior. For instance, the translated Chinese texts in multimedia-integrated layout (layout C) are reduced to shorter segments, suggesting fixations around the focused positions within the textual component and more frequent references across the Chinese texts and color photographs.

3.2 Distance Between Gaze Change Vectors and Visual Components

The result described above suggests that the transition of the focus on each page by the participants given the learning materials with different layouts can be analyzed by the gaze change vectors with their endpoints in different components assigned to different rectangular sections of the page. However, the endpoints of the gaze change vectors are not always inside the region actually occupied by any components assigned to the rectangular sections of the page for some reason. To determine which component in the page is focused on in what degree for each gaze change vector, the distance of each endpoint of the gaze change vector from the region occupied by each component included in each rectangular section is considered.

First, the region occupied by the component included in each rectangular section is extracted from the section by background elimination. Since the background of the pages is filled in the same color, the regions occupied by any components are obtained by removing the region in the color of the background. A sample result of this process for Fig. 1(c) is shown in Fig. 3(a). Eliminated background and the remained regions are shown in white and black, respectively. The regions occupied by the component included in each section are obtained as the connected regions remained in the section after the background elimination, as shown in Fig. 3(b)–(f).

(a) Herb 1 (Absinthe) in Layout A   (b) Herb 2 (Acorus) in Layout C

(c) Herb 3 (Alkekengi) in Layout B   (d) Herb 4 (Bugloss) in Layout D

(e) Herb 5 (Marrubium) in Layout C   (f) Herb 6 (Verbascum) in Layout D

Fig. 2. Examples of the representative gaze change vectors corresponding to the centroid of the clusters.

The distance of each endpoint of each gaze change vector from the region occupied by each component is obtained from the result of distance transformation for the region, which calculates the shortest distance from the region for each pixel outside the region. By comparing the distance from the regions occupied by different page components for each endpoint, the component closest to the endpoint is also obtained together with the distance from the component to the end point. The section including the component closest to $g_h^p(m)$ is denoted by $s_h^p(m) \in S$.

3.3   Frequency of Gaze Transition Across Different Visual Components

Let $\delta_h^p(m)$ and $\delta_h^p(m+1)$ denote the distance of endpoints $g_h^p(m)$ and $g_h^p(m+1)$ of gaze change vector $\gamma_h^p(m)$ from the regions occupied by the closest component assigned to rectangular sections $s_h^p(m)$ and $s_h^p(m+1)$ in the page, respectively. The frequency of transition of the focus across different components in different rectangular sections of the page describing herb h by a participant p is evaluated by F_h^p, which is defined as

(a)Result of background elimination for Fig.1(c).

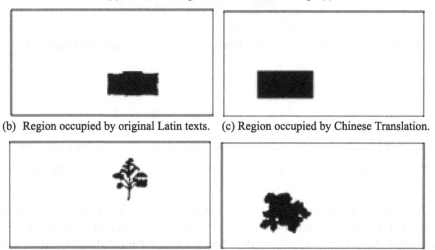

(b) Region occupied by original Latin texts. (c) Region occupied by Chinese Translation.

(d)   Region occupied by the illustration.   (d) Region occupied by the photograph.

Fig. 3. Extracting each region occupied for each component in *absinthe*.

follows:

$$F_h^p = \sum_{\substack{m=1 \\ s_h^p(m) \neq s_h^p(m+1)}}^{M_h^p-1} \left\{ \tilde{\delta}_h^p(m) + \tilde{\delta}_h^p(m+1) \right\} / \sum_{m=1}^{M_h^p-1} \left\{ \tilde{\delta}_h^p(m) + \tilde{\delta}_h^p(m+1) \right\}$$

where $\tilde{\delta}_h^p(m)$ is obtained by normalizing $\delta_h^p(m)$ into an 8-bit value within the range of $[0, 255]$ as follows:

$$\tilde{\delta}_h^p(m) = \max\left(1 - \delta_h^p(m)/255, 0\right)$$

The rate $\tilde{\delta}_h^p(m)$ should reflect how frequently the transition of focus across different visual components, which describe the same herb h with different kinds of representation in layout L presented to the participant $p \in P_L$. However, this rate varies with different participants despite some shared tendencies. To grasp the tendency for each layout if exist and difference in the tendency among different layouts, the histogram of $\tilde{\delta}_h^p(m)$ for all P_L is calculated for each page with each layout. The resultant histograms are illustrated in Fig. 4. The horizontal axis and vertical axis of each figure corresponds to the value of $\tilde{\delta}_h^p(m)$ for the page of each herb and the number of participants with the value of $\tilde{\delta}_h^p(m)$. The histograms obtained for the participants presented the learning materials with different layouts are shown in different colors.

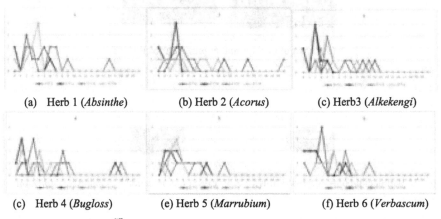

(a)   Herb 1 (*Absinthe*)   (b) Herb 2 (*Acorus*)   (c) Herb3 (*Alkekengi*)

(c)   Herb 4 (*Bugloss*)   (e) Herb 5 (*Marrubium*)   (f) Herb 6 (*Verbascum*)

Fig. 4. Histograms of $\tilde{\delta}_h^p(m)$ obtained for P_A (red), P_B (blue), P_C (yellow), and P_D (green).

By taking the medians of participants' dwelling time with each layout across different medicinal herbs, it was found that the participants spent the most time in Layout A and the least time in Layout D. According to the fixation and scan path, participants' perceived page structure of a rare book seemed to function over the distance of visual components in guiding their attention and integration.

4   Discussions and Conclusions

The preliminary findings of this study summarized descriptive information about participants' reading behaviors in terms of their eye movement. The results suggested that color photography worked as a complementary aid to participants' reading of botanical illustrations. Since the botanical illustration depicted the medicinal herb and its trait accurately for a scientific purpose [24], it reflected more faithfully the textual descriptions. Therefore, the participants of Layout A and B groups could successfully integrate the pictorial illustration with the textual information by following the textual narrative to the corresponding parts of the illustration. When color photographs are available, as in Layout C, participants' attention was quickly drawn to the contrasting traits, such as identifying flowers and leaves by color, resulting in shorter reading time and scan path. However, in Layout D, when only color photographs were shown alone, the participants were found to be distracted and even lost, owing to the lack of correspondence between textual narratives and plant traits. Participants of this group spent the least time in reading, and their scan paths were rather unstable compared to the other 3 groups. Most participants did not know what to look for due to the lack of focal depth in photographic images, and several of them also reflected in the interview on their difficulty in recognizing plant traits as novice learners in the first place. The results echoed Mason's previous study in mathematics images [25], which reported that abstract math illustrations were fixated for a longer time than concrete pictures.

Based on the understanding of how participants use and integrate different types of visual inputs in scientific reading, our further studies will keep collating data on learning performance, including memory and comprehension test scores with a larger sample size, to investigate how quality and quantity of visual inputs affect scientific reading performance.

References

1. Fennell, F., Rowan, T.: Representation: an important process for teaching and learning mathematics. Teach. Child. Math. **7**, 288–292 (2001)
2. Höffler, T.N., Prechtl, H., Nerdel, C.: The influence of visual cognitive style when learning from instructional animations and static pictures. Learn. Individ. Differ. **20**, 479–483 (2010)
3. Mason, L., Pluchino, P., Tornatora, M.C.: Using eye-tracking technology as an indirect instruction tool to improve text and picture processing and learning. Br. J. Edu. Technol. **47**, 1083–1095 (2016)
4. Mason, L., Tornatora, M.C., Pluchino, P.: Integrative processing of verbal and graphical information during re-reading predicts learning from illustrated text: an eye-movement study. Read. Writ. **28**(6), 851–872 (2015). https://doi.org/10.1007/s11145-015-9552-5
5. Mayer, R., Mayer, R.E.: The Cambridge Handbook of Multimedia Learning. Cambridge University Press, Cambridge (2005)
6. Witteveen, J.: Naming and contingency: the type method of biological taxonomy. Biol. Philos. **30**(4), 569–586 (2014). https://doi.org/10.1007/s10539-014-9459-6
7. Lin, W., Chang, H.-J.: Understanding taxonomical botanist's usage of special collection in the academic library: a bibliometrics study of NTU Tanaka collection. J. Libr. Inf. Stud. **20**, 101–129 (2022)
8. Walton, C., Morris, A.: A bibliometric study of taxonomic botany. J. Doc. **69**, 435–451 (2013)
9. Hickman, E.J., Yates, C.J., Hopper, S.D.: Botanical illustration and photography: a southern hemisphere perspective. Aust. Syst. Bot. **30**, 291–325 (2017)
10. Simpson, N., Barnes, P.G.: Photography and contemporary botanical illustration. Curtis's Bot. Mag. **25**, 258–280 (2008)
11. Berger, S.E.: Rare Books and Special Collections. Facet Publishing, London (2014)
12. McDonald, S., Stevenson, R.J.: Effects of text structure and prior knowledge of the learner on navigation in hypertext. Hum. Factors **40**, 18–27 (1998)
13. Vincent, H.: The library and the display of text. In: World Library and Information Congress: 78th IFLA General Conference and Assembly. IFLA, Helsinki, Finland (2012)
14. Bell, B., Cottrell, T.: Hands-free augmented reality: impacting the library future. In: Varnum, K.J. (ed.) The Top Technologies Every Librarian Needs to Know, pp. 13–26. American Library Association, Chicago (2014)
15. Armstrong, G., Hodgson, J., Manista, F., Ramirez, M.: The SCARLET project: augmented reality in special collections. SCONUL Focus **54**, 52–57 (2012)
16. Cheng, K.-H.: Reading an augmented reality book: an exploration of learners' cognitive load, motivation, and attitudes. Australas. J. Educ. Technol. **33**, (2017)
17. Lin, W., Lo, W.-T., Yueh, H.-P.: Effects of learner control design in an AR-based exhibit on visitors' museum learning. PLoS ONE **17**, e0274826 (2022)

18. Grasset, R., Dünser, A., Billinghurst, M.: Edutainment with a mixed reality book: a visually augmented illustrative children's book. In: Advances in Computer Entertainment Technology, Yokohama, Japan (2008)
19. Grasset, R., Dunser, A., Billinghurst, M.: The design of a mixed-reality book: Is it still a real book? In: 2008 7th IEEE/ACM International Symposium on Mixed and Augmented Reality, pp. 99–102 (2008)
20. Lin, W., Kotakehara, Y., Hirota, Y., Murakami, M., Kakusho, K., Yueh, H.P.: Modeling reading behaviors: an automatic approach to eye movement analytics. IEEE Access 9, 63580–63590 (2021)
21. Avicenna, S.: De Virtutibus Herbarum. Gioãni Andrea Vauassore, Venetia (1524)
22. https://help.tobii.com/hc/en-us/articles/212818309-Specifications-for-EyeX
23. Arthur, D., Vassilvitskii, S.: k-means++: the advantages of careful seeding. In: SODA 2007 Proceedings of the Eighteenth Annual ACM-SIAM Symposium on Discrete Algorithms, pp. 1027–1035. ACM Society for Industrial and Applied Mathematics (2007)
24. Rix, M.: The Golden Age of Botanical Art. Andre Deutsch, Carlton Publishing Group, London (2012)
25. Mason, L., Pluchino, P., Tornatora, M.C., Ariasi, N.: An eye-tracking study of learning from science text with concrete and abstract illustrations. J. Exp. Educ. 81, 356–384 (2013)

Effects of VR Technology in the Cross-Cultural Theatre Design Course

Jingyuan Shi, Weilong Wu[✉], Lin Yu, and Wu Wei

School of Film Television and Communication, Xiamen University of Technology, Xiamen,
China
wu_academic@163.com

Abstract.

Objectives. At present, major universities at home and abroad have set up theatre design-related majors, and provide professional talents with different cultural
backgrounds for the theatre design industry. The development of existing stage
technology and new media technology is becoming increasingly integrated, from
black box theatres, to large scale cabaret theatres, where new media imaging technologies such as real time projection, generative art, broadcast control software
and pre-show systems applied to the stage have become commonplace. Most students only learn through 3D modelling, graphic design and other kinds of software
pathways, lacking practical aspects of practice, and because there are students from
different geographical backgrounds and cultural and cultural backgrounds within
different classes, it is easy to lead to the learning process of the learning God audience difficult to accept the content of cross-cultural communication. The existing
theatre design courses do not meet the needs of the virtual and realistic teaching methods. Most students only learn through 3D modelling, graphic design and
other types of software, lacking practical practice. At the same time, the existence
of students from different geographical backgrounds and cultural backgrounds in
different classes can easily lead to barriers to cross-cultural communication in the
learning process. Realistic theatre design teaching scenes often require a realistic
stage to be built in a realistic theatre, and because of the large equipment and
consumables involved such as venues, choreography and lighting, such teaching
scenes are extremely expensive to set up, and more institutions often find it difficult
to achieve, or can only provide teaching scenes with lower configurations etc. In
the long run, students' learning often remains only in theory and drawings, making
it difficult to really apply them in practice. This is not conducive to the flexible
mastery of professional knowledge by students of the relevant disciplines. The use
of virtual reality technology can therefore be a good solution to this problem.

The aim of this paper is to investigate the integration and application of virtual
reality technology in the intercultural field of theatre design courses. Through
virtual reality technology, virtual reality stages from different countries, regions
and nationalities with local style characteristics can be switched at any time, while
students from different countries or regions can exchange their familiar stage
forms with each other in the virtual reality space. It examines the advantages and
disadvantages of combining the two in a cross-cultural context for teaching theatre
art and design courses.

J. Shi and W. Wu—These authors contributed equally to this study.

P.-L. P. Rau (Ed.): HCII 2023, LNCS 14024, pp. 265–277, 2023.
https://doi.org/10.1007/978-3-031-35946-0_22

Methods. Control experiment: Two students of the same year majoring in art and design are selected from a university, with the number of students in each class controlled at 25. At the same time, it is ensured that the students in both classes have the same basic professional knowledge, i.e. both classes have a certain level of theoretical and practical foundation in theatre art and design. Experiments are designed during the teaching process of the course "Stage Art Design" and are taught by the same teachers, according to the same syllabus and teaching schedule, and are assessed in the same way at the end of the course. The variables are taught in two classes, with class A set up to focus on theoretical content supplemented by design software courses. Class B is set up for practical theatre design training based on virtual reality technology, with theoretical content as a secondary foundation. At the end of the course, the same examination content and assessment requirements are used to assess the mastery of practical theatre design skills in both classes A and B.

Questionnaires: A questionnaire was set up to include ratings of students' acceptance of the different teaching methods in both classes, ratings of the different teaching methods by the lecturers, and post-course interviews to collect suggestions from students and teachers regarding the course content and the setting of the teaching methods. By analysing the data and rating the content of the opinions, the impact of using different teaching methods as variables in the same course was calculated separately.

Results. The analysis of the experimental results showed that, in the case of the control group, other variables were the same, excluding some of the subjective and objective factors that brought about the slightest influence. The use of virtual reality technology for practical teaching in theatre art and design courses, together with an appropriate amount of theoretical knowledge, has been found to be more acceptable and enjoyable to students. Teachers are more willing to integrate virtual reality technology into their courses on a regular basis.

Conclusions. Through this experiment and the end-of-course assessment, it was found that the assessment content and coursework presented in Class B, where virtual reality was used, were more innovative when anonymously graded and compared to the results in Class B, where virtual reality was used. It can be concluded that the integration of virtual reality technology into theatre design courses is more conducive to the students' mastery of the subject matter and is conducive to achieving better teaching and learning outcomes. At the same time, the use of virtual reality technology will also make the course's teaching costs and related equipment to reduce the capital investment, so that the ease of teaching professional courses to improve the operability. It will facilitate the use of similar courses in colleges and universities. However, it should be noted that in the process of promoting and using virtual reality technology, students' mastery of basic theoretical knowledge is neglected. In the teaching process need to grasp the virtual reality practical content and theoretical content pair balance. To ensure that students have a solid grasp of the theoretical basics on the basis of practical operations, more conducive to the optimal presentation of the teaching effect.

Keywords: Virtual reality technology · Theatre design Course · Cross-cultural communication

1 Introduction

Theatre is the design with "theatre design" as the signifier, precisely the design with stage equipment, lighting, curtain, sound, performance props, suspension and replacement support system, costume and make-up modeling as the signifier. As one of its key components, the stage art transforms the theatre by constantly changing the scenery, lighting and costumes, thus creating a variety of stage styles. In the modernization of society, theatre art design has become more and more diverse and open, containing very rich characteristics of the times [1]. Through the comprehensive application of visual elements, different cultural and artistic aesthetics are created, thus giving people a different aesthetic experience. In the process of continuous development of modern science and technology, the artistic elements of modern theatre are more abundant, and the artistic display effect tends to be diversified, it can be flexibly adjusted according to the changes of the stage performance content, in order to achieve the consistency of content and environmental atmosphere, and enhance the effect of theatre [2].

At present, all kinds of universities have opened stage art design-related majors or courses, aiming to cultivate this professional talent. Stage art design students mainly study the basic theory and skills of film and television, stage art design, mainly mastering stage art design such as stage art, lighting, sound, character modelling, digital media and computer 3D design and other knowledge, learning a more comprehensive stage art design and production ability, dynamic design ability and strong stage art design ability. However, at present, most of the professional courses related to theatre in colleges and universities focus on the basic knowledge of the stage and the training of drawing ability and 3D modelling design, etc. The knowledge taught in the courses is relatively single, and teachers often test students' mastery of the course content in the form of drawing assignments, neglecting the practical training of students and the cultivation of overall design thinking. Starting only with the fundamentals of theatre, spatial training, drawing exercises and theatre modelling will not better train the theatre talents needed at this stage.

The visual representation of anthropomorphic technology has done so by breaking the traditional concept of time and space and creating a novel vision. At the same time, it satisfies the psychological demands and inner desires of the public, generating an immersive and realistic experience, and its value of existence is extremely meaningful and vital [3]. The combination of virtual reality technology and theatre courses, with the advantages of virtual reality technology, to make up for the shortcomings of traditional theatre courses, so that the theatre courses follow the technological development situation, which will be more conducive to the theatre courses to adapt to future development.

2 Literature Review

2.1 Theatre Courses

The stage provides space for the actors to perform, which allows the audience's attention to be focused on the actors' performance and to obtain the desired viewing effect. The stage usually consists of one or more platforms, some of which can be raised and lowered.

One of the main components of a theatre building is the performance space in front of the auditorium. In ancient amphitheaters, the main stage was mostly extended in front of the auditorium, either below it (as in the case of the ancient Greek fan theatre stage) or above it (as in the case of the Chinese opera stage), so that the audience could watch the play from three sides. Stages in indoor theatres usually face the audience and are available as mirror-frame stages, projecting stages and center stages. The competencies required of students of theatre include theoretical knowledge of performance events (or theatre performances), stage painting, prop making (art crafts), knowledge of stage lighting, evolution of props and costume patterns, knowledge of music and repertoire, knowledge of sound control, etc. Many universities in China offer majors and directions related to theatre to train the theatre talents needed by the industry. As a number of new media technologies such as 5G and virtual reality continue to mature, theatre continues to integrate with new technologies, and traditional stage art design courses are no longer able to meet the needs of the industry.

Richard M. Isackes has concluded from his extensive teaching experience that most current classroom teaching is dedicated to creating design 'meta-objects', including drawings, model building, renderings, etc., which, although the most realistic depiction of the designed object, are, because they are detached from reality, they are not perceived by real performers, nor are they accessible to real audiences. Therefore, they have a low level of practical credibility. Stage art designers as scene-builders are neither simply designers in the visual arts nor architects in the traditional sense; rather, they are performing artists dedicated to the study of how the stage works and is artistically represented, rather than just painters of images or structures [4]. Jessica Greenberg and Brian Rague have designed an interdisciplinary course linking computer and after researching the course, they believe that students will fully understand and appreciate the importance of balancing artistic expression and technical skills as it applies to modern theatre production and design. Students will gain a solid grounding in software tools to enhance the theatre experience through the integration of audio-visual effects and interactive media. Students will gain collaboration and communication skills to work effectively with others from different disciplines [5].

There is currently a paucity of national and international research dedicated to theatre design courses, with the existing research focusing on theatre education and artistic creation methods. There is a great deal of research that emphasises the role of developing students' design thinking, as well as drawing on the experiences of successful practitioners to give students a better understanding of holistic design approaches and simple interactive experiences where technology allows. However, there is no existing research or literature that specifically examines virtual reality technology and theatre design courses. Through this study and experiment, we hope to find ways to integrate stage theory and theatre practice and to better apply them in teaching practice [6].

2.2 Virtual Reality Technology

Virtual reality technology refers to information technology that digitises images with the help of multimedia, artificial intelligence, sensors and other technologies to create a virtual space. With the application of virtual reality technology, users are able to enter virtual spaces for exploration through wearable devices, experience realistic touch and feel the presence of virtual things. Virtual reality technology can simulate any realistic environment, such as a dangerous mining site, a high-rise building operation site, a power grid maintenance site, a fire site, a traffic accident site, and allow users to participate in human-machine interaction. People can explore the virtual space with the aid of aids for a realistic visual experience and a realistic behavioural experience. Virtual reality technology also enables the sharing of virtual scenes via the Internet, allowing people to experience virtual environments together without leaving home [7–9].

In recent decades, art and design education has been striving to explore new methods and tools for better teaching and learning activities. Virtual Reality (VR) is one of the main solutions for technology-driven pedagogy [10]. As a cutting-edge science and technology, virtual reality is a product of the development of human imagination and creativity, representing the edge of advanced scientific and cultural knowledge, the development of a spirit of adventure and unlimited creativity, and its introduction into the field of education, which can enable advanced ideas and technologies to enter schools and classrooms, bringing about changes not only in teachers' teaching methods, such as classroom venues and equipment, but also in the content of teaching and learning, giving students more opportunities to actively explore knowledge. Teachers will not only be the exporters of knowledge, but will control the pace and rhythm of lessons. The practical application of this technology will lead to a dramatic change in the way students explore and receive knowledge, thus promoting innovation in the teaching and learning of the arts [11].

Dong Wang's experiments and data analysis have demonstrated the efficiency of using virtual reality in post-production and special effects painting for film and television, as well as the control of post-production costs for film and television products [12]. This experiment opens up new areas such as virtual reality in the field of artistic creation and provides experience for the experimental format of this study. Gillian Arrighi and others used the Victoria theatre in Newcastle, Australia, as the object of their research to digitally reconstruct the heritage building of the theatre with the help of virtual reality technology, enabling users to move and navigate historical and cultural content in a virtual space, by They explored the ease of use and practicality of the VR system by designing various interaction schemes, and received a good response through user experience surveys after the experiment [13]. This study was carried out for virtual reality applications in theatres, which are the same as the subject of our study, providing us with suitable examples of applications combining virtual reality with theatres. Google Expeditions is a program in which teachers can take their students around the world, to museums, mountains, historical monuments tides, oceans and outer space, without leaving the classroom. The adventure is carried out in the classroom using virtual reality technology [14]. This case better combines virtual reality with teaching tasks and provides a reference for our research on how virtual reality can be better integrated with classroom immersion. Yuefeng Pu concludes from experiments and data analysis that the application of virtual reality technology in teaching martial arts can perfectly combine book and video teaching materials, making the text and pictures in books lifelike and the movements in video demonstrations in 3D form the demonstrations are more intuitive, while action explanations and music are added to enrich the video effects. Students gain an immersive learning experience using VR equipment, stimulating their interest and enjoyment, and gradually improving the quality of martial arts movements [15]. Both the martial arts course and the theatre course are highly hands-on, and the application of virtual reality technology in the martial arts classroom provides experience in the application of the technology for our study. Remote virtual teaching technology is expected to be a new development direction for future virtual reality teaching, providing a more forward-looking research idea for our study [16].

Existing research on virtual reality technology shows that its application in various industries such as cultural industries and education has matured and achieved good results, but no case study or application has been found on its combination with theatre courses or other art and design courses for teaching.

Virtual reality is not an entirely new technology. However, a number of limitations have hindered their practical application. Continued technological advances and the availability of low-cost hardware and software have made VR more feasible and desirable in many areas, including education [17]. Virtual reality technology is currently widely used in the education industry for teaching, but there are currently no cases of virtual reality technology being used in theatre arts design but. This study will conduct experiments and analysis on the application of virtual reality technology to theatre design courses but effects and other aspects to fill the research gap in this field.

3 Experiment Design

This experiment aims to investigate whether students can better grasp the professional knowledge in a real-time interactive immersive environment by using virtual reality technology in the teaching of theatre art and design compared to traditional teaching methods, and whether the intervention of this technology can have a better teaching effect. In the experiment, a control group and an experimental group were set up, in which the control group was taught in a traditional way and in which the experimental group was taught with virtual reality technology. Two experimental groups, after being taught the theoretical knowledge of the same content at the same time, were given different practical exercises.

3.1 Experimental Participants

For this experiment, we selected 50 sophomore students of a university in China, they majoring in theatre and stage art design. All the selected students already had two years of the same professional knowledge learning experience, with no major differences in their basic conditions. Through a pre-experimental test, they were divided into two groups of 25 students each, based on their professional level, without differences, as the experimental and control groups respectively. The teacher participants were selected to be conducted by a professor with extensive experience in the subject, who participated in the whole process of the experiment, including the pre-experimental test as well as the post-experimental test proposing questions. The teacher used virtual reality technology for the practical part of the experimental group, allowing students to practise theatre design in a virtual environment, while the control group used traditional teaching methods, using computer graphics tools, to practise flat and 3D design of the stage.

3.2 Measuring Tools

The measurements for this experiment consisted of a pre-experimental quiz to reduce the differences that existed between individual subjects, and a post-experimental measurement consisting of a questionnaire and a professional test. The questionnaire includes the students' overall evaluation of the course, as well as their own acceptance, interest level and other comprehensive ratings, each set at 1–5 points. The professional test consists of a theoretical examination result and a practical work result. Both tests are based on a one-hundred-point scale. Both post-experimental tests were analysed using a t-test (known as the full independent sample t-test) for data analysis.

3.3 Experimental Procedure

Set up the experimental group and the control group before the start of the experiment, which are Class A and Class B respectively. Ensure that the two classes involved in the experiment have a total of 50 students, and that the students in the two classes have similar professional foundation abilities, both have a certain level of theoretical and practical foundation in theatre art design, and that the pre-courses in the two classes are the same. At the beginning of the experiment, the same teacher teaches the course "Stage Art Design" and the order of classes is exchanged every week between the two classes in order to exclude as much as possible the different effects of the teacher's motivation on the students. The theoretical content of the course is the same for both classes, but in terms of the teaching method, Class A adopts the traditional approach, i.e., students design and practice in the relevant theatre design software after the teacher has demonstrated on the computer, while Class B, as an experiment, uses virtual reality technology to build the stage scene with the students after the teacher has explained the theoretical knowledge. At the end of the course, the two groups of students were given a theoretical knowledge test and a practical test. A questionnaire was also administered to all students who participated in the experiment. Finally, the questionnaire and performance data were analysed separately (Fig. 1).

4 Experimental Results

4.1 Questionnaire Analysis

The t-test (known as the independent sample t-test) was used to study the differences between the participating students' ratings of the difficulty of the course, their satisfaction with the course, their interest in the course, their concentration in the course, their mastery of the course, their initiative in learning, their mastery of the course, their innovative methods of learning, their motivation to learn using the available technology or equipment, and their connection between theory and practice. From the Table 1, we can see that the different samples of students who participated in the experiment rated the difficulty of the course, the satisfaction level of the course, the interest level of the course, the concentration level of the course, the mastery level of the course, the initiative level of the course, the learning methods and innovative methods mastered by the teacher, and the use of available technology or equipment by the teacher to motivate students. This

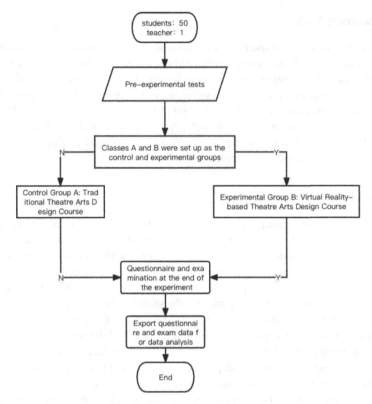

Fig. 1. The experimental process

means that the different samples of students who took part in the experiment all showed significant (p < 0.05) ratings for the difficulty of the course, their satisfaction with the course, their interest in the course, their concentration, their mastery of the course, their initiative, their knowledge of the course, and their knowledge of the course. There is variability in the ratings of learning methods and innovative approaches to the course, the extent to which teachers use available technology or equipment to motivate students, and the extent to which the course is linked to theory and practice.

The specific analysis shows that the students who took part in the experiment showed a 0.05 level of significance (t = 2.594, p = 0.013) for the difficulty level of the course, as well as a specific difference in comparison, the mean value of the traditional theatre art and design course (3.52) was significantly higher than the mean value of the virtual reality-based theatre art and design course (2.80).

The students' satisfaction with the course was significant at the 0.05 level (t = −2.213, p = 0.032), and the difference between the mean for the traditional theatre design course (2.64) and the mean for the virtual reality-based theatre design course (3.16).

The students' interest in the course was significant at the 0.01 level (t = −3.434, p = 0.001), and the difference between the mean for the traditional theatre design course (2.64) and the mean for the virtual reality-based theatre design course (3.24).

The students in the experiment showed a 0.05 level of significance (t = −2.204, p = 0.033) for the course concentration scores, as well as a specific comparison difference, with the mean for the traditional theatre arts design course (2.72) being significantly lower than the mean for the virtual reality-based theatre arts design course (3.32).

The students' level of expertise in the course was significant at the 0.01 level (t = −2.825, p = 0.007), and the difference in the specific comparisons showed that the mean for the traditional theatre arts design course (2.64) was significantly lower than the mean for the virtual reality-based theatre arts design course (3.28).

The experimental students showed a 0.05 level of significance (t = −2.457, p = 0.019) for the learning initiative scores, and the specific comparison difference shows that the mean for the traditional theatre arts design course (2.64) is significantly lower than the mean for the virtual reality-based theatre arts design course (3.36).

The students' ratings of their knowledge of learning methods and innovative approaches to the course were significant at the 0.05 level (t = −2.669, p = 0.010), and the difference in specific comparisons showed that the mean for the traditional theatre design course (2.64) was significantly lower than the mean for the virtual reality-based theatre design course (3.44).

The experimental students showed a 0.05 level of significance (t = −2.545, p = 0.015) for the extent to which the instructor used available technology or equipment to motivate students to learn, as well as a specific difference in comparison, with the mean for the traditional theatre design course (2.72) being significantly lower than the mean for the virtual reality-based theatre design course (3.52).

The students participating in the experiment showed a 0.05 level of significance (t = −2.116, p = 0.041) for the degree of connection between theory and practice, as well as specific comparative differences, with the mean for the traditional theatre design course (2.68) being significantly lower than the mean for the virtual reality-based theatre design course (3.32).

To summarise, the different samples of students participating in the experiment all showed a different level of difficulty, satisfaction with the course, interest in the course, concentration in the course, mastery of the course, initiative in learning, methods of learning and innovation in the course, the extent to which the teacher uses available technology or equipment to motivate students, and the extent to which the course is linked to theory and practice. The degree of linkage between theory and practice all showed significant differences.

4.2   Analysis of Performance

From the Table 2, it can be seen that the t-test was used to study the differences between the classes for the theoretical test scores and the two items for the work scores, and from the Table 2 it can be seen that the different class samples do not show significance (p > 0.05) for a total of 1 item for the theoretical test scores, which means that the different class samples show consistency for all the theoretical test scores and there is no difference. In addition, the class sample does not show significance (p < 0.05) for a total of 1 item for the work performance, which means that there is a difference between the class samples for the work performance. A specific analysis shows that the classes showed a 0.01 level of significance (t = −4.589, p = 0.000) for the work scores, as

Table 1. Questionnaire data t-test results

	Group	N	Average	SD	t	p
Course difficulty rating	Traditional	25	3.52	1.08	2.594	0.013*
	VR	25	2.80	0.87		
Satisfaction with the course	Traditional	25	2.64	0.76	−2.213	0.032*
	VR	25	3.16	0.90		
Degree of interest in this course pair	Traditional	25	2.64	0.57	−3.434	0.001**
	VR	25	3.24	0.66		
Course concentration score	Traditional	25	2.72	0.74	−2.204	0.033*
	VR	25	3.32	1.14		
Mastery of expertise in the course	Traditional	25	2.64	0.64	−2.825	0.007**
	VR	25	3.28	0.94		
Rating of learning initiative	Traditional	25	2.64	0.76	−2.457	0.019*
	VR	25	3.36	1.25		
Rating of learning methods and innovative approaches acquired in the course	Traditional	25	2.64	0.86	−2.669	0.010*
	VR	25	3.44	1.23		
Extent to which the teacher uses available technology or equipment to motivate students	Traditional	25	2.72	0.79	−2.545	0.015*
	VR	25	3.52	1.36		
Extent to which the curriculum is linked to theory and practice	Traditional	25	2.68	0.75	−2.116	0.041*
	VR	25	3.32	1.31		

$p < 0.05^*; p < 0.01^{**}$

well as a specific comparison of the differences shows that the mean of class A (81.56), would be significantly lower than the mean of class B (85.68).

In conclusion, it can be seen that the different class samples will not show significant differences for a total of 1 theoretical exam score, and the other class samples show significant differences for a total of 1 work score.

Table 2. Examination results t-check results

	Group	N	Average	SD	t	p
Theoretical examination results	Traditional	25	84.40	1.41	1.033	0.307
	VR	25	83.96	1.59		
Achievements in practical work	Traditional	25	81.56	3.10	−4.589	0.000**
	VR	25	85.68	3.25		

$p < 0.05^*; p < 0.01^{**}$

5   Discussion and Conclusions

Through the data analysis and research of this experiment, we can learn that in the teaching process of the stage art design course, using virtual reality technology for teaching, students are more interested in the course and have higher concentration, learning conscientiousness and initiative for learning compared with the traditional teaching mode. When students complete their theatre design work through virtual reality technology, the senses are more directly immersed in the design, thus making the design content highly consistent with the stage reality presentation, greatly improving the efficiency of the design work while minimising the differences in aesthetic perception between individuals, allowing students to design more aesthetically excellent work.

When the results of the two groups of subjects were analysed, it was found that the two classes did not show significance between the results of the theoretical examinations, while they showed significance in the achievement scores of the practical work. This data proves that virtual reality-based theatre art and design courses are more conducive to helping students to create their works, to the training of professionals and to the enhancement of their professional abilities. At the same time, the overall construction of the stage in the virtual reality environment can simulate the real stage to the greatest extent, which is conducive to enabling students to improve their design thinking and construction skills more quickly and adapt to the needs of the industry as soon as possible after graduation.

In addition, the use of virtual reality technology in the professional teaching of theatre art and design has reduced teaching costs to a greater extent, making it unnecessary for educational institutions and schools to spend a lot of money on the construction of realistic stage scenes, and virtual reality scenes can be upgraded and virtual scenes updated and upgraded at any time according to existing technology. The experience of combining virtual reality technology with theatre design courses can provide experience and a reference basis for other art and design related disciplines, and can provide virtual reality space for other teaching sections that require a lot of professional scenario practice, solving the problems of insufficient teaching space and high teaching costs for teaching institutions or schools. Combine the teaching mode of virtual reality technology with the educational concept of STEAM and design a teaching mode that is geared towards the needs of students. This teaching model consists of five components: analysing the needs of the students, analysing the learning objectives, selecting learning strategies, designing learning activities and designing learning assessments. Through teaching practice, it has been found that this model of teaching can significantly improve students' performance and inspire them to be enthusiastic about learning. Students' independent learning and expertise acquisition is significantly better than traditional multimedia teaching methods. The proposed teaching model provides an objective reference for the application of virtual reality technology in teaching [18, 19].

The use of virtual reality technology in art education has great potential to bring students closer to the possibility of using virtual 3D objects and models [20]. At present, the development of virtual reality technology has been relatively mature, but the combination with the education industry is still not close enough. In the future, it is hoped that more research and argumentation can be conducted to provide more feasible solutions and countermeasures for the combination of virtual reality technology and art and design majors. So that the two can be combined with each other to obtain better development.

Funding. This work was supported by Social Science Foundation of Fujian Province, China (Funding Number: FJ2022C071).

And supported by Xiamen Education Scientific Planning Project: Application of VR in art design courses in the post-epidemic era Innovative Teaching Reform Study (Funding Number: 22002).

And supported by High-level Talent Research Project of Xiamen University of Technology (Funding Number: YSK22018R).

References

1. Li, D.: Exploring the aesthetic style of real and imaginary scenarios in theatrical stage art design. Art Des. (Theory) **03**, 71–73 (2020). https://doi.org/10.16824/j.cnki.issn10082832.2020.03.018
2. Li, D., Liu, J.: The beauty of art in modern stage design. Architectural Structures (2021)
3. Zhang, Y., Di, L.: Application of virtual imaging technology in stage design. Digit. Technol. Appl. **07**, 137–139 (2022). https://doi.org/10.19695/j.cnki.cn12-1369.2022.07.43
4. Isackes, R.M.: On the pedagogy of theatre stage design: a critique of practice. Theatr. Top. **18**(1), 41–53 (2008)
5. Greenberg, J., Rague, B.: Digital theatre design-an interdisciplinary course connecting computing and theatre arts. In: Proceedings of the 52nd ACM Technical Symposium on Computer Science Education, p. 1262 (2021)
6. Bergner, B., Dionne, R.: Pedagogies for design thinking and experiential technologies. In: Experiential Theatres, pp. 185–193. Routledge (2022)
7. Wu, W., Zhao, Z., Du, A., Lin, J.: Effects of multisensory integration through spherical video-based immersive virtual reality on students learning performances in a landscape architecture conservation course. Sustainability **14**(24), 16891 (2022)
8. Wu, W.L., Hsu, Y., Yang, Q.F., Chen, J.J.: A spherical video-based immersive virtual reality learning system to support landscape architecture students learning performance during the COVID-19 era. Land **10**(6), 561 (2021)
9. Akdere, M., Acheson, K., Jiang, Y.: An examination of the effectiveness of virtual reality technology for intercultural competence development. Int. J. Intercult. Relat. **82**, 109–120 (2021)
10. Som, S., Mathew, D.J., Phillipson, S., Vincs, K.: Scaffolding design process in the light of art and design education: an artistic practice towards developing a hands-on learning program with the aid of virtual reality for Indian school student. ICIDR Int. J. Multidiscip. Res. **8**(2), 129–135 (2021)
11. Feng, L., Zhang, W.: Design and implementation of computer-aided art teaching system based on virtual reality. Comput.-Aided Des. Appl. **20**, 56–65 (2023)
12. Wang, D.: Application of VR virtual reality in the course of later stage and special effect production. Int. Trans. Electr. Energy Syst. **2022** (2022)
13. Arrighi, G., See, Z.S., Jones, D.: Victoria theatre virtual reality: a digital heritage case study and user experience design. Digit. Appl. Archaeol. Cult. Heritage **21**, e00176 (2021)
14. Alizadeh, M.: Virtual reality in the language classroom: theory and practice. Call-Ej **20**(3), 21–30 (2019)
15. Pu, Y., Yang, Y.: Application of virtual reality technology in martial arts situational teaching. Mob. Inf. Syst. **2022** (2022)

16. Lou, M.: A virtual reality teaching system for graphic design course. Int. J. Emerg. Technol. Learn. **12**(9), 117–129 (2017)
17. Elmqaddem, N.: Augmented reality and virtual reality in education. Myth or reality? Int. J. Emerg. Technol. Learn. **14**(3), 234–242 (2019)
18. Ji, Y.: Use of virtual reality technology in animation course teaching. Int. J. Emerg. Technol. Learn. **16**(17), 191–208 (2021)
19. Shatunova, O., Anisimova, T., Sabirova, F., Kalimullina, O.: STEAM as an innovative educational technology. J. Soc. Stud. Educ. Res. **10**(2), 131–144 (2019)
20. González-Zamar, M.D., Abad-Segura, E.: Implications of virtual reality in arts education: research analysis in the context of higher education. Educ. Sci. **10**(9), 225 (2020)

Social Innovation in Design Education: The Emergence and Evolution of Design Academic Programs

Yilin Wang[(⊠)] [iD]

College of Design and Innovation, Tongji University, 281 Fuxin Road, Shanghai, China
yilinwang@tongji.edu.cn

Abstract. As the global ecological crisis and social conflicts intensify, design is widely involved in social innovation and taking on more social responsibilities. The concept of social innovation has been continuously integrated into the educational practices of design schools, driving the transformation of design education. This paper aims to explore the emergence and evolution of academic programs related to social innovation in the process of global design education reform, and to reveal the new possibilities that social innovation brings to design education. Based on several dimensions of comparative analysis, the paper proposes that building academic programs related to social innovation is becoming a global trend in the transformation of design education. Social innovation not only reinforces design education's value base, but it also provides methodological support for design education. Despite all this, these emerging educational activities are likely influenced by various social contexts and differ in specific educational techniques and organizational structures. Elaborating on the rise of social innovation in academic programs, the outcomes of this study may provide fresh perspectives for design schools to participate in the process of social innovation as well as new ideas for socially oriented design education reform.

Keywords: Design education · Social innovation · Academic programs · Higher education

1 Introduction

Today human beings face pressing crises such as climate change, pandemics, food shortages, and ecological destruction, for which existing top-down governance structures and profit-oriented market models often fail to provide solutions. As an innovation paradigm beyond commercial and technological innovations, social innovation is defined as a "new solution to a social problem which is more effective, efficient, sustainable or fairer than existing solutions [1]." Its purpose is to respond positively to societal needs and address social challenges by creating new collaborative relationships and facilitating the systemic and continuous transition.

Design is increasingly playing an active role in various areas of social innovation, which opens up new possibilities for change in design education. As such, design thinking

P.-L. P. Rau (Ed.): HCII 2023, LNCS 14024, pp. 278–290, 2023.
https://doi.org/10.1007/978-3-031-35946-0_23

has evolved beyond a cognitive style as in the traditional design professions into an organizational resource [2] that could allow companies, government departments, and third-party organizations to achieve the transformation goal.

Globally, the rise of social innovation impacts the transformation of design education while it makes new requirements for the competencies and cognitions of future designers. Some design schools have embarked on the journey of social innovation and integrated relevant concepts into emerging educational practices in a positive response to societal needs. However, there has been very little discussion about socially oriented design education practices in a systematic way. This paper examines the emergence and evolution of academic programs related to social innovation in the global context of design education reform. It aims to illuminate how design schools respond to the new demands of social and educational change by analyzing social innovation ideas presented in these academic programs.

This paper is structured as follows: it first reviews the rise of socially oriented discourses in design research and design education. Then it introduces the methodology used to investigate the academic programs in design schools, followed by unpacking the characteristics of these programs in four dimensions: training objectives, organizational arrangement, disciplinary relationships, and pedagogies. Finally, the study concludes with a perspective on how social innovation could create the potential for design education reform and suggests future research directions.

2 Literature Review

2.1 Social Design Discourses

The origin of social design could date back to the early 1970s when radical social movements and the prevailing consumerism brought about a rethinking of the existing production modes. One of the pioneers of social design, Papanek, in his book "Design for the Real World," severely criticizes the pitfalls of consumerism brought by useless designs and advocates that designers should be socially and ecologically responsible for the real needs of the third world and marginalized groups [3]. Reviewing Papanek's socially responsible design, Victor Maglin conceives a utopian prototype of the "good society" where everyone can live in dignity. He takes the good society as an action frame to inspire thinking about restructuring lifestyles by combining many forces of social change for shared social forms of life on a large scale [4].

Over the last two decades, research on strategies and pathways for social design has advanced considerably based on a consensus on pursuing social ends. In particular, approaches of participatory design and co-design provide methodological support for social design activities. Building on the Scandinavian tradition of participatory design, Björgvinsson and his colleagues [5] talk about "design things" and "infrastructuring" as key strategies for leaving design an ongoing and dynamic process. The point is to establish agonistic public spaces and meet the goal of democratic innovations. While Sanders and Stappers [6] define co-design as "the creativity of designers and people untrained in design working together in the design development process," they actually use co-design in a broad sense to describe "any act of collective creativity...shared by two or more people". According to Kleinsmann and Valkenburg [7], co-design is the design process where the actors share knowledge and build consensus on the ultimate goal. In this regard, establishing interdisciplinary cooperation is of great importance for gaining high-quality design communication and generating new knowledge.

Integrating these theoretical foundations, Ezio Manzini [8] points out that "design for social innovation" means "everything that expert design can do to activate, sustain, and orient processes of social change toward sustainability." This definition implies that design for social innovation encompasses the broad field that arises from the intersection of all the social innovation phenomena and contemporary forms of design professions. He reexamines the "small and beautiful" culture in light of the economic and technological advancements in society today and proposes a different way of life called "The SLOC scenario," which stands for small, local, open, and connected, in order to create a new perspective on how to create a sustainable networked society. He believes the SLOC scenario might function as a potent social magnet to compel social actors to make creative endeavors.

Social design has been in a discursive moment with pluralism, which includes various practical and research activities. A report by Armstrong and her colleagues identifies social design as "the concepts and activities enacted within participatory approaches to researching, generating and realizing new ways to make change happen towards collective and social ends, rather than predominantly commercial objectives" and summarizes three kinds of discourses: social entrepreneurship, socially responsible design, and design activism [9]. These social design discourses demonstrate a challenge to traditional design perspectives and greatly enrich the theoretical framework, methods, and tools for design interventions in various fields of social innovation. Emphasizing participatory approaches and knowledge integration, social design allows the actions to dynamically adapt to changing problem situations in the maintenance of an open design process, which helps ultimately accomplish the mission of social change at a systemic level.

2.2 Socially Oriented Design Education Reform

The radical social movement of Bauhaus a century ago could be seen as early practices of social innovation through design education reform. Confronted with the social contradictions of the time, Gropius proposed a unity of art and technology instead of continuing the mode of elite art education that was divorced from reality. In this way, Bauhaus reformed the curriculum by combining teaching activities and production practices to meet the goal of cultivating talents adapted to the context of mass production [10].

Moreover, the development of socially oriented design thinking, influenced by the concept of social innovation, has also driven reflections in the field of design education. The RED team from the Design Council in the UK raises the term transformation design based on human-centeredness. It covers various design disciplines, such as service design, interaction design, information design, and industrial design, with the intention of applying design principles to large complex systems and imparting design competencies for the ongoing transition [11]. Following the spirit of transformation design, Braunschweig University of Art in Germany, the Glasgow School of Art in the UK, and the University of Applied Sciences Augsburg in Germany launched new design master programs in 2015, 2016, and 2019, respectively. Similarly, Terry Irwin assimilates the theories of change into the traditional design framework and proposes a new one called transition design. With its purpose of stimulating systemic change and creating a more sustainable, equitable, and desirable future through design interventions, the transition design framework serves as the methodological basis for the educational reform at the Carnegie Mellon School of Design [12].

Not only that, design schools' engagement in social innovation is trending towards distributed networks. Under the leadership of Manzini, the DESIS network of design schools was cofounded in 2009 by Politecnico di Milano, Tongji University, Jiangnan University, and other universities, with the core values of social innovation and sustainable development. It believes that design schools could become a leading force for social change through co-creating social values with other stakeholders. Currently, nearly 60 design schools have joined the network [13]. When it comes to its organizational model, a DESIS lab is established in each university member as an activity unit. Through the initiatives of thematic clusters, design teams worldwide working on similar themes are connected for experience exchange and substantive collaborations. Specifically, DESIS labs are composed of teachers, researchers, and students, who would together bring new ideas and visions into the social dialogues through experimental research projects and teaching activities. As a result, it provides adaptable forms of organization for developing social innovation initiatives [14].

3 Methodology

This study selects the top 30 higher education institutions according to the 2022 QS World University Rankings by the subject of Art and Design as the research objects [15]. The purpose is to identify the concept of social innovation in the academic programs of these design schools and to explore their emergence and evolution. While the discussion of the social innovation concepts has always been diverse and ambiguous, this paper adopts the working definition from The Young Foundation's report that social innovations are "new solutions (products, services, models, markets, processes, etc.) that simultaneously meet a social need (more effectively than existing solutions) and lead to new or improved capabilities and relationships and better use of assets and resources [16]." From this definition, two criteria were used to determine whether the academic program embodies the idea of social innovation: one is "social purposes"; the other is "collaborative and participatory approaches."

As for the process, first, the author collected public information about the academic programs from universities' official websites, brochures, and reports. The names and descriptions of academic programs of the top 30 institutions were checked to filter out irrelevant institutions and programs using these two criteria. This step excluded five institutions that the author did not find anything to do with social innovation concepts in their program information. Also, this step further determined that the study focuses mainly on the master programs supplemented with a small number of undergraduate and non-degree programs. Next, the remaining 41 screened academic programs from the 25 institutions were then categorized into five types depending on the different ways they show the idea of social innovation (Fig. 1). After the categorization, a detailed analysis was given to compare commonalities and differences in these academic programs for a better understanding of their emergence and evolution process.

4 Results

Overall, in the top 30 higher education institutions in the QS World University Rankings by the subject of Art and Design, 41 academic programs in the 25 design schools incorporate the concept of social innovation to varying degrees and in different ways. Figure 1 depicts five types, the amount, and the percentage of each type, which are the categorization results in accordance with the names and basic information of these academic programs.

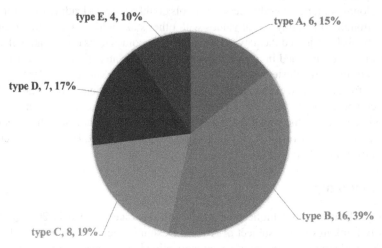

Fig. 1. The proportion of five types of academic programs related to social innovation in the 25 design schools (created by the author)

Firstly, type A is for academic programs named directly after "social innovation" or "social design." Type A comprises six programs, and the percentage is 15%, including the MA social design program by Design Academy Eindhoven, and the MFA Design for Social Innovation (DSI) program by the School of Visual Arts (SVA), etc. Relatively, these programs do not have a long history, the establishment of which is directly influenced by emergent thinking about social innovation. When SVA's DSI program, a two-year master's degree program, was launched in 2012, its founder Cheryl Heller believed that the design discipline was at a turning point when a comprehensive academic program was needed to help designers enter and play a leading role in the field of social innovation. In this case, the DSI program blends traditional and new design areas of branding, interaction, digital media, product, and game design to prepare students to become creative and visionary generalists. Also, it attempts to foster a sense of community and humanism, equipping the students to pay attention to social issues of health, equity, and justice issues and actively integrating all forces to drive systemic change ultimately [17].

As for type B, the program names do not directly include the word "social innovation" or "social design," but the program descriptions have issues related to social innovation, such as urban ecologies, future living, and social entrepreneurship. There are 16 programs in type B, accounting for the highest proportion (39%) among these five types. One thing they have in common is that they mostly attach great importance to fostering creative design cognitions and comprehensive capabilities in response to real problems, particularly around sustainability. Another point is that these programs often involve content related to other types of innovation besides social innovation, such as business and technological innovation. In other words, it acquires students to learn multidisciplinary knowledge about economics, management, politics, and biology. From this, many programs in type B are jointly organized by different schools. One example is the master's program of Creative Sustainability by Aalto University in Finland, which was co-established in 2010 by the School of Arts, Design and Architecture, School of Business, and the School of Chemical Engineering. It groups teachers and students from different fields into a diverse team and creates a collaborative environment for design education. The faculty come from three departments at Aalto University: the department of design, the department of management studies, and the department of bioproducts and biosystems. Thus, the students in this program are provided with guidance in the intersection of design, science, business, and other areas of study [18]. Taking full advantage of Aalto's multidisciplinary strengths as a comprehensive university enriches the curriculum's content. Moreover, it broadens students' horizons with a foundation for a cross-cultural understanding and diverse knowledge perspectives to deal with complex socio-technical systems.

The programs belonging to type C grow from traditional design programs with their original names, such as industrial design and service design. But they conceal the ideas associated with social innovation in the program descriptions. There are eight programs in type C, representing 19% of the total, including the master programs of industrial design at Aalto University, ArtCenter College of Design (ACCD), and the master programs of service design at Royal College of Art (RCA), University of the Arts London (UAL), Politecnico di Milano (Polimi), etc. These programs often began from the very beginning of the establishment of the design schools and have accumulated a certain amount of educational experience in their growth. Although their training modes were well adapted to the industrial market for a long time, it is time to change design education based on the new demands in the dramatically changed global context. At this moment, the entry of social innovation makes it possible for traditional programs to evolve with time. For one thing, it brings a new philosophy to design education with social awareness. And for another, the conventional design process is pushed to be updated with the latest design methods and strategies, such as community engagement, co-creation, and participatory design.

In type D programs, the idea of social innovation reflected in one academic program aligns with the idea in other programs at the design school. Actually, it permeates the overall educational framework and guides teaching and research activities as a unifying value. The goal of social innovation has been infused into the design school's organizational cultures and has become one of its core missions. Although within type D, all programs by the same institution usually present different dimensions of social innovation in their educational activities, only the most representative of these programs are included in this study for further analysis. These constitute nearly 17% and encompass MDes in Design Innovation and Citizenship and MDes in Design Innovation and

Circular Economy by the Innovation School in the GSA, Master of Design by CMU, Master of Design in the University of Technology Sydney (UTS), two master programs of PSSD and Environmental Design by College of Design and Innovation (D&I) in Tongji University, etc.

The first four types are all degree programs, occupying 90% of the total. Apart from them, only ten percent is the last type E, non-degree programs. This means that they are minor courses or short-term certificate programs. For example, ACCD's Designmatters is an interdisciplinary platform that provides students with minors on all kinds of subjects like sustainability, global health, public policy, and social entrepreneurship, as well as opportunities to engage in design research projects which enable them to employ collaborative tactics in dealing with social realities [19]. MIT School of Architecture and Planning (SA+P) has launched MITdesignX, a program dedicated to creating new solutions to address social problems at the intersection of design, business, science, and technology. It serves as a springboard for students, teachers, and researchers to collaborate with other stakeholders through a range of design and business courses tailored to their needs, with the addition of building interdisciplinary teams for collaborative learning and making [20]. In this aspect, MIT equips non-design students with design thinking and skill training and provides an institutional foundation for design students to engage in multidisciplinary cooperation.

5 Discussion

The categorization results reveal that, in general, an increasing number of design schools are taking the idea of social innovation seriously and incorporating it into their academic programs to facilitate educational reform. Yet the patterns are diverse according to different social contexts. A design school may have multiple academic programs of various types dedicated to social innovation. This section conducts a more nuanced analysis of these programs regarding their training objectives, organizational arrangement, disciplinary relationships, and pedagogies.

5.1 Training Objectives

Integrating the project descriptions of the 41 programs, the author makes a word cloud map (Fig. 2) and pulls out the keywords from the perspectives of knowledge, skills, and qualities (Table 1) to further examine the training objectives of these academic programs. As can be seen, they exhibit thorough training objectives with a broad range of social themes. Specifically, these academic programs require the improvement of interdisciplinary knowledge in politics, economics, technology, art and design, design skills such as systems thinking, leadership, management skills, teamwork, and prototyping, as well as critical, diverse, insightful, and humanistic design qualities.

It is also worth noting that most of these programs are at the graduate level, with only a few at the undergraduate level. An example is PolyU's social design, a supplementary program for senior undergraduate students, for which only the students who meet the requirements can apply. They would enter the program in the third year and complete two years of study to obtain a BA (Hons) in Social Design [21]. This reflects that the

Fig. 2. Word Cloud Map of High-Frequency Words in the Academic Program Descriptions (created by the author)

Table 1. Keyword table for the academic program descriptions (created by the author)

Knowledge	Social need, socio-cultural, complex, service, transdisciplinary, interdisciplinary, multi-disciplinary, urban, city, environment, ecosystem, ecology, technology, science, art, business, economy, industry, healthcare, transition design, methodology, theory
Skills	Systems thinking, Problem solving, leadership, research, ethnography, analyze, management, prototype, entrepreneurship, practice, study, plan, empower, imagine, model, team
Qualities	Social, innovation, transform, change, participation, collaborative, integration, sustainability, critical, community, global, creative, future, insight, human-centered, resilience, real-world, diversity, variety, responsive, social design, social innovation, positive, justice, expertise, strategic, public

concept of social innovation places higher demands on the training objectives of design education. To go further, this can be taken as two kinds of capabilities as in the "T-shaped" model, corresponding to two educational levels of the undergraduate and graduate: one is the vertical capability with respect to mastering the basic design knowledge and skills in design professions, and the other is the horizontal capability to apply knowledge across situations [22].

Traditional design education patterns, in general, focus on training proficiency in applying certain areas of design skills to fulfill market and industrial demands. In contrast, the goal of emergent programs with the notion of social innovation is an insight into the world. To put it another way, it promotes the development of a comprehensive literacy of future designers and enables them to take effective actions to make the change happen by requiring students to acquire a broader source of information, multifaceted design abilities, and humanistic social awareness to comprehend human cultures.

5.2   Organizational Arrangement

In terms of the organizational arrangement, the distribution of these academic programs in universities varies in scope and audience. Depending on the distinctive context, a particular social innovation-related academic program may operate as a university-wide platform, a stand-alone program within a design school, or a novel direction under a certain program. For example, the d.school at Stanford University serves as an inter-disciplinary platform open to the entire university, offering project-based experiential courses and workshops for undergraduate and graduate students from all seven schools. At the same time, it gives rich learning resources online, including basic tool kits and videos of symposiums [23]. In addition, the Central Academy of Fine Arts (CAFA) has restructured its courses and opened a new direction of social design in undergraduate and master's programs. In the former, it is delivered as a parallel track to the other 11 disciplines, like visual communication design, industrial design, and digital media art. In the latter, it is one of the research directions, together with others like design management studies, design thinking studies, and Chinese design culture studies [24]. Nevertheless, in most cases, an academic program with the notion of social innovation could take the form of an independent degree program. Apart from a few co-founded by multiple institutions, they are almost set up by a design school and primarily instruct the design students enrolled. The faculty members at some design schools are becoming even more varied, with backgrounds in management, political science, sociology, and communication studies. Additionally, the process of selecting the faculty places equal emphasis on professional experience and academic backgrounds, with some teachers having had extensive prior employment.

5.3   Disciplinary Relationships

How a certain design school positions social innovation in its disciplinary structure could depend on historical roots and social conditions. On the one hand, in some design schools, social innovation as a value has led to a paradigm shift in design, in line with an expanding subject scope. On the other hand, its emergence has resulted in more specialized subdivisions at the intersection of multiple disciplines. For instance, inhering the Bauhaus spirit of designing for the public and possessing the mission to move from "Made in China" to "Created in China," social innovation has been taken as part of D&I's organizational cultures and permeated all kinds of educational activities since its foundation in 2009 [25]. Over the years, D&I has grown through continuous inquiry into complex living systems in the human world. The broader interests mirror the trajectory of design in China within the modernization process from the tradition of arts and crafts to strategic innovation for social change. As evident in the professional directories published by the Chinese Ministry of Education, design has been separated from being a second-level discipline under the category of arts [26] and elevated to a first-level discipline under a new category of interdisciplinary subjects [27].

In this sense, providing a taxonomic scheme of American programs and guiding the allocation of educational resources, the Classification of Instructional Programs (CIP) reflects the disciplinary position of design in America. According to the 2020 edition of the CIP [28], most design programs about social innovation are classified under the primary category of "multi/interdisciplinary studies" (CIP Code 30) but with some subdivisional distinctions. To illustrate, MFA in Design for Social Innovation by SVA, MS in Strategic Design and Management, and MFA in Transdisciplinary Design by Parsons are all under the secondary title of "systems science and theory" [29, 30]. The master program of design for sustainability in SCAD is in another sub-category of "sustainability studies" [31]. In contrast, some of the traditional design disciplines as mature segmented fields belong to another category of the Visual and Performing Arts (CIP Code 50), such as Industrial and Product Design, Interior Design, and Graphic Design.

Therefore, the progressive entry of social innovation into design education has changed the design structure and generated new disciplinary relationships. Due to path dependency, it has developed a differentiated profile across institutions; in particular, some institutions focus more on the segmentation of sustainability, and others favor strategy and management. In general, however, these emerging programs have a wider and more comprehensive range of disciplines than the specialized traditional vocational areas. With the constant integration of new and old design disciplines, the attribute of design education as a new liberal art of technological culture is enhanced and proves its intrinsic value beyond extrinsic manifestations [32].

5.4 Pedagogies

Expanding the traditional educational approaches, these academic programs utilize a variety of pedagogies with taking social innovation into consideration to create a learning environment full of social interactions for the students. By emphasizing the notion of design activism, students are exposed to lots of hands-on experience and encouraged to use their design skills in encounters with the real world, which could help exercise creativity and develop a sense of humanism and social responsibility.

The courses are mainly in the form of a design studio with the teaching method of project-based learning, allowing the students to learn by doing. Taking significant societal concerns as the subject matter, the core of the projects usually sits in seeking the design problems in reality with uncertainty and complexity. For example, D&I in Tongji University offers a course called Sustainability Consciousness, which is intended to assist students in understanding the connection between human activities and natural systems, as well as develop insight into ecological challenges in their own lives [33]. Instead of beginning with an obvious design problem, students are asked to investigate the difficulties in their daily routines and to think critically about phenomena that are taken for granted. They need to link to their own life experience while digging out a specific problem in a complex situation and then yield alternative solutions.

Additionally, these programs introduce new methods based on localism and community engagement. While traditional design studios concentrate more on directing and critiquing students' design processes through teacher-student interaction, with professors assessing students' solutions, these new programs are more reliant on the inclusion of community resources. As a result, design schools are often active in building connectivity with local communities and inviting multiple stakeholders to participate in all aspects of the courses, including all aspects of planning, reviewing, and evaluating. Most importantly, the government, companies, and local community may act as commissioners of the project or participants in it, providing the necessary help and support for teaching and learning. Students actively communicate with them to generate new design knowledge and produce design products by means of co-creation and participatory approaches. In the process, students not only learn more facts about specific problems but also gain social experience as a kind of tacit knowledge necessary for them to grow from novice designers to design experts. For instance, the service design studio at Politecnico di Milano works on the cultural reconstruction of resilience in peripheral areas with the support of the municipality and local citizens. The educators have designed a framework derived from a social innovation process model, including three assignments: understanding the topic and framing the opportunity, generating ideas with diverse stakeholders, and developing the prototyping solutions. They propose the "action design format" that combines practical activities with theoretical research to activate students' creativity in achieving synergy between educational and societal goals [34].

6 Conclusion

In conclusion, the conception of building academic programs related to social innovation is becoming a global trend in design education reform. These programs share fundamental similarities but also differ in concrete instructional approaches and organizational structures. This study posits that social innovation opens up new opportunities for design education by sorting out relevant academic programs in design and reviewing their emergence and evolution. On the one side, social innovation can strengthen the value base for academic programs in design education. In this perspective, they go beyond typical commercial goals and dedicate themselves to addressing social demands and global concerns. On the other, social innovation promotes the development of design thinking and methodology, particularly through collaborative and participatory approaches, which enables design education to introduce resources from social innovation networks to better cultivate students' all-around qualities and generate new design knowledge. According to this point of view, design discipline could enhance its social impact by activating regional creative collectives.

This study clarifies the development of social innovation in academic programs. It could deliver a new perspective for design schools to participate in the process of social innovation and stimulate new ideas for socially oriented design education reform. Also, this paper suggests some directions for the research and practices of design education in the future. First, design educators need to consider the subject orientation of the socially oriented design. One of the most pressing questions here is how to deal with the relationship between traditional and emerging design fields. In other words, is it necessary for a design school to set up an independent design project related to social innovation to more effectively integrate social innovation into design education? Second, in order to continuously co-produce social values, it is necessary for a design school to establish an open and robust network among all stakeholders, such as the government, corporations, and local citizens. This could not only unleash the potential of design schools as a force for social change, but even more, empower the advancement of design education, providing students with an environment for social and experiential learning. Third, economic and historical circumstances would be key to developing design education in any design school. Thus, flexible academic program types must be devised to provide rich teaching and learning formats for a wider group of teachers and students to join. Fourth, given that the content of academic programs with social innovation often involves a wide range of knowledge fields and comprehensive ability requirements, it is also worth considering how to build a platform to afford institutional support for interdisciplinary cooperation and communication.

Due to the limits, the information collected for this paper could leave out some factual evidence, which may prevent a more accurate analysis. Furthermore, it seems impossible to assess some academic programs' social and educational performance since the reform process of socially oriented design education has not yet reached a mature level. The author will take this as an entry point of follow-up research and delve deeper into social innovation and design education.

References

1. Phills, J.A., Deiglmeier, K., Miller, D.T.: Rediscovering social innovation. Stanf. Soc. Innov. Rev. **6**(4), 34–43 (2008)
2. Kimbell, L.: Rethinking design thinking: part I. Des. Cult. **3**(3), 285–306 (2011)
3. Papanek, V.: Design for the Real World: Human Ecology and Social Change. HarperCollins Distribution Services, Glasgow (1974)
4. Margolin, V.: The good society project: an action frame for the 21st century. In: Ma, J., Lou, Y. (eds.) Emerging Practices: Professions, Values, and Approaches in Design, pp. 134–158. China Architecture and Building Press, Beijing (2014)
5. Bjögvinsson, E., Ehn, P., Hillgren, P.-A.: Design things and design thinking: contemporary participatory design challenges. Des. Issues **28**(3), 101–116 (2012)
6. Sanders, E.B.-N., Stappers, P.J.: Co-creation and the new landscapes of design. CoDesign **4**(1), 5–18 (2008)
7. Kleinsmann, M., Valkenburg, R.: Barriers and enablers for creating shared understanding in co-design projects. Des. Stud. **29**(4), 369–386 (2008)
8. Manzini, E.: Design, When Everybody Designs: An Introduction to Design for Social Innovation. The MIT Press, Cambridge (2015)
9. Armstrong, L., Bailey, J., Julier, G., Kimbell, L.: Social Design Futures: HEI Research and the AHRC. University of Brighton (2014)
10. Gropius, W.: The New Architecture and the Bauhaus. The MIT Press, Cambridge (1965)
11. Burns, C., Cottam, H., Vanstone, C., Winhall, J.: RED Paper 02: Transformation Design. Design Council, London (2006)
12. Irwin, T.: Transition design: a proposal for a new area of design practice, study, and research. Des. Cult. **7**(2), 229–246 (2015)
13. DESIS Network. https://www.desisnetwork.org/labs/. Accessed 19 Jan 2023
14. DESIS Network: Public and collaborative: exploring the intersection of design, social innovation and public policy. In: Manzini, E., Staszowski, E (eds.) DESIS Network (2013)
15. QS World University Rankings by Subject 2022: Art & Design. https://www.topuniversities.com/university-rankings/university-subject-rankings/2022/art-design. Accessed 28 Jan 2023

16. The Young Foundation: Social Innovation Overview: A deliverable of the project: "The theoretical, empirical and policy foundations for building social innovation in Europe" (TEPSIE), European Commission – 7 th Framework Programme, Brussels: European Commission, DG Research (2012)
17. Heller, C.: Social innovation needs design, and design needs social innovation. Stanford Soc. Innov. Rev. (2011). https://doi.org/10.48558/XWD8-3W63
18. Aalto University - Creative Sustainability Program. https://www.aalto.fi/en/creative-sustainability. Accessed 28 Jan 2023
19. Designmatters. https://designmattersatartcenter.org/. Accessed 28 Jan 2023
20. MITdesignX. https://designx.mit.edu/. Accessed 28 Jan 2023
21. PolyU Social Design (BA). https://www.sd.polyu.edu.hk/en/study-detail/social-design. Accessed 28 Jan 2023
22. Lou, Y., Ma, J.: A 3D T-shaped design education framework. In: Ma, J., Lou, Y. (eds.) Emerging Practices: Professions, Values, and Approaches in Design, pp. 228–251. China Architecture and Building Press, Beijing (2014)
23. Standford d.schoool. https://dschool.stanford.edu/. Accessed 28 Jan 2023
24. Central Academy of Fine Arts School of Design. https://design.cafa.edu.cn/en/detail.html?id=61b2eedd2e37a40012baab24. Accessed 28 Jan 2023
25. College of Design and Innovation. https://tjdi.tongji.edu.cn/?lang=en. Accessed 29 Jan 2023
26. Ministry of Education of the People's Republic of China. http://www.moe.gov.cn/srcsite/A22/moe_833/201103/t20110308_116439.html. Accessed 28 Jan 2023
27. Ministry of Education of the People's Republic of China. http://www.moe.gov.cn/srcsite/A22/moe_833/202209/t20220914_660828.html. Accessed 28 Jan 2023
28. Natural Center for Education Statistics CIP Code. https://nces.ed.gov/ipeds/cipcode/browse.aspx?y=56. Accessed 28 Jan 2023
29. SVA STEM Major CIP Code. https://assets.sva.edu/download/sva-stem-major-list-1582908213.pdf. Accessed 29 Jan 2023
30. The New School STEM Eligible Programs. https://www.newschool.edu/international-students-scholars/stem-eligible-programs/. Accessed 28 Jan 2023
31. SCAD-CIP Code Major Code Major Descriptor. https://www.scad.edu/sites/default/files/PDF/SCAD-Majors-by-CIP-Code-degrees-9-2022.pdf. Accessed 28 Jan 2023
32. Buchanan, R.: Wicked problems in design thinking. Des. Issues 8(2), 5–21 (1992)
33. College of Design and Innovation-Sustainability consciousness. https://mp.weixin.qq.com/s?__biz=MjM5MTkyMTQ5OQ==&mid=2679781074&idx=1&sn=473da68a45f5e22bdd0fd18c40d447de&chksm=bce0b2e68b973bf0fbcd699f52b42c16bf1989b67fc45af1bc4b10c17319223b5023a4d085dd&scene=21#wechat_redirect. Accessed 28 Jan 2023
34. Selloni, D.: Educating the next generation of social innovators. lessons learnt from a series of experimental service design studios at the school of design—Politecnico di Milano. In: Rehm, M., Saldien, J., Manca, S. (eds.) Project and Design Literacy as Cornerstones of Smart Education. SIST, vol. 158, pp. 3–18. Springer, Singapore (2020). https://doi.org/10.1007/978-981-13-9652-6_1

Analysis of the Effect of Applying VR Technology in Cross-Cultural Art Course

Weilong Wu[(✉)], Ya Liu, Lin Yu, and Wu Wei

School of Film Television & Communication, Xiamen University of Technology, Xiamen, China
wu_acedemic@163.com

Abstract. Objectives: In today's world, with the continuous deepening and development of human-cultural interactions, the process of communication and interaction between different cultures is becoming closer and closer. From domestic cross-regional cultural studies to transnational cultural studies, corporate management, and talent acquisition, to national strategies and cultural exports, the importance and practicality of cross-cultural communication is becoming increasingly evident. Due to the growing trend of globalization, the global communicative nature is becoming more and more prominent. In response to the needs of society, several colleges and universities across the country already offer cross-cultural arts programs. The cross-cultural Arts Program is a course that combines theory and practice. The traditional teaching model of cross-cultural art courses is teacher-centered, textbook-centered, and board-based. Time-consuming, laborious, small information capacity, information display form is rather dull and monotonous. And the traditional teaching mode of cross-cultural art courses has a single means and rarely involves modern teaching equipment, which is not conducive to broadening teachers' and students' horizons and improving teaching efficiency. This paper takes "virtual reality technology" as the core and proposes the teaching mode of "virtual reality combination" and "online and offline combination" for the practical course. The purpose is to solve a series of problems of the traditional teaching model and provide reference experience for the development and reform of other practical courses. This study uses virtual reality technology to enable students to learn more about cross-cultural art theory and understand the similarities and differences between different cultures, and achieve the purpose of "combining online and offline" and "virtual reality" teaching modes.

The cross-cultural art program is a science that studies and utilizes the relationship between art and culture and information dissemination, analyzes and summarizes various cross-cultural communication phenomena, and explores the communication and exchange between different art cultures. At the same time, cross-cultural art is highly practical, and it plays an important role in both domestic interregional and transnational cultural studies. Cross-cultural art teaching is a sunrise course, and the traditional teaching mode is mainly based on offline mode. Teachers and students conduct field research, but field research is also more limited in terms of space to meet training needs. The theoretical courses are based on teachers teaching basic knowledge, the course content is fixed, the teaching method is single, and students are not highly motivated. With the advent of the epidemic era, the offline teaching mode of cross-cultural art courses has been greatly

---

W. Wu and Y. Liu—These authors contributed equally to this study

© The Author(s), under exclusive license to Springer Nature Switzerland AG 2023
P.-L. P. Rau (Ed.): HCII 2023, LNCS 14024, pp. 291–302, 2023.
https://doi.org/10.1007/978-3-031-35946-0_24

impacted and influenced. The areas are closed due to the epidemic, and students face great risks and obstacles in their field research to meet the needs of the course objectives. At the same time, because offline field research is expensive and costly, it cannot meet the learning needs of students from different family backgrounds, and students from different cultural backgrounds have different ideas and concepts about cross-cultural art communication. In the face of the epidemic era, the different cultural backgrounds of students and the influence of their living environment, it is a question worth thinking about how to make cross-cultural art teaching play a better educational role.

Combine the virtual reality technology with the teaching process, through three-dimensional virtual simulation and virtual interactive technology to virtually show the site scenes, practice processes and results required for the course, and truly reproduce the practice process. The teaching mode of using virtual reality technology combined with the curriculum can enhance the real-time interaction between teachers and students, enrich the teaching content, overcome the equipment as well as the venue environment obstacles of the traditional practical teaching mode, and further improve the teaching quality. At the same time, the mode of combining virtual reality technology with the course brings students a different course experience in a new way, overcomes the obstacles of field research, brings students visual enjoyment, further stimulates students' interest in learning and improves learning efficiency. Therefore, the teaching mode of "virtual reality combination" can better overcome the obstacles of traditional teaching mode such as equipment and venue, and improve the quality of teaching and learning. It allows students to gain a deeper understanding of the learning content and perfectly integrates the presentation of visual effects with professional knowledge, cultivating technical and intellectual talents with high overall quality.

Methods: In this study, 20 students (10 males and 10 females) were randomly selected as the control group and 20 students (10 males and 10 females) were selected as the experimental group in a school in China. There were no major differences in basic information between the two groups, and both students had taken cross-cultural arts courses and had a preliminary understanding of cross-cultural arts programs. The control group used the traditional teaching mode, and the experimental group used virtual reality technology for teaching. A questionnaire survey on learning interest and attitude will be organized after the teaching.

Results: By comparing the teaching questionnaires of the control group and the experimental group, it can be found that the students in the experimental group were more motivated, more active in learning, and more satisfied with the class than the students in the control group. Students in the control group reported that the classroom content was boring and their participation was less active, while students in the experimental group reported that the classroom content was rich and interesting and their participation was higher. Therefore, it is hoped that more courses will be taught in this pedagogical way.

Conclusions: This study found that traditional teaching courses do not fully meet the learning needs of students, and practical courses require students to conduct more field research, and the use of virtual reality technology combined with traditional teaching can better and more effectively solve these problems and improve the quality of teaching as well as learning efficiency. The combination of virtual reality technology and cross-cultural art courses can help students better experience different cultures around the world, improve students' learning efficiency and increase their interest in cross-cultural art courses, as well as reduce the physical and financial pressure brought by field research and the hindrance of field research in the era of epidemics, and more effectively improve teaching efficiency. In addition, there are some issues that need to be noted. Most schools have very few virtual reality resources developed for teaching, and the shortage of curriculum resources is the biggest bottleneck for the promotion of virtual reality technology in some schools. However, with the rapid development of virtual reality technology, the future application of virtual reality technology in teaching is bound to bring about disruptive changes in classroom teaching methods. However, more experiments and research are needed on how to better use virtual reality technology in classroom teaching.

Keywords: Virtual reality technology · Cross-cultural arts · Virtual reality education

1 Introduction

The wave of globalization has led to a constant exchange, collision, and fusion of cultures among various nations and ethnic groups. From domestic cross-regional cultural studies to transnational cultural studies, company management, and talent introduction, to national strategies and cultural exports, cross-cultural communication is particularly important [1] order to meet the needs of the times and cultivate talents, many colleges and universities across the country have offered cross-cultural art courses. A cross-cultural art course is a course with high integration of theory and practice. The traditional teaching mode is centered on the teacher and textbook, and the teaching is mainly based on the board, which is time-consuming, laborious, with small information capacity and dull and monotonous information display form, and it is difficult to carry out a diversified display of teaching contents, and field research is also more limited to meet training needs, and teachers and students are unable to experience the charm of cross-cultural art firsthand. Under the influence of today's global epidemic, field research is hindered and cannot meet the teaching needs of the course [2], while the use of virtual reality technology can overcome the problems of equipment as well as site environmental barriers of the traditional practical teaching mode, enriching the teaching content and improving the teaching quality. This paper takes "virtual reality technology" as the core, and proposes the "virtual reality combination" course teaching mode, in order to solve a series of problems of traditional teaching, and also to provide reference experience for the development and reform of other practical courses. This study examines the effects of virtual reality technology applied to teaching and learning on students' interest and attitude toward learning through the areas of virtual reality and cross-cultural art.

The purpose of the Cross-cultural Arts Program is to increase students' sensitivity to cultural differences, increase cross-cultural communication skills, and develop specialized personnel. While cross-cultural art teaching is a sunrise course, traditional teaching is mainly in offline mode, and the theory course is based on teachers teaching basic knowledge, with fixed course content and a single teaching method. In the practical course, the site of field research is also more restricted, expensive, and costly, which cannot meet the teaching needs of the course, and will easily make students lose interest in learning and have a negative impact on their learning attitude accordingly. Students from different cultural backgrounds also have different ideas and concepts about cross-cultural art communication. In the face of the epidemic era, the different cultural backgrounds of students, and the influence of their living environment, it is a question worth thinking about how to make cross-cultural art teaching play a better educational role.

Virtual reality technology is used in the teaching process to virtually show the site scenes, practice processes, and results required for the course through 3D virtual simulation and virtual interaction technology to truly reproduce the entire process of practice [3]. Applying virtual reality technology to traditional teaching can overcome the equipment as well as site environment obstacles of traditional practical teaching mode, enhance real-time interaction between teachers and students, enrich teaching content, and can effectively improve students' learning interest and learning attitude. It also allows students to gain a deeper understanding of the learning content, to perfectly integrate the presentation of visual effects with professional knowledge, and to cultivate technical and intellectual talents with high overall quality [4].

2 Literature Review

2.1 Cross-cultural Arts and Cross-cultural Arts Program

As an important carrier of culture, artworks largely visualize the abstract behavior of communication, and it can be said that it is the materialized result of cultural communication [5]. Cross-cultural art is an art form or artwork that embodies multicultural characteristics when created by two or more individuals influenced by significantly different cultural exchanges that cross a specific cultural boundary [6]. Under the premise of cultural exchange, the differences in values, economic structures, ethnic customs, cultural symbols, language codes, etc. between different cultures collide to create artworks with unique characteristics [7]. With the widespread opening of intercultural art courses, people also feel the charm of art between different countries and nationalities, and its important role in the dissemination of art disciplines such as music, dance, drama, and fine arts, so more and more people are engaged in research about intercultural art. Sun, J. studied that applying cross-cultural studies to the field of art would break the boundaries of ethnicity and region in traditional studies and involve many issues such as artistic exchanges between different cultures, so cross-cultural art has now become a research direction of increasing interest [8]. Xia, Y. J. studied the key to the development of art based on cross-cultural contexts and concluded that in order to be based on multicultural communication and dialogue, it is necessary to both looks at oneself and pay attention to the perspective of the "other" so that art can be better developed and disseminated [9].

Under the premise of cultural exchange, it has become a trend to offer cross-cultural art courses in colleges and universities to meet the development and needs of society. Based on the importance of intercultural communication, Li, J. argues that the cross-cultural study of art is an academic practice of great relevance in order to reach the intersection and exchange of human wisdom, a method, and concept that practices the solidarity of human destiny in a disciplinary way [1]. The traditional cross-cultural art courses are mainly offline, creating a series of problems because the theoretical knowledge of cross-cultural art is abstract and more inclined to practical investigation. At the same time, because offline practice visits are costly and expensive, they cannot meet the learning needs of students from different family backgrounds, and students cannot achieve 100% of the requirements of the practice visits, and it is difficult to achieve a true and complete understanding during the learning process and to complete the comprehensive curriculum. Therefore, many researchers have started to try to solve these problems. In his study, Li, Z. proposed a "virtual-real" hybrid cross-cultural communication course experimental teaching model to build a real cross-cultural communication context for students and conduct comprehensive practical training, so as to improve the interactivity and efficiency of cross-cultural communication course experimental teaching [3], which provides ideas for subsequent researchers. The "virtual-reality" teaching model overcomes the obstacles of the traditional teaching model, so the development of the VR virtual-reality teaching model is a necessary initiative.

2.2 Virtual Reality Technology

Virtual Reality (VR) is a new technology developed in the 1990s with computer technology at its core. The principle is to use electronic glasses to immerse the wearing individual into the environment simulated by the computer [10]. Through the combination of computer graphics technology, multimedia technology, sensing technology, real-time technology, artificial intelligence, simulation technology, etc., the participants are placed in a three-dimensional virtual environment that integrates vision, hearing, touch and taste. Interacting with objects in the virtual world in a natural way with the help of special input and output devices creates a sense of immersion [11]. Thus many researchers' studies have shown that virtual reality technology is a viable tool in engineering, medicine and other scientific fields [12]. Due to the development of virtual reality technology, its role in the field of student education has gradually emerged and has had a greater impact on classroom teaching in higher education [13, 14]. The use of virtual reality technology in the field of education and the integration of technologies such as scripting design and 3D and the use of interactive devices have improved the effectiveness of teaching and learning in virtual simulation environments and the efficiency of knowledge dissemination, prompting the education of students to rise to a new level [15]. He, M. studies that virtual reality technology, which is naturally associated with art, provides a powerful support for experimental art education sessions and inspires innovation in our teaching practices [16]. Cui, H.J., Cheng, M.H. based on virtual reality technology, the progress of application in digital media art teaching proposed application strategies to bring diverse forms of creation to digital media art in order to improve students' initiative and enthusiasm for professional learning and improve learning efficiency with the support of virtual reality technology [4].In today's pandemic environment, many schools as well as training institutions have to switch from offline to online teaching, which is undoubtedly a huge blow to some subjects with strong operational and abstract theoretical knowledge. Wu W. L., Hsu Y., Yang Q. F., et al. developed a landscape architecture SV-IVR learning system using virtual reality technology to integrate into landscape architecture conservation courses, which effectively improved students' learning performance, learning attitudes, and self-regulation levels without negatively affecting students [17, 18], demonstrating the effectiveness of virtual reality technology in educational applications and its own great potential. This demonstrates the effectiveness of virtual reality technology in education and its great potential. Wang L., & Wang, Z. incorporated virtual reality technology into the vocational education curriculum to create a virtual simulation environment and concluded that it helps students to learn actively and improves teachers' teaching effectiveness and, at the same time, reduces school input costs [15].In the study of engineering education teaching, Shi, Z. pointed out that the traditional curriculum has problems such as a slow update of knowledge in teaching materials, poor ability of students to develop comprehensive systems, lack of practical projects in course content set, and poor hands-on ability of students [19], and the emergence of virtual reality technology has solved these problems. Wang, Z.Y &Wang, Y. et al. pointed out that the development of virtual reality technology, has played a positive role in the teaching effect of 5-year undergraduate students in clinical medicine, its use in medical education has a better prospect, and VR application in clinical medicine teaching has become a new trend and hot spot [20]. The intercultural art courses studied in this paper are abstract theoretical courses, and the cultural and artistic differences between different peoples and countries cannot be fully demonstrated in theory. More practical visits are needed, and offline practice is more restricted. At the same time, the development of online teaching is necessary for the present epidemic situation. We discuss whether virtual reality technology can be useful in intercultural art courses, and provide some ideas for moving from offline to online teaching in other similar courses.

3 Experiment Design

In order to determine whether virtual reality technology can play an effective role in teaching cross-cultural art courses, we targeted the integration of virtual reality technology with a cross-cultural art course in a Chinese school. The Cross-cultural Arts course is a required course for cross-cultural communication studies, and the course includes both theoretical and practical knowledge. We arranged the course for the experimental group to use virtual reality technology to learn theoretical knowledge and practical courses of cross-cultural art, and the course for the control group to have the teacher talk about theoretical knowledge, followed by a practical investigation. The purpose of our study is to investigate the effect of virtual reality technology on students' learning interests and attitudes in teaching cross-cultural art courses.

3.1 Experimental Participants

In this study, 20 students (10 males and 10 females) were randomly selected as the control group and 20 students (10 males and 10 females) as the experimental group in a school in China. There were no major differences in basic information between the two groups, and both students had taken cross-cultural arts courses and had a preliminary understanding of cross-cultural arts programs. The control group uses a traditional teaching model in which the instructor talks about the theoretical knowledge, followed by a practical examination. The experimental group used virtual reality technology for teaching. Teachers used virtual reality for classroom teaching and students used VR for learning. All teaching activities are conducted by a professor with many years of experience in education, and who has extensive theoretical and practical knowledge of teaching cross-cultural art courses, ensuring that there is no significant difference in the prior knowledge of the two groups of students. Finally, a questionnaire survey on interest in learning and attitude toward learning is organized.

3.2 Measurement Method

The research instrument for this study included a questionnaire survey on students' interests and attitudes toward learning. The questionnaire was divided into two sections, interest in learning and attitude toward learning. The Interest in Learning section contains five questions, scored on a scale of 1–5. The attitude toward learning section contains five questions, scored on a scale of 1–5.

3.3 Experimental Procedure

The experimental procedure is shown in Fig. 1. The students in the experimental group accepted the teaching mode using virtual reality technology, while the students in the control group accepted the traditional teaching mode, and both the experimental and control group students had already studied the cross-cultural art course and had a preliminary understanding of the cross-cultural art course. Finally, a questionnaire to measure interest in learning and attitude towards learning is organized.

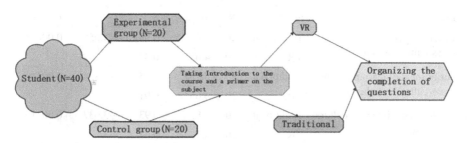

Fig. 1. The experimental process

4 Experimental Results

4.1 Analysis of Interest in Learning

An independent sample t-test was used to analyze students' interest in learning cross-cultural art courses under the traditional teaching mode and under the virtual reality technology teaching mode. As shown in Table 1, the results of the study show that the

Level of interest in cross-cultural art courses: Presents a 0.01 level of significance ($t = -4.056$, $p = 0.000$), as well as specific comparative differences can be seen that the mean of the experimental group (4.65), is significantly higher than the mean of the control group (3.65).Conscientiousness in lessons in cross-cultural art courses: Presenting a 0.01 level of significance ($t = -3.894$, $p = 0.001$), as well as specific comparative differences can be seen that the mean of the experimental group (4.65), is significantly higher than the mean of the control group (3.75).Satisfaction level of cross-cultural art courses: Presenting a 0.01 level of significance ($t = -3.637$, $p = 0.001$), as well as specific comparative differences can be seen that the mean of the experimental group (4.7), is significantly higher than the mean of the control group (3.85).Initiatives for learning cross-cultural art courses: Presenting a 0.01 level of significance ($t = -3.793$, $p = 0.001$), as well as specific comparative differences can be seen that the mean of the experimental group (4.7), is significantly higher than the mean of the control group (3.8). Level of knowledge of cross-cultural art programs: Presenting a 0.05 level of significance ($t = -2.657$, $p = 0.013$), as well as specific comparative differences, can be seen that the mean of the experimental group (4.55), is significantly higher than the mean of the control group (3.9). The total score showed a 0.01 level of significance ($t = -3.6074$, $p = 0.000$), as well as specific comparative differences, can be seen in the mean of the experimental group (4.65), which was significantly higher than the mean of the control group (3.79).In conclusion, it can be seen that students who learn with virtual reality technology show significant differences in their interest in learning from those who learn with traditional teaching mode, and the average value of those who learn with virtual reality technology is higher than those who learn with traditional teaching mode.

Table 1. Research findings on learning interest

Learning interest	group	N	average	SD	t	p
Level of interest in cross-cultural art courses	Traditional	20	3.65	0.99	−4.056	0.000**
	VR	20	4.65	0.49		
Seriousness of learning in the cross-cultural art classroom	Traditional	20	3.75	0.95	−3.894	0.001**
	VR	20	4.65	0.91		
Satisfaction with cross-cultural art courses	Traditional	20	3.85	0.93	−3.637	0.001**
	VR	20	4.7	0.47		
Initiative in learning about cross-cultural art courses	Traditional	20	3.8	0.95	−3.793	0.001**
	VR	20	4.7	0.47		
Level of knowledge of cross-cultural art programs	Traditional	20	3.9	0.97	−2.657	0.013*
	VR	20	4.55	0.51		
Total	Traditional	20	3.79	0.958	−3.6074	0.000**
	VR	20	4.65	0.57		

*$p < 0.05$** $p < 0.01$

4.2 Analysis of Learning Attitudes

An independent sample t-test was used to analyze students' attitudes toward learning in cross-cultural art courses under the traditional teaching model and under the virtual reality technology teaching model. As shown in Table 2, The results of the study show that, Student engagement in cross-cultural arts courses: Presenting a 0.01 level of significance (t = −3.3, p = 0.003), as well as specific comparative differences can be seen that the mean value of the experimental group (4.65), is significantly higher than the mean value of the control group (3.75).Degree of completion of cross-cultural art coursework: Presenting a 0.01 level of significance (t = −3.55, p = 0.001), as well as specific comparative differences can be seen that the mean of the experimental group (4.65), is significantly higher than the mean of the control group (3.8).Student-teacher interaction in cross-cultural art courses: Presenting a 0.01 level of significance (t = −3.15, p = 0.003), as well as specific comparative differences can be seen that the mean of the experimental group (4.6), is significantly higher than the mean of the control group (3.7).The extent to which you collaborate with your classmates to explore problems in cross-cultural art courses when you encounter them: Presenting a 0.01 level of significance (t = −4.12, p = 0.000), as well as specific comparative differences can be seen that the mean of the experimental group (4.7), is significantly higher than the mean of the control group (3.7).Cross-cultural art course learning atmosphere: Presenting a 0.01 level of significance (t = −4.03, p = 0.000), as well as specific comparative differences it is known that the mean of the experimental group (4.6), would be significantly higher than the mean of the control group (3.55).The total score showed a 0.01 level of significance (t = −3.63, p = 0.001), as well as specific comparative differences that show that the mean of the experimental group (4.64), would be significantly higher than the mean of the control group (3.7).In summary, it can be seen that students learning with virtual reality technology showed significant differences in their learning attitudes from those learning with the traditional teaching mode, with students learning with virtual reality technology perceiving higher motivation to learn the course than those learning with the traditional teaching mode, and higher mean values for all other learning attitudes than those learning with the traditional mode.

Table 2. Research results of learning attitudes

Learning interest	group	N	average	SD	t	p
Level of commitment to classes in cross-cultural arts programs	Traditional	20	3.75	1.07	−3.3	0.003**
	VR	20	4.65	0.59		
Cross-cultural Art Course Assignment Completion	Traditional	20	3.8	0.95	−3.55	0.001**
	VR	20	4.65	0.49		
Degree of interaction with teachers in cross-cultural art courses	Traditional	20	3.7	1.03	−3.15	0.003**
	VR	20	4.6	0.75		

(*continued*)

Table 2. (*continued*)

Learning interest	group	N	average	SD	t	p
The extent to which you collaborate with your classmates to discuss problems you encounter in cross-cultural art courses	Traditional	20	3.7	0.98	−4.12	0.000**
	VR	20	4.7	0.47		
Overall classroom learning atmosphere in cross-cultural art courses	Traditional	20	3.55	1.05	−4.03	0.000**
	VR	20	4.6	0.5		
Total	Traditional	20	3.7	1.016	−3.63	0.001**
	VR	20	4.64	0.56		

*$p < 0.05$** $p < 0.01$

By comparing the results of the questionnaire survey between the control group and the experimental group, the students in the experimental group had higher classroom interest, learning initiative, and satisfaction with classroom teaching than the students in the control group. Students in the control group reported that the class content was boring and their participation was low, while students in the experimental group reported that the class content was rich and interesting and their participation was high. Virtual reality technology has significantly increased the fun and engaging nature of learning in the course, and it is hoped that other experimental courses can be taught in this way.

5   Discussion and Conclusions

This study found that the traditional teaching course content is more fixed, the teaching method is more single compared with the virtual reality technology teaching mode, students are not highly motivated, and it is lacking in meeting students' learning needs. The practical courses require students to go on more practical visits, which are more expensive and costly. At the same time, due to the different policies around the epidemic, students face great risks and obstacles in their practical visits to meet the needs of the course objectives. The use of virtual reality technology combined with traditional teaching can better and more effectively solve these problems. It also helps students to better experience different cultures and increase their interest in cross-cultural art courses. It also reduces the physical and financial pressure brought by practical visits and the hindrance of field research in the era of epidemics, and more effectively improves learning efficiency and contributes to the cultivation of professional talents. Also, because students from different cultural backgrounds have different ideas and concepts about cross-cultural art communication. In the face of the epidemic era, the different cultural backgrounds of students, and the influence of their living environment, we propose a teaching model that combines virtual reality technology with traditional teaching. Using virtual reality technology, we can teach cross-cultural art courses very well.

Based on the results of this study, there are some suggestions for future research, Firstly, the experimental course can be more enriched, and secondly, the capacity of the questionnaire can be larger. There are also some issues to keep in mind, most schools have very few virtual reality resources developed for teaching, and the shortage of curriculum resources is the biggest bottleneck in the promotion of virtual reality technology in some schools. However, with the rapid development of virtual reality technology, the future application of virtual reality technology in teaching is bound to bring about disruptive changes in classroom teaching methods. However, more experiments and research are needed on how to better use virtual reality technology in classroom teaching.

Funding. This work was supported by 2022 Educational Teaching Reform Research Project of Xiamen University of Technology (Funding Number: JG202257).

References

1. Li, J.: Cross-cultural art history and the community of human destiny: the multipath advancement from Sullivan to Chinese scholars. Art Observ. **01**, 75–81 (2022)
2. Dong, L.H.: Living art history: cross-cultural research as a new methodology in art history: a review of "cross-cultural art history: images and their double shadows." Grand View Fine Arts **02**, 33–37 (2021)
3. Li, Z.: The Application of virtual reality technology (VR) in experimental teaching of Intercultural communication courses under the background of new liberal arts. Lab. Res. Explor. (4), 240–245 (2022). https://doi.org/10.19927/j.carolcarrollnkisyyt.2022.04.050
4. Cui, H.J., Cheng, M.H.: Digital media art teaching strategies based on virtual reality technology. J. Shanxi Univ. Financ. Econ. **S2**, 125–127 (2022)
5. Liu, C.R.: Theoretical construction of the beauty of cross-cultural art – comments on the aesthetics of cross-cultural art by Wang yichuan. Art Hundred **04**, 215–218 (2020)
6. Xiong, J.Q., Yan, J.W.: New exploration of interdisciplinary and cross-cultural art research – review of world art research: concepts and methods. J. Inner Mongolia Univ. Arts **02**, 156–161 (2022)
7. Yu, L.Q.: The objects and their validity in world art history and intercultural art history -- a response to David carrier's theory. Art Res. **4**, 110–115 (2022). https://doi.org/10.13318/j.car olcarrollnkimsyj.2022.04.011
8. Sun, J.: The cross-cultural studies in the field of art history -- review of the history of cross-cultural art: images and their double shadows. Fine Arts Study **6**, 107–111 (2020). https://doi.org/10.13318/j.carolcarrollnkimsyj.2020.06.018
9. Xia, Y.J.: Discussion on the basic structure of art history research in the cross-cultural context. Art Rev. **12**, 8–24. https://doi.org/10.16364/j.cnki.cn11-4907/j.2022.12.001
10. Akdere, M., Acheson, K., Jiang, Y.: An examination of the effectiveness of virtual reality technology for intercultural competence development. Int. J. Intercult. Relat. **82**, 109–120 (2021)
11. Huang, G., Zeng, J.S.: Research status, hotspots and trends of virtual reality technology. Educ. Informatization China **10**, 49–57 (2022)
12. Clark, D.B., Tanner-Smith, E.E., Killingsworth, S.S.: Digital games, design, and learning: a systematic review and meta-analysis. Rev. Educ. Res. **86**(1), 79–122 (2016)
13. Alhalabi, W.: Virtual reality systems enhance students' achievements in engineering education. Behav. Inf. Technol. **35**(11), 919–925 (2016)
14. Marks, B., Thomas, J.: Adoption of virtual reality technology in higher education: an evaluation of five teaching semesters in a purpose-designed laboratory. Educ. Inf. Technol. **27**, 1–19 (2021)

15. Wang, L., Wang, Z.: The application of virtual reality technology in local vocational education. China Mod. Educ. Equipment **22**, 70–73 (2022). https://doi.org/10.13492/j.carolcarrollnki cmee.2022.22.011
16. He, M.: Renmin university of china: virtual reality technology drives innovation in art experimental teaching. Online Learn. **12**, 46–47 (2022)
17. Wu, W.L., Hsu, Y., Yang, Q.F., et al.: A spherical video-based immersive virtual reality learning system to support landscape architecture students' learning performance during the COVID-19 Era. Land **10**(6), 561 (2021)
18. Wu, W., Zhao, Z., Du, A., Lin, J.: Effects of multisensory integration through spherical video-based immersive virtual reality on students' learning performances in a landscape architecture conservation course. Sustainability **14**(24), 16891 (2022)
19. Shi, Z.: Teaching reform of "virtual reality technology" from the perspective of professional certification of engineering education. Wirel. Internet Technol. **07**, 146–147 (2021)
20. Wang, Z.Y., Wang, Y., Zhai, J.B.: Application of virtual reality technology in clinical medicine teaching. Ind. Sci. Technol. Innov. **02**, 65–67 (2022)

Research on STEAM Maker Education Mode to Improve Children's Innovation Ability in Shenzhen

Cai Xia[1,2,3(✉)]

[1] Beijing Technology Institute, Zhuhai 519088, People's Republic of China
34640112@qq.com
[2] Bangkokthonburi University, Bangkok 10170, Thailand
[3] The Institute of Greater Bay Area Development, Beijing Institute of Technology, Zhuhai, China

Abstract. Since entering the 21st century, innovation has become the development tendency, the emergence of the term "Maker" has led the development of the global maker movement. The original meaning of the word "maker" is "creator". While nowadays, "Makers" put more emphasis on interest-based practices that can be turned into products but are not for-profit. "Maker" education is a new education model based on innovation and entrepreneurship education which can improve students' creative thinking, cultivate their hands-on ability and practical spirit. STEAM education model is short for science, technology, engineering, art, and mathematics, which was first put forward in the United States in 1980. From the practical perspective, many researchers suggest that the STRAM education model is benefit for improving the national competencies, improving the science awareness in the whole society, and making students to get higher income and greater job security. Shenzhen has firmly grasped the opportunity of maker education and issued several policies and regulations, but it also needs to be further improved. By reviewing the existing literature, this paper suggests that for the construction of maker education in Shenzhen, they should construct systematics curriculum, make full use of "5E" model, establish a sound evaluation system, and focus on cultivating comprehensive ability.

Keywords: STEAM model · Maker Education · Innovation Ability

1 Introduction

Since entering the 21st century, innovation has become the development tendency, especially the cultivation of innovation ability for children and teenagers has become a hot topic in the field of education. The emergence of the term "Maker" has led the development of the global maker movement. With the continuous progress of the global maker movement, it has brought new development opportunities for the innovative reform of education. STEAM education model integrates modern information technology, gradually forming a complete educational research model from the United States and has been widely recognized in the world. Although "maker" education has not been unified in a clear definition, it is widely recognized in the field of education. The development of STEAM model is also widely applied in the field of education in our country.

The original meaning of the word "maker" is "creator". In the earliest days, "maker" refers to the independent creators of small-batch production based on the background of industry 4.0 and the Internet era. In the continuous development, the word "maker" has been endowed with more connotations. And "maker education" is an educational concept aiming at cultivating future makers. STEAM education model integrates science, technology, engineering, art, and mathematics. With the continuous improvement of STEAM model, how to apply STEAM model to carry out maker education has become a hot research topic in the field of education. However, due to the differences in social background, regional differences and student characteristics, how to establish a sound STEAM evaluation system based on the current social background and make the cultivation of innovation consciousness become the normal state of education is important research on the localization of STEAM model maker education.

Shenzhen has firmly grasped the opportunity of maker education. In order to better improve maker education in primary and secondary schools, Shenzhen has issued a number of policies and regulations. From the perspective of curriculum, Shenzhen encourages students to actively identify problems in maker education and cultivate craftsman spirit. A maker target is designed for primary school, middle school, and high school. The curriculum focuses on three contents: information technology maker, art design maker and creative production maker. In the course implementation process, STEAM education strategy is integrated to strengthen the integration of interdisciplinary resources and strive to help students out of the classroom and develop in an all-round way.

This paper aims to explore how the STEAM-based maker education system can improve individual's innovation ability in terms of improving the innovation capacity in the whole society. This paper will review the content of STEAM model, maker education and related theories, and find out the effect of STEAM maker education model on improving children's innovation ability in Shenzhen by studying the existing literature. In addition, it will provide suggestions to schools or educational institutions based on relevant content.

2   Literature Review

2.1   "Maker" Education

In 2015, the word "maker" was included in the government work report. The original meaning of maker is creators, which mainly refers to those creative implementers based on interests, good at cooperation and sharing, and capable of continuous innovation (Anderson 2012). But in general, there are essential differences between "makers" and "creators". "Makers" put more emphasis on interest-based practices that can be turned into products but are not for-profit.

"Maker" education is a new education model based on innovation and entrepreneurship education. This model can improve students' creative thinking, cultivate their hands-on ability and practical spirit, and pay attention to systematics learning and personalized knowledge construction in the teaching process (Halverson and Sheridan 2014). Traditional innovation education focuses on thinking training, while "maker" education focus more on the practice oriented. Toombs et al. (2014) analyzed six cases and found that to become a real "maker", sensitivity should be enhanced, attitude of maker should be cultivated, and community awareness should be developed. Meanwhile, they found that the process of becoming a maker has an important relationship with the operation of the maker space itself. Nilsson (2012) divided makerspace into infrastructure and community construction. The former is mainly about the construction of makerspace, while the latter invites people from different backgrounds to participate in makerspace activities. Nilsson (2012) also believes that organizations should identify user needs in this process and attract more people with different interests to join the space.

In practice, the United States was the first to start the practice of "maker" education. At present, nearly 100 universities in the United States have opened Maker Spaces, such as Massachusetts Institute of Technology, Stanford University, Hawaii Pacific University, etc. (Kleinknecht et al. 2015). Led by the United States, "maker" education has become popular all over the world. The Netherlands' fab Class--"maker" club has clear rules and regulations and gathers physics, chemistry, mathematics, information technology, and other courses to stimulate students' learning enthusiasm and creativity. On the other hand, "maker" education in China is based on learning from other countries' education models and relevant theories and cases. Some scholars believe that creation is the way to learn, and the result of learning is the product. Zheng Yanlin (2015) proposed that from the level of consciousness, we should attach importance to the value of "maker" education, pay attention to the overall design of "maker" education, and strive to create a maker space. In practice, some developed areas in our country have begun to perfect the education of makers, as represented by Wenzhou, Beijing, Shanghai and so on.

In general, foreign research on "maker" education is more systematics and perfect. In our country, "maker" education is still mainly focused on the research of one aspect. So far, the theory is relatively trivial. Although systematics ideas have been formed, there is still a long way to go before the establishment of a perfect education system for makers. Therefore, how to localize "maker" education, reduce blind technology worship, and strengthen the integration with existing learning is an important issue in the development of "maker" education at present.

2.2 STEAM Model

STEAM education model is short for science, technology, engineering, art, and mathematics, which was first put forward in the United States in 1980. From the definition point of view, there are different definitions of STEAM education in academic. Some scholars believe that STEAM education is a complete integration of five disciplines (Clapp and Jimenez 2016; Glass and Wilson 2016; Guyotte et al. 2015; Liao et al. 2016; Wynn and Harris 2012), while others believe that STEAM education is a cross-disciplinary education consists of some of the five disciplines (Clary 2016; Gates 2017; Gershon and Ben-Horin 2014; Grinnell and Angal 2016), and a small number of scholars believe that STEAM education is the embedding and integration of art into STEM education (Ghanbari 2015; Kant et al. 2015; Kim and Bolger 2017).

The STEAM education model can be divided into three stages. The first stage is the study of the relationship between STS (science, technology, and Society), aiming to improve the scientific culture of the whole society. The second phase is STEM education, which raises the focus of mathematics and science education in the United States, believing that STEM education can keep it in the leading position in the world. In the third stage, Yakman and his team added art to the STEM model in 2006, enriching the STEAM education model. From the perspective of the training objectives of STEAM education model, in the early 21st century, OECD summarized the successful literacy of learners into four dimensions: knowledge, skills, characteristics and original learning (Fadel et al. 2017). In 2002, the P21 Alliance of the United States proposed 4C ability system, including communication ability, corporation, critical thinking, creativity and innovation (EDLeader21, 2019), and STEAM education added the innovation dimension in 2007.

The importance of STEAM education can be seen at the national, regional, and individual levels. Firstly, STEAM education mode is conducive to improving the overall scientific and technological strength of the country and maintaining national competitiveness (Department of Commerce, 2012). Secondly, STEAM education helps to improve the knowledge of all citizens about science and further enhance the scientific literacy of all citizens (Bencze and DiGiuseppe 2006). Thirdly, students with STEAM education are more likely to get higher income and greater job security in their jobs. Therefore, high quality STEAM education not only enables students to acquire comprehensive knowledge, but also enables students to achieve greater success in work and society.

3 Practical Suggestions

3.1 Construct Systematics Curriculum

STEAM model is a relatively new interdisciplinary education framework. Teaching organizations need to give full consideration to the practice of science, technology, engineering, and mathematics in teaching and add art elements. Yakman (2008) proposed the STEAM Interdisciplinary Teaching framework (Fig. 1). Curriculum construction based on this framework can be interactive in the five areas. The relationship between the five elements of STEAM is explained as science and technology explained through engineering and art, all of which are based on mathematical elements (Yakman 2008). We need to help students transfer knowledge between these disciplines through the construction of systematics courses, so that students can acquire higher-order thinking and innovation ability. Students who participate in STEAM model not only learn knowledge in a single field, but more importantly, become life-long holistic. This will help them better understand other disciplines, perspectives, and cultures.

Shenzhen has explained the practical curriculum of Maker education in the Guide to the Construction of Maker Education Curriculum for Primary and Secondary Schools in Shenzhen. Curriculum design revolves around thinking training, aesthetic training, tool training as the carrier, let students immerse in the reality needs. Through the analysis of practical problems, students can understand how to apply knowledge. However, in terms of the overall curriculum design, it still tends to be isolated and separate curriculum design, unable to integrate various courses well, which has a negative impact on students

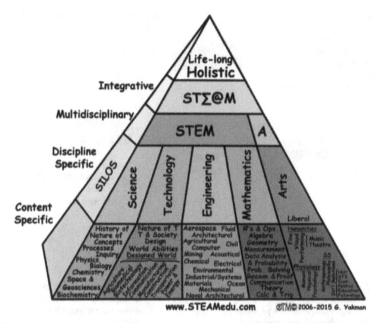

Fig. 1. STEAM: A framework for teaching across the disciplines (Yakman 2008)

to solve complex problems and new problems. Therefore, in terms of overall curriculum design, Shenzhen needs to combine STEAM model to carry out systematic and holistic curriculum construction, with the ultimate goal of cultivating life-long holistic.

3.2 Make Full Use of "5E" Model

The view on learning in constructivism theory clearly points out that learning in the process of education in which individuals actively construct knowledge rather than passively accept knowledge taught by teachers. Constructivism student theory holds that students are the subject of learning, and learning is a process in which individuals process information and build new knowledge with the help of other individuals. Based on the above theory, creating learning situation is the first step of construction. Therefore, in the STEAM education model, learning situations need to be constructed according to certain social background. In this process, education should apply the "5E" model in teaching (Fig. 2). The 5E framework model is a cyclic approach to learning designed to guide students to perfect learning activities by engaging, exploring, explaining, elaborating, and evaluating the five activities.

5E teaching model is useful to help students explore practice, which can help students focus on scientific content and provide a scientific way of thinking (DeBoer 1991). Starting from the theory of social construction, 5E model can cultivate students' scientific thinking mode and scientific thoughts in work (Skamp and Peers 2012). The 5E model begins with engage, requiring students to be able to participate in discussions and ask questions at the end. Secondly, students enter the explore stage, where they explore related concepts through collaboration and practical activities. Thirdly, the students went

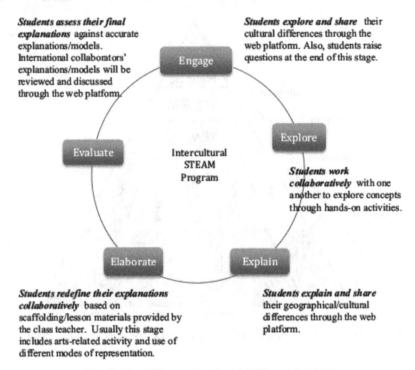

Students assess their final explanations against accurate explanations/models. International collaborators' explanations/models will be reviewed and discussed through the web platform.

Students explore and share their cultural differences through the web platform. Also, students raise questions at the end of this stage.

Students work collaboratively with one another to explore concepts through hands-on activities.

Students redefine their explanations collaboratively based on scaffolding/lesson materials provided by the class teacher. Usually this stage includes arts-related activity and use of different modes of representation.

Students explain and share their geographical/cultural differences through the web platform.

Fig. 2. The 5E Instructional model (Chu et al., 2019)

into the explain part, where they explained the differences that they felt to each other. Fourthly, the students went into the elaborate part, and modified the related concepts explored in the first stage according to the teaching materials provided by the teacher. Finally, they enter the evaluate stage to accurately evaluate the problems raised earlier. After completing the evaluate phase, they re-enter the engage part of the next problem, and finally form a closed-loop mode of learning. Therefore, this model is also considered suitable for education with cross-cultural background.

In summary, when using STEAM model for maker education, educators should make full use of 5E model and let students participate in 5E activities. Based on constructivism theory, learning is a process in which individuals actively build knowledge. When designing maker education, Shenzhen should make it clear that learning is a process for students to establish a knowledge system, rather than a process of passively absorbing knowledge taught by teachers. Therefore, the curriculum construction of maker education should follow the 5E model, which makes students fully engage in the process of discovering problems, explore each other freely, and try to explain the existing problems. At the elaborate stage, teachers will provide teaching resources, and ultimately, students will evaluate the problem-solving result. Only by following the 5E model in the overall course design can students' innovation ability be better cultivated. Therefore, building 5E model under STEAM education mode is conducive to cultivating students' innovation ability and realizing the purpose of "maker" education.

3.3   Establish a Sound Evaluation System

STEAM education is a very important educational content. It is of great significance for teaching activities to integrate STEAM systematics learning engineering and purpose and build STEAM comprehensive learning evaluation system. Emily et al. (2014) raised theoretical model of STEAM Common Measurement System (Fig. 3). In this model, STEAM learning process and evaluation system are constructed from four dimensions: school level supports, professional development, educator practice and student learning. From the model, academic identity, motivational resilience, higher-order cognitive skills and application of conceptual knowledge are not only the main goal of STEAM education, but also the main index of STEAM evaluation system. The STEAM Common Measurement System model is student-centered and coordinates schools, teachers and students to carry out STEAM learning process. On the School level supports, transformational leadership provide support for interdisciplinary instructional planning throughout the STEAM system. STEAM collaboration, professional development and learning resource supply at the teacher level provide support for STEAM system practice activities.

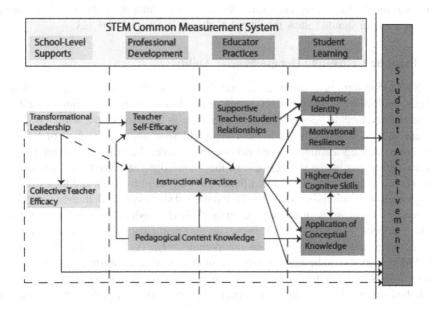

Fig. 3. STEAM comprehensive learning evaluation system (Emily et al., 2014)

In this model, the four evaluation objectives given by STEAM common measurement System are crucial. First of all, the application of conceptual knowledge is very important in this module. In contrast to traditional views of education, the STEAM model argues that education should focus more on the process of understanding and thinking, rather than on metrics such as definitions or algorithms. The STEAM model focuses on the application of concepts and understanding of knowledge rather than memorization. Sliva (2009) believes that what is more important for students is what they can do with knowledge, rather than the knowledge themselves. Secondly, higher-order cognitive skills mean that students should have the ability to solve problems, which includes discovering, analyzing and solving complex problems, applying knowledge and skills to solve a new problem or situation, and evaluating an appropriate solution. Thirdly, academic identity and motivational resilience can help students work hard and persist in difficulties and setbacks. These include high quality student participation in academic work (Skinner et al. 2009), adaptive strategies in the face of difficulties and setbacks (Skinner and Wellborn 1997).

At present, the evaluation principles of maker education in Shenzhen mainly focus on the principle of process, comprehensiveness, diversification, and incentive. In the evaluation content, the core layer pays attention to students' problem finding and scheme planning ability, the middle layer pays attention to students' tool skills and practical operation ability, and the outer layer pays attention to students' communication and resource collaboration ability. As can be seen from the model in Fig. 3, a complete evaluation of the STEAM maker education system should include four dimensions, as well as a target evaluation of maker education. Only by the overall evaluation based on STEAM Common Measurement model can we improve the construction of maker education more effectively. Therefore, Shenzhen's evaluation of the STEAM maker education model should follow the complete theoretical model in Fig. 3.

3.4 Focus on Cultivating Comprehensive Ability

The STEAM system is a robust, economically, and socially adaptable framework that includes multidisciplinary practices aimed at developing more innovation capacity of Citizens. Therefore, to conduct "maker" education in STEAM mode, attention should be paid on the cultivation of individual comprehensive ability. The goal of STEAM is to foster lifelong learning for individuals, who, under the influence of internal and external influences, make the best use of the knowledge that they are exposed to for understanding. However, due to the differences between individuals and their different backgrounds, education should not be about imparted stereotypical definitions, but about how to solve problems with knowledge. In the STEAM mode, based on the five subject fields of science, technology, engineering, art and mathematics, individuals can better view complex and emerging problems comprehensively. As shown in Fig. 1, the entire STEAM system should be built as a system of courses that are intrinsically linked and allow students to delve deeper into specific topics of interest to them. These fields can be studied separately or divided into special groups in different fields, which will be helpful to educational practice and of great significance to the cultivation of students' comprehensive ability.

In the design of the overall goal of maker education, Shenzhen mainly sets goals from three dimensions: craftsman spirit, maker ability and industrial knowledge. Interdisciplinary integration is also considered in the course setting. The guide requires that at least one topic of study should be completed in each semester, which cannot meet the requirements of STEAM maker education model. When carrying out maker education, the design of course content, experiment activities and practice activities should take full account of the cultivation of students' comprehensive ability. Instead of simply stacking the contents of different disciplines, the contents of various disciplines should be fully integrated. Only by cultivating students' comprehensive ability can they further improve their ability to solve complex problems and their persistence in the face of setbacks, thus improving their overall innovation ability.

4 Conclusion

"Makers" put more emphasis on interest-based practices that can be turned into products but are not for-profit. "Maker" education is a new education model based on innovation and entrepreneurship education which can improve students' creative thinking, cultivate their hands-on ability and practical spirit. STEAM education model is short for science, technology, engineering, art, and mathematics. From the practical perspective, many researchers suggest that the STRAM education model is benefit for improving the national competencies, improving the science awareness in the whole society, and making students to get higher income and greater job security.

Shenzhen has firmly grasped the opportunity of maker education and issued several policies and regulations, but it also needs to be further improved. By reviewing the existing literature, this paper suggests that for the construction of maker education in Shenzhen, they should construct systematics curriculum, make full use of "5E" model, establish a sound evaluation system, and focus on cultivating comprehensive ability. Only by taking these measures can Shenzhen further improve the quality of STEAM maker education.

References

Anderson, C.: Maker: The New Industrial Revolution (2012)

Cheek, D.W.: Thinking Constructively About Science, Technology, and Society Education. State University of New York Press, New York (1992)

Chu, H.E., Martin, S.N., Park, J.: A theoretical framework for developing an intercultural steam program for Australian and Korean students to enhance science teaching and learning. Int. J. Sci. Math. Educ. **17**, 1251–1266 (2019)

Clapp, E.P., Jimenez, R.L.: Implementing STEAM in maker-centered learning. Psychol. Aesthet. Creativity Arts **10**(4), 481 (2016)

Clary, R.: Science and art in the national parks: celebrating the centennial of the US national park service. Sci. Teach. **83**(7), 33 (2016)

DeBoer, G.: A History of Ideas In Science Education: Implications for Practice. Macmillan, New York (1991)

EDLeader21.Framework for 21st Century Learning [EB/OL]. http://www.p21.org/about-us/p21-framework. Accessed 24 Apr 2019

Saxton, E., Burns, R., et al.: A common measurement system for K-12 STEM education: adopting an educational evaluation methodology that elevates theoretical foundations and systems thinking. Stud. Educ. Eval. **40**, 18–35 (2014)

Fadel, B.C., Trilling, B., Bialik, M.: Four-Dimensional Education: The Competencies Learners Need to Succeed. CreateSpace Independent Publishing Platform (2015)

Foundation N S: Shaping the future: Strategies for revitalizing undergraduate education. In: Proceedings from the National Working Conference (1996)

Gates, A.E.: Benefits of a STEAM collaboration in Newark, New Jersey: Volcano simulation through a glass-making experience. J. Geosci. Educ. **65**(1), 4–11 (2017)

Gershon, W.S., Ben-Horin, O.: Deepening inquiry: what processes of making music can teach us a bout creativity and ontology for inquiry based science education. Int. J. Educ. Arts **15**(19/20), 1–37 (2014)

Ghanbari, S.: Learning across disciplines: a collective case study of two university programs that integrate the arts with STEM J1. Int. J. Educ. Arts **16**(7), 1–21 (2015)

Glass, D., Wilson, C.: The art and science of looking: collaboratively learning our way to improved STEAM integration. Art Educ. **69**(6), 8–14 (2016)

Grinnell, S., Angal, S.: Luminous lighting. Sci. Child. **53**(6), 54 (2016)

Guyotte, K.W., et al.: Collaborative creativity in STEAM: narratives of art education students 'experiences in trans disciplinary spaces. Int. J. Educ. Arts **16**(15), 1–38 (2015)

Halverson, E.R., Sheridan, K.: The maker movement in education. Harv. Educ. Rev. **84**(4), 495–504 (2014)

Hughes, J.M.: Digital making with "At-Risk" youth. Int. J. Inf. Learn. Technol. (2017)

Kant, J., Burckhard, S., Meyers, R.: Engaging high school girls in native American culturally responsive STEAM activities. J. STEM Educ. **18**(5), 15–25 (2018)

Kim, D., Bolger, M.: Analysis of Korean elementary pre-service teachers' changing attitudes about integrated STEAM pedagogy through developing lesson plans. Int. J. Sci. Math. Educ. **15**(4), 587–605 (2017)

Kleinknecht, E., Gilmore, T., Vander Zanden, A.: Promoting social change through game education: a program evaluation. In: Poster Presented at the Annual Meetings of the Western Psychological Association, Las Vegas, NV (2015).

Liao, C., Motter, J.L., Patton, R.M.: Tech-savvy girls: learning 21st-century skills through steam digital art making. Art Educ. **69**(4), 29–35 (2016)

Nilsson, E.M.: The making of a maker-space for open innovation, knowledge sharing and peer-to-peer learning. Fut. Learn. Spaces **293** (2012)

Silva, E.: Measuring skills for 21st-century learning. Phi Delta Kappan **90**(9), 630–634 (2009)

Skamp, K., Peers, S.: Implementation of science based on 5E learning model: insights from teacher feedback on trial primary connections unit. In: Australasian Science Education Research Association Conference, University of Sunshine cost, 27–30 June, 2012 (2012). https://primaryco nnections.org.au/about/history/research-and-evaluation/research-articles

Skinner, E.A., Wellborn, J.G.: Children's coping in the academic domain. In: Wolchik, S.A., Sandler, I.N. (eds.) Handbook of children's coping with common stressors: Linking theory and intervention, pp. 387–422. Plenum, New York (1997)

Skinner, E.A., Kindermann, T.A., Furrer, C.J.: A motivational perspective on engagement and disaffection: conceptualization and assessment of children's behavioral and emotional participation in academic activities in the classroom. Educ. Psychol. Measur. **69**, 493–525 (2009)

Toombs, A., Bardzell, S., Bardzell, J.: Becoming makers: hackerspace member habits, values, and identities. J. Peer Prod. **5**(2014), 1–8 (2014)

Wynn, T., Harris, J.: (2012) toward a STEM + Arts curriculum: creating the teacher team. Art Educ. **65**(5), 42–47 (2012)

Yakman, G.: STEAM Education: an overview of creating a model of integrative education. **3**, 1–28 (2008)

Yakman, G.: STΣ@M Education: an overview of creating a model of integrative education. In: Proceedings of the Pupils Attitudes Towards Technology 2008 Annual, Netherlands (2008)

Yanlin, Z.: American colleges and universities to implement education and guest of path analysis. Open Educ. Res. **21**(3), 21–29 (2015). https://doi.org/10.13966/j.carolcarrollnkikfjyyj.2015.03.003

Exploring Design Factors of Teaching Aids in Design Based Learning

Liang Yin[✉]

Beijing Institute of Technology, Zhuhai, China
yl401402@hotmail.com

Abstract. The paper presents a research on how to apply Design Based Learning in STEAM curriculum at primary schools, with a particular focus on exploring the design factors of teaching aids that may support children's learning. Building on insights from literature regarding the role of teaching aids in design practices, several design factors have been identified and guidelines for teaching aids design have been developed too. In the end, we design some teaching aids based on these guidelines in order to test its validity. The result show that the teaching aids with certain design factors could support children's design practices in learning.

Keywords: Design Based Learning · Children · Design Factors · Teaching Aids

1 Introduction

"Design-related activities are important in the primary school because they enable children to understand the world, because they play an important part in children's intellectual and emotional development, and because they make an important contribution to children's work in all parts of the school curriculum." [1]
Design Council of UK, 1987, P140

Design not only shape the physical world but also our mindset as design could be viewed as a process of learning in K-12 classroom. The so-called Design-Based Learning (DBL) are related approaches to learning that apply the tenets of design thinking in a project-based learning context [2], especially in the STEAM curriculum. DBL encourages children to construct knowledge by themselves and learn from partners. Meanwhile, the design-related learning activities in the primary school is more than a separate subject, they are something for which provide opportunities across the school curriculum. These learning activities include planning, devise tests, experiments and making products to solving problems and it can give rise to thinking, questioning and discussing.

Recent years, DBL increasingly employs technology-based teaching aids, e.g., Littlebits and LEGO education kits, etc., to support STEAM curriculum [3]. These teaching aids play an important role in DBL as children need to learn though the interaction with toolkits. Meanwhile, children also need teaching aids as scaffolding tools to express their ideas. The design factors [4] of these toolkits inform the emotions, cognitive load and attitude of learners, and finally shape their learning activities. This research aims to explore the design factors of teaching aids and try to develop guidelines for teaching aids design based on these factors.

1.1 Design Factors of Teaching Aids

Design Factors (DF) are the design methods and elements applied by designers in configuring products [4]. DF have both positive and negative impacts on users, and may shape their behavior. In the case of DBL, DF of learning environment may shape the learning activities of learners. DF comprises a set of design features of teaching aids, for example, "good affordance of product styling features" "overload information on the surface" are DF of teaching aids which could bring positive and negative impacts on DBL of children.

1.2 Design Based Learning in Primary School Curriculum

DBL is an inquiry-based pedagogy which integrates design thinking and design practices into classroom teaching, by engaging students in the process of idea generation, developing and evaluating the artifacts, systems and solutions they designed [5]. DBL has been considered as an instructional approach engaging students in real-life problems solving while reflecting on learning process [6]. It also has been defined as an educational approach grounded in the processes of inquiry and reasoning towards generating innovative artifacts, systems and solutions [7]and it employs the pedagogical insights from not only the problem-based learning but also the scenario of problems solving as design assignments [8].

Through compare with different type of DBL pedagogies, like Learning by Design [9], Design Inquiry of Learning and Design Based Understanding, I summarize some shared character of DBL as below:

Shared Features	Characters of DBL in Primary School
Open-ended	• No unique solution is given • Search alternatives and solutions • Students define the problem, the goals and the specifications • No specification is given. Students are requested to determine own procedures and testing plan • Incomplete information is provided at the start. Process of consultation and questioning help to arrive to a fully developed specification • Freedom in task implementation to encourage diversity in design approaches • Project proposal based on project planning and implementation • Case reasoning approach to solve problems • Design methodology involved in set up of project activities
Hands-on Experiences	• Students apply theory in practical schemes • Learn from iterations • Design methodology embedded in projects • Encouraging reflection based on experiencing

(continued)

(continued)

Shared Features	Characters of DBL in Primary School
Authentic Scenarios	• assignments represent real-world problems with realistic scenarios • Link project activities to real social challenges
Multidisciplinary	• The content of curriculum is integrated t from multidiscipline • Tutors form different disciplines involved in project

In conclusion, DBL needs learning environment with authentic scenarios and open-ended learning tasks, meanwhile, children need well designed toolkits to help them get hands-on learning experiences.

1.3 Teaching Aids for DBL

DBL could benefit both instructors and students in primary school through providing effective teaching aids. Noel and Liub [10] claimed that learning design could bring opportunities for a paradigmatic shift in primary-level education and design thinking with toolkits as teaching scaffolding could help pupils master learning and innovation skills. On teachers' side, Davis [11] argued that the inclusion of design education in the preparation of well design educational setting, which include space, toolkits and learning tasks, could offer strategies for improving teaching and classroom learning.

In maker space, like Fablab, teaching aids enable children to engage in digital fabrication of various applications while children learn related knowledge and skills about electronics and programming. These toolkits, like littleBits, lego WeDo, could help children to capture their imaginations and express their ideas. Science DBL means learning through dealing with various authentic challenges, providing children toolkits with DBL opportunities may support low-threshold "making" of diverse solutions for various problems [12]. Many designers designed such toolkits as teaching aid for DBL (see Fig. 1), mainly be used in STEAM curriculum.

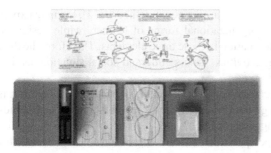 

Fig. 1. Two Teaching Aid designed for DBL: BOOKi (left) designed by Prof. Ding Junfeng; Teaching With Design (right) designed by Prof. Caylee Raber

2 Methodology

This research aims to explore how teaching aids can inform learning experience of children in DBL. In order to answer research questions in three stages, a multi-method methodology has been applied as below:

Stage	Research Question	Method	Data Collection	Data Analysis
One	How teaching aids could inform learning experience of children in DBL? What are the key themes and contributing factors of teaching aid design?	Literature Review Thematic Analysis	66 recent articles that from the experts' perspectives represent the most relevant contributions to DBL and teaching aids	Through thematic analysis to identify 17 themes of in DBL domain
Two	What are the key design factors of teaching aids in DBL? How these design factors inform DBL with educational design perspective?	Thematic Analysis	Interviews Documents	open coding selected coding
Three	What are the guidelines of teaching aid design for DBL?	Action Research	Observation Field research Questionnaires	Qualitative data analysis based on the feedback of interviews

3 Explore the Design Factors of Teaching Aids

Method: In order to identify the design factors of teaching aids, thematic analysis based on literature review has been applies according to Braun's 6-step framework of thematic analysis [13].

Scope of theme: According to the learning network theory [14], learning experience is shaped by task, setting and organizational forms of learners while design affects learning indirectly through intervention in these three elements. Therefore, the thematic analysis focus on the learning activities, task, setting and social situation, as they are objects of educational design[1].

Coding scheme: Coding on each segment of data is depended on whether it is relevant to or captured something about research question: What are the key themes and contributing factors of teaching aids for DBL?

With a learning network perspective, 17 main themes have been selected through literature review as below:

---

[1] Some themes are excluded, like teachers' attitudes, parents support and local culture, as they do not affect learners directly and not belong to the three objects of educational design. Some themes related to educational policy and school management are excluded too as they are hard to change as designers in China, even they are part of educational design.

Dimension	Theme	Examples
Task	Authentic learning tasks	authentic learning tasks stimulate meaningful and complex learning [15, 16]; Placing high value on authentic, real-world goals for learning could encourage children to inquire actively [17]
	Opportunity to conduct design project by pupils themselves	primary science and technology education should give children the opportunity to plan and devise tests, experiments, and finished products for themselves [1]
	Relevant and meaningful assignment	The design practices of children is highly dependent on the assignment at hand, relevant and meaningful assignments are imperative to design based learning [18]
	Dilemma challenge	In order to encourage children to take designerly stance towards inquiry, dilemma challenge is needed for design projects: there is no unique, 'correct' view of the problem, and there are numerous possible intervention points [19],
	Openness of design question	openness of the concrete framing was maintained so as to allow the students to develop their ideas freely [20];
	Adapted Design Thinking	Design thinking could diversify the curriculum of informal school age children education [21]; Design Thinking is an approach to learning that focuses on developing children's creative confidence through hands-on projects [22]; Design-based projects embed students analogically to engineering design with design thinking [23]; design-oriented scientific thinking [24]
	Empowerment	Empowerment of children by giving them a voice in design could facilitate the development of meaningful technologies [20]

(continued)

(continued)

Dimension	Theme	Examples
	Iterations/ Backwards Thinking in design approaches	Iterative tinkering can help children build confidence in their own capabilities and explore the world they live in [25–27]; Discussion based on existing knowledge and life experiences contribute to radiant thinking capability [28]; the growth of understanding takes place through iteration between designing and making process [29]
	Assistance for transforming ideas	all children needed a considerable amount of assistance from teachers to sort out ideas and to transform their ideas into outcomes [30]; Children tend to have more difficulty in verbalizing their thoughts, especially when it concerns abstract concepts and actions (Piaget, 1971, 1973), so assistance once necessary for children should be provided in time [20]
	Considering individual difference in design project	The progression was influenced by children's abilities at different ages which need to be considered [30, 31]; tutors need to show respect for individual differences when responding the challenges (Cowley et al., 1995)
	Multiple evaluation	Innovation cannot be evaluated simply in terms of how much students learn on some criterion measure, it is necessary to use a variety of evaluation techniques, including standardized pre-and post-tests and ongoing evaluations of the class-room milieu [32]

(continued)

(*continued*)

Dimension	Theme	Examples
	Transpositional Consideration/Empathy	(Transpositional Consideration) could direct the students' attention away from their own personal ideas to develop relevant concepts for a specific context [20] Getting "into character" and answering those questions as they think the body object would[2]
	Designerly stance towards wicked problem	Designerly stance towards inquiry as an important part of design literacy, children with designerly stance tend to avoid simplified and finalized solutions in design project [19]
Physical Setting	Toolkits	D3 PROCESS TOOLKIT[3] could empower young people through design; 3-D Body and History Wall of the DBL course in San Andres Timilpan[4] facilitate backwards thinking of children; 'Hello Life' toolkit is designed by information design students at the University of Pretoria aiming to help children create awareness of hygiene and infection risks [33]; LEGO™ help 5th grade students construct scientific conceptions about simple machines [34]; Integrating design tools into science education naturally offers students dynamic learning opportunities [35]; youth will be more able to frame design problems holistically when they are aware of the affordances and constraints of the design tools [36]

(*continued*)

---

[2] Source: https://www.cpp.edu/~dnelson/classroom.html.

[3] Source: http://www.thecommonstudio.com/d3toolkits.

(*continued*)

Dimension	Theme	Examples
	Maker setting	(maker setting) present new opportunities for children to better acquire skills [19, 37]; (maker space) provide physical computing platforms for children [38]; (maker space) enable bottom-up ideation processes, and allow children to better grasp digital technology [39]
	Narrative learning environment/ Situated learning scenario	a shared narrative environment might be fruitful when designing with children [40]
	Local setting	Introducing a child to a natural or built area in the neighborhood can open a world of wonder for them to explore outside of school hours expanding the time horizon of learning [26]; Learning that takes place in local settings contributes to improved thinking and problem solving skills [41]
	Authentic setting	Design projects within authentic settings simulate engineering practices and encourage students work with multidisciplinary perspective [42]; engineering design provides children an authentic context for science investigation and therefore enables their cognitive load of science investigations to be shared within a system [43]
Organizational Forms	Role-exchanging	Children are no longer testers or information givers, they work as experts of their daily life and conduct the design research......this provides more insights [44]; thinking about on designed objects and their context could help children recognize the role of the related social context [45, 46]

(*continued*)

(*continued*)

Dimension	Theme	Examples
	(Team) Inclusive	An inclusive setting could make every child feel safe and have a sense of belonging [47]; forming meaningful connections among students could build an inclusive learning environment which facilitates positive interaction [48]

In conclusion, teaching aids should provide leaners certain learning task, toolkits and help mangers to form organizational forms. Well designed teaching aids could help learners fully immerse in authentic scenarios, express their ideas correctly and easily.

4 Guidelines for Teaching Aids Design

4.1 Guidelines Based on Design Factors

Based on the identified DF, interview with professors and feed back from stokeholds, some guidelines of teaching aids design have been developed as below:

1. The teaching aids need to be used in a maker setting with various toolkits. These toolkits should have good affordance, low acceptance hurdle and easy to use.
2. Graphical information is needed and could provide authentic learning tasks and open-ended learning questions.
3. The physical learning environment should fit the DBL, the character of learning activities of children.
4. Teaching aids could help children exchange their ideas, express their imagines and support design practices, like experiencing, analyzing and applying.

4.2 Apply Guidelines on Teaching Aids Design

In order to test the validity of guidelines, we conducted a design practice with an aim to design toolkits for children, help them to learn Chinese traditional culture through design. We designed some teaching aids as below:

1. Toolkits for self-designed woodcut (see in Fig. 2):
2. Toolkits for self-designed stitchwork (Fig. 3):

The design practices proved that the guidelines for teaching aids design could help designers to design toolkits for DBL. Through apply the DF in teaching aids design, the effectiveness of teaching aids could be enhanced.

Fig. 2. Toolkits for children to design woodcut by themselves. (Designed by Zhan Hongqian, Qian Haitao and O Xiaofeng)

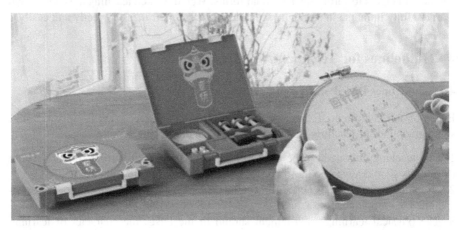

Fig. 3. Toolkits for children design stitchwork (designed by Wang Junjie and Zhong Xuanqi)

5 Conclusion

Well-designed teaching aids could enable children to gain first-hand learning experience in DBL. In teaching aids design, designers should think about the DF from three domains: Task, Physical Setting and Organizational Form. Meanwhile, some guidelines could help designers to apply DF in teaching aids design.

Meanwhile, user-centered design method could be used to design toolkits, but designers should consider different learning styles and interests of learners. When the users are children, designers also need to think about the age appropriate and how to create learning opportunities for children in DBL.

References

1. Design council: design and primary education. Stud. Des. Educ. Craft Technol. **19**(3) (1987)
2. Zhang, F., Markopoulos, P., Bekker, T.: Children's emotions in design-based learning: a systematic review. J. Sci. Educ. Technol. **29**(4), 459–481 (2020). https://doi.org/10.1007/s10 956-020-09830-y

3. Zhang, F., Markopoulos, P., Bekker, T.: The Role of Children's Emotions during Design-based Learning Activity (2018)
4. Li, C., Lee, C.-F., Xu, S.: Stigma threat in design for older adults: exploring design factors that induce stigma perception. Int. J. Des. **14**(1), 51–64 (2020)
5. Silk, E.M., Schunn, C.D., Cary, M.S.: The impact of an engineering design curriculum on science reasoning in an urban setting. J. Sci. Educ. Technol. **18**(3), 209–223 (2009)
6. Mehalik, M., Schunn, C.: What constitutes good design? A review of empirical studies of design processes. Int. J. Eng. Educ. **22**(3), 519 (2007)
7. van Diggelen, M.R., Doulougeri, K.I., Gomez-Puente, S.M., Bombaerts, G., Dirkx, K.J.H., Kamp, R.J.A.: Coaching in design-based learning: a grounded theory approach to create a theoretical model and practical propositions. Int. J. Technol. Des. Educ. **31**(2), 305–324 (2019). https://doi.org/10.1007/s10798-019-09549-x
8. Gómez Puente, S.M., Van Eijck, M., Jochems, W.: A sampled literature review of design-based learning approaches: a search for key characteristics. Int. J. Technol. Des. Educ. **23**(3), 717–732 (2013)
9. Kolodner, J.L., Crismond, D., Gray, J., Holbrook, J., Puntambekar, S.: Learning by design from theory to practice. In: Proceedings of the International Conference of the Learning Sciences, pp. 16–22 (1998)
10. Noel, L.-A., Liub, T.L.: Using design thinking to create a new education paradigm for elementary level children for higher student engagement and success. **22**(1) (2017). n1
11. Davis, M.: Making a case for design-based learning. Arts Educ. Policy Rev. **100**(2), 7–14 (1998). Heldref Publications, Washington, DC
12. Bekker, T., Bakker, S., Douma, I., Van Der Poel, J., Scheltenaar, K.: Teaching children digital literacy through design-based learning with digital toolkits in schools. Int. J. Child-Comput. Interact. **5**, 29–38 (2015)
13. Braun, V., Clarke, V.: Using thematic analysis in psychology. Qual. Res. Psychol. **3**(2), 77–101 (2006)
14. Carvalho, L., Goodyear, P.: Design, learning networks and service innovation. Des. Stud. **55**, 27–53 (2018)
15. Van Merriënboer, J.J., Kirschner, P.A.: Ten Steps to Complex Learning: A Systematic Approach to Four-Component Instructional Design. Routledge, Abingdon (2017)
16. Gómez Puente, S.M., van Eijck, M., Jochems, W.: A sampled literature review of design-based learning approaches: a search for key characteristics. Int. J. Technol. Des. Educ. **23**(3), 717–732 (2012)
17. Krajcik, J.S., Blumenfeld, P.C.: Project-based learning (2006). na
18. Fritsch, J., Iversen, O.S., Dindler, C., Nielsen, C., Nørregaard, P.: NetWorking news: a method for engaging children actively in design. In: IRIS, 2003 (2003)
19. Christensen, K.S., Hjorth, M., Iversen, O.S., Blikstein, P.: Towards a formal assessment of design literacy: analyzing K-12 students' stance towards inquiry. Des. Stud. **46**, 125–151 (2016)
20. Iversen, O.S., Smith, R.C., Dindler, C.: Child as protagonist: expanding the role of children in participatory design. In: Proceedings of the 2017 Conference on Interaction Design and Children, ACM, 2017, pp. 27–37 (2017)
21. Freimane, A.: Case study: design thinking and new product development for school age children. In: Proceedings of the 3rd International Conference for Design Education Researchers, p. 187 (2015)
22. Kwek, S.: Innovation in the classroom: design thinking for 21st century learning (2011). Accessed 20 Sep 2015
23. Schunn, C.D.: Engineering educational design, Educational Designer (2008)
24. Li, W.-T., Ho, M.-C., Yang, C.: A design thinking-based study of the prospect of the sustainable development of traditional handicrafts. Sustainability **11**(18), 4823 (2019)

25. Gabrielson, C.: Tinkering: Kids Learn by Making Stuff. Maker Media, Inc., Sebastopol (2015)
26. Kozak, S., Elliott, S.: Connecting the dots: Key strategies that transform learning for environmental education, citizenship and sustainability, Learning for a Sustainable Future (2014)
27. Wiggins, G., Wiggins, G.P., McTighe, J.: Understanding by design, Ascd 2005 (2005)
28. Yelland, N.: Pedagogical prompts: designing experiences to promote deep learning. In: Cope, B., Kalantzis, M. (eds.) A Pedagogy of Multiliteracies, pp. 288–304. Palgrave Macmillan, London (2015). https://doi.org/10.1057/9781137539724_16
29. Hutchinson, P.: Children designing & engineering: contextual learning units in primary design and technology. J. Ind. Teach. Educ. 39, 122–145 (2002)
30. Hill, A.M., Anning, A.: Comparisons and contrasts between elementary/primary'school situated design'and'workplace design'in Canada and England. Int. J. Technol. Des. Educ. 11(2), 111–136 (2001)
31. Kolodner, J.L.: Learning by design™: iterations of design challenges for better learning of science skills. Cogn. Stud. 9(3), 338–350 (2002)
32. Collins, A.: Toward a design science of education. In: Scanlon, E., O'Shea, T. (eds.) New Directions in Educational Technology. NATO ASI Series, vol. 96, pp. 15–22. Springer, Berlin, Heidelberg (1992). https://doi.org/10.1007/978-3-642-77750-9_2
33. Bennett, A.G., Cassim, F., Van der Merwe, M.: How design education can use generative play to innovate for social change: a case study on the design of South African children's health education toolkits. Int. J. Des. 11(2), 57 (2017)
34. Marulcu, I., Barnett, M.: Fifth graders' learning about simple machines through engineering design-based instruction using LEGO™ materials. Res. Sci. Educ. 43(5), 1825–1850 (2012). https://doi.org/10.1007/s11165-012-9335-9
35. Keane, L., Keane, M.: STEAM by design, design and technology. Education 21(1), 61–82 (2016)
36. Tan, V., Peppler, K.: Creative design process in making electronic textiles. In: Proceedings of the 14th International Conference on Interaction Design and Children, ACM, 2015, pp. 327–330 (2015)
37. Martinez, S.L., Stager, G.: Invent to Learn. Constructing modern knowledge press, Torrance, CA (2013)
38. Blikstein, P., Krannich, D.: The makers' movement and FabLabs in education: experiences, technologies, and research. In: Proceedings of the 12th International Conference on Interaction Design and Children, ACM, 2013, pp. 613–616 (2013)
39. Dittert, N., Krannich, D.: Digital fabrication in educational contexts–ideas for a constructionist workshop setting, FabLab Mach. Mak. Invent. 173–180 (2013)
40. Dindler, C., Eriksson, E., Iversen, O.S., Lykke-Olesen, A., Ludvigsen, M.: Mission from Mars: a method for exploring user requirements for children in a narrative space. In: Proceedings of the 2005 Conference on Interaction Design and Children, ACM, 2005, pp. 40–47 (2005)
41. Department for Education and Skills: Learning outside the classroom Manifesto (2006). DfES Publications
42. Roth, W.-M.: Authentic School Science: Knowing and Learning in Open-Inquiry Science Laboratories. Springer Science & Business Media, Dordrecht (2012). https://doi.org/10.1007/978-94-011-0495-1
43. Wendell, K.B.: The Theoretical and Empirical Basis for Design-Based Science Instruction for Children, Unpublished Qualifying Paper, Tufts University (2008)
44. Baek, J.-S., Lee, K.-P.: A participatory design approach to information architecture design for children. Co-Design 4(3), 173–191 (2008)
45. Brockbank, A.: Facilitating Reflective Learning Through Mentoring and Coaching, Kogan Page Publishers, London (2006)

46. Davis, M., Hawley, P., McMullan, B., Spilka, G.: Design as a catalyst for learning. In: ERIC 1997 (1997)
47. Gould, P., Sullivan, J.: The inclusive early childhood classroom: easy ways to adapt learning centers for all children (1999)
48. Kelly, A., Kimbell, R., Patterson, V., Saxton, J., Stables, K.: Design and Technological Activity; a Framework for Assessment, Assessment of Performance Unit, Department of Education and Science (1987)

Design of Intelligent Real-Time Feedback System in Online Classroom

Tianyi Yuan, Zhecheng Wang, and Pei-Luen Patrick Rau^(✉)

Department of Industrial Engineering, Tsinghua University, Beijing 100084, China
rpl@mail.tsinghua.edu.cn

Abstract. This study aimed to develop an online classroom real-time feedback system called AIClass, which provides personalized learning experiences based on cultural background, personal status, and learning effectiveness. Through user research, the study identified the needs and pain points of potential users and designed corresponding functions with prototypes. The key modules of the system included personalized voice features, data capture, real-time feedback, and voice interaction in complex environments. The system combined new technologies and specific scenarios, which may help stakeholders solve relevant problems in the future. However, the system has not undergone extensive user testing, and its effectiveness needs to be proven. Additionally, the current technical environment and other issues still present challenges such as hardware limitations, network delays and cost, and ethical concerns. Overall, this study provided valuable insights and a promising approach to optimize online learning experiences, with the potential to improve learning outcomes for students and reduce labor costs for educators.

Keywords: Online Classroom · Artificial Intelligence · Learning Experience

1 Introduction

1.1 Background

The use of robots in the classroom is not a new concept [1]; however, with the rapid advancements in technology, there is growing interest in the practical application of robots and artificial intelligence (AI) in educational tasks. Robots and AI are increasingly being utilized to facilitate learning, provide feedback, and offer guidance to students. In the near future, significant changes are expected to occur in the field of education, and human teachers may need to shift their focus towards managing organizational work, designing and selecting AI teaching forms and content [2]. Notably, as basic knowledge transfer primarily involves teacher-to-student communication [3], AI agents may replace human teachers in online education. For example, universities may incorporate machine teachers into courses in specific disciplines such as artificial intelligence and basic knowledge teaching. Although it may take time for AI teaching systems to gain acceptance in the educational field, the potential benefits are enormous. Previous studies have identified several valid factors such as immediacy and reliability of robot teachers [2]. However, there is a lack of knowledge regarding how robot teachers should communicate or interact. Hence, understanding this phenomenon from the students' perspective is crucial in developing effective AI teachers and systems. Prior to conducting empirical research, it is therefore essential to explore students' demands for the AI teaching system through heuristic interviews and design.

1.2 Literature Review

There has been a growing trend towards incorporating online courses in higher education. This trend has been further accelerated by the COVID-19 pandemic, which has led to an increase in the adoption of online education by educational institutions worldwide. With the development of technology, it is anticipated that machine teachers will be increasingly employed in various roles, such as teaching assistants and tutors [4]. AI teaching technology, as a technology that interacts with humans, assists in the learning process in multiple ways and influences humans from an emotional, cognitive, and behavioral perspective [5]. AI teaching technology can create a teacher's image in the form of materialization or virtualization, or build a teacher's existence only in the form of voice and text. Scholars have begun to compare the reliability of human and AI agents, while also studying differences across disciplines [6].

Unlike figurative AI-agent teachers, non-figurative teachers are based on interactive dialogues through auditory or textual methods and are not materialized in physical space. Currently, some detached AI-agent teachers are being used in educational settings, such as Duolingo, which created a series of chatbots to help language learners practice their language. There are also researchers using AI-powered robots to perform repetitive administrative tasks, such as answering students' teaching questions about lesson plans, course modules, and assignment deadlines [7].

To understand how students perceive machine teachers, it is necessary to address this issue within the theoretical framework of how humans perceive machines. The Computer as Social Actor (CASA) paradigm [8] is a theoretical perspective that focuses on society and communication technologies. According to CASA, when humans interact with computers, they interact in a way that is similar or highly consistent with how they interact with other humans. While people often state that they interact differently with computers/AI than with humans and prefer to collaborate and communicate with humans, A. Edwards et al. found that after actual interaction with AI, people perceive the interaction better than initially expected [9]. Although people initially have different expectations about the process and flow of human-computer interaction, once they participate in the actual interaction, they may perceive the process of the interaction similarly. The CASA paradigm may be relevant to social presence, which can be interpreted as an objective existence with social attributes that can be subjectively perceived [10]. In an online learning environment, social presence can promote a positive and effective learning experience [4]. Therefore, people's perceptions and attitudes towards AI teachers may be related to their perceived social presence.

2 User Research

We interviewed 12 undergraduate students with online course experience and 3 teachers with online course design experience to understand the basic user needs and pain points. Combined with existing research, traditional online courses have pain points in the following aspects and need to be improved:

(1) Audio and video quality: Online audio and video quality is often diminished during transmission, as compared to offline learning environments.
(2) Prompts and feedback: Users frequently lack the necessary prompts and feedback to effectively navigate and engage with the course material.
(3) Social presence: Online courses often lack the sense of atmosphere, social presence, companionship, and supervision that students typically experience in offline learning environments. Students participating in online courses are often situated in relatively private spaces, with limited opportunities for interaction with others in the same course.
(4) Lack of engagement: Some users may be less willing to express themselves in online courses, while others may be more likely to do so. The threshold for expression has shifted due to concerns about personal privacy and the need for additional interactive functionality. Students often feel disengaged from online courses, as they lack the personal interaction and engagement that traditional in-person courses provide.
(5) Attention: Maintaining focus and concentration can be challenging in online learning environments, with many users reporting increased difficulty concentrating and a higher likelihood of becoming drowsy. Online courses may lack the structure and organization of traditional in-person courses, leading to confusion and difficulty in keeping up with course materials and deadlines.
(6) Interpersonal interaction: Interacting with teachers and classmates can be more difficult in online courses, as users lack the ability to intuitively see and engage with others in the same physical space. Online courses often lack opportunities for students to interact with each other and with the instructor, leading to a lack of feedback and limited opportunities for collaboration.
(7) Privacy and image: Some users may feel uneasy about personal privacy concerns, particularly when required to use a camera during online courses. There is a fear that such interactions could lead to the exposure of sensitive personal details, potentially interfering with the learning process.
(8) Limited personalization: The teacher may not always be able to perceive the needs of each individual student, and students may be unable or unwilling to express their own needs during the course. Online courses often lack personalized learning experiences that cater to individual student needs and preferences.

3 System Design

3.1 Advantages of AI in Online Courses

Online AI teaching is advantageous compared to human teachers and teaching assistants due to its ability to provide all-round personalized services for each student. While human teachers may struggle to observe and consider the individual feelings of students in online courses, AI can collect, capture, store, and quickly analyze a large amount of data, allowing it to create tailored learning experiences for each student. Additionally, AI can offer immediate feedback, adapt to the learning style of each student, and provide support 24/7, which is not possible with human teachers. These advantages make AI teaching an attractive option for online education, as it can enhance student engagement and improve learning outcomes. However, despite these advantages, the impact of AI teaching on student learning attitudes and cognition remains unclear, highlighting the need for further research in this area.

3.2 The Overview of Design

The designed AIClass (AIC) framework, as illustrated in Fig. 1, incorporates the interaction and information transmission processes among teachers, AI, and students.

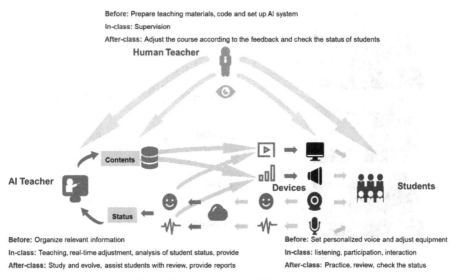

Fig. 1. The overview of AIClass system.

3.3 The Main Functional Modules of AI Online Teaching

Privacy and Permissions. To ensure that AI can interact and customize with users, it requires access to various aspects of personal privacy content, including voice, expression, personal information, preferences, chat records, among others. However, to build trust and protect users' privacy, the system must be designed with caution, ensuring that student privacy is protected, and their consent is obtained.

(1) Informed consent. Informed consent is critical, and the product must present a detailed privacy protection policy document in a prominent position to users. Functional permissions must be clearly communicated to users, and their consent should be requested before granting access.

(2) Switch functions. To provide users with greater control over their privacy, the product should include a function selection switch. This will enable users to enable or disable certain functions, such as information capture, information recommendation, personalized service, depending on their preferences and needs.

(3) Privacy protection. The product should strictly encrypt and protect user information. This will prevent any unauthorized access and disclosure of personal information, which can be detrimental to the user's privacy and trust in the system.

Personalized Voice Features. As an AI product designed to provide teaching assistance services, personalization is essential to ensure the product meets the individual preferences of students. This includes determining the type of relationship the AI should have with the user and what qualities the AI's voice should possess. Additionally, students should have the autonomy to choose their preferred voice features. The specific functions are described as follows, as shown in Fig. 2:

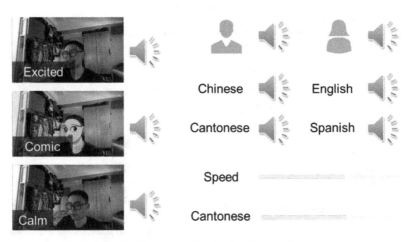

Fig. 2. The personalized voice characteristics.

(1) Select AI voice features. The product mainly interacts with users through voice, and provides the function of selecting AI voice features. Students can adjust AI's voice characteristics (speech speed, tone, timbre, emotion, etc.), AI's language habits (using dialect, Mandarin, Mandarin with local accent, etc.). Moreover, students should be able to define the role relationship between AI assistants and themselves, such as friends, teachers, or classmates, within a limited range. The characteristics of AI teachers should be defined by students themselves to confirm a friendly but not intimate image of AI teachers.

(2) Select personal voice features. Users may need to use a "fake" voice assistant to talk online because of the noisy environment, inconvenience and other factors. The AI product should also provide the ability for users to set their personal voice image using an audio generator or recording their voiceprints to create a unique voice. In addition, the product includes the voice correction functions, such as converting the

user's vague voice into a clear voice, filtering the noise, and automatically correcting some wrong pronunciation.

(3) Learning and evolution. To improve personalization, the AI should have a learning function that adjusts the sound according to the user's language habits and learning style. For instance, if a student is individualistic, the AI should use "he" and "she" instead of "they" in the teaching environment. If a student is not accustomed to close interpersonal relationships, the AI should enhance the sense of seriousness of the script. It is crucial to obtain the consent of users when learning more complex behaviors and habits to provide personalized services effectively.

Data Capture and Response. As an intelligent assistant, AIC recognizes the user's state to provide personalized feedback and adjustments accordingly.

Data Capture. With the user's consent, the system captures and analyzes the user's facial features and voice information through the camera and microphone to recognize their emotions based on their facial expression, movement, tone, eye movement, and head movement, shown in Fig. 3.

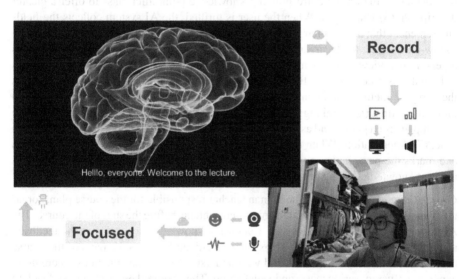

Fig. 3. The data capture and interaction mode.

Real-Time Feedback. The system modifies the teaching method according to real-time feedback and after-school feedback from students. The main interaction modes are shown in Fig. 3. The system gives real-time feedback to users based on their emotions and attention. By combining the information capture function, it provides personalized feedback. For instance, when the user's attention is low, the system raises its voice tone and sends out a reminder, or when the user is frustrated with their learning, the system's voice tone becomes gentle and encourages the user. The AI can then respond to the user's state in the following ways, as shown in Fig. 4:

(1) Sleepiness: When the user is feeling sleepy, the AI system recognizes their state and reminds them through voice to take appropriate breaks and rest if possible. (2)

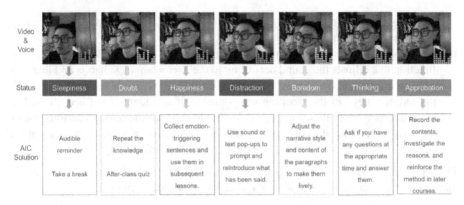

Fig. 4. Facial emotion recognition and feedback.

Doubt: When the user is puzzled, the AI teacher repeats the previous knowledge point or provides a quiz on the corresponding knowledge point after class to offer a clearer description. (3) Happiness: When the user is thrilled, the AI system collects the fields and sentences that trigger their emotions and strengthens similar teaching methods in the follow-up courses. (4) Distraction: When the user is distracted, the AI system prompts a general overview of the content just discussed using voice or text pop-up windows to help the user connect. (5) Boredom: When the user is bored, the AI system adjusts the narrative methods and content of corresponding paragraphs to make it livelier and more interesting. (6) Thinking: When the user is thinking, the AI system allows them to contemplate for a period and asks if they have any thoughts or doubts after an appropriate time. (7) Approbation: When the user expresses approbation, the AI system identifies and marks the paragraphs in which the user expressed their approval, and strengthens relevant knowledge points or teaching methods in subsequent courses.

Course Content Adjustment. The human teacher responsible for the course plans, organizes, and supervises the knowledge points and contents before the start of the course. The AI system adjusts the key nodes and structure of knowledge according to the feedback and opinions of human teachers. The system intelligently marks the parts of the course that are difficult, easy to confuse, and well understood based on situations where users express confusion, seriousness, and satisfaction. The system then provides feedback to the human teachers through marked key paragraphs for adjustment. The feedback considers whether to adjust the explanation method or increase knowledge points, presented in Fig. 5.

Reward. As an AI teaching assistant, AIC should not only provide support to students during the course, but also offer timely positive feedback and rewards after the course. This includes recording and providing feedback on classroom concentration, class participation, after-class feedback, and other relevant information. Specific actions include:

(1) Encouragement and appreciation. Real-time recording of students' course concentration and class participation, followed by encouragement or score bonuses for consistent high-concentration behavior. Additionally, the system should record student

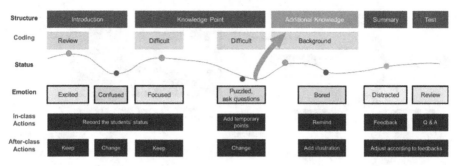

Fig. 5. Real-time feedback and course content adjustment.

feedback and needs, and thank them for effective feedback, which will be reflected in their feedback and grades.

(2) Other rewards. To implement the action of providing rewards for concentration and contribution, AIC could incorporate a point system into the online learning platform, awarding points for consistent high concentration and active participation in class discussions. These points could then be redeemed for various rewards, such as access to exclusive study materials, personalized feedback from instructors, or even discounts on future courses.

(3) Participatory classroom. AIC could also collect student feedback and suggestions after each class. The system could analyze the feedback and identify areas where the course could be improved, and then incorporate these changes into future classes. Students who provide effective feedback could be noted as contributors to the class. By offering timely positive feedback and rewards, AIC can motivate students to stay engaged and committed to their online learning journey.

In-Class Status Record and Feedback. The product should record and summarize students' learning status, which will enable students to reflect on their performance and teachers to adjust course content according to the students' needs. After class, the system should provide users with a detailed report on their class status, including emotional state, class participation, question answering, unfamiliar knowledge points, and other relevant information. This will facilitate user review and reflection. Additionally, the system should evaluate and rank students' classroom participation, enthusiasm, answer accuracy, and other indicators. It should also sort out the doubts and questions raised by students throughout the course, providing feedback on key knowledge points. Finally, the system should provide different exercises to different users, asking them to repeat content related to their inattentive/snap time in the course to ensure their mastery of the material, as shown in Fig. 6.

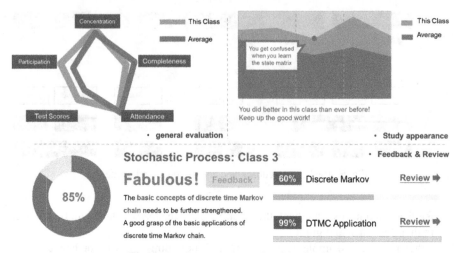

Fig. 6. In-class status record and feedback.

4 Conclusion

AIC aims to leverage AI and related technologies to enable students to unleash their full learning potential. In the era of cloud learning, AIC seeks to leverage the benefits of hardware devices, AI, intelligent algorithms, information collection, cloud computing, and other technologies to address the challenges of online courses and voice interaction, and provide personalized, real-time, and interactive learning experiences to all students.

While the application of AI in teaching systems requires careful consideration of both technological and ethical aspects, the research design offers innovative ideas for future developments in online teaching. It is anticipated that AI-assisted online teaching will soon reduce the labor cost of online education and provide personalized, interactive, and more widely accessible services to students.

References

1. Cooper, M., Keating, D., Harwin, W., Dautenhahn, K.: Robots in the classroom-tools for accessible education (1999)
2. Edwards, C., Edwards, A., Spence, P.R., Lin, X.: I, teacher: using artificial intelligence (AI) and social robots in communication and instruction. Commun. Educ. **67**(4), 473–480 (2018)
3. Kellermann, K.: Communication: inherently strategic and primarily automatic. Commun. Monogr. **59**(3), 288–300 (1992)
4. Vasagar, J.: How robots are teaching Singapore's kids. Financial Times (2017). https://www.ft.com/content/f3cbfada-668e-11e7-8526-7b38dcaef614
5. Kim, J., Yang, H., Kim, J.: Being social during the big dance: social presence and social TV viewing for March Madness in public and private platforms. Soc. Sci. J. **58**(2), 224–236 (2021)
6. Hughes, G.B.: Students' perceptions of teaching styles in mathematics learning environments. Math. Teach. Res. J. Online **3**(2), 1–12 (2009)

7. Wolhuter, S.: AI in education: how chatbots are transforming learning. WeAreBrain (2019). https://www.wearebrain.com/blog/ai-data-science/top-5-chatbots-in-education

8. Reeves, B., Nass, C.: The media equation: how people treat computers, television, and new media like real people. Cambridge, UK, vol. 10, p. 236605 (1996)

9. Edwards, A., Edwards, C., Westerman, D., Spence, P.R.: Initial expectations, interactions, and beyond with social robots. Comput. Hum. Behav. **90**, 308–314 (2019)

10. Guerin, B.: Social facilitation. Editions de la Maison des Sciences de l'Homme (1993)

Cross-Cultural Health and Wellness Design

Research on the Digital Memory Retention Service System for the Elderly–A Case Study of East China

Jiaru Chen[ID] and Jun Wu[✉][ID]

School of Art and Design, Division of Arts, Shenzhen University, Shenzhen 518061, Guangdong, People's Republic of China
2200505019@email.szu.edu.cn, junwu2006@hotmail.com

Abstract. Due to the rapid development of technology, multiple means of recording and sharing make the method of memory retention go beyond oral and handwritten. However, in contemporary times, many elderly people are excluded from the internet world due to the limitation of ability. The users of the existing memory retention service are mainly young people, while the elderly are in the phase of hard following. Older people are at a stage where they need the company of others, need to think about the meaning of life, and want to preserve their stories. Improving the degree of social participation of the elderly and meeting their spiritual needs of preserving life stories are also important ways to respond to the active aging policy. Today, China has become one of the countries with the largest elderly population in the world, and has been actively responding to the active aging policy for many years. By means of information collection and interview, this study discusses the current situation of the elderly using digital memory retention services, and intends to build a digital memory retention service system centered on the elderly group, hoping to contribute to the relevant researches on population aging and sociocultural sustainability.

Keywords: Memory Retention · the Elderly · Service Design · sociocultural sustainability · collective memory

1 Introduction

The contemporary world is characterized by informational flows and spread by the internet [1]. Information technology has dramatically changed the way we live and work. In the field of memory retention, it can be found that in addition to the traditional method of memory retention, more and more people begin to use audio and video to record their memories [2].

In the past, the main ways for the elderly in China to retain and share their personal memories are oral sharing and handwritten articles. Some publishing houses or private shops also offer the service of ghostwriting autobiographies. But now, With the help of their families, some elderly people choose to record videos and send them to online platforms, which are well received by young people. The contents shared by the elderly

P.-L. P. Rau (Ed.): HCII 2023, LNCS 14024, pp. 339–353, 2023.
https://doi.org/10.1007/978-3-031-35946-0_28

are mainly based on specific people, special places and important historical events which will become part of the collective memory of our society. The process of memory sharing involves many interactions between people and products. However, problems such as cumbersome function, difficult operation, less feedback and low sense of participation generally exist in these processes. Therefore, it is necessary to systematically analyze the process of digital memory retention from the perspective of service design.

The study uses service design strategies to analyze the psychological demands of the elderly when retaining digital memory and will finally build a digital memory retention service system to help the elderly retain and share life experiences. At the individual level, research on the retention of individual memory is an important step to meet the spiritual needs of the elderly and to realize the goal of active aging. At the collective level, it is also helpful for us to continue thinking about the sustainable development of social culture and collective memory in the future.

2 Background Summary of the Study

2.1 Current Situation of Elderly People Using Smart Devices

Theoretically, the development of information technology provides convenience and new possibilities for the lives of vulnerable groups [3–5]. In fact, we have to recognize that due to the generational differences, elder people use the Internet less frequently, they are left out by information technology [1, 3, 4]. Therefore, problems such as cumbersome process, being afraid of operation, less feedback and low sense of participation appear when the elderly use some memory retention technologies or services [6–8]. This study tries to analyze existing digital memory retention methods in China, and to build an optimized digital memory retention system for the elderly. By analyzing the process and willingness of the elderly using existing services, this study explores the possible ways to enhance the social participation of the elderly so as to improve the quality of their life.

2.2 Active Aging Policy in China

World Health Organization (WHO) described the goal of active aging in 2002 as the process of optimizing opportunities for health, participation and security in order to enhance quality of life as people age [9]. It also notes that these policies and programs should be based on the rights, needs, preferences, and capacities of older people. The core of "Active Ageing" lies in social participation [10]. Improving the social participation of the elderly can help the elderly gain dignity and meet their spiritual needs for the meaning of life.

Due to the actual national conditions, China has been actively responding and implementing the policy of active ageing [11, 12]. Nowadays, China has become one of the countries who have the largest elderly population in the world [13], and its aging population has entered a stage of rapid development. In China, by the end of 2021, the number of elderly people aged 60 and above has reached 267 million, accounting for 18.9% of the total population. It is estimated that in the near future, the total number of elderly people aged 60 and above will exceed 300 million, accounting for more than 20% of the total population [14]. At the same time, the number of Internet users in China and its Internet penetration are also increasing [15]. As of December 2021, the number of Internet users in China reached 1.032 billion, the number of elderly netizens aged 60 and over reached 119 million [16]. This means that more than half of the elderly in China are being left behind during the digital process, and are gradually marginalized due to the lack of voice in this digital society [17].

At the same time, with the rapid development of China's economic construction, the elderly gradually have spiritual needs for respect, self-realization and social identity under the premise that their material life is guaranteed [18], which are manifested as the needs for service design, sustainable design and technological intervention [17]. The East China not only has a high-speed economic and technological development, but also ranks in the forefront of the aging problem with an aging rate of over 14% in many provinces [19]. Therefore, studying problems in the process of digital memory retention service in East China can not only meet the spiritual needs of the elderly and expand their social participation, but also meet the needs of China's national conditions and provide reference experience for the global active aging.

2.3 The Significance of Digital Memory Retention for the Elderly

The aged like to retell or record their life stories and experiences. Recording helps the elderly to seek personal value. Meanwhile, sharing the content of the record is one of the ways in which the elderly can rebuild their connection with society. In 1925, Maurice Halbwachs, a French sociologist, enlarged individual memory to the level of social groups, he put forward the concept of collective memory: "The process and results of sharing past events among members of a specific social group" [21]. The transmission of collective memory requires social interaction, in which people can recall, identify, locate and analyze memories. Collective memory is not only a real story, but also a common sentiment and standard narrative formed by the group members. Nowadays, through some video websites, people can easily share their memories, so that memories can be preserved for a long time at the social level [5, 20].

3   Research Process Based on Service Design

3.1   Current Situation of Memory Retention Services for the Elderly

Most old people like to tell their stories to the younger generation, or even to tell stories of their elders, and so the memories continue through conversations from generation to generation. But this way of memory retention is not reliable, for some old people who have the ability to write or have the opportunity to get someone else to ghostwrite, paper and pencil records become a more reliable choice. Newspaper contributions and autobiographies can bring greater self-satisfaction to the elderly. Memories passed on by conversations focus more on inter-generational communications and the continuation of family memory, while the memories recorded by papers have the possibility of being widely shared due to its mass reproduction attribute, and have more chances to become a part of local chronicles and the social collective memory.

With the continuous improvement of the living condition, memory retention methods are constantly digitized. The emergence of cameras, mobile phones, computers, and Network Attached Storage has made memory storage more vivid and accurate while the media of memory has extended to pictures and images. At the same time, the development of short videos and social platforms has made the forms of memory sharing more extensive. On platforms commonly used by the young people, such as Bilibili, Tiktok and Weibo, there are also elderly people sharing their life stories who have a lot of fans, and their videos can reach one million views. However, because of their limited abilities, they may not be able to publish content without the help of their children. Besides, although many elderly people can use basic functions such as photography or video chat, they have limited ability to use content creation platforms, which forms a large digital divide between the elderly and the young people.

In this information society, the elderly are constantly marginalized and their social participation is constantly reduced. It is this digital divide that makes the social image of the elderly become lonely and silent. How to make their stories heard is what inspired this study. This study attempts to optimize and reconstruct the existing digital memory retention service system, hoping to connect this digital divide through system design, making memory retention a bridge to enhance inter-generational communication.

3.2 Research Framework of Digital Memory Retention Service Design

By designing service contact points between service providers and recipient, service design solves problems systematically [22]. Service design is user-centered and focuses

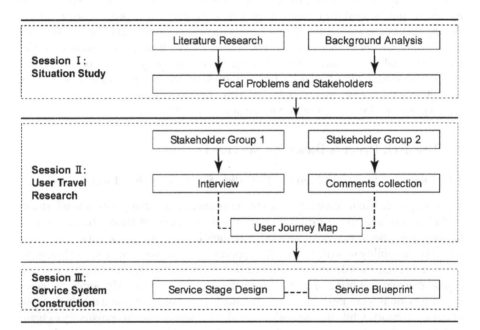

Fig. 1. The research framework of digital memory retention service system for the elderly.

on customers' behavior and situation [23]. It also needs to integrate products, processes and other key factors. Therefore, this study proposes a research framework (see Fig. 1).

3.3 Researches on Stakeholder Groups

Users of digital memory retention systems can be divided into older groups (recording subjects and memory sharing) and younger groups (assisting in recording, communicating and interacting). Among them, there are big differences in the elderly group's understanding of technology-related concepts and needs, and it is often difficult to match the feelings of the elderly with the scale data in the questionnaire when using quantitative research methods [24]. This study focuses on the spiritual needs of the elderly and hopes to build a content-oriented service system for emotional communication. Therefore, in the early research, communication with the elderly and site observation is essential. Therefore, this study mainly adopts the methods of in-depth interview and field observation to understand the preference of the elderly when using digital services to record life stories and to explore their desire to communicate and share with others. Finally, the study will summarize the experience from the results, so as to construct the overall service framework of memory retention service.

Interview Design and Implementation. According to the research purpose, several aspects of the interview outline were drawn up: the willingness to record and share their life stories; the preferred memory retention content and retention reasons; the use of digital memory retention methods and related services. This interview avoids overly formal communications, but chooses the form of daily chat to understand the life stories of the elderly and their views on communication with people and our society, so as to avoid making the elderly feel uncomfortable. After inviting 6 doctors in related majors to conduct group focus interviews, the interview outline of this study is determined as follows:

1. Is there anything you would like to share or record?
2. What kind of recording method do you usually choose when you record some ideas or events? Why?
3. Do you usually use photos, videos, notes, recordings and other ways to record your life? How does it feel?
4. Do you share your story with your relatives and friends? Why?
5. Do you share your stories with strangers and interact with others? Why?
6. If you want to design a service to help you record your life in the future, what would you recommend?

The Selection of Interviewees. According to the World Health Organization, people become elderly at the age of 60 [25]. The international standard for the starting age of the elderly in developing countries is 60 years old. With reference to international standards, people's physiological conditions and China's retirement age, China's Law on the Protection of the Rights and Interests of the Elderly stipulates that the starting age of the elderly is 60 years old [26]. Therefore, in East China, 10 people aged 60 and above were selected for this paper. The following Table 1 gives a summary of the interviewees' information.

Table 1. Summary of 10 interviewees' information

Interviewee	Gender	Age (years)	Professional field
A1	Woman	61	Liberal art
A2	Woman	62	Science
A3	Woman	63	Engineering
A4	Woman	68	Others
A5	Woman	78	Engineering
A6	Woman	87	Liberal art
A7	Man	60	Art
A8	Man	60	Science
A9	Man	62	Art
A10	Man	68	Others

Analysis of Interview Results. In order to better connect individual memory, to condense collective memory, and to build a content-oriented digital memory retention service system, it is necessary to understand the elder's willingness to record and share as well as their preference for the content they want to record. The first topic of the interview was: Is there anything you would like to share or record? By observing and recording the content the aged chose to talk about, the experimenter summarized the topic and sorted out the results as shown in the following Table 2.

Table 2. The willingness of the elderly to record and share.

Interviewee	Age	Professional field	willingness to record	willingness to share	Chat topic
A1	61	Liberal art	√	√	Daily life/Career related/Food
A2	62	Science	√	X	Daily life/Career related/Travel
A3	63	Engineering	√	√	Plants/Travel/Food
A4	68	Others	√	√	Daily life
A5	78	Engineering	√	√	Plants/Music/News
A6	87	Liberal art	√	√	Daily life/News
A7	60	Art	√	√	Plants/Music
A8	60	Science	√	√	Daily life/Career related

(*continued*)

Table 2. (*continued*)

Interviewee	Age	Professional field	willingness to record	willingness to share	Chat topic
A9	62	Art	√	√	Career related
A10	68	Others	√	X	Plants/Travel

√: Yes, X: No

As can be seen from Table 2, all the interviewees have things they want to record. But there are two of them say they have nothing to share. A2 indicates that "I don't like to share because of my personality"; A10 stands for "What do I have to share, what do I have to share at my age". Among the topics recorded/shared by the ten old people, the theme with the highest frequency is Daily life (A1, A2, A4, A6, A8), followed by Plants (A3, A5, A7, A10) and Career related (A1, A2, A8, A9). It can be seen that although some elderly people are not good at sharing with others due to personality reasons, most of them are willing to record their personal stories and share them with others, and the topics they are willing to record/share are mainly related to daily life stories, plant planting and career experiences.

In order to understand the recording methods preferred by the elderly and to know their feelings about using the existing digital memory retention services, the second topic of the interview was: What kind of recording methods do you usually choose when you record some ideas or events? Why? And the third topic was: Do you usually use photos, videos, notes, recordings and other ways to record your life? How does it feel? The interview results are shown in Table 3 below.

As can be seen from Table 3, all the ten interviewed old people have experience in using digital memory retention service, and two of them have the habit of keeping paper records. Among the ten interviewees, only one (A4) mentioned that she seldom uses relevant apps because of her poor eyesight. She only uses functions such as taking photos, sending and receiving text messages. All the other elderly people have experience in using relevant applications, among which six elderly people (A1, A2, A3, A6, A8, A9) have clear positive comments on this, and think that the existing corresponding services are convenient and fast, which can connect with others and enrich their lives. Four of the ten old people (A5, A7, A8, A10) answered that the convenience of using relevant services depends on whether they learn to use relevant services, indicating that the elderly need others to teach them relevant operations.

Table 3. The memory retention methods of the elderly interviewed

Interviewee	Hand-write	Digital service	Feelings of using existing digital memory retention services
A1	X	Camera Wechat	simple, quick, fun, and can give full play to their creativity

(*continued*)

Table 3. (*continued*)

Interviewee	Hand-write	Digital service	Feelings of using existing digital memory retention services
A2	X	Camera	improve your mental agility and enrich yourself
A3	X	Camera Wechat	fast, realistic, fashionable and convenient
A4	√	Camera Message	bad eyes, hard to see, amuse oneself
A5	X	Camera Wechat	can't use certain functions sometimes, want someone to teach me how to operate it
A6	√	Camera Wechat	can connect with my friends and get to know each other
A7	X	Recording Camera	feel very convenient only if you understand
A8	X	Camera Website	feel convenient to use, because I know all about it
A9	X	Camera Wechat	for casual use and to learn something
A10	√	Camera Wechat	to pass the time, I would use it if I was taught

√: Yes, X: No

In addition to memory recording, memory sharing in daily social interaction is also one of the important forms of memory retention. In the Internet community, memory recording and sharing are often inseparable. Therefore, in order to further explore the elder's attitude towards memory sharing, Questions 4 and 5 are set to understand the elder's use of memory sharing services. The interview results are shown in Table 4.

Table 4. Memory sharing methods of the elderly interviewed

Interviewee	Share with friends and family	Share with strangers	Interviewee	Share with friends and family	Share with strangers
A1	√	√	A6	√	X
A2	X	X	A7	√	√
A3	√	X	A8	√	√
A4	√	X	A9	√	X
A5	√	X	A10	√	√

√: Yes, X: No

As can be seen from Table 4 only one (A2) of the ten interviewed old people did not share their thoughts with others, and said, "I have seen many classmates and friends post their life photos and life experiences on the platform, I also like to see their works, but I never post my works, maybe because of personality reasons, I do not like to send out, they are all private. Maybe everyone thinks differently. I'm very conservative." Other elderly people are willing to share, mainly with family and friends. Four elderly people are willing to post on the platform, because "anyway, it is a public platform, and anyone who likes to watch it can watch it". Other elderly people only share with people they know, mainly because of "fear of being cheated when communicating with strangers".

At the end of the interview, the sixth topic is set as: If you want to design a service to help you record your life in the future, what are your suggestions? To ask the elderly to provide relevant advice on this type of service. Most of the old people think that their imagination is not enough to make any good suggestions, but they hope to follow the young people's thinking to adapt to more advanced services, while also show that "simple functions are good". Some old people also mentioned that they hoped we can improve the security and reliability of the service and protect personal privacy (A1); It is hoped that the platform will punish those who use the service maliciously, and will create a good network community environment (A7), they also hope that someone can provide corresponding use instructions (A10).

3.4   Existing Digital Memory Retention Service Process for the Elderly

According to the results of the above researches, the user journey map of the memory retention service for the elderly is drawn (see **Error! Reference source not found.**). It can be found that there are many problems in this service process that need to be considered in the subsequent framework design.

The Need for Operational Instruction. According to the above research, the elderly usually use photos, videos and other ways to record their lives. For them, simple operations can be mastered, but there are still many functions they do not understand and cannot use without learning. This is because the existing digital memory retention services mainly serve young people, and the elderly are in the stage of following the younger group to use the services, so the use of the services is extremely limited. In the process of interview, many old people mentioned that they must learn to operate conveniently, and hoped that they could learn from young people, while the young people also expressed their encouragement and admiration for the old people's active learning of new things.

Intergenerational Communication and Digital Feedback. Elderly people are willing to share their stories with their families and friends. Many young people also say that they like to hear stories shared by experienced elder people, they are also willing to help and support the elderly in actions. This suggests that memory retention within the family has a positive effect on inter-generational communication, and inter-generational communication also promotes digital feedback, which facilitates memory retention (Fig. 2).

Requirements on the Form of Content Sharing. Some older people with more open personalities will share their videos and ask for suggestions for improvement when they

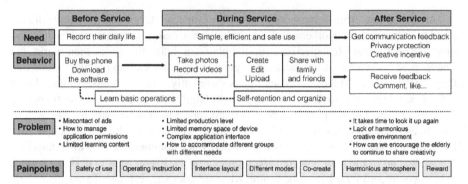

Fig. 2. Existing digital memory retention service process for the elderly.

are interviewed. After observation, it can be found that many of the content recorded by the elderly is interesting, but the video production is slightly rough. Due to the decline of their physical function, it is impossible to ask them to improve the editing of daily recorded videos. However, the improvement of video form is helpful for video transmission and sharing. This can also be seen from the comments of the young people, nowadays, a part of the young audience is very strict with the video created by the elderly.

The Overall Atmosphere and Security of the Service. In addition, the elderly also mentioned in the interview that they could not judge whether they could trust the platform, and the creation environment of the existing platform was not friendly enough. These issues are also reflected in the survey of young people. In the process of subsequent service design, it is necessary to consider how to provide a safe and friendly creation environment for the retention of old people's memory.

4   Digital Memory Retention Service Design for the Elderly

4.1   The System Map of the Digital Memory Retention Service for the Elderly

The personal stories recorded by the elderly are a memorial to themselves and their families; The life experience shared by the elderly is a spiritual wealth that can enlighten more people. The gap in the use of new media leads to the gap between the elderly and the young in digital application, which in turn leads to the difference in identification between different age groups. By building a content-oriented service system (see Fig. 3), the digital memory retention service system for the elderly establishes a flexible feedback mechanism at family, social and other levels, breaks through the barrier of time, promotes inter-generational understanding and reflection, and re-establishes emotional connection.

A System Centered on Older Users. In addition, the elderly also mentioned in the. The platform carries out early publicity and promotion by releasing the produced toolkits or user manuals to different communities. As the main target of the service, the elderly can use existing smart devices to photograph, to record or to scan their handwriting.

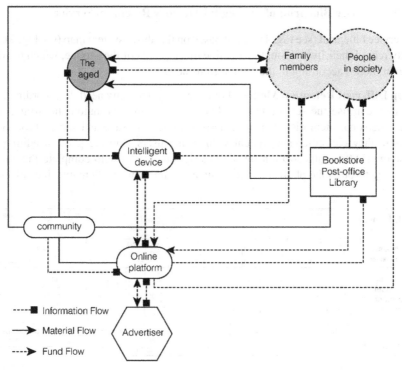

Fig. 3. System map of the digital memory retention service for the elderly.

After that, they can choose to retain or publish it. The online server will display the easily processed information to the user, and will also classify different information into different topics for the convenience of subsequent indexing.

The Two-Sided Identity of the Young Group. The identities of the young people in the system are not only the relatives of the elderly, but also ordinary people in the society. They are not only the family members who help the elderly to complete the memory retention, but also the strangers who use the service to learn more about the life stories of the elderly.

The System Connects Elderly Users with Our Society. With the consent and authorization of the elderly and their relatives, the system collects and processes a large number of elderly user information, forms an information network according to their relationships, and displays them in the form of physical books, newspapers, audio and video in offline scenes such as bookstores and post offices for publicity. At the same time, such physical objects edited by the system will also be mailed to the corresponding elderly. Relevant users can also view the audio, video and e-book edition at any time through the application.

4.2   The Service Blueprint of the Digital Memory Retention Service

The service blueprint (see Fig. 4) is built based on the above system map (see Fig. 3). The elderly record their lives through the online touch points of the service, which provides different modes according to the their various need.

Set Up Different Retention Modes. For the elderly who only need the recording function, they can use the service to complete the recording and automatic arrangement of their personal memories. For the elderly who need to save and share, through this platform, they can co-create content with young users who are good at editing and typesetting. After authorization by the elderly, others can help complete the content processing through the platform, and obtain a certain number of creative incentives.

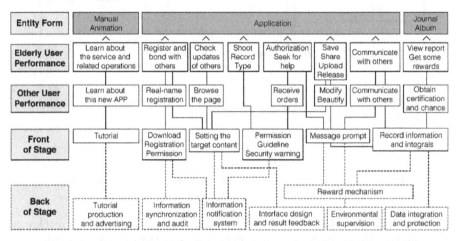

Fig. 4. Service blueprint of the digital memory retention service for the elderly.

Build Opportunities to Realize Intergenerational Communications. As a content-oriented system, it completes the social retention process of old people's memory by constructing the opportunity of intergenerational communication. On the online end, the system needs to build an opportunity for the elderly to narrative, and encourage the elderly group to record their personal lives through the guidance of themes and templates, such as guiding the elderly to answer specific help, share experiences about specific professional fields, and describe memories related to specific events.

In offline scenes, the system needs to create opportunities for young people to get to know this service through publicity. In this process, marketing advertisements and publicity of social activities are needed. It can cooperate with public places such as bookstores and libraries to set up experience centers which may help young people learn professional skills and life experience.

5 Conclusion

In the past, the pen-and-paper form of memory recording often required a lot of effort and was not suitable for most elderly people. The existing digital memory retention service makes memory not only exist in words and papers, but also exist in audio and videos which are easy to spread. It even gives rise to many "the elderly online celebrities", which narrows the social distance between the elderly and the young. These phenomena also reflect individuals' desire for socialization and spiritual survival.

This research is inspired by these social phenomena. Through the interview survey of the elderly in East China and the analysis of the comments of young people on the Internet, the study made the following conclusions:

1. The elderly themselves have the need to retain memories, and their memories also constitute the collective memory of this society in a certain time and space.
2. Existing memory retention services are mainly for young people, and the elderly will follow the young people in the family to use simple functions.
3. The elderly people are not resistant to the use of electronic products. They may be very willing to use such fashionable tools, but lack of opportunities to learn, so they encounter many difficulties, and then feel shy, at a loss or even intimidated.
4. For the elderly people who use memory retention services, most of them use such services to communicate with their family members and leave memorials to their family members. Therefore, they are concerned about the storage space of the phone, the subsequent arrangement, whether it is convenient to find later and whether these electronic documents can be in physical forms.
5. For the elderly people who are willing to communicate their stories with the society, good communication atmosphere and how to attract more people to read their stories are their concerns, which is also closely related to the young people in the society. According to the results of our survey, there are still a small number of young people who are too harsh on these old people who are willing to communicate.

According to the above content, the study constructs the concept of the service system. This study involves inter-generational communication, family emotion, and preservation of human intangible cultural heritage, and attempts to construct a memory retention service system centered on the elderly, hoping to be helpful to other studies in the field of cultural sustainability. This study only puts forward a new idea of memory retention service, and the number of elderly people surveyed is small. The specific details of the service process need to be further deepened in the future research.

References

1. Castells, M.: The Information Age: Economy, Society and Culture (3 volumes). Blackwell, Oxford (1998)
2. Ernst, W.: Digital Memory and the Archive (Vol. 39). U of Minnesota Press, Minneapolis (2012)
3. Norris, P.: Digital Divide: Civic Engagement, Information Poverty, and the Internet Worldwide (Communication, Society and Politics). Cambridge University Press, Cambridge (2001). https://doi.org/10.1017/CBO9781139164887

4. Kiel, J.M.: The digital divide: Internet and e-mail use by the elderly. Med. Inform. Internet Med. **30**(1), 19–23 (2005)
5. Reading, A.: Seeing red: a political economy of digital memory. Media Cult. Soc. **36**(6), 748–760 (2014)
6. Meuter, M.L., Ostrom, A.L., Bitner, M.J., Roundtree, R.: The influence of technology anxiety on consumer use and experiences with self-service technologies. J. Bus. Res. **56**(11), 899–906 (2003)
7. Lin, M.D.Y., Chuang, M.Y.: The predictability of age, working memory and computer attitude in learning an email system. Res. Appl. Psychol. **22**, 105–120 (2004)
8. Quan-Haase, A., Martin, K., Schreurs, K.: Interviews with digital seniors: ICT use in the context of everyday life. Inf. Commun. Soc. **19**(5), 691–707 (2016)
9. Active ageing: a policy framework. https://apps.who.int/iris/handle/10665/67215. Accessed 7 Feb 2023
10. Fang, J.Y.: How far is active aging from us – Thinking and exploration based on the spiritual needs of the elderly. J. Zhejiang Gongshang Univ. **36**(1), 126–136 (2022). https://doi.org/10.14134/j.cnki.cn33-1337/c.2022.01.013
11. Yang, H.: Micro research on the construction of suitable aging travel environment based on active aging strategy: a case study of Southwest Jiaotong University. Intellect **29**, 145–147 (2022)
12. Wang, L.: "Digital Legacy" and digital empowerment: the dilemma and outlet of technological ethics in the digital age. J. Kunming Univ. Sci. Technol. (Soc. Sci. Edn.) (2023)
13. Sun, J.: Research on the current situation, problems and countermeasures of the elderly's contact and use of smart media from the perspective of Digital Divide – Based on the investigation of the elderly's contact and use of smart media in Huzhou city. News Lovers (04), 31–34 (2021). https://doi.org/10.16017/j.cnki.xwahz.2021.04.008
14. Liu, C.R.: Healthy aging is the way that our country responds to aging of population with the lowest cost and best benefit. China Youth Daily, 012 (2022)
15. Chen, J.H., Wu, H.: Research on the way to bridge the digital divide of the elderly in the post epidemic era: theoretical perspective based on social support. Hubei Agric. Sci. **61**(2), 203–208 (2022)
16. Wu, X.L.: The number of Chinese netizens reaches 1.032 billion. China Consumer News, 003 (2022)
17. Shan, N., Zhang, F., Wang, T.: Research on the needs of elderly care design based on the perspective of life course and hierarchy of needs theory. Art Des. (Theory) (12), 36–38 (2020). https://doi.org/10.16824/j.cnki.issn10082832.2020.12.005
18. Xu, S.Y.: Investigation and suggestion on spiritual and cultural care for the elderly **009**(020), 371 (2019)
19. Lou, Y.X., Zhang, X.Q.: The impact of rural population aging on consumption structure and consumer price Index in East China: an empirical analysis based on data from 2010 to 2020. Collect. Rural Essays **01**, 91–97 (2022)
20. Garde-Hansen, J.: MyMemories?: personal digital archive fever and Facebook. Save as… Digit. Memories, 135–150 (2009). https://doi.org/10.1057/9780230239418_8
21. Morris, H., Bi, R., Guo, J.H.: On Collective Memory, pp. 68–69. Shanghai People's Publishing House (2002)
22. Qiang, Y., Yizi, C.: Research on the design of campus catering unmanned delivery system based on service design. Ind. Des. **2**, 26–27 (2021)
23. Editorial board of design: user experience design. Design **34**(03), 7 (2021)
24. Liu, Y., Zhong, F.: Elderly Life Inquiry Toolkit: Empathy Expanding in Elder-Friendly Technology Design. In: Rau, P.L.P. (ed.) Cross-Cultural Design. Applications in Business, Communication, Health, Well-being, and Inclusiveness, HCII 2022, vol. 13313, pp. 337–352. Springer, Cham (2022). https://doi.org/10.1007/978-3-031-06050-2_25

25. Ageing. https://www.who.int/health-topics/ageing#tab=tab_1. Accessed 7 Feb 2023
26. National People's Congress Internal Affairs Committee, & Department of Policies and Regulations, Ministry of Civil Affairs: Reading of Law of the People's Republic of China on the Protection of the Rights and Interests of the Elderly. Hualing Publishing House (2013)

A Pilot Study of Ring Fit Adventure Game System Applied to Upper Extremity Rehabilitation for Stroke

Mei-Hsiang Chen[1], Si Wai Mak[2], and Lan-Ling Huang[3]([✉])

[1] Chung Shan Medical University/Chung Shan Medical University Hospital, Taichung, Taiwan
[2] Chung Shan Medical University, Taichung, Taiwan
[3] Fujian University of Technology, Fuzhou, China
Lanlingh@gmail.com

Abstract. The intervention strategy of occupational therapy is to help stroke patients recover upper limb function and have the ability to live independently through meaningful activities. The Ring Fit Adventure gaming system is designed by the Nintendo Switch kicked off a wave of exercise craze. Whether the game system is suitable for upper extremity rehabilitation training for stroke patients remains to be further explored. Therefore, the purpose of this study is to conduct a preliminary study on the feasibility of the Switch Ring Fit Adventure gaming system applied to the upper extremity rehabilitation for stroke patients. Occupational therapist interviews and SUS usability assessments were used. The results can be summarized in three points: (1) Clinical OT experts selected 16 "Fitness Ring Adventure" fitness exercises that are suitable for stroke upper limb rehabilitation. (2) All stroke patients expressed their willingness to continue using it. (3) suggestions of new exercise game design are proposed. For example: Elbow and wrist movement, strength training, and single-handed training game. The results of this research can provide reference for the application of clinical upper extremity rehabilitation and game design industry.

Keywords: Feasibility · usability · Ring Fit Adventure Game System · upper extremity rehabilitation

1 Introduction

One of the three leading causes of death worldwide is cardiovascular disease (including ischemic heart disease, stroke) [1]. It is also one of the main causes of adult disability, not only causing a heavy burden on patients and caregivers, but also seriously affecting the quality of life [2]. "Stroke in young age is of great public health importance. The incidence has been increasing worldwide for decades," said Mohamed Teleb, MD, medical director of neurosciences at Banner Desert Medical Center. According to the Stroke Association in USA, 15% of all ischemic stroke cases occur in young people – those 18 to 55 years old [3]. The Helsinki Young Stroke Registry noted relatively low stroke rates under the age 40 with sharp increases beginning at age 40 [3]. Impairment

P.-L. P. Rau (Ed.): HCII 2023, LNCS 14024, pp. 354–365, 2023.
https://doi.org/10.1007/978-3-031-35946-0_29

of upper extremity movements is more common in stroke patients after stroke [4]. The decreasing age trend of stroke patients should reinforce the utility of rehabilitation and assist patients in regaining independent living and working ability.

With the development of technology, commercial virtual reality game systems (such as: Nintendo Wii, Kinect for XBOX360™, XaviX, Sony Play Station, HTC Vive, etc.) have been widely used in the upper limb rehabilitation treatment of clinical stroke patients. Many studies have found that virtual reality games can help improve the efficacy of upper limb rehabilitation and improve patients' enthusiasm for treatment [5–7].

Starting from virtual reality (VR), virtual reality exergaming (VR EXG) gradually enters people's lives through different modes such as Cardboard, home equipment, and various theme amusement parks. With the popularity of sports, exergames (e.g., Kinect for XBOX360™, Nintendo Switch, etc.) combined with sports training skills have become popular among the public. Among the Switch game consoles released by Nintendo, the game "Ring Fit Adventure" is the most popular and has set off a sports wave. This game requires a Switch Ring-Con. It combines a lot of resistance training, offers a variety of training modes, and can perform specific movements repeatedly. It is very suitable for upper limb exercise and muscle strength training for stroke patients.

Researches on the application of the Nintendo Switch Ring Fit Adventure game or Ring-Con to train physical actions were as follows: Kim et al. (2019) a new approach to transcranial direct current stimulation in improving cognitive motor learning and hand function with the Nintendo Switch in Stroke survivors [8]. The results showed that the tDCS (Transcranial direct current stimulation) + Nintendo Switch game group showed significant differences in Trail Making Test, Grip strength, Manual Function Test, and Box and Block Test results compared to the other groups between before and after intervention.

Putra et al. (2021) surveyed healthy men sequentially experiencing three "Fitness Boxing" Nintendo Switch™ game modes [9]: (1) single player-normal tempo, (2) single player-fast tempo and (3) versus. To investigate the immediate cardiovascular responses (blood pressure, heart rate), quantification of physical activity (PA) intensity (percentage of maximum heart rate (%HRmax), Borg's rating of perceived exertion (RPE), and the level of enjoyment using visual analog scale (VAS) while playing VR EXG. The results showed that VR EXG Nintendo Switch™ "Fitness Boxing" can elicit immediate cardiovascular responses and provides an enjoyable moderate to vigorous PA intensity in healthy male adults, and can be used to meet the weekly PA recommendations. However, there are very few clinical studies on the feasibility of using the Switch fitness ring game system in upper limb rehabilitation treatment for stroke patients, and further trials are needed to confirm.

A pilot study was designed to evaluate the feasibility of the Switch Ring Fit Adventure (RFA) game system used in upper extremity (UE) rehabilitation training. The results of the study are expected to help stroke patients recover from exercise and meet the needs of rehabilitation for stroke patients.

2   Methods

This study includes two stages, as follows: (1) Expert interview was used to assess the suitability of the RFA fitness exercises, and the usage needs of the RFA game system used for UE rehabilitation. (2) A System Usability scales questionnaire was used to evaluate the usability of the RFA game system. This study was approved by the Human Research Ethics Board of a local hospital.

2.1   Stage 1: Suitability of the RFA Fitness Exercises for UE Therapy

Expert interview was used in this stage. Three survey contents were conducted as follows: (1) Occupational therapists (OTs) were asked to experience various fitness exercises in RFA game system. (2) According to the Brunnstrom recovery stages for upper extremity (stage IV and stage V), OTs selected the fitness exercises were suitable for stroke patients. These selected fitness exercises were used for system usability evaluation in the next research stage.

Participants. The target sample for this stage was recruited from therapists working in the hospital's OT department in Taiwan. They have more than three years of full-time occupational therapy work experience.

Devices. The equipment used in this stage were as follows: the RFA game system (a total of 60 fitness exercises, including 43 fit skills, 12 minigames, and 5 simple games) with Switch Ring-Con and Leg strap (see Fig. 1). All the fitness exercises in RFA game were selected under specialist supervision (Japanese yoga instructor Kaoru Matsui and Mika Saiki). A variety of exercise styles in fit skills are available, including muscular, rhythm and yoga, and different areas of the body can be targeted – arms, stomach, legs and more.

Procedures. First, the researchers explained the purpose of this survey to the OTs and asked for their consent. Before the interview, the OTs were asked to operate and experience each fitness exercises. OTs selected and categorized fitness exercises suitable for upper extremity rehabilitation based on their specialty in occupational therapy.

During the experience process, the therapist also proposed usage needs or suggestions about the usability of the game system. After summarizing survey data under researchers, OTs were asked to identify these fitness exercises that had been categorized again.

Nintendo Switch Console   Nintendo Switch dock   Switch Ring Fit Adventure   Switch Ring-Con and Leg Strap (middle)

Fig. 1. Hardware and accessories for Switch Ring Fit Adventure game system

2.2   Stage 2: Usability of the RFA Game System for UE Rehabilitation

Based on the selected fitness exercises in the previous stage, two surveys are performed: (1) To observe usage status of the Nintendo Switch RFA game system used for stroke patients. (2) A system usability scale (SUS) questionnaire was used to investigate the usability of the Nintendo Switch RFA game system.

Usage Status of the Switch RFA Game System Used by Stroke Patient. When stroke patients used the Switch RFA game system, the researchers observe the patient's movements and operating behaviors to discover potential usage problems or needs. To minimize distraction from the patient, the researchers observed the patient using the devices from their side.

Participants. Stroke patients were recruited from occupational therapy department of hospitals in Taiwan. Inclusion criteria were as follows: (a) hemiparesis with UE dysfunction following a single unilateral stroke; (b) a history of first-time stroke (6–48 months post-stroke); (c) a need for UE rehabilitation to convalescent stages of Brunnstrom stages IV to V; and (d) ability to communicate, and to understand and follow instructions. Exclusion criteria were as follows: (a) engagement in any other rehabilitation studies during the study; and (b) serious aphasia or cognitive impairment. Each patient gave informed consent.

Devices. The Switch Ring-Con, Leg strap and the Nintendo Switch RFA game system were used in this stage. These fitness exercises used in this stage were already assessed by the clinical occupational therapist in the previous stage.

Procedures. First, the researchers explained the content of the research at this stage to the occupational therapists, and informed that the camera recording process would be used during the research. Occupational therapists introduced willing and eligible stroke patients to the researchers. Researchers explained the content of the research to the stroke patients. Each patient gave informed consent. All stroke patients were asked to complete a total of 3 training sessions in two weeks, scheduled at three 30-min sessions (excluding set-up time). During the 3 training courses, the patients were required to experience from installing the equipment to completing 16 fitness exercises. The researchers observed the patient's movements of using the Switch fitness ring device to interact with the game each time.

Usability of the Switch RFA Game System Used by Stroke Patient. Semi-structured interviews were used to investigate the usability of the Switch RFA game system for UE rehabilitation by stroke patients.

Participants. Stroke patients who had completed the Switch RFA game system over 3 sessions. (Same participants in 2.2.1).

Devices. The System Usability Scale (SUS) questionnaire [10] was applied in this research. The System Usability Scale is a standardized metric for measuring the usability of a website or other interactive system. SUS uses a short (see Table 1), 10-item questionnaire administered at the end of a usability test to calculate a website's score. Users respond to each question on a 5-point scale from "Strongly disagree" to "Strongly

Table 1. 10-item questionnaire of the System Usability Scale

S1	I think that I would like to use this system frequently
S2	I found the system unnecessarily complex
S3	I thought the system was easy to use
S4	I think that I would need the support of a technical person to be able to use this system
S5	I found the various functions in this system were well integrated
S6	I thought there was too much inconsistency in this system
S7	I would imagine that most people would learn to use this system very quickly
S8	I found the system very cumbersome to use
S9	I felt very confident using the system
S10	I needed to learn a lot of things before I could get going with this system

agree." These answers are then used to generate an extremely reliable overall usability score for the system.

Procedures. After completing 3 sessions, the patients filled out the SUS questionnaire. The researchers explained each question of the questionnaire to the stroke patients. They are asked to answer questions one by one based on their experience after use.

Data Analysis. The collected data were analyzed with an SPSS statistical software. To calculate the SUS score [11], first sum the score contributions from each item. Each item's score contribution will range from 0 to 4. For items 1, 3, 5, 7, and 9 the score contribution is the scale position minus 1. For items 2, 4, 6, 8 and 10, the contribution is 5 minus the scale position. To achieve a total score of 100, multiply the sum of the scores by 2.5 to obtain the overall value. It provides an easy-to-understand score from 0 (negative) to 100 (positive). The usability subscale has 8 items, and its score ranges from 0 to 32, so the multiplier is 100 divided by 32, which is 3.125. Similarly, for the learnability scale, a multiplier of 12.5 (100 divided by 8) is obtained.

3   Results

Three results were showed as follows:

(1) The suitability of the RFA fitness exercises, and usage needs of Switch RFA game system for UE rehabilitation by OTs.
(2) Usability of the Switch RFA game system used by stroke patient.

3.1   Suitability of the RFA Game System for UE Rehabilitation

A total of 5 clinical occupational therapists were interviewed. All of them have clinical OT worked for more than 5 years and were recruited from the Occupational Therapy Department of Chung Shan Medical University Hospital in Taiwan.

The Result of the RFA Fitness Exercises Suitable for UE Rehabilitation. A total of 16 fitness exercises were selected under OT therapists as suitable for stroke patients whose UE recovery stage reaches IV and V. Among 16 fitness exercises, 8 fitness exercises (see Table 2, left side) were suggested for the UE recovery stage IV, and the other 8 games (see Table 2, right side) were suggested for the UE recovery stage V. The fitness exercises in Table 2 are sorted from easy to difficult, according to the therapist's suggestion.

Table 2. A total of 16 fitness exercises are suitable for UE rehabilitation

Brunnstrom Stage of UE	Stages IV		Stages V	
Types of fitness exercise	Game name (Exercise style)	Game screen	Game name (Exercise style)	Game screen
Fit skills	a1. Standing twist* (Rhythm)		b1. Warrior II pose* (Yoga)	
	a2. Chair pose* (Yoga)		b2. Overhead arm spin* (Rhythm)	
	a3. Front Press* (Muscular)		b3. Overhead arm twist* (Rhythm)	
	a4. Bow pull* (Muscular)		b4. Overhead Press* (Muscular)	
	a5. Overhead side bend* (Muscular)		b5. Warrior II pose (Yoga)	
Minigames	a6. Crate crasher*		b6. Squattery wheel*	
	a7. Smack back*		b7. Bootstrap tower*	
	a8. Rhythm games*		b8. Robo-wrecker*	

* Accessorial tool is available: bandage..

Usage Needs of the Switch RFA Game System Proposed by OTs. After the fitness exercises experience (see Fig. 2), the OTs proposed six usage needs of the RFA game system be applied to UE rehabilitation. Six usage needs are characteristics of stroke patients, game interface design, controller design, assistive devices, data display, and new practice game design. Each usage needs are described as follows:

Patient Characteristics. Considering the physical characteristics and safety of stroke patients, the suitable physical conditions are proposed as follows: (A) having good cognitive ability. (B) It is necessary to consider that the patient's attention is weak. (C) The endurance of hand grip strength should be enough. (D) The game is played in a standing: the dynamic balance should be at least fair or good.

Game Interface Design. (A) After the demonstration teaching of body motions, to provide opportunities for practice for user. (B) When user cannot complete an action, he/her hope that a screen will pop up and guide the next step. (C) If a fitness exercise cannot be completed, to suggest secondary games for user. (D) It is suggested to present only one motion guide at the same time in the interface to avoid interference. (E) Adjustable game description speed. (F) The text on the game interface should be larger. (G) The content of the interface should be clearer, for example: color and black and white should be used together. When it is important, it will jump out as a colored indicator, while others will become black and white, to reduce cognitive interference. (H) The reaction speed of the game can be adjusted to suit for middle-aged and elderly people.

Controllers. *Switch ring-con.* (A) When using the Switch Ring-Con to turn left and right to a standard angle, it is recommended to provide a vibration prompt to complete. (B) The resistance is recommended to be adjustable by user. (C) The size of the buttons needs to be enlarged so that patients can easily operate them with the affected hand. (D) The actions of all operating functions can be simplified to a single controller. For example: the rotation, pressure or pulling action of the Switch Ring-Con can correspond to all operating functions. *Leg strap.* The binding is set on the leg needs to be redesigned to avoid slipping and being too tight to be comfortable when exercising.

Fig. 2. Occupational therapists using the RFA game system in therapy room.

Assistive Devices. (A) Using assistive devices (bandages, gloves) to assist patients with lower stages to hold Switch Ring-Con or design special bandages. (B) If it is necessary to change the left or right hand, you can add Velcro to assist in the removal or replacement.

Results Recorded. Since clinical treatment emphasizes treatment effect, training results are expected to correspond to activities of daily living.

New Exercises Game Design. (A) Fitness exercises for elbow and wrist movement and strength. (B) Adding one-handed fitness exercises.

3.2 Usability of the Switch RFA Game System Used by Stroke Patient

A total of 10 post-stroke patients were recruited from the Occupational Therapy Department of Chung Shan Medical University Hospital. One female and nine males, the mean age was 64.20 years (SD 6.05), and the mean time since stroke onset was 1.28 years (SD 0.65). Three patients had paretic side on the left side and the others on the right. After 3 training sessions, the patients used the equipment by themselves, and finally the patients filled out the questionnaire.

Result of System Usability Scale. A total of 10 SUS questionnaires were analysed. With regards to the overall SUS score reported by participants for the RFA game (see Fig. 3), the overall mean SUS score was 67.75 (SD 5.70) out of 100, which according to the evaluation criteria for SUS, indicates that the application delivers 'OK' (Descriptive adjective), 'High marginal' (Acceptability range), and Grade D (School grading scale) usability (see Fig. 4). These results indicate that the RFA game system design is feasible for UE rehabilitation. Among the 10 items of SUS (see Table 1), S4 and S10 belong to Learnability, and the other 8 items (S1, S2, S3, S5, S6, S7, S8, S9) belong to Usability. The overall mean SUS score of Learnability was 50.0 (SD 23.57) out of 100. The overall mean SUS score for Usability was 72.18 (SD 7.43) out of 100. Switch RFA game system used by the patients shown in Fig. 5.

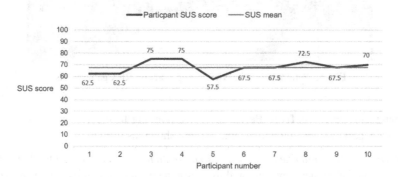

Fig. 3. SUS score of the RFA game system for each stroke patient.

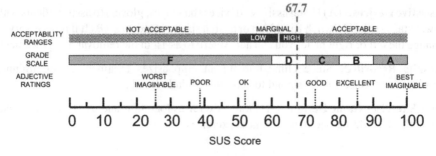

Fig. 4. Grades, adjectives, and acceptability associated with raw SUS scores.

Fig. 5. Patient using the Switch ring-con and RFA game items.

Experienced Opinions from Patients. Corresponding to the 10 questions from the SUS scale, patients presented their opinions are shown as follows:

Regarding "I would like to use this system frequently" (S1). The results showed that 9 patients indicated that they were willing to use the device frequently, and were willing to buy it and continue to use it at home.

Regarding "the unnecessary complexity of this system" (S2). One patient said that the actions and operation steps were relatively complicated. The other 9 patients thought that they could learn it more times and could operate independently.

Regarding "the ease of use of the system" (S3). 8 patients indicated that the system was not difficult to operate. The problem they encountered was that when selecting game items or menus, it was difficult for them to control the force steadily in one position, causing the indicator to fail to accurately stay on the selected option.

Regarding "the assistance of technicians to use this system" (S4). It was found that 6 patients felt that it would be better to have help from the therapist or family members to install the TV equipment, and it would be easier to understand how to operate it. The other 3 patients indicated that they did not need assistance and could operate according to the instructions of the game.

Regarding "I found the various functions in this system were well integrated" (S5). All patients considered the system to be well-integrated. The reason is that the upper and lower limbs can be trained at the same time, and there are also different game modes for diversified training.

Regarding "I thought there was too much inconsistency in this system" (S6). 5 patients said that the system operation is relatively consistent, and it is easy to operate after getting familiar with it. Another patient pointed out that there would be confusion and not knowing how to use it, for example: the fitness ring sometimes needs to be held vertically, or sometimes it needs to be held horizontally.

Regarding "most people will learn to use the system quickly" (S7). 9 patients agreed that they could learn to use it quickly.

Regarding the system is very cumbersome to use (S8). All patients thought that the operation was not cumbersome.

Regarding "I felt very confident using the system" (S9). The results indicated that all patients felt very confident using the system.

Regarding "I need to learn a lot of things before I start using this system" (S10). 2 patients thought that the preparatory work should be completed more smoothly under the guidance of the trainer, and they had difficulty reading the screen to complete the operation by themselves. The other 7 patients thought that they could learn it by following the instructions of the instructor in the game, and they were willing to learn and use it by themselves.

Summarizing the results of the SUS assessment and the participants' experiential comments, the following three findings can be presented: (A) Patients responded positively to the usability of the RFA gaming system and were willing to continue using it for upper extremity rehabilitation. (B) Patients rated the learnability of the RFA game system as moderate with varying grades of response. It may be that the patient is relatively unfamiliar with this device, and feels that there are many objects to learn or it is difficult to use it independently. (C) Some patients expressed their willingness to purchase the device for rehabilitation training at home, which provides a new reference for future game design and development.

4 Conclusion

This study aims to evaluate the feasibility of using the Ring Fit Adventure in the upper extremity rehabilitation treatment of stroke patients. This paper reports the results of the usability of the RFA game system for UE rehabilitation. Expert interviewing to professional occupational therapists about the applicability of the RFA game system and usage needs. A questionnaire survey to stroke patients about the usability of the RFA game system. In summary, the following points can be concluded:

(1) It is feasible for the RFA game system to be applied to upper extremity rehabilitation, and stroke patients have a high positive response on usability. With regards to the overall SUS score reported by participants for the RFA game, the overall mean SUS score was 67.75 (SD 5.70) out of 100. The overall mean SUS score for Usability was 72.18 (SD 7.43) out of 100.
(2) The game interface design suggestions for stroke patients are as follows: (A) When a certain action cannot be completed, the patient hopes to pop up a screen to guide the next step. (C) If a game cannot be completed, suggest that a secondary game is required. (D) The game's action description speed can be adjusted. (F) The content of the game interface should be clearer, for example: use color and black and white together to highlight key actions.
(3) New fitness exercises design. The types of exercise can be added are: (A) Elbow and wrist movements and strength training. (B) one-hand exercises.

The results of this study provide evidence as a decision-making basis for clinical rehabilitation doctors and therapists, open the integration of clinical treatment and emerging technologies, and provide reference for medical development and virtual reality game design related industries.

Acknowledgment. This study is supported by the National Science and Technology Council with grant No: MOST 111-2221-E-0400-007.

References

1. World Health Organization: https://www.who.int/zh/news-room/fact-sheets/detail/the-top-10-causes-of-death. Accessed 13 Dec 2021
2. Hatem, S.M., et al.: Rehabilitation of motor function after stroke: a multiple systematic review focused on techniques to stimulate upper extremity recovery. Front. Hum. Neurosci. **10**, 442 (2016)
3. George, M.G.: Risk factors for ischemic stroke in younger adults a focused update. Stroke **51**, 729–735 (2020)
4. Gowland, C., DeBruln, H., Basmajian, J.V., Piews, N., Burcea, I.: Agonist and antagonist activity during voluntary upper-limb movement in patients with stroke. Phys. Ther. **72**, 624–633 (1992)
5. Stewart, J.C., Yeh, S.C., Jung, Y., Yoon, H., Whitford, M., Chen, S.Y.: Intervention to enhance skilled arm and hand movements after stroke: a feasibility study using a new virtual reality system. J. Neuroeng. Rehabilitation **4**(1), 1–6 (2007)
6. Huang, L.L., Lee, C.F., Chen, M.H.: Commercial digital game devices to promote upper extremity functions for post-stroke rehabilitation: therapeutic effectiveness and usability assessments. In: The Sixth International Conference on Advances in Computer-Human Interaction Conference, pp. 250–255. (2013)
7. Baldominos, A., Saez, Y., Pozo, C.G.: An approach to physical rehabilitation using state-of-the-art virtual reality and motion tracking technologies. Procedia Comput. Sci. **64**, 10–16 (2015)

8. Kim, J.E., Lee, M.Y., Yim, J.E.: A new approach to transcranial direct current stimulation in improving cognitive motor learning and hand function with the Nintendo switch in stroke survivors. Med. Sci. Monit. **25**, 9555–9562 (2019)

9. Putra, B.A.M., Masduchi, R.H., Kusumawardani, M.K.: Cardiovascular responses, physical activity intensity, and enjoyment level of Nintendo Switch™ exergaming, comparing different tempos and playing modes: a pilot study. SPMRJ. **3**(2), 44–52 (2021)

10. Bangor, A., Kortum, P., Miller, J.: Determining what individual SUS scores mean: adding an adjective rating scale. J. Usability Stud. **4**(3), 114–123 (2009)

11. Brooke, J.: SUS: a 'quick and dirty' usability scale. In: Jordan, P.W., Thomas, B., Weerdmeester, B.A., McClelland, I.L. (eds.) Usability Evaluation in Industry, pp. 189–194. Taylor and Francis, London (1996)

The Effects of Ephemeral Social Media on COVID-19 Prevention Measures

Yu-Ting Chen[1], Yi-Hsing Han[1(✉)], and Shih-Hsien Hsu[2]

[1] National Chengchi University, Taipei, Taiwan
paulhan@nccu.edu.tw
[2] National Taiwan University, Taipei, Taiwan

Abstract. As Instagram Stories feature launched in the recent past, a few prior studies were discussing the use and the behavior intention of its Stories feature (Amancio 2017; Valiant and Setiawan 2017). During the COVID-19, social media technologies were important for disseminating information as many nonprofit health organizations sought to address public worries and the need for reliable information about the disease, leading public relations professionals and governments to view these platforms as an effective channel for strategic health communication and promoting public health preventive measures. For example, in order to connect virtually, Instagram has also added its donation sticker to more countries which helps users communicate with charities, and created a "Stay Home" shared story to encourage people who practice social distancing (Sharma and Agrawal 2020).

While most ephemeral social media studies focus on individual users' motivation to use Instagram and advertising, the effects of the ephemeral content and features of Instagram Stories about public health campaign were under-investigated. This paper follows Theory of Reasoned Action (TRA) to explore the effects of Taiwan's younger generation Instagram Stories usage (frequency, content, and features) on their intention to adopt epidemic prevention measures and subjective norms' moderating effects. A total of 819 participants completed an online survey and the results showed significant positive relationships between Stories usage and behavior intention, attitudes and behavior intention, and between subjective norms and behavior intention, with attitudes moderated by subjective norms. The implications of the role of ephemeral social media play in public health campaign were discussed.

Keywords: ephemeral social media · Instagram Stories · subjective norms · public health campaign

1 Introduction

Recent research suggests that social media is a key medium for crisis communication when it comes to public relations (Guidry et al. 2019), the integration of media by becoming a channel to gain access, verify and distribute information (Vázquez-Herrero et al. 2019), little is known about how ephemeral content usage on social media would impact

P.-L. P. Rau (Ed.): HCII 2023, LNCS 14024, pp. 366–379, 2023.
https://doi.org/10.1007/978-3-031-35946-0_30

users' engagement both online and in the real world by shaping the public's response to social and public health campaigns. Taking pandemic prevention as an example, do users take action in reality when they see the information about promoting wearing masks or washing hands on Instagram Stories?

In addition, the constant technological innovations have redefined the media outlets, social media has become networked communications that allow users to express their thoughts, communicate and interact with their peers as they create personal profiles, consume, and produce content (Boyd and Ellison 2007). Prior studies further indicated that social media replaces social interaction and how people obtain messages (Ku et al. 2013), and how the usage of Instagram Stories features affect coping behavior (Chen and Wang 2019).

As Stories feature launched in the recent past, few prior studies were discussing the use and the behavior intention of Stories feature usage from individuals (Amâncio 2017; Valiant and Setiawan 2017). During the COVID-19 pandemic, social media technologies were important for disseminating information as many nonprofit health organizations sought to address public worries and the need for reliable information about the disease (Mheidly and Fares 2020), leading public relations professionals and governments to view these platforms as an effective channel for strategic health communication and public health campaigns.

2 Literature Review

2.1 Social Media Usage and Ephemeral Content

The intention of using the Stories feature reflected its pleasure, convenience, relative advantage, and observability that users associate with (Cai 2017; Wang 2017). This huge growth of Instagram has altered the modes between audiences and brands, news agencies. Belanche et al. (2019) added that users can follow different stories, going back and forth in chronological order to previous and subsequent stories. Because of its high visual nature and user engagement rate, Instagram was considered a useful tool for social media marketing and public service. Consequently, as the role of Instagram Stories becomes increasingly significant in daily life, the importance of this topic becomes clearer.

Instagram Stories, on the other hand, is the visual platform that aims to interact privately with others (Larsson 2017), people can "share their life moments with friends through a series of (filter manipulated) pictures and videos" (Hu et al. 2014, p. 595). The media not only sees it as an appliance to communicate with sources, sharing stories, and showing audiences what happens behind the scenes (Thornton 2013), but also strengthens the interaction with young people and brand recognition. New features like Instagram Stories enable the media to experiment with diverse storytelling. According to Schmidt (2018), the Cincinnati Enquirer, the newspaper developed a direct connection with their readers by adding a Q&A feature on their Instagram Stories.

There are eight patterns identified by Amâncio (2017) in Instagram Stories and Snapchat including presenting emotions, foods, interaction, updates, people, self-images, animals, and environment. According to Robin (2008), one of the popular types of digital storytelling is presenting emotions in stories; it shows the creator's personal experiences which can be centered on life events and feel emotionally and personally meaningful to authors and the audience. There are various ways that users can display emotions, such as expressing feelings, responding to the subject vocally, or even using "haha" to show a sense of humor on the internet (Savitri and Irwansyah 2021). Moreover, since food takes a major part of their daily life, it has become a trend that people started sharing food, drinks, and even recipes with their friends on Instagram.

Stories are not only the platform features that provide information for other users to view but also enable interaction between the two by sending messages and commenting on what is happening. While any content being shared can be considered as updating, the immediacy of users uploading the events is worth noting given that users can inform their followers what they were doing or what they just did by using the update patterns on the Stories. Meanwhile, users share Stories to show who they are with, such as family, friends, or random people on the streets; a selfie is also a common practice to express their self-image and to create a digital identity online. Animals and the environment are often the popular objects to present on the internet as the surroundings show where the events occur or where characters are to help other users place themselves in the scene of the uploader (Savitri and Irwansyah 2021).

2.2 Affordance and Social Engagement

To understand how Instagram Stories users interact with the platform during the COVID-19 pandemic, this study adopts affordance to explain posting and sharing information. Affordance was defined as individuals' capabilities, objectives, values, and thoughts by Norman (1988). Moreover, Islam et al. (2020) categorized affordances into technical affordances, individual affordances, and contextual affordances by citing Norman's (1988) definition. Technical affordance refers to the technical features that social media platforms provide to the users such as sharing news and exploring information; Individuals affordance is when individuals have opportunities to promote themselves, ideologies or just for entertainment purposes; According to Islam et al. (2020), the emergence of COVID-19 has created a new condition of contextual facilitation. As new diseases, policy-related news, and health advice recommendations arise, users have been given contextual help to discuss and comment on topics.

Taylor Swift, an American singer who has been silent about her political beliefs for a long time, posted an opinion on politics on Instagram supporting the candidates in her hometown Tennessee state and encouraging millions of Instagram followers to register and vote (Nisbett and Schartel Dunn 2021). Within 24 h, there was a spike of 65,000 new registration of voters. org which was more than the number registered during September that year which made national news.

Although the impact of celebrities and influencers on elections are mixed to convince, while viewers are already acquainted with them (Chung and Cho 2017; Nisbett and Schartel Dunn 2021), there is empirical evidence that the impact of celebrities on poll numbers can be substantial. Garthwaite and Moore (2013) mentioned when Oprah Winfrey endorsed Barack Obama in 2008 which led to a bump in Obama's poll numbers. As a result, even though there are some negative comments about Swift's statements, more than two million users actually "liked" them. Nisbett and DeWalt (2016) further indicated that celebrities and influencers therefore could inspire potential voters to seek out further information. In addition, many researchers pointed out that entertainment media is a way to impact voters who have low interest and knowledge given that it is unlikely they will do their own research (Van Doorn et al. 2003). Political information may be more accessible and intelligible if it is consumed through entertainment venues such as social media.

During the 2008 U.S. presidential elections, it is shown that people got information about candidates, campaigns, and news through social media according to Pew Research 2008 (Kim and Chen 2016). Hansen et al. (2010) mentioned that people were also able to make comments, post their opinions actively during political events (Kim and Chen 2016). Lim (2008) found that a person's social network is a critical component in civic and political engagement, for instance, citizens can contact government officials, attend meetings for social issues and even participate in social movements. Additionally, it is explained that the personal connection people have on social media may encourage or ask them to participate in social activities (Lim 2008). By exposing various perspectives on social networks with their family, friends, or strangers, social media not only enables people to share news and information but also increases their actions on social issues (Kim and Chen 2016).

With the affordances provided by social technologies, people can share information with others. While social media enables users to generate content, sometimes it is hard to decide what information to publish to online users (Marwick and Boyd 2014). As sharing posts in persistent forms brings tensions to the users, the number of people using ephemeral content has grown evidently and became one of the prominent components of user experience in social media (Chen and Cheung 2019). Ephemeral content refers to a form of communication which can be synchronously delivered to engage other users, such as text, images, and video that will be removed after a certain time period. For example, Instagram Stories allows users to share ephemeral materials and interact with publishers by replying to the story.

2.3 The Effects of Stories Usage (Frequency, Features, and Content) on Attitudes

With providing immediately interactive features through polling stickers, "swipe up" function (Chen and Cheung 2019), researcher investigated the effects on advertising from the perspective of consumer involvement through the unique characteristics of Instagram Stories, and how viewing story became part of users' daily routine once they open Instagram. Yet, there is a lack of research on whether viewing Instagram Stories, a 15-s based ephemeral content, will trigger users to engage in certain activities offline. Despite the fact that people are increasingly accepting ephemeral social media content, existing literature on how they utilize the features and their effect is still in its early stages. For instance, Chen and Cheung (2019) demonstrated how user's gratification impacted their engagement with ephemeral contents; Bainotti et al. (2021) showed the contradiction between ephemeral content and archive cultures; Vázquez-Herrero et al. (2019) also found that how media produce ephemeral content for Instagram Stories to adapt their news to the platform and users' preferences.

To be specific, since Instagram launched Stories in 2016, the features have been continuously added for users to edit and share content in real-time, to name a few according to Lu (2020): (1) various types of video (i.e. boomerang, superzoom, rewind, hands-free, and stop-motion); (2) face filters that can add different materials to change one's appearance; (3) drawings and handwritings; (4) texts in different styles (i.e. adjustable size, fonts); (5) stickers such as mention, location, hashtag, GIFs, polls, emoji sliders, ask me questions stickers.

Instagram enables users to interact with the online community, and a hashtag can be considered as one of the social engagement features since it can be seen as a contribution to the social media community by everyone on Instagram. During the pandemic outbreak, hashtags like "Covid19", "StayHomeStaySafe", and "SocialDistancing" are trending on social media (Stewart 2020). According to Sharma and Agrawal (2020), users no longer can search for filters with COVID-19 themes unless they were created in collaboration with recognized health organizations on Instagram, while Instagram Search also includes educational tools and stickers that promote correct content. Moreover, any COVID-19 material and accounts from non-recognized health organizations have been excluded from the list of recommended resources. In order to connect virtually, Instagram has also added its donation sticker to more countries which helps users communicate with charities, and created a "Stay Home" shared story to encourage people who practice social distancing (Sharma and Agrawal 2020). The current study includes not only frequency of Stories usage and COVID-19 related Stories content, but also Stories features to explore their effects on attitude toward sharing COVID-19 information on Instagram Stories. Consequently, the hypothesis is proposed as below in this study:

H1: The more often participants use Instagram Stories, the more favorable attitudes they have toward sharing COVID-19 information on Instagram Stories.
H2: The more often participants use Instagram Stories Features, the more favorable attitudes they have toward sharing COVID-19 information on Instagram Stories.
H3: The more often participants perceive COVID-16 related information via Instagram Stories, the more favorable attitudes they have toward sharing COVID-19 information on Instagram Stories.

2.4 Effects of Subjective Norms

Fishbein and Ajzen (1975) proposed the Theory of Reasoned Action (TRA) that focuses on attitude and social beliefs which states that one's particular behavior could be affected by an individual's behavior intention. In order to explore the impacts on social media, the three components included in TRA were used in current study: attitude, subjective norm, and behavior intention.

TRA analyses an individual's attitude and subjective norms, resulting in a prediction of their intention to share information and take action accordingly. This further determines the way an individual shares information on social media and adopt COVID-19 related preventative measures. The general feelings and behavior of one's sharing information formed their attitudes towards information sharing. Lin et al. (2013) found that an individual's feelings and behaviors of sharing information on social media would shape his/her attitudes toward information sharing, whereas subjective norms refer to the way an individual evaluates the behavior of other people in sharing information on social media. The attitude is defined as the function of the strength of beliefs about the behavioral outcome and the evaluation of that particular behavior (Ko and Yu 2019).

According to TRA, attitude and subjective norm will influence the behavioral intention whereas attitude refers to the positive or negative assessment of a specific behavior and is decided by behavioral beliefs (the possibility of various behavioral outcomes) and behavioral evaluations (strength and weakness of the outcomes).

Prior research used TRA to examine the association between beliefs and attitudes in numerous behavioral scenarios such as investigating how guardians impact the attitudes towards online software piracy using this theory along with routine activity theory (Petrescu et al. 2018). Chen et al. (2009), Lu and Hsiao (2007), and Liang and Yeh (2011) used TRA to explore the continuance of behavioral intentions. For instance, Lu and Hsiao (2007) studied how individuals' intention to share information on weblogs is determined. In addition, existing studies are focusing on how Uses and Gratification and TRA explained the news-sharing behaviors in terms of behavioral intentions given that both are based on the expectation concept (Lin et al. 2013). Primarily, individuals obtain information to satisfy their gratification on information acquisition (Lee and Ma 2012), by sharing information, they are able to communicate with others (Choi 2016) and secure a sense of belonging (Ma et al. 2011; Lin et al. 2013). With the need to seek status (Lee and Ma 2012) among peers on social networking sites, users tend to draw attention or get recognition (Choi 2016) from others (Lin et al. 2013). A study made by Holton et al. (2014) further pointed out that users are not only using Twitter for information seeking but also sharing. Consequently, it is speculated that viewing Instagram Stories may obtain gratification along with Instagram users' evaluations which became the beliefs of behavioral outcomes. Based on TRA, subjective norms, the normative beliefs and motivations to comply with those we think they are important, will affect the behavior intention. Therefore, the current study hypothesizes that subjective norms would play a moderating role on users' intention to adopt epidemic prevention measures. Besides, we proposed the research framework of current study as Fig. 1 shows.

H4: Subjective norms would moderate the effects of attitudes on users' intention adopt epidemic prevention measures.

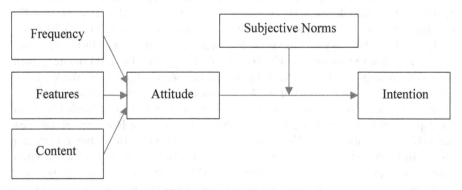

Fig. 1. Research framework

3 Survey Method

3.1 Participants and Procedure

A total of 839 subjects participated in the online survey between August and September, 2021. After eliminating 20 incomplete questionnaires, 819 responses were analyzed in total. All respondents were incentivized with the chance to win gift cards.

Respondents consented to participate in the study first and then they were instructed to fill out the filter questions that asked whether they had an Instagram account and used Instagram Stories before. Next, they were asked to respond to questions pertaining to their Instagram Stories usage, attitudes, subjective norms, and willingness to adopt COVID-19 preventive measures. Finally, they were asked to provide demographic information, including age, gender, and education.

Among 819 participants, 69.7% of them were females, and the average age was 22.6 years old ($SD = 3.13$). The majority of the participants obtained bachelor degree (77.3%).

3.2 Measures

The survey included questions referring to constructs, dimensions, and items from previous studies whose reliability and validity have been established and were adjusted according to the research background and the opinions of the pre-test results. The reliability standard of the constructs was evaluated by their Cronbach's alpha coefficients. The questionnaires captured variables regarding Instagram Stories frequency, contents, features, attitudes toward sharing information on Instagram Stories, subjective norms, and intention to adopt epidemic prevention measures.

The Usage of Instagram Stories. The first measurement of Instagram use is *frequency*. Four items were used in the questionnaire to investigate participants' frequency of using Instagram Stories ($M = 4.35$; $SD = 1.13$, Cronbach's $\alpha = .71$), such as (1) How often do you use Instagram Stories by viewing others' Stories in a week ($M = 6.58$; $SD = 1.05$); (2) How often do you reply to others' Stories in a week ($M = 4.28$; $SD = 1.77$); (3) How often do you post your own Instagram Stories in a week ($M = 3.70$; $SD = 1.63$); (4) How often do you share something (e.g., music, reposting other stories, etc.) to your Instagram Stories in a week ($M = 2.84$; $SD = 1.61$). The level of engagement was assessed ranging from 1 (never), 2 (not once this week), 3 (once this week), 4 (2–3 times this week), 5 (4–6 times this week), 6 (once a day), to 7 (several times a day).

Next, participants were asked to answer their usage on Instagram Stories *Features*, three questions were used to explore how often participants use Instagram Stories Features ($M = 3.75$; $SD = 1.48$, Cronbach's $\alpha = .35$), such as (1) How often do you skip others' Instagram Stories ($M = 3.79$; $SD = 1.29$); (2) How often do you use Instagram Stories by responding to Stories features created by others (e.g., poll stickers, emoji reactions, etc.) ($M = 3.60$; $SD = 1.33$); (3) How often do you post your own Stories with Instagram Stories features (e.g., digital filters, texts, draws and handwritings, links, etc.) ($M = 3.85$; $SD = 1.77$). Similarly, the levels of engagement were assessed ranging from 1 to 7 (1-never and 7-always). Because the reliability of Instagram Features usage was quite low, the current study decided that only the last two items were averaged as a composite score for subsequent analysis ($r = .40, p < .001$).

Furthermore, three items were used to measure the frequency of viewing COVID-19 prevention measures *content* via Instagram Stories ($M = 4.09$; $SD = 1.03$, Cronbach's $\alpha = .71$): (1) How often do you see people post information about washing hands to prevent COVID-19 on Instagram Stories ($M = 3.12$; $SD = 1.27$); (2) How often do you see people post information about wearing masks to prevent COVID-19 on Instagram Stories ($M = 4.30$; $SD = 1.44$); (3) How often do you see people post information about being vaccinated on Instagram Stories ($M = 4.85$; $SD = 1.24$). The levels of engagement were also assessed ranging from 1 to 7 (1 = never, 7 = always).

Attitudes Toward Sharing Information on Instagram Stories. Three items adopted from Fishbein and Ajzen (1975) and modified according to the current study's purposes to measure attitudes toward sharing information on Instagram Stories ($M = 4.84$; $SD = 1.03$, Cronbach's $\alpha = .83$): (1) The story about COVID-19 is informative ($M = 4.84$; $SD = 1.15$); (2) The publisher of the content on Instagram Stories is useful (i.e. CDC, celebrities, news agencies) ($M = 4.98$; $SD = 1.25$); (3) The content about COVID-19 on Instagram Stories is useful ($M = 4.71$; $SD = 1.16$). Those three items were scored from 1 to 7 (1 = strongly disagree, 7 = strongly agree).

Subjective Norms. Subjective norms refer to a function of normative beliefs and motivations to comply with those we think they are important. Three items for measuring subject norms were adopted and modified from Lu and Hsiao (2007), Ting et al. (2016), and Fishbein and Ajzen (1975) ($M = 4.15$; $SD = 1.17$, Cronbach's $\alpha = .80$): (1) People who are important to me expect me to create content on Instagram Stories ($M = 3.92$; $SD = 1.44$); (2) People who are important to me think I should use Instagram Stories ($M = 3.76$; $SD = 1.44$); (3) People whose opinion I value would approve my use of Instagram Stories ($M = 4.77$; $SD = 1.28$). Those three items were scored from 1 to 7 (1 = strongly disagree, 7 = strongly agree).

Intention to Adopt Epidemic Prevention Measures. Two items were adopted from Finset et al. (2020) about individuals' relevant behavior changes to prevent COVID-19 and one item about vaccination was also added ($M = 4.69$; $SD = 1.37$, Cronbach's $\alpha = .84$): (1) I would remember to wash my hands when I saw others posting information of washing hands to prevent COVID-19 on Instagram Stories ($M = 4.47$; $SD = 1.54$); (2) I would remember to wear masks when I saw others posting information of wearing masks to prevent COVID-19 on Instagram Stories ($M = 4.95$; $SD = 1.59$); (3) I would sign up when I saw others posting information of being vaccinated on Instagram Stories ($M = 4.66$; $SD = 1.59$). Those three items were scored from 1 to 7 (1 = strongly disagree, 7 = strongly agree).

4 Results

The most central motivation for this study was to explore the extent to which ephemeral social media content contributes to people's intention to adopt COVID-19 preventive measures during epidemic, and thereby offer a starting point for testing the theoretical claims embedded in TRA model that ephemeral format would not weaken the persuasion effects. Toward this aim, hierarchical regression and path analyses were employed.

Two hierarchical regression analyses were employed to test the four proposed hypotheses. The first hierarchical regression analysis examined the extent to which Instagram Stories Usage contribute to attitudes toward sharing COVID-19 related information on Instagram Stories. All control variables were included in the first block, followed by the Instagram Stories usage variables (Instagram Stories Frequency, Instagram Stories Features, and Instagram Stories Content) in the second block. The results support the third hypothesis, yielding a moderate significant relationship between Instagram Stories Content and attitudes toward sharing COVID-19 related information on Instagram Stories ($\beta = .38$, p < .001). The first and the second hypotheses were not supported. Instagram Stories Frequency and Instagram Stories Features were not associated with attitudes. Please see Table 1 for the results.

The second hierarchical regression analysis examined the extent to which attitudes toward sharing COVID-19 related information on Instagram Stories contributes to intention to adopt COVID-19 preventive measures during epidemic, and the extent to which subjective norms moderate this contribution. All control variables were included in the first block, followed by the main effect variables (attitudes and subjective norms) with the interaction term in the second block. The main effect variables were standardized by centering them before the interaction terms were used in order to avoid multicollinearity problems between the interaction term and its components. The results support the fourth hypothesis, yielding significant relationship between attitudes and behavior intention ($\beta = .65$, p < .001), and between subjective norms and behavior intention ($\beta = .33$, p < .01), with attitudes moderated by subjective norms ($\beta = -.32$, p < .05). See Table 2.

In addition to the direct and moderated relationships tested in the hierarchical regression models, a path analysis was used to explore the overall research model. R lavaan package was used to analyze the model-data fit. The initial model was not fit with the collected data, $\chi^2(4) = 87.08$, $p < .001$, $CFI = .83$, $TLI = .61$, $RMSEA = .16$ [.13, .19], $SRMR = .05$. After removing Instagram Stories Frequency and Instagram Stories Features and adding the path that Instagram Stories Content contributes to Intention, the final model fairly fit with the data, $\chi^2(1) = 39.46$, $p < .001$, CFI $= .92$, TLI $= .89$, RMSEA $= .08$ [.05, .09], SRMR $= .05$. (Hu and Bentler 1999). According to Hu and Bentler (1999), the Chi-square test and fit indices of current analysis showed a good fit between data and the proposed model, although the RMSEA's 90% CI upper limit exceeded .08 which may be because the sample size was relatively small. See Fig. 2.

Table 1. Results of hierarchical regression analysis for attitudes toward sharing information on Instagram Stories

Dependent variables	Attitudes toward sharing information on Instagram Stories	
Predictor variables	β	β
Block 1		
Gender	.07	.04
Age	−.01	.01
Education	−.03	−.02
Adjusted R^2	.00	
F	1.65	
Block 2		
Frequency		.03
Features		.04
Content		.38***
Adjusted R^2		.15***
ΔR^2		.15***
ΔF		25.14

$*p < .05; **p < .01; ***p < .001$

5 Discussion and Conclusion

5.1 Discussion

The current study explores the relatively new feature among social media, Instagram Stories, that whether Instagram Stories enhance users' attitudes towards social issues and contribute to the literature of the role of social media for COVID-19 preventative measures. The results have shown that ephemeral social media content contributed to participants' intention to adopt COVID-19 preventive measures during epidemic, and ephemeral content's persuasion effect was still in line with TRA model. Findings from this study have practical implications. It is essential to reveal salient behaviors of using Instagram Stories, once the behaviors are identified, public health campaigns could tailor the message –a 15-s based ephemeral content can trigger users to engage in certain activities offline, to foster a more favorable attitude toward the epidemic prevention measures.

In light of subjective norms, public health campaigns could portray preventive measures as a socially acceptable and responsible act toward the pandemic. Another theoretical contribution, whereas the literature suggests that social media use is associated with discussing essential issues as they provide real-time updates of breaking news (Small 2011), and previous studies suggested that people rely on social media as their news sources to keep themselves well-informed by receiving information from peers

Table 2. Results of hierarchical regression analysis for intention to adopt epidemic prevention measures

Dependent variables	Intention to adopt epidemic prevention measure	
Predictor variables	β	β
Block 1		
Gender	.04	.00
Age	.02	.02
Education	.02	.04
Adjusted R^2	.00	
F	.61	
Block 2		
Attitude		.65***
Subjective Norms		.33**
Attitude × Norms		−.32*
Adjusted R^2		.27***
ΔR^2		.27***
ΔF		51.97

$*p < .05; **p < .01; ***p < .001$

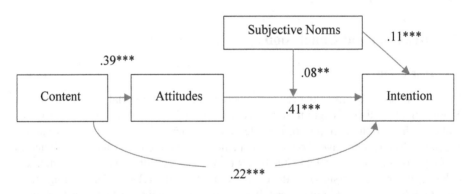

Fig. 2. The final model of current study

(Valeriani and Vaccari 2015; Ahmadi and Wohn 2018) as the ephemeral news through Instagram Stories enhance the visibility and interaction with the younger generation (Stefanou 2017; Vázquez-Herrero et al. 2019). This study fills the gap to understand whether social issues appearing on Instagram Stories would trigger users to take action, promoting health-related preventive behaviors.

5.2 Limitations and Future Research

Despite all the enlightening findings including examining a range of Instagram Stories features and exposure to health-related social issues in the same sample and exploring past experience of Instagram Stories usage, several limitations are worth noting.

First, this study discussed both frequency and features of Instagram Stories as effective variables; however, some features do not significantly predict users' attitudes and have no significant impact on intention. The survey of Stories features usage could be more specific. According to Small (2011), hashtags raised the awareness of social issues on Twitter by calling for actions, enabling Twitter users to share their stories, fears, and support toward social issues. Yet, in the current study, the scale adopted of Instagram Stories features has not been redesigned or tested to fit the research of exploring users' behaviors. Not only so, future research can explore other reasons that may affect users' attitudes toward social issues in terms of social media features usage, such as different users' degrees of immersion while viewing content on Instagram Stories.

Secondly, because the current study employed survey method, the participants could merely respond based on their impressions and recalls. Future research can use experimental design for collecting behavioral data to investigate the relationships among those variables to avoid participants' recall issues.

Finally, there may be some restrictions on the sample in this study. The majority of the participants were females (69.7%), and the imbalance of the ratio of men to women may affect the representativeness of the research results.

Also, two suggestions for future research. First, this study only focused on the Instagram Stories features, however, the ephemeral feature is also now available and popular on other social media platforms like Facebook, Snapchat, and YouTube. Future research can compare the effects of the Stories feature across these social media platforms. For example, it can also be added to the comparison to explore the differences in the exposure effects of platforms with different characteristics or to compare the difference of the effects between the posts and Instagram Stories on the same Instagram platform. Second, this study did not examine the effects of personality and other individual difference variables, and they might have played an important role on attitudes and behavior intention.

References

Guidry, J.P.D., Carlyle, K.E., LaRose, J.G., Perrin, P., Messner, M., Ryan, M.: Using the health belief model to analyze Instagram posts about Zika for public health communications. Emerg. Infect. Dis. **25**(1), 179–180 (2019)

Amancio, M.: "Put it in your Story": Digital Storytelling in Instagram and Snapchat Stories. (Master thesis). Uppsala University, Uppsala (2017)

Vázquez-Herrero, J., Direito-Rebollal, S., López-García, X.: Ephemeral journalism: news distribution through Instagram stories. Soc. Media + Soc. **5**(4), 2056305119888657 (2019)

Boyd, D.M., Ellison, N.B.: Social network sites: definition, history, and scholarship. J. Comput.-Mediat. Commun. **13**(1), 210–230 (2007)

Ku, Y.C., Chu, T.H., Tseng, C.H.: Gratifications for using CMC technologies: a comparison among SNS, IM, and e-mail. Comput. Hum. Behav. **29**(1), 226–234 (2013)

Chen, T.Y., Wang, K.T.: The influence of persuasion knowledge, third-person perception, and affect on coping behavior in the Instagram stories feature. Corporate Manag. Rev. **39**(2), 69–116 (2019)

Valiant, V., Setiawan, J.: Analyzing factors influencing behavior intention to use Snapchat and Instagram Stories. Int. J. New Media Technol. **4**(2), 75–81 (2017)

Mheidly, N., Fares, J.: Leveraging media and health communication strategies to overcome the COVID-19 infodemic. J. Public Health Policy **41**(4), 410–420 (2020)

Cai, Z.J.: A Study on User Adoption of "Stories" Based on Facebook and Instagram. (Master's thesis, National Central University, Taiwan) (2017)

Wang, S.I.: The political use of social media and civic engagement in Taiwan. J. Cyber Cult. Inf. Soc. **32**, 83–111 (2017)

Belanche, D., Cenjor, I., Pérez-Rueda, A.: Instagram stories versus Facebook wall: an advertising effectiveness analysis. Spanish J. Mark.-ESIC **23**(1), 69–94 (2019)

Larsson, A.O.: The news user on social media: a comparative study of interacting with media organizations on Facebook and Instagram. J. Stud. **19**(2), 2225–2242 (2017)

Hu, Y., Manikonda, L., Kambhampati, S.: What we Instagram: a first analysis of Instagram photo content and user types. In: Eighth International AAAI Conference on Weblogs and Social Media (2014)

Thornton, L.J.: Shared views, social capital, community ties, and Instagram. Grassroots Editor **54**(3–4), 19–26 (2013)

Schmidt, C.: The Cincinnati Enquirer wrote an audience-driven article using Instagram Stories (and it wasn't even about a hippo). Nieman Lab (2018). http://www.niemanlab.org

Robin, B.R.: Digital storytelling: a powerful technology tool for the 21st century classroom. Theory Into Pract. **47**(3), 220–228 (2008)

Savitri, S., Irwansyah, I.: The use of Instagram Stories at the age of COVID-19 pandemic. Jurnal Aspikom **6**(1), 182–196 (2021)

Norman, D.A.: The Psychology of Everyday Things. Basic Books, New York (1988)

Islam, A.K.M.N., Laato, S., Talukder, M., Sutinen, E.: Misinformation sharing and social media fatigue during COVID-19: an affordance and cognitive load perspective. Technol. Forecast. Soc. Chang. **159**, 120201 (2020)

Nisbett, G., Schartel Dunn, S.: Reputation matters: parasocial attachment, narrative engagement, and the 2018 Taylor Swift political endorsement. Atlantic J. Commun. **29**(1), 26–38 (2021)

Chung, S., Cho, H.: Fostering parasocial relationships with celebrities on social media: Implications for celebrity endorsement. Psychol. Mark. **34**(4), 481–495 (2017)

Garthwaite, C., Moore, T.J.: Can celebrity endorsements affect political outcomes? Evidence from the 2008 US democratic presidential primary. J. Law Econ. Organ. **29**(2), 355–384 (2013)

Nisbett, G.S., DeWalt, C.C.: Exploring the influence of celebrities in politics: a focus group study of young voters. Atlantic J. Commun. **24**(3), 144–156 (2016)

Van Doorn, B., Parkin, M., Bos, A.: Laughing, learning and liking: the effects of entertainment-based media on American politics. Paper Presented at Annual Meeting of the Midwest Political Science Association, Chicago, IL (2003)

Kim, Y., Chen, H.-T.: Social media and online political participation: the mediating role of exposure to cross-cutting and like-minded perspectives. Telematics Inform. **33**(2), 320–330 (2016)

Hansen, D., Shneiderman, B., Smith, M.A.: Analyzing Social Media Networks With NodeXL: Insights From A Connected World. Morgan Kaufmann (2010)

Lim, C.: Social networks and political participation: how do networks matter? Soc. Forces **87**(2), 961–982 (2008)

Marwick, A.E., Boyd, D.: Networked privacy: how teenagers negotiate context in social media. New Media Soc. **16**(7), 1051–1067 (2014)

Chen, K.J., Cheung, H.L.: Unlocking the power of ephemeral content: the roles of motivations, gratification, need for closure, and engagement. Comput. Hum. Behav. **97**, 67–74 (2019)

Sun, H.Y.: Research on the effect of Instagram stories advertising (Master's thesis, National Chengchi University, Taiwan) (2020)

Bainotti, L., Caliandro, A., Gandini, A.: From archive cultures to ephemeral content, and back: studying Instagram Stories with digital methods. New Media Soc. **23**(12), 3656–3676 (2021)

Lu, J.D.: Decoding the popularity of Instagram Stories: examining the antecedents and consequences of engagement with Instagram Stories (Master's thesis, National Chengchi University, Taiwan) (2020)

Stewart, A.: What's trending during coronavirus pandemic? A definitive guide to the most used hashtags. The National News (2020)

Sharma, D.K., Agrawal, H.: Role of social media to awareness for pandemics: special context of COVID-19. UGC Care Group-1 J. **23**(4), 189–202 (2020)

Fishbein, M., Ajzen, I.: Belief, Attitude, Intention and Behaviour: An Introduction to Theory and Research. Addison-Wesley (1975)

Lin, X., Featherman, M., Sarker, S.: Information sharing in the context of social media: an application of the theory of reasoned action and social capital theory. In: SIGHCI 2013 Proceedings, vol. 17 (2013)

Ko, H.C., Yu, D.H.: Understanding continuance intention to view Instagram stories: a perspective of uses and gratifications theory. In: Proceedings of the 2nd International Conference on Control and Computer Vision, pp. 127–132 (2019)

Petrescu, M., Gironda, J.T., Korgaonkar, P.K.: Online piracy in the context of routine activities and subjective norms. J. Mark. Manag. **34**(3–4), 314–346 (2018)

Chen, S.-C., Chen, H.-H., Chen, M.-F.: Determinants of satisfaction and continuance intention towards self-service technologies. Ind. Manag. Data Syst. **109**(9), 1248–1263 (2009)

Lu, H.P., Hsiao, K.L.: Understanding intention to continuously share information on weblogs. Internet Res. **17**(4), 345–361 (2007)

Liang, T.P., Yeh, Y.H.: Effect of use contexts on the continuous use of mobile services: the case of mobile games. Pers. Ubiquit. Comput. **15**(2), 187–196 (2011)

Lee, C.S., Ma, L.: News sharing in social media: the effect of gratifications and prior experience. Comput. Hum. Behav. **28**(2), 331–339 (2012)

Choi, J.: Why do people use news differently on SNSs? An investigation of the role of motivations, media repertoires, and technology cluster on citizens' news-related activities. Comput. Hum. Behav. **54**(3), 249–256 (2016)

Holton, A.E., Baek, K., Coddington, M., Yaschur, C.: Seeking and sharing: motivations for linking on Twitter. Commun. Res. Rep. **31**(1), 33–40 (2014)

Ting, H., Cyril de Run, E., Liew, S.L.: Intention to use Instagram by generation cohorts: the perspective of developing markets. Glob. Bus. Manag. Res. **8**(1), 43–55 (2016)

Valeriani, A., Vaccari, C.: Accidental exposure to politics on social media as online participation equalizer in Germany, Italy, and the United Kingdom. New Media Soc. **18**(9), 1857–1874 (2015)

Ahmadi, M., Wohn, D.Y.: The antecedents of incidental news exposure on social media. Soc. Media + Soc. **4**(2), 1–8 (2018)

Stefanou, E.: Guardian's Instagram serial strategy engages younger audience. INMA (2017)

Small, T.A.: What the hashtag? A content analysis of Canadian politics on Twitter. Inf. Commun. Soc. **14**(6), 872–895 (2011)

Finset, A., et al.: Effective health communication–a key factor in fighting the COVID-19 pandemic. Patient Educ. Couns. **103**(5), 873–876 (2020)

Hu, L.T., Bentler, P.M.: Cutoff criteria for fit indexes in covariance structure analysis: conventional criteria versus new alternatives. Struct. Equ. Model. **6**(1), 1–55 (1999)

The Concept and Item Selection of the Flow Ergonomics Scale 45 (FES-45): A Study on the Compassionate Meditation of Flight Attendants

Wen-Ko Chiou[1]([✉]), Szu-Erh Hsu[1], Chao Liu[2], Hao Chen[3], and Po-Chen Shen[1]

[1] Department of Industrial Design, Chang Gung University, Taoyuan City, Taiwan
wkchiu@mail.cgu.edu.tw
[2] School of Journalism and Communication, Hua Qiao University, Xiamen 361021, China
[3] School of Film Television and Communication, Xiamen University of Technology, Xiamen, China

Abstract. In the past, our research team has proposed the conceptual framework of Flow Ergonomics (FE) and the Flow Ergonomics Sale (FES) 80 (FES-80). This scale is similar to the SF-36 scale, which is also used to assess the health condition and also takes into account the physical and mental aspects. However, different from the FES, it focuses on the health status of employees in their work and life. Good work quality is good for health. The FES is a multi-project scale with seven dimensions: (1) Transcendence and oneness; (2) Present attention; (3) Positive emotion and meaning; (4) Negative emotion; (5) Pleasure Life; (6) Compassion; (7) Acceptance. In this study, 100 flight attendants were recruited and tested. After the actual test, due to the feedback of too many items, the team will select the items again, put forward the development process and origin of FES 45 (FES-45), and summarized their selection logic. Compare the contents and characteristics of FES-45 with the original FES-80.

Keywords: Flow Ergonomics Scale · Reliability · Validity · Item Selection · Compassionate Meditation · Flight Attendants

1 Introduction

In the past, our research team proposed the concept of Flow Ergonomics (FE), and developed the Flow Ergonomics Scale (FES). The FE is a more complete theory of Human Factors/Ergonomics (HFE). In the past, HFE can only be divided into three categories: physical human factor, cognitive human factor, and organizational human factor. The research team found that, in response to future changes and the development of technology, HFE development must consider the physical and mental state of people, and human interaction can reduce the pressure in all kinds of life. It shows that the academic community believes that occupational health, ergonomics and product design are the three main areas of the development of HFE in Taiwan. FE is a feeling that one's mental

© The Author(s), under exclusive license to Springer Nature Switzerland AG 2023
P.-L. P. Rau (Ed.): HCII 2023, LNCS 14024, pp. 380–391, 2023.
https://doi.org/10.1007/978-3-031-35946-0_31

power is fully invested in certain activities. When FE occurs, there will be a high sense of excitement and fulfillment. The conceptualization of FE originates from the peak experience field. All people can get the best experience [1]. HFE is an important engineering technology discipline, which studies the interaction and reasonable combination of human, machine and environment, so that the designed machine and environment system can adapt to human physiological and psychological characteristics, and achieve the goal of improving efficiency, safety, health and comfort in production. The academic community believed that occupational health, ergonomics and product design were the three main areas of the development of human performance engineering in Taiwan. This study discusses this issue from the perspective of human factors of cardiac flow. The FE can be said to be a way to improve the spiritual level of human beings, and can be effectively used in the workplace and work. The conceptual framework and scale of FE is a set of innovative thinking, which will be provided to employees in all industries in the future. Therefore, it needs more inspection and adjustment to make the concept and scale more stable and practical. Through the analysis of the experimental test structure of flight attendants and the selection of items, the team proposed the development process and origin of FES 80 (FES-80) after the re-selection of items, and summarized their selection logic. Compare the contents and characteristics of FES 45 (FES-45) with the original FES-80. SF-36 is a set of tools designed to evaluate and investigate health status, which has been widely used and recognized. This study will develop the FES-45 scale according to the construction and development of the SF-36 scale. The conceptual framework proposed by FE is composed of seven dimensions: (1) Transcendence and oneness; (2) Present attention; (3) Positive emotion and meaning; (4) Negative emotion; (5) Pleasure Life; (6) Compassion; (7) Acceptance. Based on empirical research, this study conducted exploratory and confirmatory factor analysis on the sample, adjusted the conceptual model of FE factors and the FES, and then measured the reliability and validity. The FES developed in the past in this study consists of 86 items. After the actual application of flight attendants, the inappropriate items were deleted and eliminated after analysis, so as to make the FE concept and scale more suitable for use.

2 Literature Review

Flow is an absorbing psychological state spontaneously generated when individuals are occupied by challenging activities. Flow includes concentration, loss of self-consciousness, a change in the sense of time and space, and the integration of activities and consciousness [2]. Research shows that it can counteract mental illness symptoms [3]. Besides the well-studied positive effects of flow, there is also evidence of potential undesired effects, such as impaired risk perception or increased risk of becoming addicted to flow-inducing activity [4]. Flow at work is defined as an intense short-peak experience at work characterized by absorption, enjoyment and intrinsic motivation. Absorption is characterized by a state of total concentration in which the individual is completely immersed in his or her work. The notion of time is distorted, and there is a momentary loss of self. Work enjoyment refers to feeling happy and making positive evaluations of the flow experience. Intrinsic motivation at work refers to performing an activity for its own sake and satisfaction, without necessarily seeking some extrinsic reward [5]. According to Csikszentmihalyi model of the flow state [6], personal-tool-task model [7], and the input process-output framework [8], the preconditions for entering a flow state are timely progress feedback, clear task objectives, and challenge skill balance [9].

Since flow is primarily experienced in stress-relevant situations (e.g., teaching, illegal graffiti spraying), an association between flow experience and psychological and physiological stress seems logical. Concurrently, the variety and availability of job resources (*e.g.*, autonomy, social support, opportunities for development) were positively related to work-related flow experiences [10] and fostered the occurrence of future flow at work [11]. Thus, the state of flow was most often experienced in work contexts that combined an abundance of job resources with challenging job demands [12, 13]. At this time, they are absorbed in work with a sense of enthusiasm and thriving, which is necessary to cultivate flow [14, 15]. The transactional stress model describes the process of evaluating a situation with the help of various appraisal steps and conveys that individuals experience stress (threat or harm) if the demands of the situation exceed the resources of the person [16]. In this respect, the definitions of anxiety and stress in the corresponding models can be considered equivalent [14]. Flow occurs in a state between relaxation and stress, when demands can be handled positively [14, 17]. In line with these perspectives, Bakker and Woerkom [12] proposed that individuals can create their own work related flow experiences by using proactive individual strategies such as job crafting. Recent empirical findings have shown that task crafting predicted flow in millennial youth (i.e., dimension of work engagement) [18].

In the past, the construction of the FES was derived from Maslow's hierarchy model of needs [19]. The complete expression should be six levels, namely, physiological needs, security needs, belonging and love needs, respect needs, self-realization needs and transcendence needs. The need for transcendence can also be called the spiritual need or the need for transcendence and self-realization. In the past, when constructing the scale, the research team included these levels of needs, and took mindfulness, mind flow, spirituality, mind flow, happiness, and oneness as the support of the theoretical framework. Through the foundation of these theories, the model and scale were constructed.

The State Mindfulness Scale (SMS) includes two dimensions: state mindfulness reflecting body feeling and mindfulness stating psychological events. There are 15 questions about body mindfulness and 6 questions about mental mindfulness, totaling 21 questions [20].

The answer type is Likert five-point scale, "1" means completely inconsistent, and "5" means completely consistent; The total score of each sub-scale is the score of each sub-scale, and the total score of the two sub-scales is the total scale score. The sex Cronbach's alpha measured in the study was 0.95. The FE meter is used to measure the FE state of subjects, and the FE theory proposed by Csikszentmihalyi is adopted [5]. The Short Dispositional Flow Scale 2 (SDFS-2) contains 9 dimensions: a total of 9 questions. The answer type is Likert five-point scale, "1" means completely inconsistent, and "5" means completely consistent. The total score of each subscale is the score of each subscale, and the total score of the subscale is the total scale score.

The Spiritual Attitude and Involvement List (SAIL) was used to measure the spirituality of subjects [21]. This scale includes 7 dimensions: meaning, trust, acceptance, caring for others, connection with nature, transcendental experience and spiritual activities, totaling 26 questions. The answer type is Likert six-point scale, "1" means completely inconsistent, and "6" means completely consistent; The total score of each sub-scale is the score of each sub-scale, and the total score of seven sub-scales is the total scale score. The sex Cronbach's alpha measured in the study was 0.95.

The Subjective Well-Being (SWB) is composed of two parts: emotional balance and life satisfaction [22]. Therefore, this study uses the positive and negative emotion scale to measure the positive and negative emotion experience of the subjects, and the life satisfaction scale to measure the life satisfaction of the subjects [23].

The Positive and Negative Effect Scale (PANAS) includes two dimensions [24]: positive emotional experience and negative emotional experience, with 10 dimensions, totaling 20 items. The answer type is Likert five-point scale, "1" means completely inconsistent, and "5" means completely consistent; The total score of each sub-scale is the score of each sub-scale, and the total score of the two sub-scales is the total scale score. Past studies have shown that it has quite good validity [25, 26]. The Cronbach's alpha measured in this study is 0.95.

Life satisfaction, the life satisfaction scale is used to measure the life satisfaction of subjects. The Satisfaction with Life Scale (SWLS) has 5 questions in total [27]. The answer type is Likert seven-point scale, with "1" indicating complete non-compliance and "7" indicating complete compliance; The total score is the scale score. Past studies have shown that it has quite good validity [28, 29]. The Cronbach's alpha measured in this study is 0.95. The Oneness has 16 measurement items, which are divided into two dimensions [30]: spiritual integration and physical integration. The internal consistency coefficients of the two dimensions, Cronbach's alpha, are 0.91 and 0.74 respectively.

Chiou et al. proposed a FES-80 [31]. The results of the study confirmed that the FES, as a tool for evaluating specific psychological characteristics and mental state, has good reliability and validity. The FES is the first tool to measure the psychological and spiritual harmony in the workplace. Moreover, the core categories of the theoretical framework include the integration of transcendence, mindfulness and concentration, positive emotion and meaning, negative emotion, pleasure life, compassion and acceptance,

3 Methods

The participants in this study are flight attendants working in various airlines in Taiwan. We have recruited 100 airline companies in Taiwan, which shows that compassion meditation is a self-exploration activity that can help practitioners better understand themselves, release pressure, regulate emotions and improve happiness. Participants were divided into two groups: experimental group and control group. The experiment uses the compassionate meditation animation as the intervention tool, and the measurement tool before and after the experiment is the 80 item FES, and the time to answer the questionnaire is 20 min. The experimental group, through animation intervention, continued for eight weeks, and carried out animation compassionate meditation exercise three times a week. In this study, the factors were rotated to confirm that the data were suitable for factor analysis, and then the AMOS software was used for confirmatory factor analysis. It is necessary to develop simple and effective human factors tools for

FE in order not to unduly interfere with the meditation feelings of flight attendants and increase their willingness to fill in the answers. Therefore, this study selected the topic according to the above exploratory factor analysis deletion principle, and deleted the items with the absolute value of factor load less than 0.4 to achieve the simple and effective goal. Finally, it uses confirmatory factor analysis and reliability and validity test to understand the overall fitness, constituent reliability, aggregate validity and differential validity, and also tests the criterion-related validity of the scale.

4 Results

In order to verify the validity of the FES in the air service workplace and the problems caused by too many questions, this study needs to test and evaluate the reliability and validity of the FES. In order to test the validity of the FES, we conducted exploratory factor analysis (EFA) and confirmatory factor analysis (CFA) on the samples. The following indicators are used to determine the goodness of fit of the EFA model: the root mean square error approximation (RMSEA) is less than 0.08, the contrast fit index (CFI) and the non-normed fit index (NNFI) are greater than 0.90, and the chi-square value is less than 3.0 than its degree of freedom (chi^2/df). The exploratory factor analysis uses the maximum variation rotation method to determine the factor structure of the FES. Kaiser-Meyer-Olkin (KMO) test verified the sampling adequacy of the analysis, Barrett's spherical test evaluates the correlation degree between variables, and determines the factor extraction through Kaiser standard (characteristic value $\geq$ 1). The factor loads greater than 0.4 is considered to be the threshold value for the full contribution of this item to this factor. Cronbach's alpha coefficient is calculated to determine the internal consistency of the whole scale and various factors. A value $\geq$ 0.70 is considered sufficient. All statistical analyses were performed using SPSS 21.0 and LISREL 8.80 programs, with statistical significance of p < 0.05.

In order to determine the optimal factor structure of the FES, we conducted EFA analysis. The KMO result is 0.729, and the spherical test result is significant, which indicates that the FES is suitable for factor analysis. The eigenvalues of all factors are greater than 1, which accounts for 69.4% of the total variation rate. Among them, the spirituality scale and the FES contain many dimensions. Some dimensions' express themes similar to other scales. The results of factor analysis also show the unity between them. According to the results of EFA, the FES includes seven dimensions: (1) Transcendence and oneness; (2) Present attention; (3) Positive emotion and meaning; (4) Negative emotion; (5) Pleasure Life; (6) Compassion; (7) Acceptance (as shown in Fig. 1).

With regard to the reliability of the FES, the overall scale shows high internal consistency, which is determined by Cronbach's alpha value ($\alpha = 0.959$). If any item is deleted from the scale, no higher alpha value is found. The Cronbach alpha of each subscale is shown below (as shown in Table 1).

It can be seen from the above table (as shown in Table 2 and Fig. 2) that the present attention cannot significantly affect the negative emotion ($\beta = -0.156$, P = 0.159). However, the present attention has a significant positive impact on positive emotion and meaning, comparison and acceptance ($\beta = 0.451$, P = 0.000; $\beta = 0.618$, P = 0.000; $\beta = 0.623$, P = 0.000). Negative emotion has no significant impact on Pleasure life ($\beta =$

0.051, P = 0.557). But positive emotion and meaning can have a significant impact on Pleasure life (β = 0.631, P = 0.000). Compassion has a positive impact on Transcendence and oneness (β = 0.3491, P = 0.016). However, Acceptance and Pleasure life have no significant impact on Transcendence and oneness severity (β = 0.141, P = 0.206; β = 0.112, P = 0.322).

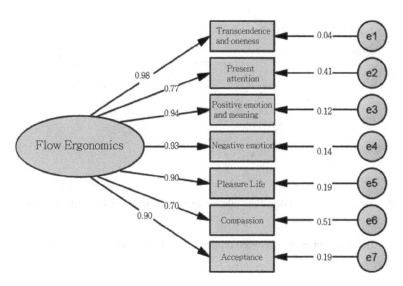

Fig. 1. CFA analysis of the fitness of each facet factor model

Table 1. Structural validity and reliability

	CR	AVE	Alpha
Transcendence and oneness	0.98	0.79	0.976
Present attention	0.80	0.52	0.774
Positive emotion and meaning	0.94	0.76	0.940
Negative emotion	0.936	0.648	0.934
Pleasure Life	0.91	0.60	0.903
Compassion	0.711	0.454	0.702
Acceptance	0.896	0.551	0.895

It can be seen from the above table that the correlation coefficients of one-in-one transcendence and focus on the present, Pleasure Life, positive emotion and meaning, sympathy and acceptance are all positive and significant at the level of 1%, which indicates that one-in-one transcendence has a significant positive correlation with these variables. Similarly, the correlation coefficient between Pleasure Life and positive emotion and meaning, sympathy and acceptance is also positive, which indicates that there

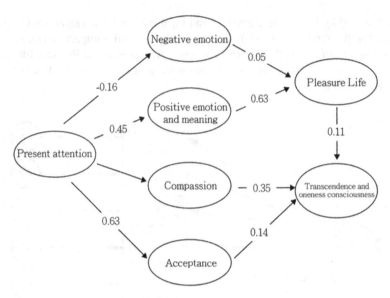

Fig. 2. An architecture model of the relationship between dimensions with path coefficients

Table 2. Correlation between dimensions and mean and standard deviation

	1	2	3	4	5	6	7
1.Transcendence and oneness	1						
2.Present attention	0.266**	1					
3.Positive emotion and meaning	0.293**	0.362**	1				
4.Negative emotion	0.297**	0.354**	0.619**	1			
5.Pleasure Life	− 0.05	− 0.13	0.02	− 0.09	1		
6.Compassion	0.344**	0.473**	0.521**	0.430**	− 0.05	1	
7.Acceptance	0.304**	0.506**	0.340**	0.376**	− 0.06	0.297**	1
Mean	6.093	3.573	3.042	3.124	1.934	3.387	3.688
SD	1.471	0.663	0.729	0.842	0.737	0.704	0.678

*: $p < 0.05$; **: $p < 0.01$

is also significant correlation between these variables. Focusing on the present also has a positive correlation coefficient with positive emotion and meaning, sympathy and acceptance, which indicates that focusing on the present has a significant correlation with these variables.

5 Discussion

The role model of SF-36 questionnaire is a self-administered questionnaire containing 36 items which takes about five minutes to complete. It measures health on eight multi-item dimensions, covering functional status, well-being, and overall evaluation of health. The evidence for the construct validity of the SF-36 was substantial. The expected distribution of scores was observed by sociodemographic characteristics, general practitioner consultation, use of hospital services, and a group of patients with chronic physical problems [32–35].

We also examined the convergent and construct validity of FES-45. Assessment of convergent validity showed that all seven FES-45 components were significantly and positively related to other measures of flow experiences in ergonomics activities. It should be noted that the negative relationship between flow and ergonomics workload found in this study is based on flow theory [36]. In contrast, Bakker [5] found in an organizational setting that job demands such as work pressure and emotional demands had a positive relationship with absorption. Employees who work under pressure and are confronted with demanding clients often lose their perspective of time, and become immersed in their work. On the other hand, experienced workers, although working under pressure, have adequate skills matching the task. From a theoretical viewpoint, this result points to the importance of the skill-challenge balance [37].

Currently, there is controversy in literature about the number of flow components, but Schiefele [38] concluded that "(a) absorption is the core component of flow, (b) there is no agreement on additional dimensions, and (c) enjoyment is a relevant aspect of flow that emerges as a separate factor or is included in the dimension of absorption". There may be many aspects that influence the reported flow-inducing activities, such as sample characteristics or the measurement method. However, our results suggest that activities in which a subject is more often involved have a better chance of inducing flow.

Through the above statistical analysis, the test of the flight attendant's scale has further established the relationship of seven dimensions. It is necessary to construct the scale with fewer questions, just like the SF-36 scale. There is a corresponding FES scale in each facet and it can fully express the FES scale. A short scale can make subjects feel more comfortable in answering. The specific adjustment of FES-45 scale varies from concept to concept, and is summarized as follows:

Transcendence and Oneness. In the original FES scale, all of them were reserved. In the dimension of Question 11, transcendence and oneness (Cronbach's $\alpha = 0.976$). Among these questions, it includes (unity consciousness and transcendence) that can make practitioners feel the connection with the environment for themselves and unity. He deleted the item in each item with α coefficient higher than 0.9.

Present Attention. In the original FES scale, it was composed of four items of cardiac flow. These four topics represent that in this dimension, focus on the current behavior, and consciously know what you need to do and understand your performance. On the whole (Cronbach's $\alpha = 0.774$), he has better performance in deleting the α coefficient of the item in each item.

Pleasure Life. In the original FES scale, all five items of life satisfaction were retained. Combining the two items of positive emotion, I feel proud and interested in my current emotion. In life, positive and pleasant emotions are added. On the whole (Cronbach's $\alpha = 0.903$), he has better performance in deleting the α coefficient of the item in each item.

Positive Emotion and Meaning. In the original FES scale, the positive emotion dimension in PANAS changed from 10 questions to 5 questions, which are happy, excited, enthusiastic, happy and optimistic. On the whole (Cronbach's $\alpha = 0.940$), which can fully express positive emotion and meaning.

Negative Emotion. In the original FES scale, the negative emotion dimension in PANAS changed from 10 to 8, including sadness, sadness, disgust, fear, guilt, fear, anger and impatience. On the whole (Cronbach's $\alpha = 0.934$), which can fully express negative emotions and meanings.

Compassion. In the original FES scale, the compassion dimension in the SAIL scale is composed of four directions. He feels the pain of others, understands the difficulty of life and feels that he is doing something meaningful. This expresses compassion, on the whole (Cronbach's $\alpha = 0.895$).

Acceptance. In the original FES scale, the mindfulness scale consists of 7 items in 15 dimensions. In these seven items, he accepts his own inner feelings and tries to detect his various thoughts and attention. On the whole (Cronbach's $\alpha = 0.895$), he has better performance in deleting the α coefficient of the item in each item.

Research Limitations and Future Studies. From the perspective of the process of compiling and deleting the scale, the final result can meet the requirements of the development of the scale, so as to make the scale stable and practical. We will propose to apply it more widely to all workplaces, so that the health of more employees will be valued. Finally, the development of this 45-item scale can better examine the degree of FE of practitioners than the 80-item scale in the first edition. In addition, the reduced number of questions will make it more convenient for the subjects to fill in, and will not bring fatigue and unpleasant feeling in filling.

This study has several limitations. In regard to the prevalence of flow, our participants were not randomly selected from the entire flight attendant's population and thus potential selection bias might have influenced the results, and the results may not be applicable to students in general. Future studies should try to determine the robustness of the findings in other samples or investigate ergonomics-related flow in more representative samples. Another limitation relates to the use of single-item measures of satisfaction with study and ergonomics workload for establishing congruent validity. Although this approach enables us to show the congruent validity of FES-45 with two distinct concepts, future studies should include other measures.

6 Conclusions

As for the level of flow human factors of air service staff, they can understand their physical and mental health, integration transcendence, mindfulness flow, positive emotion and meaning, negative emotion, Pleasure Life, Compassion, and acceptance at work.

Through the discussion of these factors, it will help to obtain the way of intervention, thereby improving their FE factor, and reducing depression, anxiety, panic and other negative emotions. At present, there are few studies to explore various factors affecting the physical and mental health of flight attendants, which highlights the importance of this study.

After exploratory factor analysis and confirmatory analysis at different stages, it was found that the 45 directions reserved could fall into the factor dimension of the original design, and the explanatory variation reached 68%. The results of confirmatory factor analysis also showed that the scale construction obtained from exploratory factor analysis is appropriate. The short scale of FES-45 will provide a more convenient answer experience for employees in the future workplace, and pay attention to the health status of employees.

References

1. Fritz, B.S., Avsec, A.: The experience of flow and subjective well-being of music students. Horiz. Psychol. **16**(2), 5–17 (2007)
2. Nakamura, J., Csikszentmihalyi, M.: The concept of flow. Flow and the foundations of positive psychology: the collected works of Mihaly Csikszentmihalyi, 239–263 (2014)
3. Riva, E., Freire, T., Bassi, M.: The flow experience in clinical settings: applications in psychotherapy and mental health rehabilitation. In: Harmat, L., Ørsted, F., Andersen, F., Ullén, J.W., Sadlo, G. (eds.) flow experience, pp. 309–326. Springer International Publishing, Cham, Switzerland (2016). https://doi.org/10.1007/978-3-319-28634-1_19
4. Zimanyi, Z., Schüler, J.: The dark side of the moon. In: Peifer, C., Engeser, S. (eds.) Advances in Flow Research, pp. 171–190. Springer, Cham (2021). https://doi.org/10.1007/978-3-030-53468-4_7
5. Bakker, A.B.: The work-related flow inventory: construction and initial validation of the WOLF. J. Vocat. Behav. **72**(3), 400–414 (2008)
6. Csikszentmihalyi, M.: Beyond Boredom and Anxiety: Experiencing Flow in Work and Play. Jossey-Bass, San Fransisco (1975)
7. Finneran, C.M., Zhang, P.: A person–artefact–task (PAT) model of flow antecedents in computer-mediated environments. Int. J. Hum. Comput. Stud. **59**(4), 475–496 (2003)
8. Šimleša, M., Guegan, J., Blanchard, E., Tarpin-Bernard, F., Buisine, S.: The flow engine framework: a cognitive model of optimal human experience. Europe's J. Psychol. **14**(1) (2018)
9. Tse, D.C., Fung, H.H., Nakamura, J., Csikszentmihalyi, M.: Teamwork and flow proneness mitigate the negative effect of excess challenge on flow state. J. Posit. Psychol. **13**(3), 284–289 (2018)
10. Mäkikangas, A., Bakker, A.B., Aunola, K., Demerouti, E.: Job resources and flow at work: modelling the relationship via latent growth curve and mixture model methodology. J. Occup. Organ. Psychol. **83**(3), 795–814 (2010)
11. Salanova, M., Bakker, A.B., Llorens, S.: Flow at work: evidence for an upward spiral of personal and organizational resources. J. Happiness Stud. **7**(1), 1–22 (2006)
12. Bakker, A.B., Van Woerkom, M.: Flow at work: a self-determination perspective. Occup. Health Sci. **1**, 47–65 (2017)
13. Demerouti, E., Mäkikangas, A.: What predicts flow at work? theoretical and empirical perspectives. In: Flow at Work, pp. 66–80. Routledge (2017)
14. Peifer, C., Tan, J.: The psychophysiology of flow experience. In: Peifer, C., Engeser, S. (eds.) Advances in Flow Research, pp. 191–230. Springer, Cham (2021). https://doi.org/10.1007/978-3-030-53468-4_8

15. Peifer, C., Wolters, G.: Flow in the context of work. In: Peifer, C., Engeser, S. (eds.) Advances in Flow Research, pp. 287–321. Springer, Cham (2021). https://doi.org/10.1007/978-3-030-53468-4_11

16. Lazarus, R.S., Folkman, S.: Stress, Appraisal, and Coping. Springer, Cham (1984)

17. Peifer, C.: Psychophysiological correlates of flow-experience. In: Engeser, S. (ed.) Advances in Flow Research, pp. 139–164. Springer, New York (2012). https://doi.org/10.1007/978-1-4614-2359-1_8

18. Mihelič, K.K., Aleksić, D.: "Dear employer, let me introduce myself"–flow, satisfaction with work–life balance and millennials' creativity. Creat. Res. J. 29(4), 397–408 (2017)

19. Maslow, A.H.: Toward a humanistic biology. Am. Psychol. 24(8), 724 (1969)

20. Lotan, G., Tanay, G., Bernstein, A.: Mindfulness and distress tolerance: relations in a mindfulness preventive intervention. Int. J. Cogn. Ther. 6(4), 371–385 (2013)

21. de Jager Meezenbroek, E., Garssen, B., van den Berg, M., Van Dierendonck, D., Visser, A., Schaufeli, W.B.: Measuring spirituality as a universal human experience: a review of spirituality questionnaires. J. Relig. Health 51, 336–354 (2012)

22. Diener, E., Lucas, R.E., Oishi, S.: Subjective well-being: the science of happiness and life satisfaction. Handb. Posit. Psychol. 2, 63–73 (2002)

23. Diener, E., Suh, E.M., Lucas, R.E., Smith, H.L.: Subjective well-being: three decades of progress. Psychol. Bull. 125(2), 276 (1999)

24. Watson, D., Clark, L.A., Tellegen, A.: Development and validation of brief measures of positive and negative affect: the PANAS scales. J. Pers. Soc. Psychol. 54(6), 1063 (1988)

25. Chen, H., Liu, C., Chiou, W.K., Lin, R.: How flow and mindfulness interact with each other in different types of mandala coloring activities? In: Rau, P.L. (ed.) Cross-Cultural Design. Methods, Tools and User Experience, HCII 2019, vol. 11576, pp. 471–486. Springer, Cham (2019). https://doi.org/10.1007/978-3-030-22577-3_34

26. Horwood, S., Anglim, J.: Problematic smartphone usage and subjective and psychological well-being. Comput. Hum. Behav. 97, 44–50 (2019)

27. Diener, E., Emmons, R.A., Larsen, R.J., Griffin, S.: The satisfaction with life scale. J. Pers. Assess. 49(1), 71–75 (1985)

28. Gigantesco, A., et al.: The relationship between satisfaction with life and depression symptoms by gender. Front. Psych. 10, 419 (2019)

29. Muñoz-Rodríguez, J.-M., Serrate-González, S., Navarro, A.-B.: Generativity and life satisfaction of active older people: advances (keys) in educational perspective. Aust. J. Adult Learn. 59(1), 94–114 (2019)

30. Garfield, A.M., Drwecki, B.B., Moore, C.F., Kortenkamp, K.V., Gracz, M.D.: The oneness beliefs scale: connecting spirituality with pro-environmental behavior. J. Sci. Study Relig. 53(2), 356–372 (2014)

31. Chiou, W.K., Liu, C., Chen, H., Hsu, S.E.: Reliability and validity assessment of the Chinese version of flow ergonomics. In: Rau, P.L.P. (ed.) Cross-Cultural Design. Interaction Design Across Cultures, HCII 2022, vol. 13311, pp. 330–341. Springer, Cham (2022). https://doi.org/10.1007/978-3-031-06038-0_24

32. Ware Jr, J.E., Sherbourne, C.D.: The MOS 36-item short-form health survey (SF-36): I. Conceptual framework and item selection. Med. Care, 473–483 (1992)

33. McHorney, C.A., Ware Johne, J.R., Anastasiae, R.: The MOS 36-item short-form health survey (SF-36): II. Psychometric and clinical tests of validity in measuring physical and mental health constructs. Med. Care 31(3), 247–263 (1993)

34. Ware, J.E., Jr.: SF-36 health survey update. Spine 25(24), 3130–3139 (2000)

35. Hawker, G.A., Mian, S., Kendzerska, T., French, M.: Measures of adult pain: visual analog scale for pain (VAS pain), numeric rating scale for pain (NRS pain), mcgill pain questionnaire (MPQ), short-form mcgill pain questionnaire (SF-MPQ), chronic pain grade scale (CPGS),

short form-36 bodily pain scale (SF-36 BPS), and measure of intermittent and constant osteoarthritis pain (icoap). Arthritis Care Res. **63**(S11), S240–S252 (2011)

36. Csikszentmihalyi, M., LeFevre, J.: Optimal experience in work and leisure. J. Pers. Soc. Psychol. **56**(5), 815 (1989)
37. Csikszentmihalyi, M., Csikszentmihalyi, M.: Toward a psychology of optimal experience. Flow and the Foundations of Positive Psychology: The Collected Works of Mihaly Csikszentmihalyi, 209–226 (2014)
38. Schiefele, U.: Response to Engeser (2012): on the nature of flow experience. Psychol. Rep. **112**(2), 529–532 (2013)

Discussion on the Usability of Inquiry Function Interface of Online Medical App

Ying-Chao Cui and Meng-Xi Chen[✉] [iD]

Shantou University, Shantou 515063, Guangdong, China
cmx12677@gmail.com

Abstract. The outbreak of novel coronavirus pneumonia has had an important impact on medical behavior of patients and promoted the development of online medical industry. With the rapid growth of online medical apps, the shortcomings in user experience have been highlighted, and the loyalties of some products' users are poorer. In this study, four online medical apps were selected to explore the influence of interface design on the usability of inquiry function interface. Twenty-four subjects were asked to use the function interfaces of expert inquiry and extremely rapid inquiry. Data was gathered through observation, interview and questionnaire. The results of this study revealed that icon design, operating procedure, information design and feedback may impact users' performance and satisfaction of online medical app.

Keywords: Online Medical · Interface Design · Usability

1 Introduction

At present, there are still many shortcomings in the preparation of medical resources in China, and many of the existing medical and health resources are concentrated in cities, of which the majority of high-quality resources converge in large and medium-sized hospitals, with a huge gap between urban and rural areas. While the aging population is increasing year by year, online medical service with low cost and high efficiency has considerable development space under the condition of increasing per capita medical expenditure.

In recent years, China has been actively promoting the development of "Internet + Medical and Health", improving the "Internet + medical and health" service system and innovating the "Internet +" public health services. Medical institutions shall be encouraged to apply Internet and other information technologies to expand the space and content of medical services and build an online and offline integrated medical service model covering pre-diagnosis, in-diagnosis and post-diagnosis.

The outbreak of novel coronavirus pneumonia has surged medical demand such as online consultation. Prior to 2019, the proportion of online medical inquires was just 2%–4%. Under the catalysis of this outbreak, the proportion of online medical inquires will be increase to about 10% [1]. Online medical service can reduce the costs of time spent attending offline visits and the risk of cross-infection. At the same time, services

P.-L. P. Rau (Ed.): HCII 2023, LNCS 14024, pp. 392–401, 2023.
https://doi.org/10.1007/978-3-031-35946-0_32

such as a free clinic and online drug purchase provided in the epidemic greatly alleviate the pressure of insufficient medical resources in physical institutions.

The main purpose of this study is to investigate the usability of inquiry function interface of online medical app, combined with theories of user experience, interface design, design aesthetics, to explore the optimal design solution for the inquiry function interfaces. We hope to be able to improve the apps' ease of use, attractiveness and flexibility to promote the development of online medical service.

2 Related Work

2.1 Online Medical App

As an emerging industry, online medical service uses mobile communication technology to provide online health services and information. At present, online medical apps can be divided into five categories according to different user needs, which are doctor-end, maternal health care, inquiry consultation, e-commerce, and hospital services. Compared with offline medical service, online medical inquiry have the advantages of saving time, rapid response and repeated inquiry. There are probably three aspects of user usage scenarios: first, known conditions or suffering from chronic diseases, requiring long-term consultation with doctors; second, smaller conditions as well as unknown disease prevention consultation, due to personal itinerary arrangements and complex offline medical processes are mostly not timely to offline hospital interviews; and third, the condition is specially shy to face-to-face consultation, such as gynecological diseases and andrological diseases. Therefore, the inquiry function of online medical app is characterized by consultation, prevention, rehabilitation, etc., and is not suitable for acute and severe diseases.

2.2 User Interface Design

The user interface is also known as called human-machine interface, which is the medium for the mutual transmission of information between the user and the machine [2]. Interface design focuses on the relationship between humans and computers and belongs to the artistic category, and its research object is also more focused on the understanding of users (such as experience, motivation, need, and availability) [3]. Understanding of users, particularly their need, is the core and starting point of this user-centered approach to experience design [4]. The interface design, including design items such as layout, text color, icons, controls and sounds, directly affects users' evaluations of the usability and satisfaction [5]. From the sensory experience and the availability of interactive operation, eight features required for a good user interface are clear, conciseness, familiarity, ease of response, consistent operation, attractiveness, efficiency, and fault tolerance [3].

2.3 Visual Perception

Rudolf Arnheim elaborated on the principle of visual perception in perceptual psychology and suggested that all mental abilities of people are active as a whole at any time, all perceptions contain thinking, all reasoning contains intuition, and all observations contain creation. The visual image is never a mechanical reproduction of perceptual materials, but a creative grasp of reality, and the image it grasps is a beautiful image containing rich imagination, creativity and acuity [6]. Thus, visual perception contains thinking activities and will not be separated from psychological perceptual activities. In other words, in watching activities, the structure, size, shape, density and space of things will be effectively encoded, so designers should design diverse artistic forms to convey ideas, so that the audience can effectively receive and understand.

3   Methods

3.1   Samples and Apparatus

The layout of the inquiry function interface for each sample is given in Table 1. The experimental samples were tested on an iPhone 12 smart phone, with a built-in iOS 14.2.1 operating system and 6.1-inch screen.

Table 1. Final samples of four expert inquiry interfaces.

Sample 1	Sample 2	Sample 3	Sample 4
Information-based interface designs, without an icon.	The interface design with icon and text.	Icon-based interface design.	Text-based interface design with icons.

3.2   Subjects

Twenty-four subjects were randomly assigned to study, all of whom were between 20 and 45 years of ages, 13 males and 11 females, and none of whom had experience using online medical apps. In addition, all subjects were educated at university, and some were above university, including 18 students and 6 working salary families, all of whom had rich experience in the use of internet equipment.

3.3 Experiment Procedure

The experimental design of this study was conducted in a between-group manner, with one sample tested from each subject and six subjects participating in each sample. First, the subjects were asked to fill in the basic data, introduce the experimental content and procedures to the subjects, and provide paper instructions on the task, while confirming whether the subjects were clear about the task again to ensure that they were not interfered by the outside during the operation. Secondly, the subjects began to perform the manipulation experiment, during which the time required for each task operation was recorded, and the use status and emotional response were observed and recorded laterally. Thirdly, subjects were requested to fill out nine questions about their satisfaction of information on the interface, ease of use, helpfulness, and so on. The questionnaire was designed based on a 7-point Likert scale anchored by 1: less satisfied and 7: much satisfied. Finally, we performed one-on-one interviews of how subjects felt after use. After the investigation, the collected data were statistically analyzed, and combined with the subject behavior and evaluation, the advantages and disadvantages of the interface were explored, and suggestions for improvement were submitted.

3.4 Task Design

In this experiment, four tasks were designed according to the inquiry function, from task 1 to task 3 mainly aimed at the expert inquiry function, and task 4 aimed at the extremely rapid inquiry function. Specific tasks are as following:

Task 1 (find department): Find the department of stomatology on the inquiry interface.
Task 2 (seek medical treatment for the disease): Without using the search box, find a doctor who treats hair loss on the inquiry interface.
Task 3 (concerned doctor): Search for fractures in the search box, find the doctor with the fastest response time under the condition of the highest number of interviews, and then follow him.
Task 4 (extremely rapid inquiry): In the function of extremely rapid inquiry, for grandma suddenly headache and vertigo symptoms, we need to find graphic consultation to inquiry the doctors belonging to Grade-A tertiary hospitals.

4 Results and Analysis

4.1 Analysis of Task Operation Time

A one-way analysis of variance (ANOVA) was performed by the IBM Statistical Package for the Social Sciences (SPSS) software to analyze the collected data. The results generated from the descriptive statistics and one-way ANOVA of task operation time are presented in Table 2, with significant differences in the task operation time of each of the four tasks ($P = 0.000 < 0.05$). Moreover, Sample 1 is the sample with the slowest operation in every task.

Task 1 (find department): The results of post-hoc multiple comparison of task 1 operation time are shown in Table 3. It can be seen that there are significant differences in the task completion time between Sample 2 and Sample 1, Sample 2 and Sample 3,

Table 2. Descriptive statistics and one-way ANOVA of task operation time.

	Sample 1	Sample 2	Sample 3	Sample 4	F	P
Task 1	29.93 (6.56)	10.76 (2.94)	25.39 (11.68)	12.97 (5.42)	9.656	.000*
Task 2	88.76 (12.38)	21.03 (2.52)	38.70 (20.79)	30.33 (9.01)	32.614	.000*
Task 3	96.29 (9.53)	31.77 (2.82)	71.47 (24.58)	31.25 (5.27)	33.394	.000*
Task 4	138.24 (14.44)	89.01 (30.14)	97.19 (14.87)	39.26 (10.39)	27.387	.000*

$\alpha = 0.05$, *$P < 0.05$.

Sample 4 and Sample 1, and Sample 4 and Sample 3. The use of Sample 2 (M = 10.76, SD = 2.94) and Sample 4 (M = 12.97, SD = 5.42) to find dentistry was significantly faster than the use of Sample 1 (M = 29.93, SD = 6.56) and Sample 3 (M = 25.39, SD = 11.68). It is mainly because the expert inquiry interface of Sample 2 (Table 1) and Sample 4 (Table 1) presents different departments in a way of monochromatic line icons combined with black text, it is simple and distinct, and the overall visual effect is unified. Although Sample 3 (Table 1) shows the familiar everyday elements of users with colored facial icons and has certain recognition and affinity, the departmental text is gray, and the words are thin and difficult to read. In addition, the name "Oral and Maxillofacial Department" is complex and specialized, increasing the thinking time and error rate of subjects. Department name of Sample 1 (Table 1) is located in the "See Expert" module and is only described in words. Slide left and right to find the department, or click the "All Doctors" button to display all departments. The steps are complicated and not easy to understand, resulting in that the subjects do not know where to click to find other departments.

Table 3. Post-hoc multiple comparison of task 1 operation time.

	Sample 2	Sample 4	Sample 1	Sample 3
Sample 2		0.610	0.000*	0.003*
Sample 4			0.001*	0.008*
Sample 1				0.299
Sample 3				

$\alpha = 0.05$, *$P < 0.05$.

Task 2 (seek medical treatment for the disease): The results of post-hoc multiple comparison of task 2 operation time are shown in Table 4. It can be seen that there are significant differences in task two completion time between Sample 2 and Sample 1, between Sample 2 and Sample 3, between Sample 4 and Sample 1, and between

Sample 1 and Sample 3. Finding physicians treating alopecia was significantly slowest using Sample 1 (M = 88.76, SD = 12.38). The main reason for this phenomenon is that the layout of the Sample 1 interface (Table 1) is complex, there is no separate department module, too much information is presented, and users can only read the doctor introduction text verbatim for judgment and selection. In addition, Sample 2 (M = 21.03, SD = 2.52) performed significantly faster than Sample 3 (M = 38.70, SD = 20.79). The reason may be that Sample 2 (Table 1) placed dermatology first in the department and was first detected by the user, while Sample 3 (Table 1) did not show dermatology in a significant position and the text recognition of the department icon was poor. During the post-experimental interview, it was found that some subjects were not aware of the department to which hair loss belonged, and the function of Sample 4 (Table 1) to find experts according to the disease could solve this problem. However, this feature has repeated information with common disease names in Sample 4 Department cards, increasing the cognitive load of users.

Table 4. Post-hoc multiple comparison of task 2 operation time.

	Sample 2	Sample 4	Sample 1	Sample 3
Sample 2		0.229	0.000*	0.029*
Sample 4			0.000*	0.277
Sample 1				0.000*
Sample 3				

$\alpha = 0.05$, *P < 0.05.

Task 3 (concerned doctor): The results of post-hoc multiple comparison of task 3 operation time are shown in Table 5. It can be seen that there were significant differences in task three completion time between other samples except for Sample 2 and Sample 4. Sample 2 (M = 31.77, SD = 2.82) and Sample 4 (M = 31.25, SD = 5.27) operated significantly faster than Sample 3 (M = 71.47, SD = 24.58), while Sample 1 (M = 96.29, SD = 9.53) was significantly the slowest. The phenomenon is mainly because the interface between Sample 2 and Sample 4 clearly shows the speed of response of each doctor. However, Sample 3 (Fig. 1) only used the label of "Quick Response" for individual doctors and mixed it with the label of other contents, with poorer recognition. The interface is slightly crowded, the size and color of the text lack obvious hierarchical division, did not form a satisfactory visual rhythm, affecting the speed of visual search. Doctors' response timing has a significant impact on patients' choice of the doctors [7], and designers should fully consider the eagerness of users to hope to find doctors who respond quickly to help solve problems. In addition, some subjects hesitated to use the words "faster" and "faster" describing the speed of response in the Sample 4 interface. The researchers found that the use of Sample 1 to find doctors was fast, and the key information of doctors used a contrasting label design. The task three operation time of Sample 1 mainly consumes the step of paying attention to the doctor, and its doctor data interface uses a five-pointed star collection icon in an imperceptible corner, which is different from the user habits of the other three samples using distinct buttons to "pay attention to" the doctor.

Table 5. Post-hoc multiple comparison of task 3 operation time.

	Sample 2	Sample 4	Sample 1	Sample 3
Sample 2		0.948	0.000*	0.000*
Sample 4			0.000*	0.000*
Sample 1				0.005*
Sample 3				

$\alpha = 0.05$, *P < 0.05.

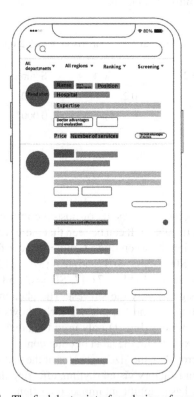

Fig. 1. The find doctor interface design of sample 3.

Task 4 (extremely rapid inquiry): The results of post-hoc multiple comparison of task 4 operation time are shown in Table 6. It can be seen that there was no significant difference in task 4 completion time between Sample 2 and Sample 3. Extremely rapid inquiry was significantly fastest using Sample 4 (M = 39.26, SD = 10.39), while it was significantly slowest using Sample 1 (M = 138.24, SD = 14.44). The main reason is that the extremely rapid inquiry interface of Sample 4 (Fig. 2a) describes the condition in a common chatting dialogue and is more cordial and familiar. Each description requires only at least 2 words and provides timely interactive feedback. Users do not have to think carefully about how to describe the condition and other problems, the process is simple and smooth, can ease tension, and quickly find a matching doctor. Sample 1, Sample 2 and Sample 3's extremely rapid inquiry interface is very similar, all require subjects to input text and upload pictures, and both Sample 1 and Sample 3 require users to input at least 10 words. The difference is that Sample 1 (Fig. 2b) requires clicking "how to describe" before a description template appears and requires the user to read it carefully, increasing the cost of time. While Sample 3s' requirements for disease description are directly displayed in the input box, users can directly read the requirements before entering, and the steps are more concise compared with Sample 1. Sample 2 has a prompt button to describe the condition, and clicking the button in turn can quickly elaborate the key points of the condition, so that the requirements for describing the condition are more intuitive, improving the efficiency of use, and avoiding the lack of key condition description.

Table 6. Post-hoc multiple comparison of task 4 operation time.

	Sample 2	Sample 4	Sample 1	Sample 3
Sample 2		0.000*	0.000*	0.465
Sample 4			0.000*	0.000*
Sample 1				0.001*
Sample 3				

*$P < 0.05$, Significant difference exists.

4.2 Analysis of Users' Satisfaction

The results generated from the descriptive statistics and one-way ANOVA of users' satisfaction are presented in Table 7. There was a significant difference in the satisfaction evaluations of the four samples ($P = 0.003 < 0.05$). Sample 4 had the highest score, followed by Sample 1, the third was Sample 2, and Sample 3 had the worst satisfaction.

Notably, regardless of the fact that Sample 1 had the longest operating time for each task, subjects ranked second in their overall satisfaction evaluation. This might be because that the presentation of the doctor 's avatar on the expert inquiry interface of Sample 1 may give the subjects more closeness, and emphasizing the hospital level with small icons in the introduction part of doctors can enhance the sense of trust and meet users' expectations. In addition, there are feedback progress bar and speech input functions on the interfaces of Sample 1, fully consider usage scenarios and users' needs, making the inquiry experience more comfortable and smooth. In summary, the results suggested that the efficiency of operation is related to usability, but that will not necessarily achieve high satisfaction.

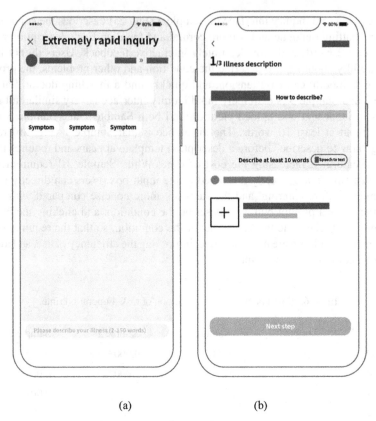

(a)   (b)

Fig. 2. The design of extremely rapid inquiry interface. (a) Sample 4, (b) Sample 1.

Table 7. Descriptive statistics and one-way ANOVA of satisfaction.

	Sample 1	Sample 2	Sample 3	Sample 4	F	P
Satisfaction	53.83 (5.85)	51.83 (3.49)	49.17 (5.23)	59.83 (0.75)	6.643	0.003*

*P < 0.05, Significant difference exists.

5 Conclusions

This study mainly investigated how the design of inquiry function interface affect the usability of an online medical app. It is found that all of the layout, text, icon, figure, information structure and feedback are very important factors. Therefore, the following suggestions are put forward for the above four aspects:

(1) Icons containing emotionality bring users closer to the online medical app and increase stickiness in use. Therefore, the icons on inquiry function interface should select the appropriate visual style and the content of text on the basis of functional differentiation.
(2) Based on users' needs and expectations, removing the unnecessary operating procedures to make the online medical process simple.
(3) The information design on inquiry function interface should consider users' visual perception. To create a visual focus for the high-priority information.
(4) To improve affordance and provide clear and timely feedback to make it easier for users to understand.

Acknowledgements. This work was funded by Philosophy and Social Science Planning Project of Guangdong Province [GD22XYS31], and STU Scientific Research Initiation Grant [STF22003].

References

1. Sina Finance. https://baijiahao.baidu.com/s?id=1657788426130034324&wfr=spider&for=pc. Accessed 10 Sept 2022
2. Zhu, S.J., Zhu, S.S.: User Experience and Product Innovation Design. Mechanical Industry Press, Beijing (2019)
3. Li, S.D.: Overview of Interactive Design. Tsinghua Press, Beijing (2009)
4. User Research and Experience Design Department of Tencent Company: Beside You, Design for You. Electronic Industry Press, Beijing (2016)
5. Chen, C.H., Chen, M.X.: Effects of the design of overview maps on three-dimensional virtual environment interfaces. Sensors **20**(16), 4605 (2020)
6. Rodolf, A.: Art and Visual Perception. Sichuan People's Press, Chengdu (2006)
7. Lu, Q., Li, Y.S., Chen, J.: Study on the influencing factors of medical behavior of patients in online medical community. Libr. Inf. Technol. Work **63**(08), 87–95 (2019)

Analysis and Validation of the Reliability and Validity of the Flow Ergonomics Scale (FES-45): Study on Mindfulness Meditation of Animation Employees

Szu-Erh Hsu[1]([✉]), Hao Chen[2]([✉]), Chao Liu[3]([✉]), Po-Chen Shen[1]([✉]), and Wen-Ko Chiou[1]([✉])

[1] Department of Industrial Design, Chang Gung University, Taoyuan City, Taiwan
`h410@hotmail.com`, `174673015@qq.com`, `wkchiu@mail.cgu.edu.tw`
[2] School of Film Television and Communication, Xiamen University of Technology, Xiamen, China
`shinn.b21@gmail.com`
[3] School of Journalism and Communication, Hua Qiao University, Xiamen 361021, China
`victory666666@126.com`

Abstract. In the past, our team improved the first version of the Flow Ergonomics (FE) Scale (FES) and proposed the FES-45 version. The scale after reducing the number of questions was not used in the actual test. Therefore, the research team will conduct the test with practitioners from different industries. The research will validate the model again and confirm whether the correlation between categories is consistent. In order to further verify the effectiveness of the model, this study will use FES-45 to test the animation employees, and use SPSS 22.0 and AMOS 22.0 to analyze the data. The questionnaire collected 100 valid questionnaires and tested their reliability and validity. In this paper, exploratory and confirmatory factor analysis are carried out respectively, and the reliability of the results of the grounded theory is verified by structural equation model. The study considers that the model of FE is reasonable, and the improved scale of FES-45 is more effective; The number of deleted questions will not make the subjects feel too much when filling in, and will reduce the fatigue and discomfort caused by filling in too long.

Keywords: Flow Ergonomics Scale · Reliability · Validity · Mindfulness Meditation · Animation Employees

1 Introduction

In recent years, affected by the epidemic, many studies have shown that the problems related to unemployment and physical and mental health have increased, and the physical and mental health of employees in the workplace has received high attention. In such an era, economic recession and widespread unemployment have led to many mental diseases, chronic diseases and use. During this period, the patients suffering from stress, anxiety and despair were also higher than the general level, and the prevalence of depression and anxiety increased significantly.

© The Author(s), under exclusive license to Springer Nature Switzerland AG 2023
P.-L. P. Rau (Ed.): HCII 2023, LNCS 14024, pp. 402–412, 2023.
https://doi.org/10.1007/978-3-031-35946-0_33

On the other hand, in addition to improving the environmental safety of employees, the company has also become an important goal of the company's sustainable development to improve employees' centripetal force and sense of work safety, and promote the quality of life, physical and mental health. Investing in the health of employees is the company's biggest profit. If we want to increase productivity, we must pay attention to the health of employees. A large number of data show that good work is good for health [1]. The Flow Ergonomics (FE) Scale (FES) developed and validated in the past in this study focuses more on understanding the impact of employees' physical and psychological health and environment in the workplace.

The research team used to propose a conceptual framework for the FE, and put forward the results of the revision of FES 45 (FES-45) in the study of animation guided compassionate meditation of flight attendants. In order to make the scale more stable and adapt to employees from all walks of life, this study will guide mindfulness meditation research through animation of employees, so that the scale will be more consistent with the way that the public practitioners evaluate the degree of FE. Based on empirical research, this study conducted exploratory and confirmatory factor analysis on the sample, adjusted the conceptual model and the FES, and then measured the reliability and validity. This study will use the FE-45 scale to observe whether it is necessary to delete items after the application of animation employees. Through the final verification and analysis, the concept and scale of FE will be more suitable for the use of various workplaces and practitioners.

2 Literature Review

2.1 Maslow's Highest Hierarchy of Needs and Related Inventories

Maslow [2] proposed that the complete expression of the demand hierarchy model should be six levels, namely, physiological needs, security needs, belonging and love needs, respect needs, self-realization needs and transcendence needs. The need for transcendence can also be called the spiritual need or the need for transcendence and self-realization. Koltko-Rivera [3] believed that Maslow expanded the demand class from five to six. In addition to the needs of physiology, security, sense of belonging and love, respect and self-realization, there is also the need for transcendence. Among them, the needs of self-realization and transcendence are all about the transformation of consciousness. Garcia-Romeu [4] believed that people can achieve self-transcendence to the maximum extent, such as altruism or spiritual improvement. In the past, when constructing the scale, the research team incorporated these levels of needs and supported the theoretical framework of mindfulness, mind flow, spirituality, mind flow, happiness, and oneness transcendence. Through the foundation of these theories, the model and scale were constructed. Mindfulness scale is used to measure the state mindfulness of subjects. The State Mindfulness Scale (SMS) developed by Lotan et al. [5] is used. The FE meter is used to measure the FE state of the subjects. The FE theory proposed by Csikszentmihalyi [6] is adopted. The Short Dispositional Flow Scale 2 (SDFS-2). The Spiritual Attitude and Involvement List (SAIL) was used to measure the spirituality of subjects [7]. The Subjective Well-Being (SWB) is composed of two parts: emotional balance and life satisfaction [8]. The part of emotional balance adopts the Positive and

Negative Effect Scale (PANAS) developed by Watson et al. [9]. The Oneness Beliefs Scale developed by Garfield et al. [10].

Chiou et al. [11] put forward a new category for the theoretical framework and scale of human factors. The seven dimensions are (1) the "consciousness of integration" of the scale of integration; (2) the "focus on the present", "clear goal" "Control task"; (3) "positive emotion and meaning" in the emotional scale; (4) "negative emotion" in the emotional scale; (5) "happy life" in the life satisfaction scale and part of the emotional scale; (6) "acceptance" in the mindfulness scale; (7) "compassion" in the spiritual scale.

2.2 Flow

Flow is defined as a rewarding state in which one is completely absorbed and can work on an optimally challenging task [6]. Flow can be characterized by the following three core components: absorption, perceived demands-skill balance, and enjoyment during task performance [12]. Flow is a positive and intense mental state of short duration in which a person performing an activity is fully immersed in a feeling of energized focus and full devotion to the present moment and is enjoying it intensely [13]. Different from work engagement, flow is the optimal experience caused by a specific activity, including engagement, absorption, and enjoyment [14]. It is associated with several positive outcomes, such as improved performance, well-being, positive affect, creativity, and physical health [15, 16]. Work engagement, however, is the overall attitude towards work and thus differs with flow in terms of time dimension [14]. In the work context, the flow state is similar to other experiences studied empirically in sports and in the arts [17]. Work-related flow can be experienced in any type of work because its occurrence depends more on the quality of the experience than on the nature of the activity [18].

The flow channel model illustrates that flow is experienced if skills and demands balance. Furthermore, boredom occurs if the skills exceed the challenges, and anxiety occurs if the challenges exceed the skills [6]. In line with the Transactional Stress Model, Peifer et al. [19] modified the original flow channel model by adding states they refer to as relaxation and stress. Work-related flow levels were generally higher than the levels of flow experienced in active or passive leisure activities [20]. The occurrence of flow at work is related to the perception that an individual has about his or her ability to respond to challenging demands at work [21]. Šimleša et al. [22] argued that, in order to experience flow, the individual must also remain focused on the task and motivated to work hard, which is the most central process. Flow can be triggered during work tasks when tasks are seen as opportunities for growth and employees are equipped with the necessary skills or resources for dealing with such demands [23]. However, the physiological pattern during flow suggests that it is a state of (at least moderately) increased physiological arousal, which underlines an association with stress and a potential relationship with burnout symptoms [19, 24, 25]. Proactive individual job redesign optimizes the level of job demands and job resources with individual needs at work [26]. By shaping their own work experience, employees create opportunities to use abilities (*e.g.*, skills, talents, competencies), to exert passions (*e.g.*, intrinsic motivations) and to build meaning at work that is aligned with their personal values [27, 28].

2.3 Flow Ergonomics

FE is a feeling that one's mental power is fully invested in certain activities. When cardiac flow occurs, there will be a high sense of excitement and fulfillment. The conceptualization of cardiac flow originates from the peak experience field. In 1968, Maslow began to study the peak experience. The peak of all experiences is self-realization. The conclusion is that everyone can get the best experience [29]. Human factors engineering is an important engineering technology discipline, which studies the interaction and reasonable combination of human, machine and environment, so that the designed machine and environment system can adapt to human physiological and psychological characteristics, and achieve the purpose of improving efficiency, safety, health and comfort in production. The academic community believed that occupational health, ergonomics and product design were the three main areas of the development of human performance engineering in Taiwan. This study explores this issue from the perspective of human factors of cardiac flow. The flow of human factors can be said to be a way to improve the spiritual level of human beings, and can be effectively used in the workplace and work [30, 31].

The theoretical framework is based on the core category of FE, including oneness transcendence, mindfulness flow concentration, positive emotion and meaning, negative emotion, happy life, environmental connection and acceptance. Chiou et al. [11] proposed the FES. The research team revised the model and scale in 2022 after the actual application and validation of the field of flight attendants, and put forward the FES-45. This scale includes seven dimensions: (1) Transcendence and oneness; (2) Present attention; (3) Positive emotion and meaning; (4) Negative emotion; (5) Pleasure Life; (6) Compassion; (7) Acceptance. Total 45 questions, Cronbach's alpha value (α = 0.959). The answer type is Likert five-point scale, "1" means completely inconsistent, and "5" means completely consistent; The total score of each subscale is the score of each subscale, and the total score of the subscale is the total scale score.

3 Methods

This study was conducted in the Human Factors/Ergonomics (HFE) Research Room of Chang Gang University, and conducted an 8-week experiment with 100 animation practitioners. They were divided into two groups, the experimental group and the control group, with 50 persons each; The 50 people in the control group were animation practitioners, who filled in the pre-test questionnaire first, and then filled in the post-test questionnaire eight weeks later; During this eight-week period, no intervention will be made; The experimental group filled in the pre-test questionnaire before the experiment, followed by animated mindfulness exercises for the next eight weeks, three times a week, and then filled in the post-test questionnaire after eight weeks. The scale test consists of the FES and the Job Creation Force Scale. This study is divided into two parts. The human factors scale of cardiac flow is rotated to obtain data suitable for factor analysis, and then the AMOS software is used for confirmatory factor analysis. In order not to unduly interfere with the meditation feelings of animation practitioners and increase the willingness to fill in the answers, it is necessary to develop simple and effective human factors tools for flow of mind. Therefore, this study selected the topic according to the above exploratory factor analysis deletion principle, and deleted the items with the absolute value of factor load less than 0.4 to achieve the simple and effective goal; Finally, it uses confirmatory factor analysis and reliability and validity test to understand the overall fitness, constituent reliability, aggregate validity and differential validity, and also tests the criterion-related validity of the scale.

4 Results and Discussion

The FES is a new seven-dimensional integration of mindfulness scale (SMS), the Flow (SDFS-2), the spirituality scale (SAIL), the oneness scale (Oneness), the emotional scale (PANAS), the life satisfaction scale (SWLS).

This study needs to test and evaluate the reliability and validity of the FES. In order to test the validity of the FES, we conducted exploratory factor analysis (EFA) and confirmatory factor analysis (CFA) on the samples. The following indicators are used to determine the goodness of fit of the EFA model: the root mean square error approximation (RMSEA) is less than 0.08, the comparison fit index (CFI) and non-normed fit index (NNFI) are greater than 0.90, and the chi-square value is greater than its degree of freedom (χ^2/df) less than 3.0. The exploratory factor analysis uses the maximum variation rotation method to determine the factor structure of the human factors scale for cardiac flow. Kaiser-Meyer-Olkin (KMO) test verified the sampling adequacy of the analysis, Barrett's spherical test evaluates the correlation degree between variables, and determines the factor extraction through Kaiser standard (characteristic value $\geq$ 1). The factor loads greater than 0.5 is considered to be the threshold value for the full contribution of this item to this factor. Cronbach's alpha coefficient is calculated to determine the partial consistency of the whole scale and various factors. A value ≥ 0.70 is considered sufficient (as shown in Table 1). All statistical analyses were carried out using SPSS 22.0 and AMOS 22.0 programs, with statistical significance of p < 0.05.

It can be seen from the following table that the correlation coefficients of one-in-one transcendence and focus on the present, happy life, positive emotion and meaning, sympathy and acceptance are all positive and significant at the level of 1%, which indicates that one-in-one transcendence has a significant positive correlation with these variables. Similarly, the correlation coefficient between happy life and positive emotion and meaning, sympathy and acceptance is also positive, which indicates that there is also a significant correlation between these variables (as shown in Fig. 1). Focusing on the present also has a positive correlation coefficient with positive emotion and meaning, sympathy and acceptance, which indicates that there is a significant correlation between focusing on the present and these variables (as shown in Table 2).

It can be seen from Table 3 that the present attention cannot significantly affect the negative emotion ($\beta = -0.096$, P = 0.398). However, the present attention has a significant positive impact on positive emotion and meaning, comparison and acceptance ($\beta = 0.589$, P = 0.000; $\beta = 0.747$, P = 0.000; $\beta = 0.476$, P = 0.000). Negative emotion has no significant impact on Pleasure life ($\beta = -0.007$, P = 0.945), but positive emotion and meaning can have a significant impact on Pleasure life ($\beta = 0.538$, P = 0.000). Comparison and Acceptance have a significant impact on Transcendence and oneness ($\beta = 0.488$, P = 0.007; $\beta = 0.361$, P = 0.004). However, Pleasure life has no significant impact on Transcendence and oneness ($\beta = -0.074$, P = 0.501).

Table 1. Structural validity and reliability

	AVE	CR	Alpha
Transcendence and oneness	0.463	0.771	0.778
Present attention	0.668	0.908	0.905
Positive emotion and meaning	0.653	0.938	0.936
Negative emotion	0.485	0.861	0.851
Pleasure Life	0.378	0.643	0.625
Compassion	0.450	0.850	0.845
Acceptance	0.463	0.771	0.778

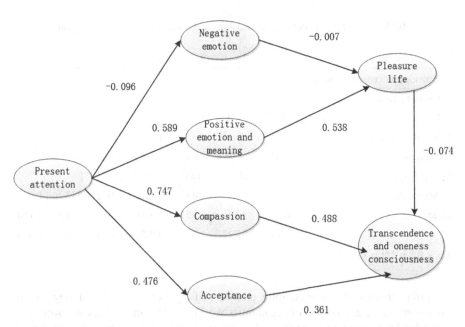

Fig. 1. An architecture model of the relationship between dimensions with path coefficients

In attempting to be comprehensive, existing general health questionnaires such as the sickness impact profile may be too long or require interviews, or both. In primary care or community settings the contact time with patients is often short, and thus to be practical and acceptable to the population the questionnaire must be brief, easy to use, and preferably self-administered. These features are also important for researchers, who may want to add a generic health measure to a disease specific questionnaire. The role model of SF-36 questionnaire seemed to meet these criteria, taking just five minutes to complete. This quantitative evidence, and the favorable impression for face to face interviews, suggests that the SF-36 questionnaire is an acceptable measure of the health of a general population [32–35].

The Work-Related Flow Inventory is a well-known and validated instrument for measuring flow at work [36]. Therefore, the aim of the present study was to validate FES-45, aimed at measuring ergonomics-related flow. The key findings can be summarized as follows. First, as expected, the results indicate that the flow dimensions can be distinguished in an ergonomics setting. The results of the CFA on the data of animation employees demonstrated that FES-45 has the same structure as the original FES, with three separate factors, namely, absorption, enjoyment, and intrinsic motivation for studying. All model fit indices reached their corresponding criteria satisfactorily. In addition, all AVE values were acceptable both for factorial and discriminant validity and were also acceptable for the internal consistency type of reliability of the scales. This indicates that the seven-factor model of ergonomics-related flow has good internal reliability and structural validity.

Table 2. Correlation between dimensions and mean and standard deviation

	1	2	3	4	5	6	7
1. Transcendence and oneness	1						
2. Present attention	.325**	1					
3. Positive emotion and meaning	.278**	.630**	1				
4. Negative emotion	.401**	.503**	.558**	1			
5. Pleasure Life	−.058	−.067	0.03	−0.04	1		
6. Compassion	.531**	.446**	.444**	.390**	0.052	1	
7. Acceptance	.517**	.311**	.243*	.211*	0.042	.523**	1
Mean	6.799	3.445	3.851	3.310	2.031	4.217	3.750
SD	1.278	0.727	1.039	0.927	0.899	0.883	0.676

*: $p < 0.05$; **: $p < 0.01$

Further studies and more complex measures of ergonomics workload may provide insights into different aspects of ergonomics workload. The animation employees may be overloaded for various reasons, such as having a too heavy work load, feeling overwhelmed by the quantity of materials, time pressure, or insufficient skills for ergonomics activities. This research examined flow as a phenomenon with seven underlying dimensions which were, in turn, operationalized as continuous variables. Although a global flow score on FES-45 may be used by calculating the mean score on all items, we were interested in investigating the specific relationships of flow components with criterion variables and therefore calculated scores for absorption, enjoyment and intrinsic motivation.

The importance of intrinsic motivation for experiencing flow was also indicated in the first studies of flow: flow was firstly noted in preferred activities such as chess playing, dancing, or sports [6]. However, further studies have shown that flow is also experienced at work [36, 37], and, even more, it has been found that flow can be more often found at work than in a leisure setting, which was explained by the inability to create a situation

Table 3. Path test

			Estimate	S.E	C.R	P
Negative emotion	<---	Present attention	−0.096	0.129	−0.846	0.398
Positive emotion and meaning	<---	Present attention	0.589	0.14	4.095	***
Compassion	<---	Present attention	0.747	0.173	3.684	***
Acceptance	<---	Present attention	0.476	0.125	3.628	***
Pleasure life	<---	Negative emotion	−0.007	0.131	−0.069	0.945
Pleasure life	<---	Positive emotion and meaning	0.538	0.195	4.414	***
Transcendence and oneness consciousness	<---	Compassion	0.488	0.382	2.712	0.007
Transcendence and oneness consciousness	<---	Acceptance	0.361	0.236	2.919	0.004
Transcendence and oneness consciousness	<---	Pleasure life	−0.074	0.129	−0.673	0.501

**: Correlation is significant at the 0.01 level (2-tailed).
*: Correlation is significant at the 0.05 level (2-tailed).

with a challenge-skill balance [38]. Additionally, Csikszentmihalyi [39] suggested that "the best moments usually occur when a person's body or mind is stretched to its limits in a voluntary effort to accomplish something difficult or worthwhile".

5 Conclusions

The purpose of this study is to evaluate the reliability and validity of FES-45 scale in the study of meditation practice of animation industry employees. Both the overall reliability and the reliability of each subscale indicate that the α value of this study is at a high level. From the effectiveness results, the goodness of fit index values of the CFA model in this study are higher than the ideal threshold, and the total variance interpretation rate of the EFA in this study is higher. FES-45 scale is composed of 7 dimensions and 45 items in total, with good reliability and validity. These seven factors are different, and the α coefficient shows a high internal consistency of all seven factors. Overall, the results of this study confirmed the reliability and validity of the FES as a tool for evaluating specific psychological characteristics and psychological status. FES-45 is a tool for measuring mental health and mental transcendence in the working environment and state. This study conducted an empirical study on the validity and reliability of the Taiwan FES-45. The measurement results show that the scale has good internal consistency and validity, and is worthy of further application in various workplaces.

To sum up, our results confirm the seven-factor structure of ergonomics-related FES-45 adapted from WOLF [36, 40, 23] for work-related flow. There is also evidence to support the convergent and construct validity of the scale. Therefore, the results provide justification for the use of FES-45 in a university context to assess study related flow experiences. Additionally, FES-45 is not a time-consuming inventory. As a whole, the present findings indicate that FES-45 can be effectively and efficiently used in an academic setting for measuring flow in ergonomics-related activities.

6 Research Limitations and Future Studies

Since the number of people in the animation industry in Taiwan is relatively less than that in Japan, the United States and other countries, many of the talent outflows in the animation industry are easily limited when recruiting subjects. The model and scale of research will be more stable and clear if we can recruit employees from other industries. In future research, the scale can be extended to domestic and foreign industries, or more industry categories, and more owners and employees can understand their employees' mental health and work status, so that owners can also timely intervene and care, establish good customer relationships, and achieve a win-win situation.

References

1. Waddell, G., Burton, A.K.: Is Work Good for Your Health and Well-Being? (2006)
2. Maslow, A.H.: Toward a humanistic biology. Am. Psychol. **24**(8), 724 (1969)
3. Koltko-Rivera, M.E.: Rediscovering the later version of Maslow's hierarchy of needs: self-transcendence and opportunities for theory, research, and unification. Rev. Gen. Psychol. **10**(4), 302–317 (2006)
4. Garcia-Romeu, A.: Self-transcendence as a measurable transpersonal construct. J. Transpers. Psychol. **42**(1), 26 (2010)
5. Lotan, G., Tanay, G., Bernstein, A.: Mindfulness and distress tolerance: relations in a mindfulness preventive intervention. Int. J. Cogn. Ther. **6**(4), 371–385 (2013)
6. Csikszentmihalyi, M.: Beyond Boredom and Anxiety: Experiencing Flow in Work and Play-San Fransisco, CA: Jossey-Bass (1975)
7. de Jager Meezenbroek, E., Garssen, B., van den Berg, M., Van Dierendonck, D., Visser, A., Schaufeli, W.B.: Measuring spirituality as a universal human experience: a review of spirituality questionnaires. J. Relig. Health **51**, 336–354 (2012)
8. Diener, E., Lucas, R.E., Oishi, S.: Subjective well-being: the science of happiness and life satisfaction. Handb. Positive Psychol. **2**, 63–73 (2002)
9. Watson, D., Clark, L.A., Tellegen, A.: Development and validation of brief measures of positive and negative affect: the PANAS scales. J. Pers. Soc. Psychol. **54**(6), 1063 (1988)
10. Garfield, A.M., Drwecki, B.B., Moore, C.F., Kortenkamp, K.V., Gracz, M.D.: The Oneness beliefs scale: connecting spirituality with pro-environmental behavior. J. Sci. Study Relig. **53**(2), 356–372 (2014)
11. Chiou, W.-K., Liu, C., Chen, H., Hsu, S.-E.: Reliability and validity assessment of the Chinese version of flow ergonomics. Paper presented at the cross-cultural design. interaction design across cultures. In: 14th International Conference, CCD 2022, Held as Part of the 24th HCI International Conference, HCII 2022, Virtual Event, June 26–July 1, 2022, Proceedings, Part I (2022)
12. Peifer, C., Engeser, S.: Theoretical Integration and Future Lines of Flow Research. In: Advances in Flow Research, pp. 417–439. Springer, Cham (2021)

13. Csikszentmihalyi, M.: Flow and the psychology of discovery and invention. HarperPerennial, New York **39**, 1–16 (1997)
14. Norsworthy, C., Jackson, B., Dimmock, J.A.: Advancing our understanding of psychological flow: a scoping review of conceptualizations, measurements, and applications. Psychol. Bull. **147**(8), 806 (2021)
15. Rivkin, W., Diestel, S., Schmidt, K.H.: Which daily experiences can foster well-being at work? a diary study on the interplay between flow experiences, affective commitment, and self-control demands. J. Occup. Health Psychol. **23**(1), 99 (2018)
16. Hirao, K., Kobayashi, R., Okishima, K., Tomokuni, Y.: Flow experience and health-related quality of life in community dwelling elderly Japanese. Nurs. Health Sci. **14**(1), 52–57 (2012)
17. Salanova, M., Bakker, A.B., Llorens, S.: Flow at work: evidence for an upward spiral of personal and organizational resources. J. Happiness Stud. **7**(1), 1–22 (2006)
18. Demerouti, E., Mäkikangas, A.: What predicts flow at work? theoretical and empirical perspectives. In: Flow at Work, pp. 66–80. Routledge (2017)
19. Peifer, C., Schulz, A., Schächinger, H., Baumann, N., Antoni, C.H.: The relation of flow-experience and physiological arousal under stress—can u shape it? J. Exp. Soc. Psychol. **53**, 62–69 (2014)
20. Engeser, S., Baumann, N.: Fluctuation of flow and affect in everyday life: a second look at the paradox of work. J. Happiness Stud. **17**, 105–124 (2016)
21. Bakker, A.B.: Flow among music teachers and their students: the crossover of peak experiences. J. Vocat. Behav. **66**(1), 26–44 (2005)
22. Šimleša, M., Guegan, J., Blanchard, E., Tarpin-Bernard, F., Buisine, S.: The flow engine framework: a cognitive model of optimal human experience. Europe's J. Psychol. **14**(1), 232–253 (2018)
23. Bakker, A.B., Van Woerkom, M.: Flow at work: a self-determination perspective. Occup. Health Sci. **1**, 47–65 (2017)
24. Peifer, C., Schächinger, H., Engeser, S., Antoni, C.H.: Cortisol effects on flow-experience. Psychopharmacology **232**(6), 1165–1173 (2014). https://doi.org/10.1007/s00 213-014-3753-5
25. Peifer, C., Zipp, G.: All at once? the effects of multitasking behavior on flow and subjective performance. Eur. J. Work Organ. Psy. **28**(5), 682–690 (2019)
26. Tims, M., Bakker, A.B., Derks, D.: Development and validation of the job crafting scale. J. Vocat. Behav. **80**(1), 173–186 (2012)
27. Peifer, C., Syrek, C., Ostwald, V., Schuh, E., Antoni, C.H.: Thieves of flow: how unfinished tasks at work are related to flow experience and wellbeing. J. Happiness Stud. **21**, 1641–1660 (2020)
28. Peifer, C., et al.: The symphony of team flow in virtual teams. using artificial intelligence for its recognition and promotion. Front. Psychol. **12**, 697093 (2021)
29. Fritz, B.S., Avsec, A.: The experience of flow and subjective well-being of music students. Horiz. Psychol. **16**(2), 5–17 (2007)
30. Dul, J., et al.: A strategy for human factors/ergonomics: developing the discipline and profession. Ergonomics **55**(4), 377–395 (2012)
31. Holden, R.J., et al.: SEIPS 2.0: a human factors framework for studying and improving the work of healthcare professionals and patients. Ergonomics **56**(11), 1669–1686 (2013)
32. Ware, J.E., Jr., Kosinski, M., Keller, S.D.: A 12-item short-form health survey: construction of scales and preliminary tests of reliability and validity. Med. Care **34**, 220–233 (1996)
33. McHorney, C.A., Ware, J.E., Jr., Lu, J.R., Sherbourne, C.D.: The MOS 36-item short-form health survey (SF-36): III. tests of data quality, scaling assumptions, and reliability across diverse patient groups. Med. Care **32**, 40–66 (1994)
34. Brazier, J.E., et al.: Validating the SF-36 health survey questionnaire: new outcome measure for primary care. Br. Med. J. **305**(6846), 160–164 (1992)

35. Ware, J.E., Kosinski, M., Keller, S.: SF-36 physical and mental health summary scales. *A User's Manual, 1994* (2001)
36. Bakker, A.B.: The work-related flow inventory: construction and initial validation of the WOLF. J. Vocat. Behav. **72**(3), 400–414 (2008)
37. Demerouti, E.: Job characteristics, flow, and performance: the moderating role of conscientiousness. J. Occup. Health Psychol. **11**(3), 266 (2006)
38. Csikszentmihalyi, M., LeFevre, J.: Optimal experience in work and leisure. J. Pers. Soc. Psychol. **56**(5), 815 (1989)
39. Csikszentmihalyi, M.: Toward a psychology of optimal experience. In: Flow and the foundations of positive psychology, pp. 209–226. Springer, Dordrecht (2014). https://doi.org/10.1007/978-94-017-9088-8_14
40. Bakker, A.B., Geurts, S.A.: Toward a dual-process model of work-home interference. Work. Occup. **31**(3), 345–366 (2004)

Empirical Research on User Stickiness of Fitness Application Based on the Theory of Continuous Use of Information System—Take Keep as an Example

Yuhang Jiang, Qiwen Chen, Jingxuan Ren, and Zhining Song[✉]

Hunan University, Changsha 410082, Hunan, People's Republic of China
676514534@qq.com

Abstract. Mobile fitness app is a new product in the Internet era, which provides convenient fitness help for sports enthusiasts. The purpose of this study is to explore the influencing factors of users' long-term willingness to use mobile fitness App-Keep, and to produce a design guide for the design and marketing of Keep. Based on the Expectation confirmation model of IS continuance (ECM-ISC), this study combines the important variables of the Technology Acceptance Model (TAM) and the Expectation Confirmation Theory (ECT), and then combines the characteristics of Keep app, constructs a model that affects its continuous use intention, and then makes statistical analysis of the questionnaire data. Verifying the influencing factors and mechanism of user stickiness does not lead to the following conclusions: (1) The perceived ease of use of mobile fitness application Keep has a positive impact on perceived usefulness, while the perceived ease of use has no significant impact on user satisfaction; (2) Perceived usefulness, perceived interestingness and perceived quality have a direct and significant impact on user satisfaction, thus enhancing users' willingness to continue using; (3) Perceived usefulness plays a complete intermediary role in the relationship between perceived ease of use and satisfaction, while it plays a partial intermediary role in the relationship between perceived interest and satisfaction. In this paper, a conceptual model of user stickiness in mobile health applications is constructed and verified theoretically. The practical level provides product strategy tips for Keep app and even all mobile health applications to form better user stickiness.

Keywords: User stickiness · Keep · Information system continuous use model · Mobile health applications

1 Introduction

In recent years, with the promotion of national policies, the national fitness enthusiasm is high, and more and more people are involved in the fitness cause. However, due to the limitation of epidemic situation, online fitness has become the most popular exercise mode for people today, and the multifunctional fitness application (MFAs) represented by Keep has ushered in the skyrocketing growth rate and profit rate. According to the

P.-L. P. Rau (Ed.): HCII 2023, LNCS 14024, pp. 413–431, 2023.
https://doi.org/10.1007/978-3-031-35946-0_34

data of Keep prospectus, the online fitness market in China will reach 369.7 billion yuan in 2021, with a compound annual growth rate of 14.3% from 2015 to 2021. The online fitness market is expected to continue to grow in the future, and the market scale will reach 896.5 billion yuan by 2026 [1].

Online fitness industry contains a huge blue ocean of consumption, covering fitness equipment, sports shoes and clothing, fitness food, sports software, smart wearable devices and many other fields [1]. As a form of online fitness, MFAs has a variety of functions, including fitness courses, diet management, fitness data, dynamic sharing, and sales of sports products. It provides users with one-stop full-process fitness services and meets the needs of users for low-cost exercise with fragmented time. Compared with traditional gyms, Keep and other fitness apps have the characteristics of free use time and space, and users can train anytime and anywhere. At the same time, the social attribute of Keep is also an important factor to attract many people to exercise online.

Different from the vigorous development in the field of practice, academic circles still lack sufficient attention to the application of mobile fitness [3]. Most scholars' research focuses on the profit model and commercial layout of mobile fitness applications, and lacks in-depth exploration of user stickiness in the field of mobile medical health. In order to improve the understanding of user behavior in mobile fitness application and promote the sustainable development of business model, we should study "application stickiness". However, few mathematicians have explored user stickiness in mobile fitness applications, and some scholars (Yin Meng 2020) have analyzed MFA users' intention of continuous use and in-app purchase from two aspects of tool stickiness and social stickiness [2]. At the same time, some scholars (Aoshang Li 2019) introduced two variables, namely perceived usefulness and habit, based on goal setting theory to explore how health goals affect the continuous use of sports fitness apps [4]. Others (Cong Liu 2020) combined the expectation confirmation theory, technology acceptance theory model, information system success model, information system continuous use theory model and the characteristics of sports fitness app to build a model of sports fitness app's willingness to continue to use, and analyzed the factors affecting the willingness to continue to use sports fitness app [5].

It is very meaningful to study the reasons and influencing factors behind the user stickiness of mobile fitness applications for the design, operation, management and commercial expansion of MFA. Specifically, 74% of health app users stopped using an app within ten times, and 26% of health apps only used it once after downloading [6]. In addition, enhancing user stickiness is very important for enterprises to improve profits and develop business. The longer users stick to an app, the more energy and emotion they put into it, and the more likely they are to develop into customers who buy more goods and services. However, with the increase of online fitness users, most of them are mobile fitness applications, but it is difficult to realize online realization, instead, a large number of them will be diverted to offline. In a sense, this is also a way of losing online users. Keep's difficulty in commercialization has also been proving this point: from the prospectus released by Keep, it can be seen that in the first three quarters of 2019, 2020 and 2021, Keep has been in a state of loss [7]. Therefore, the biggest challenge for MFA is to improve user stickiness.

In this paper, Keep users will be taken as the research object, and a model of Keep users' willingness to continue to use will be constructed by combing the existing literature. Then, the proposed research variables will be quantitatively analyzed by questionnaire survey and mathematical statistics, so as to test the proposed model of Keep users' willingness to continue to use, and then the related factors affecting the users' willingness to continue to use mobile fitness applications will be deeply discussed, and finally the relevant design strategy guidance will be put forward according to the research results.

2 Research Methodology

In order to make a scientific and complete analysis of the factors that affect the stickiness of mobile health App-Keep user groups, this study is based on the characteristics of the target user groups, considering the feasibility and standardization of different research methods of mobile application, the following three research methods are selected:

2.1 Document Analysis

In this study, we first use the book analysis method to search the relevant keywords with the help of Chinese and English databases such as Web of Science, CNKI, Sciencedirect, etc., select a wide range of applications for "Continuous use", "User stickiness", "Mobile App"-related research content to read and comb, and then focus on keywords, the research focused on the keywords of "Fitness App", "Keep", "Willingness to use continuously" and so on. At the same time, it browsed a large number of relevant web pages and public opinion introductions, the present research situation, research theory and different research methods of fitness app, especially Keep app user stickiness and continuous use intention were investigated.

2.2 Questionnaire Method

By using the method of questionnaire to investigate the users of Keep app, combining the aim of this study and the dimension of the model, and referring to the mature problems in the literature and the design of the scale, the questionnaire of this study is made, the questionnaire is in the form of Likert's five-point scale, rating each research question on a scale of one to five to obtain the data needed for model validation. And then the initial distribution of questionnaires, collect some data for analysis after adjusting the problem. Finally, the modified questionnaire is sent out and collected through various ways to eliminate the invalid questionnaire data and input the valid data into the statistical software.

2.3 Empirical Analysis

By using SPSSAU and Amos 26.0 analysis software to sort out the information obtained from the analysis, with the help of reliability and validity testing, correlation analysis, model fitting and other analytical methods, in this paper, we study the related factors of user stickiness of mobile fitness App-Keep, and use the data analysis results to test and support the theory and model of this study.

3 Literature Review and Theoretical Discussion

This research mainly focuses on the analysis of the factors that make users sticky in the process of using Keep app's core function module: training course-training sharing-training record. In order to design the analysis model of this paper as scientifically as possible, from the study of the use of psychology and use behavior to explore the use of mobile fitness app users to analyze the role of factors. Because it is very important for users to Keep using behavior, and Keep app is an information system that integrates content learning and sharing, information search, order and service, etc., therefore, the research focuses on the technology acceptance model, the theory of expectation confirmation and the model of the continuous use of information system, for the late establishment of the research model to lay a good foundation.

3.1 User Stickiness

User stickiness first appeared in the field of e-commerce, and then it was widely used in the field of Internet. Haiping Wang [8] thinks that stickiness is the extra cost that users bring when they change their consumption behavior, and they will Keep their original behavior unchanged. Wu [9] and other researchers have studied online games, describing the stickiness of game users as the willingness of players to repeatedly return to the game and prolong each stay. Li [10] believes that user stickiness refers to the willingness and behavior of users to use for a long time. At present, there are two kinds of researches on user stickiness, one is the research on the formation mechanism of user stickiness based on technology acceptance model and expectation confirmation model. The other is to study the influencing factors of user's sticky behavior by mining user's behavior data with big data [11].

3.2 Technology Acceptance Model (TAM)

Technology Acceptance Model (TAM) was developed from a psychological theory that describes computer user behavior based on beliefs, attitudes, attention, and user behavior (Davis et al. 1989) [12]. The model proposes two main determinants: perceived usefulness and perceived ease of use. They are influenced by external factors, including system design features, task features, organizational structure and other measurable variables, which have a positive impact on perceived usefulness and perceived ease of use. At the same time, perceived usability affects perceived usefulness, and both affect user's attitude, which, together with perceived usefulness, affects user's intention to use, and ultimately has a positive impact on user behavior. Since TAM was put forward, many scholars have carried on the research and the application to it, the research and the application in different fields are accompanied by the expansion and the perfection of the model, and with the improvement of the model, the TAM theory has also expanded the scope of application.

3.3 Expectation Confirmation Theory (ECT)

When people study and predict user behavior to increase user stickiness, they usually combine expected confirmation theory with other theories, and then integrate it into the continuous use model of information system, by means of structural equation modeling (SEM) and other methods to verify the object of study, to prove that the model of continuous use of information systems for the study of user behavior of the authenticity and accuracy of continuous use. Therefore, this research will continue this train of thought, based on the information system continuous use model, fusion Technology Acceptance Model (TAM) and Expectation Confirmation Theory (ECT)to introduce relevant variables, extend the information system continuous use model, the influencing factors of Keep users' stickiness were investigated by questionnaire and structural equation modeling. In theory, this research extends the continuous use model of information system to multi-function mobile fitness application field, in order to reveal and predict the behavior rule of mobile fitness application users, it can provide some theoretical reference for MFAS to observe users' psychological needs and enhance users' stickiness.

3.4 Information Systems Continue to Use the Model

Since the concept of continuous use of information system was put forward, it has been widely used in various information systems by domestic and foreign scholars, such as various portals, social platforms, management systems, online learning platforms. At the outset, Bhattacherjee argued that the willingness of users to continue using information systems is similar to whether consumers continue to buy products or services, therefore, he created a new Expectation Confirmation Model of Information System Continuance [16] based on the theory of Expectation Confirmation, which integrates the degree of Expectation Confirmation into the explanatory framework of user's Information Continuance behavior.

In recent years, the continuous usage model of information system has become more and more popular in the field of mobile application, the empirical research has also proved the validity of ECM-ISC model in explaining the continuous use behavior of information system users, ECM-ISC model is also gradually improving, more universal. Domestic scholars Xiaofeng Yang and Boyi Xu (2009) agree that the success of an information system depends to a large extent on the continued use of an object, the ECM-ISC model was constructed and validated by introducing two internal variables, trust perception and entertainment perception, and four external influencing factors, such as social influence [17]. This is the earliest research and application of ECM-ISC model in our country, and also leads a lot of research to adapt to their own research topic. Chunmei Gan et al. (2018) analyzed the community platform, and the results showed that: in the socialized Q & a community, user satisfaction, perceived usefulness, entertainment satisfaction, and information satisfaction have significant effects on users' intention to use [18]. These empirical analyses fully demonstrate that the introduction of research-appropriate and innovative variables does play a role in the long-term use intention of users. The integration and optimization of ECM-ISC model by different researchers also shows the applicability of expanding ECM-ISC model.

ECT-ISC model brings great innovation, not only consummates the theory of expectation confirmation, but also enriches the technology acceptance model. Therefore, the use of ECT-ISC theory helps us to explore the mobile fitness application user stickiness factors and the mechanism behind (see Fig. 1):

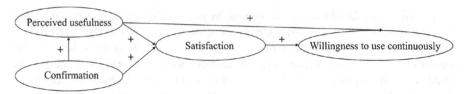

Fig. 1. Continuous use of information systems model

When people study and predict user behavior to increase user stickiness, they usually combine expected confirmation theory with other theories and then integrate it into the continuous use model of information systems, by means of structural equation modeling (SEM) and other methods to verify the object of study, to prove that the model of continuous use of information systems for the study of user behavior of the authenticity and accuracy of continuous use. Therefore, this research will continue this train of thought, based on information system continuous use model, fusion technology acceptance model (TAM) and expected confirmation theory model (ECT) to introduce relevant variables, extend information system continuous use model, the influencing factors of Keep users' stickiness were investigated by questionnaire and structural equation modeling. In theory, this research extends the continuous use model of information system to multi-function mobile fitness application field, in order to reveal and predict the behavior rule of mobile fitness application users, it can provide some theoretical reference for MFAS to observe users' psychological needs and enhance users' stickiness.

4 Research Hypothesis and Research Model

4.1 Study Assumptions

Perceived Quality and Satisfaction of Mobile Fitness App-Keep. Information quality is the quality of the output of the form of information produced by the information system used (Rai et al. 2002). The better the information quality, the more appropriate the decision-making, the more positive impact on user satisfaction. One of the important purposes of the mobile health app is to provide users with all kinds of fitness and health-related information, users are often made to feel that they are contributing to better health management, that is, the more satisfied users are with their use.

Based on the above analysis and discussion, the following hypotheses are proposed:

H1: The perceived quality of mobile fitness App-Keep has a positive effect on user satisfaction.

Perceived Ease of Use, Perceived Usefulness and User Satisfaction of Mobile Fitness App-Keep. Based on the Technology Acceptance Model (TAM) and expectation validation model adopted in this study, combined with previous studies, such as Oliver (1980) in the proposed expectation validation model, it is clearly pointed out that perceived usefulness has a positive impact on user satisfaction, Cho (2016) demonstrated that perceived ease of use affects perceived usefulness by examining the adoption behavior of healthy apps [19], according to Liao, Chen, Yen (2007), users' perception of system usefulness and ease of use has a positive effect on satisfaction [20], and the more satisfied users are, the more willing they are to continue using the system. And various studies have shown that user perceived ease of use can directly contribute to perceived usefulness [20].

Based on the above analysis and discussion, the following hypotheses are proposed:

H2: perceived usefulness of mobile fitness App-Keep has a positive effect on user satisfaction;
H3: Perceived ease of use of mobile fitness App-Keep has a positive effect on user satisfaction;
H4: User Satisfaction has a positive effect on the intention of continuous use of mobile fitness application Keep;
H5: perceived usability of mobile fitness App-Keep has a positive effect on perceived usefulness.

Perceived Entertainment and User Satisfaction of Mobile Fitness App-Keep. Perceived entertainment refers to the degree of pleasure and excitement that users get from using a mobile fitness app [21]. Previous studies have shown that entertainment satisfaction and fun have a significant impact on user satisfaction and intention to use. Basak and Calisir have studied Facebook and found that entertainment satisfaction can have a significant effect on user satisfaction, which in turn affects intent to use consistently [22]. When mobile fitness apps can improve the negative emotions users experience during a healthy workout in interesting ways, users will be more likely to feel satisfied and want to continue using them.

Based on the above analysis and discussion, the following hypotheses are proposed:

H6: the perceived entertainment of mobile fitness App-Keep has a positive effect on user satisfaction.

The Persistence of Mobile Fitness App-Keep and the Stickiness of Users. Qing Zhao et al. [23] analyzed the forming mechanism of the sticky behavior of the network users, and showed the conceptual model of the sticky behavior of the network users, the network sticky behavior is a kind of over-use behavior produced by the users on the basis of continuous use, which follows the psychological changes, therefore, the stickiness behavior of users can be predicted by the intention of continuous use.

Based on the above analysis and discussion, the following hypotheses are proposed:

H7: the continuous use intention of mobile fitness App-Keep has a positive effect on the stickiness of users.

4.2 Construction of Research Model

This research refers to the relevant literature in the fields of information system, mobile application and so on, and is mainly based on the Expectation confirmation model of IS continuance (ECM-ISC), the key variables of Technology Acceptance Model (TAM) and Expectation Confirmation Theory (ECT) are combined with the characteristics of Keep app and the previous research, it is concluded that entertainment satisfaction, social satisfaction and information satisfaction are the main marketing factors for the continuous use of information system users, and the following models are finally established (see Fig. 2):

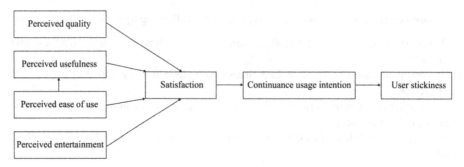

Fig. 2. Keep user stickiness influence factor concept model

5 Methods

5.1 Questionnaire Design

The questionnaire of this study consists of three parts: basic questions, measurement scales and basic information. Among them, the basic questions investigate the experience of using Keep app, including the frequency of use and common functions. The second part of the measurement scale draws on the mature scales of domestic and foreign scholars, as shown in Table 1, where the perceived usefulness scale where perceived usefulness refers to the research results of Fred D. Davis and Bhattacherjee Aetal [16], with three entries; perceived ease of use refers to the research of Fred D. Davis [25], with four entries; perceived entertainment refers to the research of Ji- Won Moon and Xueqin Zhao [26] for a total of 3 entries; perceived quality refer to the study of Bailing Liu [27] for a total of 2 entries; satisfaction refer to the study of Oliver R L and Xueqin Zhao [26] for a total of 3 entries; continuance usage intention refer to the study of Bhattacherjee A [16] for a total of 2 entries; user stickiness refer to the study of Lin [10], with a total of 2 items. A 5-point Richter scale (totally disagree - totally agree) was used for all scales. The third part of the basic information was to investigate the demographic characteristics of the subjects such as gender and age.

5.2 Statistical Method

The data were statistically analyzed using SPSSAU online and analysis software AMOS 26.0. The demographic characteristics of the sample were first analyzed by SPSSAU online; and then the reliability, convergent validity, and discriminant validity of each variable were tested using SPSSAU online; in the hypothesis testing section, structural equation analysis was performed using AMOS 26.0 software to analyze the fit of the theoretical model.

Table 1. Measurements and sources of each variable.

Latent Variable	Manifest Variable	Source of Measurements
Perceived Usefulness (PU)	**PU1.** I think Keep course training has helped me with my exercise	Fred D. Davis, 1989; Bhattacherjee A, 2001
	PU2. I think Keep helps me with my exercise program	
	PU3. Compared to other exercise and health apps, I think Keep provides me with more useful information or knowledge, or more in accord with my training wishes	
Perceived Ease of Use (PEOU)	**PEOU1.** I think the information provided by Keep is easy to understand	Fred D. Davis, 1989
	PEOU2. I think using the Keep functions is unthinkable for me	
	PEOU3. I know how to search and find useful sports resources on Keep	
	PEOU4. I know how to use the exercise resources found on Keep	
Perceived Entertainment (PE)	**PE1.** Keep has stimulated my interest in sports	Ji-Won Moon, 2001; Xueqin Zhao, 2019
	PE2. The process of using Keep is very pleasant	
	PE3. Overall Keep has given me a lot of fun	
Perceived Quality (PQ)	**PQ1.** I think the exercise resources on Keep are better than other platforms	Bailing Liu, 2018
	PQ2. I think the exercise resources on Keep can meet my individual needs	
Satisfaction (SA)	**SA1.** I think it is wise to use Keep	Oliver R L, 1980; Xueqin Zhao, 2019
	SA2. I am satisfied with the decision to use Keep	

(continued)

Table 1. (*continued*)

Latent Variable	Manifest Variable	Source of Measurements
	SA3. Using Keep has helped me solve some problems and makes me feel satisfied	
Continuance Usage Intention (CI)	**CI1.** I would like to use Keep as often as possible	Bhattacherjee A, 2001
	CI2. I would like to continue using Keep as a workout management software, rather than using something else instead	
User Stickiness (US)	**US1.** I prefer to use Keep over other exercise and health software	Lin C C, 2007
	US2. I think of looking for solutions on Keep as soon as a relevant need arises	

5.3 Data Collection Process

The study was distributed through the online platform from September 22 to September 27 in 2022, a total of 279 questionnaires were distributed and 279 questionnaires were collected, the questionnaire recovery rate was 100%, excluding those who did not answer seriously and those who had not used Keep's sample data, finally 222 valid questionnaires were obtained, the questionnaire efficiency rate was 80.0%.

Among the 222 valid questionnaires, the majority of female subjects accounted for 63.5% and male subjects accounted for 36.5%; most of the subjects were between 20 and 29 years old, accounting for 78.8%, while those under 20 years old accounted for 20.3% and those over 29 years old accounted for only 0.9%. According to the "Keep in-depth report" released by Guohai Securities on April 22 in 2022, 58% of female users and 42% of male users used Keep in 2021, female users are more concerned about personal body shape, and 74% of users are less than thirty years old, so the effective sample of this study is reasonable although it has the characteristics of youthfulness and more female subjects. In terms of the education level of the sample, most of the subjects had a bachelor's degree, accounting for 72.5%, those with a master's degree and above accounted for 25.2%, and those with high school/junior high school and below accounted for 2.3%, which was a smaller sample. The investigation of subjects' experience of using Keep app revealed that most of the subjects used Keep for the functions of training sessions, exercise records and training plans, and 32.9% of the subjects used it for one year or more. Overall, the number of valid samples in this study is sufficient and the structure is generally reasonable.

6 Results

6.1 Reliability and Validity Analysis

Table 2. Variable reliability and convergent validity tests.

Latent variable	Question number	Standard load factor	Cronbach α	AVE	CR
Perceived Usefulness (PU)	PU1	0.754	0.808	0.584	0.808
	PU2	0.747			
	PU3	0.79			
Perceived Ease of Use (PEOU)	PEOU1	0.766	0.871	0.636	0.875
	PEOU2	0.825			
	PEOU3	0.815			
	PEOU4	0.781			
Perceived Entertainment (PE)	PE1	0.79	0.879	0.717	0.884
	PE2	0.869			
	PE3	0.878			
Perceived Quality (PQ)	PQ1	0.902	0.879	0.785	0.879
	PQ2	0.87			
Satisfaction (SA)	SA1	0.894	0.916	0.784	0.916
	SA2	0.898			
	SA3	0.863			
Continuance Usage Intention (CI)	CI1	0.846	0.834	0.718	0.836
	CI2	0.849			
User Stickiness (US)	US1	0.918	0.847	0.745	0.854
	US2	0.805			

The confirmatory factor analysis (CFA) was conducted for a total of 7 factors and 19 analysis items. The valid sample size of this analysis is 222, which exceeds the number of analysis items by 10 times, and the sample size is moderate. The results of the reliability analysis on the seven variables of perceived usefulness, perceived ease of use, perceived entertainment, perceived quality, satisfaction, continuance usage intention, and user stickiness showed that (see Table 2), the Clonbach Alpha values of perceived usefulness, perceived ease of use, perceived entertainment, perceived quality, satisfaction, continuance usage intention, and user stickiness were 0.808 to 0.916, all greater than 0.80, with good reliability. The results of the confirmatory factor analysis showed that the explained variance of each variable was above 70%, the factor loadings of each question term were 0.747–0.918 (>0.70), the AVE values of each latent variable were 0.584–0.785 (>0.50), and the CR values of each latent variable were 0.808–0.916

(>0.80), indicating that the model had good convergent validity. In addition, the square roots of AVE were all greater than the absolute values of the correlation coefficients of the latent variables in their rows and columns, indicating that the model had good discriminant validity (see Table 3).

Table 3. Discriminant validity tests.

	PU	PEOU	PE	PQ	SA	CI	US
Perceived Usefulness (PU)	0.764						
Perceived Ease of Use (PEOU)	0.657	0.797					
Perceived Entertainment (PE)	0.682	0.617	0.847				
Perceived Quality (PQ)	0.704	0.672	0.661	0.886			
Satisfaction (SA)	0.755	0.684	0.711	0.728	0.886		
Continuance Usage Intention (CI)	0.673	0.581	0.716	0.676	0.811	0.848	
User Stickiness (US)	0.641	0.572	0.679	0.728	0.728	0.789	0.863

6.2 Evaluation of the Overall Fitness of Structural Equation Model

The structural equation model construction using AMOS 26.0 is shown in Fig. 3; the analysis results show (see Table 4) that X2/df = 2.502, GFI = 0.854, RMSEA = 0.082, SRMR = 0.042, IFI = 0.939, CFI = 0.939, NFI = 0.903, and AGFI = 0.804, except for the value of GFI are on the low side (some scholars also consider GFI > 0.8 as an acceptable level), the rest of the indicators are within the critical criteria, indicating that the structural model fit is good and path analysis can be performed.

Table 4. Initial structural equation model fitting indicators.

Common indicators	χ2/df	GFI	RMSEA	RMR	CFI	IFI	NFI	AGFI
Judgement Criteria	<3	>0.9	<0.10	<0.05	>0.9	>0.9	>0.9	>0.8
Value	2.502	0.854	0.082	0.042	0.939	0.939	0.903	0.804

6.3 Results of Testing the Research Hypothesis

From Table 3, H1, H2, H4, H5, H6, and H7 are supported by the data, except for H3 which does not pass the test. Although perceived ease of use does not have a significant positive relationship with satisfaction, perceived ease of use can positively affect perceived usefulness. In addition to this, when we performed model fitting and hypothesis testing, we found that perceived entertainment and perceived quality also have a positive

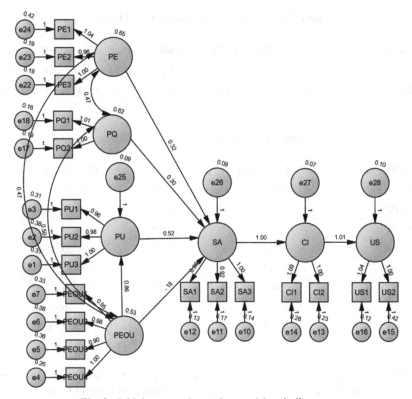

Fig. 3. Initial structural equation model path diagram.

Table 5. Initial structural equation model fitting indicators.

Hypothetical path	Coefficient	CR	Conclusion
PEOU→PU	0.858	11.666	***Supported
PU→SA	0.521	2.968	**Supported
PE→SA	0.322	4.479	***Supported
PQ→SA	0.302	2.968	**Supported
PEOU→SA	−0.179	−0.809	Not Supported
SA→CI	1.002	15.837	***Supported
CI→US	1.012	12.58	***Supported

effect on perceived usefulness to some extent. Therefore, we added the hypothesis H8 that the perceived entertainment of mobile fitness app-Keep has a positive effect on the perceived usefulness, and H9 that the perceived quality of mobile fitness app-Keep has a positive effect on the perceived usefulness (Table 5).

Table 6. Reconfiguration structural equation model fitting indicators.

Common indicators	χ2/df	GFI	RMSEA	RMR	CFI	IFI	NFI	AGFI
Judgement Criteria	<3	>0.9	<0.10	<0.05	>0.9	>0.9	>0.9	>0.8
Value	2.331	0.862	0.078	0.042	0.946	0.947	0.91	0.814

Table 7. Reconfiguration structural equation model fitting indicators.

Hypothetical path	Coefficient	CR	Conclusion
PEOU→PU	0.286	2.578	**Supported
PE→PU	0.328	4.217	***Supported
PQ→PU	0.281	2.725	**Supported
PE→SA	0.258	3.155	**Supported
PQ→SA	0.245	2.74	**Supported
PU→SA	0.447	3.253	***Supported
SA→CI	1.001	15.971	***Supported
CI→US	1.012	12.683	***Supported

The model after the additional hypothesis was reconstructed (see Fig. 4) and fit analysis was performed, see Table 6, the structural model fit is good for path analysis. From Table 7, all hypotheses are supported by the data.

6.4 Results of Mediating Effect Tests

Bootstrap method was used to test the mediating effect of perceived usefulness (see Table 8), and the test was repeated 2000 times. Based on the Bias-Corrected interval estimation method, the mediating effect was significant if the upper and lower bounds of the indirect effect did not contain 0 at the 95% confidence interval. From Table 4, in the paths "PEOU→PU→SA" and "PE→PU→SA" and "PQ→PU→SA", the confidence intervals of the Bias-Corrected method at 95% confidence level are [0.615, 0.950] with [0.314, 0.824] and [0.291, 0.923], excluding 0. The indirect effects are significant.

7 Result Discussion

After hypothesis testing, there is a positive effect of perceived ease of use on perceived usefulness of the mobile fitness app Keep, i.e., hypothesis H5 holds. The perceived ease of use of the mobile fitness app Keep, i.e., the features of the app such as easy to understand, easy to operate, easy to learn, and easy to use will have a positive impact on the perceived usefulness of the app. In the survey results, more than half of the users found Keep's features easy to understand. They were better able to search for useful exercise resources, and the courses were convenient to set up. Apps that are easy to learn

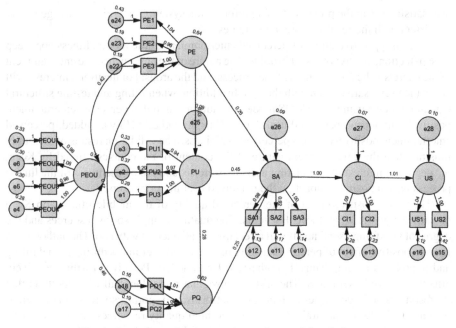

Fig. 4. Reconfiguration structural equation model path diagram.

Table 8. Mediating effect tests.

Hypothetical path	Total Effect	Probability-value of Two-sided Test	Bias-Corrected 95%CI	
			LLCI	ULCI
PEOU→PU→SA	0.959	0.001	0.615	0.95
PE→PU→SA	0.232	0.001	0.314	0.824
PQ→PU→SA	0.236	0.001	0.291	0.923

to operate have higher perceived usefulness, while apps that are complex to operate will greatly reduce users' perceived usefulness [5]. Perceived ease of use has no significant effect on satisfaction, which is not consistent with the presupposition, i.e., hypothesis H3 is not valid. The reason may be that the object of study in this paper is a mobile fitness app. This type of app is used in the process of users spend most of their time interacting with the content of exercise classes. The simple and convenient app operation cannot yet significantly affect user satisfaction.

There is a positive effect of perceived usefulness of the mobile fitness app Keep on satisfaction, and hypothesis H2 holds. The usefulness of exercise information of app and the degree of users' willingness to train will affect the satisfaction of users with app. ECM-ISC's research shows that perceived usefulness is the main factor influencing user satisfaction in the process of using information systems, and this study is generally consistent with the results of previous studies [16].

There is a positive effect of perceived entertainment of the mobile fitness app Keep on satisfaction, and hypothesis H6 holds. The nature of the app, such as the entertainment of the exercise, the pleasantness of the process, and the arousal of the user's interest, will affect the user's satisfaction with the app. In addition, when fitting and testing structural equation models using the AMOS model, the author found that perceived entertainment positively influenced perceived usefulness. Thus, hypothesis H8 was added: perceived entertainment positively affects perceived usefulness. The validation results of this study illustrate that the entertainment nature of the content of the courses offered by Keep, the degree of interest in stimulating users to exercise, and the pleasantness of the fitness process have a positive impact on the perceived usefulness of users.

There is a positive effect of the perceived quality of the mobile fitness app Keep on satisfaction, i.e., hypothesis H1 holds. The quality of app's sports resources and the degree of satisfying users' needs will affect users' satisfaction with app. The author again found a positive effect of perceived quality on perceived usefulness during model fitting and hypothesis testing. Thus, hypothesis H9 was added: Perceived quality positively affects perceived usefulness. The survey shows that more than half of users think that the resources on Keep are better than other platforms, and sports resources can meet their own needs. It shows that training courses and high quality resources tailored to users' individual needs have a great impact on the usefulness of the app, thus significantly affecting user satisfaction.

Satisfaction with the mobile fitness app Keep has a positive effect on continuance usage intention, and continuance usage intention has a positive effect on user stickiness. Hypotheses H4 and H7 hold. The continuance usage intention is the mediating variable, and the continuance usage intention plays a fully mediating role in the relationship between satisfaction and user stickiness. Research based on ECM-ISC theory shows that satisfaction has a positive effect on the continuance usage intention of exercise and fitness app users, which is in line with previous research [16]. Satisfaction positively affects user stickiness through continuance usage intention, demonstrating that the expectation confirmation model works well in explaining Keep users' continuance usage intention and also demonstrating that user stickiness behavior can be predicted by their continuance usage intention [24].

Perceived usefulness was derived as an important mediating variable during model fitting and hypothesis testing. Perceived usefulness fully mediates the relationship between perceived ease of use and satisfaction, while it partially mediates the relationship between perceived entertainment and satisfaction. It shows that the satisfaction of perceived ease of use cannot yet directly and positively influence user satisfaction, but the fitness app can positively influence perceived usefulness by improving the ease of understanding, ease of operation, ease of learning and convenience of the use process, thus enhancing the user stickiness of the platform and leaving loyal users for the platform.

8 Practice Inspiration

From the perspective of information system continuance theory, this paper takes fitness app Keep as an example to derive the factors influencing user stickiness in fitness application area, which has greater significance to the development and op-timization of mobile fitness app. According to the discussion of the results of this paper, mobile fitness app operators can start from the following strategies to im-prove user stickiness:

Provide training courses and programs that meet individual needs. Research has demonstrated that perceived usefulness positively affects satisfaction. Perceived usefulness is an important criterion for users to judge whether to use the mobile fitness app or not, and is an important factor in determining whether users will use the mobile fitness app again or continue to use it. Mobile fitness applications need to provide targeted and diversified fitness courses based on users themselves and usage scenarios, in line with users' training wishes. For example, to grasp the diverse needs of different users in time and better enrich the content and types of courses, so as to enhance users' perceived usefulness of their sports courses, and then improve users' satisfaction.

Create an easy-to-use mobile fitness application. The perceived ease of use of the sports and fitness app has a positive effect on perceived usefulness and indirectly on user satisfaction and continuance usage intention. The mobile application using needs a fast, flexible, easy and friendly interactive interface to make the functions simple and easy to understand. In addition, try to simplify the search of sports resources, make the information of sports resources and sports courses intuitive and easy to understand, and enhance the ease of learning for users, so as to quickly meet their training wishes and needs.

Create a strong sense of interaction and enjoyable fitness experience. Studies have shown that increasing perceived entertainment can promote perceived usefulness and satisfaction. The entertainment of the sport is conducive to attracting new users, and the strong sense of interaction and enjoyable fitness experience is conducive to retaining mild exerciser. Mobile fitness applications attach importance to stimulating the interest of users in sports and adding entertainment sports modules, which can not only improve the participation and activity of users using app, but also promote the retention rate of users to a certain extent.

Provide scientifically effective, high-quality exercise resources. There is a positive effect of perceived quality on perceived usefulness and satisfaction. Users pay more attention to the quality level of sports videos and sports courses. Therefore, mobile fitness applications, in terms of the introduction of sports resources, should audit the scientificity and validity of sports resources, develop strict and standard platform course audit specifications, and supervise the teaching videos uploaded by exercise bloggers [5]. The quality of exercise resources is strictly controlled in the context of adapting to the user's training goals.

9 Shortcomings and Prospects

The limitations of this study are mainly reflected in three aspects: First, the data structure of the sample is unreasonable, in which the undergraduate and master's degree populations are predominant, resulting in a low interpretation of other populations. The scope of the survey should be expanded in the future to include different groups of users of mobile fitness applications to enhance the comprehensiveness of the study. Second, the perceived ease of use of mobile fitness applications in this study does not significantly affect satisfaction, which is inconsistent with previous studies, and this part needs to be discussed and studied in detail in the follow-up. Third, other mediating variables can be considered in the future and add moderating variables. The current study concluded that perceived usefulness fully mediates the relationship between perceived ease of use and satisfaction, while it partially mediates the relationship between perceived entertainment and satisfaction. Continuance usage intention plays a fully mediating role in the relationship between satisfaction and user stickiness. In addition, there may be some mediating effect between other influencing factors. Besides perceived usefulness, influencing factors such as perceived quality, can have a direct impact on satisfaction, while user income and using frequency of mobile fitness applications have the potential to act as important moderating variables that directly affect satisfaction and continuance usage intention, which in turn leads to changes in user stickiness.

It is believed that further research in the future can expand and improve the model and enrich the related theory.

References

1. Xie, Y.: Online fitness: embracing digital healthy living. Mod. Commer. Bank. (13), 32–36 (2022). (in Chinese)
2. Yin, M., Tayyab, S.M.U., Xu, X.Y., Jia, S.W., Wu, C.L.: The investigation of mobile health stickiness: the role of social support in a sustainable health approach. Sustainability 13(4) (2021). https://doi.org/10.3390/SU13041693
3. Li, Y., Li, X., Cai, J.: How attachment affects user stickiness on live streaming platforms: a socio-technical approach perspective. J. Retail. Consum. Serv. 60 (2021). https://doi.org/10.1016/j.jretconser.2021.102478
4. Li, A.: Research on the usage behavior of fitness app user from a health goals perspective. Harbin Institute of Technology (2019). https://doi.org/10.27061/d.cnki.ghgdu.2019.000007. (in Chinese)
5. Liu, C.: Research on the continuance usage intention of sports and fitness app. Chengdu Sport University (2020). https://doi.org/10.26987/d.cnki.gcdtc.2020.000006. (in Chinese)
6. Yang, X., Ma, L., Zhao, X., Kankanhalli, A.: Factors influencing user's adherence to physical activity applications: a scoping literature review and future directions. Int. J. Med. Inform. 134 (2020). https://doi.org/10.1016/j.ijmedinf.2019.104039
7. Zou, S.: Home fitness is on fire again: go to the tuyere and leave after scraping. Reporters' Notes (19), 36–40 (2022). https://doi.org/10.3969/j.issn.1004-3799(s).2022.19.009. (in Chinese)
8. Wang, H.: A review of research on factors influencing online consumer behavior. Consum. Econ. 25(5), 92–95 (2009). (in Chinese)
9. Jen-Her, W., Wang, S.-C., Tsai, H.-H.: Falling in love with online games: the uses and gratifications perspective. Comput. Hum. Behav. 26(6), 1862–1871 (2010). https://doi.org/10.1016/j.chb.2010.07.033
10. Lin, C.C.: Online stickiness: its antecedents and effect on purchasing intention. Behav. Inf. Technol. 26(6), 507–516 (2007). https://doi.org/10.1080/01449290600740843

11. Wang, J., Liu, W.: Study on the factors influencing the sticky behavior of online course users. Distance Educ. China (03), 61–67+75 (2022). https://doi.org/10.13541/j.cnki.chinade.2022. 03.006. (in Chinese)

12. Davis, F.D.: Perceived usefulness, perceived ease of use, and user acceptance of information technology. MIS Q. (03), 319–339 (1989). https://doi.org/10.2307/249008

13. Bentham, J.: An introduction to the principles of morals and legislation. Kitchener. Batoche Books **10**, 236 (2000)

14. Oghuma, A.P., Libaque-Saenz, C.F., Wong, S.F., Chang, Y.: An expectation-confirmation model of continuance intention to use mobile instant messaging. Telematics Inform. **33**(1), 34–47 (2016). https://doi.org/10.1016/j.tele.2015.05.006

15. Wang, W., Gan, C.: Study on factors influencing continuance intention of academic bloggers. Sci. Res. Manag. **35**(10), 121–127 (2014). https://doi.org/10.19571/j.cnki.1000-2995.2014. 10.016. (in Chinese)

16. Bhattacherjee, A.: Understanding information systems continuance: an expectation-confirmation model. MIS Q. **2**(3), 351–370 (2001). https://doi.org/10.2307/3250921

17. Yang, X., Xu, B.:A research on citizens' continuance usage model of the e-government portal. J. Intell. (05), 19–22 (2009). https://doi.org/10.3969/j.issn.1002-1965.2009.05.005. (in Chinese)

18. Gan, C., Jiayi, X., Zhu, Y.: An empirical study of users' continuance intention to use social Q&A communities. Inf. Sci. **36**(02), 107–112 (2018). https://doi.org/10.13833/j.issn.1007-7634.2018.02.020. (in Chinese)

19. Cho, J.: The impact of post-adoption beliefs on the continued use of health apps. Int. J. Med. Inform. (87),75–83 (2016). https://doi.org/10.1016/j.ijmedinf.2015.12.016

20. Liao, C., Chen, J.-L., Yen, D.C.: Theory of planning behavior (TPB) and customer satisfaction in the continued use of e-service : an integrated model. Comput. Hum. Behav. **23**(06), 2804–2822 (2007). https://doi.org/10.1016/j.chb.2006.05.006

21. Eighmey, J., McCord, L.: Adding value in the information age: uses and gratifications of sites on the World Wide Web. J. Bus. Res. **41**(3), 187–194 (1998). https://doi.org/10.1016/S0148-2963(97)00061-1

22. Basak, E., Calisir, F.: An empirical study on factors affecting continuance intention of using Facebook. Comput. Hum. Behav. (48), 181–189 (2015). https://doi.org/10.1016/j.chb.2015. 01.055

23. Zhao, Q., Zhang, L., Xue, J.: The formation mechanism of internet user stickness behavior&its empirical analysis. Inf. Stud.: Theory Appl. **35**(10), 25–29 (2012). https://doi.org/10.16353/ j.cnki.1000-7490.2012.10.019. (in Chinese)

24. Wang, M., Mingxin, L., Shi, J., Yang, H.: Research on the influencing factors of video website user stickiness based on ECT theory and flow theory—taking bilibili as an example. Technol. Intell. Eng. **7**(01), 80–92 (2021). https://doi.org/10.3772/j.issn.2095-915x.2021.01.007. (in Chinese)

25. Davis, F.D., Bagozzi, R.P., Warshaw, P.R.: User acceptance of computer technology: a comparison of two theoretical models. Manag. Sci. **35**(8), 982–1003 (1989). https://doi.org/10. 1287/mnsc.35.8.982

26. Zhao, X., Wang, S.: Research of customers' continuance intention on WeChat mini program. Mod. Inf. **39**(6), 70–80+90 (2019). https://doi.org/10.3969/j.issn.1008-0821.2019.06.008. (in Chinese)

27. Liu, B., Wei, X., Xia, H.: A study on the continued use intention of mobile shopping from the perspectives of characteristics for individuals and applications. J. Manag. Sci. **31**(2), 59–70 (2018). https://doi.org/10.3969/j.issn.1672-0334.2018.02.005. (in Chinese)

Modeling and Verification of the Biomechanical Characteristics of Human Upper Limb Muscles

Ting Jiang[1], Zheng Zhang[2], Changhua Jiang[1], Hao Li[1], Teng Zhang[2], Zhen Zhang[2], Xiang Xu[2], Yueqi An[2], Weifeng Gao[2], Chunhui Wang[1], and Jianwei Niu[2(✉)]

[1] National Key Laboratory of Human Factors Engineering, China Astronaut Research and Training Center, Beijing 1000942, China
[2] School of Mechanical Engineering, University of Science and Technology Beijing, Beijing, China
niujw@ustb.edu.cn

Abstract. The skeletal muscle model is an important tool to study the law of human movement and muscle force, and the joint movement of human upper limbs is extremely complex. In this paper, we model the human upper limb based on OpenSim and the main force muscle, simplify the human upper limb skeletal muscular system, and design experiments based on the two basic movements of pushing and pulling to evaluate the effectiveness of the model, which proves that the model simulation results are highly correlated with the experimental results. Finally, a human upper limb model with three joints, eight groups of major muscles and ten marking points was established, which can simplify the simulation of human movement and is very helpful for studying human upper limb movement.

Keywords: Biomechanics · Musculoskeletal Model · OpenSim · surface EMG

1 Introduction

As an important tissue of the human body, the strength level of muscles reflects the health of the human body. In terms of medical treatment, the recovery of muscle function of patients mostly depends on the subjective experience of doctors and lacks scientific theoretical support. In the field of athlete training, muscle strength can help trainers discover the rationality of athletes' power movements, to achieve targeted training. In industrial production, muscle analysis can help managers assess muscle fatigue and injury during workers' labor, to adjust work intensity and staffing.

However, there is currently a lack of rapid and accurate assessment of muscle condition. General muscle strength testing experiments use force sensors to calculate muscle force indirectly, which is complex and cannot be accurate to every muscle. Another mainstream method is to model the human skeletal muscular system, and then biomechanical solve the muscle force through kinematic data and external force data, and now there are mature professional software, such as AnyBody, OpenSim, etc. With the development of motion capture technology, this type of software has become more widely used. Therefore, the goal of this study is to build an easy-to-use model of the human upper limb skeletal musculoskeletal system based on OpenSim.

A large number of scholars have studied human bone muscle models. When dissecting human muscles and examining the microstructure of muscles, it can be seen that the skeletal muscles of the upper limbs are mainly bundle-like, and due to the presence of pinnate angles, the muscle force generated during movement is equal to the component of the contraction force of muscle fibers. The Hill muscle model theory [1] views the human muscle as a spring-like system composed of a parallel elastic structure and a pressure structure; Tandem elastic structures represent tendons and other muscular system soft tissues. In this model, the muscle is represented as a structure with active and passive properties, which can simulate changes in physiological parameters as the angle of the joint changes. Zajac [2] et al. added a tendon conduction model to the Hill model to characterize the influence of tendon structure on the force transmission process. In 2012, Gunther [3] et al. added the inertia factor of the muscle itself to the force solving equation on the basis of the Hill model to improve the sensitivity of the model to changes in external forces in the musculoskeletal system, and Haeufle [4] et al. added an additional structure-damping on the basis of the Hill's study to make the model more consistent with the real situation when the joint angle changes.

The EMG signals can reflect the excitement of the corresponding muscles to a certain extent, and the muscle force produced by muscle contraction has a high correlation, Fleischer [5] believes that calculating muscle strength through myoelectric signals is the most accurate measurement method. Erkocevic [6] et al. collected the EMG signal of a muscle tissue, and calculated the wavelength, RMS, ZRC and other eigenvalues of the EMG signal to study the relationship between the above eigenvalues and grip strength, and the results showed that there was a high Pearson correlation between the rms value of the EMG signal and grip strength.

2 Methods

2.1 Upper Limb Model Building

In OpenSim, a musculoskeletal model is made up of joints, bones, and muscles. Joints connect multiple bones, in which muscles attach to bones and drive joint movement through the force generated by the muscles.

Upper Limb Joint Settings
The joints of the human upper limb mainly include the shoulder blade, carpal bone, collarbone, humerus, ulna, and radius, and with the help of anatomical research results, this paper adds the inertia parameter properties of the hand, radius, ulna and humerus, shoulder blade and carpal segment in the model. Among them, the mass attributes of the hand, radius, ulna and humerus, scapula and carpal segments refer to the research results of Brand [7]. The center of mass and inertial tensor properties of upper limb limbs refer to the Blackwell's research results [8], which are based on the human limb attributes of men at the 50th percentile (Table 1, Table 2).

Since this study mainly explores the characteristics of the ability to exert force on the shoulder and elbow joints of the upper limbs under typical tasks, this study mainly

Table 1. Upper limb segment mass and center of mass parameters

Segment name	Mass (kg)	Centre of mass (m)		
		Rx	Ry	Rz
Collarbone	0.156	20.011	0.006	0.054
scapula	0.703	20.054	20.035	20.043
humerus	1.997	0.018	20.14	20.012
ulna	1.105	0.009	20.095	0.024
radius	0.233	0.033	20.181	0.015
carpal	0.001	0	0	0
hand	0.5819	20.003	20.042	20.001

Table 2. Upper limb segment inertia parameters

Segment name	Inertia (kg·m^2)		
	I_{xy}	I_{xz}	I_{yz}
collarbone	20.02	20.00007	0.00005
scapula	0.00045	0.00041	0.00024
humerus	20.00035	20.00023	0.00123
ulna	0.00032	20.00008	0.00109
radius	0.00003	0	0.00006
carpal	0	0	0
hand	0	0	0.00001

focuses on the shoulder and elbow joints of the human upper limbs, and does not consider the internal and external rotation movements of the elbow, and the degrees of freedom of the upper limb joints include shoulder flexion/extension, adduction/abduction, internal rotation/external rotation, elbow flexion, wrist flexion/extension, and wrist adduction/abduction.

Upper Limb Muscle Settings

Hill [9] proposed a mechanical model of muscle structure composed of contractile element (CE), series-elastic element (SE) and parallel-elastic element (PE) and used this to reflect the function of muscles. Among them, the contractile unit CE represents actin fibers that can slide relative to each other, and the tone of the fibers is related to the number of transverse bridges; Parallel elastic unit PE indicates the intrinsic elasticity of actin fibers, transverse bridges, and connective tissues; The tandem elastic unit SE represents the tendon tissue formed by the extension of the muscle fiber membrane and exhibits nonlinear elastic mechanical properties. In OpenSim modeling, the muscle-tendon model is simplified to a nonlinear spring (SE)-active contractile element (CE)-passive spring (PE) model. In this study, Hill-type muscle-tendon was used to describe 8 muscle groups representing the main muscle groups of the upper limbs. A dynamic muscle model described [10] using Schutte to define its muscular attribute characteristics for each muscle-tendon. To align it with the upper limb kinematics model, the normalized isometric force-length curve of active muscle force and the normalized force-strain curve of tendons are set to the normalized curve defined by Delp et al. [11]. In order to make the normalized model representative of a single muscle-tendon, the fiber length, muscle peak force, and pinnate angle parameters of the muscle group refer to the research results of Holzbaur et al. [12] (Table 3).

Table 3. Upper extremity muscle parameters

Muscle name	Abbreviation	Fiber length (cm)	Peak force (N)	pennation angle
Anterior Deltoid	DELT1	9.8	1218.9	22
Lateral Deltoid	DELT2	10.8	1103.5	15
Posterior Deltoid	DELT3	13.7	201.6	18
Infraspinatus	SUPRA	6.8	499.2	7
Pectoralis Major	PMAJ	14.4	444.3	17
Latissimus Dorsi	LAT	25.4	290.5	25
Triceps	TRI	13.4	771.8	12
Biceps	BIC	11.6	525.1	0

Opensim [13] Model Building

In this study, the open-source software OpenSim was used for model creation. In the model, rigid bodies connected by joints are used to represent the skeletal system. In the musculoskeletal system, joints define the way two limbs move relative to each other. Joint restraints can limit body movement. Muscles are represented by a series of lines connecting rigid bodies, and the amount of muscle force depends on the muscle pathways that make up the length of myofibers and tendons, the rate of change in myofiber length, and the level of muscle activation. The main content of this study is the dynamics of the arm, which does not involve the relative movement of the body and uses the right arm as a modeling object. OpenSim models usually start from the ground as a generalized coordinate system, which has the advantage of quantifying the movement of the body relative to the ground, so the right arm model selects the ground as a reference frame, first defines the ground, the gravitational acceleration is -9.8 m/s^2, the length unit is m, and the unit of force is N.

For the kinematics of the model, OpenSim uses Simbody, an open-source multibody dynamics solver. In Simbody and OpenSim, the bones are the main part of the model, and the bones are connected sequentially by joints. Joints define coordinates and kinematic transformations that control the motion of an object relative to its parent. In the model, all the bones are contained in the BodySet. Therefore, you should begin modeling by first defining a set of bone rigid bodies to represent the system, and then use joints to connect the bones. Subsequently, the joints are defined. Joints are equivalent to the bone connections of the human body, which define the mutual movement between rigid bodies. This paper defines the shoulder, elbow, and sternoclavicular joints as free joints. In the definition of joints, this paper uniformly uses the skeletal coordinate system to define the elbow joint, defines the center of mass and inertia of the joint in the reference frame, and specifies the position fixed in this skeletal joint coordinate system.

On this basis, the muscles in the model need to be defined, including muscle physiological parameters, dynamic parameters, muscle paths, and muscle geometry wrapping settings. The Millard 2012 Equilibrium Muscle model was selected for this paper. The previous section determined the physiological parameters of the muscle and added geometry on the basis of the dynamic parameters. The primary role of geometry wrapping is to define the contact surface between muscle and bone to produce more precise changes in muscle length.

In sports biomechanics, the data-driven model of marker points using motion capture is an effective model-driven method, which can accurately determine the movement posture of the human body, and on this basis, the joint torque and muscle force simulation analysis are carried out. The motion capture marker points required by OpenSim are generally stored in TRC files, and the motion capture data is obtained by tracking the optical marker points attached to the human body by synchronous cameras. In order to obtain the posture of the human body in motion, the movement marker point data will be established and associated with the human body, and the virtual model of the upper limb uses 10 marker points and fixed on the right arm and torso of the upper limb, so that the posture information of the human body during movement can be determined.

Open the finished model file in the OpenSim GUI, The established model includes degrees of freedom, bone, joint, and muscle properties (Fig. 1). The model can be driven by motion capture data for reverse dynamics, reverse kinematics, and static optimization analysis.

2.2 Upper Limb Model Validation

On the basis of constructing the upper limb model, in order to evaluate the effectiveness of the upper limb bone muscle model, this study carried out the typical action force experiment of equal length pushing and pulling, and the EMG data of the main muscle of the upper limb were collected in the experiment, and the biomechanical modeling was carried out to solve the muscle activation degree according to the kinematic data and external force data collected by the experiment, and the correlation analysis between the model simulation results and the muscle activation degree results of electromyography was carried out to verify the effectiveness of the upper limb model.

Subjects

Ten healthy male subjects were selected to participate in the experiment. To ensure the validity of the experimental data, the following requirements are put forward for volunteers: age 25–35 years old, weight 50–85 kg, height 1.65–1.80 m. Subjects were asked to be right-handed, and subjects had no history of skeletal muscle injury. All

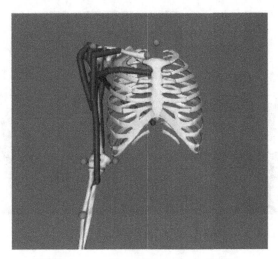

Fig. 1. OpenSim skeletal muscle model

subjects were informed of the purpose of the study and not for commercial purposes. This study was accredited by the school's ethics review committee.

Experimental Equipment

Experimental equipment includes BTE Primus RS mechanical measurement equipment, Biovison surface electrodes equipment, NDI Optorak dynamic capture acquisition system. Among them, BTE Primus RS mechanical measuring equipment was used to collect the subject's hand operating force during typical exercise, and Biovison surface electromyography measurement equipment was used to collect the EMG signals of the main upper limb muscles (Anterior Deltoid, Lateral Deltoid, Posterior Deltoid, Pectoralis Major, Triceps, Biceps, Latissimus Dorsi, Infraspinatus). The NDI Optotrak motion capture system was used to collect data on subjects' motion attitude during typical operations.

Experimental Pose

The experiment was divided into isometric static pushing and pulling operations. The subjects were required to keep their feet forked during the force process, and the left foot in front and the right foot in the back kept the center of gravity stable during the movement. Then adjust the center of the BTE joystick hinge to the same height as the subject's shoulder, the angle between the joystick and the vertical direction is 30°, and the vertical plane where the subject and the center of the joystick hinge are located is flush, maintaining 10 cm from the joystick. Adjust the joystick length so that the end of the joystick is at the same height as the subject's lumbar vertebrae, and the subject grasps the joystick in the palm of his hand (Fig. 2).

Experimental Process

Before the experiment, subjects attached electrodes to the main muscles of the upper limbs, such as the anterior deltoid fascicle, the middle deltoid fascicle, the posterior

Fig. 2. Static push-pull action pose

deltoid fascicle, the pectoralis major, the triceps, the biceps, the latissimus dorsi, and the infraspinatus muscle (Fig. 3).

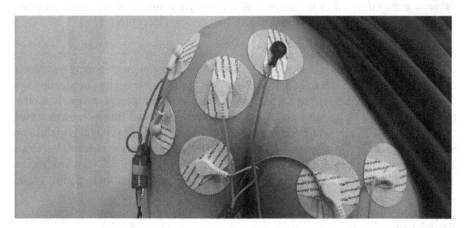

Fig. 3. Surface electrode attachment schematic

Once the electrode is attached, NDI Optorak motion is used to capture the relative position of the torso and right arm. There are four marker points on each marker point, two of which are fixed to the upper arm and forearm position of the subject's arm, and the other marker point is fixed to the subject's torso.

After the subjects finished wearing the equipment, the experiment was carried out according to the requirements of the main test, and the experiment was divided into static isometric pushing and pulling typical operations. The subjects first carried out static pushing operation, and after the physical fitness was fully restored, the static pulling operation was carried out. Among them, the push operation first requires the subjects to exert force according to the established posture of the experiment and adopt the isometric force test method. The power level is set to 30 N, 50 N, 70 N, and the maximum force level. The subjects in turn exerted force according to the set force level and maintained for 6 s, and each group of force required the subject to rest for 5 min to continue the next level test, and the subject was required to push the joystick forward with the help of arm strength during the force generation process.

The pull operation attitude is consistent with the push operation attitude, and the isometric test method is also adopted, and the force level is set to 30 N, 50 N, 70 N, and maximum force operation. The subjects maintained their strength for 6s according to the established force level in turn and took a 5-min break for each group for the next set of tests. During the force generation, subjects were asked to hold the lever and pull the lever back with the help of only the strength of the right arm.

Experimental Data Analysis

Data analysis is divided into surface EMG data activation analysis and model-based simulation muscle activation analysis. According to the test project process, the activation degree of eight main force muscles under four different force application methods in static push-pull operation was analyzed.

Surface EMG Data Activation Analysis

Firstly, the data preprocessing of the original sEMG signal mainly includes three steps: 50 Hz notch to remove power frequency interference, 30 Hz zero-phase shift high-pass filtering to remove motion artifacts, and low-pass filtering of data after full-wave rectification.

The above preprocessing method was used to process the surface EMG signal at the static push and static pull force levels, and the maximum value of the maximum voluntary contraction surface EMG signal was found, and the maximum value was regarded as the signal at 100% muscle activation. The normalized EMG signal was obtained, and the normalized EMG signal was used to solve the nerve activation intensity $u(t)$, and the nerve activation intensity was a recursive model, and the single nerve activation intensity $u(t)$ was related to the nerve activation intensity $u(t-1)$ and $u(t-2)$ of the previous two times. α is the gain coefficient, d is the electrode delay time, β_1 and β_2 are the recursion coefficients (Eq. (1)).

$$u_j(t) = \alpha e_j(t-d) - \beta_1 u_j(t-1) - \beta_2 u_j(t-2) \tag{1}$$

$$\beta_1 = C_1 + C_2 \tag{2}$$

$$\beta_2 = C_1 * C_2 \tag{3}$$

$$\alpha = \beta_1 + \beta_2 + 1.0 \tag{4}$$

The nonlinear model was used to solve the muscle activation degree a(t) according to the nerve activation degree u(t), where A is the nonlinear coefficient, representing the nonlinear degree of nerve activation intensity u(t) and muscle activation intensity a(t) (Eq. (5)).

$$a_j(t) = \frac{e^{Au_j(t)} - 1}{e^A - 1} \tag{5}$$

Model-Based Simulation Muscle Activation Analysis

The simulation muscle activation solution based on the Opensim model mainly includes model scaling, reverse kinematics solution, reverse dynamic solution, and static optimization to solve muscle force. The static kinematic data were used to scale the upper limb model to be consistent with the physical properties of the subject's limb segment. Based on the scaled model, with the collected kinematics data as input, the angle of the upper limb joint expressed in the form of Euler angle during movement can be obtained through OpenSim Inverse Kinematics solution. Based on the reverse kinematics solution, by adding hand operation force and performing Inverse Dynamics solution, the upper limb joint torque under different motion conditions of the subject under different sports conditions can be obtained considering external force factors. Combined with the kinematic data representing the change of joint angle calculated in the first two steps and the reverse dynamic data reflecting the change of joint torque, the static optimization algorithm is used to solve the main force muscle activation degree of the upper limb muscle group (Fig. 4).

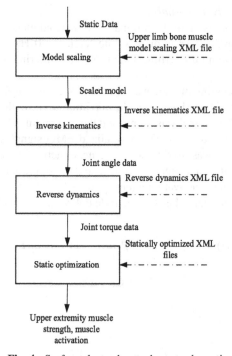

Fig. 4. Surface electrode attachment schematic

3 Results

The data obtained are divided according to the different stages of the force level during the experiment, and the average value of each stage is calculated. The surface EMG calculates muscle activation and the model simulates muscle activation of one of the subjects are shown in the table (Table 4, Table 5).

Table 4. The surface EMG calculates muscle activation

Muscles	30 N	50 N	70 N
DELT1	0.020936	0.026155	0.127053
DELT2	0.013202	0.015689	0.073118
DELT3	0.036697	0.047887	0.251177
LAT	0.024847	0.025364	0.08532
PMAJ	0.035286	0.038799	0.140311
BIC	0.01404	0.026351	0.411499
TRI	0.178924	0.22423	0.518048
SUPRA	0.012797	0.019227	0.072575

Table 5. The model simulates muscle activation

Muscles	30 N	50 N	70 N
DELT1	0.022032	0.022471	0.041865
DELT2	0.014843	0.020756	0.064073
DELT3	0.037371	0.038412	0.109357
LAT	0.025537	0.0256	0.103493
PMAJ	0.035946	0.042616	0.128705
BIC	0.014298	0.016798	0.056385
TRI	0.179731	0.18971	0.252407
SUPRA	0.013638	0.017959	0.040916

4 Discussion

The muscles data collected by 10 subjects during isometric pushing and pulling operations at different operating force levels were calculated and the muscle activation index obtained by model simulation was calculated based on surface EMG surface muscle electrolysis for Pearson correlation analysis (Table 6, Table 7).

Table 6. The static pulling operation is based on surface EMG data and model simulation Pearson analysis results.

Muscles	r	p
DELT1	0.92	0.03
DELT2	0.94	0.01
DELT3	0.83	0.02
SUPRA	0.88	0.01
BIC	0.88	0.02
TRI	0.89	0.03
LAT	0.88	0.01
PMAJ	0.93	0.04

Table 7. The static pushing operation is based on surface EMG data and model simulation Pearson analysis results.

Muscles	r	p
DELT1	0.91	0.03
DELT2	0.88	0.04
DELT3	0.86	0.03
SUPRA	0.78	0.04
BIC	0.85	0.01
TRI	0.90	0.01
LAT	0.89	0.04
PMAJ	0.71	0.01

For static pulling operations, the activation degree of the main muscle deltoid anterior tract, middle deltoid muscle and pectoralis major muscle of the shoulder joint was greater than 0.9 ($p < 0.05$), and the verification level of the activation of the other main force muscles was higher than 0.8 ($p < 0.05$). Based on the above correlation analysis, the correlation between the model-based solution results and the surface electrolytic results of the main exertion muscles of the upper limbs was greater than 0.8 in the static pulling operation (Fig. 7).

For static pushing operations, the correlation between the activation degree of the infraspinatus muscle and the pectoralis major muscle was verified to be lower than 0.8 ($p < 0.05$), while the correlation level was higher than 0.8 ($p < 0.05$) for the most powerful muscles of the shoulder and elbow joints of the upper limbs, and the activation of the anterior deltoid bundle and triceps longhead was higher than 0.9 ($p < 0.05$). Based on the above correlation analysis, it is shown that the level of muscle activation of the main

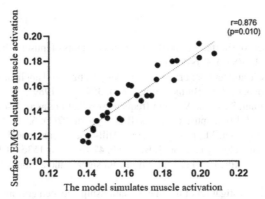

Fig. 7. Static pull operation LAT muscle electrolysis activation degree and model simulation activation degree

force of the shoulder and elbow joints of the upper limb passed the correlation test during the static push operation (Fig. 8).

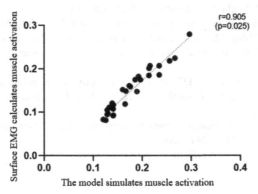

Fig. 8. Static push operation DELT1 muscle electrolysis activation degree and model simulation activation degree

5 Conclusions

Based on the above analysis, the simulated muscle activation results of typical upper limb power muscle model have a strong correlation with the results of muscle activation based on surface EMG data, which verifies the effectiveness of constructing upper limb bone muscle model. Based on the biomechanical modeling of typical dynamic operations, the upper limb bone muscle model accurately solves the upper limb joint torque through the dynamic motion biomechanical modeling, which provides an effective basis for the study of upper limb muscles.

References

1. Hill, A.V.: The heat of shortening and the dynamic constants of muscle. Proc. R. Soc. London. Ser. B-Biol. Sci. **126**(843), 136–195 (1938)
2. Zajac, F.E.: Muscle and tendon: properties, models, scaling, and application to biomechanics and motor control. Crit. Rev. Biomed. Eng. **17**(4), 359–411 (1989)
3. Günther, M., Schmitt, S., Wank, V.: High-frequency oscillations as a consequence of neglected serial damping in Hill-type muscle models. Biol. Cybern. **97**(1), 63–79 (2007)
4. Haeufle, D.F.B., Günther, M., Bayer, A., et al.: Hill-type muscle model with serial damping and eccentric force–velocity relation. J. Biomech. **47**(6), 1531–1536 (2014)
5. Fleischer, C.: Controlling exoskeletons with EMG signals and a biomechanical body model (2007)
6. Bøg, M.F., et al.: Investigation of the linear relationship between grasping force and features of intramuscular EMG. In: Dremstrup, K., Rees, S., Jensen, M.Ø. (eds.) 15th Nordic-Baltic Conference on Biomedical Engineering and Medical Physics (NBC 2011), IFMBE Proceedings, vol. 34, pp. 121–124. Springer, Berlin (2011). https://doi.org/10.1007/978-3-642-21683-1_30
7. Brand, J.: A three-dimensional regression model of the shoulder rhythm. Clinical Biomechanics, 2001
8. Blackwell, C.L., Bradtmiller, B., Parham, J.L.: 2010 Anthropometric Survey of US Marine Corps Personnel: Methods And Summary Statistics (1989)
9. Hill, A.V.: The revolution in muscle physiology. Physiol. Rev. **12**(1), 56–67 (1932)
10. Schutte, L.M.: Using Musculoskeletal Models to Explore Strategies for Improving Performance In Electrical Stimulation-Induced Leg Cycle Ergometry. Stanford University (1993)
11. Delp, S.L., Loan, J.P., Hoy, M.G., et al.: An interactive graphics-based model of the lower extremity to study orthopaedic surgical procedures. IEEE Trans. Biomed. Eng. **37**(8), 757–767 (1990)
12. Holzbaur, K.R.S., et al.: Moment-generating capacity of upper limb muscles in healthy adults. J. Biomech. **40**(11), 2442–2449 (2007)
13. OpenSim Homepage. https://simtk.org/projects/opensim

Modeling of Human Elbow Joint Force Based on MVT Test

Hao Li[1], Weifeng Gao[2], Changhua Jiang[1], Shoupeng Huang[1], Teng Zhang[2], Zhen Zhang[2], Xiang Xu[2], Yueqi An[1], Zheng Zhang[2], Jianwei Niu[2], and Chunhui Wang[1(✉)]

[1] National Key Laboratory of Human Factors Engineering, China Astronaut Research and Training Center, Beijing 1000942, China
chunhui_89@163.com
[2] School of Mechanical Engineering, University of Science and Technology Beijing, Beijing, China
niujw@ustb.edu.cn

Abstract. Human biomechanics has practical value in the fields of medicine, sports and bionics. In order to explore the influencing factors of the maximum force exertion ability of human joints, the elbow joint in the human upper limb joint was selected as the research object, and a mathematical model of the maximum force exertion ability of the human elbow joint was established. In this paper, elbow angle, direction of movement, adjacent joint (shoulder) angle and type of movement (isometric and isokinetic motion) were selected as independent variables, and maximum torque and muscle activation were selected as dependent variables. The elbow data were collected from 31 men through elbow bend/extension isometric and isometric MVT tests. Then, the basic statistical indicators such as mean, standard deviation, maximum and minimum values of the dependent variable were calculated, and draw a bar chart for data visualization. Finally, the experiments have found that under different conditions, the maximum force and muscle activation values of the elbow joint are significantly different. From the analysis of the results, it can be seen that the angle of the adjacent joint and the type of movement can significantly affect the ability of the elbow joint to exert force. The direction of movement and the angle of the adjacent joint can significantly affect the activity of the main force muscles of the upper limb.

Keywords: human biomechanics · Elbow joint · torque · MVT test

1 Introduction

In recent years, the biomechanical model of the human upper limb has become a hot topic. Whether it is in medicine, sports or bionics, it has practical value. In this paper, elbow joint movement is used as the starting point to establish a model of the maximum force capacity of human elbow joint.

In the study of upper limb joints, Ramsay et al. modeled the human elbow and wrist joints through the commercial software SIMM, and used polynomial fitting to obtain the polynomial regression equation of the corresponding muscle strength arm at the elbow and wrist joints [1]. Alvarez et al. proposed a joint angle measurement method combining an inertial sensor (accelerometer and gyro-scope) and a magnetic sensor. This method calculates the angles of wrist flexion, wrist lateral shift, elbow flexion, flexion internal rotation, shoulder flexion, shoulder abduction, and shoulder internal rotation respectively [2]. Marion Hoff-mann et al. developed a surface mesh model of the shoulder muscles that im-proves the accuracy of calculating shoulder muscle length and muscle strength arm from a musculoskeletal model [3]. In order to measure the elbow angle, G. Ligorio et al. proposed a four-step functional calibration method based on the two-degree-of-freedom elbow joint model, which can realize real-time estimation of elbow angle with the help of magnetic inertial sensor [4]. Kengo Onuma et al. proposed A method for measuring muscle strength in restraining valgus joint angulation [5]. In order to study the relationship between joint angle and muscle activation, J.E. Kasprisin et al. conducted concentric isokinetic, eccentric isokinetic and isometric maximum voluntary contraction experiments of elbow flex-ors [6]. Alexander Ellwein et al. using a three-dimensional elbow simulator to compare the lateral collateral ligament reconstruction [7]. Caitlin E. Hill et al. studied the effect of multidirectional elastic bands on forearm muscle activity and wrist extension during submaximal gripping in patients with lateral elbow tendinopathy [8].

These studies are able to predict the corresponding muscle activity for specific tasks, however, to make these models more applicable, it is necessary to measure real subjects. A better way to assess joint maximum strength is to focus on joint strength within spatial boundaries, rather than individual muscles. Therefore, the result can also be directly used in simpler models such as RAMSIS for force and attitude prediction based on joint torque. In this paper, the effects of elbow angle, direction of movement, adjacent joint (shoulder) angle and type of movement (isometric and isokinetic motion) on the maximum joint torque and muscle activation of the elbow joint were analyzed.

2   Method

In order to perform the elbow joint force capacity test, the experimental equipment is BTE Primus RS, Biovison surface electromyograph and Martin ruler. The number of test volunteers in this experiment is 31 people, all male volunteers. The average height of the volunteers is 175.9 cm (SD = 3.1), and the average weight is 74.2 kg (SD = 5.6). The test indicators of the experiment are the maxi-mum torque of the elbow joint and the degree of muscle activation.

2.1   Experimental Content

The experiment is divided into elbow joint isometric and isokinetic maximum force test. The horizontal setting of the elbow joint experiment is shown in 0 (Table 1).

2.2   Isometric Strength Experimental Process

The isometric strength test is used to obtain maximum muscle strength (MVC). In this experiment, BTE Primus RS simulation mechanical test evaluation training system is used to perform isometric muscle strength test.

Table 1. Elbow joint maximum torque experimental project parameter setting

Number	Experimental projects	Joint range of motion	Forward flexion angle of the shoulder joint
1	Elbow flexion/extension isometric MVT test	45°/90°	0°
2			30°
3			60°
4			90°
5	Elbow flexion/extension isokinetic MVT test	0°–135°	0°
6			30°
7			60°
8			90°

The measurement method is as follows:

(1) General requirements: Before the test, volunteers attach electromyography sheets, and the adherent muscles are the middle deltoid, posterior deltoid, biceps, triceps, pectoralis major, latissimus dorsi, and infraspinatus. During the measurement, the foot needs to be fixed to the ground. In addition, the left foot needs to be forward and the right foot backward to maintain the center of gravity. Warm-up must be performed before all measurements begin.
(2) Force application method: Try to keep the position unchanged during the measurement of the motion torque of the single joint. Quickly and smoothly apply the maximum force within 2 s and maintain it for 6 s;
(3) Number of repetitions: Repeat measurement of each force 2 times;
(4) Measurement duration requirements: The single duration of shoulder and elbow single joint exercise is 10 s;
(5) Interval and rest requirements: Rest for 30 s after each measurement, and rest time not less than 3 min after 3 repeated measurements.

2.3 Isokinetic Strength Experimental Process

The isokinetic strength test is used to obtain maximum muscle force (torque). In this experiment, the BTE Primus RS simulation mechanical test evaluation training system is used to perform isokinetic muscle strength test.

The measurement method is as follows:

(1) General requirements: Volunteers wear sneakers and must warm up before all measurements begin.
(2) Force application method: Quickly and smoothly apply the maximum force after starting and continue to apply force until the equipment stops;
(3) Number of repetitions: Repeat measurement of each force 2 times.
(4) Interval and rest requirements: Rest for 3 min after each measurement, and rest time not less than 3min after the end of 2 repeated measurements.

2.4 Data Processing and Analysis

There are several data analysis methods:

(1) MVC: For isokinetic motion, the moving average method is used to filter the force curve, and then the force curve data during the whole test process is taken; For isometric motion, the maximum operating force within 2–5 s in the isometric 100% MVC test is extracted, and the maximum force application capacity of isometric motion at other angles is solved by taking the isometric motion and isokinetic motion force data as the mapping relationship.

(2) Basic statistical indicators: Calculate the average, standard deviation, maximum and minimum values of the force application ability of each movement direction of the joint, and compare the difference of the average value under different movement angle ranges;

(3) Relationship between single joint angle and maximum joint torque: According to the isokinetic motion, isometric motion angle and moment data curve obtained in the experiment, the variation law of maximum joint torque with joint angle in each direction of joint movement is analyzed and summarized by polynomial fitting method.

(4) The relationship between the maximum joint moment and the single joint angle: Analyze the influence of shoulder angle on elbow flexion/extension ability, and analyze the influence of elbow angle on shoulder flexion/extension and adduction/abduction. On this basis, the influence model of elbow angle on shoulder joint force ability and the influence model of shoulder angle on elbow joint force application ability are established by data fitting and other methods.

(5) Muscle activation index: The collected original EMG signal is filtered by bandpass 20–500 Hz, and the muscle activation index is extracted after removing the power frequency and its odd harmonics. The activation of the main force muscles of the upper limbs in different exercise states under different operating postures is analyzed.

3 Result

3.1 Elbow Maximum Torque Test Results

The statistical results of the maximum joint moment during the isometric movement and isokinetic movement of the elbow joint are shown in 0. Under different exercise conditions, the average range of maximum joint torque of elbow flexion and extension of 31 volunteers is (26.9–42.9) Nm and (19.0–38.7) Nm, respectively. Under different sports conditions, the average maximum joint moments of elbow flexion and extension of 31 volunteers are (25.4–34.3) Nm and (26.4–33.4) Nm, respectively (Table 2).

3.2 Elbow Maximum Torque Data Analysis

The angle of the elbow joint significantly affects the ability to exert force on the elbow joint in the direction of extension movement, but does not significantly affect the ability to exert force on the elbow joint in the direction of flexion motion. The statistical results and proportional relationship of the maximum joint torque of elbow isometric movement

Table 2. Statistical results of average joint torque of shoulder joint (unit: Nm)

Action	Movement Direction	Elbow angle	Forward flexion angle of the shoulder joint	Mean	Standard deviation	Maximum	Minimum
Elbow isometric exercises	Flexion	45°	0°	41.2	8.1	56.6	25.9
			30°	39.3	8.8	58.4	23.7
			60°	36.4	10.3	65.0	21.4
			90°	28.8	7.7	45.9	17.0
		90°	0°	42.9	8.4	62.2	24.6
			30°	34.4	7.5	51.8	21.6
			60°	30.9	10.5	59.5	17.6
			90°	26.9	10.7	58.0	11.7
	Extension	45°	0°	35.5	9.4	59.9	18.2
			30°	35.8	9.4	55.4	16.3
			60°	38.3	9.9	51.2	19.5
			90°	38.7	11.3	69.0	19.0
		90°	0°	35.4	8.0	47.0	21.4
			30°	30.8	7.8	43.2	16.6
			60°	26.6	6.7	38.8	16.8
			90°	19.0	7.1	35.2	8.0
Elbow isokinetic movement	Flexion	/	0°	34.3	9.3	60.1	18.5
			30°	30.9	3.9	35.3	20.6
			60°	26.4	2.5	29.4	18.5
			90°	25.4	5.5	34.8	15.7
	Extension		0°	33.4	7.8	51.0	18.1
			30°	29.9	4.7	33.8	15.1
			60°	28.5	5.4	34.2	17.7
			90°	26.4	4.5	34.4	20.4

under different elbow angles are shown in 0. In the elbow extension isometric exercise, the paired t-test results showed that there is a significant difference in the maximum joint torque ($p < 0.05$) between 45° and 90° of the elbow joint, and the elbow joint 45° is 33% higher than that of 90°. In shoulder flexion isometric movements, the paired t-test results showed that there is no significant difference in maximum joint moment between 45° and 90° elbow ($p > 0.05$) (Figs. 1 and 2).

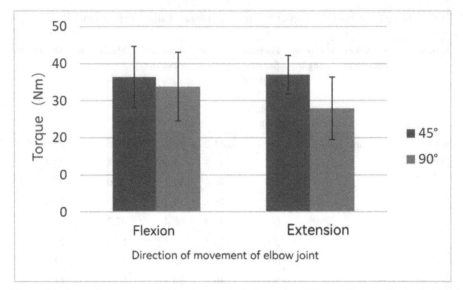

Fig. 1. Maximum joint torque of elbow isometric movement at different elbow angles (unit: Nm). The direction of movement has no significant effect on the elbow joint exertion ability, and there is no significant difference between the maximum torque of elbow flexion and stretching. The maximum joint moment data of elbow isometric movement in different directions of movement are shown in 0. The results of paired t-test showed that there is no significant difference in the ability to apply force in the two directions of flexion and extending the elbow joint ($p > 0.05$).

The adjacent joint angle can significantly affect the elbow joint application ability, and the maximum elbow moment at different shoulder flexion angles is different. Taking the isometric movement with an elbow angle of 90° as an example, see 0, with the increase of shoulder flexion angle (within the range of 0°–90°), the maximum joint torque of elbow flexion and stretching decreases. The maximum joint torque of elbow flexion with shoulder angle of 90° is 37% lower than that of shoulder angle of 0°, and the maximum joint torque of elbow extension exercise with shoulder angle of 90° is 46% lower than that of shoulder angle of 0°, and the results of paired t-test show that there is a significant difference in the maximum joint torque of elbow joint ($p < 0.05$) when the shoulder angle is 0° and 90° (Fig. 3).

The type of exercise significantly affects the ability of elbow joint to exert force, and the ability of elbow joint flexion exercise under isometric exercise is higher than that of isokinetic exercise, and the force exertion ability of stretching exercise is lower than that of isokinetic exercise. In isokinetic movement, the elbow joint needs 1 s–2 s to reach the maximum force capacity at the beginning of the conversion of the direction of movement, and at the same time, it will be affected by fatigue factors at the end of the movement, therefore, the maximum joint moment of the middle position of the elbow isokinetic movement (that is, the elbow angle 45°) is selected and compared with the isometric movement, the results are shown in 0. The results of paired t-test showed that there are significant differences between the maximum joint torque of isokinetic and isometric motion in the direction of elbow flexion and extension ($p < 0.05$), and the

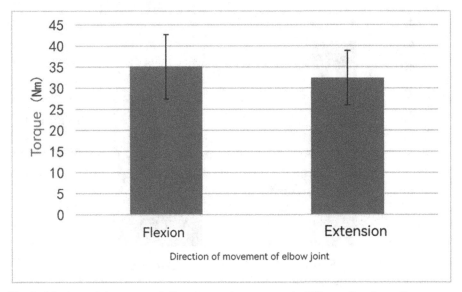

Fig. 2. Maximum joint torque of elbow isometric movement in different directions of movement (unit: Nm)

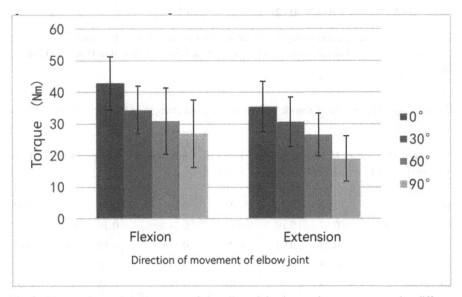

Fig. 3. The maximum joint moment of the elbow joint isometric movement under different shoulder angles when the elbow joint is 90° (unit: Nm)

maximum joint torque of elbow flexion is 17% higher than that of isometric exercise, and the maximum joint torque of elbow extension is 8% lower than that of isokinetic motion (Fig. 4).

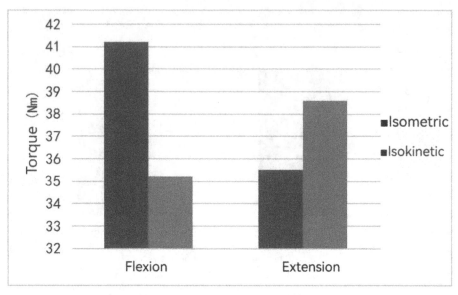

Fig. 4. Maximum joint torque of elbow joint in different exercise types (unit: Nm)

3.3   Elbow Surface Electromyography Test Results

The statistics of the activation degree of the main force muscles of the upper limbs during the isometric and isokinetic movement of the elbow joint are shown in 0 and 0 (Tables 3 and 4).

Table 3. Statistical results of muscle activity of the main strength of the upper limbs in elbow isometric exercise

Movement Direction	Shoulder joint angle	Middle deltoid	Posterior deltoid	Pectoralis major	Infraspinatus	Biceps	Triceps	Latissimus dorsi
Flexion	0°	0.26	0.2	0.04	0.26	0.39	0.02	0.02
	30°	0.57	0.18	0.03	0.24	0.39	0.02	0.09
	60°	0.23	0.09	0.06	0.47	0.35	0.01	0.01
	90°	0.08	0.37	0.04	0.55	0.23	0.01	0.01
Extension	0°	0.06	0.25	0.04	0.1	0.43	0.5	0.01
	30°	0.25	0.47	0.03	0.77	0.55	0.55	0.1
	60°	0.06	0.72	0.04	0.51	0.17	0.23	0.02
	90°	0.34	0.49	0.06	0.55	0.27	0.06	0.04

Note: the angle of forward flexion of the elbow joint is 45°

Table 4. Statistical results of muscle activity of the main force of the upper limb in elbow isokinetic exercise

Movement Direction	Shoulder joint angle	Middle deltoid	Posterior deltoid	Pectoralis major	Infraspinatus	Biceps	Triceps	Latissimus dorsi
Flexion	0°	0.10	0.08	0.03	0.07	0.14	0.54	0.12
Extension	0°	0.10	0.30	0.02	0.13	0.11	0.60	0.12

3.4 Elbow Surface Electromyography Data Analysis

There are differences in the main force muscles of the upper limbs under different elbow joint movement directions. The average muscle activity of the elbow joint in the two directions of movement is shown in 0. By comparing the muscle activity of the same muscle in different directions of movement, it can be seen that in the elbow joint flexion exercise, the main force muscles are the middle deltoid, posterior deltoid, infraspinatus, and biceps. In extension exercise, the main muscles are the middle deltoid, posterior deltoid, infraspinatus, triceps and biceps (Figs. 5, 6 and 7).

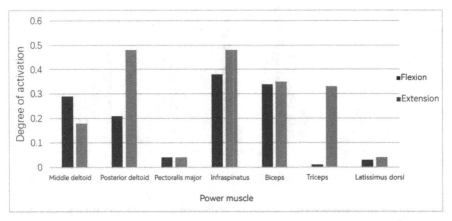

Fig. 5. Muscle activity of the main force of the upper limbs during the isometric movement of the elbow joint

Adjacent joint angle can significantly affect the activity of the main force muscles of the upper limb, and there are differences in the activity of the main force muscles of the upper limb at different elbow flexion angles, but it does not reflect a clear regularity. The muscle activity of the main exerting muscles of lower upper limb movements at different elbow angles is shown in 0, 0.

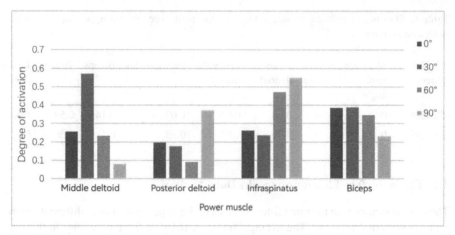

Fig. 6. Elbow extension isometric movements at different shoulder angles mainly exert muscle activity of muscles

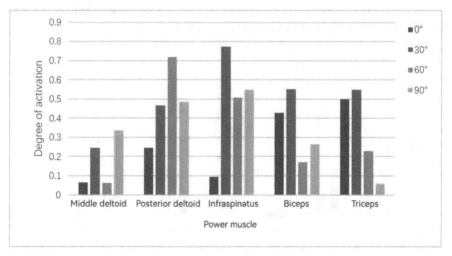

Fig. 7. Elbow extension isometric movements at different shoulder angles mainly exert muscle activity of muscles

4   Discussion

The mathematical model of the maximum force exertion ability of the human elbow joint established in this paper is collected from real subjects and has great applicability. By focusing on the forces of the joints in the spatial range, rather than individual muscles, the result can also be directly used in simpler models such as RAMSIS.

In this paper, the torque of the elbow joint and the activation degree of the main force muscles under different working conditions are measured. Through data analysis, it is not difficult to find the following points: shoulder angle can significantly affect the joint force application ability in the direction of some elbow joint movement; The direction of movement had no significant effect on the ability to exert force on the elbow joint. The angle of the adjacent joint can significantly affect the ability of the elbow joint to exert force, and the maximum joint moment of the elbow joint at different adjacent joint angles is different. The type of exercise can significantly affect the elbow joint force application ability, under isometric exercise, the elbow joint flexion exercise force application ability is higher than that of isokinetic exercise, and the extension exercise force application ability is lower than that of isokinetic exercise.

In this experiment, only 31 participants are collected, and the amount of data is small, and there is a certain degree of contingency. In this experiment, only the flexion and extension of the elbow joint are considered, and the next step is to consider the torque and muscle degree of the elbow joint under more complex movements.

5 Conclusion

In this paper, by collecting real data of human body, a mathematical model of the maximum force exertion ability of human elbow joint is established, which has great applicability. By collecting the torque and muscle activation of the elbow joint during flexion and extension under different working conditions, the influencing factors of the maximum force exertion ability of the human body are analyzed. Next, the joint torque-joint angle function can be obtained by data fitting. Combined with the mathematical model of the maximum force capacity of the shoulder joint, the biomechanical model of the human upper limb can be constructed.

References

1. Ramsay, J.W., Hunter, B.V., Gonzalez, R.V.: Muscle moment arm and normalized moment contributions as reference data for musculoskeletal elbow and wrist joint models. J. Biomech. **42**(4), 463–473 (2009)
2. Alvarez, D., Alvarez, J.C., Gonzalez, R.: Upper limb joint angle measurement in occupational health. Comput. Methods Biomech. Biomed. Engin. **19**(2), 159–170 (2016)
3. Hoffmann, M., Haering, D., Begon, M.: Comparison between line and surface mesh models to represent the rotator cuff muscle geometry in musculoskeletal models. Comput. Methods Biomech. Biomed. Engin. **20**(11), 1175–1181 (2017)
4. Ligorio, G., Zanotto, D., Sabatini, A.M., Agrawal, S.K.: A novel functional calibration method for real-time elbow joint angles estimation with magnetic-inertial sensors. J. Biomech. **54**, 106–110 (2017)
5. Onuma, K., Yanai, T.: A method for measuring muscle strength in restraining valgus joint angulation: Elbow varus muscle strength against valgus loading. J. Biomech. **147**, 111427 (2023)
6. Kasprisin, J.E., Grabiner, M.D.: Joint angle-dependence of elbow flexor activation levels during isometric and isokinetic maximum voluntary contractions. Clin. Biomech. **15**, 743–749 (2000)
7. Ellwein, A., et al.: Biomechanical comparison of lateral collateral ligament reconstruction with and without additional internal bracing using a three-dimensional elbow simulator. Clin. Biomech. **81**, 105236 (2021)

456   H. Li et al.

8. Hill, C.E., Heales, L.J., Stanton, R., Holmes, M.W., Kean, C.O.: Effects of multidirectional elastic tape on forearm muscle activity and wrist extension during submaximal gripping in individuals with lateral elbow tendinopathy: A randomised crossover trial. Clin. Biomech. **100**, 105810 (2022)

Position-Aware Tooth Segmentation and Numbering with Prior Knowledge Injected

Changlin Li$^{(\boxtimes)}$, Jian He, Gaige Wang, Kuilong Liu, and Changyuan Yang

Alibaba Group, Hangzhou, China
{lichanglin.lcl,jiange.hj,gaige.wgg,kuilong.lkl,
changyuan.yangcy}@alibaba-inc.com

Abstract. Tooth segmentation and numbering are the most fundamental tasks in oral analysis as they are the prerequisite for many popular oral businesses such as root canal therapy and whitening. Despite the growing attention in this research field, the results are still far from satisfactory. Existing methods either employ a complicated multi-stage framework or couple tooth segmentation and numbering together simply by using multi-class segmentation, which is neither convenient to use nor accurate enough. To this end, we propose a single-stage multi-task framework to perform tooth segmentation and numbering in an end-to-end and decoupled fashion. Furthermore, We also involve the prior knowledge of the oral structure in the network and leverage adversarial learning to further improve the accuracy. Extensive experiments on two real-world datasets demonstrate that our proposed method achieves state-of-the-art performance.

Keywords: oral health · computer vision · tooth segmentation

1 Introduction

Oral health is vital in human life. To diagnose the oral health of the patients, clinicians need to take oral images from Cone-beam Computed Tomograhpy (CBCT) and carefully inspect the images to recognize oral diseases, which is challenging and time-consuming. To make this process more efficient and accurate, the oral diagnostic automation system has been designed to handle several important tasks, including tooth detection and numbering [45], tooth segmentation [16,21], caries detection [18,23], osteoporosis diagnosis [5,24], and endodontic treatment [35]. Amongst all these tasks, tooth segmentation and numbering are the most fundamental as they are the starting point of oral analysis. Tooth segmentation requires recognizing the teeth area from the oral image, and tooth numbering needs to identify each teeth instance and assign unique ids to them, as Fig. 1 and Fig. 2 show. Due to the importance of these two tasks, researchers have made great efforts in this area.

C. Li and J. He—Contribute equally to this work.

© The Author(s), under exclusive license to Springer Nature Switzerland AG 2023
P.-L. P. Rau (Ed.): HCII 2023, LNCS 14024, pp. 457–475, 2023.
https://doi.org/10.1007/978-3-031-35946-0_37

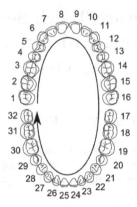

Fig. 1. Universal numbering system [2]. This is a dental practitioner's view. Tooth number 1 is in the rear upper tooth on the patient's right. Each tooth has a unique number.

Earlier works [6,16,21] in this field mainly focus on a single task instead of both, which requires extra effort to design models for the other task. To fill this gap, [3,34,40] couple them together as a multi-class segmentation task, where the number of categories is 33 to represent 32 teeth and background. Despite the satisfying inference speed, these methods suffer from low accuracy. [45] designs a two-state framework to generate initial bounding boxes for teeth and then cropped tooth images in the second stage to classify their ids. This method is not practical as it is time-consuming and hard to employ due to the involution of multiple stages. Furthermore, all the above methods ignore the essential prior geometry knowledge of teeth, which leads to failures in corner cases in the dental diagnosis process, such as missing teeth and artifact addition.

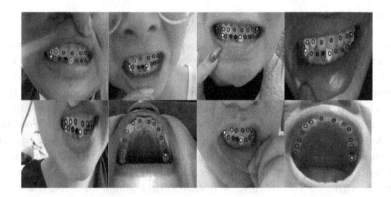

Fig. 2. Visualization of segmentation (with individual mask) and numbering (with circle) result for PAPK dataset

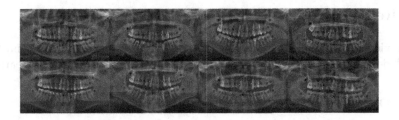

Fig. 3. Visualization of prediction result for DNS Panoramic Images dataset

To this end, we propose a **P**rior **K**nowledge guided **P**osition-**A**ware network, dubbed as PAPK-Net, to tackle the tooth segmentation and numbering tasks in a single-stage end-to-end fashion. The overall architecture is shown in Fig. 4. Unlike the previous works, PAPK-Net decouples the two tasks and learns them jointly by generating segmentation masks and heatmaps in two separate heads. Such design has several advantages: 1) It takes the oral images as input and outputs the predictions that can be directly employed in the downstream applications, which is easy to use; 2) The segmentation and numbering are optimized jointly as multi-tasks, which can help the backbone learn more robust feature representations. We further involve prior knowledge in the network to better handle challenging sets. The teeth are arranged symmetrically in the mouth and have bell shapes. We consider this as valuable prior knowledge and carefully design a generative adversarial network (GAN) to inject it into the framework. Specifically, the predicted segmentation mask and heatmaps produced by the generator will be paired with the oral images as the input of the discriminator, which will judge whether the geometric shape naturally matches the oral images. Finally, we introduce a tooth augmentation strategy, which simulates the corner cases in oral diagnosis by adding artifacts to the normal tooth during training.

To evaluate our framework, besides the known public tooth dataset DNS panoramic Images dataset [16], we further carefully collected a new dataset with a much larger size, named PAPK dataset. Extensive experiments on these datasets demonstrate that our method achieves state-of-the-art performance.

Our contributions can be summarized as follows:

- We propose PARK-Net, which solves tooth segmentation and numbering in an end-to-end fashion through multi-task learning. Extensive experiments demonstrate that our method achieves the best performance.
- We came up with an effective way to incorporate prior knowledge into PARK-Net via adversarial learning.[1] Ablation study suggests the potential of the proposed model under insufficient data scenario.
- We present a deficient tooth augmentation strategy to adaptively learn the corner cases.
- We collect a new large-scale tooth dataset named PARK dataset, which can benefit the whole community.

---

[1] "Adversarial learning" here refers to the process for the GAN model to discriminate between correct and mismatched pairs.

2   Related Works

We review three main areas of related work: object detection and segmentation, tooth detection and segmentation, and knowledge incorporation in deep learning.

2.1   Object Detection and Segmentation

Region-based Convolutional Neural Network (R-CNN) series [10,11,39] are milestones for deep learning-based object detection, while fully convolutional networks (FCN) [31] break new ground for semantic segmentation and has brought great progress to many fields such as autonomous driving [50,53] and medical image analysis [7,40]. Mask R-CNN [13] further enhances R-CNN with its outstanding performance on instance segmentation, where the instance segmentation branch benefits from the high-quality proposals generated from the ROI align [13] layer. Generally, object detection and segmentation algorithms in deep learning can be broadly categorized into two categories from different aspects. Depending on whether anchor exists in the network, We have anchor-based [37–39] and anchor-free [22,36,44] models. Similarly, we distinguish one-stage models [28] from two-stage models by checking if the regional proposal network included [39].

Although the anchor mechanism with the region proposal network together can significantly boost object detection and segmentation performance, the inference speed is far from satisfactory, which is caused by the exhaustive computation resources consumed by anchors and region proposals. As a result, one-stage anchor-free object detection models [44,46,49] are proposed to improve the speed while keeping similar or even better performance on the general object detection benchmark. It has become a more popular approach and has been applied in different domains such as automated perception system [8,52].

2.2   Tooth Numbering and Segmentation

Tuzoff et al. [45] proposed a CNN-based architecture for both tooth detection and numbering tasks. The tooth detection module processed the radiograph to generate the boundaries of each tooth. The tooth numbering module classifies detected teeth according to the FDI notation [1]. The author further utilized the heuristic algorithm to improve the performance based on the rules of teeth spatial arrangement. [45] can not perform end-to-end training, and inappropriate heuristics may drive the results to undesirable traits.

Cui et al. [7] introduced a two-stage method to segment and recognize each tooth in CBCT images. In the first stage, edge maps will be extracted from CBCT images. In the second stage, edge maps are concatenated with original images as the input of the 3D regional proposal network to generate region proposals, where a spatial relation module is introduced to inject spatial distribution. [34] instead employed a multi-class Mask-RCNN model with the post-processed inference result to complete the numbering task in one shot.

Kim *et al.* [19] proposed a technique that combined a R-CNN model with heuristic methods to detect and number the teeth in a dental panoramic radiograph image. Tooth regions are first detected by a pre-trained Faster R-CNN model. Then each tooth region is cropped and combined with positional value as a whole input, feeding into another CNN classification model to determine tooth numbering. [45] proposed a Faster R-CNN model to detect tooth bounding boxes first and then cropped them out to classify their number, which shared a similar design.

Chung *et al.* [6] proposed a method to recognize teeth in panoramic X-ray images with a center point based object detection model to identify each tooth, followed by bounding box regression applied to a patch cropped from the tooth center. A distance regularization penalty is employed on the 32 points to smooth the variation of distances between teeth to remove the outliers. However, the model designed in this paper cannot generate tooth segmentation results, and the tooth center point regression branch is not powerful enough to tackle complicated cases.

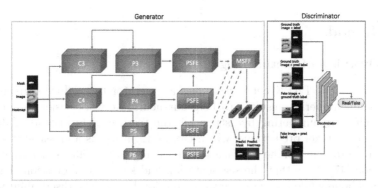

Fig. 4. The overview of our GAN architecture. It consists of the *Generators* (in Sect. 3.2) and *Discriminators* (in Sect. 3.3). The oral images and heatmaps are concatenated and passed to a discriminator to determine if the given heatmaps belong to the corresponding images. The segmentation mask follows the same configuration.

2.3 Knowledge Incorporation in Deep Learning

Prior knowledge targets to constrain the output of deep learning models and reduce the number of unreasonable outliers, which can remarkably improve the deep learning models, especially when the amount of available data is small. Xiao *et al.* [48] proposed a method that incorporated class similarity knowledge into CNN models using a graph convolution layer to improve classification accuracy. Jiang *et al.* [17] exploited an explicit knowledge module to incorporate external knowledge and an implicit knowledge module to learn knowledge without explicit definitions or being summarized by the human in an object detection model. Xu *et al.* [51] utilized color information from the reference image as prior knowledge to help restore and colorize old photos.

Here we explore Generative adversarial networks(GANs) [12] to model object relations. GANs have an outstanding ability to mimic data distributions from real data. Generally, GAN is composed of a generator and a discriminator. The training procedure of GAN is a minimal-maximum game. The discriminator tries to distinguish generated samples from mixed samples to minimize classification loss, while the generator tries to generate high-quality samples to cheat the discriminator to maximize classification loss. Luc *et al.* [32] trained a convolutional semantic segmentation network along with an adversarial network that discriminates segmentation maps coming either from the ground truth or from the segmentation network. Ghafoorian *et al.* [9] proposed EL-GAN in lane detection to make the semantic segmentation network output to be more realistic and better structure-preserving.

In our scenario, an oral region is approximately a rigid object, where the number of the tooth is 32 at most in general. And no matter how oral pose rotates, the basic shape and spatial relation between teeth are maintained, which is valuable prior knowledge we should make good use of.

3   Methods

3.1   Overview of Methodology

As Fig. 4 depicts, PAPK-net first applies a generator to produce segmentation masks and numbering results. To help our neural network easier to converge, we simplify the numbering by estimating the teeth centers instead of directly making dense pixel predictions, which can be regarded as a classical keypoints regression problem similar to face landmark regression [43] and human pose estimation [47]. Note that the segmentation and keypoints regression share the same backbone while having separate prediction heads. The discriminator aims to classify the image-mask-regression pairs to capture the prior knowledge of the oral structure.

3.2   Generator

The generator is a multi-task model to predict mask and heatmap with the oral image, as shown in Fig. 4. Context feature is very important to determine precise tooth location. Thus, we convert convolution layers (C3-C5 in Fig. 4) into dilation convolution. By doing so, we enlarge the receptive field of the feature maps. We additionally change the stride of the pooling layer before C3 from 2 to 1 to double the scale of output feature maps.

Position-Aware Feature Extraction. Positional-sensitive is of great importance in coordination-related computer vision tasks, where it helps neural networks learn spatial relations and constraints. For our tasks, with the support of that positional information, valuable insights can be obtained to determine the correct tooth number between neighbor teeth, as well as the shape of each tooth.

However, we notice that the conventional convolution neural networks are not position-sensitive since the same filters are applied to the whole feature map.

To introduce positional information, We follow a similar design in CoordConv [29], where feature maps are concatenated with normalized pixel coordinates within the range of $[-1, 1]$ and then passed to the following layers. By attaching coordinates to the feature map, the tooth spatial distribution can be utilized to help distinguish neighbor teeth and assign them the correct numbers.

Prediction Heads and Multi-scale Feature Fusion. We utilize Feature Pyramid Network (FPN) [27] to obtain four feature maps in different scales, where three heads following each of them in parallel. Those heads are center regression, segmentation (adapted from [30]), and mask IoU prediction. In detail, the tooth center regression head will predict the location of the corresponding tooth center by regressing tooth heatmaps. The coordinates of the highest intensity in the heatmap represent tooth spatial locations, and the index of the corresponding heatmap represents tooth identity. In the meantime, the segmentation branch generates segmentation maps to present each tooth mask.

To evaluate the quality of the generated mask, we introduce a mask score prediction branch inspired by Mask Scoring R-CNN [15]; this branch will predict the intersection over union(IoU) between generated segmentation masks and ground truth masks. As human teeth may not all be visible in digital photos, we add another branch to predict the visibility of certain teeth at the top of the FPN.

For multi-scale feature fusion (MSFE), we upsample feature maps generated from all of the segmentation/keypoint heads to the same scale and merge them to refine prediction. MSFE learns the coefficients to fuse different features via soft attention, following the similar design in keypoint-FPN [25].

Loss Functions for Generator. The loss for the generator (also referred to "base network") is defined as follows:

$$L_{center} = \sum_{i=1}^{N} \sum_{j=1}^{K} (z_{ij} - \hat{z}_{ij})^2 \tag{1}$$

$$L_{inseg} = 1 - \frac{1}{K} \sum_{j=1}^{K} \frac{2 \sum_{i=1}^{N} s_{ij} \hat{s}_{ij}}{\sum_{i=1}^{N} s_{ij} + \sum_{i=1}^{N} \hat{s}_{ij}} \tag{2}$$

$$L_{vis} = \sum_{i=1}^{N} \sum_{j=1}^{K} -c_{ij} * log\hat{c}_{ij} \tag{3}$$

$$L_{IoU} = \sum_{i=1}^{N} \sum_{j=1}^{K} \left\| IoU_{ij} - I\hat{o}U_{ij} \right\|^2 \tag{4}$$

$$L_b = L_{center} + L_{inseg} + L_{vis} + \mu L_{IoU} + \lambda L_{reg} \tag{5}$$

where L_{center} is Mean Square Error(MSE) loss for heatmap regression in tooth numbering task. L_{inseg} is dice loss for tooth segmentation. L_{vis} is Binary Cross Entropy(BCE) loss for tooth visibility prediction. L_{IoU} is Mean Square Error between the predicted IoU and ground truth IoU. L_{reg} is a weight decay term. μ is a coefficient for L_{IoU} term, λ is a coefficient for weight decay loss term, we set $\mu = 0.01$ and $\lambda = 0.0005$ in our experiment. K is the category number, N is the total image number. i,j refers to i_{th} image j_{th} category ground truth. z_{ij}, $\hat{z}_{ij}$, s_{ij}, $\hat{s}_{ij}$, c_{ij} and $\hat{c}_{ij}$ refers to predict and ground-truth for tooth center, segmentation, and visibility results.

We use dice loss instead of cross-entropy loss because of a heavy class imbalance in the pixel classification task, where dice loss has shown its insensitivity to the class imbalance issue. Additionally, it is also important to point out that we compute loss for visible teeth only.

3.3   Implicit Knowledge Incorporation

As can be observed from Table 2, the generator itself as a single model can already achieve good performance. However, it is still possible to make improvements. For example, the predicted tooth centers suffer from displacements and overlaps, indicating the need to impose more powerful spatial constraints on predictions. The spatial constraints follow the physical shape of the oral, where each tooth follows the neighbor horizontally in bell-shaped curves, which is a common spatial relationship across all human beings.

PAPK-net considers this as valuable prior knowledge and models it by forming four input pairs to learn the prior knowledge via GAN. Here discriminators identify whether a given input pair is fake or not. If the given person's image matches its ground truth, then it is a true sample, else not. During the whole process, the discriminator tells the generator what a true sample is. In turn, the generator learns the feature and generates higher quality fake "ground truth" to fool the discriminator. By playing the min-max game, GAN final converges and high-quality masks/heatmaps can be generated accordingly. Please refer to Fig. 4 for a complete picture.

The quality of the predicted pair from GAN can be evaluated from two aspects: 1. to what extent does the generator's output look like GT heatmap, where it tells the similarity between the generated sample and the reality 2. To what extent does the generator's output mismatch with the random target, where we can tell how dissimilar the generated results and the random samples are. Those two aspects work together to ensure the high quality of the generated samples.

Further, there are two advantages we use GAN. i). We avoid explicitly fabricating some sophisticated loss functions to refine the output for certain cases. ii). Adversarial loss is appropriate to learn data under a variety of conditions. Thus we no longer need to develop loss functions separately.

3.4   GAN Loss

We adopt a vanilla GAN loss in the conditional setting in this phase, which is defined as:

$$
\begin{aligned}
L_{adv}^{D} = L_{bce}(D(x_1, GT_1), 1) \\
+ L_{bce}(D(x_1, G(x_1)), 0) \\
+ L_{bce}(D(x_2, GT_1), 1) \\
+ L_{bce}(D(x_2, G(x_1)), 0)
\end{aligned}
\tag{6}
$$

$$
L_{adv}^{G} = L_{bce}(D(x_1, G(x_1)), 1)
\tag{7}
$$

where L_{bce} denotes BCE loss, G and D denote generator and the discriminator respectively, x_1 denotes conditional input oral image, while GT_1 denotes corresponding ground truth heatmaps(segmentation masks).

Total loss functions for generator G are defined as:

$$
L^{G} = \mu L_{adv}^{G} + L_b
\tag{8}
$$

μ is set to 0.005 in our experiments.

3.5   Deficient Tooth Augmentation

By manually inspecting our datasets, we find some cases where the deficient tooth (missing tooth and artifact additions) is present. Although those cases are quite limited in a normal tooth dataset, they are abundant in datasets related to oral disease. Previous literature rules those scenarios out for simplicity purposes, unavoidably resulting in an incomplete solution.

Here we adopt a deficient tooth augmentation(DTA) strategy, which is inspired and adapted from [26]. The purpose of the DTA is to train the model to recognize extreme cases in tooth segmentation and numbering task. In detail, we simulate two cases, 1). few teeth missing and 2). implanting of artifact addition, including braces and dental fillings. Two kinds of data augmentation are available to manually simulate the scenarios mentioned above. 1). A tooth is randomly selected from each given image, and all ground truth associated with it is removed to simulate a tooth-missing scenario. 2). A tooth is randomly selected from each given image and filled with a rectangular patch at its center with an intensity of 255 to simulate cases of dental filling and other artifact addition. Both augmentations are called with a probability of 0.2 in our implementation. Here we provide visualization results to validate the effectiveness of DTA in Fig. 5.

Implementation Details for DTA. To implement case 1, we remove the associated mask and keypoint from the selected tooth. We additionally set the tooth area in the original image as zero intensity to mask out the selected tooth to simulate the tooth missing scenario. To implement case 2, we consider two specific artificial additions, which are braces and dental fillings. We design them as squares and rectangles respectively, where the center of both is the keypoint

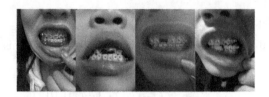

Fig. 5. Visualization of DTA result for PAPK Images dataset. By introducing DTA, PAPK-net is able to identify missing tooth and artifact additions (namely braces) and correctly assign the corresponding number to each tooth. Best viewed by zooming in.

coordinate of the tooth. For braces, we fill the square with a filling threshold mentioned before. The side of the square is decided by the minimum height and width of the tooth, multiply by the factor of 0.6. For the dental filling, we compute the filled tooth area as 0.8 of the tooth's height multiplied by the tooth's width and then fill the area by the filing threshold.

4   Experiments and Result

4.1   Network Training and Inference

All the models are implemented with Tensorflow and trained on an Nvidia GeForce 2080Ti GPU.

Details About Training PAPK. To achieve a satisfying performance, we separate two stages to train PAPK-net. In stage one, we train the generator by an Adam optimizer [20] with a learning rate of 0.0004. In stage two, we train the discriminator for 20 epochs at the beginning of the training process. At the same time, we freeze the parameters of the generator with the consideration that a weak discriminator may disturb the process to train the generator. After that, we unfreeze the generator and train the generator and discriminator altogether. During stage two, we use the Adam optimizer to tune our models, where the learning rate is fixed to 0.00001 for both the generator and discriminator.

Data Augmentation. Images are augmented during the training stage with horizontal flip, color adjustment, geometry transformation, and random crop, then resized to a predefined resolution. We additionally introduced DTA for more generalized scenarios.

Network Inference. We apply a gaussian smooth operation to each output heatmap during the inference before calculating the maximum value index. For the segmentation result, we use a threshold of 0.5 to obtain the binary segmentation mask. We additionally report inference speed for PAPK-Net; it takes 19 ms/23 ms to process an image of 256×256 size with VGG-16 [41]/Resnet-50 [14] backbone.

4.2   Datasets

We conduct experiments on two datasets, which are the PAPK dataset and the DNS Panoramic Images dataset [40].

PAPK Dataset. To assess the performance of PAPK-Net on digital photography, we collect 11200 images in total with manually labeled masks as well as tooth centers and name it "PAPK" dataset, where each image contains an open mouth with several teeth exposed, ranging from 6 to 31 with 16.76 teeth per image on average. The width and height range from 500 to 6528 pixels and 500 to 8184 pixels, respectively. We randomly split dataset into three parts, with 9002 training images, 1119 validation images, and 1079 testing images. Teeth are numbered following predefined order as in Fig. 1[2]. Please refer to supplementary material for a detailed discussion of PAPK dataset.

Since the oral dataset is hard to collect and the images taken by distinct machines have specific domain gaps, a model must be able to learn with limited data. To demonstrate the capability of the PAPK-net learning robust features even with insufficient data, we randomly sampled 750 images from the PAPK training set (around **8%** of data) to form a tiny training set while keeping the same evaluation set. We name this dataset PAPK-tiny. An ablation study will be performed on PAPK-tiny to show the robust performance of PAPK-net in insufficient data scenarios.

DNS Panoramic Images dataset. This dataset modifies the UFBA-UESC Dental Images Deep data set [16] which contains 1500 panoramic dental X-ray images by adding more instance annotations and including numbering information. Finally, the dataset contains 543 panoramic images. We split the whole dataset into the training/validation/test set according to the ratio of 8:1:1. It requires special attention that the small instances account for only 0.5% of all annotations, which results in insufficient entries for small objects and very low AP_{small} in the quantitative results.

4.3   Evaluation Metric

Three evaluation metrics will be used in our experiments: 1. Average normed distance (AND) between predicted tooth centers and ground truth centers, 2.Accuracy for tooth numbering (Acc_{id}), 3. Mask average precision (Mask AP) for tooth segmentation. To make it clear, we demonstrate how to calculate these metrics below with equations:

$$AND = \frac{\sum_{j=1}^{N} \frac{\sum_{i=1}^{K} Dis(pred_i, GT_i)}{K}}{N} \qquad (9)$$

$$Acc_{id} = \frac{\sum_{j=1}^{N} \frac{\sum_{i=1}^{K} f(Dis(pred_i, GT_i))}{K}}{N} \qquad (10)$$

---

[2] https://en.wikipedia.org/wiki/Universal_Numbering_System#/media/File:
Universal_Numbering_System.svg.

Table 1. The quantitative result on DNS Panoramic Images dataset. In the experiment, we select Mask Average precision (AP) and average normed distance (AND), and accuracy (Acc_{id}) as the primary metrics to measure the overall performance. Low AP_{small} is due to insufficient small instances present in the dataset. Texts in red show the estimated metrics.

Method	Backbone	resolution	AP	AP_{50}	AP_{75}	AP_{small}	AP_{mid}	AP_{large}	AND	Acc_{id}
MRCNN-FCN [33]	ResNet-50	256 × 256	32.2	76.1	12.9	0.0	28.9	41.2	0.030	73.1
MRCNN-FCN [33]	ResNet-50	800 × 600	50.3	81.9	**60.7**	0.0	**49.2**	52.8	0.016	91.5
MRCNN-PRend [33]	ResNet-50	256 × 256	31.0	76.4	11.4	0.0	28.6	39.6	0.025	80.9
MRCNN-PRend [33]	ResNet-50	800 × 600	49.1	78.0	59.8	0.0	47.2	52.3	0.016	91.4
Prados *et al.* [34]	ResNet-101	256 × 256	34.1	82.7	13.6	0.0	30.7	42.8	0.027	77.0
PAPK-Net	VGG-16	256 × 256	36.5	86.5	18.4	0.0	27.3	44.8	0.017	89.6
PAPK-Net	ResNet-50	256 × 256	44.7	94.0	31.3	0.0	37.0	53.8	0.011	98.1
PAPK-Net	ResNet-50	800 × 600	**51.2**	**94.7**	51.6	0.0	44.7	**56.5**	**0.010**	**98.5**

Table 2. The quantitative result on PAPK dataset. In the experiment, we select Mask Average precision (AP) and average normed distance (AND), and accuracy (Acc_{id}) as the primary metrics to measure the overall performance. Texts in red show the estimated metric. (Refers to Column AND and ACC from row #1 to #7). Best viewed in color.

Method	Backbone	resolution	AP	AP_{50}	AP_{75}	AP_{small}	AP_{mid}	AP_{large}	AND	Acc_{id}
MRCNN-FCN [33]	ResNet 50	256 × 256	23.3	34.5	31.2	3.6	23.3	29.2	0.037	67.5
MRCNN-FCN [33]	ResNet 50	800 × 600	38.8	49.0	44.6	**28.3**	38.3	44.8	0.025	79.8
MRCNN-PRend [33]	ResNet-50	256 × 256	24.0	35.5	28.1	4.6	23.9	30.0	0.036	68.0
MRCNN-PRend [33]	ResNet-50	800 × 600	32.6	41.8	37.8	23.4	32.1	37.8	0.027	77.4
Prados *et al.* [34]	ResNet-101	256 × 256	30.5	43.7	36.4	5.0	29.4	39.1	0.028	75.2
Yolact [4]	ResNet-50	256 × 256	19.2	33.9	20.6	4.1	18.0	25.4	0.044	63.1
Yolact [4]	ResNet-50	800 × 600	26.2	36.3	30.8	18.2	25.6	31.6	0.030	73.7
PAPK-Net	VGG-16	256 × 256	42.4	80.3	41.4	14.2	39.9	52.0	0.025	77.2
PAPK-Net	ResNet-50	256 × 256	**51.6**	**86.5**	**52.9**	19.5	**49.3**	**59.2**	**0.017**	**89.5**

$$f(x) = \begin{cases} 1 & x < thr \\ 0 & x >= thr \end{cases} \tag{11}$$

Dis is the Euclidean distance function, $pred_i$ and GT_i are the predicted tooth center and ground truth tooth center, respectively. K is the number of visible teeth, N is the total number of images, f is a threshold function to decide if the predicted tooth center is right, and thr is the average ratio between tooth width and image width in both datasets. For Mask AP and Acc_{id}, a higher value indicates better performance; for AND, a lower value indicates better performance.

4.4   Quantitative Result

We report quantitative results in Table 1 and Table 2 on DNS Panoramic Images dataset and PAPK dataset. Here we select mean average precision (MAP), AND, and Acc_{id} as the primary metrics for a balanced comparison. Previous literature

Table 3. Ablation study on PAPK dataset.

methodmetrics	AND	Acc_{id}	$MaskAP$
Only backbone	0.398	37.2	16.6
+FPN	0.389	37.5	21.0
+Tooth numbering	0.025	77.1	44.5
+MSFF	0.021	83.8	44.8
+PSFE	0.019	88.7	46.7
+MaskIoU	0.018	88.7	50.4
+DTA	0.018	88.9	50.8
PAPK-Net (with GAN)	0.017	89.5	51.6

such as [3] [34] implement tooth numbering by multi-class detection or segmentation, which is different from ours. To properly compare, We make estimations for AND and Acc_{id} metrics (**with corresponding scores labeled in red text**) by calculating the center of the predicted bounding box or segmentation mask. Please note that this is an approximation for benchmarking purposes only. We additionally provide visualization results on both datasets (see Fig. 2 and Fig. 6) for reference purposes.

Typical multi-class instance segmentation models [33] as well as decoupled multi-stage models [34] are selected to compare. From Table 2, PAPK-Net with Resnet-50 backbone ranks first amongst all segmentation benchmarks (typical double-stage method MRCNN-FCN and single-stage method Yolact) with the mask average precision of 51.6, which beats all other models by a large margin. In the meantime, PAPK-Net also ranks first in tooth numbering tasks, with the best score of 89.5 in terms of Acc_{id}. In Table 1, we observe a similar trend.

Yet PAPK-net is not perfect. We observe the higher score for metric AP_{75} and AP_{mid} reported from MRCNN-FCN and MRCNN-PRend in DNS panoramic dataset as compared with the proposed. The reason is due to 1) The modality of the data differs, thus the data distribution varies; 2) We specially tune anchors for MRCNN-based methods to make sure that anchors fit the dataset. However, as the PAPK-net is anchor-free, it cannot benefit from the anchor design. As the purpose of the PAPK-net is to resolve tooth segmentation and numbering tasks end-to-end instead of pushing every metric to state-of-art, we would like to leave this challenge to future research.

In addition, we train HRNet [42] and other challenging benchmarks on the DNS Panoramic Images dataset to compare the performance of the tooth numbering task, where PAPK-Net achieves the best performance compared with other baselines. The details are reported in the supplementary material for reference purposes.

4.5 Ablation Study

Here we conduct a comprehensive study on the PAPK dataset to show how each component of PAPK-Net contributes to the overall superior performance. We add each of these modules once at a time, then train the modified network again. Evaluation metrics will be computed on the test data set for reference purposes.

FPN (Baseline). In this experiment, we directly train two 32-class segmentation models to classify each pixel into 32 classes; one of them uses P5 in the backbone of Fig. 4 and another model uses four pyramids to segment objects. From Table 3 we can see that the single-scale model could only get 16.59 AP on the PAPK dataset, while based on our multi-level prediction, we further achieve 21.0 AP.

Tooth Numbering Branch. In this experiment, a tooth center regression branch is added to the FPN-based model. As expected, we observe a large performance gain on both segmentation and numbering tasks. The tooth center regression task decouples the numbering from 32-class instance segmentation, reducing the task's difficulties.

Multi-scale Feature Fusion. To validate the performance of MSFF module, we add it on FPN to get fused results to benchmark the performance. As Table 3 shows, model without MSFF gets 0.025 AND and 77.1% Acc_{id} on the dataset. On the other hand, with the help of MSFF, PAPK-net gets 0.021 AND and 83.8% Acc_{id}, which is nearly 7 points boost in Acc_{id} and 0.004 AND drop. Thanks to the soft attention, MSFF is able to fuse the results from different scales by importance and thus leads to a satisfying performance gain.

Position-Sensitive Feature Extraction. In this experiment, we add position-sensitive feature extraction(PSFE) module to the baseline. As Table 3 shows, without PSFE PAPK-net gets 0.021 AND and 83.8% Acc_{id}. Instead, when the PSFE module is introduced, we get 0.019 AND and 88.7% Acc_{id}, which suggests the effectiveness of PSFE on both the tooth segmentation and numbering task.

Mask IoU Prediction Branch. In this experiment, we evaluate the mask IoU branch. As Table 3 shows, Mask AP increases by 3.7% when the MaskIoU branch is added, yet the tooth numbering task benefits little from the Mask IoU branch.

Deficient Tooth Augmentation. In this experiment, we introduce deficient tooth augmentation to help resolve extreme cases in the dental diagnostic process. We observed a marginal improvement (0.4) in terms of AP. Please check Fig. 5 for the visualization result of DTA module.

Prior Knowledge Guided Refinement. In this experiment, the discriminator is introduced in addition to the generator for adversarial learning purposes. Table 3 shows the effectiveness of the prior knowledge where PAPK-net achieves performance gain in all three metrics.

PAPK in Insufficient Data Scenario. One interesting question is, whether PAPK-net can remain top performance with only a tiny proportion of training

Table 4. PAPK in insufficient data scenario. Experiments are conducted on PAPK-tiny (8% of training set but the same validation set as PAPK). Texts in red show the estimated metric.

metrics	AND	Acc_{id}	$MaskAP$
MRCNN-FCN [33]	0.047	60.1	15.5
PAPK-Net	0.034	73.1	21.5
PAPK-Net (with GAN)	0.032	75.8	23.9

data, which is useful for the case where it is not possible to gather a large dataset as PAPK.

Table 4 answers this question. From the table, PAPK-net is able to outperform MRCNN by a large margin. In the meantime, adding GAN to PAPK can gain additional two percents boost of AP. The performance gain mainly comes from prior knowledge, which is implemented in an adversarial way and motivates the generator to learn better about the geometry of the tooth as well as the oral structure in return. By working together, generators and discriminators can reach higher accuracy.

5   Limitations

While the proposed PAPK-Net achieves state-of-art performance on two benchmark datasets, there still remains a plethora of avenues for future work.

In the post-analysis of DNS dataset, we observe some failure cases and visualize them below. From the observation, the PAPK-Net is not able to recognize and segment the corner tooth occasionally (check the figure to the right in the first row and the figure to the left in the second row). The model may be confused between adjacent teeth, resulting in incorrect pixel assignments. So the performance gap remains and it is still possible to further improve the performance of PAPK-Net.

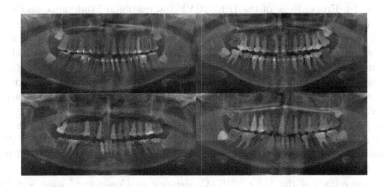

Fig. 6. Visualization for some failure cases on DNS dataset

Another limitation comes from the dataset itself. The extreme cases are limited in both benchmark datasets and we have no oral diseases related images. So PAPK-Net is not able to maintain the same level of precision for those data. However, as we introduce DTA, the performance for extreme cases could be better.

Based on those limitations, we provide some future research directions. 1). Research and develop a more robust and precise model for tooth segmentation and numbering task. 2). Extend the research scope and include more clinical cases for more generalized and powerful oral analysis-related algorithm design.

6 Conclusion

We propose an end-to-end deep learning model called PAPK-Net to accomplish tooth segmentation and numbering tasks on real-world datasets. PAPK-Net incorporates prior knowledge into the learning process to generate more realistic tooth segmentation and numbering results while alleviating the demand for training data. Position-aware convolution is introduced to attach spatial information to learnable features to better distinguish different teeth. These two techniques are integrated into PAPK-Net to form a concise model. Extensive ablation studies are conducted to analyze the contribution of each component in PAPK-Net. As we are able to decouple tooth numbering from segmentation, PAPK-Net provides a promising direction for future research in oral-based applications.

References

1. Dentistry-designation system for teeth and areas of the oral cavity (first revision). J. Pierre Fauchard Acad. **8**(2), 71–3 (1994)
2. Bernstein, R.: Tooth numbering systems. N. Y. J. Dent. **55**(4), 159 (1985)
3. Bilgir, E., et al.: An artificial intelligence approach to automatic tooth detection and numbering in panoramic radiographs. BMC Med. Imaging **21**(1), 124 (2021)
4. Bolya, D., Zhou, C., Xiao, F., Lee, Y.J.: YOLACT: real-time instance segmentation. In: Proceedings of the IEEE/CVF International Conference on Computer Vision, pp. 9157–9166 (2019)
5. Chu, P., et al.: Using octuplet Siamese network for osteoporosis analysis on dental panoramic radiographs. In: 2018 40th Annual International Conference of the IEEE Engineering in Medicine and Biology Society (EMBC), pp. 2579–2582. IEEE (2018)
6. Chung, M., et al.: Individual tooth detection and identification from dental panoramic X-ray images via point-wise localization and distance regularization. Artif. Intell. Med. **111**, 101996 (2021)
7. Cui, Z., Li, C., Wang, W.: ToothNet: automatic tooth instance segmentation and identification from cone beam CT images. In: Proceedings of the IEEE/CVF Conference on Computer Vision and Pattern Recognition, pp. 6368–6377 (2019)
8. Fan, L., et al.: Embracing single stride 3d object detector with sparse transformer. In: Proceedings of the IEEE/CVF Conference on Computer Vision and Pattern Recognition, pp. 8458–8468 (2022)

9. Ghafoorian, M., Nugteren, C., Baka, N., Booij, O., Hofmann, M.: EL-GAN: embedding loss driven generative adversarial networks for lane detection. In: proceedings of the European Conference on Computer Vision (ECCV) Workshops (2018)

10. Girshick, R.: Fast R-CNN. In: Proceedings of the IEEE International Conference on Computer Vision, pp. 1440–1448 (2015)

11. Girshick, R., Donahue, J., Darrell, T., Malik, J.: Rich feature hierarchies for accurate object detection and semantic segmentation. In: Proceedings of the IEEE Conference on Computer Vision and Pattern Recognition, pp. 580–587 (2014)

12. Goodfellow, I., et al.: Generative adversarial nets. Adv. Neural Inf. Process. Syst. **27** (2014)

13. He, K., Gkioxari, G., Dollár, P., Girshick, R.: Mask R-CNN. In: Proceedings of the IEEE International Conference on Computer Vision, pp. 2961–2969 (2017)

14. He, K., Zhang, X., Ren, S., Sun, J.: Deep residual learning for image recognition. In: Proceedings of the IEEE Conference on Computer Vision and Pattern Recognition, pp. 770–778 (2016)

15. Huang, Z., Huang, L., Gong, Y., Huang, C., Wang, X.: Mask scoring R-CNN. In: Proceedings of the IEEE/CVF Conference on Computer Vision and Pattern Recognition, pp. 6409–6418 (2019)

16. Jader, G., Fontineli, J., Ruiz, M., Abdalla, K., Pithon, M., Oliveira, L.: Deep instance segmentation of teeth in panoramic X-ray images. In: 2018 31st SIBGRAPI Conference on Graphics, Patterns and Images (SIBGRAPI), pp. 400–407. IEEE (2018)

17. Jiang, C., Xu, H., Liang, X., Lin, L.: Hybrid knowledge routed modules for large-scale object detection. arXiv preprint arXiv:1810.12681 (2018)

18. Karimian, N., Salehi, H.S., Mahdian, M., Alnajjar, H., Tadinada, A.: Deep learning classifier with optical coherence tomography images for early dental caries detection. In: Lasers in Dentistry XXIV, vol. 10473, p. 1047304. International Society for Optics and Photonics (2018)

19. Kim, C., Kim, D., Jeong, H., Yoon, S.J., Youm, S.: Automatic tooth detection and numbering using a combination of a CNN and heuristic algorithm. Appl. Sci. **10**(16), 5624 (2020)

20. Kingma, D.P., Ba, J.: Adam: a method for stochastic optimization. arXiv preprint arXiv:1412.6980 (2014)

21. Koch, T.L., Perslev, M., Igel, C., Brandt, S.S.: Accurate segmentation of dental panoramic radiographs with U-nets. In: 2019 IEEE 16th International Symposium on Biomedical Imaging (ISBI 2019), pp. 15–19. IEEE (2019)

22. Law, H., Deng, J.: CornerNet: detecting objects as paired keypoints. In: Proceedings of the European conference on computer vision (ECCV), pp. 734–750 (2018)

23. Lee, J.H., Kim, D.H., Jeong, S.N., Choi, S.H.: Detection and diagnosis of dental caries using a deep learning-based convolutional neural network algorithm. J. Dent. **77**, 106–111 (2018)

24. Lee, J.S., Adhikari, S., Liu, L., Jeong, H.G., Kim, H., Yoon, S.J.: Osteoporosis detection in panoramic radiographs using a deep convolutional neural network-based computer-assisted diagnosis system: a preliminary study. Dentomaxillofacial Radiol. **48**(1), 20170344 (2019)

25. Li, P., Zhao, H., Liu, P., Cao, F.: RTM3D: real-time monocular 3D detection from object keypoints for autonomous driving. arXiv e-prints arXiv:2001.03343 (2020)

26. Liang, Y., Han, W., Qiu, L., Wu, C., Shao, Y., Wang, K., He, L.: Exploring forensic dental identification with deep learning. Adv. Neural Inf. Process. Syst. **34** (2021)

27. Lin, T.Y., Dollár, P., Girshick, R., He, K., Hariharan, B., Belongie, S.: Feature pyramid networks for object detection. In: Proceedings of the IEEE Conference on Computer Vision and Pattern Recognition, pp. 2117–2125 (2017)
28. Lin, T.Y., Goyal, P., Girshick, R., He, K., Dollár, P.: Focal loss for dense object detection. In: Proceedings of the IEEE International Conference on Computer Vision, pp. 2980–2988 (2017)
29. Liu, R., Lehman, J., Molino, P., Such, F.P., Frank, E., Sergeev, A., Yosinski, J.: An intriguing failing of convolutional neural networks and the coordconv solution. arXiv preprint arXiv:1807.03247 (2018)
30. Long, J., Shelhamer, E., Darrell, T.: Fully Convolutional networks for semantic segmentation. arXiv e-prints arXiv:1411.4038 (2014)
31. Long, J., Shelhamer, E., Darrell, T.: Fully convolutional networks for semantic segmentation. In: Proceedings of the IEEE Conference on Computer Vision and Pattern Recognition, pp. 3431–3440 (2015)
32. Luc, P., Couprie, C., Chintala, S., Verbeek, J.: Semantic segmentation using adversarial networks. arXiv preprint arXiv:1611.08408 (2016)
33. Pinheiro, L., Silva, B., Sobrinho, B., Lima, F., Cury, P., Oliveira, L.: Numbering permanent and deciduous teeth via deep instance segmentation in panoramic x-rays. In: Rittner, L., M.D., E.R.C., Lepore, N., Brieva, J., Linguraru, M.G. (eds.) 17th International Symposium on Medical Information Processing and Analysis, vol. 12088, pp. 95–104. International Society for Optics and Photonics, SPIE (2021). https://doi.org/10.1117/12.2606211
34. Prados-Privado, M., García Villalón, J., Blázquez Torres, A., Martínez-Martínez, C.H., Ivorra, C.: A convolutional neural network for automatic tooth numbering in panoramic images. Biomed. Res. Int. **2021**, 3625386 (2021)
35. Prados-Privado, M., Villalón, J.G., Martínez-Martínez, C.H., Ivorra, C.: Dental images recognition technology and applications: a literature review. Appl. Sci. **10**(8), 2856 (2020)
36. Redmon, J., Divvala, S., Girshick, R., Farhadi, A.: You only look once: unified, real-time object detection. In: Proceedings of the IEEE Conference on Computer Vision and Pattern Recognition, pp. 779–788 (2016)
37. Redmon, J., Farhadi, A.: YOLO9000: better, faster, stronger. In: Proceedings of the IEEE Conference on Computer Vision and Pattern Recognition, pp. 7263–7271 (2017)
38. Redmon, J., Farhadi, A.: YOLOv3: an incremental improvement. arXiv preprint arXiv:1804.02767 (2018)
39. Ren, S., He, K., Girshick, R., Sun, J.: Faster R-CNN: towards real-time object detection with region proposal networks. Adv. Neural. Inf. Process. Syst. **28**, 91–99 (2015)
40. Silva, B., Pinheiro, L., Oliveira, L., Pithon, M.: A study on tooth segmentation and numbering using end-to-end deep neural networks. In: 2020 33rd SIBGRAPI Conference on Graphics, Patterns and Images (SIBGRAPI), pp. 164–171. IEEE (2020)
41. Simonyan, K., Zisserman, A.: Very deep convolutional networks for large-scale image recognition. arXiv preprint arXiv:1409.1556 (2014)
42. Sun, K., Xiao, B., Liu, D., Wang, J.: Deep high-resolution representation learning for human pose estimation. In: Proceedings of the IEEE/CVF Conference on Computer Vision and Pattern Recognition, pp. 5693–5703 (2019)
43. Sun, Y., Wang, X., Tang, X.: Deep convolutional network cascade for facial point detection. In: Proceedings of the IEEE Conference on Computer Vision and Pattern Recognition, pp. 3476–3483 (2013)

44. Tian, Z., Shen, C., Chen, H., He, T.: FCOS: fully convolutional one-stage object detection. In: Proceedings of the IEEE/CVF International Conference on Computer Vision, pp. 9627–9636 (2019)
45. Tuzoff, D.V., et al.: Tooth detection and numbering in panoramic radiographs using convolutional neural networks. Dentomaxillofacial Radiol. **48**(4), 20180051 (2019)
46. Wang, Xinlong, Kong, Tao, Shen, Chunhua, Jiang, Yuning, Li, Lei: SOLO: segmenting objects by locations. In: Vedaldi, Andrea, Bischof, Horst, Brox, Thomas, Frahm, Jan-Michael. (eds.) ECCV 2020. LNCS, vol. 12363, pp. 649–665. Springer, Cham (2020). https://doi.org/10.1007/978-3-030-58523-5_38
47. Wei, S.E., Ramakrishna, V., Kanade, T., Sheikh, Y.: Convolutional pose machines. In: Proceedings of the IEEE Conference on Computer Vision and Pattern Recognition, pp. 4724–4732 (2016)
48. Xiao, X., Ji, C., Mudiyanselage, T.B., Pan, Y.: PK-GCN: prior knowledge assisted image classification using graph convolution networks. arXiv preprint arXiv:2009.11892 (2020)
49. Xie, E., Sun, P., Song, X., Wang, W., Liu, X., Liang, D., Shen, C., Luo, P.: Polar-Mask: single shot instance segmentation with polar representation. In: Proceedings of the IEEE/CVF Conference on Computer Vision and Pattern Recognition, pp. 12193–12202 (2020)
50. Xu, R., Tafazzoli, F., Zhang, L., Rehfeld, T., Krehl, G., Seal, A.: Holistic grid fusion based stop line estimation. In: 2020 25th International Conference on Pattern Recognition (ICPR), pp. 8400–8407. IEEE (2021)
51. Xu, R., et al.: Pik-Fix: restoring and colorizing old photo. arXiv preprint arXiv:2205.01902 (2022)
52. Xu, R., Xiang, H., Xia, X., Han, X., Li, J., Ma, J.: OPV2V: an open benchmark dataset and fusion pipeline for perception with vehicle-to-vehicle communication. In: 2022 International Conference on Robotics and Automation (ICRA), pp. 2583–2589. IEEE (2022)
53. Zhang, L., et al.: Hierarchical road topology learning for urban map-less driving. arXiv preprint arXiv:2104.00084 (2021)

Research on Short Video Health Communication in Medical and Health Institutions Under the Background of "Healthy 2030"

Chao Liu[1], Zi-Qiong Shi[1], Jing-Wen Zhuo[1], Hao Chen[2], and Wen-Ko Chiou[3](✉)

[1] School of Journalism and Communication, Hua Qiao University, Xiamen 361021, China
[2] School of Film Television and Communication, Xiamen University of Technology, Xiamen, China
[3] Department of Industrial Design, Chang Gung University, Taoyuan City, Taiwan
wkchiu@mail.cgu.edu.tw

Abstract. Health communication is an important means to build a healthy China, realize the "Healthy Fujian 2030 Action plan", "Healthy Quanzhou 2030 action plan", and improve the national health literacy. As an important medium of health communication in the new media era, short video plays an important role in mass communication. Based on the current situation of short video health communication in medical and health institutions, combined with the media interaction behavior between short videos produced by medical and health institutions and audiences, this study analyzes the existing problems of short video health communication in medical and health institutions at the level of information acquisition and reception, and explores the causes of existing problems in short video health communication in medical and health institutions. To find solutions to the dilemma under the mode of knowledge, belief and action, and explore ways to improve the effectiveness of health communication in medical and health institutions.

Keywords: Health ccommunication · Short video · Medical institutions · Communication path

1 Introduction

China proposed the "Health China Action" in the report of the 19th National Congress, and in order to implement this strategic deployment, the Fujian Provincial Government proposed the "Health Fujian 2030 Action Plan" and the Quanzhou Municipal Government proposed the "Health Quanzhou 2030 Action Plan". In the context of this series of policies, the public's concern for health has gradually increased, and new requirements for health communication have been put forward. The "Healthy China Action" stresses the need to accelerate the transformation from a focus on "treatment of diseases" to a focus on "people's health", and improve people's health literacy [1]. The improvement of public health literacy is inseparable from the effective popularization of health knowledge. Medical and health institutions are important carriers to disseminate health knowledge. With the change of the audience's habit of receiving information,

P.-L. P. Rau (Ed.): HCII 2023, LNCS 14024, pp. 476–485, 2023.
https://doi.org/10.1007/978-3-031-35946-0_38

short video health communication has grown into a blowout type, and it has become an inevitable trend to shift from the traditional single form to multi-mode content production and communication [2]. By June 2022, China's online medical users had reached 300 million, an increase of 1.96 million from December 2021, accounting for 28.5% of the total netizens. The number of short video users in China reached 995 million, an increase of 20.7 million compared with December 2021, which accounted for 94.6% of the total netizens [3]. Short video industry has shown a blowout trend of development, short video has become one of the most important ways to spread and popularize health knowledge. Medical and health institutions try to produce original short video works and build their own short video platforms, but it is more common to enter popular Internet short video platforms such as TikTok [4, 5].

In the era of intelligent media, short video, as a new form of communication, has its own communication characteristics and rules. For medical and health institutions, how to give full play to the value of short video, make accurate and popular visual narration of authoritative health knowledge and realize effective communication, so as to improve public health literacy and contribute to "Healthy Fujian 2030 Action plan" and "Healthy Quanzhou 2030 Action plan" is an issue worthy of attention and thinking. Therefore, it is necessary to further explore the problems, causes and solutions in the process of health communication of short video in medical and health institutions.

2 Difficulties Faced by Short Video Health Communication in Medical and Health Institutions

Strengthening the health communication efficiency of medical and health institutions is an important way to promote the "Healthy Fujian 2030 Action Plan" and "Healthy Quanzhou 2030 Action Plan", and also an important measure to improve the health communication structure of medical and health institutions. Therefore, it is necessary to understand the development status and existing problems from practice.

2.1 The Content of Communication is Not New and Lacks Pertinence and Innovation

Since the advent of social media in the late 1990s, it has permeated every aspect of our personal and professional lives. The popularity and use of social media has transformed public health services. More and more healthcare organizations have realized the importance of active participation in social media. Social media has become immersed in every aspect of our lives. The healthcare and health institutions sector is no exception, and public health departments are now using social media to provide healthcare services and health literacy. Provincial health commissions in China have begun to use short video sharing platforms, such as TikTok and WeChat public accounts, to interact with local residents and exchange health-related information [6, 7]. According to the current situation of short video communication, it is not difficult to find that the more targeted and innovative the information content, the more it can meet the needs of certain groups of people or individuals for information, and the easier it is to be obtained and accepted, the better the effect of information communication. Short video platforms will allocate a basic traffic pool to each user from the algorithmic mechanism of content distribution. In order for medical and health institutions to push their released videos, original videos are the first prerequisite. If the contents are identified by the AI as similar, they will be not be recommended. Video content in addition to the original also need to have a certain creativity, if the user stay for a long time and good feedback, like, comment, forward and other operations, the video will be recommended twice, and even pushed to a higher traffic pool, into the browsing list of more users. On the contrary, if the user stays for a short time, gives poor feedback or is reported in the early stage of the video push, the video will be less recommended or even stop recommended [6]. According to the progress report of China's disease prevention and control work of National Health and Family Planning Commission, in recent years, the number of deaths caused by chronic diseases such as cerebrovascular disease and malignant tumors has accounted for 86.6% of the total deaths. As chronic diseases are closely related to life style, the media is filled with a lot of information about healthy life style. However, in the process of actual transmission in medical and health institutions, the audience does not accept or even avoid [8]. In real life, the elders often send health information to the younger generation, remind and urge them to change unhealthy living habits, but the younger generation turns a blind eye and even has to shield the same health content everywhere. When the audience not only does not take action after receiving the message, but also avoids the message from the beginning. When the content disseminated by the medical and health institutions lacks pertinence and effectiveness, the information transmitted by the health information with high repetition rate and sameness is easy to droplets [9].

Health information droplets can be understood as, for public space information dissemination, more and more like injecting a drop of water in the sea, which people may turn a blind eye to. Without the ability to accurately target people, the health information, knowledge and advocacy spread by these organizations can easily bubble into the air and dissipate instantly [10]. For example, compared with 10 years ago, the public's awareness of "the harm of second-hand smoke" has been significantly improved, but smokers' quitting behavior is not obvious. In 2016, there were still 316 million smokers in China; Most people know that reasonable diet and exercise are good for health, but the problem of obesity in our country remains high, with one third of the population overweight. Thus, if there is no targeted and innovative communication, the communication effect is worrisome [11].

In healthcare, the adoption of social media is often too stuffy and not fresh enough. Although social media has been widely adopted by patient-care providers, many health communication institutions focus on patient empowerment, health promotion, doctor-patient relationship building, and public health testing. Medical and health institutions do not pay attention to the special properties of short video platforms of new media. Since medical and health institutions focus on the quality of medical services provided to citizens, they are very cautious about the operation of social media, making its communication effect lag behind that of other public sectors [12].

2.2 The Form of Communication is Not Flexible, and the Method of Communication is Single and Boring

Health communication in short video platforms can be divided into science, documentary, entertainment and public opinion. Influenced by traditional publicity modes and concepts, the short videos released by official accounts of many medical and health institutions are regular, mostly mechanized science explanation products. The form of video communication is not flexible and the content is not interesting. As a result, it is difficult for the videos released by health and medical accounts to enter the short video traffic pool at a higher level and get high attention [13].

Fear appeal is often a technique commonly used by the media. Medical and health institutions try to attract the audience's attention through words with a sense of urgency such as "death" and "cancer", but there is a phenomenon that fear appeal fails. The reasons are as follows: first, it only provides threats but does not contain specific and effective information to help audiences change their unhealthy behaviors. For example, the media repeatedly emphasize the harm of smoking, but fail to inform the concrete and feasible solutions, resulting in the failure to promote the change of the audience's behavior; Secondly, the positioning of fear appeal is inaccurate. It is well known that "smoking is harmful to health", but blindly listing all possible consequences will not only fail to attract the attention of the audience, but also make the audience ignore this fear appeal as a cliche [14].

Nowadays, users prefer the presentation of short videos, and how to integrate difficult medical terms into short videos has become a creative challenge for healthcare institutions. Promoting the image of health professionals and knowledge of common diseases is the current theme of healthcare institutions' publicity, which does effectively bring the public closer to the daily life of doctors. But the drawbacks are also quickly presented, because the main characters of the videos of major health care institutions are professional doctors and nurses, Who do not have a strong performance nature, they are not strong enough to attract the public in the short video platform. Therefore, if you want to have vivid, image and interesting video effect presentation, you need to recruit professional actors to create short videos for health care institutions. However, when the public finds out that it is not professional health care professionals but actors who explain health knowledge, they will question the content of their videos [15].

2.3 The Communication Mechanism is Not Sound, and False Information and Infringing Information Emerge One After Another

The internal management of the major short video communication websites is not in place, and false information is common. In TikTok, Weibo and other major short video websites, it is common to see some short health communication videos with false information in the title. In addition, health knowledge publicity has special requirements, the content must ensure the authority and authenticity, and the comprehensive quality of the propagandists is very high. At present, a small number of "New media" still continue to spread incorrect and inappropriate information about medical and health care and doctor-patient relationship intentionally or unintentionally for various reasons. Just take the short video rumors as an example: In November 2021, Social Survey Center of

China Youth Daily conducted a questionnaire survey on short video rumors among 2006 respondents on the online platform. The survey results showed that 87.7% of respondents had encountered short video rumors online, among which 43.4% believed that there were more short video rumors in the field of life and health. Short video production teams in medical and health institutions not only need to deal with copywriting, video shooting and post editing, but also need to have certain basic medical knowledge. Such interdisciplinary talents are extremely lacking in major medical and health institutions, which leads to an endless stream of false information infringement information in the existing short video of health communication [16].

For example, during the COVID-19 pandemic, a great deal of health information and opinions about the COVID-19 pandemic have been pouring out, with various kinds, but it is difficult to distinguish the truth from the fake. Young people like to get information through the Internet, WeChat, TikTok and other social media, while older people get information through TV and newspapers. We have to admit that during the COVID-19 pandemic, the demand for authentic and effective information has been increasing. In the face of sudden outbreaks, health communication is a key means and an important channel to save lives and control the epidemic. This is the time for our major health institutions to step up and achieve accurate and sound health communication with the public, so as to promote social stability and reduce public panic during the pandemic. This is because medical and health institutions are more authoritative than media practitioners on online platforms. However, due to the imperfect communication mechanism of medical and health institutions, false information is also emerging in an endless stream, which strikes the public's trust and dependence on the health communication of short video of medical and health institutions [10].

3   Short Video Health Communication in Medical and Health Institutions is Faced with Multiple Difficulties

In the process of short video health communication in medical and health institutions, there are some problems, such as the content of communication is not novel, the form of communication is not flexible, and the communication mechanism is not sound. The reasons are mainly analyzed in the following three aspects.

3.1   Medical and Health Institutions Are Traditional and Old-Fashioned, and Their Communication Interaction is Weak

The short video operation groups of major medical and health institutions are influenced by traditional propaganda modes and concepts, and their communication channels and methods are too traditional and old-fashioned. It should be known that all major short video platforms attach great importance to user experience and user feedback, but the short video health communication of medical and health institutions is mostly one-way knowledge output, lacking communication and interaction with the audience. As a result, It is also impossible to timely detect the audience's receiving effect and absorption degree of health information, so it is difficult to accurately locate the needs of users and timely adjust the communication strategy. In this way, the information released is easy to fall into the sea and become inefficient communication. As mentioned above in the analysis of the predicament of health communication in short videos of medical and health institutions, the information communication facing public space is like injecting a drop of water into the sea, which may be ignored by people, while the "sea" will not increase or decrease. This profoundly changes the traditional transmission and receiving relationship: in the past era, the listener had to try to identify the speaker's message, but now the speaker has to find the listener in the ocean of information, and has to call for the attention of the other party. Instead of cutting out a "health tip" or a "health checklist" from a newspaper, public health authorities, NGO, commercial medical institutions and the media began to take the initiative to investigate and screen the target population. Even if the target population is precisely targeted, the health information, knowledge and advocacy spread by these medical and health institutions can easily become droplets, fill the air and dissipate instantly [17].

3.2 Short Video Platform has Strong Entertainment and Low Exposure Rate of Healthy Content

As mentioned in the previous analysis of the problem, today's short video platforms allocate a base traffic pool to each user based on the algorithmic mechanism of content distribution. In order to make the released video be pushed, the original video is the first premise. If the machine recognizes the same content, it will be recommended by low traffic, or even only visible by oneself. In addition to originality, entertainment of short video platform is also strong. In addition to originality, video content also needs to have some creativity. If users stay for a long time and give good feedback, like, comment, forward and other operations, the video will be recommended for a second time, and even pushed to a higher traffic pool, and enter more users' browsing list. On the contrary, if the user stays for a short time, gives poor feedback or is reported in the early stage of the video push, the video will be coolly recommended or even stopped [18].

Influenced by traditional propaganda models and concepts, many short videos released by official accounts of hospitals are regular. The traditional stiff output of health knowledge lacks entertainment, and gets less traffic and low exposure rate. A lot of content is left on the surface, without profound popularization education, lack of theoretical support, the form of publicity of knowledge experts is also lack of innovation, only a formality. The video content is not innovative enough, so it is difficult for the videos released by health and medical accounts to enter the traffic pool at a higher level and get high attention [19].

3.3 The Health Information Censorship Mechanism has Flaws and Omissions, Resulting in Many Errors and False Information

In the face of rapidly changing information groups, the deficiencies and omissions of the health information censorship mechanism have been gradually exposed. New media bring new challenges to health communication. Health information can be rapidly and widely transmitted through new media means, but at the same time, there are problems such as unclear sources of information, information quality cannot be guaranteed, and the form and type of media information, social media indicators, etc., will also have different degrees of impact on the audience [20].

For example, Transmission and Regulation: The Impact of Social Media Videos on Childbirth on Women's attitudes towards Natural Childbirth was set up to test the persuasive effect of information types and social media indicators on women's attitudes towards natural childbirth. Or "When Players Become Patients: The Impact of Media Narrative on Stigma perception of Video Game Disorder", from the perspective of media narrative, explores the impact of media information forms on adolescents' stigma perception of video game disorder, using the experimental method of communication. It holds that different forms of media information can affect the severity, controllability and social distance of the cognition of video game disorder, and further points out that medicalized expression using media narrative as the carrier may deepen the stigma of the disease. A large number of literatures have described the adverse effects of the absence of health information censorship mechanism leading to wrong information, the inflow of false information leading to the wrong perception of the audience, the stigmatization of diseases and so on [21].

4 Strategies to Break the Dilemma of Short Video Health Communication in Medical and Health Institutions

4.1 Instant Interaction to Close the Distance

Short video platforms, represented by TikTok, have social media properties, with their typical advantages of immediacy and two-way interaction. While watching short videos, audiences can realize instant interaction with short video producers and other audiences through such functions as "like", "forward", "comment" and "reply". Such instant interaction not only enhances the interest and entertainment of the viewing process of short videos, but also deepens the audience's understanding and knowledge of the content of short videos.

In order to get out of the dilemma of short video health communication in medical and health institutions, doctor-patient communication and online communication should be emphasized in short video health communication. Some studies use affective exchange theory to predict the need for emotion. Studies have shown that high-intensity interaction, timely care, and doctor-patient emotional empathy can build a good doctor-patient relationship. Therefore, medical and health institutions should avoid emotional deprivation, attach importance to doctor-patient communication and doctor-patient empathy, improve the interaction between medical and health institutions and the public, so as to improve the stickiness between short video health communication of medical and health institutions and users [22].

The content of medical science popularization is characterized by professionalism and abstractness, and ordinary people may have various questions in the process of accepting it. Producers of medical popular science should make full use of the characteristics of short video platforms in the communication process to maintain immediate interaction with the audience, encourage content creators to communicate with the audience more, help the audience better understand the content of short video of medical popular science, and narrow the distance between the communication subject and the audience. At the same time, interactive behaviors such as "like", "forward" and "comment" by the audience should also be encouraged to accelerate the fission and transmission of short videos of medical popular science, so as to promote the medical popular science knowledge to be understood and accepted by more people. In this way, the communication mode of medical science popularization can realize the transformation from one-way education to two-way interaction, and change the public's obscure and rigid understanding of traditional medical science popularization [23].

4.2 Content is King, Medical Media Integration

Dr Wen-Hong Zhang, who is known for his frequent quotes during the epidemic, once said with a smile to reporters, "You can understand every Chinese character I speak, but you won't know what it means." In fact, this sentence also explains the important strategy for the popularization of short medical science videos, that is, the popularization and popularization of the video content telling way and language style. The unique typography, text, pictures and other diversified communication methods in the content will bring good viewing feelings to the readers. The disseminators will explain the complex and difficult professional medical knowledge to the audience in the form of easy to understand. The popular science knowledge is practical and interesting, which will greatly enhance the acceptability of popular science videos.

In the era of information explosion, people are more inclined to choose the "fool" way of information acquisition. Short videos of medical science popularization need to present professional and abstract medical science content to the audience easily in a short time, reducing the audience's thinking link. At the same time, if we can give consideration to the interestingness of the video expression form and realize the cross-border integration of specialization and entertainment, it will be more conducive to improving the acceptance rate of the audience and achieving better communication effect [24].

4.3 Strict Censorship and Establishment of Authority

Health information should be strictly examined to build an authoritative health communication path. In his speech at the Munich Security Conference, Dr. Tedros Adhanom Ghebreyesus, Director-General of the World Health Organization (WHO), stressed that health organizations and health institutions are not only fighting epidemics, but are fighting information epidemics. Therefore, major medical and health institutions should strictly examine the mass information groups to ensure the authenticity and authority of information, so as to build an authoritative health communication path of short video health communication in medical and health institutions. The pseudo health information in the short video platform often induces the elderly to receive wrong health knowledge, resulting in wrong health cognition and even wrong health behavior, which brings unevaluable physical and mental damage to the elderly. In the face of the confusion of health information and health knowledge on short video platforms, it is necessary to strengthen the examination of the content released on the platform, increase the publicity of health science knowledge, and strictly control the source of health information transmission at the level of "knowledge". China Medical We-Media Alliance and other medical and health we-media alliance cooperate with new media platforms such as Tencent Platform to establish a professional communication and cooperation mechanism to combat medical rumors and fake popular science information: identify and verify online rumors with the help of the big data screening technology of new media platform; Then, healthcare professionals should speak out in the first time, and carry out targeted, authoritative and popular interpretation or refuting rumors on the new media platform, which can eliminate the relevant misunderstanding or panic of the public, so as to build a better communication environment [25].

Funding.. This research was supported by Social Science Fund of Fujian Province (No. FJ2022BF070), and Quanzhou Social Science Foundation (No. 2022E11).

References

1. Tan, X., Liu, X., Shao, H.: Healthy China 2030: a vision for health care. Value Health Reg. Issues **12**, 112–114 (2017)
2. Chen, P., Li, F., Harmer, P.: Healthy China 2030: moving from blueprint to action with a new focus on public health. Lancet Public Health **4**, e447 (2019)
3. Ju, B., Sandel, T., Fitzgerald, R.: Understanding Chinese internet and social media: the innovative and creative affordances of technology, language and culture. Se Mettre en Scène en Ligne' [Presenting Oneself Online] (2019)
4. Liu, C., Chiou, W.K., Chen, H., Hsu, S.E.: Effects of animation-guided mindfulness meditation on flight attendants' flow ergonomics. In: Rau, P.L.P. (eds.) Cross-Cultural Design. Applications in Business, Communication, Health, Well-being, and Inclusiveness. HCII 2022. Lecture Notes in Computer Science, vol. 13313, pp. 58–67. Springer, Cham, (2022). https://doi.org/10.1007/978-3-031-06050-2_5
5. Liu, C., Chen, H., Zhou, F., Long, Q., Wu, K., Lo, L.M., et al.: Positive intervention effect of mobile health application based on mindfulness and social support theory on postpartum depression symptoms of puerperae. BMC Women's Health **22**(1), 1–14 (2022)
6. Pedersen, E.A., Loft, L.H., Jacobsen, S.U., Soborg, B., Bigaard, J.: Strategic health communication on social media: insights from a Danish social media campaign to address HPV vaccination hesitancy. Vaccine **38**(31), 4909–4915 (2020)
7. Chen, H., Liu, C., Zhou, F., Chiang, C.H., Chen, Y.L., Wu, K., et al.: The effect of animation-guided mindfulness meditation on the promotion of creativity, flow and affect. Front. Psychol. **13**, 894337 (2022)
8. Davis, M., Lyall, B., Whittaker, A., Lindgren, M., Flowers, P.: A year in the public life of superbugs: news media on antimicrobial resistance and implications for health communications. Soc. Sci. Med. **256**, 113032 (2020)
9. Liu, C., Chen, H., Zhou, F., Chiang, C.H., Chen, Y.L., Wu, K., et al.: Effects of animated pedagogical agent-guided loving-kindness meditation on flight attendants' spirituality, mindfulness, subjective wellbeing, and social presence. Front. Psychol. **13** (2022)
10. Mheidly, N., Fares, J.: Leveraging media and health communication strategies to overcome the COVID-19 infodemic. J. Public Health Policy **41**, 410–420 (2020)
11. Tong, W.Y., Ru, H.K., Jian, Z., Ling, A.F., Lin, S.Y., Wei, W.X., et al.: The association between exposure to second-hand smoke and disease in the Chinese population: a systematic review and meta-analysis. Biomed. Environ. Sci. **36**(1), 24–37
12. Liu, P.L.: COVID-19 information on social media and preventive behaviors: managing the pandemic through personal responsibility. Soc. Sci. Med. **277**, 113928 (2021)

13. Zhang, L., Jung, E.H.: WeChatting for health: an examination of the relationship between motivations and active engagement. Health Commun. **34**, 1–11 (2018)
14. Park, J., Son, J.Y., Suh, K.S.: Fear appeal cues to motivate users' security protection behaviors: an empirical test of heuristic cues to enhance risk communication. Internet Res.: Electron. Netw. Appl. Policy **32**(3), 708–727 (2022)
15. Anderson, R.J., Bloch, S., Armstrong, M., Stone, P.C., Low, J.T.: Communication between healthcare professionals and relatives of patients approaching the end-of-life: a systematic review of qualitative evidence. Palliat. Med. **33**(8), 926–941 (2019)
16. Tzourio, C., Texier, N., Ouazzani, K., Mebarki, A., Montagni, I.: Acceptance of a Covid-19 vaccine is associated with ability to detect fake news and health literacy. Eur. J. Public Health **2021**(5), 1–8 (2021)
17. Hermes, S., Riasanow, T., Clemons, E.K., Böhm, M., Krcmar, H.: The digital transformation of the healthcare industry: exploring the rise of emerging platform ecosystems and their influence on the role of patients. Bus. Res. **13**(3), 1033–1069 (2020). https://doi.org/10.1007/s40685-020-00125-x
18. Choi, Y., Wen, H., Chen, M., Yang, F.: Sustainable determinants influencing habit formation among mobile short-video platform users. Sustainability **13**(6), 3216 (2021)
19. Chen, H., Liu, C., Hsu, S.E., Huang, D.H., Liu, C.Y., Chiou, W.K.: The effects of animation on the guessability of universal healthcare symbols for middle-aged and older adults. Human Factors (2021)
20. Yang, J., Tian, Y.: "Others are more vulnerable to fake news than I Am": third-person effect of COVID-19 fake news on social media users. Comput. Hum. Behav. **125**(1), 106950 (2021)
21. Bratu, S.: The fake news sociology of COVID-19 pandemic fear: dangerously inaccurate beliefs, emotional contagion, and conspiracy ideation. Linguis. Philos. Invest. **19**, 128–134 (2020)
22. Luk, T., Wong, S., Lee, J., Chan, S., Lam, T., Wang, M.: Exploring community smokers' perspectives for developing a chat-based smoking cessation intervention delivered through mobile instant messaging: qualitative study. JMIR mHealth uHealth **7**(1), e11954 (2019)
23. Yoon, C., Jeong, C., Rolland, E.: Understanding individual adoption of mobile instant messaging: a multiple perspectives approach. Inf. Technol. Manage. **16**(2), 139–151 (2014). https://doi.org/10.1007/s10799-014-0202-4
24. Tandoc, E.C., Lim, D., Ling, R.: Diffusion of disinformation: how social media users respond to fake news and why. Journalism **21**(3), 381–398 (2020)
25. Wang, R., He, Y., Xu, J., Zhang, H.: Fake news or bad news? Toward an emotion-driven cognitive dissonance model of misinformation diffusion. Asian J. Commun. (2), 1–26 (2020)

A Flow Study on Virtual Reality Games to Help Autistic Youngsters with Healthy Activities

Ta-Wei Lu[1,2]([⊠]), Mo-Li Yeh[2], and Liang-Chun Lu[2]

[1] National Taiwan University of Arts, New Taipei City 220307, Taiwan R.O.C.
twlu@mail.lhu.edu.tw
[2] Lunghwa University of Technology and Science, Taoyuan City 333326, Taiwan, R.O.C.
1101moli@gmail.com, ryan@mail.lhu.edu.tw

Abstract. This study designed and produced a virtual reality game - "Catch and Throw" for teenagers between 17 and 19 years of age with autism and conducted a flow experiment to collect data from users to define that the levels of difficulty in game design can be the critical influence of their flow status.

The traditional activity in school tends to look past students with special needs who also want to participate in sports like ordinary people. Due to the slow development of most autistic physical movements, they usually grow with low mobility, physical strength, and a lack of rhythm. The behavioral characteristics of autism include social interaction and language communication impairment. Studies have confirmed that exercise can improve the physiological functions of autism, such as mediating neurotransmitters, strengthening the connection of the nervous system, and changing the behavioral characteristics of autism through physiological effects.

After interviewing the youngsters with autism and their caretakers, we found that the lack of feedback in the existing exercise process affects their motivation. After a series of discussions, we agree that virtual reality games could involve physical movement with playability is a good solution for them to do exercise.

To motivate users and for them to engage in the game proactively, we refer to the flow theory. This study applies theory to practice by adjusting the difficulty of the challenges in the game to match up with the user's ability. Using the questionnaire method, we analyze the data and prove that controlling the users' flow levels can maximize their flow experience and engagement with the activity.

In this study, we design and create a VR game for autism and apply the flow method. As a result, we enable users to get longer excise duration, better activity experience, and better health outcomes.

Keywords: Autism · Virtual Reality Game · Flow Experience

1 Research Background

Conventionally, when it comes to special education, people pay more attention to teaching subjects but ignore those special people who also want to participate in sports like ordinary people. Due to the slow development of most autistic body movements, they

P.-L. P. Rau (Ed.): HCII 2023, LNCS 14024, pp. 486–504, 2023.
https://doi.org/10.1007/978-3-031-35946-0_39

usually come with poor essential motor ability, lack of physical strength and sense of rhythm, difficulty in expressing and social interaction, and difficulty acquiring regular and complex movements; autistic people do not like athletics and sports. However, suppose teachers will adjust or simplify the activities' content and use the updated equipment during the teaching process. In that case, it is easy to find that students are willing to participate in athletics and sports activities.

The behavioral characteristics of autism include social interaction and language communication barriers. Studies have confirmed that exercise can improve the physiological functions of autism, such as mediating neurotransmitters and strengthening the nervous system connection. Changing the behavioral characteristics of autism through physiological influences can improve their adaptability. In addition to increasing the amount of exercise, this study will also have the potential to have a particular impact on improving the adaptability of autism.

2   Research Purpose

Through the activities from our previous experiences, we learned that game mechanisms could attract people to sports activities. In virtual reality, through the combination of sports and games, special education students can be assimilated into the virtual environment without worrying about the difficulty of expression and social interaction obstacles caused by ordinary sports.

Unlike ordinary people, autistic people need more specialized counseling methods to achieve the best results. The education methods for ordinary people may not be suitable for them. This study promotes the adaptation of sports through the relationship between flow and virtual reality game design to achieve sports effects. The long-term goal of this study is to help improve the quality of education for special education students and develop their potential.

3   Literature Review

Psychologist Csikszentmihalyi [1] proposed the concept of "Flow" from a psychological point of view, describing the state of people's complete immersion in a particular activity or situation, forgetting self, forgetting time, and forgetting all other irrelevant things, and defined it as a feeling of entirely devoting one's mental energy to a particular activity. There will be a high sense of excitement and fulfillment when flow occurs. One will be highly focused on doing something one likes without any irritability or boredom caused by confusing, repetitive, and complicated tasks. Human beings aim to pursue happiness, which is the basis of flow theory. People find fun and continuous satisfaction in different activities, and these activities will bring them into a state of "Flow." When people feel happy, "Flow experience" comes with it.

The main argument of "Flow Experience" is that if it is in human nature only to seek freedom and relaxation, no one is willing to participate in activities that engage challenges and stand up to tasks. However, even without the offering of money or other external motivation, there are still many people who continue to engage in certain activities because of it. After interviewing many outstanding artists, scientists, and athletes in his research, it was found that they all had "Flow Experiences" that allowed them to concentrate on the process of being willing to accept the challenges, forgetting the existence of time, and getting pleasure and satisfaction from activities, so they never get tired of it [2]. "Flow Experiences" is why individuals continue to engage in certain activities. It is a subjective and temporary experience [1, 3]. From the design perspective of the game content in this project, this knowledge is also transformed into techniques to attract users to continuously interact with the content to increase the "playability" and the "engagement" of the game.

Most games have rules that provide individuals with good leverage on their goals. In the game, individuals explore the game through strategic decisions and various representations of the game content and control the game's resources through the interface to achieve the preset goals in the game [4].

The main point of the game design, in this case, is to adjust the possible actions through such skills, emphasizing the best sense of control. The design of challenges should not be too easy, and as such, it will not bring players a feeling of boredom; at the same time, the overcoming of obstacles and the oppression of competing with time will not be too overwhelming, causing players to have too much anxiety and panic. The process of the game arranges visual, auditory, and interactive richness and feedback while maintaining the balance of skills and challenges and keeping players guided in the "Flow Channel" (see Fig. 1).

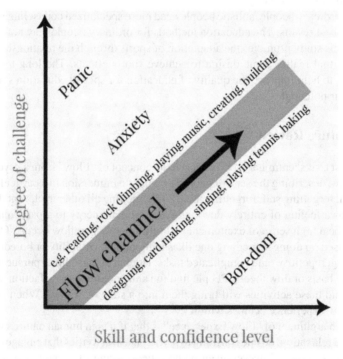

Fig. 1. Flow Channel [5]

According to flow theory, players enter a state of flow when the challenges they face are very close to being difficult. Just like trained athletes, dancers, and famous chess players, when they match a specific challenge with good ability, they can enter a state of flow. If their skills are much more excellent than the challenge provided by a particular activity, they will be bored; if their skills are far below the level of challenge provided, they will be frustrated and very anxious [6, 7].

To allow players to achieve a flow experience so that players do not feel bored because the challenge is too easy or feel frustrated because the challenge is too difficult, too complicated, or acquired skills do not meet the ability of the player, game design has to perfectly meet the delicate balance between player skill and game challenge. When the player enters a state of flow, it is characterized by a loss of self-awareness, a distorted perception of time, and pleasurable feelings. Csikszentmihalyi [1] pointed out: "Games are an excellent embodiment of flow."

4 The Process of Creating the Game for Research

4.1 Expert Interview

Through interviews with experts, we gather elements of making game content and formulate gameplay methods. Experts interviewed for this study include the ROC Foundation for Autistic Children and Adults in Taiwan, Taiwan Healthy Life and Sports Association, the occupational therapist of Happy Mount Sanatorium, adaptive sports coaches of Power-Sunny Adjustment Exercise Studio, New Taipei Municipal Tur Ya Kar Elementary and Middle School Counseling Office, Consultants of Lunghwa University of Science and Technology Counseling and Career Development Center.

Through expert interviews, this study has obtained the following conclusions:

1. Through goal-oriented, structured, progressive, and interrelated training exercises can significantly improve the motor skills of autistic people.
2. By practicing the correspondence between vision, proprioception, and vestibular system, sensory integration can be improved.
3. The lifestyle of autistic people can be changed through the form of gameplay and repeated systematic training methods.
4. Besides improving physical movement ability, it can promote social interaction and improve interpersonal relationships.

The following is a summary of interviews with experts and guidelines for game design:

1. Adaptive sports are an excellent direction to help people with autism to be healthy. The virtual reality game production plan is to stand on the shoulders of giants and continue to move forward.
2. The development of many sports relies on the group's strength, but autistic people have difficulties in social skills, and their frustration tolerance is extremely low.
3. The mirror neuron function of autistic people is low. When watching other people's actions, their brains may not necessarily be activated to imitate them.

4. Insufficient abstract thinking often requires direct experience to understand the environment's needs.
5. Most sports rules are complicated and must be simplified.
6. Reducing the game's difficulty should also give back a considerable sense of accomplishment.
7. Generate attraction through theme specificity and user preferences.
8. People with autism will have tactile discomfort and must first feel safe through demonstrations.
9. Most patients need help with balance, and more attention should be paid to activities or operations.
10. Avoid taboos, such as adverse effects caused by loud sounds and intense light.
11. It is not necessary to increase the amount of exercise as the goal at the beginning; one can start with being able to sweat and boost heart rate to 130.
12. VR adaptive exercise can increase muscle endurance, coordination, and balance.
13. Focus on security.
14. More than 95% of autistic people can easily be attracted by the "games" theme.
15. For sports, it must be the amount of exercise, and there is no need to learn any special skills.
16. When the habit is established, one may accept sports in the future.

4.2   Game Content

This is a virtual reality reaction training game made with unreal engine 4. When players enter the game, they can choose the difficulty level to suit their reaction speed. After the selection, the player clicks the button on the VR handlebar to enter a scene where a lamb will throw pillows at the player from time to time. The player must pick up the pillow and throw it to the lamb within the specified time. The way to pick up the pillow is to use the VR handlebar in the player's hand and click the trigger to pick up the pillow on the ground or throw it. After the time, the score will pop up to count how many pillows the player has thrown and hit the lamb to calculate the player's reaction speed. The higher the score, the better the player's reaction ability. In addition, the game is played in a fixed-point mode to avoid collision damage caused by players moving around (see Fig. 2, Fig. 3).

Fig. 2. Menu Screen   **Fig. 3.** Gameplay Screen

5   Research Method

In this study, through the questionnaire survey method, the subjects are 37 autistic students from freshman to sophomore who belong to moderate to mild patients on the spectrum. The structural equation was used to construct the variable model. The questionnaire data was input through SmartPLS to obtain the path coefficient and factor analysis between the variables.

PLS-SEM is a structural equation model based on variance, which is solved by using the Partial Least Squares method, using the linear combination of observed variables to define the principal component structure, and then using the principle of regression analysis model to test the relationship between the prediction and explanation of principal components.

5.1   Path of PLS-SEM

In the PLS-SEM model, there are only one-way arrow paths and no two-way arrow paths like in CB-SEM model. The path value is called the path coefficient. The path diagram can more intuitively describe the relationship between variables. PLS-SEM model construction consists of Measurement Model and Structural Model. The measurement model describing the relationship between latent variables and indicators is called the Outer Model. The research model structure is set as follows (see Fig. 4):

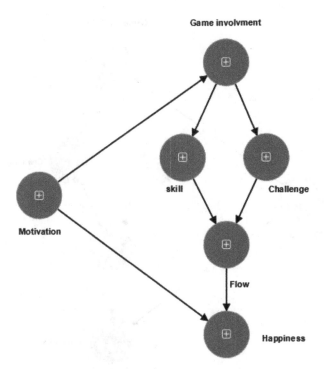

Fig. 4. Model Structure

5.2 The Hypotheses

Based on the above model, the hypotheses of this research are proposed and tested.

H1: Game motivation affects game involvement.

H2: Game motivation affects happiness.

H3: The degree of game involvement affects game skills.

H4: Game involvement affects the game challenge.

H5: Skills affect the flow.

H6: Challenges affect the flow.

H7: Flow affects happiness.

According to the above hypotheses, the operational definition questionnaire for each facet is shown in Appendix A.

6 Data Analysis Process and Results

6.1 PLS-SEM Path Analysis

The path coefficient shows the causal relationship among the latent variables in the structural model, which belongs to the direct effect and can also be interpreted as the causal relationship in behavior, sometimes called influence (see Fig. 5).

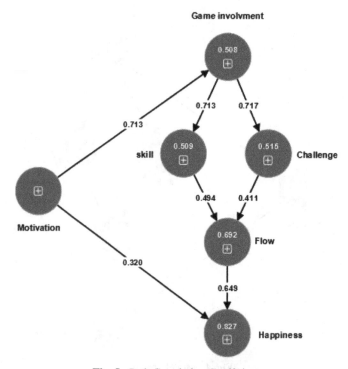

Fig. 5. Path Correlation Coefficient

Outer Loading. Outer Loading refers to the factor loadings of the indicator variable (item) on the construct (latent variable). When evaluating the model, the primary reference is the outer loading. When the value of the outer loading is more significant than 0.7, it is one of the criteria for judging the convergent validity of the model. The outer loading is obtained by the least square method and regression analysis with the construct (latent variable) as the independent variable and the items in the model as the dependent variable. Hulland [8] deems that the standardized outer loading of exploratory research should be greater than 0.5 to be acceptable. This study achieved Hulland's [8] standardized outer loading greater than 0.5, indicating that the convergence reliability of the index reached the standard, as shown in Table 1.

Table 1. Outer Loading

Item No	Motivation	Item No	Flow	Item No	Skill
1	0.7	21	0.775	41	0.948
2	0.837	22	0.765	42	0.959
3	0.658	23	0.824	43	0.951
4	0.722	24	0.909		**Challenge**
5	0.525	25	0.78	44	0.871
6	0.534	26	0.805	45	0.85
7	0.786	27	0.692	46	0.792
8	0.753	28	0.718		
9	0.629	29	0.74		
10	0.824	30	0.768		
11	0.811		**Happiness**		
12	0.7	31	0.681		
	Game Involvement	32	0.826		
13	0.735	33	0.829		
14	0.758	34	0.885		
15	0.769	35	0.773		
16	0.793	36	0.775		
17	0.647	37	0.874		
18	0.785	38	0.767		
19	0.652	39	0.849		
20	0.626	40	0.804		

6.2 Quality Criteria

After the model has completed the PLS measurement convergence, it can display the evaluation model quality of relevant model indicators, which include R^2, f^2, Cronbach's α, composite reliability (CR), average variation extracted (AVE), variance inflation factor (VIF) and model fit index.

Hair et al. (2014) pointed out that academically the value of **R^2** is relatively varied in different research fields. It is generally required that 0.25 is regarded as a slightly weak explanatory value, and when the R2 value is close to 0.5, the model has a moderate explanatory value. When it is close to 0.75, the explanatory value of the model is very significant. According to the results, the model has above moderate explanatory value (see Fig. 6).

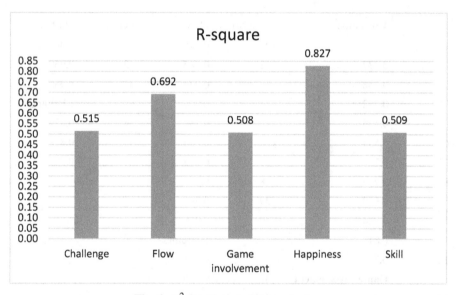

Fig. 6. R^2 Coefficient of Determination

f^2 Effect Size: f^2 effect size shows the effect of exogenous variables on endogenous variables. It is mainly used to delete specific exogenous variables in the model to see the variation in **R^2** and evaluate whether exogenous variables significantly influence endogenous variables. (see Fig. 7).

Cohen [9] stated the **f^2**-value evaluation principle:
$0.02 < \mathbf{f^2} \leqq 0.15$ *represents* a small effect,
$0.15 < \mathbf{f^2} \leqq 0.35$ *represents* a medium effect.
$\mathbf{f^2} > 0.35$ *represents* a significantly larger effect, so the result shows:
Flow on Happiness: 1.137 (**$f^2 > 0.35$**) *represents* a large effect.
Game involvement on challenge:1.06 (**$f^2 > 0.35$**) *represents* a large effect.
Game involvement on skill: 1.037 (**$f^2 > 0.35$**) *represents* a large effect.

Game motivation on game involvement: 1.033 ($f^2 > 0.35$) *represents* a large effect.
Game motivation on happiness: 0.277 ($0.15 < f^2 \leq 0.35$) *represents* a medium effect.
Skill on Flow: 0.422 ($f^2 > 0.35$) *represents* a large effect.
Challenge on flow: 0.292 ($0.15 < f^2 \leq 0.35$) *represents* a medium effect.

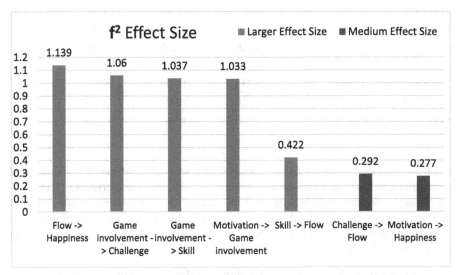

Fig. 7. f^2 Effect Size

Construct Reliability and Validity: Construct reliability and validity, such as Cronbach's α inter-rater reliability index, composite reliability (CR), and average variation extracted (AVE), are used to evaluate indicators that reflect the reliability and convergent validity of the measurement model for evaluating internal consistency.

Hair et al. [10] suggested that using the construct reliability to evaluate internal consistency while measuring the model is more appropriate.

Scholars Fornell & Larcker [11] suggested that the construct reliability of latent variables should be greater than 0.7. The construct reliability values of all latent variables in this study are more significant than 0.7, so the items in the construction have high internal consistency. The average variation extracted (AVE) is the average variation explanatory value of each index variable of the latent variable to the latent value. The construct reliability and validity results of this study are presented in Table 2.

6.3 Bootstrapping

PLS-SEM does not emphasize the normal distribution for characteristics of the data, so the significance of outer loadings, weights, and path coefficients in the model is tested through the bootstrapping method in the nonparametric statistics analysis method. The whole process is applied by using random sampling with replacement, and the existing observation sample is regarded as the population and carry out sampling repeatedly.

Table 2. Construct Reliability & Validity

	Cronbach's alpha	Composite reliability (rho_a)	Composite reliability (rho_c)	Average variance extracted (AVE)
Challenge	0.789	0.801	0.876	0.703
Flow	0.928	0.930	0.939	0.608
Game Involvement	0.870	0.888	0.897	0.523
Happiness	0.940	0.944	0.949	0.653
Motivation	0.912	0.926	0.924	0.509
Skill	0.949	0.956	0.967	0.908

When the number of samples drawn reaches the preset number of samples, the sampled observations are used as a sub-sample, and the distribution characteristics of each sub-sample are estimated. This process will be executed until a specific number of sub-samples is completed (5000 sub-samples are set in this study). The operation will be stopped, and the analysis and statistics will be performed. The model structure testing and analysis values are shown as follows.

Path Coefficients- Mean, STDEV, t Value, p-Value: According to the test results, the t-value and p-value of the coefficient test results between each path are extremely significant, as shown in Table 3.

Table 3. Path Coefficients- Mean, STDEV, t Value, p-Value

	Original sample (O)	Sample mean (M)	Standard deviation (STDEV)	T statistics (|O/STDEV|)	P values	2.50%	97.50%	Bias
Flow -> Happiness	0.649	0.642	0.086	7.511	0***	0.448	0.793	0.008
Skill -> Flow	0.494	0.474	0.128	3.868	0***	0.215	0.718	0.02
Challenge -> Flow	0.411	0.442	0.131	3.143	0.002***	0.175	0.687	0.031
Motivation -> Happiness	0.32	0.33	0.082	3.894	0***	0.181	0.505	0.01
Motivation -> Game Involvement	0.713	0.731	0.06	11.927	0***	0.608	0.847	0.018

(continued)

Table 3. (*continued*)

	Original sample (O)	Sample mean (M)	Standard deviation (STDEV)	T statistics (|O/STDEV|)	P values	2.50%	97.50%	Bias
Game Involvement -> Skill	0.713	0.724	0.067	10.654	0***	0.578	0.843	0.011
Game Involvement -> Challenge	0.717	0.737	0.069	10.425	0***	0.599	0.872	0.02
*** p < 0.001	*** t = 3.28							
** p < 0.01	** t = 2.58							
* p < 0.05	* t = 1.96							

According to the above results, the hypothesis of H1 – H7 is all positive and well-established (see Fig. 8).

The average variance extracted (AVE) - Mean, STDEV, t value, p-value of the test as shown in Table 4.

According to the test, the R^2 value test also showed a very significant effect, indicating that the research model has above medium explanatory value, as shown in Table 5.

According to the test results, Cronbach's Alpha value of the test is also extremely significant, as shown in Table 6.

7 Conclusion

In this study, we observed that during the gameplay, over time, players mastered game-playing skills and transformed their interactive behavior from a cognitive process of conscious assessment and execution to a subconscious, intuitive response process. Players gradually improve the way to handle the relative difficulty presented on the level and get a better sense; eventually, the player learns enough skills to break through the level and complete the goal. During this process, players extricate themselves from the sense of oppression and awkwardness in unfamiliar gameplay situations and can gradually control the gameplay smoothly and elegantly. At the same time, they receive the satisfaction of meeting the challenges and the scores or skills required for passing the level in the game.

Through the statistical results of the questionnaire in this study, we found that the characteristics of the situation in the gameplay make individuals prone to flow experience

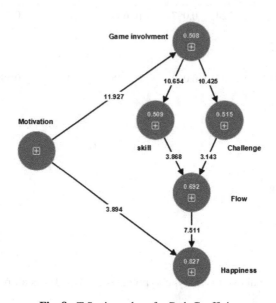

Fig. 8. T Statics values for Path Coefficient

Table 4. Average variance extracted (AVE)- Mean, STDEV, t value, p-value

	Original sample (O)	Sample mean (M)	Standard deviation (STDEV)	T statistics (|O/STDEV|)	P values
Happiness	0.653	0.66	0.058	11.168	0***
Flow	0.608	0.613	0.054	11.288	0***
Skill	0.908	0.907	0.028	32.962	0***
Challenge	0.703	0.709	0.076	9.248	0***
Motivation	0.509	0.521	0.063	8.146	0***
Game Involvement	0.523	0.528	0.073	7.133	0***
*** p < 0.001					

in the game. In the game, individuals are more willing to engage in actions based on intrinsic motivation proactively and can effectively improve learners' concentration. It is a suitable environment for self-directed learning and skill exploration.

Table 5. R-Square adjusted- Mean, STDEV, t value, p-value

	Original sample (O)	Sample mean (M)	Standard deviation (STDEV)	T statistics (IO/STDEVI)	P values
Happiness	0.817	0.831	0.057	14.372	0***
Flow	0.674	0.702	0.071	9.45	0***
Skill	0.495	0.515	0.098	5.048	0***
Challenge	0.501	0.536	0.104	4.812	0***
Game Involvement	0.494	0.525	0.089	5.525	0***
R-Square -Mean, STDEV, t value, p-value					
Happiness	0.827	0.841	0.054	15.407	0***
Flow	0.692	0.718	0.067	10.275	0***
Skill	0.509	0.529	0.095	5.339	0***
Challenge	0.515	0.549	0.101	5.087	0***
Game Involvement	0.508	0.538	0.087	5.844	0***
*** p < 0.001					

Table 6. Cronbach's Alpha - Mean, STDEV, t value, p-value

	Original sample (O)	Sample mean (M)	Standard deviation (STDEV)	T statistics (IO/STDEVI)	P values
Happiness	0.94	0.94	0.016	57.103	0***
Flow	0.928	0.927	0.018	52.957	0***
Skill	0.949	0.948	0.017	55.903	0***
Challenge	0.789	0.786	0.078	10.173	0***
Motivation	0.912	0.912	0.022	41.137	0***
Game Involvement	0.87	0.864	0.043	20.067	0***
*** p < 0.001					

The questionnaire statistics show that the direct correlation between game motivation and happiness is low. However, through the path of game involvement with the correspondence between skill and challenge difficulty, it can directly affect the player's flow and improve happiness.

This study found that the design of the game mechanism can significantly increase the intensity of physical activity motivation for people with autism. In the future, it is hoped that it will inspire more rigorous ways to track virtual reality games that improve physical and mental health.

Appendix A: Questionnaire

(**1** = Strongly Disagree; **2** = Disagree; **3** = Neutral; **4** = Agree; **5** = Strongly Agree).

Game Motivation:

Innovative items:		1	2	3	4	5
1	Playing games can bring creativity and imagination					
2	Playing games creates new discoveries and curiosity					
3	Playing games can learn new concepts and knowledge					
4	Playing games invokes me to brainstorm					

Social items:		1	2	3	4	5
1	Playing games allows me to meet all kinds of people					
2	Playing games can build and increase friendship					
3	Playing games can show my strengths to others					
4	Playing games can have a good time with friends					

Competency items:		1	2	3	4	5
1	Playing games can improve operating skills and abilities					
2	Playing games can improve self-challenging ability					
3	Playing games gives me a sense of accomplishment					
4	Play games to show off my skills to others					

Avoidance items:		1	2	3	4	5
1	Playing games can keep me away from family stress and tension					
2	Playing games can keep me away from the stress and tension of your studies					
3	Playing games can keep me away from social stress and tension					
4	Playing games can keep me away from emotional stress and tension					

Game Involvement:

Attraction items:		1	2	3	4	5
1	I think playing games is an important leisure activity					
2	I think the advantages of playing games outweigh the disadvantages					
3	I think I like playing games more than any other activity					
4	I think playing games makes me feel good when I'm stressed					

Self-expression items:		1	2	3	4	5
1	I like to discuss game content with my friends					
2	I will take the initiative to pay attention to the latest news of the game					
3	I think I can overcome various problems encountered in the game					
4	I think games make other people enjoy interacting or reaching out to me					

Centrality:		1	2	3	4	5
1	I spend most of my time playing games					
2	I play games whenever I am free					
3	I will spend time on games					
4	I'll save my money and spend it on games					

Flow:

Feedback items:		1	2	3	4	5
1	When playing a game, if I make a mistake, I always know immediately whether I can pass the level					
2	When playing games, if I can break through the difficulties, I will know how to play the next level better					
3	When playing a game, I always know whether my performance meets my expectations					
4	When playing the game, my improvement in skill can often be clearly felt					

Concentration items:		1	2	3	4	5
1	When playing games, I can always stay in state of concentration					
2	When playing games, I'm often engrossed					
3	When playing games, I often pay attention to every detail of them					
4	When playing games, I can often get away from the annoyance in my life					

Self-Realization items:		1	2	3	4	5
1	I really enjoy the joy of playing games					
2	Most games can satisfy me					
3	Playing games can bring me emotional satisfaction					
4	Playing games can increase my self-confidence					

Sense of Time items:		1	2	3	4	5
1	When playing games, I feel like time flies by very fast					
2	When playing games, I often don't know how long I've been playing					
3	When playing games, when someone tells me I've been playing for too long, I still feel like I don't have enough time					
4	When playing games, if there is no reminder from other people, I often don't pay attention to the time					

Happiness:

Physiologically oriented items:		1	2	3	4	5
1	Playing games keeps me energetic					
2	Playing games can help me get my strength back					
3	Playing games can keep excited emotional					
4	Playing games keep my wits about me					

Psychologically oriented items:		1	2	3	4	5
1	Playing games can make me feel that life is colorful					
2	Playing games can put me in a good mood					
3	Playing games improves my gaming skills					
4	When playing games, I use my skills to overcome difficult challenge					

Emotionally oriented items:		1	2	3	4	5
1	Playing games can relax me physically and mentally					
2	Playing games can relieve my stress					
3	Playing games helps me emotionally					
4	Playing games helps me relieve tension					

Education-oriented items:		1	2	3	4	5
1	Playing games can broaden my perspectives					
2	Playing games helps me understand other people					
3	Playing games helps me try new things					
4	The experience of playing games can help me challenge the next game					

Social Oriented items:		1	2	3	4	5
1	Playing games gives me the opportunity to interact with other people					
2	Playing games allows me to understand my own and other people's thoughts					
3	Playing games allows me to have a common topic with my friends					
4	I will exchange game information with my friends					

Aesthetics-oriented items:		1	2	3	4	5
1	Whether the game's soundtrack is appropriate is very important to me					
2	It's important to me that the game's font size is appropriate					
3	It is very important to me whether the picture quality of the game is beautiful					
4	Whether the visual style of the game meets my requirements is very important to me					

Challenge:

Challenge items:		1	2	3	4	5
1	Playing games is a challenge for me					
2	Playing games is a test of my abilities					
3	Playing games can improve my abilities through accumulating experience					
4	Playing games makes me want to perform at my best					

Skill:

Skill Items:		1	2	3	4	5
1	Playing games allows me to express my best ability to deal with the interface					

(continued)

(continued)

Skill Items:		1	2	3	4	5
2	I have comprehensive of skills to play the game					
3	The game offers me the best opportunity to test my control and skills					
4	Games push the limits of my ability to play games					

References

1. Csikszentmihalyi, M.: Flow: the psychology of optimal experience. J. Leis. Res. **24**(1), 93–94 (1990)
2. Csikszentmihalyi, M.: Finding Flow: The Psychology of Engagement with Everyday Life, 1st edn. HarperCollins, New York, NY (1997)
3. Webster, J., Trevino, K.L., Ryan, L.: The dimensionality and correlates of flow in human-computer interactions. Comput. Hum. Behav. **9**(4), 411–426 (1993)
4. Costikyan, G.: Uncertainty in Games (Playful Thinking), 2nd edn. The MIT Press, Cambridge, MA (2015)
5. Lopez, S.J., Snyder, C.R.: The Oxford Handbook of Positive Psychology, 3rd edn. Oxford University Press, Oxford, UK (2016)
6. Jackson, S.A.: Factors influencing the occurrence of flow state in elite athletes. J. Appl. Sport Psychol. **7**(2), 138–166 (1995)
7. Jackson, S.A., Csikszentmihalyi, M.: Flow in Sports: The Keys to Optimal Experiences and Performances, 1st edn. Human Kinetics, Champaign, IL (1999)
8. Hulland, J.: Use of partial least squares (PLS) in strategic management research: a review of four recent studies. Strateg. Manag. J. **20**(2), 195–204 (1999)
9. Cohen, J.: Set correlation and contingency tables. Appl. Psychol. Meas. **12**(4), 425–434 (1988)
10. Hair, J.F., Jr., Sarstedt, M., Hopkins, L., Kuppelwieser, V.G.: Partial least squares structural equation modeling (PLS-SEM): an emerging tool in business research. Eur. Bus. Rev. **26**(2), 106–121 (2014)
11. Fornell, C., Larcker, D.F.: Structural equation models with unobservable variables and measurement error: algebra and statistics. J. Mark. Res. **18**(3), 382–388 (1981)

Research on Transformation and Redesign of Nucleic Acid Sampling Booths in Communities: A Case Study of Shenzhen Communities

Wenzhe Luo⬥ and Jun Wu(✉)⬥

School of Art and Design, Division of Arts, Shenzhen University, Shenzhen 518061, Guangdong, People's Republic of China
junwu2006@hotmail.com

Abstract. During the terms of COVID-19, nucleic acid sampling booths are extremely important medical facilities in cities, and millions of residents undergo nucleic acid sampling and testing every day. With the changes of policies in epidemic prevention and control, a large number of nucleic acid sampling booths have been stopped using and left idle in every corner of the cities. Some people regard nucleic acid sampling booths as a feature of the times and hope to abandon and destroy those numerous industrial products. Meanwhile, some people think that nucleic acid sampling booths are still valuable medical resources in cities. The nucleic acid sampling booths can be transformed and designed through scientific and reasonable methods, and change them into what residents need and love products. This research focuses on the transformation and design of communities' nucleic acid sampling booths, aiming to summarize and excavate the needs and values of communities and residents in the process of transforming, and explore nucleic acid in combination with community medical and design theories. Finally, this research explores the practical directions of transforming nucleic acid sampling booths into convenient medical stations combining the theories of primary care and redesign.

Keywords: Primary Care · Nucleic Acid Sampling Booths · Convenient Medical Stations · Transformation and Redesign Methods

1 Introduction

Since the outbreak of the COVID-19, epidemic diseases have affected all aspects of urban residents' life and work which is mainly related to five major themes, namely, environmental quality, socioeconomic impacts, management and governance, (4) transportation and urban design and medical system of city [1]. Under the influence of many factors, their negative effects account for a large proportion, including the decline of urban economy, the decline of commodity trade circulation, the hindrance of commodity exports, the rise of urban unemployment rate, the decline of employment rate, overcapacity, the decline of water consumption of residents, and so on [2]. In a much recent report by

Indian Council of Medical Research, the apex medical body in India, the risk is 1.09 times higher in urban areas and 1.89 times higher in urban slum-like conditions vis-a-vis the rural areas [3]. These problems have made urban poor and marginalized groups more vulnerable to pandemics [4]. The pandemic of COVID-19 has made people question and criticize the rationality of large-scale urban development. At the same time, the pandemic has negative impacts on social mobility and interaction within public urban spaces [5]. Some people worry that the high density of cities may be a risk factor, making epidemics spread uncontrollably and unexpectedly. In fact, the population density of cities cannot explain the geographical distribution pattern of confirmed cases after researching [6]. Cases can be minimized, and health can be enhanced when residents change the lifestyle and follow the directions from public health organization. The large-scale spread of the epidemic has exposed the fragility and resilience of the urban system from the whole to the local level. On the other hand, it has also created a driving force for urban promoters to change global resilient cities and regional planning [2]. Numerous strategies such as safe water, green environment, adaptive strategies of climate, comprehensive community planning, de-density inside buildings, and primary care have become the solutions for future urban architecture and environment design [7]. Due to rapid economic development, people's material conditions have been greatly improved, and health issues have gradually become the focus of social attention. The relevant measures between communities and medical institutions for residents' cleanliness and sanitation safety need to mobilize the available urban resources and partners to the greatest extent to ensure that sufficient quantities of safe water and disinfectant are provided to satisfy the sanitation of urban residents. Focusing on supply throughout the outbreak response; cities need to sustain this investment to promote community safety, healthy long-term growth to prevent future pandemic outbreaks [8]. From the perspective of urban epidemic resistance, China is global role model and pioneer representative in actions and measures during the pandemic. The city's resilience plays a key role when the government manages the flow and risk pressure from the COVID-19. In terms of improving primary care, China has maximized the adequacy of infrastructure and the improvement of urban management, which has greatly improved the efficiency of the control of the COVID-19 and enhanced the city's resilience [9]. During the COVID-19 epidemic, nucleic acid sampling booths are extremely important and widely used in Chinese cities and communities. Millions of residents millions of residents undergo nucleic acid sampling and testing every day. The measures isolate the patients which effectively hinder the spread of the epidemic [10]. With the changes of policies in epidemic prevention and control, a large number of nucleic acid sampling booths have been stopped using and left idle in every corner of the cities. In order to maximize the use of urban resources and avoid waste, more and more cities have transformed and designed the nucleic acid sampling booths into convenient-mobile spaces in view of the actual needs from residents [11]. Based on the above research background, how to transform, design and reuse the nucleic acid sampling booths are the themes of this study. The purpose of the study is as follows:

1. Focus the research perspective on the transformation and redesign of nucleic acid sampling booths in urban villages and communities;
2. Explore the needs of residents in the process of transformation and redesign of nucleic acid sampling booths;

3. Explore the practical direction of the transformation of Shenzhen community nucleic acid sampling booths into convenient medical stations combining the theories of primary care and redesign.

2 Literature Review

2.1 Status and Needs of Primary Care

Primary care service is closely related to residents' health and plays an important bridge between health care, economy and society. Complete primary care can help residents meet their basic medical needs [12]. A healthy community benefits everyone who lives in it. Primary care is an important way to achieve healthy communities. Public health aims to protect and improve the health of communities by addressing the structures and systems, and to support the community residents who live and work there to make healthy decisions. To study primary care and health problems, we need to collect data and resources to solve community health and sanitation problems [13]. However, with the increasing demand for urban medical and health care, primary care institutions have problems such as small scale and poor facilities, which are far from the requirements of modern hospitals. This contradiction between supply and demand has caused great obstacles to the reform of primary care and community health, and the social concern about medical institutions has gradually emerged [14]. Why primary care is important to community health? About half of Americans have a chronic illness. Many residents do not have access to health resources due to socio-economic factors beyond their control. In a medical emergency, an elderly diabetic with no family and no driver's license and a pregnant woman with toxemia who lives more than 50 miles from the hospital are at high risk in the community. This makes primary care and sanitation particularly important [15]. Residents need to cooperate with and accept management strategies and medical services provided by Medical Organizations in the process of long-term struggle, detection and treatment against epidemic diseases. At the same time, all communities consume a lot of human, material and financial resources in the organization of medical services, and its medical services activities are also deeply affected by the environment and residents [16]. Therefore, based on sanitation and health of residents, the construction of primary care is urgent, complicated and heavy task.

2.2 Status and Needs of Primary Care

During the COVID-19 pandemic, prevention and control are key measures to curb the rapid spread of the virus. However, the practical implementation is very difficult, and some of these measures may be harmful to the living conditions of members of many communities. In addition, due to the weak primary care system, the community may severely lack of detection, isolation and treatment are diseased, the ability of tracking and isolating contacts. Public health and social measures in these communities need to be balanced against other risks affecting their communities, such as low-income populations, health care services, social networks and food safety issues. Residents need to act pragmatically and take advantage of local structures and systems, particularly through social mobilization and strong community participation [8]. On May 9, 2022, The State

Council proposed to further confirm "Sifang" responsibilities and "Sizao" requests [17]. "Sifang" responsibilities refers to the responsibility of the territory, department, unit and individual. "Sizao" requirements refer to the requirements of early detection, early reporting, early isolation and early treatment [18]. A number of departments across Tulane University are actively responding to the 2019–2020 outbreak of COVID-19. Researchers in the School of Public Health and Tropical Medicine, School of Medicine, National Primate Research Center, and Science and Engineering are addressing the disease on several fronts, from immediate response and containment, modeling to anticipate the disease spread and so on [19]. Nucleic acid sampling booths are important medical facilities in cities. Millions of residents undergo nucleic acid testing services every day. Nucleic acid testing is an indispensable procedure for confirming COVID-19 [20]. Nucleic acid sampling booths mainly free medical staff from the heavy nucleic acid sampling work. Compared with the previous open-air sampling, the nucleic acid sampling booths improved the sampling environment for medical staff and ensured the safety of the sampled personnel. Nucleic acid sampling booths have the following three advantages: First, the built-in ultraviolet lamp can disinfect the sampling booths in the early stage of work, creating a sterile and safe sampling environment. Second, the intercom system is configured to facilitate the medical sampler to communicate with the external staff in time, so as to better complete the sampling work. Third, the fresh air positive pressure system keeps the positive pressure inside the sampling booth higher than that outside, effectively preventing the virus from entering the sampling booth through the air. Nucleic acid sampling kiosk detection channel has special gloves, and equipped with HD tempered glass for observation, to achieve zero contact with the sampled person, effectively avoid cross infection. The universal wheel installed at the bottom of the sampling booth can be moved at any time according to the sampling situation, so as to complete the nucleic acid sampling work more efficiently. The sunshade at the top of the sampling pavilion effectively prevents direct sunlight or other factors from affecting the samples. The internal and external sampling Windows of the booth are illuminated by LED lights to facilitate nucleic acid sampling by medical staff at night [21].

2.3   The Functions of Nucleic Acid Sampling Booths in the Communities

The traditional nucleic acid testing mainly uses tents to build temporary sampling sites. It is vulnerable to weather, especially severe weather such as strong winds, torrential rain and high temperatures. Sampling becomes more difficult. In addition, the way medical workers and those being sampled are tested face-to-face leads to a high risk of infection. However, the use of contactless, mobile nucleic acid sampling booths can effectively solve this problem and further enhance the capacity of epidemic prevention and control. Most nucleic acid sampling booths are portable, allowing for flexible use and easy deployment. At the same time, some nucleic acid sampling booths are also equipped with intelligent registration system. Residents only need to complete the work of health code scanning, personnel information entry, temperature measurement, etc. Then residents can take samples for convenience [22].

With the changes of policies in epidemic prevention and control, a large number of nucleic acid sampling booths have been stopped using and left idle in every corner of the cities. Some people raised whether nucleic acid sampling booths could be converted into breakfast shops and street stalls in the future. If it works, it could boost employment. In this regard, some retail workers think that the reconstruction of sampling booths should be carried out in accordance with the relevant government planning. On the other hand, if you do cater or retail purposes, it also involves the relevant business license, health conditions, qualifications of practitioners, etc. However, the small size of the nucleic acid sampling booths also needs to be considered whether it can hold the goods [23]. Some people regard nucleic acid sampling booths as a feature of the times and hope to abandon and destroy those numerous industrial products. Meanwhile, some people think that nucleic acid sampling booths are still valuable medical resources in cities. The nucleic acid sampling booths can be transformed and designed through scientific and reasonable methods and change them into what residents need and love products. The advantages of this method on the one hand can save social resources, reduce waste. On the other hand, it can also design and transform this service space with mobile and portable type to meet the needs of daily urban residents. Many people expect that the idle nucleic acid testing booths can have more diversified functions, such as fever clinic, treatment stations, Spring Festival Goods Stalls, civilized tourism traffic guidance stations, voluntary service stations, convenience service stations, community sharing stations, rest station for workers, people's life liaison stations, express delivery station, urban management service station, Love Rafting Library, miniature fire stations [24] (Fig. 1).

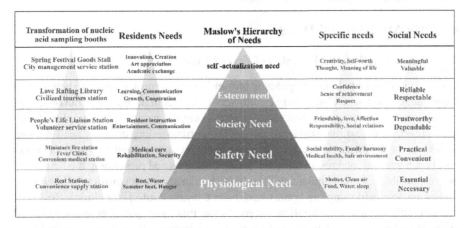

Fig. 1. Research framework.

3 Research Methods

3.1 A Subsection Sample

In this study, the reconstruction of idle nucleic acid sampling booths in various cities was selected as the research object. Analyze, compare and study cases. Combining the transformation and redesign of nucleic acid sampling kiosk with Maslow's hierarchy of needs theory [25], this study expounds the needs of community residents achieved during the transformation and redesign of nucleic acid sampling booth. A hierarchical model of community residents' needs for nucleic acid sampling booth transformation was constructed. Taking the transformation and redesign of nucleic acid sampling booth in Funan Community, Futian Street, Futian District, Shenzhen as the exploration objective, the direction of promoting the high-quality development of primary care and health construction by the transformation and redesign of nucleic acid sampling booth was explored. The following three points are the main points of this study.

4. Explore the current idle situation of nucleic acid sampling booths in the community, as well as the views of residents on the transformation and redesign of nucleic acid sampling booths, what difficulties exist at present and what problems can be optimized.
5. Study the current situation and influence of the modified nucleic acid detection booths in the community, compare and analyze their advantages and disadvantages, and put forward the design scheme that can be optimized and improved for the community nucleic acid sampling booths.
6. Through the relationship between communities, residents and nucleic acid sampling booths, it proposed the renovation design and research scheme of nucleic acid sampling booths based on practicability, functionality, controllability, modularity, lightweight and recyclable, and proposed the renovation scheme of convenient medical station applicable to communities.

4   Case Analysis and Design

4.1   Transformation and Redesign of Fever Clinic

With the changes of policies in epidemic prevention and control, in order to better serve the residents, the Yuepu Community Health Service Center in Baoshan District of Shanghai has recently transformed and redesigned the original nucleic acid sampling booth into a fever clinic, so that residents can get the corresponding drugs in need without arriving at the health service center. The fever clinic is equipped with two medical workers at each window, one responsible for asking questions and prescribing medicine, and one responsible for taking medicine [26]. In the Futian and Baoan districts of Shenzhen, several nucleic acid sampling booths have been converted into fever clinics. Residents can smoothly complete registration, diagnosis and treatment, payment, dispensing and other procedures. This reduces the risk of cross infection. According to Biqin Chen, director of the Funan Community Health Center in Futian District, Funan Community Health was the first to transform and redesign nucleic acid sampling booths into fever clinics in Futian district on December 12. Patients can complete the procedures of seeing a doctor, charging, dispensing medicine, examination and treatment, which can be completed in 5 to 10 min at the fastest. The nucleic acid sampling booths can accommodate 3 medical workers at the same time. Internal air conditioning, disinfection equipment, positive pressure ventilation system and other electrical equipment are very complete which can meet the needs of the fever clinic and residents [23]. Some nucleic acid sampling booths in Suzhou have been transformed into fever clinics. When residents arrive, they can get medical treatment through a window and fill prescriptions at a pharmacy in the back. According to official data, 1,519 medical service centers have been built in 8 cities (counties) in Wuxi, among which 499 have been rebuilt from nucleic acid sampling booths, 514 have been set up using the booths of community neighborhood committees (villagers' committees), and 506 have been built by other means (Fig. 2).

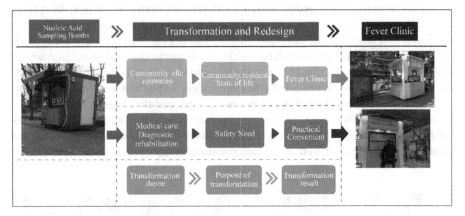

Fig. 2. Transformation and Redesign of Fever Clinic.

4.2 Transformation and Redesign of Love Rafting Library

In order to maximize the conservation of social resources, Suzhou city is trying to play a role in the transformation and redesign of nucleic acid sampling booths. In Xiangcheng District, Suzhou, the first 18 civilized service stations, which were transformed and redesigned from nucleic acid sampling booths, were officially put into operation [27]. In Zhonghailongwan Community, Suzhou City, many donating books donated by residents are displayed in the Love Rafting Library transformed by nucleic acid sampling booth. Converted from an unused nucleic acid sampling booth. The love rafting bookstore is open only on weekends and can be borrowed or donated by the surrounding residents. According to the relevant person who is in charge of the community, there are numerous teachers and students in the community. Residents are supportive of the conversion of the nucleic acid sampling booth into Love Rafting Library. The management made a presentation to the owners' group at that time. Many families have donated the books they read to make it easier for everyone to read and create more value [28]. Rules and instructions are posted inside the Love Rafting Library, and community volunteers help register the information. After understanding the status quo of occupation, age, family and environment of local residents, the nucleic acid sampling booth was transformed and redesigned according to the hidden needs of local residents. This design method according to local conditions is quite scientific. It can be concluded that the transformation of nucleic acid sampling booths should be analyzed according to the different conditions of different regions, and the transformation should be carried out according to the specific needs after the investigation of local human characteristics and environmental status. At the same time, the corresponding rules and instructions are specified and displayed in the interior space, such as the detailed rules of borrowing and donation, the opening hours of the Love Rafting Library, and the specific requirements of volunteer work. In divergent thinking, there must be logical guidance, and at the same time, information screening and concentration should be carried out. Through centralized orientation and systematic comparison, the best and reasonable scheme can be sorted out from numerous schemes. Through continuous design evaluation and transformation practice, the optimal scheme to meet the needs of the community and the design objectives is found [29]. As a civilized post station of the city, Love Rafting Library can well meet the needs of the city for civilization, and also enrich the needs of communication and interaction among residents. Under the condition of excess nucleic acid sampling booths resources, it maximizes the use and transformation of urban convenient mobile space resources, well taps the hidden needs of community residents, and creates and develops the value of more nucleic acid sampling booths. This proves the great potential of nucleic acid sampling booths in transformation and redesign and presents high-quality cases for reference and research in urban cultural, humanistic and emotional interactions (Fig. 3).

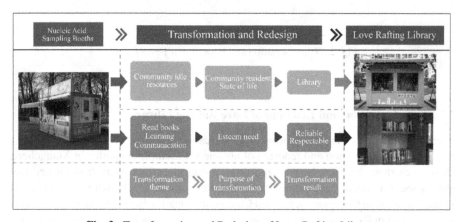

Fig. 3. Transformation and Redesign of Love Rafting Library.

4.3 Transformation and Redesign of Rest Station for Workers

In Yulan Park on the east side of Huanhu Road in Zhongjing Community, nucleic acid sampling booths has been transformed and redesigned into Rest Station, attracting many maintenance workers, cleaners and security guards from surrounding parks to rest and supply, chat and talk in this mobile space, shielding the vigorous summer sun. The Rest Stations provide daily services such as hot water, charging, and sanitation boxes for workers [30]. "When we see a sign for a rest stop, we all come in and sit down". Park maintenance worker Aunt Xu said, "You can store tools here and there are all kinds of services. It's very sweet. Now a lot of people are very caring for us. It is so warm for me". The transformation actions and strategies of nucleic acid sampling booths in Suzhou have shown a kind of warm cultural feelings in every corner of the city. According to local conditions, it maximizes the utilization of abandoned urban resources, saves resources and makes the best use of materials. The reconstructed nucleic acid sampling booths are distributed in various places of Xiangcheng, creating great value. In the Rest Station, workers can enjoy a moment of peace and joy outside of working hours. It is like a home for workers during working hours. Every worker is welcome to take a rest at any time. At the same time, after getting a high-quality rest, it can also improve the working efficiency of workers and reduce the unnecessary consumption of extra working time [31]. In the process of transformation and redesign of nucleic acid sampling booths, designers should pay more attention to the practicability, functionality, controllability, implementability and recyclability of products. In the external and internal space should also be the main visual design, can let people identify. "When we see a sign for a rest stop…" means that people can recognize the renovation pavilion through the concrete symbol. The function of the external space should be emphasized. In the function of the internal space also want to do see can be used, simple and practical (Fig. 4).

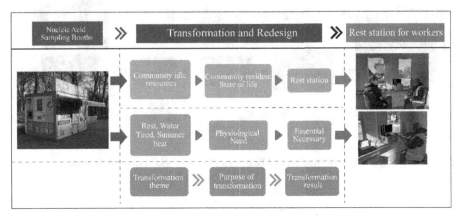

Fig. 4. Transformation and Redesign of Rest Station for Workers.

4.4   Transformation and Redesign of People's Life Liaison Station

Around some residential areas of the city, nucleic acid sampling booths have been transformed into People's Life Liaison Station. It is used to collect feedback, opinions and suggestions from the masses to help solve the vital interests of the people and the people's livelihood. In some places of lacking delivery cabinets, nucleic acid sampling booths have been transformed into "Delivery Stations" to provide temporary storage for community residents' online shopping. Shang Xiangke, deputy head of the publicity department of Sangseong District Party Committee, said the transformation of nucleic acid sampling booths follows the principle of adapting to local conditions and making the best use of materials. "At present, our civilized post includes 11 functions, such as learning from Lei Feng volunteer post, Love Supply Station, Rest Station and Health House and so on. Based on the actual situation of different nucleic acid sampling booths, such as the area and material, and based on the needs of the masses, relevant functional combinations will be selected for transformation, and other functions will be explored and expanded in accordance with the actual situation". It can be concluded that according to the cultural characteristics, living habits, social communication and emotional needs of community residents, nucleic acid sampling booths should be transformed and redesigned in terms of function, operation, safety, convenience, interaction and practicality. This makes the function and function of nucleic acid sampling booths have infinite daydream. People can think of it as a light, mobile, small urban space for the convenience of the city and the community. In this space, the transformation and reuse of different forms and functions can be carried out to enrich the daily work and life experience, solve and expand the complex social problems of the city and the way of resource utilization (Fig. 5).

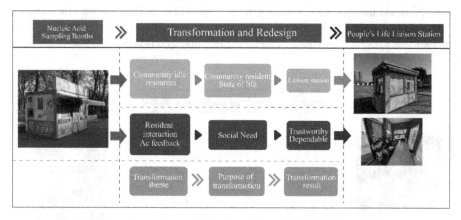

Fig. 5. Transformation and Redesign of People's Life Liaison Station.

4.5 Transformation and Redesign of Spring Festival Goods Stall

The Spring Festival Goods Stall is an example of nucleic acid sampling booth transformation and redesign with cultural integration [32]. In the theme activity of the New Year Market in Nanmen Business Circle, 30 nucleic acid sampling booths were transformed into Spring Festival Goods Stall, which displayed on the west sidewalks of Dongdajie and at the gate of Panmen Scenic Spot. Culture can be divided into three levels: spiritual culture in metaphysics, living culture in action, and physical material culture [33]. In 2003, Leong proposed the three-layer theory of cultural product design: external level, intermediate level and internal level, which respectively represent tangible material, behavior and customs, and intangible spiritual ideology [34]. The nucleic acid sampling booth was transformed into a Spring Festival Goods Stall and provided free of charge to the enterprises and merchants around the South Gate business Circle as the Spring Festival Goods Stall. This practice not only provides convenience for the surrounding old residents to buy Spring Festival goods, but also promotes the consumption of enterprises and merchants to set off a jubilant festival atmosphere. The Spring Festival Goods Stall activities are divided into five themes: agricultural and sideline products, trade promotion, catering and Spring Festival goods crafts, and cultural and creative publicity. In the market, you can buy Spring Festival goods and feel the cultural characteristics and festive atmosphere of the local city and residents. The Spring Festival Goods Stall provides a reference for the design method and creation mode of multilevel creative play for the transformation of nucleic acid sampling booth, and also contributes to the practical experience of cultural level design and transformation of nucleic acid sampling booth. In cultural transformation and redesign, designers pay attention to the cultural component, story and artistic value, as well as the viewer or user's interpretive ability or creative behavior [35]. Through the material carrier, culture is displayed in the important cultural festivals of residents, affecting the cultural breadth and depth of experiencers and consumers, deepening the connotation of spiritual civilization, and influencing the emotions and cognition of residents, which plays a role in integrating into the local material life and cultural characteristics [36] (Fig. 6).

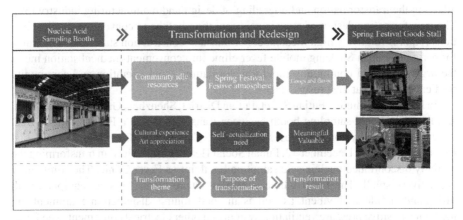

Fig. 6. Transformation and Redesign of Spring Festival Goods Stall.

4.6 Transformation and Redesign of Nucleic Acid Sampling Booths in Shenzhen Villages and Communities

For a long time, urban villages have been regarded by some people as a synonym for chaos, disorder and clutter. Often listed as the object of urban rectification, but in the transformation again and again to maintain strong vitality, in the city's steel forest between roots and continuation. It not only breaks away from the interpersonal relationship and production mode embedded in the traditional rural society, but also maintains a separate area from the modern city, showing a possibility of transcending the dual opposition between city and township. Facts have proved that urban villages, as a kind of production and living space, have not been forgotten in the tide of urban governance and reconstruction and thus become a footnote in the process of urbanization. Instead, they are gradually perceived, experienced and remembered by the public and become an important symbol of urban history, humanity and culture and the accumulation of charm [37].

Primary care and health service stations are the most basic medical and health service institutions and plays an important role in the development of Chinese health undertakings. In its construction, we should not only pay attention to the improvement of hardware facilities, but also pay attention to the improvement of interaction and working environment. As an important part of the construction of community health service station, the design of convenient-medical station not only needs to consider the functionality, aesthetics, practicability and efficiency of the design, but also needs to pay attention to its visual-psychological rationality and interactive experience [38]. The transformation, redesign and high-quality development of nucleic acid sampling booths are promoted through transformation and design innovation, which also drives the continuous progress of the design itself from concept to method to realization method. However, economic cost, practical situation and insufficient design ability are still the bottleneck problems affecting the transformation and upgrading of design and manufacturing industry [39]. The transformation design of nucleic acid sampling booths to convenient-medical stations requires relatively high medical conditions and construction standards. The transformation of Funan Shekang mobile fever clinic into convenient-medical station meets the urgent needs of community rapid transformation, rapid operation and community medical treatment at the present stage.

In Funan Community, Futian Street, Futian District, Shenzhen, Guangdong Province, an idle nucleic acid sampling booth has been transformed into a Fever Clinic to treat patients from nearby communities. According to Chen Biqin, director of Funan Social Health Center, since December 12, Funan Social Health took the lead in transforming the partially discontinued nucleic acid sampling booth into a Fever Clinic. The community is relatively small. The Fever Clinic is only 4 square meters in size, equipped with lifting and mobile deployment, as well as air conditioning, disinfection equipment and medicine, positive pressure ventilation system and other electrical equipment. The Fever Clinic can accommodate both a doctor and a patient for one-to-one treatment, as well as taking medicines home nearby, and currently each doctor sees more than 160 patients a day. However, there are also some problems in the first batch of Fever Clinic, such as poor working environment for doctors, small space, unclear medical process information and rough texture. The modification of nucleic acid sampling booth in Funan Community, Futian Street, Futian District, Shenzhen City, Guangdong Province was discussed. In this study, the transformation and design of nucleic acid sampling booth were optimized in combination with the aforementioned case study and the actual needs of the community, aiming to explore the transformation of nucleic acid sampling booth towards the direction of high quality, heavy experience, high quality and demand solution. At present, the nucleic acid sampling kiosk idle to be transformed has the following four advantages: (1) it is convenient for the public; (2) Friendly medical care; (3) the distribution point is more; (4) light and reusable. On the other hand, there are the following disadvantages: (1) simple facilities, rough reconstruction work, poor product experience; (2) the epidemic customization, one-time fixed investment is high, late use is difficult and high cost; (3) lack of systematic and complete information and interactive process [40] (Figs. 7 and 8).

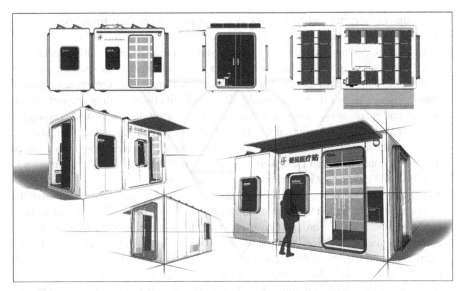

Fig. 7. Nucleic acid sampling booth – convenient-medical station renovation design.

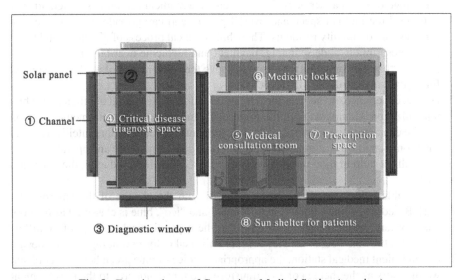

Fig. 8. Functional area of Convenient-Medical Station (top view).

The transformation of nucleic acid sampling booth into a convenient medical station in Funan Community, Futian Subdistrict, Futian District, Shenzhen has the following six characteristics:

1. The community medical system, social health centers and existing medical stations are complementary to build a multi-level and multi-echelon hierarchical diagnosis and treatment service system for fever, so as to better cope with the risk of regular

community epidemics and daily serious and serious diseases, and provide better health protection for community residents.

2. Antibacterial system. Convenient-Medical Station installed good antibacterial system. The positive pressure fresh air system can realize stepless speed regulation through the chip control EC fan, keeping the air pressure in the convenience medical station always higher than the outside 30 pa, effectively preventing the outside air flow in, and ensuring the safety of the doctor. At the same time, the system is equipped with a real-time pressure digital display device, which can automatically alarm the abnormal pressure with sound and light. G4+H14 dual filtration system is adopted in the workstation, which can ensure the filtration efficiency of 0.3 μm particles is 99.999% and effectively isolate external viral aerosols.

3. Health and safety system. The filter system can also realize intelligent detection of the filter element life. When the filter element needs to be replaced, the automatic alarm can give a warning. In order to ensure the cleanliness and safety of the cabin, the convenient medical station is also equipped with a UV sterilizing device for timing sterilizing, and the device has the function of delay opening, which can leave enough time for medical staff. The station is equipped with infrared human sense protection system module, which can automatically turn off the kill function when the human body enters, to protect medical staff from ultraviolet radiation damage [41].

4. Full range of medical services. The convenience medical station has systematically optimized the internal space and overall pattern and can provide one-stop medical services for community residents. The whole medical process of diagnosis and treatment, prescription, code scanning, payment and medicine distribution can be completed within the community, so as to improve the convenience of medical treatment for community residents with fever.

5. Human experience. In the functional transformation of the pursuit of efficiency, while humanization. Compared with the traditional clinic, the convenient medical station has the characteristics of small scale, full function, standardization, intelligence and easy construction. The community residents can go to experience and operate and can also call for help in time through the one-button call button, reducing the operation cost.

6. Reasonable color tone. Behavior is adjusted with the change of the environment [42]. Based on people's cognition of "water" and "ice", blue is classified as the cool color system, which is further extended to the psychological feelings of "indifference", "calm" and "cold". In view of this universal color psychology, in the design of convenient medical station, the appropriate choice of blue green between cool and warm colors as the theme color of transformation, is conducive to the development of community patients' mental health. According to Kandinsky, green has a "human, self-satisfied peace, which has a solemn, supernatural infinite mystery". The psychological expression of green caters to the psychological needs of patients. Therefore, in the outdoor and indoor space design of convenience medical station, green plants that are harmless to human body can also be used to decorate, and plants full of vitality and soft appearance can also give people positive guidance, healthy and upward hint [38].

5 Conclusion

With the changes of epidemic policies, more and more cities and communities have transformed a large number of idle nucleic acid sampling booths in order to reduce the waste of social resources. Through the above research, it can be concluded that the nucleic acid sampling booths can provide transformation and adaptive-functional services according to the needs of communities and residents. Taking Funan Community, Futian Street, Futian District, Shenzhen as an example, the convenient-medical station designed by optimizing the fever clinic transformed from a nucleic acid sampling booth. The transformation and redesign of a large number of idle nucleic acid sampling booths into convenient-medical stations have enabled communities which are far away from urban infirmaries and hospitals to obtain timely medical services and emergency treatment. The transformation and redesign of the nucleic acid sampling booths can provide first aid and medical services for the elderly, if it is transformed into medical service stations for the elderly. The prefabricated and modularized convenient-medical stations have the characteristics of small scale, complete functions, standardization, intelligence, reuse, less operation and easy construction. The practices of transformation and redesign are important measures of reform and innovation from the supply side of service facilities. The primary care environment extends from urban hospitals to communities, from indoors to outdoors. it is suitable for the construction of various urbanization processes such as urban blocks, communities, and tourist attractions. Through the above measures, we will build a foundation and provide guarantees for the construction of primary care and residents' health and play a certain role in the high-quality development of community medical care and health and the improvement of the happiness index of residents.

This study transformed and redesigned the nucleic acid sampling booth into a convenient-medical station based on previous transformation cases and design experience. How to transform and redesign the abandoned nucleic acid sampling booths to better serve communities and residents can not only save resources, avoid waste, but also meet the needs of community life through design, which is an important research topic.

References

1. Sharifi, A., Khavarian-Garmsir, A.R.: The COVID-19 pandemic: impacts on cities and major lessons for urban planning, design, and management. Sci. Total Environ. **749**, 142391 (2020)
2. Banai, R.: Pandemic and the planning of resilient cities and regions. Cities **106**, 102929 (2020)
3. Swarajya. ICMR serosurvey: Just 0.73 per cent of population had evidence of past exposure to coronavirus. Swarajya (2020). https://swarajyamag.com/insta/icmr-serosurvey-just-073-per-cent-of-population-had-evidence-of-past-exposure-to-coronavirus
4. Mishra, S.V., Gayen, A., Haque, S.M.: COVID-19 and urban vulnerability in India. Habitat Int. **103**, 102230 (2020)
5. Askarizad, R., Jinliao, H., Jafari, S.: The influence of COVID-19 on the societal mobility of urban spaces. Cities **119**, 103388 (2021)
6. Khavarian-Garmsir, A.R., Sharifi, A., Moradpour, N.: Are high-density districts more vulnerable to the COVID-19 pandemic? Sustain. Cities Soc. **70**, 102911 (2021)

7. Ahsan, M.M.: Strategic decisions on urban built environment to pandemics in Turkey: lessons from COVID-19. J. Urban Manage. **9**(3), 281–285 (2020)

8. World Health Organization. Overview of public health and social measures in the context of COVID-19: interim guidance, 18 May 2020 (No. WHO/2019-nCoV/PHSM_Overview/2020.1). World Health Organization (2020)

9. Chen, J., Guo, X., Pan, H., Zhong, S.: What determines city's resilience against epidemic outbreak: evidence from China's COVID-19 experience. Sustain. Cities Soc. **70**, 102892 (2021). (in Chinese)

10. Wu, J., et al.: Detection and analysis of nucleic acid in various biological samples of COVID-19 patients. Travel Med. Infect. Dis. **37**, 101673 (2020). (in Chinese)

11. COVID sampling booth turned into fever consulting room. http://www.sz.gov.cn/en_szgov/news/latest/content/post_10349135.html/. Accessed 10 Feb 2023

12. What is Community Health and Why Is It Important? https://www.rasmussen.edu/degrees/health-sciences/blog/what-is-community-health/. Accessed 10 Feb 2023

13. What is Community Health? https://www.elmhurst.edu/blog/what-is-community-health/. Accessed 10 Feb 2023

14. Wang, L., Zhang J.: Research on multiple supply model of community medical service under the background of urbanization. Econ. Trade Pract. (22), 32 (2018). (in Chinese)

15. Why Community Health Is Important for Public Health? https://publichealth.tulane.edu/blog/why-community-health-is-important-for-public-health/. Accessed 10 Feb 2023

16. Ke, L.: Analysis and thinking on the influencing factors of the improvement of urban community medical service system - based on the survey of the current situation of community medical service and residents' needs in Wuhan. Mod. Commer. Trade Ind. (09), 83–84 (2010). (in Chinese). https://doi.org/10.19311/j.cnki.1672-3198.2010.09.049

17. Hua, Q., Gao, J.: Compacting the "Four Party Responsibility", firmly holding the hard won achievements in prevention and control, building a strong line of defense against the epidemic, and providing a strong security guarantee for people's health. Zhumadian Daily, 001 (2022). (in Chinese)

18. Xiao, L., Zhang, Y., Hu, X., Liu, T., Liu, Y.: Analysis of the global prevalence of novel coronavirus variants. Chin. J. Front. Health Quarantine (01), 10–12 (2022). (in Chinese). https://doi.org/10.16408/j.1004-9770.2022.01.004

19. Tulane University. https://sph.tulane.edu/covid-19/. Accessed 10 Feb 2023

20. Su, Y., et al.: Innovative design research on the structure of mobile gas film nucleic acid sampling booth. Build. Struct. (S2), 313–318 (2022). (in Chinese). https://doi.org/10.19701/j.jzjg.22S2646/. Accessed 10 Feb 2023

21. What are the main functions of mobile nucleic acid sampling kiosks?. (in Chinese). https://zhuanlan.zhihu.com/p/577394164/. Accessed 10 Feb 2023

22. Jasiński, A.: COVID-19 pandemic is challenging some dogmas of modern urbanism. Cities **121**, 103498 (2022)

23. Le, Y., Lin, Z., Wang, Z., Lu, R.: How to reuse massive resources in the transformation of nucleic acid sampling booth. China Business Daily, A10 (2022). (in Chinese)

24. Nucleic acid detection booth, super "change change"!. (in Chinese). https://mp.weixin.qq.com/s/ldjbQKLv_6sKzVtK-mb0jA/. Accessed 10 Feb 2023

25. Lester, D.: Measuring Maslow's hierarchy of needs. Psychol. Rep. **113**(1), 15–17 (2013)

26. Luo, L., Zou, Z.: Layout of mobile nucleic acid sampling stations (kiosks) in Shenzhen communities. Shenzhen Special Zone News, A01 (2022). (in Chinese)

27. Micro transformation, smart upgrade and great use! Nucleic acid sampling booth, a "transformation" civilization station!. (in Chinese). https://mp.weixin.qq.com/s/6Z2o2maTWix6216j17axqw/. Accessed 10 Feb 2023

28. The idle nucleic acid kiosks on the street have been withdrawn! Renovation and reuse are the most recommended. https://mp.weixin.qq.com/s/8Qp8lkXEAGjabpLMShQmmA. Accessed 10 Feb 2023

29. Wang, X.: Complementary Design thinking and methods – research on complementary design methods based on the field of visual communication design. Jiangsu Phoenix Fine Arts Publishing House. Jiangsu (2019). 60, 64, 70, 119, 217

30. Nucleic acid detection kiosk, super "change"!. https://mp.weixin.qq.com/s/ldjbQKLv_6sK zVtK-mb0jA. Accessed 2023/2/10

31. Lan, Y.: Urban village community: a case study of farmers' urbanization organization and lifestyle. https://mp.weixin.qq.com/s/B2wpsScX4qbKMWjFGuSbvQ. Accessed 10 Feb 2023

32. How can idle nucleic acid sampling kiosks be "re-employed"? https://mp.weixin.qq.com/s/ wowP0YSfeDvCbKlYzbh8kQ. Accessed 10 Feb 2023

33. Zheng, Y.: Construction of cultural design mode: discussion on the application of china traditional culture in product modeling mode. Institute of Innovative Design, National Taipei University of Technology (2004)

34. Baird, K., Jia Hu, K., Reeve, R.: The relationships between organizational culture, total quality management practices and operational performance. Int. J. Oper. Prod. Manage. 31(7), 789–814 (2011)

35. Lu, D., Zhang, J.: Concept and design process of user's continuous design. J. Design 12(2), 1–13 (2007)

36. Yang, C., He, M., Lu, D.: A gestalt-oriented modeling creation model. J. Design 16(4), 19–34 (2011)

37. China Social Sciences in 2022. China Social Sciences (12), 204–208 (2022)

38. Wang, L., Visual psychology in interior design of community health service stations. China Rural Health Manage. (02), 156–157 (2018)

39. Hao, N., Liu X.: Research on the transformation path of manufacturing design based on the concept of life cycle. Packag. Eng. (22), 47–56 (2022)

40. GODESIGN. https://www.puxiang.com/galleries/1e6efd5bbd1d180b04c886ed425d6045? favorite=true/. Accessed 10 Feb 2023

41. Shenzhen street nucleic acid testing houses have been transformed into "mobile fever clinics". https://www.chinanews.com.cn/sh/2022/12-20/9917956.shtml/. Accessed 10 Feb 2023

42. Kaufka, K.: Principles of Gestalt Psychology, no. 12, p. 23. Peking University Press, Beijing (2010). translated by Li Wei

Reproduction of Internal States by Video-Stimulated Recall of Enjoyable Activities

Kanako Obata, Hirotada Ueda, Kei Shimonishi, Kazuaki Kondo,
and Yuichi Nakamura$^{(\boxtimes)}$ ⓘ

Academic Center for Computing and Media Studies, Kyoto University,
Sakyo, Kyoto, Japan
{obata,yuichi}@media.kyoto-u.ac.jp

Abstract. Engaging in enjoyable activities with intimate persons have positive effects on both the physical and mental states of a person. For instance, co-eating or chatting with family members or friends tends to elicit positive emotions and feelings. This research aims to analyze the effects of recalling enjoyable experiences, and to gain insights into developing methods for effectively reproducing positive internal state. For this purpose, we conducted preliminary experiments in which original activities were recorded by videos and a heartbeat monitor, and these videos were presented to some participants after a certain number of days with facial expressions and heartbeats measured in the same ways as the original activities. The results show that facial expressions and heart rate features effectively characterize the internal states in the original experiences and when reviewing the recordings. Moreover, the results suggest that there are conditions for evoking internal states similar to the original experiences.

Keywords: reproduction of internal states · video recall · heart rate · smile

1 Introduction

When we look at photos or videos of our activities with friends or intimate people, we typically feel happy and at peace. The effect is presumably provided by the mechanism by which recall of our experiences significantly induces our emotions and feelings. This research focuses on measuring the effects of the mechanism; to what extent can videos or photos can evoke what types of effects.

This research is motivated by severe social demands for monitoring and preserving mental health from depression, isolation, frail, etc. Reminiscence therapy, one of the dementia treatments, utilizes the effects of early recollection of memories [1]. It aims to improve psychological well-being by retrieving self-efficacy, self-esteem, and the importance of existence by recollecting the early days, typically days at a young age.

P.-L. P. Rau (Ed.): HCII 2023, LNCS 14024, pp. 522–534, 2023.
https://doi.org/10.1007/978-3-031-35946-0_41

One type of the activities we are focusing on is "eating with intimate people," i.e., co-cooking or co-eating. These activities undoubtedly benefit our mental health, not only during the time of activities but also when we reflect on these experiences. Thus, we can anticipate that providing photos or videos records of those activities will have a positive impact.

To analyze those effects, first, we need to measure the internal states both during actual experiences and when recalling them, and then analyze the recalled experiments by comparing the measuring results. For this purpose, we use facial expressions and heartbeats, and confirm the conditions for good effects. Second, we need to determine which portions of the records are more effective to draw good response, i.e., good internal states [3] as stated in episodic memory recall [2]. With these analyses, we can effectively design the use of activity records.

As preliminary experiments, we recorded chatting, co-cooking and co-eating activities and reviewed and analyzed the effects. Thorough experiments, we obtained good clues that support the above framework of inducing good internal states, and obtained some ideas for conditions under which this mechanism works effectively.

2   Activity and Internal States

2.1   Enjoyable Activities

We focus on the activities of chatting, cooking, and eating with intimate persons. We have an enjoyable time chatting and eating special meals together at Christmas time, the new year's day, and other festival seasons. Memories of those experiences are typically recalled triggered by similar dishes or photos, and we retrieve a happy feeling at those activities. This suggests that watching or hearing enough records of those activities would induce good internal states. Hereafter, this process of watching to recall experiences will be referred as the "reviewing process."

To use review processes, we need to consider negative conditions that those records do not provide good effects, e.g., photos or videos are less stimulus and boring, or sometimes even embarrassing. We also need to consider the situation in which a person does not have enough time to watch the records. Considering those backgrounds, we investigated which part of activities (records) cause good effects to the internal states.

2.2   Relationship of Internal States Between Original Expedience and Reviewing Process

We focus on positive internal states, e.g., happy, pleased, delighted, etc. that are most desirable emotions for maintaining mental well-being. Hereafter, we represent them by "positive state". This positive state can be specified by positive valence, and the rightmost area in Russel's circumplex model [4] may represent this state. This area typically causes facial expressions such as smiling, which is occasionally superseded by laughing.

The area does not correspond to a high arousal value in the circumplex, which means that the sympathetic nervous system is not highly active, and that the parasympathetic nervous system is more active than it. This state is considered free from severe stress and strain, and is rather related to a relax mood or feeling. The state is partially measured by heart rate features.

From the above consideration, we employed smile ranking through activities and a video-reviewing process. Smile is easily recognized by humans and possibly by computer vision. We first attempted human rating; however, we are considering automatic smile rating in the future [6,7]. The other measurement is on the heartbeat. Some feature indices of heartbeat e.g., LF/HF, SDNN, and RMSSD, are closely related to the activation of the sympathetic nervous and the parasympathetic nervous systems. The heart rate features are supposed to provide supplemental information to smile ranking by the estimation of a stressed or relaxed state.

The following important points should be clarified:

- How can we reliably measure positive states using facial expressions and heart rate features?
- What are the internal state relationships between the original experience and the reviewing process?
- What are the individual differences among the participants?
- How does the reviewing condition (including the internal state) affect the reviewing results?
- How long does the effect last?

Each of the above points includes a variety of factors, and we first deal with the first and second points in this article.

3   Measurements

We record the states of the participants using videos and a heart rate monitor during original activities and reviewing processes.

3.1   Recording Method

For video recording, we mainly use omnidirectional cameras (GoProMAX) to capture the faces of the participants and important objects such as dish and drink, as shown in Fig. 1(a). If necessary, two or more cameras were placed to capture the faces of the participants and environments. Speeches and other important sounds are recorded and included in the videos. Figure 1(b) shows the recording method for video reviewing. An omnidirectional camera is placed to capture the face of the participant and video content.

Heartbeats are recorded using wearable heart rate monitors (myBeat WHS-1) during both the original activities and reviewing processes. These sensors (monitors) also record acceleration in three dimensions, which is used for data synchronization with the video data[1].

---

[1] The wearing participant jumps while being captured by the video.

(a) original activity   (b) video reviewing

Fig. 1. (a) Original activity and video capturing. Omnidirectional camera(s) is placed to capture the faces of the participants and the environment. (b) Video-reviewing process. Omnidirectional camera(s) is placed to capture the face of the participant and the video monitor.

level 0   level 1   level 2   level 3   level 4   level 5

Fig. 2. Example of smile rating. Facial expressions are classified -1 (negative), 0 (neutral) to 5 (smile with the highest intensity)

3.2 Smile Index

Facial expressions in reviewing video records potentially represent the internal states [5]. For this purpose, a human rater scores facial expressions every second ranging from ?1 to 5, with "0" representing neutral, "5" representing the maximum smile, and ?1 representing negative. Figure 2 shows sample images of facial expressions.

The rating was done by a single person in the following experiments; however, multiple raters will be preferable for future experiments [6,7]. In the current experiments, we do not detect and remove fake smiles, and this is left for future work. Rating results are processed by moving averages to reduce the effects of fluctuations and quantization errors. We use the resultant sequence of the averaged ranks as "smile-index," To analyze the relationships of two facial expression sequences, e.g., person A and B, we calculated the correlation between two sequences of facial expression changes for 10 s.

3.3 Heart Rate Variability

RRI (interval between R waves) has been intensively analyzed. The high-frequency component of RRI (HF) is mainly related to the parasympathetic nervous systems; the low-frequency component of RRI (LF) is related to both the sympathetic and parasympathetic nervous systems. However, because RRI is significantly affected by body movements and other artifacts, LF/HF is commonly used as an index of the activation of the parasympathetic nervous system.

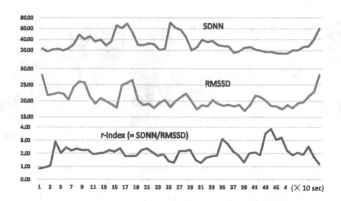

Fig. 3. Sample of heartrate variability (SDNN, RMSSD, r-index (=SDNN/RMSSD))

Thus, a smaller LF/HF value suggests a relaxed mental state, and a larger value suggests a stressed or strained internal state.

LF and HF are indices in the frequency domain, which cannot be reliably calculated in a short period. Alternatively, SDNN and RMSSD are frequently used as indices that are tightly related to the activation of the sympathetic and parasympathetic nervous systems [8,9]. They are calculated as follows.

$$SDNN = \sqrt{\frac{\sum_{i=1}^{N}(I_i - \widetilde{I})^2}{N}} \tag{1}$$

$$RMSSD = \sqrt{\frac{\sum_{i=2}^{N}(I_i - I_{i-1})^2}{N-1}} \tag{2}$$

where I_i represents the i-th RRI of heartbeat, and $\widetilde{I}$ represents the average of RRIs.

RMSSD is considered the index of the superiority of the parasympathetic nervous system to the sympathetic nervous system, which may correspond to the HF element. SDNN is related to the activation of both nervous systems. These indices are also significantly affected by body movements, postures, and speaking acts. The ratio of SDNN and RMSSD (SDNN/RMSSD) is devised to cancel those artifacts by dividing SDNN by RMSSD, both of which values are increased by body movements [10,11]. Hereafter, we represent the ratio as "r-index" ($r =$ SDNN/RMSSD).

It is common to calculate SDNN and RMSSD for 3- to 5-min epochs, and the person being measured is typically requested to stay still (at rest) during the measurement. Our purpose is to measure the internal states of a person while he/she is engaged in activities, such as chatting, cooking, and eating. The internal state in such situations is expected to change more quickly than the above resting case. To deal with this condition, we calculate these indices every 30-s epoch. Figure 3 shows a sample in our experiments. SDNN, RMSSD, and r-index (=SDNN/RMSSD) changed based on both body motions and internal

Table 1. The idea of categorizing internal states by facial expression and heart rate features. P denotes "positive," R denotes "relaxed," S denotes "stressed," m denotes "possible effects of movement," and $*$ denotes "uncertain," that is, "cannot be estimated."

smile-index	small r-index		large r-index	
	large SDNN	small SDNN	large SDNN	small SDNN
large smile-index	$P \oplus Rm$	$P \oplus R$	$P \oplus m$	$P \oplus S$
small smile-index	$* \oplus Rm$	$* \oplus R$	$* \oplus m$	$* \oplus S$

states, and this does not show unacceptable fluctuations. We intensively analyze the proper use of the measurement of these indices in a short epoch such as a 30-s epoch.

3.4 Analysis Using Two Modalities

We analyze videos and heartbeats that are simultaneously recorded in the original activities and their reviewing processes. The meaning of heart rate indices is partially deduced from video recordings by examining motion and speech conditions.

Considering the characteristics of each feature index, we have following classification of internal states as shown in Table 1

- Large smile-index represents positive internal states. However, it does not always express relaxed states. We need to assess heart rate features to clarify it.
- Low r-index suggests relaxed internal states.
- If the r-index is large, we need to check the SDNN value. If the SDNN value is large, we assume that this portion expresses body movements and does not provide clues for a stressed or relaxed state. If the SDNN value is small, it suggests a stressed internal state.

We can use SDNN as a representative of SDNN and RMSSD because both simultaneously become large with body movements. If the SDNN (or RMSSD) value is small, it implies small and negligible body movements. Consequently, a state with a large r-index and small SDNN is considered stressed or strained. In contrast, a state with a large r-index and SDNN does not provide clues for either a stressed or relaxed state, because a large SDNN does not necessarily mean body movements. It is assumed that a small r-index value represents a low LF/HF index and indicate relaxed rather than stressed states.

Hereafter, the feature values f of the i-th participant in the original experience and a reviewing process are denoted as $f_i^o(t)$ and $f_i^r(t)$, respectively. t represents the timeline of the original experience and its record. f can be smile-index (Si), r-index (Ri), SDNN, RMSSD, etc. $\widetilde{f}_{i \neq k}^o(t)$ represents average of f^o for all participants, except the k-th participant.

Fig. 4. Experiment 1: chatting with an intimate friend

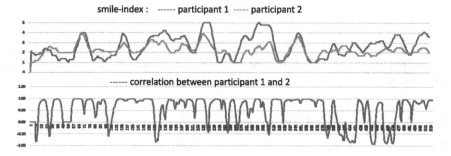

Fig. 5. Smile-index changes in experiment 1

4 Preliminary Experiments

4.1 Recorded Activities

We recorded the following activities.

Experiment 1. Figure 4 shows sample images of the activity of chatting with an intimate friend. We did not notice any significant body movements, such as standing up or walking, from the participants while they sat in front of the table. One participant wore a heart rate monitor. The length of chatting was approximately 25 min. The reviewing process was done by one of the participants alone without communicating with others, as shown in Fig. 1(b). The reviewing process was performed 3 weeks after the original activity.

Experiment 2. Four participants in the same office cooked pancakes together, as shown in Fig. 1(a). Throughout the activity, they chatted, cooked, and ate pancakes, the effects of which were recorded. Each participant wore a heart rate monitor. Two of the participants reviewed the video recording. The reviewing process was performed approximately 5 weeks after the original activity. All reviewing processes were performed by one participant alone without communicating with others.

4.2 Smile and Heart Rate Features

First, we show the measurement results and the analysis results of the original activities. The upper row of Fig. 5 shows smile-index changes through Experi-

smile-index : ------ participant 1 ----- participant 2   participant 3 ----- participant 4

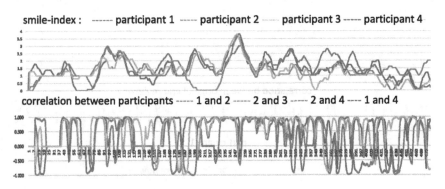

correlation between participants ----- 1 and 2 ----- 2 and 3 ----- 2 and 4 ---- 1 and 4

Fig. 6. Smile-index changes in experiment 2

smile index: ------ original ----- reviewing

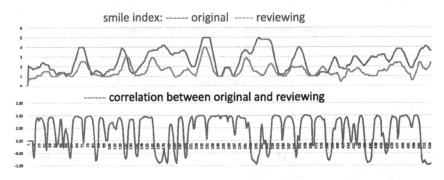

------ correlation between original and reviewing

Fig. 7. Smile-index changes during the reviewing process in Experiment 1

ment 1. As shown in the figure, the smile-indices of both participants are relatively high on average, and peaks intermittently appeared. The correlation between the smile-indices of the two participants throughout the experiment is approximately 0.6, as described in the lower row of Fig. 5. It is mostly positive, which implies that the chatting activity was fun for both participants and that they felt sympathy.

The upper row of Fig. 6 shows smile-index changes through Experiment 2. Similar to Experiment 1, smile-index peaks appear intermittently; however, the intensity is relatively low compared with Experiment 1. The lower row of Fig. 6 shows detailed correlation between participants. The correlation shows more complicated changes in which negative values frequently appeared, presumably due to sophisticated communications among four participants while attention was frequently paid to the cooking tasks such as success or failure of each process.

Figure 7 shows the smile-index during the reviewing process in Experiment 1. In the original activity, body motions significantly affected the indices; however, in a reviewing process, body movements are negligible, and the indices are expected to represent mostly internal states. The lower row of the figure depicts the correlation to the original activity. Mostly, similar facial expressions appeared

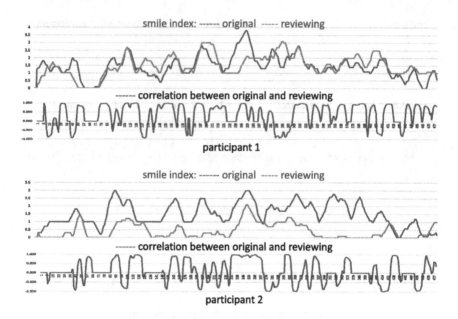

Fig. 8. Smile-index changes during the reviewing processes in Experiment 2

as the original activity even though some portions have a lower correlation, and the reason for this is discussed below.

Figure 8 shows the smile-index during the reviewing process in Experiment 2. The baseline of the intensity is stable and lower than that of the original activity, especially for participant 2; however, there are some significant peaks almost aligned with the peaks of the original activities.

Figure 9 and 10 show the heart rate features through Experiments 1 and 2. The figures show that SDNN and RMSSD have almost the same trend and peak positions, with a correlation of approximately 0.9. This supports the above discussion in Sect. 3.4 that we can use either of them to detect trends and peaks. Different from those indices, r-index has a lower baseline and intermittent spikes that suggest the activation of the sympathetic nervous system. In the experiments, many of those peaks correspond to situations with significant body movements or intensive chatting.

Each SDNN, RMSSD, and r-index correlation between participants is low, with the majority of them being close to zero. Examples of details are shown in Fig. 9(b) and Fig. 10(b). Positive and negative portions alternated, implying that raw heart rate features are not systematically synchronized.

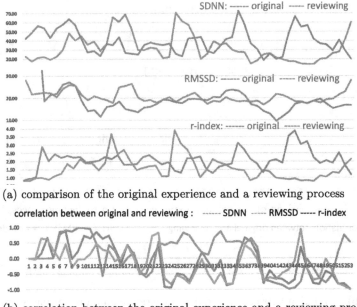

(a) comparison of the original experience and a reviewing process

(b) correlation between the original experience and a reviewing process

Fig. 9. Heart rate features in Experiment 1

4.3 Relationship Between the Original and Reviewing

Before discussing the relationships, we first categorize the situations in the original activities. The following are four typical situations that cause peaks (local maxima) of smile-index or local extrema of r-index.

Suppose that we are focusing on one participant, denoted by X, and others are denoted by Y_i.

(A) body movements or discussion of Y_i created a lively mood
(B) body movements or discussion of X created a lively mood
(C) body movements or discussion of X and one or more Y_i created a lively mood
(D) body movements or discussion of X or Y_i had no significant effect on mood

As shown in the above examples, smile-index peaks in the original activities typically resulted in smile-index peaks in a reviewing process. Generally, smile-index has a significant correlation between the Original experience and a reviewing process, that is, denoted as correlation(Si_i^o, Si_i^r). The lower parts of Fig. 5 and Fig. 6 show examples. Correlation between self smile-index in the original experience and that in a reviewing process (correlation(Si_i^o, Si_i^r) = 0.59 in Fig. 5 case) is slightly higher than the correlation to other members (correlation($Si_{k \neq i}^o$, Si_i^r) = 0.42 in Fig. 5 case). This suggests that smile reproduction strongly depends on the self internal states of the original experiment rather than the atmosphere in the original experiment.

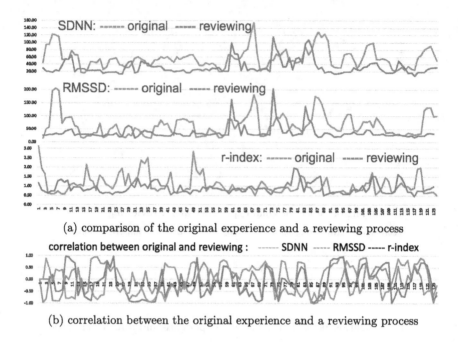

(a) comparison of the original experience and a reviewing process

(b) correlation between the original experience and a reviewing process

Fig. 10. Heart rate features in Experiment 2

More precisely, the above categories (A) and (C) are the most frequent Types, where larger peaks are reproduced in a reviewing process. Category (B) also occasionally reproduces smile-index peaks in a reviewing process; however, the frequency is less, and the peak values are typically lower than those of category (C). Smile-index peaks in a reviewing process always have corresponding peaks in the original experiences. We did not observe smile-index peaks without the corresponding peaks in the original experiences.

Looking at heart rate indices, the correlation between the original and reviewing process is approximately 0, which is similar to that between participants. However, some extrema indicating relaxed/stressed states in the original experience may have induced relaxed/stressed states during a reviewing process, as indicated by the red/green solid lines on the graph in Fig. 11. These are typical examples of the above categories (A) and (C) for relaxed states, (D) for stressed or strained states, or unrelated to positive internal states. Counter samples that do not follow this idea are at the dotted orange lines in the same graph, and the situation corresponds to (B). This is probably because watching the participant's behaviors objectively is sometimes embarrassing, which may cause stress. One of the participants introspected that he/she felt embarrassed in watching his/her big smiles/laughs. In this regard, when one participant's behaviors amused the others, the person and others may exhibit different trends. For example, the person has a higher r-index (stressed or strained), whereas the others have a lower r-index (relaxed).

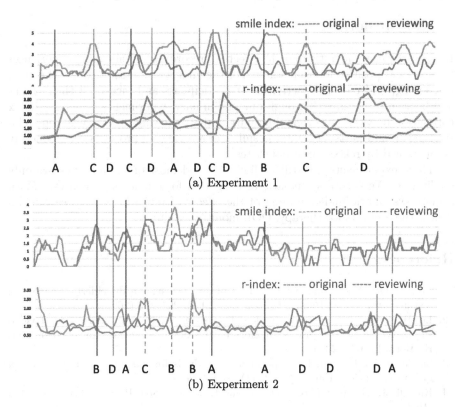

Fig. 11. Relationship on internal states between the original experience and a reviewing process in (a) Experiment 1 and (b) Experiment 2 (Color figure online)

Next, let us consider the mutual relationships between facial expressions and heart rate features. The red solid lines in Fig. 11 correspond to $P \oplus R(m)$, and the green solid lines correspond to $* \oplus S$ given in Table 1. If those conditions are satisfied, the same internal states tend to be induced, as demonstrated in the example. The orange solid lines represent $P \oplus S$, which correspond to the above categories (B) or (C) in which the participant's actions elicited a positive mood and smiles. In such cases, smiles may also appear, but they tend to be weaker than in the typical cases of (C).

The orange dotted lines represent $P \oplus m$. Although smiles may appear in a reviewing process of such portions, smiles tend to be significantly weaker, and internal states show stressed states such as $P \oplus S$ or $* \oplus S$. Most of these types correspond to the cases that we already discussed in the above cases, that is, the participant was slightly embarrassed. Another possibility is that the participant recalled the sophisticated situations, e.g., the participant pretended to smile (a wry smile) a little bit in the original experiment.

In addition, intense smiles frequently occur ($P \oplus Rm$) just after some stressed situations in which r-index is relatively high ($* \oplus S$). This can be also a good clue to finding portions that reproduce positive internal states.

5   Conclusion

In this article, we investigated the effects of recordings of enjoyable experiences to reproduce positive internal states. For the analyses, we recorded the chatting, co-cooking, and co-eating activities of participants and measured their smiles and heart rate features. Through our preliminary experiments, the smile-index correlation between the original activity and a reviewing process was kept relatively high, and parts with intense smiles in a reviewing process were frequently accompanied by relaxed internal states.

These experiments are still preliminary, and most of the analyses are only qualitative. We need a systematic investigation for quantitative analysis. With a more systematic understanding of the effects of reviewing processes, we can expect those effects for therapy, QOL monitoring, etc.

References

1. Lin, Y., Dai, Y., Hwang, S.: The effect of reminiscence on the elderly population: a systematic review. Public Health Nurs. **20**(4), 297–306 (2003)
2. Le, H., Clinch, S., Sas, C., Dingler, T., Henze, N., Davies, N.: Impact of video summary viewing on episodic memory recall - design guidelines for video summarizations. In: CHI 2016 (2016)
3. Siedlecka, E., Denson, F.: Experimental methods for inducing basic emotions: a qualitative review. Emot. Rev. **11**(1), 87–97 (2019)
4. Russell, J.: A circumplex model of affect. J. Pers. Soc. Psychol. **36**, 1161–1178 (1980)
5. Haj, M., Daoudi, M., Gallouj, K., Moustafa, A., Nandrino, J.: When your face describes your memories: facial expressions during retrieval of autobiographical memories. Rev. Neurosci. (2018)
6. Hideo, J., Jacopo, S., Nicu, S., Joemon, J.: Looking at the viewer: analysing facial activity to detect personal highlights of multimedia contents. Multimed. Tools Appl. **51**, 505–523 (2011)
7. Kondo, K., Nakamura, T., Nakamura, Y., Sato, S.: Siamese-structure deep neural network recognizing changes in facial expression according to the degree of smiling. In: The 25th International Conference on Pattern Recognition (ICPR 2020) (2021)
8. Otzenberger, H., Gronfier, C., Simon, C., et al.: Dynamic heart rate variability: a tool for exploring sympathovagal balance continuously during sleep in men. Am. J. Physiol. **275**(3), H946–H950 (1998)
9. Balocchi, R., Cantini, F., Varanini, M., Raimondi, G., Legra-mante, J., Macerata, A.: Revisiting the potential of time-domain indexes in short-term HRV analysis. Biomed. Tech. **51**(4), 190–193 (2006)
10. Sollers, J., Buchanan, T., Mowrer, S., Hill, L., Thayer, J.: Comparison of the ratio of the standard deviation of the R-R interval and the root mean squared successive differences (SD/rMSSD) to the low frequency-to-high frequency (LF/HF) ratio in a patient population and normal healthy controls. Biomed. Sci. Instrum. **43**, 158–163 (2007)
11. Wang, H.-M., Huang, S.-C.: SDNN/RMSSD as a surrogate for LF/HF: a revised investigation. Model. Simul. Eng. **2012**, Article ID 931943 (2012)

An Intervention Design Study for Mobile Phone Addiction in Sleep Scenarios

Yunxiang Shi[✉], Jingnan Zhang, Lanke Li, and Wenbo Qu

Hunan University, Changsha 410082, China
yunxiang@hnu.edu.cn

Abstract. The study explores the problem of mobile phone addiction in sleep scenarios and analyzes the possibility of designing interventions to address the problem of mobile phone addiction. Literature research, case studies, questionnaire research and mass media research are used to explore how to mitigate the negative effects of mobile phone addiction on sleep from a design perspective. Based on relevant research in the field of behavioral interventions, a strategy for applying active intervention operationalization to design interventions for mobile phone addiction in sleep scenarios is proposed. Based on this strategy, a night light is designed to stop users' excessive use of mobile phones in sleep scenes. In conclusion, this study has a certain reference value and guidance for future design in this field.

Keywords: Mobile Phone Addiction · Anti-addiction · Product Design · Self-regulation

1 Introduction

With the rapid development of information technology, mobile phones have become an important part of life. According to the 50th Statistical Report on the Development of the Internet in China, as of June 2022, the number of Internet users in China was 1.051 billion, and the Internet penetration rate reached 74.4%. From daily social interaction to leisure and entertainment, from transportation to information access, mobile phones have become the link between humans and the world, delivering a constant stream of information and exciting pleasure.

At the same time, more and more people are spending more and more time on their mobile phones than they can control, leading to addictive dependency. Mobile phone addiction is becoming a worldwide phenomenon [1], and its adverse effects have attracted the attention of many researchers. Studies have shown that mobile phone addiction can have a negative impact on an individual's academic performance and interpersonal relationships, and is closely linked to lower life satisfaction and psychological problems such as anxiety, depression and even suicidal ideation [2–4]. In addition, mobile phone addiction also has a serious impact on sleep quality and sleep status, especially in young people, causing sleep delay or other negative effects on physical and mental health [5].

P.-L. P. Rau (Ed.): HCII 2023, LNCS 14024, pp. 535–545, 2023.
https://doi.org/10.1007/978-3-031-35946-0_42

2 Literature Review

2.1 Overview of Mobile Phone Addiction

As for the criteria for judging mobile phone addiction, foreign scholars tend to judge mobile phone addiction from two perspectives: excessive use (including time and frequency of use) and post-use reactions (i.e., psychological, physiological and social relationships), while domestic scholars rely on the criteria for judging behavioral addiction and prefer mobile phone addiction as a psychological disease. In other words, at present, domestic and foreign scholars do not have a unified standard of judgment [6]. In this paper, cell phone addiction is defined as a person who has difficulty controlling his or her own behavior and is excessively dependent on mobile phones, with a continuous and strong sense of craving and dependence on mobile phones, which has a certain negative impact on the user's physiological, psychological and social behaviors, and when he or she cannot use the mobile phone normally, he or she will have emotional addictive behaviors such as anxiety, irritability and breakdown.

Mobile phone addiction has four characteristics: (1) excessive use, long time and high frequency of use; (2) withdrawal avoidance, using mobile phone as a refuge and difficult to use appropriately; (3) impaired function, difficult to control behavior, damage to physical and mental health, anxiety and sense of loss, and behavioral disorders; (4) tolerance, uncontrollable craving for Internet access, and in an obsessive state [7].

State of Addiction. In terms of academic and work performance, there is a lack of concentration, reduced thinking ability, and an aversion to school or work, which adversely affect school or work; in terms of physiological health, playing mobile phones for a long time is likely to cause somatic discomfort, such as tinnitus, eye strain, headache, spinal disease and other health problems, and sleep disorder is one of the common symptoms of mobile phone addicts [8]; In terms of mental health, less contact with social Insufficient emotional needs can lead to poor interpersonal relationships, easily generate feelings of loneliness and emptiness, experience less access and lower value, easily generate low self-esteem, and increase stress due to staying awake for long periods of time, thus promoting the generation of psychological problems such as depression [9]. That is, cell phone addiction promotes the generation of psychological problems such as depression, anxiety, loneliness, and irritability [10]; in terms of social functioning, cell phone addicts are more likely to have cognitive biases, procrastination, inattention, and behavioral execution problems [11]. In real life, they show more low self-esteem, fear of socializing, and are also prone to adverse situations such as deteriorating interpersonal relationships [12].

2.2 Causes of Addiction

Mobile phone addiction is mainly related to two aspects: individual characteristics and environmental characteristics. Individual characteristics include self-control ability, personality traits, psychological needs, etc. Research shows that poor self-control is more likely to become addicted; low self-esteem, low self-esteem, sensitivity and introversion are more likely to become addicted to mobile phones; users have needs for information acquisition, entertainment, communication, emotional affiliation, etc. Environmental characteristics include family environment, i.e. lack of communication and unmet emotional needs in the family environment due to fast-paced and stressful life, so they choose to join the Internet. In terms of social environment, the use of mobile phones has become common, and the functions of mobile phones are gradually diversifying, so that consumers can shop, order food, communicate, entertain, study and other aspects of content on their mobile phones, which leads to an increase in the use of time.

3 Definition of Sleep Procrastination and Related Studies

Sleep procrastination is the failure to go to bed on time and the decision to postpone bedtime when there are no external factors that interfere with the freedom to schedule bedtime. Sleep procrastination is associated with self-regulation, mobile phone addiction, stress and compensatory psychology. Studies have found that delayed sleep is more likely to occur in people with poor self-regulation. Some people who self-regulate too much during the day because they are busy with work, school or other things may also become less disciplined about going to sleep on time at night, resulting in sleep procrastination.

Sleep procrastination is different from common sense procrastination, which refers to the things that should be done but one does not want to do. People have a neutral or positive attitude towards sleep and do not hate it per se, but they procrastinate because they are tempted or disturbed by external things and have no way of stopping for a while, resulting in a weakened sense of wanting to sleep [13]. Procrastination not only delays sleep but also affects sleep quality. This is partly because sleep does not occur at the planned time, i.e. self-regulation fails, and negative emotions such as remorse and guilt affect sleep quality.

Studies have shown that mobile phones affect sleep quality. The higher the level of mobile phone addiction or dependence, the worse the quality of sleep. Playing mobile phone before bedtime, mobile phone will have electronic field and blue light generation, which has a certain harmful effect on eyes, leading to poor sleep and daytime sleepiness [14]. Mobile phone content continues to stimulate the brain, making mental activity, not only affect the time to fall asleep will also cause people to produce excitement, leading to a decline in sleep quality. Long periods of unconscious playing with mobile phones can cause confusion in work and rest.

4 How to Intervene the Theoretical Basis of Addiction

As an important cognitive factor, the source of psychological control affects individual values and behaviors. Meanwhile, the behaviors also continuously strengthen the source of psychological control, which forms the inherent reaction and specific behavior pattern after repeated practice verification. According to existing studies, psychological locus of control, as a personality characteristic of human beings, has certain different effects on mobile phone addiction in different dimensions: Internal control is negatively correlated with mobile phone addiction, and it is negatively correlated with the prominent behavior of mobile phone addiction. Mobile phone addiction is positively correlated with opportunity and influential others in all dimensions, and individuals with external control tendency of opportunity and influential others are more likely to have mobile phone addiction tendency. Therefore, the psychological control source can be used as the theoretical basis for effective intervention of mobile phone addiction [15].

Relevant studies show that the sources of psychological control are divided into internal control and external control tendencies, which are converted into each other with the assistance of training or other means. From the perspective of psychological control, the theory of source of psychological control divides people into two categories: internal control and external control. People with internal control tendencies are usually self-aware, able to control their own behavior, and have a positive attitude towards things. Those with external control tendency are more likely to have a negative attitude when they are stimulated by external factors. This paper explores the psychological factors of addiction to mobile phones from the psychological level of those with external control tendencies, introduces the theory of psychological control source into product design, and provides the psychological basis and starting point for the design output of mobile phone addiction users.

Developing a mental model of the target user is fundamental to interaction design. Based on the basic model of mobile phone anti-addiction interaction design strategy, starting from the reaction inhibition disorder and planning disorder of mobile phone addicts, combined with the mental model of mobile phone addicts, a mobile phone anti-addiction interaction strategy conforming to the cognition of mobile phone addicts is designed. The designer model is simulated from the perspective of designer through user research, hoping to approach the mental model of addicted mobile phone users. As the basis for anti-addiction interaction design of mobile phones, the mental model of mobile phone addicts is analyzed through user research and market research, and in-depth analysis is made through psychological control source, and then the mental model of mobile phone addicted users is constructed.

In the early stage of design, the mental model of mobile phone addicts is fully studied, so as to get closer to the psychological expectations of mobile phone addicts, and products with good user experience are designed so that mobile phone addicts can operate easily and quickly according to their existing cognition.

Anti-addiction interactive design strategy is a series of actions, thinking and choices in the design process. This strategy is to build the "S-P" model of mobile phone addiction prevention on the basis of the mental model of mobile phone addiction. Starting from the reaction inhibition disorder and planning disorder of mobile phone addicts, combined with the mental model of mobile phone addicts, an interactive strategy of mobile phone addiction prevention is designed in line with the cognition of mobile phone addiction [16].

5 Design Intervention Advantage

5.1 Sleep Delay and Self-regulation

Self-regulation refers to an individual's ability to flexibly plan, direct, and monitor personal behavior to achieve goals, and to consciously and actively adjust their motivation and behavior to achieve their desired goals over time and in response to changing circumstances. Self-regulation is an important influence on procrastination. Most studies have focused on the relationship between students' mobile phone addiction and college students' academic procrastination or procrastination in general, and concluded that mobile phone addiction positively predicts irrational procrastination. Based on the self-regulatory resource theory, individuals who consume more self-regulatory resources during the day and lack sufficient resources to resist late sleep behavior fail to self-regulate and experience sleep procrastination.

The study found that a proportion of subjects who tended to delay sleep hoped to go to bed on time, but did not. Evidence that sleeping procrastinators may experience difficulties in translating sleep intention into behavior. From the time-limited self-regulation theory hypothesis, time, behavioral dominance and self-regulatory ability all have an effect on sleep procrastination behavior. When the self-regulation theory fails, external help or intervention is needed to enter sleep when the sleep intention played becomes weaker or loses its effect.

5.2 Behavior-Change Strategies

The main advantage of behavioral design can be the implicit incorporation of interventions into artifacts, reducing the likelihood of conscious recognition and the possibility of negating awareness of the intended effect. Contrast this with persuasive design's usual focus on positive, technically facilitative strategies in which interventions are offered to users that drive counterproductive effects. Behavioral design aims at automatic response, eliminating possible counterproductive effects through implicit effects, while preserving freedom of choice [17]. Behavior can be described as: antecedent (trigger) > behavior > consequence (outcome). Design interventions can target: conscious and unconscious thought systems based on dual process theory.

Based on the above background, the general information strategy is broken down into: pure information strategy and positive motivation strategy. Pure information emphasizes awareness of the problem, and how future behavior will affect this. Positive motivation encourages people to perform specific actions. Both types emphasize freedom of choice. The key to implicit intervention is that both information and positive motivation can be achieved through physical cues, such as pictures, objects, or written materials. Cues change the context and background of the behavior and provide a trigger for change. Cues can be delivered in a variety of ways and can be formulated for conscious or unconscious decision making.

This illustrates the different routes available in designing behavior change. Each rout highlights a different strategy, as well as different behavioral (antecedent-consequence) and cognitive goals (conscious-unconscious). These can be further modified by the way influence is exerted versus the type of artifact used. Thus, behavior change design poses a multidimensional problem that contains many interactive elements that are also culture and context dependent.

5.3 Application of Behavioral Intervention Design Strategies

A brief behavioral sleep intervention trial showed that ADHD symptoms, behavior, daily functioning, quality of life, and working memory were effectively improved six months after a randomized intervention for sleep onset moments [18]. It was found that a significant proportion of subjects with a tendency to delay sleep time subjectively wanted to fall asleep on time. From the time-limited self-regulation theory hypothesis, time, behavioral dominance and self-regulatory ability all have an effect on sleep procrastination behavior [19]. When self-regulation fails, external help is needed to enter the sleep state when the role played by sleep intention becomes weaker. Therefore, the aim of the design intervention is to help those who are experiencing difficulties in converting sleep intention into behavior, to enter the sleep state.

6 Design Practice

6.1 User Research and Insights

Questionnaire Research. The Pittsburgh Sleep Quality Index (PSQI) and the Mobile Phone Addiction Index (MPAI) were adapted to create a research questionnaire that was distributed using the Questionnaire Star platform. The participants of this survey were mainly 20–30 years old, and 104 valid questionnaires were collected. Descriptive statistics, reliability analysis, t-test, and correlation analysis were conducted using SPSS 26.0 to understand the overall situation of mobile phone addiction, sleep delay, sleep quality, and correlation. The results of the study were as follows.

(1) Sleep habits

The respondents generally went to bed later than the optimal sleep time of 11 p.m. in the past month, and the length of sleep was shorter than the normal time of 8 h. Only 11.54% of the population fell asleep before 23:00 at night, and 38.49% of them chose to sleep after 1:00 in the morning. In terms of sleep duration, only 25.96% of the population reached the normal sleep duration of 8 h.

(2) Sleep quality

Statistics show that 45.19% of people said that they had medium to high quality sleep in the past month, and the average sleep quality accounted for 1/3 of the total number of people. 40.00% of the people said that the delayed sleep caused by playing mobile phone will affect the state of the next day, and 28.57% said that the delayed sleep will affect both the quality of sleep and the state of the next day.

(3) Mobile phone management

According to the analysis of the results, 68.57% of the population will choose to use the mobile phone before going to sleep without message notification and use purpose. In the questionnaire, 10% of the people have the tendency to be addicted to mobile phones, among which 85.71% of the people choose to focus on the entertainment aspect and 80.00% of the subjects focus on the social aspect of mobile phone use.

(4) Self-control

The results show that 82.69% of people usually plan their bedtime habits at night, and 53.49% of them choose to plan their time before lights out at night. However, only 20.93% of people will go to sleep strictly according to the original planned time, and 84.88% of people will choose to delay 10-60min to really fall asleep. Delayed sleep 81.4% of respondents said they have a habit of using their smartphones before bedtime, which leads to a delay in going to sleep.

Analysis of the survey results led to the following conclusions.

(1) Respondents generally stay up late, as evidenced by late bedtimes and short sleep duration.
(2) There is a significant positive correlation between cell phone addiction and sleep procrastination, and mobile phone addiction reduces the ability to self-regulate, resulting in sleep delay.
(3) There is a significant positive correlation between mobile phone addiction and sleep quality.
(4) There is a positive correlation between sleep procrastination and sleep quality; mobile phone addiction affects sleep procrastination, which in turn reduces sleep quality.
(5) The respondents' self-restraint ability is at a medium level, and some of them want to take the initiative to restrain themselves with external objects or people.

Interview Research. Ten young people aged between 18 and 30 were selected for semi-structured interviews, among whom 5 were studying in school and 5 were already working, so as to have an in-depth understanding of the sleep dilemma of young users and their expectations of mobile anti-addiction products in sleep scenes.

According to the content of the user interview, many keywords in the process of answering and communicating are extracted and summarized as follows: 7 of the above 10 interviewees choose to sleep late due to course assignments and work tasks. Through the interview on their sleep process, it is found that there are problems such as sleep procrastination, addiction to mobile phones and other electronic products, poor sleep quality and so on. The respondents have certain sleep management methods, such as using sleep guide APP and listening to novels to fall asleep, and also use sleep aid earplugs, sleep pillows, sleep aid aromatherapy and other tools. Respondents mentioned that some sleep management apps are not effective and some functions need to be paid for.

Based on the above research and analysis, this practice will start from the application of behavior change strategies in intervention design, and design products aimed at the problem of mobile phone addiction before going to bed, so as to reduce sleep procrastination and improve the sleep quality of users.

6.2   Design Concept

The analysis of user research shows that there is significant overuse of mobile phones among young people, which exacerbates sleep procrastination, and that a large proportion of those affected by this problem have weak self-regulatory skills and are unable to overcome or resolve the problem by themselves. Based on theoretical research on behavioural interventions, it is clear that a simpler and more effective way to intervene by design is to operationalize active interventions that prevent users from using their phones excessively at bedtime by actively isolating manipulation or interference in the context of avoiding the negative effects of mobile phone addiction on sleep. Therefore, after discussing and thinking about this design path, the team decided that it would be more natural for the intervention to occur by superimposing it on the product needed for the sleep scenario, so the team chose a night light as the design object, using the night light to prompt the user to put down the phone at the required time.

In terms of design details, the team collected relevant ideas on keywords such as 'time', 'rule' and 'reminder', and chose 'hourglass' as the final product appearance reference. "The hourglass is traditionally perceived as a symbol of the passing of time and the finite nature of time, which plays a positive psychological role. In order to make the intervention of asking the user to put down the mobile phone appear more powerful, wireless charging and identification functions are added to the design solution to monitor whether the user puts down the mobile phone or not, which can also bring convenience to life during sleep, as shown in Fig. 1.

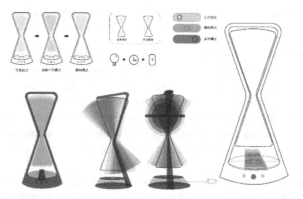

Fig. 1.   Concept of the sleep light.

6.3   Design Display

The anti-addiction night light in the sleeping scene has the function of intervening users' excessive use of mobile phones based on the lighting function, as shown in Fig. 2. Before the user goes to sleep, the small night light is kept in a weak static state. 15 min before the set sleep time, the user is reminded of information through the mobile APP, as shown in Fig. 3. If the user is at rest at this time, place the mobile phone at the bottom of the night light to charge and automatically end the intervention function of the night light. 15 min later, if the user does not place the mobile phone at the bottom of the night light and is at rest, the night light will change from a weak static state to a strong blinking state until the user places the mobile phone at the bottom of the night light. The small night light is changed from a strong blinking state to a light still state. At this point, the small night light intervention process is complete, as shown in Fig. 4.

Fig. 2. The schematic diagram of the sleep light product.

Fig. 3. APP user interface of the sleep light product.

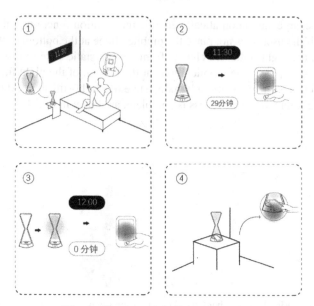

Fig. 4. The sleep night light using steps.

7 Conclusion

This paper investigates the problem of mobile phone addiction in sleep scenes, and proposes a feasible way of design intervention from the perspective of behavioural interventions. By using the "hourglass" as the main intention of the design, the user is given a psychological hint that time is passing, and wireless charging is added to the design practice to facilitate the design practice incorporates features such as wireless charging, which facilitates daily life and also serves as a monitoring function. This product system design practice confirms the effectiveness of design interventions in solving the problem of mobile phone addiction in sleep scenarios, and provides some research value and guidance for future design in this field.

References

1. He, J.B., Chen, C.R., Bao, Y.C., Lei, Y.J.: A probe into mobile phone dependence in adolescents: measurement, harmfulness and genesis mechanism. Chin. J. Clin. Psychol. **20**(6), 822–825 (2012)
2. Chen, L., Yan, Z., Tang, W., et al.: Mobile phone addiction levels and negative emotions among Chinese young adults: the mediating role of interpersonal problems. Comput. Hum. Behav. **55**, 856–866 (2016)
3. Seo, D.G., Park, Y., Kim, M.K., Park, J.: Mobile phone dependency and its impacts on adolescents' social and academic behaviors. Comput. Hum. Behav. **63**, 282–292 (2016)
4. Li, J., Lepp, A., Barkley, J.E.: Locus of control and cell phone use: implications for sleep quality, academic performance, and subjective well-being. Comput. Hum. Behav. **52**, 450–457 (2015)

5. Liu, Q., Zhou, Z., Niu, G., Fan, C.: Mobile phone addiction and sleep quality in adolescents: mediation and moderation analyses. Acta Psych. Sinica **49**(12), 1524–1536 (2017)
6. Xu, B., Zhang, B.: A survey of mobile phone dependence and anxiety, depression and sleep quality amongst medical college freshmen. Chin. Gener. Pract. **22**(29), 3596 (2019)
7. Lin, Y.H., Chang, L.R., Lee, Y.H., et al.: Development and validation of the smartphone addiction inventory (SPAI). PLoS ONE **9**(6), e98312 (2014)
8. Beranuy, M., Oberst, U., Carbonell, X., Chamarro, A.: Problematic Internet and mobile phone use and clinical symptoms in college students: the role of emotional intelligence. Comput. Hum. Behav. **25**(5), 1182–1187 (2009)
9. Chuchu, X., Jin, X., Xinyu, W., Hai, H., Chunyan, Z.: Research progress of smartphone addiction interventions in adolescents. Chin. J. Sch. Health **43**(8), 1276–1280 (2022)
10. Li, L., Songli, M.: Impulsivity, other related factors and therapy of smartphone addiction in college students, pp. 105–106 (2016)
11. Wei, H., Ding, H., Huang, F., He, A., et, al.: The relationship between need for uniqueness and college students' mobile phone addiction: the chain mediating role of anxiety and effortful control. Chin. J. Clin. Psychol. **30**(2), 5 (2022)
12. Wang, H., Sun, H.: Effect of self-esteem on depression in college students: Mediating role of mobile phone addition. Chin. J. Health Psych. **30**(11), 1698–1702 (2022)
13. Wei, D., Zhaoliang, L.: The Impact of Short Video Addiction on Sleep Quality among College Students: A Chain Mediation Effect of Self -regulation and Bedtime Procrastination, pp. 9–10 (2022)
14. Chen, X., Jing, J., Jiang, L.: Correlation between mobile phone use behavior, mobile phone dependence syndrome, and sleep quality in medical college students. Mod. Prevent. Med. **43**(21), 3957–3960 (2016)
15. Liu, Z.: Concept and main research relationships of locus of control. Soc. Sci. Manage. Rev. (02), 59–72+112 (2013)
16. Sun, S.Q.: Research on mobile phone anti-addiction Interaction Design based on the Locus of control theory. Xi 'an University of Architecture and Technology
17. Lian, S., Feng, Q., Yan, J., Zhang, Y.: Mobile phone addiction, irrational procrastination and depression or anxiety: the protective role of mindfulness. Chin. J. Clin. Psychol **29**(18), 51–55 (2021)
18. Nauts, S., Kamphorst, B.A., Stut, W., De Ridder, D.T., Anderson, J.H.: The explanations people give for going to bed late: a qualitative study of the varieties of bedtime procrastination. Behav. Sleep Med. **17**(6), 753–762 (2019)
19. Hiscock, H.,et al.: Impact of a behavioural sleep intervention on symptoms and sleep in children with attention deficit hyperactivity disorder, and parental mental health: randomised controlled trial. BMJ (2015)

Research on the Application of Ceramic Art Therapy in University Students' Mental Health Education

Xiao Song and Mingming Zong[✉]

Beijing Technology Institute, Zhuhai, People's Republic of China
842766039@qq.com

Abstract. Art is a natural human need. The game theory about the origin of art, imitation theory, residual energy catharsis theory, all involve human nature and emotional expression. Art is the natural expression of mental state and personality characteristics. The research on art education and psychotherapy is based on the research results of RON Field, an American art educator in the middle of the 20th century. In his book Creation and the Growth of the Mind, he discusses the issue of "therapy through art education". He regards art creation as a tool to express behavior and emotion, and art as a tool to achieve self-cognition. The therapeutic essence of art education is to use creative activities as a method of self-cognition. This view has found an important theoretical basis for art therapy, and also pointed out the integration point of art therapy and art education. The goal of achieving self-realization through artistic activities and promoting the development of sound personality is consistent.

Ceramic art is a discipline that requires strong practical ability, expressive ability and creative ability. In the process of treating patients, clay can be used as a material to express behaviors and emotions, and as a method of self-cognition through making and creating activities. Ideal art therapy is also a kind of art education, which can be used not only to guide people to understand an object, but also to guide people to visually reproduce the object. The popularization of ceramic art design in Colleges and Universities education can also play a healing effect in solving the psychological problems of Colleges and Universities students. The clay making process can be used as a way for Colleges and Universities students to solve problems and express their feelings and ideas, and help students get out of the trouble caused by some environmental, memory or emotional problems. And look for the potential and emotional strength that students show in the process of making ceramic objects, which can be strengthened to support the life of Colleges and Universities students after treatment.

Researchers in universities in the form of questionnaires, research university student common psychological problems and the acceptance of ceramic art teaching way, on the basis of data analysis for ceramic art of mental health education course construction, gradually formed in view of the Colleges and Universities students mental health care system of ceramic art education, through effective teaching link, The use of ceramic art education can not only cultivate the aesthetic ability, but also cultivate the heart and temperament, so as to find and treat the mental health problems of Colleges and Universities students in time.

P.-L. P. Rau (Ed.): HCII 2023, LNCS 14024, pp. 546–556, 2023.
https://doi.org/10.1007/978-3-031-35946-0_43

Keywords: Art therapy · Ceramic art therapy · Colleges and Universities · Mental health education

1 Introduction

In recent years, college students' mental health education has increasingly become a difficulty in college education. Especially in the wake of the COVID-19 pandemic in 2020, According to a survey conducted by relevant researchers on the mental health status of college students, the mental health level of college students is relatively low during the epidemic period. Compulsion, interpersonal relationship and anxiety are the top three psychological questions in the survey results.How to further enhance college students' mental health education and improve the effectiveness of crisis intervention has become a realistic and urgent research topic.

The research team is composed of teachers with many years of experience in pottery education and mental health education.The researchers observed that some students with mental disorders refocused on their studies after taking ceramic art and design courses, They gradually began to be willing to communicate with teachers and classmates around them, and their personalities were more lively and cheerful than before.Researchers believe that the clay material provides an effective method for communication, allowing learners to listen to the natural wisdom of the body through hand-making. In the process of making, ceramic art stimulates one's creativity due to its own design needs, and makes learners full of vitality. Through observation, the researchers hope to help students with psychological disorders treat their own inner experience more kindly by focusing on ceramic art design and production in a new way, so that they can get healing in the process of making ceramic art and design works from the experience of the body, and take a firm step towards change.

2 Literature Review

2.1 Focusing-Oriented Therapy

Focusing is a mind-body integration exercise that encourages people to bring a welcoming, friendly attitude to the experience that is relevant to the problem, situation, or experience they are facing. Listening opens the door to physical wisdom – the next steps one will take toward growth and healing. Instead of jumping straight to conclusions or falling into habitual thinking patterns, focusing offers a new perspective on how the whole of your being is experiencing the present situation in the present moment – your mind, body, and spirit [1].

Focusing-Oriented Therapy (FOT) [2], "Focus" for short is one of the most important branches of the modern development of human-centered therapy, also known as experience-oriented therapy. Focused psychotherapy originated from the research of psychotherapy and counseling conducted by Carl Ranson Rogers to find effective treatment methods. Later, the famous American philosopher and psychologist Dr. Gendlin formally founded the classic focus in 1980, and the focus further developed. New forms of focus oriented psychotherapy, dream focus, child focus, whole body focus, internal relationship focus, regional focus, community work focus, and interactive focus were also developed successively. It has greatly enriched the theory, practice and application of humanistic psychological orientation therapy [3].

2.2 Psycho-Educational Orientation

Psycho-educational orientation approach is a kind of psychotherapy based on behaviorism theory, cognitive theory and developmental psychology theory, which implements intervention treatment for people with behavioral, cognitive or emotional disorders. It mainly includes art therapy, cognitive behavioral art therapy and developmental art therapy.

Cognitive Behavioral therapy (CBT), as a traditional means of psychotherapy, still has some problems after long development. Margarita Tartakovsky summarized the most critical points: Cognitive behavioral therapy (CBT) model fixation is inflexible, it only changes patients' negative thoughts to positive ones, and CBT does not believe that people's subjective consciousness and emotions will affect the therapeutic effect. Tartakovsky adds that CBT ignores the patient's experiences and especially the formative process of childhood. After nearly 30 years of development, cognitive Behavioral Art therapy (CBAT) has gradually been accepted by experts in the field of art therapy. It makes up for the shortcomings of CBT by integrating art into CBT and emphasizing the interaction and emotional experience with patients [4].

2.3 Art Therapy

Art therapy is also known as art psychotherapy. Broadly speaking, it plays the role of a mediator in human spiritual life. People get relief when appreciating art and get vent in artistic creation. In a narrow sense, art therapy is the method and process of diagnosing, treating or rehabilitating certain diseases in the artistic interaction with the treated under the guidance of professionals. Art therapy is to convey and express the inner world through art, so as to release negative emotions and make people optimistic, cheerful and healthy. The unique way of art therapy, which cannot be banned by other forms of therapy, has its own unique advantages. Most psychotherapy is directly expressed through language and other means, while art, such as painting or music, can indirectly express the inner bad emotions through certain works, and then with the help of psychiatrists and professional therapists, Recognize the cause of your thoughts and emotions and let go of depression and anxiety [5].

Art therapy combines visual art, creative processes, and psychotherapy to promote well-being – emotional, cognitive, physical, and spiritual. The unique way of art therapy, which cannot be banned by other forms of therapy, has its own unique advantages. Most psychotherapy is directly expressed through language and other means, while art, such as painting or music, can indirectly express the inner bad emotions through certain works, and then with the help of psychiatrists and professional therapists, Recognize the cause of your thoughts and emotions and let go of depression and anxiety.

2.4 Focusing-Oriented Art Therapy

Focusing - oriented art therapy combines the theories and methods of focusing - oriented psychotherapy and art therapy. This therapy begins by building the client's sense of safety, then builds the therapeutic relationship, incorporating various empathic reflexes – such as experiential listening, artistic reflexes, and mirror functions. The counselor helps the client bring a welcoming, friendly, accepting, focused attitude to the inner experience of their problems, problems, or experiences. The client listens to the body, gets an experience, waits until there is an inner symbol or image that describes the experience, and then expresses it through artistic means [6].

First, focus on the orientation of art therapy. The core content of "Focus" is collaborative art therapy to achieve psychological comfort in a quiet and comfortable environment. It is basically the same as the six steps of focusing: the first step is to create space, the second step is to choose a question and gain experience, the third step is to use a word, sentence, picture, gesture or sound as a symbol of sharing inner emotions, the fourth step is to interact, the fifth step is to ask, and the sixth step is to accept and integrate.Cindy, a patient with rectal cancer, underwent four weeks of focused art therapy based on her own events, and drew her expressions. Focused art therapy, a useful intervention to prevent permanent trauma and provide emotional support to patients and their families during invasive treatments, is now widely used in the treatment of cancer patients and children with autism [3].

2.5 Expressive Art Therapy

Different from the single art form of art therapy, art therapy integrates different art forms such as music, dancing, painting and drama, emphasizes non-verbal, physical and emotional expression and expression, integrates various organ stimulation modes, and provides opportunities and environment for participants to actively explore their own potential, self-expression and personal interests [7].

In the early 1980s, Lelis University referred to the psychotherapy of painting, music, literature, crafts, drama and other art forms as "expressive art therapy" and developed it as an independent field. The core feature of expressive art therapy is that the form of artistic creation can more effectively assist the client to express the repressed and hidden emotions, and assist the client to restructure and retell the past experience. It includes two work orientations: "artistic psychotherapy" and "artistic creation is therapy". The former believes that artistic creation is an important tool in psychotherapy, focusing on the non-verbal communication and analysis between therapist and client in the process of artistic creation. The latter believes that the process of creation is the process of therapy. In the process of therapy, more attention is paid to the creative environment and the expression of the creator. The two work orientations are not contradictory in practice, and should be selected according to the treatment object and specific situation [8].

Traditional psychological counseling and treatment techniques, due to the difficulty of the expression of the visitors, poor communication and the situation of the dilemma, to a certain extent, the expression of the needs of some visitors and their own heart, affecting the process of psychological counseling and psychotherapy. Expressive art therapy is characterized by "non-verbal communication". Art forms such as painting and music provide more media for visitors to express themselves. The potential unconscious emotions, memory, self and needs projected in artistic creation can be expressed more smoothly and completely.Nowadays, expressive art therapy techniques and media continue to develop and enrich, and gradually become a powerful supplement to the traditional working methods of mental health education in colleges and universities.

2.6 Handicraft Art Therapy

Manual creation art is a three-dimensional image creation process through the close combination of human hand, eye and brain, with the help of certain material materials. It needs to combine the brain's image thinking with abstract thinking, so as to arouse people's thinking, explore people's creativity and expressive force, and stimulate people's interest. The ultimate purpose of handmade art is to create different forms of works with different materials, so as to activate the thinking and cultivate students' aesthetic and pleasant feeling. If the course of manual creation art is included in the teaching system of higher vocational colleges, it can not only promote students' intelligence, improve their artistic quality, but also benefit students' physical and mental health. Manual creation can express and present the innermost thoughts with the help of certain carrier and creative techniques, and express the inner emotions with three-dimensional things by means of suggestion or symbol, so as to help professional therapists find the core basis for solving psychological problems [9].

3 Methods

3.1 Selection of Research Objects

In this study, participants were recruited from Beijing Technology Institute, Zhuhai, for psychological evaluation of depression and anxiety. Finally, 30 current students with anxiety and depression but no diagnosis of mental symptoms were selected as intervention objects and randomly divided into two groups with 15 predecessors in each group. With the progress of the course, 3 students from each group left the group and 24 students participated in the whole course. At the same time, the control group members were recruited in the school, and 24 students with anxiety and depression but no diagnosis of mental symptoms were selected.

3.2 Intervention Methods

In this study, 2 (experimental group/control group) × 2 (pre-test/post-test) experimental design was adopted. Members of the experimental group were tested before and after and interviewed, and had 90 min of ceramic art design course intervention for 9 consecutive weeks. The team leaders are: professional teachers from the Mental Health Education and Counseling Center of Beijing Institute of Technology Zhuhai, who have been engaged in the work of mental health education for college students; And teachers with years of experience in ceramic art design education. After the formal ceramic art design course, an open questionnaire survey was conducted for all experimental group members, and an in-depth interview was conducted for 4 experimental group members. The control group received no intervention.

The intervention process was carried out in the way of curriculum specific project guidance, and was carried out by hand kneading forming, mud plate forming and drawing forming. The content covers five topics, including self-examination, self-growth, getting closer to others, team strength, and life planning.

3.3 Measurement Methods

In this study, the Self-Rating Anxiety Scale (SAS) and Self-rating Anxiety Scale (SAS) were respectively adopted before and after the treatment. The Life Satisfaction Scales include four independent subscales. One is the other rating scale. Life Satisfaction Rating Soale, LSR for short; The other three components represent the self-rating scale, namely Life Satisfaction Index A and Life Satisfaction Index B, referred to as LSIA and LSIB. The self-rated Depression Scale (SDS) measured the anxiety, depression, positive psychological capital, self-esteem, perceived social support level and other multi-dimensional psychological conditions of the experimental group and control group before and after the intervention. And Tafarodi's Revised Two-dimensional Self-esteem Scale (SLCS-R) [10]. SPSS26.0 was used to analyze the data, and the descriptive statistical results of anxiety, depression, psychological capital and other indicators of members of the experimental group and control group were obtained (Table 1).

Table 1. Descriptive statistical results of pre - and post-test in experimental group and control group (M ± SD)

	Experimental group (n = 26)		Control group (n = 24)	
	pretest	post-test	pretest	post-test
anxiety	41.81 ± 5.61	38.42 ± 4.32	40.21 ± 6.69	41.00 ± 5.38
depression	20.77 ± 5.52	17.31 ± 4.99	17.71 ± 5.03	18.00 ± 4.98
Positive psychological	111.3 ± 17.68	122.3 ± 18.79	112.83 ± 12.43	110.9 ± 15.80
self-esteem	47.88 ± 3.37	54.23 ± 3.80	53.21 ± 4.23	52.33 ± 4.49
Social support	51.54 ± 16.48	59.85 ± 13.36	55.46 ± 13.49	55.83 ± 15.36

4   Results

4.1   Help College Students Effectively Relieve Anxiety and Depression

The American Psychiatric Association defines anxiety as "an expectation of future danger and misfortune, accompanied by nervousness, irritability, restlessness, and a range of physical symptoms [11]". Moderate anxiety can promote college students to complete their studies, but excessive anxiety may lead to a series of psychological and physical diseases. In this study, repeated measurement analysis of variance found that the main effect of pre and post measurements was not significant, $F (1,48) = 2.57$, $p > 0.05$. The interaction between pre and post test and group was significant, $F (1,48) = 6.16$, $p < 0.05$. The difference between pre and post test was not significant in the control group, while the difference between pre and post test was significant in the experimental group. Paired sample t test was used, $t = 3.23$, $p < 0.05$, and the score of post test was significantly lower than that of the main effect of pre and post test, $F (1,48) = 5.19$, $p < 0.05$. The interaction between pre and post test and group was significant, $F (1,48) = 7.28$, $p < 0.01$. The difference between pre - and post-test was not significant in the control group, while the difference between pre - and post-test was significant in the experimental group. Paired sample t test was adopted, $t = 3.28$, $p < 0.05$, and the score of post-test was significantly lower than that of pre - test. It can be seen that ceramic art design therapy has a significant effect on anxiety and depression of college students.

In addition, according to the subjective feedback of the experimental group members, it is found that the ceramic art design course can provide long-term and stable psychological support for participants. Participants take the initiative to adjust negative emotions in the process of making ceramic art works in a variety of ways, which effectively improves their emotional regulation ability, so as to adjust the frequency and degree of emotional fluctuations.

4.2 Therapeutic Effect of Ceramic Art Therapy on Anxiety and Depression of College Students

Positive psychological capital refers to a positive psychological state that an individual shows in the process of growth and development, including self-efficacy, resilience, hope, optimism four dimensions. Students with positive psychological capital are usually able to adjust their own state in time, and actively cope with academic, employment, emotional and other aspects of pressure. Repeated measures analysis of variance found that the main effect of pre and post measurements was significant, $F (1,48) = 6.70$, $p < 0.01$. The interaction between pre and post test and group was significant, $F (1,48) = 13.41$, $p < 0.001$. Simple effect test found that the difference between pre and post test was not significant in the control group, while the difference between pre and post test was significant in the experimental group. Paired sample t test was used, and the result was $t = -4.07$, $p < 0.001$, and the score after test was significantly higher than that before test. Through the guidance of therapists in the course, members of the experimental group were able to feel themselves in art, have a clear and comprehensive understanding of themselves, and gradually improve their cognition of others. One member said, "I am able to be more honest with my heart and feelings". "I am able to deal with other people in my life in a more tolerant manner". "My biggest change is to be more consistent and less obsessive". It can be seen that ceramic art design course can effectively improve the positive psychological capital of college students.

4.3 Awaken the Inner Self-esteem of College Students

Self-esteem is an individual's overall evaluation of their own value, including belief and emotion. It is reflected in behavior, an internal component of dignity, and an emotional self-regulation variable related to self-evaluation. Repeated measures analysis of variance found that the main effect of pre and post measures was significant, $F_{(1,48)} = 18.59$, $p < 0.001$. The interaction between pre and post test and group was significant, $F_{(1,48)} = 32.39$, $p < 0.001$. Simple effect test found that the difference between pre and post test was not significant in the control group, while the difference between pre and post test was significant in the experimental group. Paired sample t test was used, and the result was $t = -7.30$, $p < 0.001$. The score of post test was significantly higher than that of pre test. "The therapist kept telling me that I was worthy of love, which helped me stop denying myself", one of the experimental group members said during the interview. After ceramic art design therapy and self-reflection, the member broke up with her lover because she could not get approval from him. Another member said, "Every time I apply for the poverty grant, I feel very sad. After the group counseling, I found that everyone has a difficult pain and can overcome it by themselves". It can be seen that the group interaction of ceramic art design therapy helps the members to inspire each other. Students' sharing of experience and mutual support and encouragement in the course can not only help individuals to understand the views and behaviors of others towards events, but also help the subjects to improve their self-cognition, reduce their self-abasement, and enhance self-esteem and confidence.

4.4 Improve the Quality of College Students' Connection with Society

Social support means that individuals obtain general or specific support resources from others or social networks, which can help individuals cope with problems and crises in work and life. The perceptive social support Scale was used to measure the extent to which participants perceived support from various social support sources. Repeated measures analysis of variance found that the main effect of pre and post measurements was significant, $F_{(1,48)} = 5.13$, $p < 0.05$. The interaction between pre and post test and group was significant, $F_{(1,48)} = 4.28$, $p < 0.05$. Simple effect test found that the difference between pre and post test was not significant in the control group, while the difference between pre and post test was significant in the experimental group. Paired sample t test was used, and the result was $t = -3.03$, $p < 0.05$, and the score of post test was significantly higher than that of pre test.

It can be seen that ceramic art design therapy can effectively improve the closeness and quality of individual and social connection. After several sessions, members of the experimental group said that ceramic art design therapy can improve their communication with others, eliminate loneliness and reduce social fear. Most of the participants made friends during the sessions and said they would actively seek more connections in the future. "I am no longer a lonely star". "Before the event, my desire to share was at its lowest point, and now I'm open to sharing things with people around me". "What I like most is to talk about impressions together. It's very useful for getting to know each other and myself. If I have the chance, I will also form a group and try to bring people closer together in this way". It can be seen that people with more social support have a stronger sense of happiness, which will further enhance the willingness and ability of individuals to actively increase contacts.

5 Recommendations

5.1 Carry Out College Mental Health Education Based on Ceramic Art Therapy

In this study, college students suffering from anxiety or depression in Beijing Technology Institute, Zhuhai, were treated with ceramic art course, and their conditions before and after the treatment were compared to evaluate the therapeutic effect after treatment. In order to promote ceramic art therapy courses in colleges and universities in the future, regulate and relieve the depression and anxiety of college students to provide solutions. Among the 25 open-ended questionnaires collected, 24 members of the experimental group supported the regular opening of elective courses related to expressive art therapy, and fully recognized the path and method of adjusting their emotional state through scientific means in the context of art.

This study believes that ceramic art design therapy can, in a harmonious group atmosphere, through artistic expression and the cooperation of participants, deeply dig the inner needs of the growth of college students, help them establish the consciousness of self-help, mutual assistance, help, rational face the reality of setbacks and difficulties, is one of the popular and can effectively improve the level of mental health of college students. Carrying out mental health education based on ceramic art design therapy can enrich the forms and means of mental health education in colleges and universities, attract college students to participate widely, make them gradually understand themselves in art healing, and resolve individual emotional troubles and deep problems. Psychological teachers can learn from the theory and practical experience of expressive art therapy, design themed activities around the physical and mental characteristics and development needs of students at different stages, such as the establishment of health network growth groups, healing groups for patients with procrastination, etc., through more detailed ways, effectively improve the mental health literacy of college students.

5.2 Incorporating Expressive Art Therapy into the Training of Teachers' Mental Health Education Skills

At present, psychological counseling centers have been basically established in colleges and universities, equipped with professional psychological teachers and psychological counselors to help students solve relevant problems, but there are very few art therapy professionals in the teaching staff of mental health education. In this study, therapists from the Art Behavior Therapy Center of Rehabilitation Department of Beijing Hui-longguan Hospital, who have rich experience in group therapy, were hired to carry out art healing courses for college students, which achieved remarkable results in solving emotional problems and were highly recognized by the participants.It can be seen that in the future mental health education work, colleges and universities can break the space restrictions, through external art therapists and other ways to relieve the psychological pressure of college students. In addition, the Notice on Strengthening the management of students' mental health stressed the need to strengthen the mental health education and training of college teachers. In view of this, the school can hire art therapy experts and scholars to carry out basic training for relevant teachers in colleges and universities to learn primary art therapy methods, so that they can improve the mental health level of college students through art therapy in daily work and courses, explore a new path to form a joint force within and outside the school and educate the whole staff, and jointly lead the healthy growth of students.

Ceramic art design therapy creates a safe and credible communication atmosphere, and innovates the interaction mechanism between teachers and students. Art therapists give full play to the characteristics of non-language through artistic feelings and artistic creation, which effectively alleviates the anxiety and depression of college students, and guides students to constantly explore themselves, express their true emotions, improve their psychological quality and face life bravely. In today's education environment, colleges and universities can take expressive art therapy group guidance as a new model of mental health education curriculum, carry out further attempts and explorations, integrate rich forms of art activities to guide college students to enhance mental health awareness and stimulate the positive inner motivation.

6 Conclusion

Due to the dual needs of material and spiritual life, as well as the conflict between sensibility and rationality, people may have some psychological problems to varying degrees, and artistic psychology is a special problem in human nature. We can turn to art to express the unspeakable in an artistic way and explore the problem of psychological efficacy with artistic thinking. Through the research on the application of ceramic art design in college students' mental health education, the research data show that through the safe environment of art activities, students can directly express the relationship between themselves and the world and change their behavior attitude, and thus affirm the feasibility and effectiveness of curing psychological problems through art education in the school environment. This kind of dualism of body and mind has been the philosophical basis of art therapy, and also provides the integration direction of art therapy and art education [12].

References

1. Krycka, K.C., Ikemi, A., Cain, D.J., Keenan, K.R.: Shawn Focusing-Oriented–Experiential Psychotherapy: From Research to Practice. Washington: American Psychological Association Humanistic Psychotherapies: Handbook of Research and Practice, pp.251–282. Transaction Publishers, New York (2016)
2. Gendlin, E.T.: Focusing - Oriented Psychotherapy, p. P147. Guilford Press, New York (1996)
3. Rappaport, L.: Focusing Art Therapy, p. 11. China Light Industry Press. Beijing, China (2019)
4. Rosal, M.L.: Cognitive-Behavioral Art Therapy: From Behaviorism to the Third Wave, pp. 3–25. Taylor and Francis, New York (2018)
5. Cornell, W., Parker, R.: The SAGE Encyclopedia of Theory in Counseling and Psychotherapy, vol. 1, pp. 423–426. Transaction Publishers, New York (2015)
6. Holttum, S.: Research watch: art therapy: a dose of treatment, an aid to social inclusion or an unnecessary indulgence. Ment. Health Soc. Inclus. 17(2), 64–69 (2013). https://doi.org/10.1108/20428301311330108
7. Yan, Y., Lin, R., Zhou, Y.: Effects of expressive arts therapy in older adults with mild cognitive impairment: a pilot study. Geriatr. Nurs. 42, 129–136 (2021)

8. Rubin, J.A.: Approaches to Art Therapy: Theory and Technique, pp. 230–248. Taylor and Francis, New York (2016)
9. Using textile arts and handcrafts in therapy with women; weaving lives back together. Reference & Research Book News, vol. 27, pp. 78–93 (2012)
10. Tafarodi, R., Swann, W.: Two-dimensional self-esteem: theory and measurement. Pers. Individ. Differ. **31**, 653–673 (2001)
11. Feng, X.: Research on internet users' information retrieval anxiety. Libr. J. 130–140 (2008)
12. Lau, C.: Postmodern art education, p. 42. Hong Kong Arts Development Council, Hong Kong (2004)

An Evaluation of Mindfulness Product Design Based on Using KANO Model

Zijia Xu[1], Fucong Xu[1], Langyue Deng[1], Xinyue Guo[1], and Yu-Chi Lee[2(✉)] (iD)

[1] School of Design, South China University of Technology, Guangzhou 510006, China
[2] College of Management and Design, Ming Chi University of Technology,
New Taipei City 243303, Taiwan
yclee@mail.mcut.edu.tw

Abstract. Factors such as the economic recession during the COVID-19 pandemic increased depression and worrisome mental health conditions, especially among college students and workers. Mindfulness-based stress reduction (MBSR) has been proven one of the most effective treatments for reducing stress and anxiety with positive effects on the mental health of college students and workers. The available information for designing MBSR relative products is still lacking. Hence, this study aimed to apply KANO model and mixed design methods to evaluate the user needs for MBSR products. First, this study obtained the functional requirements of the current MBSR products through competitive analysis and further obtained user suggestions through a focus group. Then, a Kano questionnaire was conducted based on the above user's needs and the results classified and prioritized the functional requirements. Finally, this study provided useful information for the designers and manufacturers (three performance needs and two expectation needs extracted by the KANO model) when redesigning new-generation mindfulness meditation products.

Keywords: Mindfulness · KANO model · User requirements

1 Introduction

1.1 Background

According to a research brief published by the World Health Organization (WHO), the prevalence of anxiety and sadness surged dramatically globally in the first year of the COVID-19 pandemic. The executive summary also identifies those most impacted and outlines how the epidemic has influenced access to mental health treatments and how this has evolved. The pandemic's social isolation has resulted in stress and economic recession, which was related to restrictions on people's capacity to work, ask loved ones for help, and participate in their communities. Stressors that can cause melancholy and anxiety include loneliness, dread of illness, suffering for oneself and loved ones, bereavement, and financial concerns. Exhaustion has been a significant contributor to suicidal thoughts in health professionals. The pandemic has affected young people's mental health, and they are disproportionally at risk of suicidal and self-harming behaviors. People with pre-existing physical health concerns, such as asthma, cancer, and heart disease, were more likely to develop signs of mental illnesses. According to the data, those with mental illnesses do not seem more at risk of contracting COVID-19. However, compared to those without mental illnesses, these individuals have a higher risk of hospitalization, severe illness, and death when contracting the infection. Young persons with mental problems and those with more severe mental disorders, such as psychoses, are particularly in danger [1].

1.2   Introduction to Mindfulness Meditation

Mindfulness cognitive behavioral therapy is a cutting-edge alternative to traditional psychotherapies for severe depression because it uses the mental calmness that comes from meditation [2]. It is a mental training practice that combines meditation with mindful practice. It can be defined as a mental state that involves being entirely focused on "the now" so you can acknowledge and accept your thoughts, feelings, and sensations without judgment. Individuals may exercise greater integrity and experience spiritual sublimation and progress through seclusion, prayers, and soul-searching self-narratives.

Mindfulness meditation has recently shown benefits in lowering stress levels in various populations. Even a remote, online, group-based mindfulness program can reduce negative emotions in people [3]. Western approaches to stress reduction have recently focused on behavioral modifications, mechanistic techniques, and CBT-oriented treatments that build on ideas from cognitive behavioral therapy [4]. In contrast, eastern meditative traditions focused on present-centered attention and awareness, termed mindfulness compared to the West [5]. Existing studies indicate that mindfulness meditation can play a positive role in the reduction of stress and stress-related symptoms when carried out in a self-directed way. Reducing stress, feelings of anxiety and sadness, and improving mental and sleep quality are all positive outcomes [6]. Short-term mindfulness meditation training can also improve concentration and self-regulation [7]. Mindfulness-based stress reduction (MBSR) has been proven one of the most effective treatments for reducing stress and anxiety, with positive effects on the mental health of college students and workers [8]. The students could lessen negative thoughts or sensations by switching from an avoidant type to an approach-oriented coping technique through MBSR. This enables individuals to react to stress more constructively. The skills the student gains from the MBSR help them become more self-aware, empathic, reflective, and reflexive, all of which may improve their capacity to engage in anti-oppressive social work and form the foundational elements of sustainable long-term practice [9]. MBSR can assist workers in building emotional resilience so they can handle the rigors of their jobs. After practicing MBSR, workers can lessen perceived stress and compassion fatigue while increasing resilience (emotional self-efficacy and psychological flexibility) and the influence of well-being-related components, such as compassion satisfaction [10].

1.3   KANO Model Overview

Noriaki Kano, a professor at Tokyo Institute of Technology in Japan, first proposed Kano's model of customer satisfaction in the 1980s [14]. The Kano model is helpful for designers to classify product requirements and user demands. As part of the product design process, the designers prioritized design goals and assigned grades to various product features based on user satisfaction. By categorizing this relationship into five groups, the Kano model enhances the conventional linear view between customer satisfaction and the fulfillment of product requirements. The five demand can be classified by using KANO model:

1. Attractive Demand: What users do not expect requires exploration and insight. If not provided, user satisfaction will not be reduced; if provided, it will be greatly improved.
2. One-dimensional Demand: If provided, user satisfaction will increase; If it is not provided, user satisfaction will decrease.
3. Must-be Demand: The so-called pain points, for the user, these demands must be satisfied as a matter of course. When not provided, user satisfaction decreases significantly, but optimizing this demand does not significantly improve user satisfaction.
4. Indifferent Demand: User satisfaction will remain the same whether this demand is provided or not. Designers should try to avoid it.
5. Reverse Demand: Users do not have this demand. If provided, user satisfaction decreases.

Martzler [15] developed a more thorough application approach of the Kano model in 1996, which has now gained popularity. The Kano model requires its users to fill the Kano questionnaires. Positive and negative questions were posed regarding whether or not each potential demand had been met. The Kano evaluation form was used to calculate the survey's results.

1.4 Research Status and Aim of the Study

People are open to using a physical mindfulness product or app based on MBSR to support their mindfulness meditation. Nevertheless, only a few studies have examined the quality of mindfulness apps using validated and standardized tools [11]. Furthermore, due to the lack of physicality, people often feel less engaging to the user and, therefore, less effective. Although many MBSR products have been developed commercially in recent years, most of the existing product research has been conducted in the laboratory and is technology-driven results without focusing on user's needs [12]. Meanwhile, commercial MBSR products exhibit classic capitalist logic that negatively impacts those who practice mindfulness [13]. Therefore, it is necessary to study the design of daily mindfulness-based stress reduction products based on user needs analysis. To fill these research gaps, this study applied the KANO model primarily and mixed design methods to determine the user needs for MBSR product design.

2   Methods

2.1   Competitor Analysis

First, this study performed a competitive analysis of the top five sales MBSR physical products on Amazon [16] and the top five AppStore downloaded apps [17] from 2019 to 2022 to obtain functional requirements met by existing mindfulness meditation products.

"Tide", "Pause", "Now", "Wild Journey", and "Healthy Lab" were chosen to analyze and compare (see Fig. 1).

"Tide" mainly provides breathing training, a concentration clock, a sleep aid, meditation exercises, and a variety of optional sound scenes.

"Pause" uses the Mindful Touch as an interaction style with soothing background music designed to help users relieve anxiety and distraction.

"Now" mainly provides sleep-aid functions with sleep-aid sounds and sleep-aid training. It also provides breathing and meditation training.

"Wild Journey" mainly provides a variety of beautifully animated landscapes and fantastic nature sound effects. It also has timed, voice-guided functions to assist in mindfulness meditation and offers multi-day meditation courses to help develop mindfulness meditation habits.

"Healthy Lab" mainly provides a variety of meditation training, meditation-assisted music, sleep stories, and a focus clock function.

The primary user groups of these apps are social workers and teenage students. By weakening the professionalism of meditation content, these apps are more lifelike, and easy for users to use the fragmented time for meditation, which is beneficial for young users and beginners. These apps can be used in many scenarios, and users can come to a quiet place for a five to ten-minute meditation session. There are paid content ads in "Now", and the commercial atmosphere is heavier than the rest of the APPs.

We summarize the following functional requirements for a mindfulness meditation APP: 1) Timing function; 2) Guided meditation training; 3) Meditation music to assist mindfulness meditation; 4) Physical interaction; 5) Sleep aid function; 6) Meditation training of different levels of difficulty.

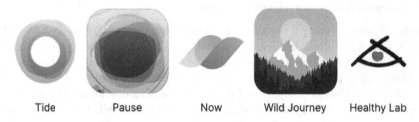

Tide   Pause   Now   Wild Journey   Healthy Lab

Fig. 1. Logo of the apps

Core   FocusZen   Breathing Buddha   Magicteam   Hathaspace

Fig. 2. Product effect picture

For evaluating the mindfulness meditation products, the "Core", "FocusZen", "Breathing Buddha", "Magicteam", and "Hathaspace" were chosen to analyze and compare (see Fig. 2).

"Core" is a handheld device that helps people focus. It vibrates to guide breathing and serve as a natural reminder, and its built-in biosensor detects heart rate and can be used with an app.

"FocusZen" is a head-mounted device that detects brainwave data. It works with an app to provide real-time feedback on sound and visualization of meditation states.

"Breathing Buddha" guides the user's breathing through lighting changes.

"Magicteam" provides eight soothing sounds to assist meditation and sleep and nine different dynamic lighting effects to create a meditative atmosphere. It is decorative, has a wireless charging function, and can be used with an app.

"Hathaspace" has a marble coating for a stylish look. It has an Aroma humidification function that diffuses essential oils to help relieve stress and calm emotions.

These mindfulness meditation products include wearable devices, handheld devices, and desktop devices, which assist mindfulness meditation by detecting body data, creating an atmosphere, and guiding meditation. We summarize the following functional requirements for the design of mindfulness meditation products: 1) beautiful appearance, with specific decorative; 2) multi-sensory experience; 3) body data detection; 4) product feedback timely; 5) the product can create a suitable atmosphere for meditation; 6) diversified use of the product; 7) can guide the user to mindfulness meditation; 8) product can help users focus on.

2.2 Focus Group

This study organized a focus group session based on the competitive analysis to obtain user-driven requirements. We also designed interview content based on the functional requirements met by existing mindfulness meditation products.

Two university students, two office workers, and two designers with mindfulness meditation experience were invited to the focus group, aged 19 to 40. A 2-h focus group discussion was conducted, focusing on the following three topics:

- When will you need mindfulness meditation?
- What kind of mindfulness meditation product have you used, and how do you practice mindfulness meditation?
- What is your evaluation of existing mindfulness meditation products and your expectations for future ones?

During the discussion, participants made the following critical statements:

- Participant A: It is ritualistic to use physical products to assist in mindfulness meditation. When I am tired at work and do not want to pick up my phone to use the app, having the physical product next to me can attract me to do mindfulness meditation. The reminders and guidance of physical products are more gentle and natural.
- Participant B: I have come across many products that help release stress or focus through physical contact, and handheld products give a greater sense of control.

- Participant C: It would be a bit strange to have the physical product in my office when I am not meditating. It can be designed as a decoration for display, and it would help soothe me outside meditation time.

The participants in this interview were optimistic about the physical products of mindfulness meditation and considered them to be a solid aid for mindfulness meditation. Participants would do mindfulness meditation before bed to aid in falling asleep or at their desks before studying at work to help focus. The main mindfulness meditation scenario is a quiet, private space. The participants do this mainly by listening to music and following instructional videos.

The results indicated the critical design recommendations:

- At least use two or more senses of humans to achieve a better immersive experience.
- Use handheld interaction to aid mindfulness meditation and perform heart rate monitoring.
- It can be used as an ornament to create a relaxing atmosphere during idle time.

2.3 User Requirements Analysis Based on KANO Model

User requirement analysis can help develop product design strategies, and we use the KANO model to classify and prioritize users' requirements in this paper.

2.3.1 Questionnaire Design and Collection

This study extracted ten functional requirement indicators from the results of competitive analysis and focus groups, which were divided into three categories: product styling, user experience, and mindfulness meditation assistance, and labeled as A1, A2, A3, B1…C3, as shown in Table 1. Then we created a questionnaire using the KANO model, and each functional requirement was set with a positive question of "have this feature" and a negative question of "don't have this feature". Each question has five levels of options, in the order of "Like it a lot", "Must-be", "Doesn't matter", "Tolerable", and "Unacceptable" (see Table 2).

In this paper, we select university students and social workers as the main survey population. From this, people with mindfulness meditation experience were screened as subjects to obtain the data with the reference value. The questionnaires were mainly distributed in online questionnaires, and 81 subjects participated in the survey. Seventy-eight valid questionnaires were finally collected after excluding invalid randomly scored questionnaires.

2.3.2 Data Analysis

Before processing the questionnaire data, we performed a reliability analysis first. The Cronbach α coefficient of the positive question was 0.858, and the Cronbach α coefficient of the negative question was 0.807. The Cronbach α coefficients for both the positive and negative questions were greater than 0.8, indicating that the study data had a high internal consistency and can be used for further analysis.

Table 1. List of functional requirements

Requirement categories	No.	Functional requirements	Explanatory notes
Product Styling	A1	Comfortable material of the product	The use of soft and comfortable materials brings better tactile sensation and reduces the user's sense of rejection
	A2	Beautiful product shape	Product appearance is simple and beautiful, with smooth lines, decorative solid
	A3	Soft color of the product	A soft and calm feeling through low saturation colors
User Experience	B1	Multi-sensory experience	The product can mobilize the user's senses through vibration, light, aroma, etc., to guide mindfulness meditation and create an atmosphere
	B2	Diversification of product use	The product can be used with apps and other methods for a diversified experience
	B3	Product can be timely feedback	The product can provide real-time feedback on changes in body data through changes in vibration frequency and other methods
	B4	Ergonomic	Wearable devices and handheld devices are ergonomically designed to bring a more comfortable experience
Mindfulness Meditation Assistance	C1	Product idle time usage	The product can be used to create a mindfulness environment through regular movement and white noise when it is idle
	C2	Can monitor body data	Monitor the user's heart rate through wearable devices and handheld devices

(*continued*)

Table 1. (*continued*)

Requirement categories	No.	Functional requirements	Explanatory notes
	C3	Timed reminder function	The product can be set to attract users to do mindfulness meditation through light and vibration reminders at specific times

Table 2. Questionnaire topic setting mode

Feature	Like it a lot	Must-be	Doesn't matter	Tolerable	Unacceptable
Have this feature					
Don't have this feature					

The questionnaire data were compared with the Kano evaluation form (Table 3) to obtain the attributes corresponding to the subjects' attitudes toward each functional requirement. Each attribute of the same feature was summed, and the highest percentage was the attribute of that functional requirement (Table 4). Q stands for the questionable result, which usually does not happen; A stands for Attractive Quality; I stands for Indifferent Quality; R stands for Reversal Quality; M stands for Must-be Quality; O stands for One-dimensional Quality.

The Better-Worse coefficients are obtained by substituting each feature's corresponding percentage of attributes into the Better-Worse coefficient calculation formula (Table 4). The calculation formula is as follows.

$$Better = (A + O)/(A + O + M + I) \tag{1}$$

$$Worse = -1 * (O + M)/(A + O + M + I) \tag{2}$$

The value of the Better coefficient is usually positive, which means that users' satisfaction will increase if a feature is provided. The closer the value is to 1, the easier it is to improve users' satisfaction. The value of the Worse coefficient is usually negative, meaning user satisfaction will decrease if a feature is not provided. The closer the value is to -1, the greater the impact on user dissatisfaction.

Excluding Reversal Quality and questionable results, a scatter plot is constructed with the Better coefficient as the horizontal coordinate and the |Worse| coefficient as the vertical coordinate. The scatter plot is divided into four quadrants by making parallel dashed lines with the horizontal and vertical coordinates at point P (the point consisting of the average of the Better coefficient and the |Worse| coefficient), respectively (Fig. 3).

The first quadrant is One-dimensional Demand. Better > 0.5, |Worse| > 0.5, indicating the feature desired by the users, with a high degree of perfection, will increase the user's satisfaction. If there is no such feature, the user's satisfaction will decrease.

Includes A1 (Comfortable material of the product), B1 (Multi-sensory experience), and C2 (Can monitor body data), three features. They should be satisfied as a priority during development and design.

The second quadrant is Attractive Demand. Better > 0.5, |Worse| <0.5, indicating the feature that users are not overly expecting. If this feature is not provided, user satisfaction will not decrease. If this feature is provided, user satisfaction will be significantly improved. Includes B4 (Ergonomic), and C1 (Product idle time usage), two features that should be explored during development and design.

The third quadrant is Indifferent Demand. Better < 0.5, |Worse| < 0.5, indicating the feature that the user does not care about, the impact on user experience is weak, whether this requirement is provided or not, user satisfaction does not change much. Includes A3 (Soft color of the product), B3 (Product can be timely feedback), and C3 (Timed reminder function), three features. Features in this quadrant are usually not considered.

The fourth quadrant is Must-be Demand. Better < 0.5, |Worse| > 0.5, indicating the feature that users feel must be satisfied. If this feature is not provided, user satisfaction will be significantly reduced, but optimizing this feature will not significantly improve user satisfaction. Includes A2 (Beautiful product shape), and B2 (Diversification of product use), two features. Features in this quadrant are core user requirements and must be implemented.

According to the definition of the Kano model for the description of each requirement attribute, the priority order of requirement attribute implementation should be: basic need > performance need > excitement need > indifferent need. The features in the same quadrant were ranked according to the distance from each point to the origin of the coordinate. The farther away means, the more significant the impact on user satisfaction and the higher the importance, and finally, the functional requirement priority ranking can be obtained: B2 > A2 > B1 > A1 > C2 > C1 > B4 > A3 > B3 > C3 (see Table 5).

Table 3. Kano evaluation form

		Positive question				
		Like it a lot	Must-be	Doesn't matter	Tolerable	Unacceptable
Negative question	Like it a lot	Q	A	A	A	O
	Must-be	R	I	I	I	M
	Doesn't matter	R	I	I	I	M
	Tolerable	R	I	I	I	M
	Unacceptable	R	R	R	R	Q

Table 4. Statistical results of the questionnaire data

No.	M	O	A	I	R	Q	Better	IWorseI
A1	16.05%	35.8%	12.35%	30.86%	1.23%	3.7%	50.65%	54.55%
A2	33.33%	3.7%	25.93%	32.1%	1.23%	3.7%	31.17%	38.96%
A3	6.17%	3.7%	30.86%	54.32%	1.23%	3.7%	36.36%	10.39%
B1	11.11%	34.57%	20.99%	28.4%	1.23%	3.7%	58.44%	48.05%
B2	35.8%	7.41%	8.52%	33.33%	2.47%	2.47%	27.27%	45.45%
B3	8.64%	7.41%	17.28%	61.73%	1.23%	3.7%	25.97%	16.88%
B4	20.99%	6.17%	37.04%	30.86%	2.47%	2.47%	45.45%	28.57%
C1	2.47%	7.41%	45.68%	39.51%	1.23%	3.7%	55.84%	10.39%
C2	3.7%	35.8%	20.99%	35.8%	2.47%	1.23%	58.97%	41.03%
C3	2.47%	3.7%	9.75%	69.14%	1.23%	3.7%	24.68%	6.49%

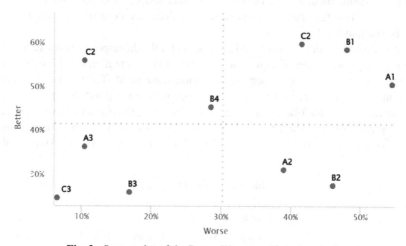

Fig. 3. Scatter plot of the Better-Worse coefficient analysis

3   Results and Discussion

3.1   Demand Analysis

In terms of product styling, Beautiful product shape > Comfortable material of the product > Soft color of the product. Respondents focus on the appearance of mindfulness meditation products. They think a beautiful shape is necessary for mindfulness meditation products and prefer simple, beautiful, smooth lines and decorative designs. In addition, respondents expect the product material to be soft and comfortable, which can bring a better tactile experience and reduce the feeling of rejection in the process of use. Respondents are not very concerned about the softness of the product colors but

Table 5. Prioritization of functional requirements

Attribute	No.	Distance to the origin	Priority ranking
M	B2	0.5300	1
	A2	0.4989	2
O	B1	0.7567	3
	A1	0.7444	4
	C2	0.7184	5
A	C1	0.5680	6
	B4	0.5368	7
I	A3	0.3782	8
	B3	0.3097	9
	C3	0.2552	10

believe that low saturation colors bring a soft and calm feeling and assist in mindfulness meditation.

In terms of user experience, Diversification of product use > Multi-sensory experience > Ergonomic > Product can be timely feedback. Respondents believe that diversity in product use is a must and that using the product with an app can bring a better experience. Moreover, respondents expect the product to have a multi-sensory experience and to guide mindfulness meditation by engaging the senses of sight and touch. In addition, respondents feel that the ergonomic design of the wearable and handheld devices would provide a more comfortable meditation experience. Respondents do not care if the product allowed for timely feedback but feel that having the feature affected the mindfulness meditation experience positively.

In terms of mindfulness meditation assistance, Can monitor body data > Product idle time usage > Timed reminder function. Respondents expect to use a wearable, handheld device to monitor biological data and help focus attention. Then, respondents believe that the use of the product's idle time can better assist in mindfulness meditation and make the product more attractive. Respondents think that the timed reminder function is not more useful as an aid to mindfulness meditation and that having this function or not has little effect on user satisfaction.

3.2 Design Suggestions

This paper mainly focuses on One-dimensional Demand and Attractive Demand. Design suggestions are made for the functional requirements of multi-sensory experience, comfortable material of the product, and product idle time usage.

Physical feedback, such as vibrational cues, can help improve concentration and cognition [18], and natural sounds help with physiological stress recovery [19], so lights, vibrations, sounds, and aromas can be used to engage the user's senses when designing mindfulness meditation products. The feeling of the space is related to the overall depth of meditation, and the environment can facilitate meditation [20]. Therefore, lighting, music, and aromatherapy can also promote mindfulness meditation by creating a suitable environment for meditation. In the process of mindfulness meditation, the product can change the color and brightness of the lights or the intensity and frequency of the vibrations to make cues and guide mindfulness meditation and use natural sounds and white noise as background music to assist users in relaxing. In the meditation process, voice cues may distract the user's attention, so voice cues can be provided at the beginning and end of the meditation to help the user understand the meaning of light and vibration cues [21]. Breathing exercises are common in apps and physical products. We also know from the interviewees that breathing exercises are commonly used, and continuous breathing exercises have been shown to affect mood positively [6], so we use breathing exercises as an example. When meditation begins, the product provides voice and vibration alerts to remind users of the start of training. During the process, the product can guide the user to breathe through vibration and light, such as using different colors of light to prompt the user to inhale, exhale, hold their breath, or use different frequencies of vibration corresponding to different breathing rates.

Users, mainly through the handheld, wear the way to produce contact with the product to detect body data and feel the vibration. Therefore, the product can be used lycra [22], TPU [23], and other soft materials to give users a more comfortable tactile sensation, reducing the user's sense of rejection of the product. Mindfulness meditation products are idle for longer during the day, so designers can utilize the idle time of the products to bring more added value. Such as being equipped with a wireless charging dock, allowing the product to be charged when idle, improving the range, and facilitating the product's placement. Alternatively, magnetic levitation technology also can be used so that the product is idle suspended rotation, decorative, and simultaneously creates a relaxing atmosphere through regular movement. Designers can also let the product in the idle role of fragrance diffusion to help users relax.

4   Conclusion

To obtain user needs for mindfulness meditation product design, this paper uses competitive analysis to summarize the functional requirements met by existing mindfulness meditation products at first. Then, a focus group interview is used to further capture the users' design needs. Finally, this paper uses the KANO model to categorize and prioritize design requirements for mindfulness meditation products providing two Must-be demands, three One-dimensional demands, two Attractive demands, and three Indifferent demands. In this paper, design recommendations are given for One-dimensional needs and Attractive needs. Mindfulness meditation products can be made more competitive by using multi-sensory experiences, soft materials, and product idle time. This paper offers a competitive product analysis of 10 popular physical and digital products from the previous three years and design guidance to focus on when designing new-generation mindfulness meditation products.

5 Limitations

The limitation of this paper is that the questionnaire respondents are mainly college students and workers, and the age group is focused 20–40 years old. Most of them are beginners in mindfulness meditation, and their primary purpose of mindfulness meditation is to relieve stress and improve sleep. Therefore, the design recommendations obtained were biased toward introductory mindfulness meditation. In future studies, the large group of practitioners of mindfulness meditation could be investigated to obtain the functional requirements of products with different levels of difficulty in mindfulness meditation.

References

1. COVID-19 pandemic triggers 25% increase in prevalence of anxiety and depression worldwide. https://www.who.int/news/item/02-03-2022-covid-19-pandemic-triggers-25-increase-in-prevalence-of-anxiety-and-depression-worldwide
2. Hayes, S.C., Levin, M.E., Plumb-Vilardaga, J., Villatte, J.L., Pistorello, J.: Acceptance and commitment therapy and contextual behavioral science: examining the progress of a distinctive model of behavioral and cognitive therapy. Behav Ther. **44**, 180–198 (2013). https://doi.org/10.1016/j.beth.2009.08.002
3. Mirabito, G., Verhaeghen, P.: Remote delivery of a Koru mindfulness intervention for college students during the COVID-19 pandemic. J. Am. Coll. Health 1–8 (2022)
4. Ho, D.Y., Chan, S.F., Peng, S., Ng, A.K.: The dialogical self: Converging east–west constructions. Cult. Psychol. **7**, 393–408 (2001)
5. Chan, C.L., Ng, S.M., Ho, R.T., Chow, A.Y.: East meets west: applying eastern spirituality in clinical practice. J. Clin. Nurs. **15**, 822–832 (2006)
6. van der Zwan, J.E., de Vente, W., Huizink, A.C., Bögels, S.M., de Bruin, E.I.: Physical activity, mindfulness meditation, or heart rate variability biofeedback for stress reduction: a randomized controlled trial. Appl. Psychophysiol. Biofeedback **40**(4), 257–268 (2015). https://doi.org/10.1007/s10484-015-9293-x
7. Tang, Y.-Y., et al.: Short-term meditation training improves attention and self-regulation. Proc. Natl. Acad. Sci. **104**, 17152–17156 (2007)
8. Ma, L., Wang, Y., Pan, L., Cui, Z., Schluter, P.J.: Mindfulness-informed (ACT) and Mindfulness-based Programs (MBSR/MBCT) applied for college students to reduce symptoms of depression and anxiety. J. Behav. Cogn. Ther. **32**(4), 271–289 (2022)
9. Maddock, A., McCusker, P.: Implementing the learning from the mindfulness-based social work and self-care programme to social work student practice during COVID-19: a qualitative study. Br. J. Soc. Work **52**, 4894–4913 (2022). https://doi.org/10.1093/bjsw/bcac094
10. Kinman, G., Grant, L., Kelly, S.: 'It's my secret space': the benefits of mindfulness for social workers. Br. J. Soc. Work **50**, 758–777 (2020). https://doi.org/10.1093/bjsw/bcz073
11. Schultchen, D., et al.: Stay present with your phone: a systematic review and standardized rating of mindfulness apps in European app stores. Int. J. Behav. Med. **28**, 552–560 (2021)
12. Chinareva, S., Jones, J., Tumia, N., Kumpik, D., Shah, P., Everitt, A.: Lotus: mediating mindful breathing. In: Extended Abstracts of the 2020 CHI Conference on Human Factors in Computing Systems, pp. 1–7 (2020)
13. Jablonsky, R.: Meditation apps and the promise of attention by design. Sci. Technol. Human Values **47**, 314–336 (2022)
14. Kano, N.: Attractive quality and must-be quality. Hinshitsu (Qual. J. Jpn. Soc. Qual. Control) **14**, 39–48 (1984)

15. Matzler, K., Hinterhuber, H.H., Bailom, F., Sauerwein, E.: How to delight your customers. J. Prod. Brand Manage. (1996)
16. iSellerPal. https://www.isellerpal.com/
17. https://app.diandian.com/
18. Boerema, A.S., et al.: Beneficial effects of whole body vibration on brain functions in mice and humans. Dose-Respon. **16**, 1559325818811756 (2018). https://doi.org/10.1177/155932 5818811756
19. Alvarsson, J.J., Wiens, S., Nilsson, M.E.: Stress Recovery during exposure to nature sound and environmental noise. Int. J. Environ. Res. Public Health **7**, 1036–1046 (2010). https://doi.org/10.3390/ijerph7031036
20. Costa, M.R., et al.: Nature inspired scenes for guided mindfulness training: presence, perceived restorativeness and meditation depth. In: Schmorrow, D.D., Fidopiastis, C.M. (eds.) HCII 2019. LNCS (LNAI), vol. 11580, pp. 517–532. Springer, Cham (2019). https://doi.org/10.1007/978-3-030-22419-6_37
21. Kim, E., Heo, J., Han, J.: Attention to breathing in response to vibrational and verbal cues in mindfulness meditation mediated by wearable devices. In: Kurosu, M. (ed.) HCII 2021. LNCS, vol. 12763, pp. 415–431. Springer, Cham (2021). https://doi.org/10.1007/978-3-030-78465-2_31
22. Gooch, J.W.: Lycra. In: Gooch, J.W. (ed.) Encyclopedic Dictionary of Polymers, pp. 436–436. Springer, New York (2011)
23. Gooch, J.W.: TPU. In: Gooch, J.W. (ed.) Encyclopedic Dictionary of Polymers, pp. 757–757. Springer, New York (2011)

Author Index

Printed in the United States
by Baker & Taylor Publisher Services